A PROPERTY ANTHOLOGY

Continued

PROBLEMS AND SIMULATIONS IN EVIDENCE
by Thomas F. Guernsey

A PROPERTY ANTHOLOGY
by Richard H. Chused

THE REGULATION OF BANKING
Cases and Materials on Depository Institutions and Their Regulators
by Michael P. Malloy

A SECTION 1983 CIVIL RIGHTS ANTHOLOGY
by Sheldon H. Nahmod

SPORTS LAW: CASES AND MATERIALS
by Raymond L. Yasser, James R. McCurdy and C. Peter Goplerud

A TORTS ANTHOLOGY
by Lawrence C. Levine, Julie A. Davies and Edward J. Kionka

TRIAL PRACTICE
Text by Lawrence A. Dubin and Thomas F. Guernsey
Problems and Case Files with *Video* Presentation
by Edward R. Stein and Lawrence A. Dubin

A Property Anthology

Edited with Comments by

Richard H. Chused

Professor of Law

Georgetown University Law Center

Anderson Publishing Co.

NOTE ON EDITING

All of the materials used in this anthology have been edited. Most footnotes have been deleted without elision marks. Editor's deletion of text is noted by asterisks: * * *. Materials deleted in the original are noted by periods: . . .. Matter inserted by the editor is noted by brackets: [insertion].

A PROPERTY ANTHOLOGY

Library of Congress Cataloging-in-Publication Data

A property anthology / edited, with comments by Richard H. Chused.
p. cm.
Includes index.
ISBN 0-87084-734-1
1. Real property—United States.
KF570.A2P76 1993
346.7304'3—dc20
[347.30643]

93-19310
CIP

Acknowledgment

My thanks go to David Taube, Georgetown University Law Center Class of '94, and Alan Minsk, Georgetown University Law Center Class of '93, for their work in tracking down, reading and making recommendations about materials for this anthology.

Contents

Part I

Introduction: Possession, Notice and Ownership as Defining Elements of Property

Most property courses begin with a look at the importance and meaning of possession as a defining element of legal rules that create or protect value. Two articles are excerpted below. The first, by Richard Helmholz, reviews the relationships between concepts of morality and legal recognition of one's possession as binding upon others. The second, by Carol Rose, takes an insightful journey through the cases—those discussing the capture of foxes, the unearthing of treasure trove, the existence of adverse possession and the "discovery" of North America—most often used to open introductory property courses. For a somewhat different perspective on the importance of possession, *see* Epstein, *Possession as the Root of Title*, 13 GA. L. REV. 1221 (1979).

R. H. Helmholz, *Wrongful Possession of Chattels: Hornbook Law and Case Law*, 80 NW. U. L. REV. 1221–1231, 1233–1237, 1242–1243 (1986)*

I. INTRODUCTION

It is hornbook law that possession of a chattel, even without claim of title, gives the possessor a superior right to the chattel against everyone but the true owner. The possessor has a "special" property interest in the chattel that only the chattel's owner, or someone claiming under him, can dispute. This special property interest exists even in the most extreme case: that in which the possessor has obtained the chattel by trespass, fraud, or theft. Even a wrongful possessor may reclaim the chattel from any nonowner who violates this possessory right. Such is the oft-stated rule of simple possession.

Support for this statement of the law is formidable. It boasts a strong leading case, *Anderson v. Gouldberg*, an 1892 Minnesota decision which held that a possessor of logs acquired by trespass had a right to them "against all the world except those having a better title."[3] The court's decision rested on the logically unanswerable argument that if the law were to embrace any standard but that of simple possession, the consequence would be "an endless series of unlawful seizures and reprisals in every case

[3] Anderson v. Gouldberg, 51 Minn. 294, 296, 53 N.W. 636, 637 (1892).

where property had once passed out of the possession of the rightful owner."

In addition, the rule claims the weighty authority of Justice Holmes,[5] Dean Ames,[6] and Sir Frederick Pollock.[7] They described the rule as one firmly established at common law, and they stated that it clearly demonstrated the law's longstanding preference for purely objective standards. Holmes, in particular, used the rule to show the law's indifference toward moral considerations. He argued that since the wrongful possessor could obtain rights to a chattel equal to those enjoyed by a lawful possessor, the law took an objective view of externally verifiable facts. Holmes, therefore, could use the rule to support his vision of a law cleansed of morality.

Yet doubts persist. Despite Holmes' view, morality has been a strong force in American public life, and *Anderson* has turned out to be a peculiar leading case. Although routinely and usefully included in property casebooks, *Anderson* rarely has been cited in subsequent reported cases. No citations for it appear at all after 1950, and most of the earlier cases that cited *Anderson* with approval involved a possessor with rights in addition to that of simple possession. Moreover, scholars recently have criticized Holmes' description of the law as representing largely his own subjective preferences.[12] H.L.A. Hart, for example, has observed that the desire to establish an objective standard, free from considerations of inner-blameworthiness, was "an idee maitresse, which in the end became something of an obsession with Holmes."[13] One cannot help wondering whether Holmes' endorsement of the rule of simple possession might have been wishful thinking on his part. Holmes himself said, "The first call of a theory of law is that it should fit the facts," and there is at least a possibility that his rule does not.

This Article examines whether the rule of simple possession "fits the facts" of modern case law. * * * While later cases do not indicate that *Anderson* was wrongly decided, the case law since 1892 shows three ways in which its black letter rule has been overextended.

First, the paradigmatic situation of *Anderson* almost never has arisen in actual litigation. Virtually all the cases addressing the rights of simple possession have not been contests between two wrongdoers. The argument on which *Anderson* is based—that anything but a simple possession rule would lead to an endless series of seizures by persons having no right to the chattel, although logically sound, turns out not to address the problems most often raised in actual litigation. If there are thieves involved in successive seizures of stolen goods, few of them find their way into a court of law. When they do, the thieves are apt to be defendants to criminal charges, not plaintiffs seeking to vindicate possessory rights. Most cases have involved parties whose claims to property could be weighed against each other, without relying upon who had possession first. The possibility of "endless seizures" is a specter more theoretically frightening than real.

Second, the traditional statement of the rule of simple possession entirely omits one of the most important distinctions that emerges from the case law: that between rightful and wrongful possession. The omission of moral considerations is, of course, exactly what Holmes desired. But Holmes' view does not square with the facts of a large number of subsequent cases. Courts regularly have examined the legitimacy of possession of chattels, and have refused to accord possessory rights when they have found *mala fides* or misconduct on the part of the possessor. Sometimes this has involved balancing equities between two competing possessors, neither of whom has a claim to title. More often, however, it simply has involved closing the door on wrongdoers who are seeking to take advantage of their own wrongs.

Third, although the above might suggest that the rule of simple possession rarely appears in the case law, in fact the opposite is true. Judges use it with some frequency. They do not invoke it, however, to protect wrongfully acquired possession. On the contrary, courts invoke the rule when it can be used to buttress claims of rightful possession. In other

---

[5] O.W. HOLMES, THE COMMON LAW 190 (M. Howe ed. 1963). Holmes gave judicial voice to the doctrine in Odd Fellows' Hall Ass'n v. McAllister, 153 Mass. 292, 295, 26 N.E. 862, 863 (1891).

[6] Ames, *The Disseisin of Chattels*, in LECTURES ON LEGAL HISTORY 172, 179 (1913).

[7] F. POLLOCK & R. WRIGHT, AN ESSAY ON POSSESSION IN THE COMMON LAW 91-93 (1888).

[12] See J. NOONAN, PERSONS AND MASKS OF THE LAW 65-110 (1976); R. SUMMERS, INSTRUMENTALISM AND AMERICAN LEGAL THEORY 58-59, 179-81 (1982); Atiyah, *The Legacy of Holmes Through English Eyes*, 63 B.U.L. REV. 341, 357-59 (1983); Kaplan, *Encounters with O. W. Holmes, Jr.*, 96 HARV. L. REV. 1828, 1830 (1983); Kelley, *A Critical Analysis of Holmes's Theory of Torts*, 61 WASH. U.L.Q. 681 (1983); Vetter, *The Evolution of Holmes, Holmes and Evolution*, 72 CALIF. L. REV. 343 (1984).

[13] H.L.A. HART, PUNISHMENT AND RESPONSIBILITY 242 (1968).

words, courts have not employed the rule of simple possession to protect simple possession. Hornbook law could usefully be amended to take account of what the rule actually does.

II. REPLEVIN, TROVER, AND CONVERSION

The actions of replevin, trover, and conversion must provide the primary test of the simple possession doctrine. The rule of simple possession holds that a possessor who can allege no more than prior possession can recover a chattel against anyone but the rightful owner. The cases, however, show that in practice the law is considerably more complex. Few of the cases decided since 1892 have involved the paradigmatic case of two equal wrongdoers. When the situation has arisen, courts most often have held that "one trespasser or wrongdoer can not maintain trover against another." They have forbidden either party to bring suit.

The few courts that have applied the hornbook rule in cases of wrongful possession have dealt with unusual facts. A recent New York case, for example, involved a soldier who had taken some of Adolf Hitler's effects at the end of World War II and kept them openly for many years. His chauffeur stole the effects from him, and the former soldier sued to recover them. The court invoked the rule of simple possession to allow the soldier to prevail.[24] The facts of this case were, to say the least, out of the ordinary. Even if the former soldier's possession were tainted by the means of acquisition, he was not what most judges would think of as a thief.

Such direct contests between two thieves have been very rare in reported litigation. In the great majority of cases in which a wrongdoer has attempted to assert possessory rights, his opponent has not also been a wrongdoer. The opponent instead has had some legitimate claim to custody of the chattel, even if it did not amount to a claim to title. In such cases the wrongful possessor virtually always has lost. Courts have distinguished between rightful and wrongful possession and have accorded legal protection only to the former. * * *

Cases involving money acquired illegally provide one illustration. In a Montana case, the owner of slot machines sued to recover money confiscated by the police.[26] The court held that the machines' owner could not recover the money from the police, even though no statute permitted forfeiture of the money: "[T]he power of our courts, either at law or in equity, cannot be invoked in aid of one showing a violation of the law to . . . secure to the violator the fruits of his outlawry." * * *

In these cases, a wrongdoer has sought the aid of the courts to recover from a third party property he had unambiguously possessed. The third party has neither been the owner nor claimed under the owner. But neither has he been a wrongdoer. Often the third party has been a governmental agency or a stakeholder. In such situations, the possessors have invoked the doctrine that the law looks no further than the fact of prior physical possession. The courts, however, have rejected the doctrine and instead have applied fundamental concepts of morality and fair dealing to deny the possessor's claim. The recurring theme found in the resulting case law is this: What a man has acquired illegally he cannot replevy.

* * *

The common policy justification for denying the wrongful possessor's claim is simple and pervasive in the case law: courts should not allow wrongdoers to take advantage of judicial resources. The policy is based upon what courts characterize as "the dignity of the law," and it is much the same policy that also has resulted in the well-established rule that courts will not enforce illegal contracts. This policy prevents application of the doctrine of simple possession in replevin cases. It would require courts to sanction what they consider wrongdoing. They hold, contrary to the black letter rule, that "no court should be required to serve as paymaster of the wages of crime, or referee between thieves."[42]

Despite this seemingly conclusive rejection of the rule, recent cases exist in which American judges have invoked the doctrine that even wrongful possession deserves the protection of the law. In fact, such cases are not infrequent. Judges clearly find the doctrine useful, and research into the case law does not suggest that the rule plays no part in the current work of the courts. But its function in the decided cases normally has not been to protect possession acquired by wrongdoing. Its function has been the protection of lawful possession against inequitable claims.

The most frequent cases have involved possessors with a legitimate, but limited, interest, such as a

---

[24] Lieber v. Mohawk Arms, Inc., 64 Misc. 2d 206, 314 N.Y.S.2d 510 (Sup. Ct. 1970) * * *.

[26] Dorrell v. Clark, 90 Mont. 585, 4 P.2d 712 (1931).

[42] Stone v. Freeman, 298 N.Y. 268, 271, 82 N.E.2d 571, 572 (1948) * * *.

bailee of a chattel. If a wrongdoer takes the chattel from the bailee's possession, or damages it through negligence or design, the wrongdoer may set up bailee's lack of title as a defense. This is an attempt to escape the consequences of the defendant's acts by showing a defect in the title of someone in lawful possession. The rule of simple possession provides a sufficient answer to this plea.

In one typical case, a court permitted the state of Montana to maintain an action of replevin to recover a road roller a state employee had converted wrongfully.[46] The road roller had come into the state's possession from the federal government, and the defendant urged that the state failed to obtain authorization for the transaction under state law. He argued that title remained in the federal government, so that the state lacked the right to sue. The court, however, dismissed this argument, citing with approval Justice Holmes' views on possession. The court conceded that "the state is not the absolute owner of the disputed road roller." Nevertheless, the court held that "the controlling fact here is that the state did come into the lawful possession." Citation of the hornbook rule allowed the Montana court to treat the matter as an easy case, because the greater (wrongful possession) necessarily included the lesser (legitimate possession).

* * *

Indeed, it is noteworthy how often judges couple the recitation of the hornbook rule protecting wrongful possession with a finding that the plaintiff in the case before them had a legitimate right to the chattel. No incongruity occurs to them. Thus, one finds the rule that the law protects even wrongful possession joined with express findings that a plaintiff had acquired the chattel "in a lawful manner," or that he had held "peaceable possession of the property," or that he was "rightfully and not wrongfully entitled to the chattel." How ironic to see the doctrine of the skeptic Holmes pressed into the service of morality.

III. THE LAW OF FINDERS

Cases involving finders of lost or abandoned chattels provide a second test of the status of wrongful possession. They make a particularly good test, since very often the only claims that arise in finders cases are possessory claims. In these cases, courts must concentrate upon the circumstances under which the finder's simple possession ought to prevail over everyone but the true owner. Moreover, the cases are valuable because they take a uniform position on the issue of wrongful possession. Although the law of finders contains contradictory decisions and artificial distinctions, the cases are consistent on the subject of wrongful possession.

Most finders cases do not involve two wrongful possessors. The paradigmatic case represented by *Anderson* is not at issue. Instead, the typical case involves a person who discovers a lost chattel while on property where he has a right to be and takes the chattel into his control. *Armory v. Delamirie*,[58] the leading English case, arose in just such a situation. The chimney-sweep's boy found a jewel while cleaning a chimney. The court held the boy was entitled "to keep it against all but the rightful owner."[59] Today, cases of underwater divers who have discovered treasure in old ships sunk off the American coast have raised the same legal questions and most have reached the same result. Courts have awarded possessory rights to the divers who first reduced sunken treasure to their unequivocal control. In such cases, no serious competing claims emerge at the time of finding because the goods have been abandoned. Moreover, the finder has done nothing wrong by seeking out the treasure. His initiative, labor, and pluck rather deserve praise. Courts, therefore, find it easy to invoke the doctrine that the mere possessor has valid rights against everyone but the chattel's owner.

When the facts become more tangled, however, the limitations of the hornbook rule appear. Nothing changes the reaction of courts more quickly than wrongdoing on the part of the finder. Thus, courts have held that one cannot become the "finder" of a book of traveller's checks, or of shopping carts left in the vicinity of a supermarket, because the "finder" could have ascertained quite easily that another person had a good claim to them. The "finder" is a wrongdoer. The same holding is reached when the discovery occurs in the course of a trespass. The wrongfulness of the trespass disqualifies the "finder" from claiming the item discovered. Of one such "self-confessed thief," an Ohio judge remarked that "to talk of his 'finding' the money under the circumstances is just pure twaddle."[64] * * * A Pennsylvania judge, dealing with three boys who had entered an

---

[46] State ex rel. Olsen v. Sundling, 128 Mont. 596, 281 P.2d 499 (1955).

[58] 1 Str. 505, 93 Eng. Rep. 664 (K.B. 1722).

[59] * * * *[S]ee also* Hannah v. Peel, [1945] 1 K.B. 509.

[64] Niederlehner v. Weatherly, 73 Ohio App. 33, 38, 54 N.E.2d 312, 314, aff'd, 142 Ohio St. 366, 51 N.E.2d 1016 (1943).

unused building and discovered $280 made the same point. Refusing their claim as finders of the money, he held that "they should get none inasmuch as they had no business being in the building."[66] In other words, trespassers cannot "find" in any sense the law will credit.[67] It does not matter that the owner of the property has no title to the chattel. What matters in the cases is that a trespassing finder can acquire no rights in the fruits of his wrong.

* * *

Good-faith possession, therefore, has played a vital role in the finders cases. * * * Courts have shaped the law of finders to encompass this ethical factor. Judicial decisions regularly go beyond the rule of simple possession and treat wrongful possession quite differently from lawful possession. Rightful conduct is the first step in qualifying as a finder. Only when such conduct exists will American courts invoke the rule that simple possession is protected by the law.

IV. POSSESSION AND THE STATUTE OF LIMITATIONS

A third test of the rule of simple possession arises out of cases invoking the statute of limitations to defeat the rights of chattel owners. According to hornbook law, the possessor of a chattel belonging to someone else has a valid possessory interest in the chattel, which will ripen into full ownership after the passage of a statutorily fixed number of years. The law provides the owner with that period of time to reclaim the chattel, but if he fails to act within that time, title passes to the possessor by operation of law. The passage of time alone cures the defect in the possessor's title. * * * Under this view, wrongful conduct by the person claiming under the statute of limitations is irrelevant if that person has held nonpermissive possession for a sufficient length of time.

American case law has not, however, evolved quite this way. Courts have not looked simply to the fact of possession and the passage of time in deciding cases in which the statute of limitations is involved. Courts do sometimes expressly invoke the rule of simple possession as a title-clearing mechanism. It is essential that they be able to do so: otherwise the possibility of perpetually unownable property might arise. But courts rarely invoke the rule to protect the wrongful possessor. Only when other factors favoring the possessor coincide with unambiguous possession does the statute of limitations in practice convert possession into title. The working principle that best explains the pattern of case law is the distinction between clear wrongdoing and honest, if mistaken, possession.

The distinction between wrongful and honest possession lies behind the many statutes that toll the statute of limitations when the defendant fraudulently has concealed the existence of the cause of action from the owner or when the cause of action itself is based upon the defendant's fraud. American legislatures have given concrete shape to the maxim that no man should profit from his own wrong by enacting statutes precluding use of statutes of limitations when they would allow defendants to hide behind their own fraudulent acts. The thief is not the only sort of defendant caught by such statutes, but he is one of them. "Theft," said one Minnesota court, "is an aggravated case of fraud or wrong where every effort is made to conceal the property taken . . .. In such case the courts hold the statute does not start running until discovery so that legal redress may be possible against the wrongdoer."[83] The rule is based on "good morals" and "the plainest principles of justice."

Even without express statutory authorization, American courts rarely have permitted dishonest possession to ripen into title. To avoid applying the statute of limitations, courts have employed a variety of theories. One frequently invoked is equitable estoppel. Courts have held that a defendant is estopped to invoke the statute of limitations when it would enable him to take refuge behind the shield of his own wrong. Thus, when someone knowingly withholds property from its rightful owner, he will be estopped to set up the statute of limitations when the owner sues to recover the property. The flexibility of the doctrine and the incantation-like sound of the words "equitable estoppel" allow courts to set aside the plain language of the statute of limitations when the interests of justice seem to require it.

A second device used to avoid awarding title based upon wrongful possession is judicial manipulation of the phrase "accrual of the cause of action." It plausibly can be argued that no cause of action has accrued until someone has a meaningful chance to assert it. When a thief has taken personal property,

---

66 Bussler Estate, 12 B. Fiduc. 281 (1962).

67 The leading case is Barker v. Bates, 30 Mass. (13 Pick.) 255 (1832); *see also* * * * Favorite v. Miller, 176 Con. 310, 407 A.2d 974 (1978) * * *.

83 Commercial Union Ins. Co. v. Connolly, 183 Minn. 1, 5-6, 235 N.W. 634, 636 (1931).

for example, the rightful owner lacks any real chance to reclaim it. Until he discovers who has taken his property, courts hold that no cause of action has accrued within the meaning of the statute of limitations. Such an interpretation of "accrual of a cause of action" prevents dishonest possessors from successfully asserting title under the statute of limitations.

A third judicial device for evading the statute of limitations depends directly upon considerations of fairness. An early case from New Hampshire presents a typical set of facts. The plaintiff lost a pocketbook in 1871.[88] The defendant found the purse and spent the money inside, even though he knew it belonged to the plaintiff. The plaintiff discovered what had happened twelve years later and sued to recover the money appropriated. By then the statute of limitations had long since run, and the defendant set up the statute as a bar. The New Hampshire court, however, summarily rejected the defense. Even though the state had not enacted an exception to its statute of limitations for fraudulent concealment, the court held that the defendant's "willful silence" amounted to constructive fraud and "constitute[d] a sufficient answer to the plea." The defendant's possession and use of the pocketbook for the statutory period was not enough to "cure the vice" of the initially wrongful appropriation.

Although the New Hampshire case is old, its rationale has not weakened over time. A modern New Hampshire court emphatically rejected a similar plea: "It is well established that our courts will not countenance fraudulent conduct."[90] Nor is New Hampshire alone. Other American courts have continued to reject statute-of-limitations defenses when they would protect dishonest possessors. Even when the statute of limitations contains no exception for fraudulent concealment, most judges enforce the rule that it would be "shocking both in morals and to common sense" to confer title on a wrongful taker simply because he escapes detection for long enough.[92]

But this is not the whole story. American courts have found the doctrine of simple possession useful when the wrongdoer has sold the chattel to a bona fide purchaser, who subsequently holds it for the statutory period. In this situation, courts often have awarded title to the bona fide purchaser. The result certainly is correct. Clear title must be established at some future point; title eventually must pass out of the original owner. Otherwise, no one could ever gain secure title. The rule that the law protects even wrongful possession helps to make this result possible.

The clearest illustration of the rule's utility involves cases in which a wrongful taker has sold the chattel to a bona fide purchaser and the statute of limitations does contain a fraudulent concealment exception. The question in such cases becomes whether the purchaser falls within the exception. If a court holds that his possession is fraudulently concealed, title will not pass to him no matter how long he holds the chattel. It is a difficult case. On the one hand, he will very likely have "concealed" the chattel from its owner just as completely as the wrongdoer did. On the other hand, his conduct will lack the element of conscious fraud or wrongdoing that would have kept the statute of limitations from operating in favor of the original taker. Does his possession retain the character it had in the hands of the thief, or does he take a new, untainted possessory interest?

In this situation, American courts have called upon the hornbook rule of simple possession when the equities have favored the bona fide purchaser. For title to accrue to the purchaser, three things generally must exist: (1) honesty on the part of the purchaser; (2) open use by him for the statutory period; and (3) failure on the part of the owner to take reasonable steps to secure his rights. The heralded recent case of *O'Keeffe v. Snyder*[96] expressly laid down this test, although in fact the result is less innovative than the New Jersey Supreme Court announced. The test it adopted is very much like what American courts have long done in practice.

* * *

It cannot be said that the American cases involving bona fide purchasers of stolen goods have been altogether harmonious. Courts within the same jurisdiction may reach seemingly contradictory results, sometimes allowing the statute of limitations as a bar, sometimes not. Nevertheless, virtually all the cases in which courts have allowed possession to ripen into title have involved good-faith takers of the property. There must be a title-clearing mechanism for chattels, and the bona fide purchase largely serves that function. The evident wrongdoer, the out-and-out thief, and the willful defrauder cannot set up the statute of limitations as a defense to actions brought to recover the chattel or its value. * * * [I]t is not the

---

[88] Quimby v. Blackey, 63 N.H. 77 (1884).

[90] Lakeman v. La France, 102 N.H. 300, 303, 156 A.2d 123, 126 (1959).

[92] Lightfoot v. Davis, 198 N.Y. 261, 267, 91 N.E. 582, 584 (1910) * * *.

[96] 83 N.J. 478, 416 A.2d 862 (1980).

simple passage of years that cures the "vice" of wrongful possession. It is honesty.

* * *

VI. CONCLUSION

* * *

The conclusion that emerges from the accumulation of evidence, therefore, is that a gap exists between the decided cases and the hornbook rule that possession of chattels, however acquired, prevails against anyone but the rightful owner. First, ordinary statements of the rule exaggerate the frequency of disputes between two wrongdoers. Most cases involving purely possessory claims are not like *Anderson v. Gouldberg*. Second, when possessory claims arise in litigation, courts regularly reject them if they stem from wrongful possession. Courts examine the quality of possession as well as the fact of possession. Third, the most common use of the hornbook rule in judicial opinions has been to permit courts to disregard technical flaws in one person's title when those flaws might permit a wrongful possessor to prevail. Without recognizing the apparent incongruity, American courts have used an apparently amoral rule to buttress moral claims.

In light of this gap between theory and practice, the hornbook rule of simple possession should be qualified as a statement of the law normally applied by modern American courts. The paradigmatic case of two equally guilty possessors has arisen so rarely, and the unwillingness on the part of judges to close their eyes to ethical considerations has been so persistent, that flat statements of the rule can easily mislead. The attempt to remove morality from the law of possession simply has not "fit the facts" of many cases decided since Holmes wrote in 1892.

On the other hand, the doctrine of simple possession itself surely could not be abandoned without real inconvenience. Courts have applied it in contests between equal wrongdoers and cited it in other situations too frequently to suggest that commentators should give it up. In actual litigation, however, the rule admits of an exception when the prior possessor of a chattel is a wrongdoer and the other litigant is not. In such cases, courts regularly have preferred the merit of honest conduct to the logic of the rule of simple possession. The exception to the rule has arisen often enough that commentators should now recognize its existence.

Note

Helmholz argues that most cases involving the first possession rule are decided on moral grounds: those wrongfully taking possession may not claim rights against prior possessors. In *Anderson v. Gouldberg*, Anderson cut down the logs from the land of another before Gouldberg took the timber. May Anderson, a trespasser, make any claim that he is morally superior to Gouldberg? If not, why not require Gouldberg to make payment for the value of the logs he took, but tender the funds to the true owner of the logs rather than to Anderson? Or, alternatively, why not require Gouldberg to pay the value of the logs to the state?

Carol M. Rose, *Possession as the Origin of Property*, 52 U. Chi. L. Rev. 73–79, 81–88 (1985)*

How do things come to be owned? This is a fundamental puzzle for anyone who thinks about property. One buys things from other owners, to be sure, but how did the other owners get those things? Any chain of ownership or title must have a first link. Someone had to do something to anchor that link. The law tells us what steps we must follow to obtain ownership of things, but we need a theory that tells us why these steps should do the job.

John Locke's view, once described as "the standard bourgeois theory,"[1] is probably the one most familiar to American students. Locke argued that an original owner is one who mixes his or her labor with a thing and, by commingling that labor with the thing, establishes ownership of it.[2] This labor theory is appealing because it appears to rest on "desert," but it has some problems. First, without a prior theory of ownership, it is not self-evident that one owns even the labor that is mixed with something else. Second, even if one does own the labor that one performs, the labor theory provides no guidance in determining the scope of the right that one establishes by mixing one's labor with something else. Robert Nozick illustrates this problem with a clever hypothetical. Suppose I pour a can of tomato juice into the ocean: do I now own the seas?[5]

A number of thinkers more or less contemporary to Locke proposed another theory of the basis of ownership. According to this theory, the original owner got title through the consent of the rest of humanity (who were, taken together, the first recipients from God, the genuine original owner).[6] Locke himself identified the problems with this theory; they involve what modern law-and-economics writers would call "administrative costs." How does everyone get together to consent to the division of things among individuals?

The common law has a third approach, which shares some characteristics with the labor and consent theories but is distinct enough to warrant a different label. For the common law, possession or "occupancy" is the origin of property. This notion runs through a number of fascinating old cases with which teachers of property law love to challenge their students. Such inquiries into the acquisition of title to wild animals and abandoned treasure may seem purely academic; how often, after all, do we expect to get into disputes about the ownership of wild pigs or long-buried pieces of eight? These cases are not entirely silly, though. People still do find treasure-laden vessels, and statesmen do have to consider whether someone's acts might support a claim to own the moon, for example, or the mineral nodes at the bottom of the sea. Moreover, analogies to the capture of wild animals show up time and again when courts have to deal on a nonstatutory basis with some "fugitive" resource that is being reduced to property for the first time, such as oil, gas, groundwater, or space on the spectrum of radio frequencies.

With these more serious claims in mind, then, I turn to the maxim of the common law: first possession is the root of title. Merely to state the proposition is to raise two critical questions: what counts as possession, and why is it the basis for a claim to title? In exploring the quaint old cases' answers to these questions, we hit on some fundamental views about the nature and purposes of a property regime.

Consider *Pierson v. Post*,[16] a classic wild-animal case from the early nineteenth century. Post was hunting a fox one day on an abandoned beach and almost had the beast in his gunsight when an interloper appeared, killed the fox, and ran off with the carcass. The indignant Post sued the interloper for the value of the fox on the theory that his pursuit of the fox had established his property right to it.

---

[1] Richard Schlatter, Private Property: The History of an Idea 151 (1951).

[2] John Locke, *Second Treatise of Government* § 25, in Two Treatises of Government 327 (P. Laslett rev. ed. 1960) (1st ed. London 1690).

[5] Robert Nozick, Anarchy, State and Utopia 175 (1974). The example rests on the argument that Locke's labor theory of property means that one acquires property by mixing what one owns (one's labor) with what one does not own. Nozick substitutes the can of tomato juice for one's labor.

[6] See, e.g., Hugo Grotius, On the Law of War and Peace bk. 2, ch. 2, PP 1, 4–5 (Kelsey trans. 1925) (1st ed. Amsterdam 1646) * * *.

[16] 3 Cai. R. 175 (N.Y. Sup. Ct. 1805).

The court disagreed. It cited a long list of learned authorities to the effect that "occupancy" or "possession" went to the one who killed the animal, or who at least wounded it mortally or caught it in a net. These acts brought the animal within the "certain control" that gives rise to possession and hence a claim to ownership.

Possession thus means a clear act, whereby all the world understands that the pursuer has "an unequivocal intention of appropriating the animal to his individual use." A clear rule of this sort should be applied, said the court, because it prevents confusion and quarreling among hunters (and coincidentally makes the judges' task easier when hunters do get into quarrels).

The dissenting judge commented that the best way to handle this matter would be to leave it to a panel of sportsmen, who presumably would have ruled against the interloper. In any event, he noted that the majority's rule would discourage the useful activity of fox hunting: who would bother to go to all the trouble of keeping dogs and chasing foxes if the reward were up for grabs to any "saucy intruder"? If we really want to see that foxes don't overrun the countryside, we will allocate a property right—and thus the ultimate reward—to the hunter at an earlier moment, so that he will undertake the useful investment in keeping hounds and the useful labor in flushing the fox.

The problem with assigning "possession" prior to the kill is, of course, that we need a principle to tell us when to assign it. Shall we assign it when the hunt begins? When the hunter assembles his dogs for the hunt? When the hunter buys his dogs?[21]

Pierson thus presents two great principles, seemingly at odds, for defining possession: (1) notice to the world through a clear act, and (2) reward to useful labor. The latter principle, of course, suggests a labor theory of property. The owner gets the prize when he "mixes in his labor" by hunting. On the other hand, the former principle suggests at least a weak form of the consent theory: the community requires clear acts so that it has the opportunity to dispute claims, but may be thought to acquiesce in individual ownership where the claim is clear and no objection is made.

On closer examination, however, the two positions do not seem so far apart. In *Pierson*, each side acknowledged the importance of the other's principle. Although the majority decided in favor of a clear rule, it tacitly conceded the value of rewarding useful labor. Its rule for possession would in fact reward the original hunter most of the time, unless we suppose that the woods are thick with "saucy intruders." On the other side, the dissenting judge also wanted some definiteness in the rule of possession. He was simply insisting that the acts that sufficed to give notice should be prescribed by the relevant community, namely hunters or "sportsmen." Perhaps, then, there is some way to reconcile the clear-act and reward-to-labor principles.

The clear-act principle suggests that the common law defines acts of possession as some kind of *statement*. As Blackstone said, the acts must be a *declaration* of one's intent to appropriate.[23] This possibility is illustrated in a later nineteenth-century case involving possession of land. *Brumagim v. Bradshaw*[24] involved two claimants to a considerable amount of land that had become, by the time the litigation was brought, the residential and commercial Potrero district of San Francisco. Each party claimed ownership of the land through a title extending back to an original "possessor" of the land, and the issue was whether the first of these purported possessors, one George Treat, had really "possessed" the land at all. If he had not, his successors in interest could not claim ownership through him, and title would go to those claiming through a later "first possessor."

Those who claimed through Treat put a number of facts before the jury to establish his original possession. They noted particularly that Treat had repaired a fence across the neck of the Potrero peninsula—to which the other side rejoined that outsiders could still land in boats, and that, in any event, there was a gap in the fence. The Treat claimants also alleged that Treat had made use of the land by pasturing livestock on it—though the other side argued that the land had not been suitable for cattle even then,

[21] For a similar problem concerning ownership of oil and gas, having to do with uncertainties about the point at which to attribute "possession" to one who claims a fugitive resource, compare Hammonds v. Central Ky. Natural Gas Co., 255 Ky. 685, 689, 75 S.W.2d 204, 206 (1934) (gas withdrawn from earth and then pumped back for storage is comparable to animal returned to wild and may thus be tapped by a neighbor), with Westmoreland & Cambria Natural Gas Co. v. DeWitt, 130 Pa. 235, 250, 18 A. 724, 725 (1889) (oil and gas in the ground are "possessed" if all equipment is in place to tap at any time).

[23] 2 William Blackstone, Commentaries on the Laws of England, at *9, *258.

[24] 39 Cal. 24 (1870).

because San Francisco was expanding in that direction. The court ruled that the jury should decide whether Treat's acts gave sufficient notice to the public that he had appropriated the property. If so, he had "possessed" it and could pass it on as an owner.

This instruction would seem to come down clearly on the side of the "clear act" theory of possession. Yet that theory seems to leave out some elements of the evidence. The fence question, to be sure, bore on whether Treat's acts informed the public of his claim. But the parties' arguments over whether Treat's use was "suitable" seemed to reflect concern over an aim of rewarding useful labor. If suitable use were a relevant issue, why did the court's jury instruction ignore the value of rewarding labor?

The answer to this question may well be that suitable use is also a form of notice. If outsiders would think that a large area near a growing city was abandoned because it was vacant except for a few cows, they might enter on the land and claim some prime waterfront footage for themselves. In other words, if the use that Treat made was unsuitable, his use would not give notice of his claim to others. Thus, to ask whether Treat used the land suitably is just another way of asking whether he informed others of his claim, particularly those others who might have been interested in buying the land from Treat or settling it for themselves. Society is worst off in a world of vague claims; if no one knows whether he can safely use the land, or from whom he should buy it if it is already claimed, the land may end up being used by too many people or by none at all.

Possession now begins to look even more like something that requires a kind of communication, and the original claim to the property looks like a kind of speech, with the audience composed of all others who might be interested in claiming the object in question. Moreover, some venerable statutory law obligates the acquiring party to keep on speaking, lest he lose his title by "adverse possession."

Adverse possession is a common law interpretation of statutes of limitation for actions to recover real property. Suppose I own a lot in the mountains, and some stranger to me, without my permission, builds a house on it, clears the woods, and farms the lot continuously for a given period, say twenty years. During that time, I am entitled to go to court to force him off the lot. But if I have not done so at the end of twenty years, or some other period fixed by statute, not only can I not sue him for recovery of what was my land, but the law recognizes him as the title owner. The doctrine of adverse possession thus operates to transfer property to one who is initially a trespasser if the trespasser's presence is open to everyone, lasts continuously for a given period of time, and if the title owner takes no action to get rid of him during that time.

Here again we seem to have an example of a reward to the useful laborer at the expense of the sluggard. But the doctrine is susceptible to another interpretation as well; it might be designed, not to reward the useful laborer, but to require the owner to assert her right publicly. It requires her to make it clear that she, and not the trespasser, is the person to deal with if anyone should wish to buy the property or use some portion of it.

* * *

Why, then, is it so important that property owners make and keep their communications clear? Economists have an answer: clear titles facilitate trade and minimize resource-wasting conflict. If I am careless about who comes on to a corner of my property, I invite others to make mistakes and to waste their labor on improvements to what I have allowed them to think is theirs. I thus invite a free-for-all over my ambiguously held claims, and I encourage contention, insecurity, and litigation—all of which waste everyone's time and energy and may result in overuse or underuse of resources. But if I keep my property claims clear, others will know that they should deal with me directly if they want to use my property. We can bargain rather than fight; through trade, all items will come to rest in the hands of those who value them most. If property lines are clear, then, anyone who can make better use of my property than I can will buy or rent it from me and turn the property to his better use. In short, we will all be richer when property claims are unequivocal, because that unequivocal status enables property to be traded and used at its highest value.[39]

Thus, it turns out that the common law of first possession, in rewarding the one who communicates a claim, does reward useful labor; the useful labor is

---

[39] See RICHARD POSNER, ECONOMIC ANALYSIS OF LAW 27-31 (2d ed. 1977). For critiques of this analysis, see Kennedy & Michelman, *Are Property and Contract Efficient?*, 8 HOFSTRA L. REV. 711, 717-20 (1980); Michelman, *Ethics, Economics and the Law of Property*, 24 NOMOS 3 (1982); for critiques of these two articles, respectively, see Baker, *Starting Points in Economic Analysis of Law*, 8 HOFSTRA L. REV. 939, 957-65 (1980); Demsetz, *Professor Michelman's Unnecessary and Futile Search for the Philosopher's Touchstone*, 24 NOMOS 41 (1982).

the very act of speaking clearly and distinctly about one's claims to property. Naturally, this must be in a language that is understood, and the acts of "possession" that communicate a claim will vary according to the audience. Thus, returning to *Pierson v. Post*, the dissenting judge may well have thought that fox hunters were the only relevant audience for a claim to the fox; they are the only ones who have regular contact with the subject matter. By the same token, the mid-nineteenth century California courts gave much deference to the mining-camp customs in adjudicating various Gold Rush claims; the Forty-Niners themselves, as those most closely involved with the subject, could best communicate and interpret the signs of property claims and would be particularly well served by a stable system of symbols that would enable them to avoid disputes.

The point, then, is that "acts of possession" are, in the now fashionable term, a "text," and that the common law rewards the author of that text. But, as students of hermeneutics know, the clearest text may have ambiguous subtexts. In connection with the text of first possession, there are several subtexts that are especially worthy of note. One is the implication that the text will be "read" by the relevant audience at the appropriate time. It is not always easy to establish a symbolic structure in which the text of first possession can be "published" at such a time as to be useful to anyone. Once again, *Pierson v. Post* illustrates the problem that occurs when a clear sign (killing the fox) comes only relatively late in the game, after the relevant parties may have already expended overlapping efforts and embroiled themselves in a dispute. Very similar problems occurred in the whaling industry in the nineteenth century: the courts expended a considerable amount of mental energy in finding signs of "possession" that were comprehensible to whalers from their own customs and that at the same time came early enough in the chase to allow the parties to avoid wasted efforts and the ensuing mutual recriminations.

* * *

There is a second and perhaps even more important subtext to the "text" of first possession: the tacit supposition that there is such a thing as a "clear act," unequivocally proclaiming to the universe one's appropriation—that there are in fact unequivocal acts of possession, which any relevant audience will naturally and easily interpret as property claims. Literary theorists have recently written a great deal about the relativity of texts. They have written too much for us to accept uncritically the idea that a "text" about property has a natural meaning independent of some audience constituting an "interpretive community" or independent of a range of other "texts" and cultural artifacts that together form a symbolic system in which a given text must be read. It is not enough, then, for the property claimant to say simply, "It's mine" through some act or gesture; in order for the "statement" to have any force, some relevant world must understand the claim it makes and take that claim seriously.

Thus, in defining the acts of possession that make up a claim to property, the law not only rewards the author of the "text"; it also puts an imprimatur on a particular symbolic system and on the audience that uses this system. Audiences that do not understand or accept the symbols are out of luck. For *Pierson's* dissenting judge, who would have made the definition of first possession depend on a decision of hunters, the rule of first possession would have put the force of law behind the mores of a particular subgroup. The majority's "clear act" rule undoubtedly referred to a wider audience and a more widely shared set of symbols. But even under the majority's rule, the definition of first possession depended on a particular audience and its chosen symbolic context; some audiences win, others lose.

In the history of American territorial expansion, a pointed example of the choice among audiences made by the common law occurred when one group did not play the approved language game and refused to get into the business of publishing or reading the accepted texts about property. The result was one of the most arresting decisions of the early American republic: *Johnson v. McIntosh*,[49] a John Marshall opinion concerning the validity of opposing claims to land in what is now a large part of Illinois and Indiana. The plaintiffs in this case claimed through Indian tribes, on the basis of deeds made out in the 1770's; the defendants claimed under titles that came from the United States. The Court found for the defendants, holding that the claims through the Indians were invalid, for reasons derived largely from international law rather than from the law of first possession. But tucked away in the case was a first-possession argument that Marshall passed over. The Indians, according to an argument of the claimants from the United States, could not have passed title to the opposing side's predecessors because, "[b]y the law

---

[49] 21 U.S. (8 Wheat.) 543 (1823).

of nature," the Indians themselves had never done acts on the land sufficient to establish property in it. That is to say, the Indians had never really undertaken those acts of possession that give rise to a property right.

Although Marshall based his decision on other grounds, there was indeed something to the argument from the point of view of the common law of first possession. Insofar as the Indian tribes moved from place to place, they left few traces to indicate that they claimed the land (if indeed they did make such claims). From an eighteenth-century political economist's point of view, the results were horrifying. What seemed to be the absence of distinct claims to land among the Indians merely invited disputes, which in turn meant constant disruption of productive activity and dissipation of energy in warfare. Uncertainty as to claims also meant that no one would make any productive use of the land because there is little incentive to plant when there is no reasonable assurance that one will be in possession of the land at harvest time. From this classical economic perspective, the Indians' alleged indifference to well-defined property lines in land was part and parcel of what seemed to be their relatively unproductive use of the earth.[55]

Now it may well be that North American Indian tribes were not so indifferent to marking out landed property as eighteenth century European commentators supposed. Or it may be that at least some tribes found landed property less important to their security than other forms of property and thus felt no need to assert claims to property in land. But however anachronistic the *Johnson* parties' (ultimately mooted) argument may now seem, it is a particularly striking example of the relativity of the "text" of possession to the interpretative community for that text. It is doubtful whether the claims of any nomadic population could ever meet the common law requirements for establishing property in land. Thus, the audience presupposed by the common law of first possession is an agrarian or a commercial people—a people whose activities with respect to the objects around them require an unequivocal delineation of lasting control so that those objects can be managed and traded.

But perhaps the deepest aspect of the common law text of possession lies in the attitude that this text strikes with respect to the relationship between human beings and nature. At least some Indians professed bewilderment at the concept of owning the land. Indeed they prided themselves on not marking the land but rather on moving lightly through it, living with the land and with its creatures as members of the same family rather than as strangers who visited only to conquer the objects of nature.[59] The doctrine of first possession, quite to the contrary, reflects the attitude that human beings are outsiders to nature. It gives the earth and its creatures over to those who mark them so clearly as to transform them, so that no one else will mistake them for unsubdued nature.

We may admire nature and enjoy wildness, but those sentiments find little resonance in the doctrine of first possession. Its texts are those of cultivation, manufacture, and development. We cannot have our fish both loose and fast, as Melville might have said,[61] and the common law of first possession makes a choice. The common law gives preference to those who convince the world that they have caught the fish and hold it fast. This may be a reward to useful labor, but it is more precisely the articulation of a specific vocabulary within a structure of symbols approved and understood by a commercial people. It

---

55 * * * From the perspective of a hunting people, however, definite property in land may seem undesirable and indeed may cause insecurity. A recent example is the series of complicated land settlements that have arisen under the Alaska Native Claims Settlement Act of 1971, 43 U.S.C. §§1601-1624 (1982). Some Native American corporations have objected to selection of specific lands as tribal property because they think this may prevent them from following the migratory herds that supply their livelihood. See Parfit, *Alaska's Natives Are Bringing Off the Biggest Corporate Takeover*, SMITHSONIAN MAG., Aug. 1981, at 30 * * *.

59 This attitude is reflected in a letter from an elderly Indian chief to President Franklin Pierce in 1855, described in C. HAAR & LIEBMAN, PROPERTY AND LAW 15 (1977). After stating that the Indians did not see the land as something to be owned, the letter went on: "We know that white man does not understand our ways[,] . . . for he is a stranger who comes in the night and takes from the land whatever he needs. The earth is not his brother but his enemy, and when he has conquered it he moves on." * * *.

61 HERMAN MELVILLE, MOBY DICK ch. 89 ("Fast-Fish and Loose-Fish") (1st ed. London 1851). This chapter describes some litigation over ownership of a whale that had been harpooned but got away, harpoon and all, only to be harpooned and taken by a second crew. The legal question involved the point at which the whale stopped being a "loose-fish" and became a "fast-fish"—that is, the point at which the whale became someone's property. Melville goes on to describe a number of items (including serfs and mortgages) as "fast-fish" and a number of other items (America at Columbus' arrival, ideas, the rights of man) as "loose-fish."

is this commonly understood and shared set of symbols that gives significance and form to what might seem the quintessentially individualistic act: the claim that one has, by "possession," separated for oneself property from the great commons of unowned things.

Note

How would Helmholz describe the outcome in *Pierson v. Post*? Does your moral evaluation of the behavior of the fox hunter and interloper depend, as Rose perhaps suggests, upon the cultural meaning of notice?

Part II

Property Over Time: The Changing Perceptions of Property as a Political Institution

A. The Founding Decades

1. Property, Politics and Gender in the Early Republic

Property ownership was intimately linked with concepts of virtue and citizenship during the early years of the republic. Though not required by the Constitution, all the new states limited access to the ballot to men holding some property. In a further effort to insure that propertied men controlled the government, direct election of the United States Senate was precluded. Article I, Section 3, Clause [1] of the original Constitution provided that "The Senate of the United States shall be composed of two Senators from each State, chosen by the Legislature thereof, for six Years; and each Senator shall have one vote." Various state constitutions had similar provisions limiting membership in their legislatures to those holding property and providing for indirect election of their upper house or governor. The entire United States Senate was not directly elected until the adoption of the 17th Amendment in 1913.

These governing structures were in part justified by an ideology of republicanism linking attainment of appropriate civic virtues to the ownership of property. Thus the landless, paupers, women and children, who depended upon others for their well being, lacked the free will necessary for making political decisions. The close ties between property ownership and the ballot began to loosen shortly after the Constitution took effect. Despite this change, the ideological connections between ownership and civic responsibility live on today.

The excerpts below include an analysis of Thomas Jefferson's theories of property and republicanism by Stanley Katz, an excerpt from a letter written by John Adams on the reasons for excluding women from then standard definitions of republican citizenship, a review by Robert Steinfeld of the early movement to reduce property limitations on the franchise, and a modern critique of the inherent inequalities built into property based definitions of citizenship by Jennifer Nedelsky. For further reading, *see* Frank Michelman, *Tutelary Jurisprudence and Constitutional Property*, in LIBERTY, PROPERTY AND THE FUTURE OF CONSTITUTIONAL DEVELOPMENT (Ellen Frankel Paul and Howard Dickman, eds.) 127 (1990); FORREST MCDONALD, NOVUS ORDO SECLORUM: THE INTELLECTUAL ORIGINS OF THE CONSTITUTION (1985); Elizabeth Mensch, *The Colonial Origins of Liberal Property Rights*, 31 BUFF. L. REV. 635 (1982).

Stanley N. Katz, *Thomas Jefferson and the Right to Property in Revolutionary America*, 19 J. L. & ECON. 467, 474–476, 479–488 (1976)*

In the early stages of his career Jefferson was firmly wedded to the notion that land ownership and the tilling of one's own soil was not only good economics but good politics. It was only by independent labor * * * that a man could divest himself of subordination to superiors and cultivate that inner strength upon which republicanism depended. As Jefferson wrote to John Jay in 1785:

> Cultivators of the earth are the most valuable citizens. They are the most vigorous, the most independent, the most virtuous, and they are tied to their country and wedded to it's liberty and interests by the most lasting bands. As long therefore as they can find emploiment in this line, I would not convert them into mariners, artisans or any thing else.

Jefferson is here operating in the context of John Locke's theory of private property, according to which the earth and its fruits were given to mankind in common but a man's person and labor were his alone, and his property was whatever he produced by dint of his personal labor. * * *

According to Locke man extracts his property from a common stock.[18] * * * Locke imposed two limitations upon man's capacity to appropriate property to himself: first, there must be "enough, and as good left in common for others" and second, no one must take more than he can use. Locke recognized that these limitations were significant in the context of English society, but he speculated that conditions might be far different across the Atlantic. He argued that where growing population and "the use of Money" rendered land scarce the limitations on property holding might prove oppressive, but where land abounded and there was little commerce:

> there Men will not be apt to enlarge their Possessions of Land, were it never so rich, never so free for them to take. For I ask, What would a Man value Ten Thousand, or an Hundred Thousand Acres of excellent Land, ready cultivated, and well stocked too with Cattle, in the middle of the in-land parts of *America*, where he had no hopes of Commerce with other Parts of the World, to draw Money to him by the Sale of the Product? It would not be worth the enclosing, and we should see him give up again to the wild Common of Nature whatever was more than would supply the Conveniences of Life to be had there for him and his family. Thus in the beginning all the World was *America*.

Jefferson frequently expressed himself in similar terms. * * * [F]or Jefferson, America was the perfect environment for the operation of the Lockeian theory of property shorn of its limitations, for in America the endless abundance of land in the inexhaustible continent rendered it unthinkable that either more accumulation or unavailability could deprive each man of his due share of the natural stock of plenty. But we must remember that for Jefferson it was not so much the provision for one's natural wants, although that was obviously important, but the maintenance of a moral standard which was the most important product of a society composed of small, free holding farmers. It was the virtue and judgment produced by such independent labor that rendered them capable of becoming republicans, and therefore rendered America capable of republican government.

This is as good a moment as any to explain that Jefferson rationalized the existence of slavery in his early political theory largely by ignoring the problem. His best suggestion, in the *Notes*, was that emancipated slaves should be colonized in "other parts of the world," since he believed that: "Deep rooted prejudices entertained by the whites; ten thousand recollections, by the blacks, of the injuries they have sustained; new provocations; the real distinctions which nature has made . . . will divide us into parties, and produce convulsions which will probably never end but in the extermination of the one or the other race." He would also doubtless have agreed with his friend St. George Tucker who, in 1806, declared that the preamble of the Declaration of Independence was framed with a "cautious eye" to the subject of slavery, "and was meant to embrace the case of free

[18] JOHN LOCKE, TWO TREATISES OF GOVERNMENT, bk. II, ch. 5, par. 26–27, at 185 (1698).

citizens, or aliens only; and not by a side wind to overturn the rights of property. . . ."

* * *

Jefferson * * * [saw a] symbiotic relationship between the wide accessibility of arable land, the prevention of undue aggregations of landed property, and the close relationship of government to the governed. It was to secure such ends that Jefferson proposed legislation in 1776 in his effort to secure the Revolution by rooting out the last vestiges of the entrenched aristocracy and footing the new government on a broad and propertied base. * * *

Jefferson's reasoning about property might have carried him much further than it did. His point was that republicanism required a wide distribution of land and that in America with its apparently endless resources of landed wealth, the problem was primarily one of distributing unallocated lands in small parcels. While some of his reforms, such as the abolition of primogeniture and entail, would have the long range result of winnowing down the extent of the great landed estates, he did not propose anything which would immediately have a destructive impact on existing property holdings. His general sympathies, and his labor theory of property, might, however, have carried farther in the direction of redistribution, and so they did for a brief moment in his career. The occasion was his visit to France during the 1780's, when he for the first time experienced the impact of the property rules of the Old Regime on a society which lacked America's unsettled frontier. In a famous letter of October 1785 written from Fontainebleau, Jefferson mused on the inequality of the European division of property, which he thought "absolutely concentered in a very few hands. . . ." He attributed European poverty to the fact that the nobility had enclosed great tracts of land and withdrawn them from production "mostly for the sake of game."

He remarked that the abolition of primogeniture would be one way of moving toward this result, as would progressive taxation: ". . . to exempt all from taxation below a certain point, and to tax the higher portions of property in geometrical progression as they rise." He concluded:

> Whenever there is in any country, uncultivated lands and unemployed poor, it is clear that the laws of property have been so far extended as to violate natural right. The earth is given as a common stock for man to labour and live on. If, for the encouragement of industry we allow it to be appropriated, we must take care that other employment be furnished to those excluded from the appropriation. If we do not the fundamental right to labour the earth returns to the unemployed. It is too soon yet in our country to say that every man who cannot find employment but who can find uncultivated land, shall be at liberty to cultivate it, paying a moderate rent. But it is not too soon to provide by every possible means that as few as possible shall be without a little portion of land. The small landholders are the most precious part of a state.

This was the same line of thought which later led Jefferson to try out on Madison the proposition which he supposed to be ". . . self evident, '*that the earth belongs in usufruct to the living.* '" * * * [B]ut Jefferson never pursued the thought after his return to the United States in 1789.

There were probably two reasons why Jefferson did not espouse such a radical, redistributive line of thought. In the first place, it ran squarely athwart one of the cardinal principles of his political thinking, namely, that the state should exercise no more than the minimum powers necessary to maintain social order. Taxation, confiscation or any other broadly redistributive program would necessitate precisely the kind of governmental action which Jefferson was pledged to avoid. Second, and probably more important, Jefferson did not think that such radical surgery upon the body politic was necessary. For, in a country in which all men had land upon which they could labor and in which they participated freely in governmental process, redistribution was not necessary. We can understand this best by a brief examination of the assumptions which underlay the republican thinking of Jefferson and his contemporaries.

* * * American revolutionaries were committed to the idea that the public good, the people's welfare, was the end of government and it was axiomatic for them that freedom of political participation in representative assemblies was the best way to achieve public good in a free government. Republicans, did, of course, believe in a government which included an executive and an upper house, but they had confidence that a properly constructed government would promise a new era of stability and cooperation between rulers and ruled in spite of their personal experience of the incredible turbulence of eighteenth-century American politics.

At the heart of this faith was the assumption that the people, especially when set against their rulers, were a homogeneous body whose interests when candidly considered are one. * * * The corollary to this line of thinking was that organized political parties were inimical to the public interest and in fact signs of ill-health in a republican society. On the contrary, the republican assumption was that political representatives would act in an entirely disinterested spirit.

* * *

But Americans were realistic enough to perceive that republicanism created a severe theoretical problem—the nature of obedience in a political state. Obedience was of course not a problem in the monarchical system under which they had lived, for English political theory demanded obedience to the Crown in Parliament, and British government had clear sanctions for enforcing its authority. In a republic, however, where authority came from below, obedience would have to be self-imposed, since government was explicitly denied any coercive principle existing independently of popular sovereignty. * * *

The republican conundrum was thus how to change the flow of authority, from top-down to bottom-up; the republican solution was that obedience must be internalized.

> . . . each man must somehow be persuaded to submerge his personal wants into the greater good of the whole. This willingness of the individual to sacrifice his private interests for the good of the community—such patriotism or love of country—the eighteenth century termed "public virtue."[38]

This notion of public virtue was at the core of republican political thought, and it in turn rested on the assumption that individuals living in a republican society would be willing to exercise a highly self-conscious form of self-restraint, subordinating their private interests to the good of the state. The basic premise of republicanism was thus the assertion, astonishing to modern ears, that "Once men correctly perceived their relation to the commonwealth they would never injure what was really their personal interest to protect and sustain." Republicanism thus rested on public virtue, which in turn rested on private virtue, which itself rested upon the faith that individuals could bring themselves to subordinate their narrow self-interest to the interest of the community at large.

* * *

I hope it is also clear from the preceding discussion that widespread landholding and the predominance of farming in the economy might well be seen as essential to republicanism, as it was precisely this sort of individual industry which produced the virtue upon which the republican state depended. Jefferson was not the only one to perceive this connection. * * * Innumerable examples of this connection between property, virtue, and republicanism could be cited, although most of them appear in the very early years of the Revolution, for the truth of the matter is that pure republican theory had only a very brief moment of triumph in America. The years 1776–1787 may be thought of as the republican years, although by the early 80's, under the pressure of depression and despair at the seeming ineffectiveness of the government under the Articles of Confederation, the forces of American political realism began to reassess the social situation and to develop the principles upon which the constitution of 1787 and the modern American political tradition were to be founded. Seventeen-seventy-six in particular, and the late 1770's in general, constituted the "Jeffersonian moment" in American history.

Of course, one immediately associates Alexander Hamilton with the more modern view, but it is worth pointing out that the former republican and Jefferson's close friend James Madison also rejected the tenets of pure republicanism. In responding to Jefferson's plan for revision of the Virginia constitution in 1783, Madison sketched out his understanding of the relationship between property and government. He spoke of ". . . the two cardinal objects of Government, the rights of persons, and the rights of property." Arguing that the rights of persons would be protected by the lower house of the legislature and the rights of property by the upper, he stressed the need for a "middle way" to be taken.

> Give all power to property, and the indigent will be oppressed. Give it to the latter and the effect may be transposed. Give a defensive share to each and each will be secure.

* * * Madison went on to argue that a minority of citizens in a republic would be committed to the preservation of property rights, and that therefore the function of a constitution must be to protect property at that critical time of state-formation ". . . when the bulk of the people have a sufficient interest in possession or in prospect to be attached to the rights of property, without being insufficiently attached to the right of person." He thus opposed giving government over either to the rich or the poor and favored that sort of constitution which would balance rights of individuals and of property.

---

[38] GORDON S. WOOD, THE CREATION OF THE AMERICAN REPUBLIC 68–70 (1969).

At the federal convention in 1787 he returned to this theme, speculating that in the future there would be a "great majority" of Americans who would be without either landed or any other type of property. His fear was that this propertyless class ". . . will either combine under the influence of their common situation; in which case, the right of property & the public liberty, [will not be secure in their hands] or which is more probable, they will become the tools of opulence & ambition, in which case there will be equal danger on another side." This analysis led him to favor the constitution of 1787 and to give short shrift to those who believed in equality and poverty, or at least minimal possession, as the basis of republicanism. In the tenth *Federalist* he attacked republican theorists who: ". . . have erroneously supposed that by reducing mankind to a perfect equality in their political rights, they would at the same time be perfectly equalized and assimilated in their possession, their opinions, and their passions." * * *

The position was of course elaborated with even more directness and clarity by that exemplar of federalism, Alexander Hamilton.

> We may preach [he commented in 1782] till we are tired of the theme, the necessity of disinterestedness in republics, without making a single proselyte. The virtuous declaimer will neither persuade himself nor any other person to be content with a double mess of porridge, instead of a reasonable stipend for his services. We might as soon reconcile ourselves to the Spartan community of goods and wives, to their iron coin, their long beards, or their black broth. There is a total dissimulation in the circumstances, as well as the manners, of society among us; and it is as ridiculous to seek for models in the simple ages of Greece and Rome, as it would be to go in quest of them among the Hottentots and Laplanders.

Hamilton was above all a realist, and he felt that politics must come to terms with existing and potential economic and social divisions in American society. At the federal convention he noted that: "The difference of property is already great amongst us. Commerce and industry will still increase the disparity. Your government must meet this state of things, or combinations will in process of time, undermine your system." And at the New York ratifying convention in 1778, he stood republicanism upon its head:

> As riches increase and accumulate in a few hands; as luxury prevails in society; virtue will be in a greater degree considered as only a graceful appendage of wealth, and the tendency of things will be to depart from the republican standard. This is the real disposition of human nature: It is what, neither the honorable member nor myself can correct. It is a common misfortune, that awaits our state constitution, as well as all others.

* * * Here, as so often, Hamilton was following the psychological and political realism of David Hume, who had advised legislators ". . . to comply with the common bent of mankind and give it all the improvements of which it is susceptible," while warning that ". . . that policy is violent which aggrandizes the public by the poverty of individuals." The emergence of this psychological realism and the rapid destruction of the briefly flourishing revolutionary faith in republican virtue, necessitated entirely new principles for the establishment of government.

In his thoughtful analysis of this transformation, Gerald Stourzh concludes that this emerging era of Federalist political thought

> . . . asserted the primacy of the private passions for individual self-preservation, self-enrichment, and self-aggrandizement in three respects. First, on the level of psychology, these selfish passions were assumed to be fundamental to human nature. . . . Second, on the level of morality, the self-interest of the individual was made that yardstick of the public good. . . . Third, on the level of political and social theory, the private passions were believed to work to the advantage of the body politic.[50]

If Stourzh is correct, what we see after 1787 is a second revolution in American political thought occurring within the lifetime of the original revolutionary generation. The simple faith of the Jeffersonian republican in the capacity of the individual to repress his desires in deference to the common good was replaced by the notion that it was not only inevitable that individuals should pursue their own self-interest, but that indeed it was possible to construct a modern republican government in such a way that the multiplicity of private interests would in the end conduce to the general welfare. How this theory was worked out is of course principally the

---

[50] Gerald Stourzh, Alexander Hamilton and the Idea of Republican Government 73 (1970).

history of the Constitutional Convention of 1787 and of the work of the Hamiltonian Federalists in the early years of the new nation. I trust it is clear how thoroughly this modern theory of politics reverses Jeffersonian concepts about the individual right to property and about the function of property in the political process.

* * * Thomas Jefferson was able to accommodate himself to the new system and his ideas changed markedly in response to it. At the very least, he came to appreciate the political and economic advantage, if not the virtue, of commerce and urban growth, and his presidency clearly indicates that he disabused himself of the feasibility of truly minimal government, but all that came well after our brief era of revolutionary republicanism.

* * *

Americans, we have long been told, venerate Washington, love Lincoln, and remember Jefferson. In trying to understand why Jefferson remains such an ambiguous figure for us, it may be helpful to think of him in a rather unusual way. When Bernard Bailyn was at the [University of Chicago] Law School last week, he was asked by one of our students why he had chosen to write the biography of Thomas Hutchinson, the unhappy man who had been the last royal governor of Massachusetts.[52] He replied that he had fixed upon Hutchinson because he was "a loser," and went on to argue that the historical virtue in such a study was that it enabled one to imagine what the world would have been like if men such as Hutchinson had prevailed in 1776. Only by considering the historical losers, Professor Bailyn suggested, can we conceive what the alternatives were at any given moment in the past. It occurred to me, listening to this exchange, that it would be helpful to think of Thomas Jefferson as "a loser," for there is little doubt that Jefferson the republican symbolizes an alternative rejected in American history. Jefferson was, after all, the man who in the Declaration of Independence rewrote Locke's "life, liberty and property" into "life, liberty and the pursuit of happiness." It is both fascinating and a little sad to imagine what might have happened if the Jefferson of 1776 had prevailed.

---

[52] BERNARD BAILYN, THE ORDEAL OF THOMAS HUTCHINSON (1974).

Note

In *Johnson v. McIntosh,* the United States Supreme Court refused to recognize the validity of a title to land passed from a Native American to an Englishman. Is there a way of describing early nineteenth century attitudes toward land claims of Native Americans in terms of civic republicanism? What do you make of that portion of Justice Marshall's opinion in *Johnson v. McIntosh* which states that "the Indian inhabitants are to be considered merely as occupants, to be protected, indeed while in peace, in the possession of their lands, but to be deemed incapable of transferring the absolute title to others?" Would a civic republican explain the status of women and Native Americans in a similar way?

Letter From John Adams to James Sullivan, May 26, 1776, IN IX THE WORKS OF JOHN ADAMS (C. ADAMS, ED.) 375–379 (1856)

* * *

It is certin, in theory, that the only moral foundation of government is, the consent of the people. But to what extent shall we carry this principle? Shall we say that every individual in the community, old and young, male and female, as well as rich and poor, must consent, expressly, to every act of legislation? No, you will say, this is impossible. How, then, does the right arise in the majority to govern the minority, against their will? Whence arises the right of the men to govern the women, without their consent? Whence the right of the old to bind the young, without theirs?

But let us first suppose that the whole community, of every age, rank, sex, and condition, has a right to vote. This community is assembled. A motion is made, and carried by a majority of one voice. The minority will not agree to this. Whence arises the right of the majority to govern, and the obligation of the minority to obey?

From necessity, you will say, because there can be no other rule.

But why exclude women?

You will say, because their delicacy renders them unfit for practice and experience in the great businesses of life, and the hardy enterprises of war, as well as the arduous cares of state. Besides, their attention is so much engaged with the necessary nurture of their children, that nature has made them fittest for domestic cares. And children have not judgment or will of their own. True. But will not these reasons apply to others? Is it not equally true, that men in general, in every society, who are wholly destitute of property, are also too little acquainted with public affairs to form a right judgment, and too dependent upon other men to have a will of their own? If this is a fact, if you give to every man who has no property, a vote, will you not make a fine encouraging provision for corruption, by your fundamental law? Such is the frailty of the human heart, that very few men who have no property, have any judgment of their own. They talk and vote as they are directed by some man of property, who has attached their minds to his interest. * * *

[P]ower always follows property. * * * [T]he balance of power in a society, accompanies the balance of property in land. The only possible way, then of preserving the balance of power on the side of equal liberty and public virtue, is to make the acquisition of land easy to every member of society, to make a division of land into small quantities, so that the multitude may be possessed of landed estates. If the multitude is possessed of the balance of real estate, the multitude will have the balance of power, and in that case the multitude will take care of the liberty, virtue and interest of the multitude, in all acts of government. * * *

The same reasoning which will induce you to admit all men who have no property, to vote, with those who have, for those laws which affect the person, will prove that you ought to admit women and children; for, generally speaking, women and children have as good judgments, and as independent minds, as those men who are wholly destitute of property; these last being to all intents and purposes as much dependent on others, who will please to feed, clothe, and employ them, as women are upon their husbands, or children upon their parents. * * *

Depend upon it, Sir, it is dangerous to open so fruitful a source of controversy and altercation as would be opened by attempting to alter the qualifications of votes; there will be no end of it. New claims will arise; women will demand a vote; lads from twelve to twenty-one will think their rights not enough attended to; and every man who has not a farthing, will demand an equal voice with any other, in all acts of state. It tends to confound and destroy all distinction, and prostrate all ranks to one common level.

Note

Divorce was available in very limited circumstances in most states by the first decade of the nineteenth century. Would a civic republican of that time favor divorce?

Robert J. Steinfeld, *Property and Suffrage in the Early American Republic*, 41 STAN. L. REV. 335, 337–341, 351–353, 355–357, 360–362, 364, 366–370 (1989)*

By the middle of the eighteenth century, all the American colonies save one had adopted property qualifications for the suffrage. Colonists explained the disfranchisement of the propertyless in their midst in part by observing that such people "had no wills of their own." Under colonial restrictions all the propertyless, regardless of whether they were wage earners or recipients of poor relief, occupied the same political status. After the Revolution, as many states began to enfranchise some of those who owned no property, mainly wage earners and leaseholders, under taxpaying or manhood suffrage provisions, they began simultaneously to disfranchise others such as paupers. In such states, the undifferentiated propertyless of the colonial era were being separated into two distinct categories.

Some of the propertyless would henceforth be qualified to vote, some would not. Of those who would not, it was no longer sufficient merely to say that they could not vote because, being propertyless, they "had no wills of their own." Something more had to distinguish them from the others who were being enfranchised. In other words, as some of the propertyless were enfranchised and others were explicitly disfranchised, it became necessary to redefine not only the former but also the latter. Much more was involved than the simple persistence of traditional attitudes in the new era.

As the traditional undifferentiated propertyless were divided into two groups, the new political-cultural categories of independent wage earner and dependent pauper emerged together, defining each other by mutual contrast. Whatever qualities now seemed to define paupers as dependent, it was the absence of those qualities which made it seem possible to view propertyless wage earners as independent.

It was no accident that this division of the traditional world of the propertyless began to occur at this particular moment in American history. The movement toward distinguishing among the traditional propertyless developed as one response to the contradictory legacy of the American Revolution. That legacy had left American political culture embracing fundamentally inconsistent premises. To state the dilemma in its simplest terms: On the one hand, Americans continued to adhere to the classical republican notion that only property ownership conferred independence on a man. On the other hand, they had also come to believe that "all men were by nature equally free and independent and had certain inherent and unalienable rights." One view pointed toward a world in which all men, whether or not they owned property, were assumed by nature to be free and independent, and capable of political discretion. The other assumed that the polity was divided at bottom into two groups, those who owned property and those who did not. According to this view, the propertyless should never exercise political authority precisely because they were not free and independent agents.

These two views led to contradictory visions of political order. What we must understand, however, is that at bottom most Americans simultaneously believed some version of both. New York City and Philadelphia artisans of the era may have agitated for a broadening of the suffrage on the ground that all men were by nature equally free and independent,[11] but there can be little question that most of them also believed that only property ownership conferred real independence on a man.

As Americans struggled over the question of broadening the suffrage in the decades after the Revolution, they simultaneously struggled with these deeply inconsistent premises. The division of the traditionally undifferentiated propertyless into two new categories defined as binary opposites of one another represented an accommodation of these fundamental, yet inconsistent, premises of American life.

---

[11] *See* * * * E. FONER, TOM PAINE AND REVOLUTIONARY AMERICA 142–44 (1976); S. WILENTZ, CHANTS DEMOCRATIC: NEW YORK CITY AND THE RISE OF THE AMERICAN WORKING CLASS, 1788-1850, at 65–66, 70–71 (1984); H. ROCK, ARTISANS OF THE NEW REPUBLIC: THE TRADESMEN OF NEW YORK CITY IN THE AGE OF JEFFERSON 49–51 (1979).

To fully understand the genesis of these developments, however, we must go back to an earlier point in time. We must begin by considering the position of the propertyless in early modern Anglo-American society. We must also develop an understanding of the complex connections which existed in that society between property ownership and self-government. Only then can we grasp the problem which confronted Americans as they struggled over the question of broadening the franchise. And only then can we understand the kind of answer which pauper exclusions represented.

* * *

In a comment which Americans frequently cited, Blackstone * * * wrote of the franchise that

> [t]he true reason of requiring any qualification, with regard to property, in voters, is to exclude such persons as are in so mean a situation that they are esteemed to have no will of their own. If these persons had votes, they would be tempted to dispose of them under some undue influence or other. This would give a great, an artful, or a wealthy man, a larger share in elections than is consistent with general liberty.[18]

Blackstone emphasized that those without property lacked autonomy and would inevitably fall under the sway of others. Since, in his view, only "free agents" could be allowed to vote, the propertyless could not be enfranchised.

In the colonies, John Adams expressed a nearly identical view. "Such is the frailty of the human heart," he wrote,

> that very few men who have no property, have any judgment of their own. They talk and vote as they are directed by some man of property, who has attached their minds to his interest . . .. [They are] to all intents and purposes as much dependent upon others, who will please to feed, clothe, and employ them, as women are upon their husbands, or children on their parents.[21]

But such views were also held at the other end of the eighteenth century political spectrum. Even many *radical* English whigs firmly believed that the propertyless were not fit to exercise political authority. Joseph Priestley, for example, wrote that "those who are extremely dependent should not be allowed to have votes . . . because this might . . . be only throwing more votes into the hands of those persons on whom they depend."[22]

As we now know, eighteenth century whig thought played a critical role in American political culture during the Revolutionary period. American whigs, like their English counterparts, continued to regard the politically relevant "people as a unitary, property-holding, homogeneous body—not the vile populace or rabble of the country . . .."[23] To eighteenth century whigs, in fact, property represented much more than material possessions. It represented "the attributes of a man's personality that gave him a political character."[24]

* * *

In the decades after the Revolution, most Americans accepted the idea that only people who governed themselves were entitled to claim membership in the "self governing people." People controlled and dominated by others simply could not be trusted with the important task of selecting magistrates and legislative representatives. As Gordon Wood has noted, "most of the constitution-makers in the early years of the Revolution assumed, although with increasing defensiveness, that 'sufficient discretion,' making a man 'a free agent in a political view,' was a prerequisite to the right to vote."[55]

If most Americans believed that only the free and independent should participate in self-government, they also continued to believe that only property ownership conferred genuine independence on a man. What is difficult to justify is separating political rights from economic status when both of these propositions are taken seriously. Together, these propositions point directly to the conclusion that political rights must be based on property ownership. The propertyless, because they remain dependent on and subject to the government of men who control resources, cannot be included among the truly self-governing. They will continue to be dependent on and subject to the government of the wealthy.

But the Revolution had also spawned ideas and generated movements which began to make the close identification of political rights with property owner-

---

[18] 1 W. BLACKSTONE, COMMENTARIES ON THE LAWS OF ENGLAND *171 (1765) [hereinafter COMMENTARIES]. * * *

[21] 9 J. ADAMS, THE WORKS OF JOHN ADAMS, 376–77 (C. Adams ed. 1864) (letter from John Adams to James Sullivan, May 26, 1776).

[22] J. PRIESTLEY, AN ESSAY ON THE FIRST PRINCIPLES OF GOVERNMENT, 13 (2d ed. 1771). * * *

[23] G. WOOD, THE CREATION OF THE AMERICAN REPUBLIC, 1776–1787, at 62 (1969).

[24] *Id.* at 219.

[55] *Id.* at 169.

ship deeply problematic. Almost as soon as the Revolution broke out, groups of artisans and mechanics began to agitate for suffrage reform. They claimed the maxim "[t]hat all men are by nature equally free and independent, and have certain inherent rights" for themselves. And under the banner of equality of right, they began to insist that property owning qualifications betrayed the fundamental precepts of the Revolution. But as they pressed for the separation of political rights from property ownership, claiming that all men regardless of their status were entitled to these rights, not very many of them would have denied that it was only property ownership which made a man genuinely independent. How then could men who owned no property legitimately claim the political privileges of the self-governing?

The debate over suffrage which was initiated during these years continued for decades. Its structure was relatively simple. Those who sought to maintain property qualifications appealed to the traditional view that property ownership was necessary for personal independence, and hence a prerequisite for political participation. Those who wished to replace formal property owning qualifications with taxpaying qualifications or manhood suffrage appealed to the proposition "that all men are by nature equally free and independent and have certain inherent rights."

But the suffrage reformers' task was not as straightforward as this simple contrast of positions might at first suggest. They vigorously asserted that "by nature all men are equally free and independent." But most of them did not dispute that only property ownership conferred real independence on a man. And most also agreed that the dependent should not be permitted to participate in the self-governing people, even under a broadened suffrage. As a result, when they argued for a broadened suffrage, reformers were faced with the task of reconciling underlying beliefs which appeared flatly contradictory. In order to do so, they had to offer a way of thinking about independence which did not turn on property ownership, but which recognized the indisputable fact that property ownership did bring power, and did confer a degree of personal independence. The process of accommodating these contradictory basic beliefs is the story of how the struggle to extend the suffrage produced a distinctively nineteenth century, hybrid republican-liberal regime of political rights.

* * *

In 1829, [for example,] Virginia still required that voters own freehold land. Persons had to own twenty-five acres with a twelve-foot by twelve-foot house, or unsettled land of fifty acres, to be qualified to vote. As was the case with so many of the constitutional conventions called during these post-Revolutionary decades, the suffrage quickly emerged as one of the principal issues in the 1829–30 Virginia convention.

In October, suffrage reformers presented to the convention "The Memorial of the Non-Freeholders of the City of Richmond."[62] The memorialists urged the adoption of a broader franchise. They began their argument from the first principles of post-Revolutionary political theory, including the idea that all power derived from the people, that no man deserved special privileges, and that under the great compact by which their polity was ordered, government and taxation required popular consent. Foremost among these principles, they contended, was the idea "[t]hat all men are by nature equally free and independent, and have certain inherent rights . . .."

* * *

But the Virginia reformers' appeals to abstract principles of natural equality and freedom did not mean they were arguing for universal suffrage. They were not. And that left them open to the gibes of their opponents. "[W]hy," defenders of the status quo taunted reformers, "exclude any from the right of suffrage? . . . Why are not women, and children, and paupers, admitted to the polls?" Some reformers had difficulty answering this question, suggesting only that "we are all agreed" that women, children, paupers, and slaves were not entitled to vote, and that it was inappropriate to test the principle of equality by such "extreme cases."[66]

---

[62] PROCEEDINGS AND DEBATES OF THE VIRGINIA STATE CONVENTION OF 1829–30, TO WHICH ARE SUBJOINED, THE NEW CONSTITUTION OF VIRGINIA AND THE VOTES OF THE PEOPLE 25 (Richmond 1830).

[66] *Id.* at 414. One reformer argued:

> Mr. Chairman, it has been said . . . that we derive a rule from the law of nature and the Bill of Rights, in relation to suffrage, that is in its terms universal, and that we ourselves abandon it, and thereby prove its fallacy: the females, including one half of the population, are disfranchised at one fell swoop; minors, convicts, paupers, slaves, &c., which together, compose a large majority of every community . . .. For this argument, I have a short answer; it will not do to test any rule by extreme cases. I presume it cannot be necessary for me to assign a reason for the exceptions . . . [because, after all,] [i]n the foregoing exceptions we are all agreed.

Other reformers, however, offered what they considered substantial reasons for these exclusions. They argued that the abstract proposition that "all men were by nature equally free and independent" did not mean that all people were, in fact, independent. And in good republican fashion, they affirmed that they only wished to extend the privilege of self-government to those who were independent. But their definition of independence was now quite different from the classic republican one. "[I]t is said," Mr. Cooke of Frederick declared,

> that if it be true that "all men are by nature equally free," then all men, all women, and all children, are . . . entitled to the right of suffrage . . ..
>
> Sir, no such absurdity can be inferred from the language of the Declaration of Rights. The framers of that instrument . . . did not express the self-evident truth that the Creator of the Universe, to render woman more fit for the sphere in which He intended her to act, had made her weak and timid, in comparison with man, and had thus placed her under his control, as well as under his protection. That children, also, from the immaturity of their bodies and their minds, were under a like control. They did not say . . . that the exercise of political power, that is to say, of the right of suffrage, necessarily implies free-agency and intelligence; free-agency because it consists in election or choice between different men and different measures; and intelligence, because on a judicious choice depends the very safety and existence of the community. That nature herself had therefore pronounced, on women and children, a sentence of incapacity to exercise political power. They did not say all this; and why? Because to the universal sense of all mankind, these were self-evident truths. They meant, therefore, this, and no more: that all members of a community, of mature reason, and free agents by situation, are originally and by nature, equally entitled to the exercise of political power, or a voice in the Government.[67]

This answer was particularly good because it reconciled several of the most basic premises of the reformist position. On the one hand, reformers said that the right to the suffrage "has its origin in every human being . . . it is inherent, and appertains to him in right of his existence; his person is the title deed . . ." On the other hand, they proposed to continue excluding many from the suffrage. But they were not free to argue, as the defenders of the property qualification were, that social status or economic position disqualified these kinds of persons. It was, after all, the reformers' contention that the suffrage right inhered "in every human being," that personhood "is the title deed."

A crucial part of their attack on the status quo had been that property ownership was a purely private matter, holding no significance for legal and political rights.

The suffrage reformers instead justified the continued exclusion of so many from the franchise on the basis of natural or individual incapacity. This preserved the idea that only the self governing were entitled to participate in politics, but it added a new twist. Dependence was no longer associated with propertylessness, but dictated by nature and character and embodied in legal relationships of dependence, like husband and wife, parent and child, and pauper and town. The law of nature guaranteed the suffrage to all, reformers urged, "unless it be those on whom the same natural law has pronounced judgment of disability [i.e., women and children], or those who have forfeited it by crime or profligacy . . .." It was precisely because of their perceived natural and individual disabilities that women, children, and paupers continued to be placed under the legal control of those who protected and provided for them.

* * *

Thus, the reformers noted that in a commercial society, no clear boundary between economic dependence and independence could be drawn at the property line. Very few men were completely independent, and the economic position of most was neither absolute dependence nor independence, but some relative level of economic vulnerability. In such a society, the reformers argued, the true measure of independence should be whether a man "manage[d] . . . his private affairs." In other words, the real question in separating the self-governing from the dependent should be whether a man had the legal right to dispose of himself or whether that right of control lay in another.

* * *

This new way of thinking about personal independence was plausible to many Americans in this period precisely because of the implicit and familiar contrast between people who controlled themselves

---

[67] *Id.* at 55-56.

and the many adults who still did not enjoy that right. In the relationships of "legal dependence" still common in the early nineteenth century, not only wives and children, but also paupers, lacked the right of legal disposal of their own persons. They were not self-governing, in that they were legally obligated to obey the reasonable commands of their providers. In particular, they could not dispose of their energies according to their own desires; their labor was the property of their providers.

* * *

In contrast to these legally dependent persons, those who had the legal right to control themselves, though they were otherwise propertyless, began to appear autonomous in a way which also made them appear qualified to participate in government. By this time, as we have seen, wage earners were included among the legally autonomous. They entered employment through "contracts," and were understood to retain the legal control and disposal of their own persons under all circumstances. The employment relationship no longer took the form of a legal relationship of dependence. Wage earners were no longer legally analogous to wives, children, and paupers, but stood as their binary opposites: wage earners legally autonomous; wives, children, and paupers legally dependent and bound.

* * *

As reformers won in more and more states, expanding the suffrage and bringing more working men into the political process, the idea of legal self-government as a way of understanding independence and dependence, and of allocating political rights, began to supplant the very different classical republican understanding of personal independence. In this new Jacksonian world of the nineteenth century, the crucial distinction between the independent and the dependent began to turn on whether a man legally disposed of his own labor, and supported himself and his dependents, or whether he was forced into dependence on poor relief.

* * *

These developments did not mean that wage earners had stopped believing that only property ownership made men truly independent, or that property conferred power. On the contrary, increasingly they denounced their employment as wage slavery. What these developments meant, rather, was that American culture and experience now embraced two contradictory versions of the independence/dependence distinction. One drew the line at property ownership, the other at self-ownership. In a sense, the two versions had long played roles in Anglo-American culture, but now their positions were reversed. The one, based on property ownership, which had previously been "established," was being disestablished. The other, based on self-ownership, was being established in its place.

Increasingly, political rights were being linked, even if sometimes indirectly, to self-ownership rather than to property ownership. Property ownership, in turn, was relegated to the realm of the "private." Property might confer independence and give power, but that was only a matter of private relationships between individuals in civil society. The power of property to govern was being disestablished, and by virtue of disestablishment became more difficult to see and attack. In the official realm, the realm of legal and political rights, less and less turned on property ownership. Legal autonomy and the political right of self-government were beginning to be guaranteed to virtually all men who could support themselves by their own labor.

* * *

But while this conceptual universe divorced dependence from propertylessness, it simultaneously acknowledged the intimate connection between the two, as indeed it had to, if it was to serve as a plausible depiction of social and political life. It reaffirmed the unarguable truth that property and independence were connected. But it did so by projecting this truth through the prism of a narrowed legal understanding of dependence. The propertyless were dependent only insofar as they were so utterly destitute that they had to accept public assistance. Only paupers were genuinely propertyless; they had been deprived of even the property in their own labor. The rest of the propertyless were independent, self-supporting citizens precisely because they possessed valuable property in their own labor. In the contractual realm of civil society, wage earners dealt with the propertied as full juridical equals.

Recast in this way, the indisputable truth that property ownership was necessary for self-government began to appear compatible with the proposition that all men were entitled to govern themselves. The dangerous truth that propertylessness involved subjection to other men had been partially neutralized. The utterly destitute segment of the propertyless, the genuinely dependent, were, by definition, those who had failed even to enter into contractual relationships with the propertied. Their destitution placed them entirely outside the boundaries of civil society, as wards of the public. In this form, the politically charged connection between propertylessness and subjection could be carried forward more safely. There was no possibility, however, in a universe in which all capable men were thought to be entitled to govern themselves, that the problem of property ownership could be permanently laid to rest. It was and would remain one of the most basic and intractable problems in American political culture.[103]

As the nineteenth century wore on, wage earners vigorously insisted that the power of property made them slaves to their employers. They could appeal to deeply entrenched republican beliefs to support their claims, but their argument was now more difficult and more contradictory. For decades wage-earners had argued that they merited the vote precisely because they were among the self-governing, and that they were among the self-governing because they owned and disposed of themselves. Their propertylessness, they had contended, made no difference. Having prevailed in that contention, having won the franchise, and having gained legal autonomy in the employment relationship, it became paradoxically difficult for wage-earners to argue that their propertylessness subjected them to the rule of other men.[109]

Throughout much of the nineteenth century, labor had to contend with this basic contradiction. Equally important, working men had to contend with a parallel, contradictory sense of freedom and unfreedom in their own lives. They celebrated their independence, and considered themselves free and self-governing men, even though they owned no property; and yet they also experienced their propertylessness as wage slavery. As a consequence of the "disestablishment" of property, labor found itself in the unenviable position of having to argue and live out these contradictory propositions. Together with the greater difficulty involved in "seeing" the disestablished power of property, labor's contradictory experience operated simultaneously to reinforce and bring into question the assumptions upon which the nineteenth-century social universe increasingly rested. The position of labor subtly legitimated the existing order even as it stood as testimony to its utter falsity.

---

[103] For an excellent discussion of this problem during the Civil War era, see generally D. MONTGOMERY, BEYOND EQUALITY: LABOR AND THE RADICAL REPUBLICANS, 1862–1872 (1967).

[109] Needless to say, this universe was not created unilaterally by laboring men. Rather, it was the product of a complex process which had seen laboring people achieve some of their transformative political-legal and social objectives, but fail completely to achieve others. During the Revolution, for example, radical artisans in Pennsylvania had agitated for the adoption of so-called agrarian laws. These laws would have limited the amount of property any one individual could legally accumulate. And such legislation did find support in aspects of classical whig thought. Had agrarian laws achieved wide acceptance after the Revolution, the universe of the nineteenth century might have looked quite different. In a more egalitarian republic, independence and property ownership might have continued to be linked. On the demand for agrarian laws in the period of the Revolution, see Nash, Smith & Hoerder, *Labor in the Era of the American Revolution: An Exchange*, 24 LABOR HIST. 414, 430–32 (1983). * * *

Note

Steinfeld's suggestion at the end of his article that it was difficult for wage earners to argue that working for a living made them both self-governing and the slaves of their employers was also relevant to slavery. For example, it is possible that general acceptance of the idea that earning wages made a man independent was a necessary prerequisite for freeing the slaves later in the nineteenth century. Does this also help explain why, after the Civil War, women were not given suffrage along with freed male slaves?

Jennifer Nedelsky, *Law, Boundaries and the Bounded Self*, in LAW AND THE ORDER OF CULTURE (ROBERT POST, ED.) 162, 163–169, 176–184 (1991)*

I

One of the ways of understanding both the power and the perversity of American constitutionalism is to examine its origins. * * *

During the 1780s the newly independent confederation of states seemed to pose problems for which the revolutionary conceptions of politics were inadequate. The new governments had solved the problem of "no taxation without representation," but many men of property felt that their rights were still not secure. During the revolution they had proclaimed that "a man is a slave if his property can be taken without his consent." By the 1780s that consent had been ensured through representation, but the new representative governments were themselves threatening property. The depreciating currency and debtor relief laws promulgated by virtually every state were widely seen as violations of property rights—and thus illegitimate even though passed by duly elected representatives. For many of the great statesmen of the time, the threats these laws posed came to be understood as part of a more general problem. Their important (and now trite) insight was that democracy solves some problems of tyranny but brings its own: the tyranny of the majority.[2]

The forms of representation that the colonists had demanded to secure the rights of Englishmen turned out to threaten those very rights. Property in particular turned out to be just as vulnerable to debtor relief measures in the republic as it had been to unjust taxation under the monarchy. Indeed, many thought this would always be so: property would be inherently vulnerable in a republic because the many would always be poor and the few rich; what would prevent the many from using their numerical power in the legislature to take the property from the few? The problem of designing a republican government that could provide security for property was a central one for the Federalists, whose views prevailed at the Constitutional Convention of 1787. It was an immediate problem that had to be solved if the republic was to survive, and, for the most thoughtful Framers, it became the defining instance of the larger problem of securing rights against the threat of majority oppression. Ironically, it is because this original preoccupation with property was not limited to a crass concern with protecting the interests of the rich that it has had such a lasting and destructive legacy. Originally invoked as the defining instance of the larger problem of securing justice and liberty in a republic, property indeed came to define the terms of that problem for at least one hundred fifty years.[4]

There were many complex consequences to this original focus on property. To begin with, the problem of property arose for the Framers because their conception of it was inseparably tied to inequality. The link to inequality was liberty. Property was important for the exercise of liberty, and liberty required the free exercise of property rights; this free exercise would inevitably lead in turn to an unequal distribution of property. Property thus posed a problem for popular government because this inequality required protection; those with property had to be protected from those who had less or none. Without security, property lost its value. And the threat to security was inevitable, for (the Framers presumed) it was in the very nature of a productive system of private property that many, perhaps most, would have none.[5] It was this inequality, which the

---

[2] The reference to *democracy* is an anachronistic usage. That term was used disparagingly by almost all the leading Framers. They used the term *republic.* I use *democracy* here because it captures the basic issues more easily for the modern reader.

[4] In 1937 (one hundred and fifty years after 1787), *West Coast Hotel v. Parrish,* 300 U.S. 379, signaled the end of the era beginning with *Lochner v. New York,* 198 U. S. 45 (1905), in which the Supreme Court had struck down social welfare legislation in the name of property and contract. But the Framer's basic paradigm of rights as limits has endured even though property no longer holds a central place.

[5] *See* JENNIFER NEDELSKY, PRIVATE PROPERTY AND THE LIMITS OF AMERICAN CONSTITUTIONALISM (1990). * * * [Editor's Note: This book is a more complete version of the property arguments made by Nedelsky in the article excerpted here.]

Framers both feared and accepted as natural, that skewed their conception of republican government.

The republic the Framers envisioned required the security of a right to which the majority posed a constant and inevitable threat. Defense against such a threat was a problem quite different from that arising from the general insight that in a republic the majority may oppress the minority. It is one thing to say that everyone's rights are vulnerable to the possibility of majority oppression. It is another to say that an essential ingredient of the republic is the protection of rights that the majority will never fully enjoy, will always want more of, and will therefore always want to encroach upon. The vulnerability of property bred a fear and, perhaps, contempt of the propertyless, who were to be the vast bulk of the people. With fear came an urgent sense of the need to contain the people's threatening power.

Given the historical context, we can understand both the focus on property and the insistence that it stood for broader issues and deeper values. The Framers who focused on property were not crass materialists of either the self-interested or philosophical variety; they were not devoted to property for its own sake. Their preoccupation with property had its origins in the connections they presumed between property and other basic human goods, in particular liberty and security. Property came to be not merely a link to those basic values but the symbolic focal point for the effort to make republican government compatible with both liberty and security. Property was a powerful symbol of these goals because it could both crystallize complex aspirations and problems and provide a practical focus for dealing with them. Property was an effective symbol in part because it was not *merely* a symbol but a concrete means of having control over one's life, of expressing oneself, and of protecting oneself from the power of others, individual or collective. In addition, the need for security in order for property to serve those purposes expressed the important link between security and liberty: although the two values are not the same, and can be in tension with one another; some level of security is necessary for liberty to have meaning.

Property effectively captures this link between liberty and security in that it literally loses its meaning without security. We mean by property that which is recognized to be ours and cannot be easily taken from us—hence the connection between property and what are seen as the sources of its security (and thus, in part, its meaning); law and government. Property is a right that requires collective recognition and enforcement. In ways quite different from freedom of conscience, it requires the involvement of the collective for definition and defense and thus is peculiarly vulnerable to collective power—at the same time that one of the basic purposes of property is to provide a shield for the individual against the intrusions of the collective. Property defines what the society, or its representative the state, cannot touch (in the ordinary course of things). It defines a sphere in which we can act largely unconstrained by collective demands and prohibitions. But the definition and protection of that sphere must reside with the collective itself. Property thus captures the essence of the problem of self-limiting government. But a focus on property also provides a distorted image of the problem.

Property (at least as the Framers understood it) must distort because it makes inequality rather than liberty, or individual autonomy, the central problem of government. (Note that what follows is not an argument that there must be equality of property. It is an argument about what happens when property, conceived of as inherently unequal, becomes the central symbol for the protection of individual rights.) The Federalists presumed that the threat inequality posed to property captured the inevitable threat democracy posed to individual freedom and security. But the Federalists were wrong: not all rights, all components of liberty, must be enjoyed unequally. Perhaps even property need not be enjoyed unequally, but the Framers' conception of property had inequality—and thus fear, anger, and resentment—built into it. The centrality of inequality skewed the Federalists' comprehension of the basic problem of republican government. They failed to see that protecting the rights of the propertied few against the demands of the many is not the same as protecting individuals from the ever-present possibility of collective oppression. The cost of the Framers' insight is that they cast the general problem in the terms of the particular—and we have continued to think in those terms.

The tension between the individual and the collective does not inevitably concern inequality, power, and domination, but the problem of protection of unequal property does. In accepting vast economic inequality as a given, and the contours of property rights as obvious, the Framers were in fact focusing on protecting the few from the many, not the individual from the collective of which he or she is a part. The Framers' focus on property turned attention away from the real problem: the need for an ongoing collective formulation of individual rights in a political culture that respects both democratic decision making and individual freedom, and that recognizes the need to sustain the inevitable tension between them. The Framers recognized this tension, but they were preoccupied with one dimension of it: insulating property from democratic decision making. Rights became things to be protected, not values to be collectively determined. The most thoughtful Framers transformed a widespread fear about threats to property into a sophisticated analysis of the inherent problem of majority oppression. But in doing so they also transformed this general problem into a question of how to contain the power of the people.

The 1787 Constitution did indeed "insulate" property rather than set up rigid boundaries to protect it. Its solution was a carefully structured system of institutions that would minimize the threat of the future propertyless majority in large part by minimizing their political efficacy. This undermining of democracy was justified in part by an articulation of competing categories of civil and political rights. Civil rights, with property as the leading example, were the true ends of the government; political rights were merely means. It was therefore no sacrifice of basic principle to tailor the means to the end. But this conceptual hierarchy remained institutionally fluid in the Constitution of 1787; there was no clear answer to how the priority of civil over political rights was to be enforced. There were few formal declarations of rights as limits to the power of the federal government (or as we would put it today, few rights specified as limits to the legitimate scope of democratic decision making).[7] Rather, the Constitution the Framers wrote protected civil rights in more subtle ways by channeling the power of the people in order to minimize their threat to property and civil rights generally.

By 1800 this channeling seemed insufficient to contain the threats posed by Jeffersonian democracy. With the rise of judicial review the conceptual hierarchy of civil over political rights hardened into an institutional one: the judiciary wielded the power to strike down the outcomes of the democratic process in the name of constitutionally protected rights. Those rights were proclaimed as clear boundaries to the legitimate power of the state, boundaries to be defined and defended by the judiciary.

We are now coming to my central point. The vision of constitutionalism sketched above—the tension between democracy and individual rights, the hierarchical distinction between civil and political rights, the notion of rights as boundaries—not only has the dark underpinning of inequality but rests on a flawed conception of the individual, a conception captured, amplified, and entrenched by its association with property. The boundaries central to American constitutionalism are those necessary to protect a bounded or "separative" self; the boundaries around selves form the boundaries to state power. Now, the boundedness of selves may seem to be a self-evident truth, but I think it is a wrong-headed and destructive way of conceiving of the human creatures for whom law and government are created.

II

Much of our constitutional protection can be understood as a (misguided) attempt to protect individual autonomy. The primary content of this underlying conception of autonomy is protection from the intrusion of the collective. The autonomy the American system is designed to protect can be achieved by erecting a wall of rights around the individual. Property provided an ideal symbol for this vision of autonomy, for it could both literally and figuratively provide the necessary walls. The perverse quality of this conception is clearest when taken to its extreme: the most perfectly autonomous man is the most perfectly isolated.

Everyone is familiar with, or at least would immediately recognize as intelligible, the image of rights as boundaries defining the sphere within which human autonomy (or freedom or privacy) resides. Certainly within Anglo-American legal theory that image is routine. These images abound, for example, in Charles Reich's famous "new property" article in which he tries to expand the traditional meaning of property to cover government largess:

> The institution called property guards the troubled boundary between individual man and the state. . . . Property draws a circle around the activities of each private individual or organization. Within that circle, the owner has a greater degree of freedom than without.

[7] Of course, the Bill of Rights was not included in the 1787 Constitution. It was added as amendments in 1789. And the Bill of Rights had a purpose and rationale different from the rest of the Constitution. It was aimed at the Anti-Federalists' fear of tyrannical rules, not the Federalists' fear of the people. Nevertheless, it fit quite comfortably within the Federalist conceptual framework: it defined rights as limits to the legitimate authority of government. The irony is that the Bill of Rights has taken on the significance it has in our system because of the establishment of judicial review, the final consolidation of the Federalist conception of constitutional government.

> Outside, he must justify or explain his actions, and show his authority. Within, he is master, and the state must explain and justify his interference.[11]

Reich wants to redefine property so that it can continue to define protective spheres, but ones that are appropriate for a regulatory state.

* * *

[T]he image of protective boundaries as essential to the integrity and autonomy of the self is deep and pervasive in our culture. Must my challenge to the rhetoric of boundaries then extend beyond the peculiarities of the property-based boundary forms of American constitutionalism? Yes—at least because * * * I do not accept the position that we should simply remove the perversions of the original focus on property by replacing it with other rights to serve as boundaries, and more broadly still because the boundaries of American legal discourse effectively capture a wider (and deeper) phenomenon. So I must pose my question more broadly: What is wrong with boundary imagery.

* * * As I see it, individual autonomy is a capacity, not a static human characteristic to be posited as a presupposition of legal or political theory. This capacity must be developed; it can flourish or become moribund. What is essential to the development of autonomy is not protection against intrusion but constructive relationship. The central question for inquiries into autonomy (legal or otherwise) is then how to structure relationships so that they foster rather than undermine autonomy. The boundary metaphor does not direct our attention to this question. Instead it invites us to imagine that the self to be protected is in some crucial sense insular, and that what is most important to the preservation of such a self is drawing boundaries around it that will protect it from invasion (or at least that is the most crucial thing the law can do.)

* * *

What actually makes human autonomy possible is not isolation but relationship, first with parents, then teachers, friends, and, potentially, agents of the state (although, in fact, many relationships with the state, such as the receipt of welfare, are structured so that they undermine rather than foster autonomy).

* * *

III

* * *

Will * * * new images of the boundary help? Yes, to the extent that they focus the mind on connection and patterns of relationship. But in the traditional legal spheres we are still better off without them. The imagery associated with boundary is too well established, too wall-like, too closely tied to a separative self. We have thought of the problems of the self and the collective in boundarylike terms for so long that they invite no new modes of inquiry; they shield our understanding of reality. * * * In constitutional discourse troubling problems of the meaning of democracy and the process of defining basic values masquerade as boundary issues. The concept of boundary has become more of a mask than a lens.

One of the things the language of boundaries masks is power. We can see that most clearly by returning to our starting point of property. Although property rights are no longer important constitutional boundaries, property is itself conceived in boundary terms and continues to be seen as an important source of autonomy. Everyone is familiar with notions that property gives us control, property allows us to express ourselves by shaping the space around us, property provides privacy and security, owning a house gives a sense and impression of permanence. And in almost every case it seems as though the physical contours of the property are essential to these desirable experiences. But, of course, property really is a set of legal rules and norms that structure power and relationships. The boundaries the law defines and enforces are a means of wielding power, of shielding power and of shielding from power. The rules of property tell us who has to ask whom for what, and how much power or powerlessness they will have in their request. As Robert L. Hale explained a long time ago, the power to exclude that our legal structure of property gives us is the starting point of all contracting, all negotiation over use of, access to, and exchange of property and labor.[35]

The focus on the naturally bounded, thinglike quality of "property" obscures the fact that the power we derive from it in no way inheres in the object but is allocated to us by the state. The power to exclude exists because it is backed by the power of the state, and all the other dimensions of property and its

---

[11] Charles Reich, *The New Property,* 73 YALE LAW JOURNAL 733, 771 (1964). [Editor's Note: An excerpt from Charles Reich's *The New Property* is reprinted *infra* in Part 2(D).]

[35] Robert L. Hale, *Coercion and Distribution in a Supposedly Non-Coercive State,* 38 POLITICAL SCI. Q. 470 (1923).

relation to autonomy and security flow from that power. The boundary metaphor permits us to indulge in focusing on the experiences we can have in, on, and with our property (whose value I do not deny) and ignore the patterns of relationship shaped by the power to exclude. Private property permits us to flaunt power at the same time that we deny its state-created nature. And that denial has of course sustained the distorted quality of the prevailing discussions of the "free market" versus state "interference" via regulation. A discourse of property that always kept at its center the relationship structured by property backed by the power of the state at its center could not sustain the myth of the free market. Our focus on boundary turns our attention away from relationship and thus away from the true sources and consequences of the patterns of power that property constitutes.

* * *

IV

Having pointed to the problems the boundary metaphor gives rise to, I must come finally to the most basic question: Can we do without it? Is there not something *essentially* bounded about us that makes us routinely invoke boundary metaphors to describe those things we experience as basic to our selfhood—like property, privacy, protection against the power of others, individually and collectively? I think not. What is true is that the dominant notion of selfhood is that of the "separate self," and we take that notion so much for granted that our boundedness seems natural and essential.

* * *

Catherine Keller * * * offers a sweeping, brilliant exposition of Western culture and the centrality in it of sexism and the "separative self." * * * In Keller's view we cannot fully understand the genesis or power of * * * selfhood unless we see its connection with sexism: "Separation and sexism have functioned together as the most fundamental self-shaping assumptions of our culture." And until we recognize their interdependence, "the old world view will retain the momentum of unconsciousness." * * *

Keller * * * provide[s] an alternative image of selfhood * * *. She tries both to explain the fierce resistance to such an alternative—"creative connectivity then appears as chaos and confinement, as an undifferentiated heap, a constrictive—maternally monstrous—mix of matters"—and to take seriously what "differentiation *in* relation" or integrity without oneness might mean. She * * * envision[s] a self that is "an event, a process, and no fixed substance, no substantive."[53]

In the course of constructing an alternative, Keller helps us understand the relationship between the separative self and the problems of power and domination—and the ways those problems are in turn linked to the boundaries of constitutionalism, property, and privacy. * * * [T]he separative self is on an endless and doomed search for security, a security that seems possible only in power and domination. Thus, the sought-after walls of protection (like property) are those that entail domination.

* * *

These links between the separative self, control, and domination offer a new perspective on the distortions of inequality that the focus on property brought to American constitutionalism. The way the Framers' sense of the need to control the threat of the people distorted the democratic institutions they designed no longer looks like an anomaly born of a particular historical preoccupation with property. Rather, property appears as a logical preoccupation for separative selves, providing the sought-after illusion of security through power, domination, and isolation. And property can crystallize the fears of loss of control, of intrusion, and of the threat of impending chaos if things are not under control. An emerging democracy stirs up (not entirely unwarranted) fears of the collective (and, in 1787, repeated references to the need for a strong, *manly* republic untainted by feminine vices). Property focuses these fears in ways that are paradigmatic of the efforts of separative selves to protect themselves through boundaries: the protection of those boundaries is inevitably tied to fear and domination and to the inequalities of power necessary for security through domination. The protections the Framers sought from property (and for property) were inseparable from domination. But from this perspective, the inequality and fear of the people that shaped American constitutionalism is not anomalous but characteristic of the protection in boundaries sought by separative selves.

* * * If we accept Keller's (and others) accounts of the depth of the separative self (and its fears and illusions) in our mythology as well as our philosophy, our psychology (both as discipline and as self-con-

---

[53] CATHERINE KELLER, FROM A BROKEN WEB: SEPARATION, SEXISM, AND SELF (1986).

sciousness) as well as law, we know we need more than a good theory to change things. In this case I am not thinking of political action (which is of course required) but of new symbols, myths, and metaphors to replace the old.

* * *

Recall the claim that started my inquiry here: we need new ways of conceiving of the tension between the individual and the collective for which boundary is not an apt metaphor. * * * Boundary mediates. Our new conception will focus on the complexities of the interpenetration of individual and collective. Boundaries and mediation imply a separation and opposition that does not capture the complex, fertile, and tension-laden interconnection between self and others that a transformed constitutionalism must respond to.

* * *

V

There is something profoundly and I think irreducibly mysterious about the combination of individuality and "enmeshedness," integrity and integration that constitutes the human being. * * * [O]ur boundary-setting rights protect us from the seemingly overwhelming responsibility that would flow from a recognition of unity. This is, I think a frightening form of the "oceanic feeling," intimations of which have reached us.[61] We fear being "invaded," "taken over," not just by threats but by demands—the overpowering demands of those in pain and hunger all around us. We wall ourselves off from their cries—genuinely do not hear them most of the time, even though we "know" they are there—by telling ourselves that we are "within our rights," that rights define our obligations as well as our entitlements, and that as long as we have violated no one's rights, we are doing nothing wrong in our daily nonresponsiveness.

That particular form of freedom would, I think, be radically transformed if we were to come to see ourselves as "inseparable from all other beings in the universe."[62] The fear of such a transformation is old, deep, and not crazy. I think we see it lurking under the Framers' assertions of the illegitimacy of redistributing property as well as in modern attacks on the welfare state. Throughout American history anxieties about redistributive legislation have been accompanied by cries of "Where will it all end?" If such a redistribution (in the form of paper money, or a progressive income tax, or workers' compensation, or socialized medicine) is permitted, what boundaries can we count on? Won't the demands of the collective become insatiable, finally devouring us and the orderly society that keeps chaos and the collective at bay?

* * * We will need new ways of capturing the mystery of human creativity, the spontaneous combustion of human action. But the puzzle of a nonsubmerged selfhood amidst connective responsibility cannot be solved by walls of rights. We need to take our traditional concepts like property and ask what patterns seem true to both integrity and integration. Those questions do not necessarily preclude a concept of property, but they imply a focus not on limits but on forms of interaction and responsibility for their consequences.

In rejecting the categories of the past, we should never underestimate the task. The American Constitution is only a particularly vivid modern form of an age old effort to use the concept of boundary to mediate, to "grasp," to "bring under control" the illusive mysteries of human freedom and connection. Without the boundary metaphor, the structure of legal conceptions of freedom disintegrates. But some of that disintegration is already underway. At least in the academic legal community there is no consensus on the basic meaning of law or of the values it is supposed to protect. New metaphors are a genuine option because they are in fact emerging. We are in a period of flux where our presuppositions are in doubt. It is therefore possible to exercise some deliberate choice about the frame of reference through which we see the world. We can try to transform our own language, push it in the direction of the barely articulated "intimations" that have reached us. Disintegration entails promise. If we can let go of our walls of rights, the reintegration is likely to be far fuller and more promising.

---

[61] SUSAN GRIFFIN, PORNOGRAPHY AND SILENCE (NEW YORK, 1981); QUOTED IN KELLER, FROM A BROKEN WEB, 155.

[62] *Id.*

Note

If we take Nedelsky's notion of lack of boundaries about ourselves seriously, does that require significant alteration of our notions of ownership? For example, in *Pierson v. Post*, would Nedelsky be uncomfortable with the idea that either one or the other of the litigants should end up owning the fox? Why not share the bounty in a case where norms of ownership are unclear? Or what about *Armory v. Delamirie*, where a chimney sweep found a jewel. As between the chimney sweep and the owner of the chimney, who should get the jewel? Why not share it too? Is there something about the American legal system, in addition to standard notions of individual ownership, which has traditionally rejected remedies of sharing? Does the notion of boundaries help explain the lack of sharing rules in many areas of property? For other views on sharing, *see* the materials in Part IV(C), the last section of this anthology.

2. A Major Property Development of the Early Republic: Exclusion of Native Americans From Republican Concepts of Property

Women, of course, were not the only people living here at the turn of the nineteenth century who were automatically excluded from republican governing structures. As Carol Rose noted at the end of her article, *Possession as the Origin of Property*, excerpted in the first section of this volume, *Johnson v. McIntosh*:

> is a particularly striking example of the relativity of the "text" of possession to the interpretative community for that text. It is doubtful whether the claims of any nomadic population could ever meet the common law requirements for establishing property in land. * * * At least some Indians professed bewilderment at the concept of owning the land. Indeed they prided themselves on not marking the land but rather on moving lightly through it, living with the land and with its creatures as members of the same family rather than as strangers who visited only to conquer the objects of nature.

Rose's notion that tribes were nomadic was misplaced for a significant number of Native Americans by 1820. Many of those living in the southeast, for example, had adopted agrarian, yeoman farmer life styles under pressure from Jefferson. The Cherokees and other groups adopted Constitutions much like that of the United States. Their later removal during the 1830's, despite the Supreme Court's declaration in *Worcester v. Georgia*, 31 U.S. 515 (1832), that the states were without authority to control tribal lands, forcefully ended any pretensions that Native American lands were to be protected under the same republican ideologies governing the majority culture.

That is made quite clear by the work of Robert Williams, excerpted below. The literature on the Native American land cases is enormous. Some items worth your attention include Norgren, *Lawyers and the Legal Business of the Cherokee Republic Courts of the United States, 1829–1835,* 10 LAW & HIST. REV. 253 (1992); Singer, *Sovereignty and Property, 86 NW. U. L. REV.* 1 (1991); Townsend, *Congressional Abrogation of Indian Treaties: Reevaluation and Reform,* 98 YALE L. J. 793 (1989); Williams, *The Algebra of Federal Indian Law: The Hard Trail of Decolonizing and Americanizing the White Man's Indian Jurisprudence,* 1986 WISC. L. REV. 219; Chambers, *Judicial Enforcement of the Federal Trust Responsibility to Indians*, 27 STAN. L. REV. 1213 (1975); and Burke, *The Cherokee Cases, A Study in Law, Politics, and Morality*, 21 STAN. L. REV. 503 (1969). Related materials may be found in histories of public land policies. The best such history is Paul W. Gates, A HISTORY OF THE PUBLIC LAND POLICIES (1965).

ROBERT WILLIAMS, THE AMERICAN INDIAN IN WESTERN LEGAL THOUGHT 287–290, 292–294, 305–308, 312–313, 316–317 (1990)*

The Colonists' War for America

On the eve of the colonies' Revolution, at least three competing discourses respecting the legal status and rights of the frontier Indian tribes were contending for legitimacy in American colonizing legal theory. Each was acted on in one way or another by individuals who invested fortunes on the chance that their preferred theory of Indian land rights would win out and they would profit handsomely from their perspicacity.

The British Crown's discourse of empire asserted a Norman-derived royal-prerogative right to control the disposition of Indian lands on the frontier in the Proclamation of 1763. Virginia and the other landed colonies asserted their controlling rights to the West on the basis of their Crown charters and their purer legal discourse of the natural-law-based Saxon Constitution realized by their colonies' governments. And finally, a large group of frontier speculators who cared for neither the Crown's nor the landed colonies' pretensions claimed that under natural law and natural right, the Indians themselves as sovereign princes of the soil they occupied could sell land to whomever they wished.

Of course, these divergent discourses on Indian legal status and rights were all derivative of the larger and more direct question (in the minds of the ministers at Whitehall and the colonists themselves) regarding rationalization of the land-acquisition process on the colonial frontier. As far as American colonizing legal theory during the Revolutionary period was concerned, that was virtually the only arena in which the Indian's legal status was seriously debated. Their natural rights, if any, were of only indirect concern, for they were but a supplement to the larger, manifest goals pursued by European-descended Americans on the frontier of their destiny. What directly concerned whites was the Indians' ability or inability to pass a vested title to land without the positive sanction of a European-derived sovereign entity. Only when it became apparent to Indian tribes that their own survival required a less accommodating stance toward the whites' invitations to enter the market economy for land would American colonizing legal theory directly confront the issue of the rights and status of Indians in land they did *not* desire to surrender to the whites. And that particular confrontation would not occur with notable inconveniencing frequency until after the Revolution and the adoption of a policy by the United States of simply removing the tribes by military force from their lands to make way for white settlement. Only then would American legal theory directly confront the question of whether Indians had natural rights in lands that they *refused* to sell to whites, and the answer of course was that they did not.

The Patriots' Discourses

Few legislative bodies in American history have so mired themselves in corrupted self-interest parading as principle as did the Revolutionary-era American Continental Congress. In the nearly decade-long debate on the status of the western lands under the proposed Articles of Confederation, delegates from the "landed" states, particularly Virginia, continued to insist on the inviolability of their charter-based rights in the West. At the same time, numerous delegates to the Congress from the "landless" states, such as Maryland, Pennsylvania, and New Jersey, acquired or even increased their interests in various land-speculation ventures on the frontier. They hoped that the Congress would secure control of the West under the Articles of Confederation and would affirm the validity of their Indian-derived grants.

Large fortunes would be determined by the answer to the question of whether the "landed" states or the central government would supervise the process of land acquisition and distribution on the frontier. And many of the largest fortunes were to be won or lost by a number of the congressional delegates themselves, entrusted with the responsibility for deciding this vital question of national interest.

By far the most powerful syndicates at the Congress, in terms of the number of delegates holding shares, were the Indiana Company and the Illinois-Wabash Company. The Indiana Company had been organized by Samuel Wharton from the ruins of the "suffering" traders-Vandalia colony project. The Illinois-Wabash Company was the combination of two separate ventures resulting from the frontier land-speculation activities of the Indian traders William Murray and Louis Viviat prior to the outbreak of the Revolution.

In 1773, the trader Murray had set out for the interior country with the intention of making several large purchases of land directly from the frontier tribes. Reaching the Illinois country on June 11, 1773, Murray first encountered Captain Hugh Lord, commander of the English garrison at Fort Gage at Kaskaskia. Lord was under strict orders from London to enforce the prohibition of the Proclamation of 1763 against Indian land sales to colonial speculators. Murray, however, directly challenged the captain's authority to prevent a free English subject from making purchases directly from the Indians * * *. Lacking authority to arrest Murray, who like most traders would readily bring suit against any military officer who violated his "English liberties," Lord merely warned the Indian trader that he would not allow him to *settle* any of the lands, as this was expressly forbidden by royal orders.

On July 5, 1773, Murray purchased two prime tracts of land from the Illinois Indians, one at the junction of the Ohio and Mississippi rivers and the other at the Illinois and Mississippi rivers, for the combined price of $24,000. Murray's partner, Louis Viviat, then acquired two additional tracts of upper Ohio lands from the Piankeshaw Indians in 1775.

These definite purchases by Murray and Viviat on behalf of the Illinois-Wabash Company prior to the outbreak of the Revolution would later form the basis of a lawsuit, *Johnson v. McIntosh,*[6] brought in the United States Supreme Court in 1823 by the successors in interest to the land syndicate. In its refusal to recognize the validity of Murray's and Viviat's Revolutionary-era purchases from the frontier tribes, Chief Justice John Marshall's opinion in *Johnson v. McIntosh* provided Western legal thought and discourse with its single most important textual interpretation of the law governing the rights of indigenous tribal peoples in the territories they occupied. Marshall's influential discourse of conquest in *Johnson,* accepted as the settled law on indigenous peoples' rights and status in all the European-derived settler-colonialist states of the West, merely provided a *post hoc* legal rationalization for the Revolutionary-era political compromise on the frontier lands question. That compromise, embodied in a feudally derived, fictive doctrine of discovery and conquest, vested superior title to the frontier Indian lands in the United States government. Thus Marshall's decision in *Johnson,* recognizing the Doctrine of Discovery as governing the frontier land-acquisition process in the United States, had little to do with "law" as the Western legal tradition prefers to define that term. Politics and the Founders' brokered definition of "public good," which did not include the Indian tribes, determined the rights and status of American Indian nations in the lands they occupied on the frontier.

The Players and the Play

The Illinois-Wabash Company, Samuel Wharton's "suffering" traders-Vandalia syndicate, and several other lesser ventures represented at the Continental Congress had all acquired huge tracts of western land directly from the frontier tribes prior to the outbreak of revolt. The delegates who held substantial shares in these ventures worked diligently to ensure that the new Congress, despite Virginia's and the other landed states' vigorous protests and defenses of their charter rights, would assume complete control of the western frontier territories as a national domain and would recognize the validity of their Indian grants. They refused to agree to any draft of the Articles of Confederation that did not vest Congress with the authority to determine the vital western lands question.

The land-speculating delegates in Congress often voiced their opposition to the expansive frontier claims of the landed colonies in terms of the necessary balance of landholding power in a federation of supposedly equal states. However, other delegates, with less personal interest in the matter, doubted that the issue delaying agreement on the Articles of

6 21 U.S. (8 Wheat.) 543 (1823).

Confederation, the proposed constitution for the new federation of state sovereignties, was solely one of small states' fears of being engulfed by larger ones. John Adams commented in the spring of 1776 that the goal of a confederated union was being delayed by "that avarice of Land, which has made upon this Continent so many votaries to Mammon, that I sometimes dread the Consequences."[8] One member of Congress voiced the fear that competition between the states for land in the West would result in wars and convulsions, tearing the continent "in pieces."[9]

* * *

The "Plain Facts" of the "Public Good"

The Virginians who insisted on maintaining their state's control over western lands believed that they were fighting far more than the greed of the speculators. To radicals such as Thomas Jefferson, the Declaration of Independence signified that the peoples of the individual states, not the British Crown, were to be the ultimate source of sovereignty. As the colonists were fighting and dying in a revolution against the potentially aggrandizing coercive power of Great Britain, the Virginians were not about to place control of the western lands in the hands of another aggrandizing central government.

Many of the radicals who opposed vesting too much authority in the Congress of the new confederation firmly believed that to establish thirteen distinct centers of power was a far better method of preserving liberty than to plant a seed in one power that might grow to choke off liberty for all the citizens of the individual states. * * * Because power corrupted, it was unwise to place too much power in one centralized body. Thus the Articles' overriding structural premise of dispersal of sovereignty represented the temporary triumph in American political theory of the radicals' distrust of centralized power.

With respect to the West, the completed version of the Articles that was passed on to the states for formal ratification in early 1778 assured that no state could be deprived of its territory for the benefit of the United States. Congress at best could arbitrate territorial disputes between states, but it could neither make nor enforce a specific decision. Virginia, most contented with this proposed version of the Articles, was the only state ready to ratify without qualification or criticism by the appointed date, March 20, 1778. "Landless" Maryland, the state most discontented with the proposed Articles, presented the strongest list of objections. The Marylanders demanded that the Articles be amended to give Congress the power to determine and define the limits of the states claiming lands in the West. And Congress also had to recognize, in the words of the Marylanders, their state's right to a share of the country lying westward "of the frontiers of the United States, the property of which was not vested in individuals at the commencement of the present war."

This odd formulation by the Marylanders can be better understood in light of the fact that a large percentage of Maryland's most prominent citizens had heavily invested in western land-speculating ventures based on Indian purchases prior to the "commencement of the present war." Governor Thomas Johnston, Samuel Chase, Charles Carroll, William Paca, and many other Marylanders held outright or secret shares in the Illinois-Wabash Company, and in other ventures as well. Thus Maryland's peculiar demand probably reflected the personal financial interests of controlling members in that state's delegation. Maryland's western land speculators were required to maintain that Indian nations possessed the sovereign capacity to sell their lands and "vest" a title in individual purchasers—namely, those Marylanders who held interests in Indian grants acquired prior to the "commencement of the present war."

Virginia's George Mason, himself a land speculator and close political ally of Jefferson, perceived clearly the motivation behind the Marylanders' objections and their odd formulation implicitly recognizing the natural rights of Indians to vest land titles in individual purchasers. The demand that Congress be given the right to control only those western lands not "vested" prior to the war demonstrated, in Mason's opinion, "the secret and true cause of the great opposition to Virginia's title to her chartered territory." The "cause" was the Indian purchases held by "Governor Johnston and several of the leading men of Maryland." Mason asked sarcastically, "Do you observe the care Governor Johnston . . . has taken to save his Indian purchase?"[21]

* * *

The Norman Yoke Revived to Decide the Rights and Status of American Indian Tribes

The lobbying efforts of the speculators before Congress and the pamphlet-reading public continued

[8] M. Jensen, *The Articles of Confederation* 122 (1940).
[9] *Id.* at 113.

[21] M. Jensen, *supra* note 8, at 205.

for * * * years, while Virginia refused to remove its stipulation to cession of the Old Northwest demanding that Congress void Indian-derived claims of the non-Virginia land companies. Then in late 1783, a political compromise satisfactory to the Virginians and to Congress (but certainly not to the Indians or to the speculators) was finally brokered. Congress would accept Virginia's cession of its claims north of the Ohio, but it would not specifically invalidate all private land purchases from the natives in the territories, as originally demanded by Virginia. Congress, however, agreed not to investigate the question of conflicting claims in the region. Given this agreement and the additional promise by Congress that the lands should be used for the common benefit of the states, the Virginians were satisfied that their cession did not require a provision against private purchases from Indians. Nor were they at all concerned about the theoretical implications of Congress's assumption of the English Crown's devolved sovereignty over the Northwest. Congress had essentially acceded to Virginia's demands, and the Virginians (aware that politics is the art of compromise) knew that national authority over the Northwest Territory had in reality devolved from Virginia, and not from some Norman tyrant.

In 1784, Congress formally accepted the Old Northwest cession from Virginia, thus effectively closing the door on the land-speculating companies. At the same time, a new door opened for Congress itself, as it sought under the Northwest Ordinance of 1785, "with utmost faith . . . observed toward the Indians, their lands and property," to utilize the western lands to pay off the nation's enormous war debt.

The Constitutional Convention of 1787 merely ratified the bargain struck in 1784. With little debate, the convention's new constitution for the nation vested exclusive authority in Congress to regulate trade and commerce and to make treaties with Indian tribes. This was a far simpler and clearer declaration of legislative authority over Indian tribes than the superseded Articles of Confederation had contained. The Constitution's broad statement of power seemed to imply that Congress's authority over Indian tribes, and thereby Indian lands, was unlimited in scope, applying in the Old Northwest as well as elsewhere throughout the American frontier.

Significantly, however, North Carolina and Georgia did not cede their western land claims to the United States until 1790 and 1802, respectively. Georgia, in particular, extracted significant concessions from the federal government in the process—concessions that would ultimately lead to what Charles Warren has described as the most serious crisis in the history of the United States Supreme Court, the Cherokee Nation cases of the early 1830s.[83]

Furthermore, those former colonies which retained significant Indian populations and Indian-occupied lands after the Revolution, most notably Massachusetts and New York, continued their historical practice of unilaterally purchasing territory directly from Indian tribes located within their defined state borders. These purchases were made despite Congress's apparently exclusive constitutional jurisdiction over Indian commerce and the series of nonintercourse acts passed soon after ratification of the Constitution, which specifically prohibited "any person or persons, or . . . state whether having the right of pre-emption to such lands or not," to purchase lands from "any nation or tribe of Indians within the United States" without the consent of the federal government. Thus while the new Constitution's text implicitly sought to affirm the feudal principle that the British Crown's prerogative powers over Indian lands had *devolved* to the sovereignty of the United States, a significant faction of the American polity apparently believed that the principle applied only to that part of the western frontier ceded by the individual states to the federal government as part of the national domain. There the federal government was free to exercise its Norman-derived prerogative rights and to acquire the Indian estate by war, duress, or sometimes even peaceful purchase. The states, however, despite the Constitution and subsequent acts of Congress intended to assert the national government's unilateral control over all Indian affairs under the Constitution, continued to exercise their similarly Norman-derived, charter-based rights of preemption over Indian lands within their defined borders. The only seeming consensus on Indian rights in the decades immediately following ratification of the Constitution was that Indian tribes did not have the natural-law right to sell the lands they occupied to whomever they pleased. The Norman Yoke was revived after the Revolution to settle the law on Indian rights and status in the frontier lands. Only a European-derived government could exercise

---

[83] C. Warren, *The Supreme Court in United States History* 189 (1928).

the Norman-derived rights of conquest over Indian lands devolved from the English Crown.

In time, of course, as the final state cessions were accepted by Congress and as the national domain came to comprehend an entire continent to be won from the Indian, these assertions of the states' superior rights over Indian lands lost much of their legal significance. But most significantly, of the three competing legal discourses on Indian rights and status that had been in circulation during the Revolutionary era—the centralizing feudal discourse of the Crown's right of conquest in Indian lands, the charter-based discourse of the "landed" colonies, and the natural-law based discourse of the speculators defending the right of the Indians to own and freely sell their lands—only one had failed to retain its currency in American colonizing discourse just a decade later, when the new Constitution was signed. The notion that under natural law and natural right, the Indians themselves, as sovereign princes of the soil they occupied, could sell to whomever they wished was denied by all white men of common sense in America. This discarded discourse did not adequately address the Founders' perceptions of the new nation's public good in Indian lands. Those who had won the war for America chose instead to explain their territorial rights in America by the convenient Norman-derived fiction of a superior claim in European-derived governments to the lands of the Indians.

Thus the Norman Yoke had not been completely thrown off by the Revolution; its feudal vestiges had been preserved in United States colonizing discourse in the definition of the legal status and rights of Indian tribes in their lands. The Indians' rights, natural or otherwise, of sovereignty in their soil were to be unilaterally determined by an alien, Norman-derived tyrant.

Such was the nature of the compromised discourse respecting the western lands that was accepted by the Founders for the public good as they came to understand that term in the period between the Revolution of 1776 and the Constitution of 1787. Their discourse of natural rights, which had energized and legitimated their resistance to Norman tyranny, was compromised so as not to include the American Indians. The principle liberating thematics of the revolutionary era, which envisaged America as a land freed of the Norman Yoke where property secured liberty and governments secured property, was restricted to Europeans by an act of state accepting the United States government's superior sovereignty over the Indian frontier in furtherance of the public good.

Johnson v. McIntosh and United States Colonizing Legal Theory

Thus in 1823, when the successors in interest to the Illinois-Wabash Company's claims based on Murray's and Viviat's Revolutionary-era frontier purchases finally had their chance to argue for the validity of their Indian-derived deeds before the Supreme Court, Chief Justice John Marshall found himself conveniently confronted by a *fait accompli.* The Indians of the Old Northwest had been forced to cede their claims to their lands to the United States during the course of various frontier military campaigns. These wars and skirmishes culminated in General Anthony Wayne's victory at the decisive Battle of Fallen Timbers in 1794. By subsequent treaty, the western tribes ceded their claims to the Northwest Territory, which included the Revolutionary-era purchases of the Illinois-Wabash Company's Indian deeds. In fact, in 1818 the federal government had sold the same lands described under the Illinois-Wabash Company's Indian deeds to the defendant in the company's lawsuit, William McIntosh. All that remained for the Supreme Court in *Johnson v. McIntosh*, therefore, was formally to legitimate the outcome of this forty-year-old compromise by which the speculators' Indian deeds and the Indians' natural rights had been silently ignored.

* * *

Chief Justice Marshall's Discourse of Conquest

Chief Justice Marshall, * * * writing for a unanimous Supreme Court in *Johnson v. McIntosh,*[105] sought to avoid the extremes of old passions that were no longer immediately relevant to the needs and concerns of the nation in 1823. Ignoring the moral dimensions of the controversy presented by *Johnson v. McIntosh,* Marshall instead focused his opinion exclusively on the need for rationalizing the process of land acquisition in a country originally inhabited by a savage people but gradually overtaken by a foreign invader. The disenchanted nature of this rationalized inquiry—its segregation of transcending questions of "justice" or "morality" from its discussion of a sovereign will driven by utilitarian concerns and expressed in positive law—is indicated by Marshall's succinct formulation of the sole issue before the Court in *Johnson v. McIntosh*: "The inquiry, therefore, is, in a great measure confined to the power

---

[105] 21 U.S. (8 Wheat.) 543 (1823).

of Indians to give, and of private individuals to receive, a title which can be sustained in the courts of this Country."

Marshall's opinion admitted, in Lockean fashion, that this inquiry was confined by boundaries demarcated by the actual conduct of individuals in a state of nature agreeing on the rules of property acquisition for their new society. The role of subsequently established courts of justice was to enforce those agreements according to the principles that "our own government has adopted in the particular case, and given us as the rule of our decision." A court could not engage in speculation on the justness of those principles or their harmony with any type of hypothesized higher law. According to Marshall, "[T]he right of society, to prescribe those rules by which property may be acquired and preserved is not, and cannot be drawn into question . . . . The title to lands, especially, is and must be admitted to depend entirely on the law of the nation in which they lie."

The dominant themes of Marshall's denial of Indian natural-law rights in *Johnson* are clearly established in those early evasions of judicial accountability for the positive law established by European-derived governments for acquiring lands in America. History and the decisions made and enforced by those Europeans who invaded America respecting Indian land rights determined the inescapable framework for Marshall's legal discourse. His judicial task was merely to fill in the details and rationalize the fictions by which Europeans legitimated the denial of the Indians' rights in their acquisition of the Indians' America.

Thus Marshall's opinion in *Johnson* turned immediately to the discourse of compromise which silently denied Indian natural-law land rights and which had triumphed after the Revolution—that is, the discourse of the Norman Yoke and its fiction that European monarchs acquired feudally conceived rights of conquest upon their discovery of the infidel-held territories of America. Marshall's opinion in *Johnson* held that under the "Doctrine of Discovery," assertedly recognized as part of the Law of Nations by virtually every European colonizing nation, discovery of territory in the New World gave the discovering European nation "an exclusive right to extinguish the Indian title of occupancy, either by purchase or by conquest." This title, which England had acquired under the Doctrine of Discovery, had devolved to the United States as a result of its victory in the Revolutionary War. Marshall's opinion in *Johnson* therefore held that the Murray-Viviat purchases of lands from the western Indian tribes without the approval or sanction of either the discovering European nation or its successor in interest, the United States, could not be recognized as valid in a United States court.

* * *

Marshall's discourse of conquest in *Johnson* settled the law on the rights and status of American Indians in the lands of the United States. Acknowledging the outcome of a political compromise that had been concluded forty years earlier, *Johnson*'s acceptance of the Doctrine of Discovery sought to absolve the Supreme Court of any injustices arising from the Founders' denial of natural rights to the American Indians. It is not surprising, therefore, that Marshall made only passing reference to the medievally derived premises supporting the Doctrine of Discovery in *Johnson v. McIntosh*—"the character and religion of . . . [America's] inhabitants afforded an apology for considering them as a people over whom the superior genius of Europe might claim an ascendancy." But Marshall and the other justices were well aware of the historical paternity of this bastardized principle sired by Europe's Law of Nations and legitimated by the United States Supreme Court. As was clearly recognized by Marshall's close friend and fellow Supreme Court justice, Joseph Story, the assumptions supporting the Doctrine of Discovery permitted European nations to claim

> an absolute dominion over the whole territories afterward occupied by them, not in virtue of any conquest of, or cession by, the Indian natives, but as a right acquired by discovery. Some of them, indeed, obtained a sort of confirmatory grant from the papal authority. But as between themselves they treated the dominion and title of territory as resulting from the priority of discovery . . . . The title of the Indians was not treated as a right of property and dominion, but as a mere right of occupancy. *As infidels, heathens, and savages, they were not allowed to possess the prerogatives belonging to absolute, sovereign, and independent nations.* The territory over which they wandered, and which they used for this temporary and fugitive purpose, was, in respect to Christians, deemed as if it were inhabited only by brute animals.[135]

---

[135] Joseph Story, *Commentaries*, § 152, reprinted in M. Lindley, *The Acquisition and Government of Background Territory in International Law* 29 (1926) (emphasis added).

The acceptance of the Doctrine of Discovery into United States law held profound implications for future relations between the federal government and the Indians. The Doctrine of Discovery's discourse of conquest was now available to legitimate, energize, and constrain as needed white society's will to empire over the North American continent. The doctrine confirmed the superior rights of a European-derived nation to the lands occupied by "infidels, heathens, and savages," encouraged further efforts by white society to acquire the Indians' "waste" lands, and vested authority in a centralized sovereign to regulate the Indians' dispossession according to national interest, security, and sometimes even honor.

Perhaps most important, *Johnson* 's acceptance of the Doctrine of Discovery into United States law preserved the legacy of 1,000 years of European racism and colonialism directed against non-Western peoples. White society's exercise of power over Indian tribes received the sanction of the Rule of Law in *Johnson v. McIntosh*. The Doctrine of Discovery's underlying medievally derived ideology—that normatively divergent "savage" people could be denied rights and status equal to those accorded to the civilized nations of Europe—had become an integral part of the fabric of the United States federal Indian law. The architects of an idealized European vision of life in the Indians' New World had successfully transplanted an Old World form of legal discourse denying all respect to the Indians' fundamental human rights. While the tasks of conquest and colonization had not yet been fully actualized on the entire American continent, the originary legal rules and principles of federal Indian law set down by Marshall in *Johnson v. McIntosh* and its discourse of conquest ensured that future acts of genocide would proceed on a rationalized, legal basis.

Like all the other great theorists and systematizers of the European legal tradition, Marshall had performed a bold and reconciling act of critical anamnesis in *Johnson*. He had articulated a conqueror's legal discourse that drew on the most ancient discursive traditions of Western legal thought but was nonetheless capable of serving the contemporary needs of his European-descended countrymen's vision of progress. The Doctrine of Discovery, the primordial mythic icon of Europe's medieval, feudal past, had been preserved and brought to readability in a modern form that spoke with reassuring continuity to a nation that was about to embark on its own colonizing crusade against the American Indians who remained on the North American continent.

B. Before and After the Civil War: From Property as Dominion to Property as Contract

1. The Rise of Property as Contract

Two major historical movements over the course of the nineteenth century led to enormous changes in the way property was conceptualized. First, industrialization and urbanization left rules based on agrarian ideals out of date and unworkable. Models of property based on civic responsibility emerging from the absolute dominion over and governance of a community living upon land became untenable. Emergence of wage labor, large scale business enterprises and improved methods of communication and travel increased the importance of large markets and contractual undertakings between strangers. Second, the Emancipation of slaves after the Civil War further invigorated the idea that contracting for one's labor was a central feature of citizenship. The overall effect was to merge many aspects of property and contract law into a single set of ideas agreed to by widely disparate sectors of the body politic. Both wage laborers and large industrialists clung to the vocabulary merging free contract for labor with property.

The two articles in this section trace some of these changes, starting with Morton Horwitz's now classic formulation of nineteenth century legal history, THE TRANSFORMATION OF AMERICAN LAW,

1780–1860. His work is followed by a late nineteenth century justification of "private property" rights by Judge, later Chief Justice and President, William Howard Taft, who used the post-Civil War amendments designed to guarantee full citizenship to African Americans as the basis for support of *laissez faire* theories of property and contract. Taft's work is a dramatic example of how most portions of the late nineteenth and early twentieth century political spectrum used the language of contract to frame arguments about property.

For additional reading on the relationships between property and contract in the late nineteenth century, *see* Stephen A. Siegel, *Understanding the Nineteenth Century Contract Clause: The Rule of the Property-Privilege Distinction and "Takings" Clause Jurisprudence*, 60 So. Cal. L. Rev. 1 (1986); Note, *Tortious Interference With Contractual Relations in the Nineteenth Century: The Transformation of Property, Contract and Tort*, 93 Harv. L. Rev. 1510 (1980). Other important work on the history of property law in the nineteenth century has been done by Gregory Alexander in *The Dead Hand and the Law of Trusts in the Nineteenth Century*, 37 Stan. L. Rev. 1189 (1985).

Morton J. Horwitz, The Transformation of American Law, 1780–1860, at 31–34, 47–53 (1977)*

II. The Transformation in the Conception of Property

The productive development of land and natural resources at the beginning of the nineteenth century drew into question many legal doctrines formulated in an agrarian economy. In the eighteenth century, the right to property had been the right to absolute dominion over land, and absolute dominion, it was assumed, conferred on an owner the power to prevent any use of his neighbor's land that conflicted with his own quiet enjoyment. Blackstone, in fact, asserted that even an otherwise lawful use of one's property could be enjoined if it caused injury to the land of another, "for it is incumbent on a neighboring owner to find some other place to do that act, where it will be less offensive." Not until the nineteenth century did it become clear that, because this conception of ownership necessarily circumscribed the rights of others to develop their land, it was, in fact, incompatible with a commitment to absolute dominion. Logical difficulties had been easily concealed by experience, since the prevailing ideal of absolute property rights arose in a society in which a low level of economic activity made conflicts over land use extremely rare. As the spirit of economic development began to take hold of American society in the early years of the nineteenth century, however, the idea of property underwent a fundamental transformation—from a static agrarian conception entitling an owner to undisturbed enjoyment, to a dynamic, instrumental, and more abstract view of property that emphasized the newly paramount virtues of productive use and development. By the time of the Civil War, the basic change in legal conceptions about property was completed. * * *

Property Rights in the Nineteenth Century: The General View

Two potentially contradictory theories of property rights underlay eighteenth century legal doctrines for resolving conflicts over uses of property. The first, an explicitly antidevelopmental theory, limited property owners to what courts regarded as the natural uses of their land, and often "natural" was equated with "agrarian." For example, in cases involving the conflicting claims of two riparian owners, courts

*Reprinted by permission of the publishers from The Transformation of American Law, 1780-1860, by Morton J. Horwitz, Cambridge, Mass.: Harvard University Press, Copyright © 1977 by the President and Fellows of Harvard College.

usually gave precedence to appropriation of water not only for domestic purposes but often for agriculture and husbandry as well.

Natural uses of land were probably favored also by strict liability in tort: any interference with the property of another gave rise to liability; only the lowest common denominator of noninjurious activity could avoid a suit for damages. The frequency with which eighteenth century courts solemnly invoked the maxim *six utero tuo, ut alienum non laedas*[4] is a significant measure of their willingness to impose liability for injury caused by any but the most traditional activities.

The second theory of property rights on which courts drew in the eighteenth century, though it appeared in a variety of legal forms, amounted to a rule that priority of development conferred a right to arrest a future conflicting use. Sometimes this rule was simply stated by the long-standing maxim "first in time is first in right." More refined formulations required that the first user be engaged in his activity for a period of time sufficient to ripen into a prescriptive property right against interfering activities.

At first glance, the rule of priority seems more compatible with economic development, since it gives at least the first user freedom to develop his land as he wishes. By contrast, doctrines based on natural use confer on all landowners equal power to maintain the traditional order of things and thereby to impose a continuing pattern of nondevelopment. Before the nineteenth century, however, the theory of property was harnessed to the common antidevelopmental end. Where two neighboring parcels of land were underdeveloped, each owner could claim a right, based on priority, to prevent further development. Thus, depending on the level of economic development from which one begins to measure priority, the consequences of the theories of natural and prior use may be the same; since the lowest level of development is also the earliest, each party acquires a prior right to the land in its natural state.

Furthermore, just as the theory of priority could be reduced to one of natural use, so could the natural use doctrine claim to enforce a rule of priority. If the starting point for judgment is not the first introduction of a new use on the land but rather the prior state of inactivity before the new use appears, then once again the doctrines of priority and natural use yield the same result. Indeed, when in the name of economic development the inevitable attack on eighteenth century property doctrine begins, these two are regularly lumped together by their opponents as part of one theory.

Though the two theories can be merged, they can also be made to have profoundly different consequences. If priority is measured not from a common denominator of natural use but from the time that a new technology appears, the theory of natural use continues to enforce its antidevelopmental premises, but a rule of priority now confers an exclusive property right on the first developer.

The potential for conflicts between the two theories first began to surface in the nineteenth century. There are, for example, no cases before then dealing with conflicts over use of water in which an English or American court acknowledges that different consequences follow from a rule of "natural flow" as opposed to one of "prior appropriation." Courts were induced to distinguish between the two rules in such cases only when the judges began trying to break away from the antidevelopmental consequences of common law doctrine.

Once priority and natural use had taken on different operational meanings, the common law had moved into the utilitarian world of economic efficiency. Claims founded on natural use began to recede into a dim preindustrial past and the newer "balancing test" of efficiency came into sharp focus. As priority came to take on a life of its own distinct from doctrines of natural use, it was put forth not as a defense against encroachments of modernity but as an offensive doctrine justified by its power to promote economic development. In a capital-scarce economy, its proponents urged, the first entrant takes the greatest risks; without the recognition of a property in the first developer—and a concomitant power to exclude subsequent entrants—there cannot exist the legal and economic certainty necessary to induce investors in a high risk enterprise.

Though the strength of its hold varied among particular areas of the law, in general, priority became the dominant doctrine of property law in the early stages of American economic growth. Its development paralleled that of pervasive state-promoted mercantilism in the early nineteenth century American economies; while it was displaced almost immediately in some areas of the law, in others it continued to stand firm well into this century.

---

[4] Use your own [property] so as not to harm another's.

The attack on the rule of priority reveals the basic instability of utilitarian theories of property. As property rights came to be justified by their efficacy in promoting economic growth, they also became increasingly vulnerable to the efficiency claims of newer competing forms of property. Thus, the rule of priority, wearing the mantle of economic development, at first triumphed over natural use. In turn, those property rights acquired on the basis of priority were soon challenged under a balancing test or "reasonable use" doctrine that sought to define the extent to which newer forms of property might injure the old with impunity. Priority then claimed the status of natural right, but only rarely did it check the march of efficiency. Nor could a doctrine of reasonable use long protect those who advanced under its banner, since its function was to clear the path for the new and the efficient. Some of its beneficiaries eventually reclaimed the doctrine of priority, this time asserting the efficiency of "natural monopoly" and the inevitability of a standard of priority.

Viewed retrospectively, one is tempted to see a Machiavellian hand in this process. How better to develop an economy than initially to provide the first developers with guarantees against future competitive injury? And once development has reached a certain level, can the claims of still greater efficiency through competition be denied? By changing the rules and disguising the changes in the complexities of technical legal doctrine, the facade of economic security can be maintained even as new property is allowed to sweep away the old.

The plan that the historian sees in retrospect, however, was not what the participants in this process saw. They were simply guided by the conception of efficiency prevailing at the moment. Practical men, they may never have stopped to reflect on the changes they were bringing about, nor on the vast differences between their own assumptions and those of their predecessors.

* * *

The Mill Acts: Property as an Instrumental Value

The various acts to encourage the construction of mills offer some of the earliest illustrations of American willingness to sacrifice the sanctity of private property in the interest of promoting economic development. The first such statute, enacted by the Massachusetts colonial legislature in 1713, envisioned a procedure for compensating landowners when a "small quantity" of their property was flooded by the raising of waters for mill dams. The statutory procedure was rarely used, however, since the Massachusetts courts refused to construe the act to eliminate the traditional common law remedies for trespass or nuisance. After the act was amended in 1795 and 1798, mill owners began to argue that it provided an exclusive remedy for the flooding of lands. As a result, the mill acts adopted in a large number of states and territories on the model of the Massachusetts law were, more than any other legal measure, crucial in dethroning landed property from the supreme position it had occupied in the eighteenth century world view, and ultimately, in transforming real estate into just another cash-valued commodity. The history of the acts is a major source of information on the relationship of law to economic change. For reasons of convenience the discussion that follows concentrates on the Massachusetts experience, which, though particularly rich, is not atypical.

Under the 1795 Massachusetts statute, an owner of a mill situated on any nonnavigable stream was permitted to raise a dam and flood the land of his neighbor, so long as he compensated him according to the procedures established by the act. The injured party was limited to yearly damages, instead of a lump sum payment, even if the land was permanently flooded, and the initial estimate of annual damages continued from year to year unless one of the parties came into court and showed that circumstances had changed. The act conferred extensive discretion on the jury, which, in addition to determining damages, could prescribe the height to which a dam could be raised as well as the time of year that lands could be flooded. Unlike the statutes in some states, such as Virginia, the Massachusetts law authorized the mill owner to flood neighboring lands without seeking prior court permission. Thus, except for the power of the jury to regulate their future actions, there was no procedure for determining in advance the utility of allowing mill owners to overflow particular lands.

The exclusive remedial procedures of the mill acts foreclosed four important alternative avenues to relief. First, they cut off the traditional action for trespass to land, in which a plaintiff was not required to prove actual injury in order to recover. In a mill act proceeding, a defendant could escape all liability by showing that, on balance, flooding actually benefited the plaintiff. Second, the statutory damage formula removed the possibility of imposing punitive damages in trespass or nuisance. The common law view had been that unless punitive damages could be imposed, it might pay the wrongdoer to keep it up forever; and thus one individual will be enabled to take from another his property against his consent, and detain it from him as long as he pleases. A third form of relief at common law allowed an affected landowner to resort to self-help to abate a nuisance. Indeed, there are a number of reported cases in which mill dams not covered by the protection of the mill acts were torn down by neighbors claiming to enforce their common law rights. Finally, the acts foreclosed the possibility of permanently enjoining a mill owner for having created a nuisance.

In the early nineteenth century the need to provide a doctrinal rationale for the extraordinary power that the mill acts delegated to a few individuals was acute. Not only had the use of water power vastly expanded in the century since the original Massachusetts act, but there was also a major difference between the eighteenth century grist mill, which was understood to be open to the public, and the more recently established saw, paper, and cotton mills, many of which served only the proprietor. In *Stowell v. Flagg,*[86] Chief Justice Parker said, "The Statute was made for the relief of mill owners from a multiplicity of suits," because the legislature found that the common law remedy would "so burthen the owner of a mill with continual lawsuits and expenses" when he overflowed his neighbor's land. Parker was not troubled by the statutory mode of compensation through annual payment of damages, which, in effect, compelled the landowner to make a loan to the mill owner and thereby enabled the mill owner to amortize any permanent damage he caused. Nor did he point out that under the common law there was no private right to flood adjoining land, even upon making just compensation.

By viewing the statute as entirely remedial, Parker did not have to portray the enterprise as sufficiently public in nature to bring it within the power of eminent domain. Troubled by the enormous potential for unplanned economic change that the mill acts made possible, however, Parker did suggest that the 1798 statute was "incautiously copied from the ancient colonial and provincial acts, which were passed when the use of mills, from the scarcity of them, bore a much greater value, compared to the land used for the purpose of agriculture, than at present."

Parker's language seems to imply that the only public purpose required in order to justify an extensive invasion of private rights was an increase in total utility—and that such a calculation was within the exclusive domain of the legislature. If the legitimacy of a taking was a function only of the relative values of the adjoining properties, any compelled transfer would be lawful so long as compensation was required. It is more likely, however, that Parker was merely questioning the prudence of the legislative judgment, while never doubting that mills were public in terms of whom they served.

By 1814 the significance of the growing separation between public and private enterprise was only beginning to penetrate the judicial mind. Some still conceived of mills as a form of public enterprise in which competition was impermissible. Business corporations were only beginning to upset the old corporate models, in which the raison d'etre of chartered associations was their service to the public. Nor is there any evidence that the increasingly private nature of mills, which was painfully evident to everyone fifteen years later, had as yet caused judges the slightest conceptual difficulty. * * *

The dramatic growth of cotton mills after 1815 provided the greatest incentive for mill owners to flood adjoining land and, in turn, brought to a head a heated controversy over the nature of property rights. The original mill dams were relatively small operations that caused some upstream flooding when proprietors held back water in order to generate power. With the growth of large integrated cotton mills, however, the flooding of more lands became necessary not only because larger dams held back greater quantities of water but also because of the need to generate power by releasing an enormous flow of water downstream. In light of this fact, the Massachusetts legislature amended the mill act in 1825 to allow the flooding of "lands . . . situated either above or below any mill dam." Two years later, in the *Wolcott Woollen* case,[93] the Supreme Judicial Court of Massachusetts, adopting its customary posture of resignation, observed only that "the encouragement of mills has always been a favorite object with the legislature, and though the reasons for it may have ceased, the favor of the legislature continues." It thereby extended the protection of the mill act to what were essentially manufacturing establishments, even though regulating the flow and assessing yearly damages were far more difficult than in the case of upstream flooding, where the extent of damage could easily be predicted once the allowable height of the dam was determined. Even more significant, the mill owners succeeded in inducing

---

[86] 11 Mass. 364 (1814).

[93] Wolcott Woollen Mfg. Co. v. Upham, 22 Mass. (5 Pick.) 292, 294 (1827).

the court to extend the act to cover a situation that the legislature could scarcely have envisioned. Thus, a mill that had purchased land and built a new dam more than three miles upstream from its existing mill, was allowed to overflow all the land between the dam and the original mill site. In effect, the court gave mill owners virtually unlimited discretion to destroy the value of lands far in excess of any benefit they might possibly receive.

Also, in 1827,[94] the court applied another new section of the act to allow a defendant to escape damages entirely by showing that the irrigation benefits the plaintiff received from having his lands overflowed more than outweighed any injury he had incurred. Representing the culmination of a quarter century's experience under the mill acts, this marked the final break with the eighteenth century conception of property, which regarded the flooding of land as a fundamental invasion of right regardless of actual damage. * * * Under the mill act * * * mere interference with another's quiet enjoyment of land no longer possessed any independent claim to compensation. The only measure of damage was the effect on the productive value of land.

* * *

Extension of the mill act to manufacturing establishments brought forth a storm of bitter opposition. One theme—that manufacturing establishments were private institutions—appeared over and over again. One commentator, for example, pointed out that the original mill act had been enacted at the time when "the country had been in a state of slow progress from a wilderness to cultivation" and "lands were of comparatively little value, while the support of corn and saw mills . . . was . . . of vital necessity." Under these circumstances, he said, mills could have reasonably been regarded as "*public* easements." With the extension of the acts to manufacturing establishments, however, the essential question was changed to "the right to apply the property of any one against his consent to *private* uses."[100] * * * Finally, those whose lands were flooded complained bitterly that there was "no remedy worth pursuing," so that "but few of those who suffer seek any relief." "Generally," they observed, "the mills and mill seats are in the hands of the active and wealthy—able to make the sufferers repent, if they resort to the law."[102]

The nearly unanimous denunciation of the mill acts soon brought forth a degree of change. From 1830, when Lemuel Shaw began his thirty year tenure as chief justice, the Massachusetts court began a marked retreat away from its earlier reluctant, but expansive, interpretation of the act. And after 1830, when the legislature eliminated the most notorious windfall to mill owners by extending to the injured party the opportunity to recover permanent damages, the leading attraction of proceeding under the act was eliminated.

With this evidence of diminished legislative support, the Massachusetts court consistently rejected attempts to extend the statute to novel areas. Shaw's first mill act case[105] posed the question whether the protection of the act extended to mills erected on artificial canals built for the purpose of drawing water away from natural streams. This issue presented the court with the opportunity to encourage a vast geographical expansion of industry under the protective wing of the mill act by sanctioning the flooding that would result from a network of canals on which dams would be built. If the mill act applied, "the owner of a parcel of low land may erect a mill upon it and bring water to the mill from any distant pond or reservoir, through the intermediate lands, without the permission of the owners of lands, and may rely for protection upon these statutes." Although the court had seemed to sanction such a procedure only five years earlier, Shaw held that the benefits of the mill act extended only to riparian proprietors. The full import of the earlier decision was just becoming apparent as the dispute expanded beyond the fairly narrow and historically separate question of the proper means of regulating riparian owners to include the more general and necessarily controversial problem of determining the rights of landowners to use their lands.

Conceding that the mill acts "are somewhat at variance with that absolute right of dominion and enjoyment which every proprietor is supposed by law to have in his own soil," Shaw nevertheless proceeded to offer a dual justification for the acts. The legislation could be defended, he wrote, "partly upon

---

[94] Avery v. Van Deusen, 22 Mass. (5 Pick.) 182 (1827).

[100] "The Law of Water Privileges," 2 *Am. Jurist* 25, 30-31, 34 (1829).

[102] Maine Citizens Memorial To the Legislature (c. 1833, broadside J 38 (ms. Treasure Room, Harvard Law School). Maine, which separated from Massachusetts in 1820, continued to enforce the Massachusetts mill act. For another attack on the act, see "The Requisites to Dower and Who are Capable of It," 20 *Am. Jurist* 47, 60-63 (1838).

[105] Fiske v. Framingham Mfg. Co., 29 Mass. (12 Pick.) 68 (1832). But *cf.* Chase v. Sutton Mfg. Co., 58 Mass. (4 Cush.) 152 (1849).

the interest which the community at large has, in the use and employment of mills" —a theory of eminent domain—"and partly upon the nature of the property, which is often so situated, that it could not be beneficially used without the aid of this power." However artificial it may have been in the existing context, Shaw argued that the mill act "was designed to provide for the most useful and beneficial occupation and enjoyment of natural streams and water-courses, where the absolute right of each proprietor, to use his own land and water privileges, at his own pleasure, cannot be fully enjoyed, and one must of necessity, in some degree, yield to the other."

In spite of the difficulties inherent in viewing the mill act as a mere regulation of water rights, Shaw preferred to treat at least part of his case on that restrictive but historically approved function. Thus, he put great emphasis on the relativity of rights as between riparian owners while minimizing his reliance on a theory of eminent domain. This effort to limit the importance of the power of eminent domain appears to reflect a growing realization of the essentially private nature of the interests that were being served by the mill acts and a consequent unwillingness to allow the state to intervene solely to advance private ends.

While it did help to overcome some of the difficulties in applying a theory of eminent domain to essentially private activities, the main contribution of Shaw's formulation was to force courts to see that a conception of absolute and exclusive dominion over property was incompatible with the needs of industrial development. Whether the rationale for state intervention was eminent domain or a more explicit recognition of the relativity of property rights, under the influence of the mill acts men had come to regard property as an instrumental value in the service of the paramount goal of promoting economic growth.

Note

Those writing of the history of nuisance law, like Horwitz, make the general point that commercial development required changing property rules giving absolute dominion and control over property to those who might challenge industrial growth. Does *Boomer v. Atlantic Cement Company*, 26 N.Y.2d 219, 257 N.E.2d 870 (1970), the classic nuisance case used in virtually all property casebooks, seem like the sort of case that should have been decided during the last half of the nineteenth century?

William H. Taft, *The Right of Private Property,* 3 MICH. L. J. 215, 217–222, 224, 226–228, 231–233 (1894)*

As far back as we can go in the history of the common law of England, the right of property of the freeman was theoretically inviolate. Of course the serf or slave, owned by another, enjoyed no such right. But freedom, and the security of private property were linked together as the ancient liberties of the free English subject. The Norman kings were not as regardful of these liberties as they should have been, and the barons of the realm forced from King John in 1215 the written promise to preserve that which * * * all of us know as the Magna Charta. The important words of John's promise were: "No freeman shall be taken or imprisoned, or be disseised of his freehold or liberties, or free customs or be outlawed or exiled, or any otherwise damaged, nor will we pass upon him, nor send upon him but by lawful judgment of his peers or by the law of the land."

* * *

In 1791, a bill of rights was added to the federal constitution and by its fifth article congress and the general government were forbidden to deprive any person of life, liberty or property without due process

*An address delivered before the graduating class and alumni of the law department of the University of Michigan at the last commencement. * * * [Editor's Note: This footnote is in the orginal.]

of law. Following Sir Edward Coke's statement in his Institutes, the supreme court of the United States has held that the words "due process of law" are the equivalent to the words of Magna Charta "except by the lawful judgment of his peers or by the laws of the land." In 1866, after the late civil war, and for the purpose of establishing the security of life and property, so much in peril in the states which had been devastated by war and which were being subjected to radical changes in their social conditions, the fourteenth amendment to the federal constitution was adopted, providing among other things, that no state shall pass laws depriving any person of life, liberty or property without due process of law. Similar restrictions upon the power of state legislatures may be found in all the state constitutions.

* * *

I have thus reviewed the guaranties of private property contained in our fundamental law, familiar to us all, for the purpose of showing what a conservative government we live under and how strongly buttressed by written law is our American society against the attacks of anarchy, socialism and communism. While we inherited from our English ancestors the deep seated conviction that security of property and contract and liberty of the individual are indissolubly linked, as the main props of higher and progressive civilization, we have by our complicated form of government, with its many checks and balances, been able to give substantial guaranties of those rights, much further removed from the gusty and unthinking passions of temporary majorities, than has our mother country.

* * *

In this country until recent years not only have we had broad constitutional guaranties of property and contract rights, but there has been present in the breasts of our whole people a firm conviction of their sacred character. The fundamental compacts of state and nation have been merely declaratory of that which has been recognized as right and necessary by every individual, no matter how humble, and the immense advantage to our country growing out of the inviolability of property and contract rights has until recently been fully appreciated by all American citizens.

But while there has been no change in our constitutional guaranties, it cannot be denied that there has lately come a change of sentiment in certain of our people, by whom the right of private property is not now as highly regarded as formerly. Constitutional restrictions are generally not self executing but appropriate legislation must be passed for the purpose. Statute laws do not execute themselves, but, to be effective, must be administered by the firm hand of executive power. Events are happening each day which make a thoughtful man fear that if the tendency, indicated by them, is to grow in popular weight and intensity, our boasted constitutional guaranties of property rights will not be worth the parchment upon which they were originally written.

Impatience with the existing social order and contempt for the security of private property have found strongest expression among those who do manual labor for a living. By some of the more radical the wisdom of private property has been already challenged, while others manifest a resentment toward the system without formulating a purpose to destroy it. There are others, not confined to the ranks of labor, who would not admit an intention to undermine the constitutional guaranties we have just been considering and yet publicly express so strong a hatred for aggregated capital, and show so marked a disposition to obstruct in every way its lawful accretions, that much comfort and strength is given to the avowed enemies of private property. Now the institution of private property is a good thing or it is not. We who believe in it must be able to give reasons for the faith that is in us. A full discussion of the subject would be too much extended for an address like this, but it may not be out of place briefly to refer to the origin of private property, and its incalculable advantage to our race, and to point out why the laborer of all members of modern society is most interested in maintaining its absolute security.

As soon as man raised himself above the level of beasts, and began to live in a social state with his fellows, he recognized as a principle of natural justice that one should enjoy what his labor produced. * * * The certainty that a man could enjoy as his own that which he produced, furnished the strongest motive for industry beyond what was merely necessary to obtain the bare necessities of life. The knowledge that what he saved would enable him to increase and share the result of another's labor was the chief inducement to economy and self control, and this was greatly strengthened as a motive when he came to know that what he saved during his life could be enjoyed after his death by those to whom he was bound by natural affection. In other words, the institution of private property is what has led to the accumulation of capital in the world. * * * Without it the whole world would still be groping in the darkness of the tribe or commune stage of civilization with alternating periods of starvation and plenty, and no happiness but of gorging unrestrained appetite. Capital increases the amount of production and reduces the cost in labor units of each unit of production. The cheaper the cost of production the less each one had to work to earn the absolute necessities of life and the more time he had to earn its comforts. As the material comforts increase the more possible becomes happiness and the greater the opportunity for the cultivation of the higher instincts of the human mind and soul.

* * *

Labor needs capital to secure the best production, while capital needs labor in producing anything. The share of each laborer in the joint product is necessarily determined by the amount of capital in use as compared with the number of laborers. The more capital in use the higher is the reward of each laborer, while the less the capital in use, the number of laborers remaining the same, the lower the reward of each laborer. To state it in another way, the more capital in use the more work there is to do, and the more work there is to do the more laborers are needed. The greater the need for laborers the better their pay per man. Manifestly then it is to the interest of the laborer that capital should increase faster than the number of those who work. Everything which tends to legitimately increase the accumulation of wealth and its use for production will give each laborer a larger share of the joint result of capital and his labor. It will be observed that the laborer derives little or no benefit at all from wealth which is not used for production. Nothing is so likely to make wealth idle as insecurity of capital and property. It follows as a necessary conclusion that to destroy the guaranties of property is a direct blow at the interests of the working man.

* * *

What has been said should not be misunderstood. The men who have by economic organization of capital at the same time increased the amount of the country's capital increased the demand and price for labor and reduced the costs of necessities, are not philanthropists in the sense that they have done this from any motive of unselfish and disinterested love for human kind. Their sole motive has been one of gain, and with the destruction of private property that motive would disappear and so would the progress of society. The very advantage to be derived from the security of private property in our civilization is that it turns the natural selfishness and desire for gain into the strongest motive for doing that without which the upward development of mankind would cease and retrogression would begin.

* * *

I have said that the increase of capital is for the benefit of the laborer, because it increases the demand for his labor and therefore his wages. As the fruits of production are to be divided between labor and capital, their common interest to increase the fruits is manifest. But in the division of their joint product their interests are plainly opposed. Clearly in such a conflict of interest the laborers united are stronger than when acting singly. Ultimately the division of the fruits is inexorably determined by the law of supply and demand, but during the gradual adjustment, according to that law, the capitalists will gain the advantage unless labor acts as a body. On a rising market, early advantage in the increase of the demand for labor may be taken by the laborers if they act together, and a prompt raising of wages secured, when otherwise it would be grudgingly and slowly granted; while, by the same united action, they may retard their too eager employer in reducing wages on a falling market. Such organizations, when they are intelligently and conservatively conducted, do much I have no doubt to aid their members in the hard struggle for existence, and have materially increased the share of the workingman in the joint product of capital and labor. * * *

But unfortunately for capital and labor, many unions as now conducted are very different from that just described. In them, the turbulent are either in the majority or by mere violence of demonstration overawe the conservative element. The leaders are selected, not because of their clear judgment and intelligence, but because they are glib of tongue and intemperate of expression. The influx of foreign workmen bringing with them the socialistic ideas which prevail among the laboring classes of Europe, has planted in many unions the seeds of sedition and discontent with the existing order. Hence it is, that whenever a controversy arises between labor and capital resulting in a strike, lawlessness too often follows any attempt of the employer lawfully to continue his business. If this lawlessness is not repressed promptly and firmly, as often it is not, the sympathies of members of the union are awakened in behalf of lawless methods, their former law-abiding disposition is blunted and they manifest an alarming indifference to the necessity for peace and order.

Then many labor organizations appear in politics and their influence is thrown, regardless of party lines, for the candidate who loudly proclaims himself the friend of labor and proves it by denouncing the greed of capital, the slavery of the workingman and his purpose to change all this by legislation. While their members are not in a majority, the united action of such labor organizations, together with the inert partisanship of which gives to each of the great parties a certain vote whatever the issue, enables them to exercise an influence in elections far beyond their mere numbers. As there is still much human nature in man, the impulse of most persons in public life is to say and do nothing which will displease them. Thus it is that the workingman is rarely told the exact truth about his relations to capital and is too often encouraged by public men to believe that he suffers from society wrongs which should not be borne. Is it much cause for wonder, that he is skeptical about the wisdom of private property, when he is told in the halls of our national legislature that he should have the right to compel another to employ him at his own price, and that, in a bloody battle waged for him, for this purpose, against private property and its defenders, he is entitled to sympathy? Is his illogical hostility to aggregate capital very strange when in the same place he frequently hears men attacked with virulence and a torrent of epithet, simply because by industry, thrift, executive ability and sound business judgment, they have succeeded in accumulating wealth?

* * *

It seems to me enough has been stated to show that, while we have the strongest guaranties of the rights of property in our fundamental laws, there is a growing tendency to weaken the firm maintenance of those guaranties, so far at least as they relate to corporate capital; that everything which weakens this security of corporate capital cannot but affect that of individual private property; and that if the present movement against corporate capital is not met and fought, it will become a danger to our whole social fabric. I do not think the present state of social unrest is any ground for a pessimistic view of modern civilization. We are passing through an era of tremendous economic changes and the apparently alarming phenomena in the social horizon are only the necessary results of an adjustment to new conditions. But this view does not, in the slightest degree, diminish the necessity for reducing the friction of the adjustment, so that it may not be retarded, or for preventing a temporary impairment or destruction of the chief agent in the material progress of the human race, the security of private property and free contract.

How then can we stay the movement I have described against property rights? It is by telling and enforcing the truth that every laborer, and every man of moderate means has as much interest to preserve the inviolability of corporate property as he has that of his own. It is by defending modern civilization and the existing order against the assaults of raving fanatics, emotional and misdirected philanthropists, and blatant demagogues. It is by purifying politics from corruption. It is by calling to strict account our public men for utterances or conduct likely to encourage resentment against the guaranties of law, order and property and by insisting that equal and exact justice shall be done as well to a corporation as to an individual in legislative and executive action. The friends and believers in our modern civilization with its security for private property, as the best mode of a gradual elevation of the race, must make their views and voices heard above the resounding din of anarchy, socialism, populism and the general demagogy which is so wide spread to-day.

In the days of old, the charter guaranties were given it was supposed, for the benefit of the poor and lowly against the oppressions of the rich and powerful. To-day it is the rich who seek the protection of the courts for the enforcement of those guaranties. The judges of federal and other courts are sworn to administer justice fairly between the rich and poor. When the oath was formulated it was doubtless feared that the temptation would be to favor the rich. To-day, if a judge would yield to the easy course, he would lean against the wealthy and favor the many. While this seems to be a change, it is not really so. The sovereign to-day is the people, or the majority of the people. The poor are the majority. The appeal of the rich to the constitution and courts for protection is still an appeal by the weak against the unjust aggressions of the strong. Mr. Justice Miller, speaking for the supreme court in *Loan Association v. Topeka,*[2] a case where the majority of the voters of a city were seeking to impose upon its property holders against their consent, a tax to build a private factory for the use and ownership of a private individual, uses this language in reference to the right of the property owner to object to the taxing of his property for the personal advancement of another. "It must be conceded that there are such rights in every free government beyond the control of the state. A government which recognized no such rights, which held the lives, liberty and property of its citizens, subject at all times to the absolute disposition and unlimited control of even the most democratic depository of power is, after all, a despotism. It is true it is a despotism of the many, of the majority, if you choose to call it so, but is none the less a despotism."

[2] 20 Wall., 655.

The immediate burden of this conflict for the security of private property will, I suppose, fall upon the courts until by discussion and longer experience, light shall come to its opponents. The bench must rest for its strength upon the bar. * * *

And for this reason I have addressed you. As you enter upon your professional life you will be required to swear that you will support and defend the constitution of the United States and of the state of Michigan. Many of you will become foremost in the communities where you live as leaders of public sentiment. Many of you, I hope, will take part in politics. You will go to the legislature and to congress. As public teachers, as public men, as politicians, you will not cease to be lawyers or lose your allegiance to the fundamental compacts you have sworn to uphold and defend. It has seemed to me fitting, at such a time, to remind you that in those compacts there is secured as sacred the right of private property, and that unless you do everything that in you lies to maintain that security and guaranty, you will be false to the oath you take. You are about to enter a profession which a great French chancellor said was "as old as the magistrate, as noble as virtue, as necessary as justice." In ancient times the members of the profession were the bulwark of freedom and of the vested rights of property. I do not doubt that they will continue to be so in the future. The freedom of the citizen is secure. It is the right of private property that now needs supporters and protectors.

Note

Do either Horwitz or Taft take status into account in their work? For example, was the institution of marriage, like property, affected by the movement to contractual concepts? Consider two examples.

1. At the height of the merger of contract and property regimes, the United States Supreme Court decided two cases, *Lochner v. New York*, 198 U.S. 45 (1905), and *Muller v. Oregon*, 208 U.S. 412 (1908), quite differently. In *Lochner,* the Court invalidated a New York statute limiting the hours male bakers could work to sixty per week and ten per day on the theory that the statute interfered with the right of employers and employees to freely contract for their labor. Three years later, the *Muller* Court sustained an Oregon law banning employment of women in factories and laundries for more than ten hours per day. The famous Brandeis brief, filed in *Muller* in support of the Oregon regulation, contained dozens of references to studies suggesting that women's reproductive roles were endangered by hard work. Were women not deemed appropriate participants in Taft's world of property and contract? Taft, by the way, became President in 1909, and was appointed to the Supreme Court in 1921.

2. The tenancy by the entirety, discussed in *Sawada v. Endo*, 57 Haw. 608, 561 P.2d 1291 (1977), was changed or abolished in many jurisdictions in the second half of the nineteenth or the beginning of the twentieth century. Is there anything contractual about the idea that creditors have a more difficult time attaching the property of married persons than they do assets held by others?

Perhaps Amy Dru Stanley's article in the next segment of the anthology, will help you sort out these issues.

2. A Major Property Development of the Post Civil War Era: Emancipation, Free Labor and Women's Wages

Changes in property rules for women have often come after war and civil rights agitation. War time activities of women frequently extended into areas previously occupied by the men sent off to fight. Post-war attempts to return to "normal" didn't always succeed. Public concern about the status of African Americans has often been accompanied by more widespread discussions of the meaning of equality and citizenship for other groups. The Abolitionist Movement of the 1830's and 1840's was closely associated with the first women's movement. The modern rise of feminism followed closely on the heels of the Civil Rights Movement. The post Civil War era followed a similar pattern, with suffragists attempting (but failing) to make headway as the nation adopted the 13th, 14th and 15th Amendments. Property reforms favored by many feminists, however, were passed. Amy Dru Stanley describes how and why this occurred.

Amy Dru Stanley, *Conjugal Bonds and Wage Labor: Rights of Contract in the Age of Emancipation,* 75 J. AM. HIST. 471–477, 480–484, 488–493, 495, 497–499 (1988)*

Preeminent among the rights that belonged to freedom were "rights of family and rights of contract." So Charles Sumner declared to the United States Senate in the course of a very long and learned disquisition on the legal status of emancipated slaves in December 1865. Sumner gave due regard to rights of property, suffrage, and equality before the law. But the defining difference between freedom and bondage, he maintained, was freedom of contract: the right to marry and have a family, and the right to sell one's labor for a wage. Like most others of his generation, Sumner took for granted that relations of marriage and wage labor were complementary.

Sumner's argument contained a notable contradiction, however. Marriage bonds and contract rights were hardly congruent—at least where wives were concerned. Under the common law, married women had no right to contract; their labor belonged to their husbands. Sitting high above in the Senate gallery, Frances Gage, an advocate of antislavery and of woman's rights, listened closely to Sumner's oratory and objected to the lapses in his reasoning. "When I . . . found that he meant only freedom for the male sex, I learned that Charles Sumner fell far short of the great idea of liberty," Gage tartly observed. "I would not say one word against marriage. . . . But let it be a marriage of equality."[2]

The contradiction between contract rights and the marriage relation resonated at the levels both of rhetoric and of social experience. It was a central theme of woman's rights agitation, and it echoed through the halls of Congress during debates over emancipation, for the destruction of slavery and the equation of freedom with contract set in sharp relief the anomalies of the conjugal bond. In state legislatures and state courts, the disjunction between contract rights and marriage rules figured more palpably. For the wage system of labor, extolled in the wake of emancipation and made ascendant by the burgeoning of industrial capitalism, subverted time-honored assumptions of marriage law. At the heart of the contradiction lay the wife's title to her wages, a right that the wage contract presupposed, but the marriage contract denied. To state lawmakers fell the task of reconciling those competing claims.

This essay explores how the code of contract that came to prevail in the post-bellum United States came also to express a profoundly gendered conception of freedom. During years when law makers most venerated men's contract rights, they resisted fully extending the legal and ideological implications of a market economy and waged forms of labor to married women; consequently, wives' title to their labor and earnings remained circumscribed. The first part of the essay shows how congressional debates over emancipation elevated the right to work for wages to a cardinal tenet of freedom and maps the legal symmetry between slavery and marriage. The second part examines another emancipation: a series of "earnings" laws enacted by Republican-dominated state legislatures that entitled wives to keep the fruits of their labor. At first blush, the wife's right to

2 Elizabeth Cady Stanton, Susan B. Anthony, and Matilda Joslyn Gage, eds., *History of Woman Suffrage* (3 vols., Rochester, N.Y., 1889), II, 114-15. * * *

her wages may seem the counterpart of the freedom guaranteed the ex-slave. In fact, the analogy was neither so tidy nor so simple.

By analyzing marriage in the context of the demise of bonds of personal dependency, this essay provides new perspective on the ideology and politics of Reconstruction. It also documents the way law impinged on the family economy of the working classes and addresses the tension between the wage system and legal conventions of marriage. Although recent works on marriage law study the world of propertied women in detail, few historians note the enactment of legislation giving laboring wives a claim to their earnings, and those who do focus chiefly on the links between the passage of the laws and woman suffrage. This essay frames the problem differently. It deals with the wife's right to own herself, her labor, and her wages, not with her ownership of real property; and it sets her title to earnings against the counterpoint between contract rights and the paternal rules of marriage. It thereby casts new light both on ideas of freedom promulgated after the Civil War and on the cultural and legal consequences of wives' wage labor. In an age that consecrated the rules of the market, women's legal right to sell their labor and keep its fruits—no less than their ability to barter sexuality for subsistence—determined the boundaries of their freedom.[3]

In the years following the Civil War, principles of free contract became the subject of fierce public debate and social conflict, supplying a vocabulary for divergent interests and ideologies. E. L. Godkin, the editor of the *Nation*, gave classic expression to the wisdom of the age. The tendency of modern times, he said, was to substitute contract for status: "to submit our social relations more and more to the dominion of contract simply." Sundering the bonds of slavery, transforming the obligations of workers and employers, the tendency had penetrated further still, Godkin asserted, into the most private domain of husband and wife. The feminist and free love advocate Victoria Woodhull agreed. "There is neither right nor duty," she proclaimed, "beyond the uniting—the contracting—individuals." An official of the Freedmen's Bureau translated the proposition into a simple catechism for ex-slaves: "Contracts are very numerous; numerous as the leaves on the trees, almost; and, in fact, the world could not get on at all without them."[4] Such aphorisms celebrated a cultural code that identified contract with individual freedom and social progress, that found a metaphor for social relations in commercial exchange.

The intellectual roots of these contractual principles extended to antebellum debates over slavery, twisting along the paths of the common law to the liberal political thought of the seventeenth century.[5] But in the aftermath of the Civil War, those who clarified the meaning of emancipation, whether inside legislative chambers or out of doors, stated the link between contract and freedom with new urgency and precision. That enterprise and the configuration of legal tenets, economic principles, and moral assumptions to which it gave credence were rife with unsettling implications for the law of husband and wife.

The virtues of contract were elaborated with particular rigor during the debate over the Civil Rights Act of 1866. The act asserted the principle of equality before the law and the authority of the national government to guarantee the irrevocable rights of citizens, which it enumerated as those of contract, property, and personal liberty. But its immediate purpose was to strike down the southern Black Codes that restricted the liberty of black labor, and the right of contract was the cornerstone of the legislation. One congressman expostulated, "there

---

[3] On the significance of gender in historical interpretations, see Joan W. Scott, "Gender: A Useful Category of Historical Analysis," *American Historical Review*, 91 (Dec. 1986), 1053–75. Recent works that examine the role of law in shaping the lives of propertied women include Norma Basch, *In the Eyes of the Law: Women, Marriage, and Property in Nineteenth-Century New York* (Ithaca, 1982); Suzanne D. Lebsock, *The Free Women of Petersburg: Status and Culture in a Southern Town*, 1784–1860 (New York, 1984); and Richard H. Chused, "Married Women's Property Law, 1800–1850," *Georgetown Law Journal*, 71 (June 1983), 1359–1425. On the links between legal reform and woman suffrage reform, see Suzanne D. Lebsock, "Radical Reconstruction and the Property Rights of Southern Women," *Journal of Southern History*, 63 (May 1977), 195–216; and Basch, *In the Eyes of the Law*. * * *

[4] E. L. Godkin, "The Labor Crisis," *North American Review*, 105 (July 1867), 183. * * * Victoria Woodhull, "The Principles of Social Freedom," *Woodhull & Claflin's Weekly*, Aug. 16, 1973; Clinton B. Fisk, *Plain Counsels for Freedmen: In Sixteen Brief Lectures* (Boston, 1866) 47. Fisk was an assistant commissioner of the Freedmen's Bureau.

[5] On the legal and intellectual history of contract, see * * * Patrick S. Atiyah, *The Rise and Fall of Freedom of Contract* (Oxford, 1979); James Willard Hurst, *Law and the Conditions of Freedom in the Nineteenth-Century United States* (Madison, 1956); Morton J. Horwitz, *The Transformation of American Law, 1780–1860* (Cambridge, Mass., 1977), 160–210; and David Brian Davis, *The Problem of Slavery in the Age of Revolution, 1780–1823* (Ithaca, 1975), 489–501. * * *

are certain rights which belong to a freedman. He has a right to contract, he has a right to support himself." According to an Ohio legislator, it was "mockery" to grant a citizen the right to live "yet deny him the right to make a contract to secure the privilege and the rewards of labor."

Perhaps the only feature of freedom not in dispute among members of Congress was the former slaves' right to sell their labor for wages. Some conceded the point only grudgingly, yet it was generally acknowledged that emancipation made freed people into proprietors of their own persons and labor, abolishing the status, as one Maryland senator admitted, "in which one man belongs to another, which gives to that other a right to appropriate the profits of his labor." The nub of freedom, legislators of various political persuasions concluded, amounted to ownership of one's self and one's labor—the right to make contracts and to keep at least some portion of the fruits of labor.

That definition departed notably from an earlier tradition that yoked freedom to property ownership. It was contested by a handful of Radical Republicans as well as by a greater number of ex-slaves and industrial wage earners who stubbornly claimed that freedom of contract was illusory in the absence of economic independence and political rights. And some critics of postbellum society condemned the reduction of social ties to the laws of the marketplace. Still, few challenged the association, in principle at least, of freedom with contract. As Wendell Phillips put it, lauding the free labor system: "A man here makes a contract, and, if he does not keep it there's a court. If he does keep it and is not paid, there is a jury . . . That is liberty."[8]

* * *

The common law rule of coverture governed the status of husband and wife. The rule made them one person at law, creating an "indissoluble connexion" that submerged the legal identity of the wife in her husband. Like slavery, marriage was a relation of domination and dependence, premised on reciprocal exchange; the law bound the wife to serve and obey her husband in return for his support and protection. Marriage stripped her of the essential right of freedom—the right to possess her own person. Accordingly, she also lost the fundamental rights derived from self-ownership, the rights to make contracts, to acquire property, and to control her own labor and its proceeds.

* * *

The authors of Reconstruction * * * asserted the permanence of the family bond as an essential ingredient of freedom and claimed that the freeman, unlike the slave, possessed a property right in his family. "Is a freeman," demanded one senator, to be deprived of the right of "earning and purchasing property; of having a home. . . a wife and family, or of eating the bread he earns?" Such an inventory suggested that a man's claim to his wife was equivalent to his title to material things or to the means to acquire them. Legislators' affirmation of the freedman's title to his family rested on their conception of the family as an indivisible unit based on male supremacy and female dependence. That notion, deeply ingrained and unexamined, underpinned the denial of freedom of contract to wives. Whereas emancipation had fractured the reciprocity between master and slave, leaving the freedman dependent solely on himself, women were a "part of the family" and therefore needed no entitlement at law. * * * According to this argument, which relied on the family as its organizing metaphor, the legal rights of freedmen issued from the enmity between ex-slaves and ex-masters and the social distance between the races. Conversely, because women belonged to family units purportedly bound by ties of affection, such rights were denied them as individuals. To conceive the wife as a contracting individual was to subvert the animating principles of republicanism, which defined the freeman, the citizen, as a household proprietor whose rights embraced dominion over his wife, including title to her person, labor, and wages.

Statesmen, then, elevated contract into a sovereign right of citizenship and defined the right to marry and work for wages as the difference between slavery and freedom. Nevertheless, they simply extended white males' established right of contract to freed males, leaving wives of both races to whatever protection the marriage contract could afford. Indeed, the subject of marriage arose only as a reductio ad absurdum. But the undeniable logic of that argument provoked a hasty reinterpretation of the meaning of emancipation, a revision that emphasized themes of race over those that portrayed a transition from obligations of obedience and authority to rights of

---

[8] *National Anti-Slavery Standard*, Feb. 24, 1866. * * * On black workers' resistance to the contract system, see Litwack, *Been in the Storm So Long*, 414–20 (1979); on industrial wage earners' critique of the ideology of free contract, see William E. Forbath, "The Ambiguities of Free Labor: Labor and the Law in the Gilded Age," *Wisconsin Law Review* (no. 4, 1985), 767–817. * * *

self-ownership and contract. Civil War and emancipation turned the slaveholders' world upside down, yet the bonds of marriage remained intact. "It was only in marriage," Stanton bitterly observed in 1868, that woman

> must demand her rights to person, children, property, wages, life, liberty and the pursuit of happiness. All the special statutes of which we complain—all the barbarities of the law—fall on her as wife and mother. We have not yet outlived the old feudal idea, the right of property in woman.[22]

In equating freedom with contract, congressional legislators stumbled against a set of thorny questions regarding the status of married women. They chose to evade them and confined the tenets of emancipation to men. In the years that followed, however, similar legal conundrums arose to test the ingenuity of state legislators, who could not so readily dismiss them. In Congress, the conflict between contract principles and the marriage bond was purely an abstract proposition, a matter of polemic. But state lawmakers encountered it concretely, in the material and domestic needs of laboring men and women. And, at the same time, they faced an organized woman's movement agitating for wives' right to their wages.

Even as congressional legislators recoiled from the prospect, state legislators undertook to reconcile the conflicting claims of the wage contract and the marriage bond. Unimpeded by considerations of federalism, they passed "earnings" statutes that entitled wives to keep the proceeds of their own labor. Yet they hardly envisioned the enactments as part of any onrushing tide of universal freedom, nor did they intend, any more than their counterparts in Congress, to uncouple the marriage bond. The new legislation reinscribed, rather than resolved, the tension between contract rights and the marriage relation, which diluted its value to the working wives it was supposed to relieve.

By 1887 some two-thirds of the states had passed earnings laws. The statutes not only gave the wife title to her wages but also protected her wages against the claims of her husband and his creditors. Several of the laws expressly enabled her to make contracts. Though a handful of states had enacted limited earnings reforms prior to the Civil War, the two decades thereafter witnessed the great rush of legislation. The married woman, declared one law writer, "now has the right to her labor." That right was known in the law as "emancipation."[23]

The earnings legislation was not part of any sweeping plan by state assemblies to redraft the law of husband and wife. Passed in "piecemeal" fashion, it aimed to preserve "marital rights" but also to "emancipate" the wife to enter into wage contracts and facilitate her dealings with third parties in the marketplace. Treatise writers, whose statements of the law were regularly cited by lawyers and judges, conceded that the acts were "radical in their effect." However, they hastened to warn that the laws were not designed to disrupt the marriage relation — to "accomplish the aims of disorganizing revolutionists." The legislation, they commented, abounded in "unsettled and discordant" principles.[24]

* * *

Ascendant ideas of contract furnished a vocabulary to the woman's rights advocates, who drew up the most expansive justification for the wife's title to her wages. Explicitly equating chattel slavery and the bonds of marriage, they likened the wife's labor to the slave's. Like most slaves, declared a writer in the *Woman's Journal*, woman possessed the right to labor, "but she has not the control of the results of her labor." Antoinette Brown Blackwell, explaining why she supported the earnings cause, reasoned similarly. When the law tells the husband "he may take the wages of his wife, just as the master does those of the slave, and she has no right to them," then, she concluded, women must seek "redress." In opposition to the enduring inequalities of marriage law, feminists proclaimed the wife's sovereign right of contract: her right, as Anthony declared to an association of working women, to "be the controller of her own person, and her own earnings." They stressed the contradiction between the rules of marriage and

---

[22] *Revolution*, Oct. 15, 1868. * * *

[23] George E. Harris, *A Treatise on the Law of Contracts by Married Women, Their Capacity to Contract in Relation to Their Separate Statutory Legal Estates, under American Statues* (Albany, 1887), 114; Joseph Warren, "Husband's Right to Wife's Services," *Harvard Law Review*, 38 (Feb. 1925), 421-46; * * *. In 1855, for example, the Massachusetts legislature gave wives limited title to their earnings; New York passed an earnings law in 1860 as part of a comprehensive married women's act. But the major legislation affording wives the right to contract and keep their earnings came in the 1870s and early 1880s. See Chused, "Married Women's Property Law," 1424. * * *

[24] Warren, "Husband's Right to Wife's Services," 622 Harris, *Treatise on the Law of Contracts by Married Women*, i, ii, 45; Wells, *Treatise on the Separate Property of Married Women*, iii, iv, 73, 77; David Stewart, "Married Women Traders," *American Law Register* (June 1885), 360; James Schouler, *Law of the Domestic Relations* (Boston, 1905), 5.

the wife's rights as a wage earner. According to Elizabeth Osgood Willard, an especially forthright exponent of woman's legal and sexual emancipation, men had unjustly appropriated the fruits of female labor and usurped sole right "to control the time of woman and all her vital energy." "Repeal the slave code for wives," demanded an article in the *Revolution*, "the law which says, 'All that she can acquire by her labor, service or act, during coverture, belongs to her husband'. . . . Emancipate wives." Reiterating the ruling ideas put forward by congressional Republicans, woman's rights advocates claimed nothing less for wives than the freedom exercised by other hireling laborers—the freedom guaranteed to ex-slaves. "Woman has a right to herself," argued a correspondent of the *Revolution*, "a right to the use of all the powers and faculties God has given her, a right to the profits of her labor. . . . Woman has a right to all she earns by honest labor."

It is doubtful that state legislatures assigned any such emancipatory meaning to the earnings statutes, however. Though congressional Republicans openly acknowledged the revolutionary quality of the Reconstruction enactments so far as they applied to black men, silence shrouds the intent of the lawmakers who recognized wives' contract rights. Virtually no records remain of the arguments that carried the earnings statutes through Republican-dominated state legislatures in the postwar decades. Yet enough evidence exists to piece together the motives behind two statutes: a Massachusetts act of 1874 and an Illinois act of 1869. Legislators in those states do not seem to have drawn deliberate lessons from the demise of slavery. They appear to have responded to more immediate pressures, to signs of acute distress in working-class marriages and to the explanations feminists advanced for the plight of laboring wives. Married women gained legal title to their wages, noted a lawyer who wrote often for the *Woman's Journal*, "not from a sound philosophical view of the case," but simply from "expediency or necessity."

* * *

In the era of the earnings laws, * * * income for most families consisted chiefly of wage earnings—as opposed to profits, salary, rent, or interest. And the economic conditions that rendered wage work a highly precarious means of survival fell with equal weight on laboring men and their wives. It was not simply that women bore the primary burden of balancing family income with subsistence needs, performing both paid labor and unpaid housework. Rather, marriage itself had become a less certain means of support for increasing numbers of women. The dominance of commodity production and dependence on wages undercut the ideal of the husband as household provider and also magnified the significance of married women's paid work. Registering the primacy of the wage system, the earnings act, in one sense at least, directly paralleled the theory of slave labor's emancipation. Just as members of Congress viewed the freedman primarily as a wage earner, so state lawmakers took new account of the wife's waged status. The fact behind the earnings acts, commented an authority in the *American Law Review*, was that women had become members of "economic classes new to the public thought."

Contemporaries agreed that the Civil War had greatly disturbed the "traditional functions of the sexes." Nor did the features of postbellum society and economy restore their customary roles. Production slackened while prices rose, continuing an inflationary trend. New industrial methods based on division of tasks and labor-saving machinery reduced wage levels and the demand for skilled workers. Unemployment and casual labor grew increasingly common as wage-dependency left skilled as well as unskilled workers vulnerable to economic fluctuations and seasonal rhythms of production. Idle men, reported the Illinois Bureau of Labor Statistics in 1883, roved the country "driven from place to place by want, seeking work." Women sent notices to labor newspapers, seeking news of their missing husbands; some deserted wives took to the road themselves. As Helen Campbell observed in her influential study of laboring women, the chain binding humanity was not made of "one set of links for men and another for women," for a blow at one was felt by the other "by indirect transmission."

* * *

Whether because their husbands earned wages below subsistence, were unemployed or employed only intermittently, were ill or in prison, or had abandoned them, wives of wage earners were often compelled to sell their labor. According to the charity workers and public officials who made a career of inspecting the lives of the working classes, climbing tenement stairs to peer into their domestic habits, laboring wives cleaned other people's houses and toiled in manufactories, mills, and sweatshops. But more often, they did wage work in their homes, taking in washing, mending, and fancy sewing when they could find it. Or they labored beside their husbands and children in tenement house production of cigars and clothing. Although a few women found "regular washing," more depended on "chance work," that frequently amounted to as little as three hours a week.

* * *

What riveted the attention of bourgeois observers—woman's rights advocates, government investigators, and charity workers alike—was that laboring men and women were flouting the traditional terms of the marriage relation, inverting conventions of masculine and feminine prescribed by law. Some were scandalized, others sympathetic. Yet most observers, feminists excepted, paid little heed to the antecedents of the wife's entry into the market economy: her labor in independent household production, in rural putting-out industries, and in the earliest metropolitan sweatshops. Instead, they dwelled on the conspicuous importance of her earnings to family subsistence and stressed that her work for employers trespassed on her unpaid household obligations. Whether the wife's paid labor was viewed as a sign of social pathology or of sexual equality, it was apparent that the poverty and itinerancy of working-class families had stripped married women of their husbands' support and endowed them with an independent economic identity. "In our large cities thousands of women toil to support families, including often their indolent and inebriate husbands," the sociologist Lester Ward expostulated, "how false is the assertion that men perform the labor of support, while women confine themselves to maternal and domestic duties."[43] The wage system disrupted the fundamental premise of the marriage bond: the relation of male protection and female dependency. The fact that wives needed to market their labor revealed that conjugal rules of support and subordination figured mainly as inventions of the legal imagination.

By granting wives the right to their wages, the earnings statutes gave formal recognition to the erosion of the economic underpinnings of the marriage contract. In contrast to congressional Republicans who presumed both the unity of the marriage bond and its perfect accordance with the wage relation, state legislators conceded distinct legal identities to laboring husbands and wives. The earnings law "emancipated" the wife from dependence on her husband. And it also relieved the public of her charge, by ratifying her independent economic activity and granting her the legal right to own and sell at least part of her labor. Yet from clues two judges left about the intent behind the legislation, it appears that the wife's contract rights were less a token of her immutable freedom than a response to rifts and reversals within the marriage relation. The "chief benefit" of earnings laws, according to Judge John Wells of the Massachusetts supreme court, was to release married women's wages from their husbands' grasp: to confer on "women of the poorer, laboring classes" the "power to control the fruits of their own labor." Many poor women, he explained,

> are left to struggle against the hardships of life—sometimes with a family of children, abandoned by their husbands, or, still worse, with a drunken, thriftless, idle vagabond of a man, claiming all the rights of a husband, and fulfilling none of the duties of that relation.[46]

It was not merely the growing importance of monetary income—"the great accretions of personal over real property, in modern times"—that accounted for the new laws, a judge in the District of Columbia found, but principally the collapse of male support, the "unhappy recurrence of drunken or profligate husbands with patient and industrious wives."[47] The earnings statutes reflected the strains the wage system imposed on working-class families, but if judicial opinion may be trusted, legislators imputed the wife's vulnerability mainly to her husband's derelictions.

The earnings legislation closely resembled married women's property laws enacted earlier in the nineteenth century, hewing to their provisions while seeming also to duplicate their limits. Indeed, recent scholarship places the earnings acts in an unbroken line of legal reform that began in the 1830s with the first married women's property acts and continued through successive waves of legislation into the twentieth century. The property laws, such accounts stress, acknowledged married women's rights as property owners but actually represented a form of debtor relief; in securing family property against the

[43] Lester Ward, *Dynamic Sociology* (2 vols., New York, 1883), I, 644. Norma Basch suggests that the 1860 earnings reform in New York represented principally a concession to feminist demands for suffrage and that wage-earning wives were too few and too powerless to exert political pressure; see Basch, *In the Eyes of the Law*, 164–65, 195–99. At issue, however, was not simply women's ability to shape the law, but also legislators' response to the uncertainty of male support and to wives' independent economic dealings. On middle class observers' apprehensions that wives' labor infringed on their family obligations and violated codes of domesticity, see Kessler-Harris, *Out to Work*, esp. 86, 90.

[46] *Chicago Legal News*, Jan. 16, 1869, pp. 125–26 Judge Wells's observations were quoted during parliamentary debates over married women's property law in England, which were reprinted in the Chicago journal—a roundabout reference, but the most explicit legal statement of the intent behind the earnings laws.

[47] D.C. Court of Claims, cited in "Woman Forbidden to Practice Law," *Woman's Journal*, May 23, 1874.

husband's debt, they benefited the wife less than the husband or kin.[48] Like the property statutes, the earnings laws promised to shield a portion of family income against the claims of creditors and were often written into comprehensive married women's legislation.

But the property acts and the earnings acts protected radically different forms of wealth acquired by women of different social classes. The property laws regulated the domestic economic relations of the propertied classes, applying exclusively to real and personal property traditionally transferred along kin lines by gift or inheritance: land, chattels, movable goods, even business enterprises. And they recognized the wife's legal rights solely in relation to property she owned separately from her husband, leaving her otherwise, as Livermore explained, under the "somewhat violent" rule of his "control." The earnings acts, however, adjusted title to income within the families of the working classes and the poor, governing the wages that wives earned by dint of their own labor. The earnings acts not only recognized a new form of property right specific to a wage economy. In principle, they also placed the wife's legal rights on a new foundation—on the title to her own labor, rather than to separate property. The earnings laws seemed to imply that the wife owned nothing but her labor and its proceeds, an assumption that echoed those articulated in the debates over emancipation.

Unlike the property acts, the earnings acts struck at the core of the marriage relation. For the wife's right to her labor and wages presupposed what ownership of material things did not: her right to own herself. This right contradicted the central premise of marriage: the exchange of service for support that gave the husband absolute title to the labor and person of his wife.

* * *

[Though t]he earnings statutes confounded the traditional logic of the marriage relation * * * they did not overturn it entirely. Though the wife gained a contractual right to her wages, her husband retained his proprietary claim both to her person and to her domestic labor. "Nowhere," averred one law writer, "have the courts gone so far as to suffer these statutes to undo all the obligations which depend on the marriage status."[57] But to parse out just where the wife's rights ended and her obligations began was no simple task.

Especially unclear was the legal boundary between the waged labor the wife owned and the unpaid labor she owed her husband. Yet for working-class men and women, this was the critical question: Exactly what sort of labor did the earnings laws protect? The question arose in the courts in as many ways as wives made money; the litigation concerned everything from factory labor to farm labor, boarding-house management, nursing, shoe binding, and clothing manufacture. Two major issues were at stake. Who had the right to bring a suit to recover for the labor of the wife, the husband or the wife? And who had the paramount claim to her income, the wife or the husband's creditor? Underlying both questions was a more fundamental problem: Who owned her labor, the wife or her husband? As courts threaded their way through the intricacies of wage earners' economic dealings, they confronted head on the contradiction between the wife's right of contract under the earnings acts and her dependent status under the common law.

* * *

The ambiguities turned on the nature and location of her labor—whether it fell within the category of "house work," whether it was performed inside or outside the home—as well as on the use to which the earnings were put. The problem, as the New York court confessed, was that "where the husband and wife are living together, and mutually engaged in providing for the support of themselves and their family,—each contributing by his or her labor to the promotion of the common purpose," there was nothing to indicate the wife's intention to "separate her earnings from those of her husband."[60] In such perplexing situations—where labor did not neatly divide into parcels of property labeled mine and thine—the courts held that the wife's earning belonged to her husband, an interpretation that returned to the common-law rule.

* * *

Courts thus resolved the ambiguities surrounding the wife's work by presuming her labor belonged to

---

[48] See Elizabeth Warbasse, "The Changing Legal Rights of Married Women, 1800–1861" (Ph.D. diss. Harvard University, 1960); Lebsock, "Radical Reconstruction and the Property Rights of Southern Women"; Chused, "Married Women's Property Law"; and Richard H. Chused, "Late Nineteenth Century Married Women's Property Law: Reception of the Early Married Women's Property Acts by the Courts and Legislatures," *American Journal of Legal History*, 29 (1985), 3–35.

[57] Bishop, *Commentaries on the Law of Married Women*, II, 22.

[60] *Birkbeck v. Ackroyd*, 74 N.Y. 356, 359 (1878). * * *

her husband. Even as judges weighed the conflicting claims to her wages, studying her domestic habits while also sifting through her independent dealings with employers, storekeepers, and moneylenders, they assigned her a legal identity more akin to that of a bound servant than a free hired laborer. In consequence, her legal rights came to hinge, not on her title to herself and her labor, but entirely on her ability to keep her work and wages from her husband's reach, to segregate them as forms of separate property.

This legal rule not only contradicted the verities of the wage contract; it was also contrary to the domestic economy of wage earners, in which the wife's paid labor and unpaid housework intertwined. Her earnings paid for family necessities, and her home was most often the site of her labor. In working-class households in Boston, for example, married women took in washing and ironing, stringing it up to dry in two-room flats that served for "living, eating, work and sleeping." One woman did beadwork, which her husband took out to sell. In Manhattan, husbands and wives finished caps together in their homes, working fourteen and fifteen hours a day, for fifty cents a dozen. In the tenement apartments where cigar makers plied their trade, Samuel Gompers noted with horror, the "odor of tobacco hovers over everything, the infant's cradle, the marriage bed, and the food set before the children." The separate property requirement—discriminating not simply between men and women but between women of the propertied and laboring classes—gutted the value of the earnings law for working-class wives. Among husbands and wives who owned little beyond their labor, no clear line separated their work, their wages, or their belongings to shield even a fraction of the wife's income from her husband's debt.

* * *

In an age that designated contract the embodiment of freedom, the very axis of legal rights and social relations, wives' liberty to contract remained strictly hedged by the bonds of marriage. Registering the effects of the wage system in working-class homes, the earnings statutes established married women's title to their wages. But the entitlement was encased in the paternal rules of marriage; it strained, but did not sunder, the abiding conjugal relation of dominion and dependency. The legal status of the "emancipated" wife therefore differed sharply from that of the freedman. Destroying the unity of master and slave, the Reconstruction enactments gave former slaves contract rights and also made them proprietors of their own persons. But for the wife, emancipation yielded the right to contract while denying her title to herself. However rightly she might assert that she owned her labor and wages, she nonetheless had to reckon with the competing claims of the marriage bond.

* * * Indeed, it was the tenuousness of the marriage contract as a voluntary exchange of support for subordination that led to the passage of the earnings laws. However, the wife's newfound right to the fruits of her labor was not the freedom of other hirelings. Since she lacked unqualified rights of self-ownership, the law founded her claims more narrowly on her title to property or her estrangement from her husband.

Reconciling wage relations with the time-honored code of marriage, the earnings laws brought to light a new set of contradictions. Prevailing beliefs in the post-bellum United States defined freedom as the contract right both to work for wages and to have a family. But the legal rules governing the wife's waged labor implicitly denied her status as proletarian while also presupposing breach of the marriage relation. Here was a paradox no less curious than the persistence of conjugal bonds in a land of free men.

C. The Realists' "Reconstruction" of Property

1. The De-Reification of Property in the Early Twentieth Century

At least two major strains of thought led to significant alterations in the meaning of property during the first few decades of the twentieth century. First, affirmation of absolute rights in property established by contract legitimized "relational property." That is, property was not necessarily about rights in a tangible thing, but an abstraction about relationships between people creating social value. Such a notion opened up room to argue about the ability of any party to claim absolute ownership in any tangible or intangible thing. As notions of appropriate human relationships changed, property could be altered. Second, the notion that property was an idea rather than a thing also meant it could be political. Description of rights in things could be replaced by analysis of the connections between property and power. Legal rules were no longer abstract neutral concepts but part of a much larger social pattern of values, politics, culture and philosophy. Logic could not be created in law standing by itself; only by reference to economics, sociology, or some other "scientific" discipline could legal institutions be understood and improved.

The Realists reconstruction of property is portrayed here in several articles, beginning with Kenneth Vandevelde's analysis of Wesley Hohfeld. Hohfeld was a transitional figure in American legal thought. His work, like much nineteenth century legal writing, was quite formalistic; categories were quite rigidly and "scientifically" defined. But he also insisted that property was a socially constructed set of ideas, not a regime designed to protect rights in things. For additional reading on Hohfeld, *see* Joseph W. Singer, *The Legal Rights Debate in Analytical Jurisprudence From Bentham to Hohfeld*, 1982 Wisc. L. Rev. 975. For other work on the lessening influence of absolutist property norms, *see* Robert G. Bone, *Normative Theory and Legal Doctrine in American Nuisance Law: 1850–1920*, 59 So. Cal. L. Rev. 1101 (1986). Later realists, such as Morris Cohen, whose timeless article, *Property and Sovereignty,* follows Vandevelde's, worked on the foundation Hohfeld built. While he rejected much of Hohfeld's formalism, he insisted that property norms reflected human relationships and political power and looked to non-legal disciplines for realistic solutions to humanity's ills. That sort of thinking process reached a high point of refinement in the classic *Dialogue on Private Property* by Felix Cohen.

Kenneth J. Vandevelde, *The New Property of the Nineteenth Century: The Development of the Modern Concept of Property*, 29 BUFF. L. REV. 325, 328–330, 357–364 (1980)*

"There is nothing which so generally strikes the imagination and engages the affections of mankind, as the right of property. . . ." wrote William Blackstone in 1765. Two centuries after Blackstone wrote, Charles Reich's highly influential article "The New Property,"[2] argued that property is the indispensable foundation of the free individual in the modern welfare state. While the concept of property has been central to the development of both public and private law during the history of the United States, the meaning of the term "property" has changed radically.

* * *

In broad outline, the thesis is this: at the beginning of the nineteenth century, property was ideally defined as absolute dominion over things. Exceptions to this definition suffused property law: instances in which the law declared property to exist even though no "thing" was involved or the owner's dominion over the thing was not absolute. Each of these exceptions, however, was explained away. Where no "thing" existed, one was fictionalized. Where dominion was not absolute, limitations could be camouflaged by resorting to fictions, or rationalized as inherent in the nature of the thing or the owner. The result was a perception that the concept of property rested inevitably in the nature of things and that recognition of some thing as the object of property rights offered a premise from which the owner's control over that thing could be deduced with certainty. The perceived inevitability of this definition of property legitimated the concept. At the same time, the serviceability of property as a premise from which legal relations could be deduced permitted courts to use the concept to fix the boundaries of dominion between private individuals and between the individual and the state.

[2] Reich, *The New Property*, 73 YALE L. J. 733 (1964).

Property law thus appeared to settle controversies while simultaneously legitimating, and even necessitating, the result.

As the nineteenth century progressed, increased exceptions to both the physicalist and the absolutist elements of Blackstone's conception of property were incorporated into the law. Acting at times on a theory of natural law and at other times on the instrumentalist public policy of a positive state, courts increasingly sought to protect valuable interests as property even though no thing was involved. The protection of value rather than things—the dephysicalization of property—greatly broadened the purview of property law. Any valuable interest potentially could be declared the object of property rights. This dephysicalization was a development that threatened to place the entire corpus of American law in the category of property. Such conceptual imperialism created severe problems for the courts. First, if every valuable interest constituted property, then practically any act would result in either a trespass on, or a taking of, someone's property, especially if property still was regarded as absolute. Second, once property had swallowed the rest of American law, its meaningfulness as a separate category would disappear. On the other hand, if certain valuable interests were not to be considered property, finding and justifying the criteria for separating property from nonproperty would be difficult. The sense of inevitability in the definition of property had disintegrated and with it the legitimacy of the concept of property.

The absolutist conception of property also came under assault. Throughout the nineteenth century, courts discovered that interests which deserved protection, whether based on natural law or positive instrumentalism, could not be protected absolutely without unduly restricting the activity of others. Courts created less protected forms of property, but once they admitted that all property was not equally protected, the designation of an interest as property no longer provided a premise from which legal rights could be automatically deduced. The designation of an interest as property no longer settled any controversy; it merely restated the dispute. Courts, therefore, were faced with the dilemma of finding and justifying criteria for deciding upon the protection to which a particular species of property was entitled.

By the beginning of the twentieth century, the Blackstonian conception of property was no longer credible. A new conception emerged and was stated in its definitive form by Wesley Newcomb Hohfeld. This new property was defined as a set of legal relations among persons. Property was no longer defined as dominion over things. Moreover, property was no longer absolute, but limited, with the meaning of the term varying from case to case.

The new conception of property failed to solve the problems left by the destruction of the Blackstonian conception. Courts still had to decide whether a particular interest was property, and if it was, how much protection it merited. Nevertheless, the Hohfeld conception provided a vocabulary for discussion that was consistent with the new dephysicalized and limited property.

This century long evolution resulted in an inability of property concepts to settle controversies and to legitimate the results. Courts overcame their paralysis by deciding individual cases with overt recourse to political goals. But, in so doing, they abandoned the myth of judicial neutrality and with it their own legitimacy. This evolution illustrates the general transformation of legal reasoning. It is the story of a radical reconceptualization in a crucial area of American law that brought with it the destruction of the legitimacy of law that the Realist movement bequeathed to American legal thought.

* * *

III. The Conceptualization of New Property

By the end of the nineteenth century, Blackstone's conception of property as absolute dominion over things had become fatally anachronistic, and was supplanted by a new form of property. This new property had been dephysicalized and thus consisted not of rights over things, but of any valuable right. The new property had also been limited. It consisted not of an absolute or fixed constellation of rights, but of a set of rights which were limited according to the situation.

Legal commentators were acutely aware of the development of the new property. Francis J. Swayze, addressing the 1915 graduating class of the Yale Law School, described the "new kinds of property of great value."[142] These included business goodwill, trademarks, trade secrets, common law copyright, going value of businesses, franchises and equitable easements. Similarly, Dean G. Acheson observed in 1914 that "the all-absorbing legal conception of the [nineteenth] century [was] that of the property right. Everything was thought of in terms of property—

[142] Swayze, *The Growing Law*, 25 YALE L. J. 1, 10 (1915).

reputation, privacy, domestic relations—and as new interest required protection, their viability depended upon their ability to take on the protective coloring of property."[144]

Lawyers were interested in the new property because of its personal and commercial importance. But more than that, the new property struck the legal imagination because, as Acheson observed, the concept of nonphysical and limited property seemed capable of embracing every valuable interest known to the law. Among the interests that the courts held to constitute property were, in addition to those listed by Swayze, the right to use the mail system, the right of an employer to a free flow of labor, the right of an employee to free access to employment, the right of a stockholder to vote for all the directors of a corporation, the right to a tax exemption, the right to prohibit others from selling news one has gathered,[151] the right of a building owner to use an elevator, the right to membership in a stock exchange, the right to use of a church pew, and the right to control the disposition of a dead body. The increasing awareness of legal commentators that a vast body of property right was being created which did not fit Blackstone's physicalist or absolutist conceptions rendered Blackstone increasingly obsolete. The exceptions had engulfed the rule.

In a pair of articles published in 1913 and 1917, Wesley Newcomb Hohfeld presented a conceptual scheme for analyzing the new property.[156] Hohfeld identified eight fundamental legal relations which formed the constituent elements of property. Each of these fundamental legal relations was defined relative to its opposite and correlative. The juxtaposition of these relations produced the following scheme:

Jural Opposites	**right** **no right**	**privilege** **duty**	**power** **disability**	**immunity** **liability**
Jural Correlatives	**right** **duty**	**privilege** **no right**	**power** **liability**	**immunity** **disability**

Hohfeld believed that these eight legal relations were "the lowest common denominators of the law," and that any legal relationship could be expressed as the sum of some combination of these eight denominators. To say that one owned property was to say that the owner had some set of rights, privileges, powers and immunities. Moreover, one who did not one property had a set of no rights, duties, disabilities, and liabilities relative to the owner.

Hohfeld's conception of property differed from Blackstone's in two crucial respects. To begin with, Hohfeld banished the need for things from property law. The obsession of old property with things had been manifested in * * * [various] ways. First, at various times, Blackstone had equated property with things. Corporeal hereditaments (land), for example, were things while incorporeal hereditaments (rights) were reified so that they too were considered things. Hohfeld criticized the equation of property with things: "Since all legal interests are 'incorporeal'—consisting, as they do, of more or less limited aggregates of abstract legal relations—such a supposed contrast as that sought to be drawn by Blackstone can but serve to mislead. . . ." Property according to Hohfeld consisted of legal relations, not things. * * * Blackstone, at other times, equated property not with things, but with rights over things. This was the second manifestation of the old property's obsession with things. Hohfeld also disputed this definition of property by arguing that legal relations were between people, not between people and things. * * *

The second crucial difference between Hohfeld's and Blackstone's conceptions of property was that the dominion of the owner of Hohfeldian property was not absolute or fixed. Property consisted of a set of legal relations, but not necessarily any particular set. Hohfeld denounced the tendency to lump together under blanket terms the multiplicity of legal relations that might exist between the property owner and others. This was exemplified by the owner of land in fee simple, whose property actually consisted

[144] Acheson, *Book Review*, 33 HARV. L. REV. 329, 330 (1919).

[151] International News Serv. v. Associated Press, 248 U.S. 215 (1918); * * * .

[156] Hohfeld, *Some Fundamental Legal Conceptions As Applied in Judicial Reasoning,* 23 YALE L. J. 16 (1913); Hohfeld, *Fundamental Legal Conceptions as Applied in Judicial Reasoning,* 26 YALE L. J. 710 (1917).

of a complex aggregate of rights, privileges, powers, and immunities against other persons. Hohfeld urged that these different legal relations not be confused with one another. The owner might, for example, alienate some portion of his rights to the land without affecting the remaining aggregate of relations. By breaking property into its constituent parts, Hohfeld both demonstrated that property does not imply any absolute or fixed set of rights in the owner and provided a vocabulary for describing the limited nature of the owner's property.

Hohfeld's conception of the new property gained broad acceptance among other legal commentators. * * * The complete acceptance of the Hohfeldian conception of property by the American legal establishment was signaled by the promulgation of the American Law Institute's *Restatement of Property* in 1936. The word "property" is not included among the terms defined by the *Restatement*. Instead the *Restatement* defines the four constituent elements of property: rights, privileges, powers, and immunities, with their correlatives: duties, no rights, liabilities, and disabilities.[166]

Once property was reconceived to include potentially any valuable interest, there was no logical stopping point. Property could include all legal relations. Indeed Hohfeld had insisted that his eight fundamental legal relations were the "lowest common denominators" of all legal relationships. * * *

Such an explosion of the concept of property threatened to render the term absolutely meaningless in two ways. First, if property included all legal relations, then it could no longer serve to distinguish one set of legal relations from another. It would lose its meaning as a category of law. Second, the greater the variety of interests that were protected as property, the more difficult it would be to assert that all property should be protected to the same degree. The pressure to create new species of property protected in different ways would be intense, so that the designation of some interest as property would no longer indicate any fixed protection. Consequently, property would cease to distinguish one kind of legal relation from another and fail to distinguish with any clarity legally protected interests from other interests. * * *

The destruction of meaning in the concept of property destroyed the concept's apparent power to decide cases. * * * Walter Wheeler Cook noted this problem in relation to general expressions such as "property in new" or "quasi property" which he argued were too vague to be of assistance in deciding legal disputes. To Cook, the more useful questions were what rights, privileges, powers, and immunities did the news gatherer have regarding the news, and against whom did he have them?[169]

Pressure thus mounted to find some way of containing the expansion of property. The strategy adopted was to concede that while any valuable interest could be property, it would not necessarily be considered property merely because it was valuable. A court would consider such an interest to be property only if public policy so demanded. Justice Brandeis, dissenting in *International News Service v. Associated Press*,[170] summarized the new approach:

> But the fact that a product of the mind has cost its producer money and labor, and has a value for which others are willing to pay, is not sufficient to insure to it this legal attribute of property. The general rule of law is, that the noblest of human productions—knowledge, truths ascertained, conceptions, and ideas—become, after voluntary communication to others, free as the air to common use. Upon these incorporeal productions the attribute of property is continued after such communication only in certain cases where public policy has seemed to demand it.

Justice Holmes, dissenting* in the same case, restated the argument more concisely: "Property, a creation of law, does not arise from value, although exchangeable—a matter of fact. Many exchangeable values may be destroyed intentionally without compensation. Property depends upon exclusion by law from interference. . . ."

Holmes and Brandeis were saying that property was what the law said it was. But positivism was nothing new; Blackstone had a positivist streak. The real significance of the Holmes-Brandeis position

---

[166] American Law Institute, *Restatement of Property* §§1-4 (1936).

[169] Comment, *The Associated Press Case*, 28 YALE L. J. 387, 388-89 (1919).

[170] 248 U.S. 215 (1918). The issue was whether one could have property rights in news.

* [Editor's Note: Though Justice Holmes' views differed dramatically from the majority in *Associated Press*, his opinion was actually labeled as concurring in the official report of the case. That was because Holmes, like the majority, preferred to remand the case to the trial court for reconsideration of the exact form of the injunction to be issued against International News Service.]

was that they were also denying that law had produced a self-limiting definition of property. Some valuable interests were property and some were not. The basis for distinguishing the two categories was not anything in the definition of property, but public policy. Holmes and Brandeis had stopped the seemingly limitless expansion of property, but at the price of admitting that there was no inevitability in the definition of property. In effect, the determination of whether an interest was property was not one of logic, but of politics. As one writer noted, "... the difficulty that causes such a volume of disagreement is the chameleon character of the term 'property right' or 'vested right': the fact that it is not an absolute standard, but a variant which each man, layman, legislator, and judge, determines individually out of his own background."[173]

[173] Note, *The Variable Quality of a Vested Right*, 34 YALE L. J. 303, 309 (1925).

Note

International News Service v. Associated Press, 248 U.S. 215 (1918), involved allegations that INS took AP news releases in the eastern time zone and telegraphed them to its client papers in the west, enabling them to use the stories at the same time as their AP competitors. Associated Press claimed a property right in their "hot" stories and sought to enjoin use of them by INS. The Brandeis quotation used just above by Vandevelde was part of the Justice's dissent from the Court's opinion granting Associated Press the relief it sought. Justice Pitney, writing for the Court, argued that even if Associated Press did not have any rights over the news against the general public, it did have the right to prohibit its competitors from "taking" and using its stories without making any investment to gather the material. In the Court's words, International News Service erred "in applying as a test the right of [Associated Press] * * * as against the public, instead of considering the rights of * * * competitors in business, as between themselves. * * * [D]efendant, by its very act, admits that it is taking material that has been acquired by * * * organization and the expenditure of labor, skill, and money, and which is salable * * * for money, and that defendant in appropriating it and selling it as its own is endeavoring to reap where it has not sown * * *." Was Justice Pitney's bifurcation of the issues between the public and competitors as "Hohfeldian" as Justice Brandeis' views in dissent? Was the only difference that Pitney viewed protection of news distribution channels as supportive of important public policies, while Brandeis viewed such protection as endangering political discourse?

Morris R. Cohen, *Property and Sovereignty*, 13 CORNELL L. Q. 8–12, 14–30 (1927)*

Property and sovereignty, as every student knows, belong to entirely different branches of the law. Sovereignty is a concept of political or public law and property belongs to civil or private law. This distinction between public and private law is a fixed feature of our law-school curriculum. It was expressed with characteristic 18th century neatness and clarity by Montesquieu, when he said that by political laws we acquire liberty and by civil law property, and that we must not apply the principles of one to the other.

Montesquieu's view that political laws must in no way retrench on private property because no public good is greater than the maintenance of private property, was echoed by Blackstone and became the basis of legal thought in America.

* * *

Can we dismiss all this with the simple exclamation that all this is medieval and we have long outgrown it?

Well, right before our eyes the Law of Property Act of 1925 is sweeping away substantial remains of the complicated feudal Land Laws of England, by abolishing the difference between the descent of real and that of personal property, and by abolishing all legal (though not equitable) estates intermediate between leaseholds and fees simple absolute. These remains of feudalism have not been mere vestiges. They have played an important part in the national life of England. Their absurdities and indefensible abuses were pilloried with characteristic wit and learning by the peerless Maitland. The same thing had been done most judiciously by Joshua Williams, the teacher of several generations of English lawyers brought up on the seventeen editions of his great text book on Real Property Law. Yet these and similar efforts made no impression on the actual law. What these great men did not see with sufficient clearness, was that back of the complicated law of settlement, fee-tails, copyhold estates, of the heir-at-law, of the postponement of women, and other feudal incidents, there was a great and well founded fear that by simplifying and modernizing the real property law of England the land might become more marketable. Once land becomes fully marketable it can no longer be counted on to remain in the hands of the landed aristocratic families; and this means the passing of their political power and the end of their control over the destinies of the British Empire. For if American experience has demonstrated anything, it is that the continued leadership by great families cannot be as well founded on a money as on a land economy. The same kind of talent which enables Jay Gould to acquire dominion over certain railroads enables Mr. Harriman to take it away from his sons. From the point of view of an established land economy, a money economy thus seems a state of perpetual war instead of a social order where son succeeds father. The motto that a career should be open to talent thus seems a justification of anarchy, just as the election of rulers (kings or priests) seems an anarchic procedure to those used to the regular succession of father by son.

* * *

As the terms "medievalism" and "feudalism" have become with us terms of approbrium, we are apt to think that only unenlightened selfishness has up to recently prevented English land law from cutting its medieval moorings and embarking on the sea of purely money or commercial economy. This light-hearted judgment, however, may be somewhat sobered by reflection on a second recent event—the Supreme Court decision on the Minimum Wage Law. Without passing judgment at this point on the soundness of the reasoning, whereby the majority reached its decision, the result may still fairly be characterized as a high water mark of law in a purely money or commercial economy. For by that decision private monetary interests receive precedence over the sovereign duty of the state to maintain decent standards of living.

The state, which has an undisputed right to prohibit contracts against public morals or public policy, is here declared to have no right to prohibit contracts under which many receive wages less than the minimum of subsistence, so that if they are not the objects of humiliating public or private charity, they become centres of the physical and moral evils that result from systematic underfeeding and degraded standards of life. Let me repeat I do not wish here to argue the merits or demerits of the minimum wage decision. Much less am I concerned with any quixotic attempt to urge England to go back to medievalism. But the two events together show in strong relief how recent and in the main exceptional is the extreme position of the *laissez faire* doctrine, which according to the insinuation of Justice Holmes, has led the Supreme Court to read Herbert Spencer's extreme individualism into the 14th Amendment, and according to others, has enacted Cain's motto, "Am I my brother's keeper" as the supreme law of industry. Dean Pound has shown that in making a property right out of the freedom to contract, the Supreme Court has stretched the meaning of the term property to include what it has never before signified in the law or jurisprudence of any civilized country. But whether this extension is justified or not, it certainly means the passing of a certain domain of sovereignty from the state to the private employer of labor, who now has the absolute right to discharge and threaten to discharge any employee who wants to join a trade union, and the absolute right to pay a wage which is injurious to a basic social interest.

It may be that economic forces will themselves correct the abuse which the Supreme Court does not allow the state to remove directly, that economic forces will eliminate parasitic industries which do not pay the minimum of subsistence, because such industries are not as economically efficient and profitable as those that pay higher wages. It was similarly argued that slavery was bound to disappear on account of its economic inefficiency. Meanwhile, however, the sovereignty of the state is limited by the manner in which the courts interpret the term "property" in the 5th and 14th amendment to the Federal Constitution and in the bills of rights in our state constitutions. This makes it imperative for us to consider the nature of private property with reference to the sovereign power of the state to look after the general welfare. A dispassionate scientific study of this requires an examination of the nature of property, its justification, and the ultimate meaning of the policies based on it.

I

Property as Power

Anyone who frees himself from the crudest materialism readily recognizes that as a legal term property denotes not material things but certain rights. In the world of nature apart from more or less organized society, there are things but clearly no property rights.

Further reflection shows that a property right is not to be identified with the fact of physical possession. Whatever technical definition of property we may prefer, we must recognize that a property right is a relation not between an owner and a thing, but between the owner and other individuals in reference to things. A right is always against one or more individuals. This becomes unmistakably clear if we take specifically modern forms of property such as franchises, patents, good will, etc., which constitute such a large part of the capitalized assets of our industrial and commercial enterprises.

The classical view of property as a right over things resolves it into component rights such as the *jus utendi, jus disponendi,* etc. But the essence of private property is always the right to exclude others. The law does not guarantee me the physical or social ability of actually using what it calls mine. By public regulations it may indirectly aid me by removing certain general hindrances to the enjoyment of property. But the law of property helps me directly only to exclude others from using the things which it assigns to me. If then somebody else wants to use the food, the house, the land, or the plow which the law calls mine, he has to get my consent. To the extent that these things are necessary to the life of my neighbor, the law thus confers on me a power, limited but real, to make him do what I want. If Laban has the sole disposal of his daughters and his cattle, Jacob must serve him if he desires to possess them. In a regime where land is the principal source of obtaining a livelihood, he who has the legal right over the land receives homage and service from those who wish to live on it.

The character of property as sovereign power compelling service and obedience may be obscured for us in a commercial economy by the fiction of the so-called labor contract as a free bargain and by the frequency with which service is rendered indirectly through a money payment. But not only is there actually little freedom to bargain on the part of the steel worker or miner who needs a job, but in some cases the medieval subject had as much power to bargain when he accepted the sovereignty of his lord. Today I do not directly serve my landlord if I wish to live in the city with a roof over my head, but I must work for others to pay him rent with which he obtains the personal services of others. The money needed for purchasing things must for the vast majority be acquired by hard labor and disagreeable service to those to whom the law has accorded dominion over the things necessary for subsistence.

* * *

[T]he recognition of private property as a form of sovereignty is not itself an argument against it. Some form of government we must always have. For the most part men prefer to obey and let others take the trouble to think out rules, regulations and orders. That is why we are always setting up authorities; and when we cannot find any we write to the newspaper as the final arbiter. While, however, government is a necessity, not all forms of it are of equal value. At any rate it is necessary to apply to the law of property all those considerations of social ethics and enlightened public policy which ought to be brought to the discussion of any just form of government.

* * *

II

The justification of Property

1. *The Occupation Theory*

The oldest and up to recently the most influential defense of private property was based on the assumed right of the original discoverer and occupant to dispose of that which thus became his. This view dominated the thought of Roman jurists and of modern philosophers—from Grotius to Kant—so much so that the right of the laborer to the produce of his work was sometimes defended on the ground that the laborer "occupied" the material which he fashioned into the finished product.

It is rather easy to find fatal flaws in this view. Few accumulations of great wealth were ever simply found. Rather were they acquired by the labor of many, by conquest, by business manipulation, and by other means. It is obvious that today at any rate few economic goods can be acquired by discovery and first occupancy. Even in the few cases when they are, as in fishing and trapping, we are apt rather to think of the labor involved as the proper basis of the property acquired. Indeed, there seems nothing ethically self-evident in the motto that "findings is keepings." There seems nothing wrong in a law that a treasure trove shall belong to the king or the state rather than to the finder. Shall the finder of a river be entitled to all the water in it?

* * *

Despite all these objections, however, there is a kernel of positive value in this principle. Protecting the discoverer or first occupant, is really part of the more general principle that possession as such should be protected. There is real human economy in doing so until somebody shows a better claim than the possessor. It makes for certainty and security of transaction as well as for public peace—provided the law is ready to set aside possession acquired in ways that are inimical to public order. * * *

Nevertheless, it would be as absurd to argue that the distribution of property must never be modified by law as it would be to argue that the distribution of political power must never be changed. No less a philosopher than Aristotle argued against changing even bad laws, lest the habit of obedience be thereby impaired. There is something to be said for this, but only so long as we are in the realm of merely mechanical obedience. When we introduce the notion of free or rational obedience, Aristotle's argument loses its force in the political realm; and similar considerations apply to any property system that can claim the respect of rational beings.

2. *The Labor Theory*

That everyone is entitled to the full produce of his labor is assumed as self-evident by both socialists and conservatives who believe that capital is the result of the savings of labor. However, as economic goods are never the result of any one man's unaided labor, our maxim is altogether inapplicable. How shall we determine what part of the value of a table should belong to the carpenter, to the lumberman, to the transport worker, to the policeman who guarded the peace while the work was being done, and to the indefinitely large numbers of others whose cooperation was necessary? Moreover, even if we could tell what any one individual has produced—let us imagine a Robinson Crusoe growing up all alone on an island and in no way indebted to any community—it would still be highly questionable whether he has a right to keep the full produce of his labor when some shipwrecked mariner needs his surplus food to keep from starving.

* * *

Yet despite these and other criticisms, the labor theory contains too much substantial truth to be brushed aside. The essential truth is that labor has to be encouraged and that property must be distributed in such a way as to encourage ever greater efforts at productivity.

* * *

The occupation theory has shown us the necessity for security of possession and the labor theory the need for encouraging enterprise. These two needs are mutually dependent. Anything which discourages enterprise makes our possession less valuable, and it is obvious that it is not worth while engaging in economic enterprise if there is no prospect of securely possessing the fruit of it. Yet there is also a conflict between these two needs. The owners of land, wishing to secure the continued possession by the family, oppose laws which make it subject to free financial transactions or make it possible that land should be taken away from one's heirs by a judgment creditor for personal debts. In an agricultural economy security of possession demands that the owner of a horse should be able to reclaim it no matter into whose hands it has fallen. But in order that markets should be possible, it becomes necessary that the innocent purchaser should have a good title. * * *

3. *Property and Personality*

Hegel, Ahrens, Lorimer, and other idealists have tried to deduce the right of property from the individual's right to act as a free personality. To be free one must have a sphere of self-assertion in the external world. One's private property provides such an opportunity.

Waiving all traditional difficulties in applying the metaphysical idea of freedom to empirical legal acts, we may still object that the notion of personality is too vague to enable us to deduce definite legal consequences by means of it. How, for example, can the principle of personality help us to decide to what extent there shall be private rather than public property in railroads, mines, gas-works, and other public necessities?

* * *

Not the extremest communist would deny that in the interest of privacy certain personal belongings such as are typified by the toothbrush, must be under the dominion of the individual owner, to the absolute exclusion of everyone else. This, however, will not carry us far if we recall that the major effect of property in land, in the machinery of production, in capital goods, etc., is to enable the owner to exclude others from *their necessities*, and thus to compel them to serve him. Ahrens, one of the chief expounders of the personality theory, argues "it is undoubtedly contrary to the right of personality to have persons dependent on others on account of material goods." But if this is so, the primary effect of property on a large scale is to limit freedom, since the one thing that private property law does not do is to guarantee a minimum of subsistence or the necessary tools of freedom to everyone. So far as a regime of private property fails to do the latter it rather compels people to part with their freedom.

It may well be argued in reply that just as restraining traffic rules in the end give us greater freedom of motion, so, by giving control over things to individual property owners, greater economic freedom is in the end assured to all. This is a strong argument, as can be seen by comparing the different degrees of economic freedom that prevail in lawless and in law abiding communities. It is, however, an argument for legal order rather than any particular form of government or private property. It argues for a regime where every one has a definite sphere of rights and duties, but it does not tell us where these lines should be drawn. The principle of freedom of personality certainly cannot justify a legal order wherein a few can, by virtue of their legal monopoly over necessities, compel others to work under degrading and brutalizing conditions. A government which limits the right of large land-holders limits the rights of property and yet may promote real freedom. Property owners, like other individuals, are members of a community and must subordinate their ambition to the large whole of which they are a part. They may find their compensation in spiritually identifying their good with that of the larger life.

4. *The Economic Theory*

The economic justification of private property is that by means of it a maximum of productivity is promoted. The classical economic argument may be put thus: The successful business man, the one who makes the greatest profit, is the one who has the greatest power to foresee effective demand. If he has not that power his enterprise fails. He is therefore, in fact, the best director of economic activities.

There can be little doubt that if we take the whole history of agriculture and industry, or compare the economic output in countries like Russia with that in the United States, there is a strong *prima facie* case for the contention that more intensive cultivation of the soil and greater productiveness of industry prevail under individual ownership. Many *a priori* psychological and economic reasons can also be brought to explain why this must be so, why the individual cultivator will take greater care not to exhaust the soil, etc. All this, however, is so familiar that we may take it for granted and look at the other side of the case, at the considerations which show that there is a difference between socially desirable productivity and the desire for individual profits.

* * *

As * * * no individual rights can in fact be exercised in a community, except under public restriction, it has been left mainly to publicists, to writers on politics and constitutional and administrative law to consider the limitations of private property necessary for public safety, peace, health, and morals, as well as in the interest of all those enterprises like housing, education, the preservation of natural resources, etc. which the community finds it necessary to entrust to the state rather than to private hands. The fact, however, that in the United States the last word on law comes from judges, who, like other lawyers, are for the most part, trained in private rather than in public law, is one of the reasons why with us traditional conceptions of property prevail over obvious national interests such as the freedom of laborers to organize, the necessity of preserving certain standards of living, or preventing the future manhood and womanhood of the country from being sacrificed to individual profits, and the like. Our students of property law need, therefore, to be reminded that not only has the whole law since the industrial revolution shown a steady growth in ever new restrictions under use of private property, but the ideal of absolute *laissez faire* has never in fact been completely operative.

* * *

There must be restrictions on the use of property not only in the interests of other property owners but also in the interests of the health, safety, religion, morals, and general welfare of the whole community. No community can view with indifference the exploitation of the needy by commercial greed. As under the conditions of crowded life, the reckless or unconscionable use of one's property is becoming more and more dangerous, enlightened jurists find new doctrines to limit the abuse of ancient rights. * * *

Of greatest significance is the fact that in all civilized legal systems there is a great deal of just expropriation or confiscation without any direct compensation. This may sound shocking to those who think that for the state to take away the property of the citizen is not only theft or robbery but even worse, an act of treachery, since the state avowedly exists to protect people in those very rights.

As a believer in natural rights, I believe that the state can, and unfortunately often does, enact unjust laws. But I think it is a sheer fallacy based on verbal illusion to think that the rights of the community against an individual owner are no better than the rights of a neighbor. Indeed, no one has in fact had the courage of this confusion to argue that the state has no right to deprive an individual of property to which he is so attached that he refuses any money for it. Though no neighbor has such a right the public interest often justly demands that a proprietor shall part with his ancestral home to which he may be attached by all the roots of his being.

When taking away a man's property, is the state always bound to pay a direct compensation? I submit that while this is generally advisable in order not to disturb the general feeling of security, no absolute principle of justice requires it. * * * [T]here is no injustice in taxing an old bachelor to educate the children of others, or to tax one immune to typhoid for the construction of sewers or other sanitary measures. We may go farther and say that the whole business of the state depends upon its rightful power to take away the property of some (in the form of taxation) and use it to support others, such as the needy, those invalided in the service of the state in war or peace, and those who are not yet able to produce but in whom the hope of humanity is embodied. Doubtless, taxation and confiscation may be actuated by malice and may impose needless and cruel hardship on some individuals or classes. But this is not to deny that taxation and confiscation are within the just powers of the state. A number of examples may make this clearer.

* * * When slavery is abolished by law, the owners have their property taken away. Is the state ethically bound to pay them the full market value of their slaves? It is doubtless a grievous shock to a community to have a large number of slave owners whose wealth often makes them leaders of culture, suddenly deprived of their income. It may also be conceded that it is not always desirable for the slave himself to be suddenly taken away from his master and cut adrift in a sea of freedom. But when one reads of the horrible ways in which some of those slaves were violently torn from their homes in Africa and shamelessly deprived of their human rights, one is inclined to agree with Emerson that compensation should first be paid to the slaves. This compensation need not be in the form of a direct bounty to them. It may be more effectively paid in the form of rehabilitation and education for freedom; and such a charge may take precedence over the claims of the former owners. After all, the latter claims are no greater than those of a protected industry when the tariff is removed. If the state should decide that certain import duties, *e.g.* those on scientific instruments, or hospital supplies, are unjustified and proceed to abolish them, many manufacturers may suffer. Are they entitled to compensation by the state?

It is undoubtedly for the general good to obviate as much as possible the effect of economic shock to a large number of people. The routine of life prospers on security. But when the security contains a large element of injustice the shock of an economic operation by law may be necessary and ethically justified.

* * *

In our own day, we have seen the confiscation of many millions of dollars of property through prohibition. Were the distillers and brewers entitled to compensation for their losses? We have seen that property on a large scale is power and the loss of it, while evil to those who are accustomed to exercise it, may not be an evil to the community. In point of fact, the shock to the distillers and brewers was not as serious as to others, *e.g.* saloon keepers and bartenders who did not lose any legal property since they were only employees, but who found it difficult late in life to enter new employments.

* * *

With confiscations such as these in mind, it becomes clear that there is no unjustifiable taking away of property when railroads are prohibited from posting notice that they will discharge their employees if the latter join trade unions, and that there is no property taken away without due or just process of law when an industry is compelled to pay its laborers a minimum of subsistence instead of having it done by private or public charity or else systematically starving its workers.

IV

Political vs. Economic Sovereignty

If the discussion of property by those interested in private law has suffered from a lack of realism and from too great a reliance on vague *a priori* plausibilities, much the same can be said about political discussion as to the proper limits of state action in regard to property and economic enterprise. Utterly unreal is all talk of men being robbed of their power of initiative because the state undertakes some service, *e.g.* to build a bridge across a river. Men are not deprived of opportunities for real self reliance by having their streets lighted at night, by filling up holes in the pavements, by removing other dangers to life and limb and by providing opportunities for education to all. The conditions of modern life are complex and distracting enough so that if we can ease the strain by simplifying some things through state action we are all the gainers by it. Certain things have to be done in a community and the question whether they should be left to private enterprise dominated by the profit motive or to the government dominated by political considerations, is not a question of man versus the state, but simply a question of which organization and motive can best do the work.

* * *

[E]xperience has shown all civilized peoples the indispensable need for communal control to prevent the abuse of private enterprise. Only a political or general government is competent to deal with a problem like city congestion, because only the general government can coordinate a number of activities some of which have no financial motive. Private business may be more efficient in saving money. It does so largely by paying smaller wages to the many and higher remuneration to those on top. From a social point of view this is not necessarily a good in itself. It is well to note that men of great ability and devotion frequently prefer to work for the government at a lower pay than they can obtain in private employment. There is something more than money in daily employment. Humanity prefers—not altogether unwisely—to follow the lead of those who are sensitive rather than those who are efficient. Business efficiency mars the beauty of our countryside with hideous advertising signs and would, if allowed, ruin the scenic grandeur of Niagara.

* * *

The main difficulty * * * with industrial and financial government is that the governors are released from all responsibility for the actual human effects of their policies. Formerly, the employer could observe and had an interest in the health and morals of his apprentice. Now, the owners or stockholders have lost all personal touch with all but [a] few of those who work for them. The human element is thus completely subordinated to the profit motive. * * *

Let me conclude. There can be no doubt that our property laws do confer sovereign power on our captains of industry and even more so on our captains of finance.

Now it would be unworthy of a philosopher to shy at government by captains of industry and finance. Humanity has been ruled by priests, soldiers, hereditary landlords, and even antiquarian scholars. The results are not such as to make us view with alarm a new type of rules. But if we are entering a new era involving a new set of rulers, it is well to recognize it and reflect on what is involved.

* * *

It may, of course, rightly be contended that the modern captain of industry is not merely concerned with the creation of things, that his success is largely determined by his judgment and ability to manage large numbers of human beings that form part of his organization. Against this, however, there is the obvious retort that the only ability taken account of in the industrial and financial world, the ability to make money, is a very specialized one; and when business men get into public office they are notably successful. Too often they forget that while saving the money of the taxpayer may be an admirable incident, it is not the sole or even the principal end of communal life and government. The wise expenditure of money is a more complicated problem than the mere saving of it, and a no less indispensable task to those who face the question of how to promote a better communal life. To do this effectively we need a certain liberal insight into the more intangible desires of the human heart. Preoccupation with the management of property has not in fact advanced this kind of insight.

* * *

It is certainly a shallow philosophy which would make human welfare synonymous with the indiscriminate production and consumption of material goods. If there is one iota of wisdom in all the religions or philosophies which have supported the human race in the past it is that man cannot live by economic goods alone but needs vision and wisdom to determine what things are worth while and what things it would better to do without. This profound human need of controlling and moderating our consumptive demands cannot be left to those whose dominant interest is to stimulate such demands.

It is characteristic of the low state of our philosophy that the merits of capitalism have been argued by both individualists and socialists exclusively from the point of view of the production and distribution of goods. To the profounder question as to what goods are ultimately worthwhile producing from the point of view of the social effects on the producers and consumers almost no attention is paid. Yet surely this is a matter which requires the guidance of collective wisdom, not to be left to chance or anarchy.

Note

Was the Supreme Court's decision in *Village of Euclid v. Ambler Realty Co.*, 272 U.S. 365 (1928), one that Morris Cohen would have liked? Take some care in thinking about this question. You might wish to read the materials on racial covenants and zoning later in this part of the anthology before answering.

Felix S. Cohen, *Dialogue on Private Property*, 9 Rutgers L. Rev. 357, 363–374 (1954)*

C.* Can we agree * * * that this institution of property that we are trying to understand may or may not involve external physical objects, but always does involve relations between people. Unless there is some dissent to that proposition, I suggest that we consider [that] * * *[p]roperty, at least the kind of institution that we are talking about when we distinguish between a capitalist and communist country, is basically a set of relations among men, which may or may not involve external physical objects. Would you dissent from that conclusion, Mrs. Evans?

E. Well, calling property a set of relations among men is such a vague generality that I'd hardly dare dissent from it.

Property and Wealth

C. Of course you're right, and yet a generality that is true may be more useful than a more specific idea like Blackstone's that is false. But can we make our conception of property more specific without excluding any of the rights we recognize as property rights? Have you any suggestions, Mrs. Evans, to help us clarify this set of relations that we call property? Do you see any point in the suggestion of Hamilton that property is essentially an economic concept?

E. Yes, it seems to me that when we are talking about property we are really talking about economic goods or wealth.

C. Mrs. Evans, I have here some personal papers that are of no possible value to anyone else in the world. If somebody took these papers from me and I brought suit to have them returned, do you think the court would require the return of these papers?

E. Yes, I suppose it would.

C. Would you then say that these papers are my property even though they have no economic value?

E. Yes, I would.

* * *

C. Then there is such a thing as valueless property, and economic value is not essential to the existence of legal property?

E. Yes, I suppose we would have to accept that conclusion.

C. What about the other side of Hamilton's equation between wealth and property? Could there be wealth that did not consist of private property? Suppose I discover a new form of exercise that increases the life-span of diabetics. Would that discovery add to the wealth of mankind?

E. Yes, I suppose it would, if put to use.

C. And to the extent that I were willing to communicate that discovery to individuals and charge them for the teaching, the discovery would be of value to me, would it not?

E. Yes, I suppose it would.

**[Editor's Note: C. is the questioner, Felix Cohen. Other letters represent hypothetical students.]

C. And yet this bit of knowledge which I could not prevent anyone else from using or discovering would not be property, would it?

E. No, I suppose not.

C. Then it seems to me we have come to the conclusion that not only is there valueless property, but there is also propertyless value.

E. I see no way of avoiding that conclusion.

C. Would you agree that air is extremely valuable to all of us?

E. Yes, of course.

C. Why then is there no property in air?

E. I suppose because there is no scarcity.

C. Suppose there were no scarcity of any material objects.

E. I suppose then there would be no property in material objects.

C. Would you say then that private property is a function of privation?

E. Yes I suppose it is, in the sense that if there is no possibility of privation there cannot be private property.

C. And would you also say that wealth is a function of plenty?

E. Yes, if we think of wealth broadly as covering the whole field of human goods, or utilities, or enjoyments.

C. Then, wealth and property are in some ways opposites rather than identical?

E. I am not sure what that means, practically.

C. Doesn't it mean, practically, that if we could create a situation in which no man lacked for bread, bread would cease to be an object of property; and if conversely, we could create artificial scarcities in air or sunshine, and then relax these scarcities for a consideration, air and sunshine might become objects of property? Or, more generally, a society might increase the sum of its goods and enjoyments by eliminating one scarcity after another and thus reducing the effective scope of private property.

E. I suppose that is so. At least, I don't see how one can maintain that private property is identical with goods or wealth.

C. Well, that seems to leave us with a further point of general agreement. Property may exist without value; value may exist without property; private property as a function of privation may even have inverse relation to wealth; in short, property is not wealth. But what is it? We are still not beyond the vague generality that property is a set of social relations among human beings. We have still not distinguished between property relations and other human relations. Mr. Fielden, what do you think of the American Law Institute's definition of property as including any "rights, privileges, powers and immunities?" Under that definition would immunity from racial discrimination in the exercise of the franchise be a property right?

F. Yes, under that definition I suppose it would.

C. And would the right to kill in self-defense be a property right?

F. Yes, I believe so.

C. In fact, any legal relationship under the definition of the American Law Institute is property, is it not?

F. Yes, I think the definition is comprehensive enough to cover any legal relation.

* * *

The Case of the Montana Mule

C. Mr. F., there's a big cottonwood tree at the southeast corner of Wright Hagerty's ranch, about 30 miles north of Browning, Montana, and under that tree this morning a mule was born. Who owns the mule?

F. I don't know.

C. Do you own the mule?

F. No.

C. How do you know you don't own the mule? You just said you didn't know who owns the mule. Might it not be you?

F. Well, I suppose that it is possible that I might own a mule I never saw, but I don't think I do.

* * *

C. Suppose you owned a piece of unfenced prairie in Montana and the mule's mother during her pregnancy ate some of your grass. Would that make you the owner of the mule?

F. No, I don't think it would.

C. Well, then you seem to know more about the ownership of this Montana mule than you admitted a few moments ago. Now tell us who really owns the mule.

F. I suppose the owner of the mare owns the mule.

C. Exactly, but tell me how you come to that conclusion.

* * *

F. Well, it does seem to me to be in accordance with the laws of nature to say that the progeny of the mother belong to the owner of the mother.

C. Wouldn't it be just as much in accordance with the laws of nature to say that the progeny of the father belong to the owner of the father?

F. I suppose that might be so, as a matter of simple biology, but as a practical matter, it might be pretty hard to determine just which jackass was the mule's father.

C. Then as a practical matter we are dealing with something more than biology. We are dealing with human need for certainty in property distribution. * * * Do you think that property law reflects some such human demand for certainty?

F. I think it does * * *.

* * *

C. Suppose we decided that the mule should belong to the first roper. Wouldn't that be a simple and definite rule?

F. Yes, but it wouldn't be fair to the owner of the mare who was responsible for its care during pregnancy if a perfect stranger could come along and pick up the offspring.

C. Now, you are assuming that something more than certainty is involved in rules of property law, and that somehow such rules have something to do with ideas of fairness, and you could make out a good case for that proposition in this case. But suppose you are trying to explain this to a cowboy who has just roped this mule and doesn't see the fairness of this rule that makes it the property of the mare owner. Are there any more objective standards that you could point to in support of this rule? What would be the economic consequences of a rule that made the mule the property of the first roper instead of the mare-owner?

F. I think that livestock owners wouldn't be so likely to breed their mares or cows if anybody else could come along and take title to the offspring.

C. You think then that the rule that the owner of the mare owns the mule contributes to economic productivity?

F. Yes.

* * *

C. Could we sum up this situation, then, by saying that this particular rule of property law that the owner of the mare owns the offspring has appeal * * * because this rule contributes to the economy by attaching a reward to planned production; is simple, certain, and economical to administer; fits in with existing human and animal habits and forces; and appeals to the sense of fairness of human beings * * *?

F. I think that summarizes the relevant factors.

C. And would you expect that similar social considerations might lead to the development of other rules of property law, and that where these various considerations of productivity, certainty, enforceability, and fairness point in divergent directions instead of converging on a single solution, we might find more controversial problems of private ownership?

F. That would seem to be a reasonable * * * [inference.]

Ownership, Use and Sale

C. Suppose we pass, then, to a slightly more difficult problem. Mrs. Farnsworth, do you own any songs?

F. No.

C. How do you know that you don't own any songs? What does it mean to say that somebody owns a song?

F. Well, I suppose it means that the owner has a right to sing the song himself, and has a right to charge others for the privilege of singing the song, or at least for making commercial use of the song.

C. You and I have the right to sing "Auld Lang Syne" without paying anyone for the privilege, don't we?

F. Yes, I suppose so.

C. Then, the right to sing can exist even where there is no property right?

F. Yes.

C. Can a corporation sing?

F. No. I don't suppose so.

C. But a corporation can own the copyright to a song, can't it?

F. Yes.

C. Then ownership can exist without the possibility of the owner's enjoying or using what he owns.

F. Yes, I suppose so.

C. Then the criterion of use as a mark of ownership breaks down at both ends. We can have use without ownership and ownership without use. What about the other half of your criterion, the possibility of charging others for the use of something. Suppose you secure a lease on an apartment with the condition that you can't assign the lease, can't sublease the apartment, can't have pets or babies on the premises and can't take in boarders. Might you not still have a property interest even though you couldn't sell it?

F. Yes, I suppose there is such a thing as non-salable property.

C. And what about the other side of that equation. Is it possible that you can buy or sell what is not property at all, services, for example?

F. Yes, I suppose I have to retreat from the position that the right to sell is a distinctive characteristic of private property.

C. But wait, now, before you retreat too far. When you say that an owner can charge somebody else for the use of what he owns you mean, don't you, that he can charge somebody else if that person is willing to pay?

F. Yes, of course that is understood.

C. But I could charge you for walking across Brooklyn Bridge if you were willing to pay for it and that would not be proof that I had a property right in Brooklyn Bridge, would it?

F. No, but in that case I could walk across Brooklyn Bridge without paying you, and in the case of the song, if you owned the song, you could exclude me from the use of the song unless I made the payment.

Exclusion and Exclusiveness

C. Well, then, we are really talking about a right of exclusion, aren't we? What you are really saying is that ownership is a particular kind of legal relation in which the owner has a right to exclude the non-owner from something or other. That is really the point that * * * Morris Cohen * * * make[s], isn't it?

F. Yes, I think that is where * * * [he] find[s] a difference between property and other rights.

C. Do you agree, then, [with this] * * *: "By property we mean an exclusive right to control an economic good"?

F. Yes, I think that is a fair statement, except that what is controlled may be an economic evil rather than a good, or even a worthless thing, as we agreed a while ago.

C. Suppose I have acquired a non-exclusive easement to cross a piece of land. That might be a very valuable right to me, might it not, if that were the only way of reaching my house from the public streets?

F. Yes.

C. But by definition this would not be exclusive and would not be property * * *.

F. No, I suppose not.

C. And if I own a beach in common with 600 other people, I would not have an exclusive right to control the beach, would I?

F. No.

C. But aren't these non-exclusive rights property in the fundamental sense that I can exclude third parties from certain types of interference with my activities?

F. Yes * * *.

C. Can we agree, then, that the essential factor that we are reaching for here is the power to exclude, whether that power is exclusive or shared with others?

F. Yes, I think that is an essential factor. There may be others.

C. Is there any dissent from that proposition? If not, let us put this down as one more point of agreement in our analysis of the meaning of private property. Private property may or may not involve a right to use something oneself. It may or may not involve a right to sell, but whatever else it involves, it must at least involve a right to exclude others from doing something.

Now Mr. Galub, if you agree that a property right always involved a power to exclude, would you also agree that a power to exclude always involves a property right?

G. No, not necessarily.

C. The Yale football team might have the power to exclude the Princeton team from the goal line, but that would not make the goal line Yale property, would it?

G. No, I think we would have to agree more precisely on just what we mean by the power to exclude.

Property and Law

C. Does Bentham offer any help in clarifying this idea of power?

G. Yes, I think he does. He draws a distinction between physical power and the power that is derived from government. He says:

> Property and law are born together, and die together. Before laws were made there was no property; take away laws, and property ceases.

C. Then can you say that the kind of power to exclude that is essential to the institution of property is the power that exists when we can count upon agencies of the state to help us to exclude others from some activity?

G. Yes, I think that would help clarify the idea of property.

C. Would you say, then, that there is no property without sovereignty and that property relationships always involve government,—in other words, that property is a function of government or sovereignty?

G. Yes, that is what Morris R. Cohen, * * *, Hamilton, and Bentham all say, and I think they are right as far as they go.

* * *

C. Well, now, if we can agree that in order to have private property we must be able to count on governmental help in excluding others from certain activities, that tells us something important about property. But we still don't have a definition of property unless we can say that wherever there is a power to exclude others with government help of some activity there we have private property. Would such a statement be correct in your opinion?

G. I am not sure.

C. Suppose I live on a street where commercial vehicles are not permitted. If I see a truck coming down the street I can call a policeman and get the aid of the state in excluding the truck from the street. Does that mean that I have a property right in the street?

G. No, you might have a right to call upon the aid of the state in stopping all kinds of criminal activities, but that would not give you a property right in those activities.

C. Exactly. But if I could not only stop a truck from using the street in front of my house and secure the help of the state in enforcing that prohibition, but could also, on my own responsibility, grant permission to somebody to drive a truck on the street and charge him for the privilege and have the assistance of the state in enforcing such decisions, then would you say that I had a property right in the use of the street?

G. Yes, I think you would. That would be the kind of property that the owner of a toll road would have.

C. Private property, then presupposes a realm of private freedom. Without freedom to bar one man from a certain activity and to allow another man to engage in that activity we would have no property. If all activities were permitted or prohibited by general laws there would be no private property. Does that make sense to you, Mr. Galub?

G. Yes * * *. I suppose that is really what Morris Cohen is driving at * * * when he talks about private property as a delegation of sovereign power in certain limited areas. In those areas the government doesn't make a final decision but agrees to back up whatever decision the so-called owner of property makes.

C. Very clearly put, I think. Now suppose we put together all the conclusions we have been able to agree upon so far in our discussion: Private property is a relationship among human beings such that the so-called owner can exclude others from certain activities or permit others to engage in those activities and in either case secure the assistance of the law in carrying out his decision. Would that be a sound definition of private property?

G. I'm not sure what it means to say that a definition is sound or not.

C. Good. The same word may mean different things to different people. Therefore, asking whether a definition is true or false is a meaningless question. But we can ask whether a definition is useful or useless. * * * Now, * * * what do you think of our definition of property?

G. Well, I'd rather postpone any judgment as to the utility of a definition until we see how it is to be used and what help it may give us. * * *

C. Would you go further and say that a definition which distinguishes between private property and other legal relationships is more useful than a definition like that of the A.L.I.* which applies in effect to all legal relations, and is also more useful than the Blackstonian definition which applies to nothing at all in the real world.

G. Yes.

* * *

C. Do you find any ambiguities in our definition that might be cleared up by a more precise use of language?

G. I'm not sure.

Property and Contract

C. Isn't there a basic ambiguity in our use of the word "exclusion"? May that not cover two quite different things, a right against the world and a right against a specific individual based perhaps upon his own agreement? Suppose I am operating a string of 50 laundry machines in Washington, and I enter into a contract with you by which I sell you the machines and agree that I will stay out of the laundry business in Washington during the next ten years. Do you see any important difference between the rights that you would acquire over the machines and the rights that you would acquire with respect to my entering the laundry business?

G. I suppose that one important difference would be that so far as your entering the laundry business is concerned, I have a right to exclude you, but that right applies only to the person who made the contract, whereas with respect to the machines themselves, my right to exclude applies to the whole world.

C. Exactly. And while both these rights are derived from contract and might be called contractual rights, we may find it useful to distinguish those rights that apply only against the contracting party and those rights that apply against the world at large and call rights of the latter kind property rights. I don't say that this strict definition of property is universally followed, but I think generally we will find it more useful than any broader definition of property.

Now at this point, it may be useful to summarize our analysis of property in terms of a simple label.

---

* [Editor's Note: A.L.I. stands for American Law Institute, the creator of the Restatements.]

Suppose we say, that is property to which the following label can be attached:

To the world:

Keep off X unless you have my permission, which I may grant or withhold.

Signed: Private Citizen
Endorsed: The State

Note

Both Morris and Felix Cohen argue that property may not exist without the blessing of the state. Does that mean that in a case like *Neponsit Property Owners' Association v. Emigrant Industrial Savings Bank*, 278 N.Y. 248, 15 N.E.2d 793 (1938), in which beach access rights were established by use of covenants, termination of the covenants entails actions by the state triggering the Takings Clause? Or does it mean that the state must be involved in the blessing of both the creation and the destruction of "property?" *Compare Shelley v. Kraemer*, 334 U.S. 1 (1948).

2. Two Major Property Developments of the Early Twentieth Century: Covenants and Zoning for Racial Exclusion

Urban problems became a major focus of attention by 1920. Urbanization, the automobile, high rise construction methods, electricity and telephones transformed the landscape. Immigration, migration of African Americans from south to north, and suburbanization caused enormous dissension and controversy. An outpouring of reforms ensued. The Realist notion that property was a bundle of rights endorsed by the state took on new meaning as regulation of the urban economy blossomed. Tenement house controls, work place regulations, and fire and building codes, among others, appeared. Some of the reform, however, especially the norms surrounding use of covenants and zoning, was not pretty. Racism ran rampant in their early use, making quite "realist"-ic the notion that property reflects the norms of the surrounding community.

Three articles trace some of this history. The first, Timothy Jost's *The Defeasible Fee and the Birth of the Modern Residential Subdivision*, describes the problems that arose in the early use of conditioned fee simples to control land use and the gradual replacement of conditioned fees with covenants. Covenants, in turn, became a favorite device for excluding African Americans and others from purchasing property in large segments of urban America. Garrett Power, in *Apartheid Baltimore Style: The Residential Segregation Ordinances of 1910–1913,* traces the impact of racial animosity on the development of Baltimore, the city's attempt to zone by race and the rise of exclusionary real estate practices and covenant schemes. This section concludes with a short essay of mine on the history of *Village of Euclid v. Ambler Realty Co.*, which made possible the exclusively residential white suburban communities that came to ring central cities by the middle of the twentieth century. The neighborhoods approved by *Euclid* later came under serious attack in the exclusionary zoning cases reviewed later in Part III(F) of this anthology. For additional reading on the racial covenant cases, *see* Leland B. Ware, *Invisible Walls: An Examination of the Legal Strategy of the Restrictive Covenant Cases*, 67 WASH. U. L. Q. 737 (1989). For additional material on the early history of zoning *see* Garrett Power, *The Unwisdom of Allowing City Growth to Work Out its Own Destiny*, 47 MD. L. REV. 626 (1988), another in a wonderful series of pieces on the property history of Baltimore.

Timothy Jost, *The Defeasible Fee and the Birth of the Modern Residential Subdivision,* 49 Mo. L. Rev. 695–714, 719–721, 724–726, 728–739 (1984)*

I. Introduction

In the late nineteenth and early twentieth centuries, the United States experienced an unprecedented building spree. With the quickened pace of housing construction came a dramatic innovation in residential housing development: the emergence of the modern restricted residential subdivision. Across the nation, developers large and small began to build blocks of uniformly spaced and similarly constructed houses, separated from industrial and commercial uses, and largely segregated by class and race.

Developers sought new legal tools to assure the restricted character of these subdivisions. Eventually, such tools emerged: real covenants, equitable servitudes, negative easements, and finally, zoning. But at the end of the mid-nineteenth century, public land use planning was largely non-existent. Even private restrictions were still nascent, undeveloped, and most important, unfamiliar to most lawyers. The lawyers advising the subdividers and developers of the period faced a not uncommon problem: how does the legal counselor and drafter satisfy the demand for new legal tools and doctrines emanating from changing social and economic needs? The drafter of the period, and, more to the point, the drafter's client, were not interested in providing a test case to extend the common law precedents. Though creation of new legal tools through legislation was a conceivable solution, legislation was not always politically possible, and was a less common approach to legal problems in the nineteenth century than it is now. Ideally, the drafter could have received direction from the treatise writers and law review commentators, who have always purported to guide the profession. But these sources were not only far more scarce a century ago than now, they were also even more out of touch with the needs of practitioners.

In the common law tradition, lawyers of the late nineteenth and early twentieth centuries looked to the existing cases and attempted to meet the needs of their clients, the developers and subdividers, through extension or new application of the tools they found. The defeasible fee was the tool chosen by many lawyers who first considered the problem of restricting the new subdivisions their clients were developing.[5] During the late nineteenth and early twentieth centuries, the defeasible fee became a common device for restricting land use in most jurisdictions, ubiquitous in a few. Thousands, perhaps millions, of deeds were written conveying property conditional on observance of various land use restrictions.

The choice of the defeasible fee was on the whole unfortunate, indeed, a disaster. The use of defeasible fees for restricting residential subdivisions caused innumerable problems, some of which continue to plague us to the present. Moreover, defeasible fee restrictions were seldom enforced by the courts, at least through forfeiture, and thus did not directly achieve their restrictive purpose. By the third decade of the twentieth century, the defeasible fee was by and large abandoned as a land use planning device, though it continues to surface in casebooks and treatises discussing private land use planning, and of course, continues to be useful in other contexts. Litigation involving the defeasible fee, however, seems to have helped point the way to other, more functional, forms of deed restrictions that matured as the use of the defeasible fee waned. In this respect, the defeasible fee may have played an important role in the development of modern private land use planning.

This article tells the story of the emergence and decline of the defeasible fee as a land use planning device. In doing so, it also examines the beginnings of private residential land use planning in the United States. Finally, it seeks to shed some light on the phenomenon of the development and dissemination of legal knowledge and customs in a non-litigation context in the late nineteenth and early twentieth centuries. The article is based not only on cases and literature from and about this period, but also on the

---

[5] The term defeasible fee is used here in accordance with the Restatement of Property * * * to include the fee simple determinable, fee simple subject to a condition subsequent, and fee simple subject to an executory limitation. * * *

author's review of deeds from subdivisions spanning the period of 1870 to 1930 from four American cities that were undergoing rapid expansion during the period.[12]

II. Urban Growth in the Late Nineteenth and Early Twentieth Centuries

Three eras have been identified in the history of American urban development.[13] During the first phase, from colonial times until about 1860, urban growth was constrained because the principal form of transportation in cities was walking. This made it necessary for most people to live close enough to walk to the places where they worked, shopped, and obtained services. The second phase of urban growth occurred during the second half of the nineteenth and early twentieth centuries, as developments in transportation technology made distinct and more widely spread residential districts possible. First, the horse-drawn trolley car and steam-powered train, and later the electric railway and the elevated subway, radically expanded the scale of urban development. The third phase began about 1920, as the rapid proliferation of the automobile further amplified the possibilities of suburban growth and contributed to the creation of the modern metropolis. This article focuses on the second stage of development, from 1870 to 1920, during which the modern residential subdivision was born.

Though innovations in transportation technology undoubtedly played a major role in giving rise to the modern residential subdivision, several other forces also converged to conceive and give a particular form to residential subdivision development. First, other technical and economic changes gave impetus to the building boom. In particular, the perfection of balloon frame construction made possible efficient mass construction of residential dwellings in the new subdivisions. Additionally, in the late nineteenth century, the development of institutions and methods to provide capital for residential development—in particular, for financing owner-occupied, single family dwellings—permitted unprecedented levels of residential construction and purchase.

Other social and intellectual conditions gave direction to the new form of development. Traditional American distaste for city living flowered during the nineteenth century. Urban concentration of population, while perhaps necessary for economic reasons, was believed to be unhealthy and morally degrading. Urban congestion was considered a major social evil. By contrast, country living was idealized. Suburban life partook of the best of both urban and rural environments, combining at once the open air and spaciousness of the country with the sanitary improvements, comforts, and associated life of the city.

* * *

Finally, the late nineteenth century saw the emergence of American city planning, a development that had some influence on the nature of suburban growth. The era is best remembered for its grand urban designs: Burnham's plans for Chicago and San Francisco, and the plan of Burnham, Olmstead and others for Washington, D.C. However, some advocates of city planning also attended to development at the suburban level. Planned residential communities emerged in the United States as early as 1870. While speculative unplanned residential subdivision continued throughout the period, the planning movement contributed to the emergence of ordered and restricted subdivisions.

The decentralization of the nation's large urban areas, through the outward spread of residential subdivisions, began as early as the 1850's but became really significant only after 1870. By 1900, ten American cities of more than 50,000 population had decentralized and by 1930, 51 more had undergone this process. The character of the new residential neighborhoods that emerged in these decentralized urban areas varied somewhat by location, economic status of occupants, and time of construction. By the end of the nineteenth century, however, the basic model of residential development was established that would continue to the present: detached, single-family housing segregated from other uses and arranged on uniform blocks fronting on residential streets, usually laid out in a grid pattern.

III. Legal Tools for Restricting Subdivisions

Developers and home buyers desired legal control mechanisms to protect and preserve this residential environment. A home buyer was often investing his or her life savings, and was vitally concerned with the protection of this investment. Moreover, the purchas-

[12] The author reviewed deeds found in the recording offices of Franklin County (Columbus), Ohio; Suffolk County (Boston), Massachusetts; Cook County (Chicago), Illinois; and the District of Columbia. * * *

[13] C. Glaab & A. Brown, A History of Urban America (1967); S. Warner, Streetcar Suburbs (1978).

er bought not only a piece of property, but also a way of life. Controls were necessary to assure that neighboring lots were not developed for commercial use or, worse yet, industrial uses that would destroy the homeowner's peaceful enjoyment of his property and diminish the value of his investment. The purchaser of a suburban lot desired exterior open space for access to light and air, provision for that great American institution, the lawn, and room for a garden for relaxation and for a place for the children to play. Even if this open space consisted of a pitifully few feet of grass between the house and the street and a slightly larger space to the rear between the house and the alley or the rear of an adjacent lot, it was still treasured. Purchasers in the new subdivisions also sought to protect the resale value of their investment through restrictions that would assure uniformity of building size, value, and architecture.

Until 1920, most residential real estate was controlled, if at all, only through private plat and deed restrictions.[33] Until late in the nineteenth century, however, even private law deed restrictions, as we know them today, were still immature. Though a number of devices for permitting one landowner to enjoy rights in the property of another had emerged earlier in a variety of contexts, none of these devices were ideally suited for restricting residential subdivisions.

The legal restriction needed for creating and preserving residential subdivisions had to meet certain specifications. First, it had to be enforceable against all subsequent purchasers (i.e., the burden of the obligation had to run with the land). Second, the restriction had to be enforceable not only by the developer, but also by the subsequent purchasers (i.e., the benefit of the obligation had to run with the land). An initial purchaser could, of course, at the time of sale, take on obligations to the developer through a contract restricting the purchaser's development and use of his or her property. This was not adequate, however, since such a contract would not bind future owners of the restricted parcel or benefit purchasers of neighboring lots. What was needed was a device that created something more than contractual relationships between the developer and purchasers. A device was needed that would create durable property interests mutually enforceable by and against all owners of lots in the development.

The law as it existed at the outset of our period presented three tools used in other contexts, each of which met some of these specifications and could be adapted to the job of restricting property: the defeasible fee, the real covenant, and the negative easement. By the end of the nineteenth century, a fourth device, the equitable servitude, emerged as the tool preferred by the courts for subdivision restriction.

The real covenant was, by the nineteenth century, recognized by English property law in a variety of contexts. Covenants placed in deeds provided security of title. The earlier law of warranty had been, by this time, replaced by covenants of warranty, right to convey, seisin, quiet enjoyment, further assurances and against encumbrances. The benefits of these covenants of title attached to and ran with the estate of the covenantee. Covenants that attached to and ran with the estates of lessors and lessees were also utilized to govern landlord-tenant relationships.

For the covenant to be functional in creating restrictions in the residential subdivision context, however, it was necessary that the burden of the covenant obligation, as well as the benefit, attach to and run with the land in situations where privity of estate, in the sense of a landlord-tenant relationship, did not exist. This possibility was blocked in England where, by the early nineteenth century, courts had held that the burden of real covenants would not run at law in the absence of tenurial privity.[40] This restrictive definition of privity was early rejected by Judge Hare, the most influential commentator on real covenants in nineteenth century America, in favor of a broader definition, finding privity between any grantor and grantee of property. Most American courts that considered the issue concurred and permitted the burden of a real covenant to run whenever there was a grantor-grantee relationship between the initial covenantee and covenantor. Indeed, some courts permitted the burden of covenants to run even in the absence of privity of estate. * * *

The receptivity of American courts and commentators to the running of real covenants no doubt contributed to the increasingly frequent use of real

---

[33] Control over the development and use of property would, of course, be provided during the third, post-1920 stage of urban development by public zoning and subdivision controls. But zoning did not really take hold until the second decade of the twentieth century. New York, the first major city to adopt zoning, did so in 1916. * * * The legitimacy of zoning was not finally established until Village of Euclid v. Ambler Realty Co., 272 U.S. 365 (1926).

[40] *Keppel v. Bailey*, 2 My. & K. 517, 39 Eng. Rep. 1042 (1834); *Webb v. Russell*, 3 Tem. Rep. 393, 106 Eng. Rep. 639 (1789) * * *.

covenant language, by drafters of the period, in creating deed restrictions. By the early twentieth century, many deeds used the word "covenant," or specified that restrictions should "run with the land." Rarely, however, did cases address whether residential deed restrictions were enforceable as covenants at law.

This was true first, because the most controversial aspects of covenant doctrine were seldom at issue in the subdivision restriction context. The requirement that restrictions "touch and concern" burdened and benefited property, a much litigated aspect of covenant law, was not an issue because subdivision restrictions were almost exclusively negative in character, imposing limitations on the development of the burdened properties. Thus, they clearly touched and concerned affected properties by any definition. The negative nature of most subdivision restrictions also largely obviated consideration of the issue of privity, which during the nineteenth century came up as a problem almost exclusively in actions brought to enforce affirmative obligations.

Second, and more important, the paucity of decisions discussing deed restrictions as covenants is attributable to the fact that plaintiffs seeking to enforce subdivision restrictions normally brought actions for equitable relief. In these cases, the question of whether restrictions were enforceable at law as covenants was seldom dispositive. The few cases pronouncing deed restrictions to be covenants did so in the context of either saying the restrictions were not something else or as a predicate to enforcing them at equity.

Another candidate for the job of restricting residential subdivisions was the negative easement. An easement is an interest in land possessed by another which entitles the owner of the easement to limited use and enjoyment of the other's land. This interest is protected against interference by third parties and is capable of creation by conveyance. It is not subject to the will of the possessor of the servient property nor a normal incident of the possession of any other land of the owner of the dominant parcel. One common example of an easement is a right of way across the land of another. The negative easement by analogy created negative rights in the land of another. It entitled its owner to prevent the possessor of the land from using the land in specific ways otherwise within the possessor's rights. A number of early cases interpreting deed restrictions held that the restrictions created negative easements.

By the mid-nineteenth century, an extensive body of easement law existed in the United States. The negative easement was reluctantly acknowledged by English law, which recognized only four negative easements: the rights to air, light, support, and water in an artificial stream. But negative easements came to be used expansively in the United States, not only for protecting light and air, but also for enforcing setback lines and limiting noxious uses. The easement was superior to the covenant as a restricted tool because it was not subject to a requirement of privity. As deed restrictions became more complex and extended beyond establishing setback lines and limiting nuisances, however, they bore less resemblance to traditional easements and seemed increasingly fictive. Some American courts were hesitant to recognize negative easements for purposes not known to the common law. Moreover, while restrictions treated as easements were commonly enforced at equity, some courts expressed doubt whether they were enforceable at law. This suggests that such "equitable easements" were not in fact true easements. Perhaps because of these uncertainties, drafters of subdivision restrictions were less enamored with easement theory than were the courts. None of the deeds surveyed by the author denominated use restrictions as easements.

As actions for injunctions to enforce subdivision deed restrictions became more common, it became increasingly clear that courts were not particularly concerned with the legal classification of restrictions, only with whether the restrictions ought to be enforced at equity. Thus, a fourth kind of restriction enforceable at equity, variously called an equitable servitude, equitable easement, or sometimes an (equitable) negative easement, came to the fore as the primary tool the courts recognized for enforcing subdivision restrictions. Though this development is commonly traced to the English case of *Tulk v. Moxhay*,[66] American cases enforcing restrictions at equity antedate *Tulk*.[67] The theories courts put forward for equitable enforcement of restrictions varied widely. Some courts believed that they were enforcing covenants at equity, others that they were specifically enforcing negative easements, still others that they were simply enforcing a promise against successors to a promisor with notice of the promise. Theory was a good deal less important to the courts

---

[66] 2 Phil. Ch. 774 (1848).

[67] *Barrow v. Richard*, 8 Paige Ch. 351 (N.Y. Ch. 1840); *Hills v. Miller*, 3 Paige Ch. 254 (N.Y. Ch. 1832).

than were the equities of the situation being litigated. The primary concern of the courts was identifying the obligor and beneficiary of a duty respecting a parcel of land.

The willingness of these courts to enforce virtually any form of restriction at equity made relatively unimportant the form of restriction drafters used. Nevertheless, drafters of subdivision deed restrictions generally attempted to use recognized legal devices. Most commonly, they used either covenant or condition rather than easement or equitable servitude language. This may be attributable to the relatively slow recognition and exploration of equitable servitudes in the cases and commentary, caution and fear of innovation on the part of the drafters, or a desire by drafters for remedial options other than the injunction, i.e., damages or forfeiture. Avoidance of equitable servitudes in a few situations may also have been due to the reluctance of some American jurisdictions to enforce affirmative obligations through equitable servitudes.

IV. The Defeasible Fee as a Land Use Planning Tool

While the law of real covenants, negative easements, and equitable servitudes was still in a formative stage until late in the nineteenth century, the drafter of deed restrictions of that period had ready access to an elaborate law of defeasible fees developed in closely related contexts, such as charitable or public donations, industrial development, family settlements, and support arrangements. It was natural for many developers to turn first to this body of law for models for drafting residential subdivision restrictions. It is not surprising, therefore, that use of defeasible fees for deed restrictions was widespread during the period from 1870 until 1920, appearing before other forms of restriction in many jurisdictions and becoming nearly universal in some areas.

For the benefit of those whose memory of first year property is now fuzzy, a quick review of the lore of defeasible fees is in order. The 1936 Restatement of Property distinguished three kinds of defeasible fees: the fee simple determinable—created by any limitation that establishes an estate in fee simple and provides that the estate shall automatically expire upon the occurrence of a stated event; the fee simple subject to a condition subsequent—created by any condition that establishes an estate in fee simple and provides that upon the occurrence of a stated event the grantor or his successor shall have the power to terminate the estate; and the fee simple subject to an executory limitation, which establishes an estate in fee simple in a grantee but provides that upon the occurrence of a stated event the grantee will be divested in favor of another transferee other than the grantor or his successor. A fee simple determinable would be created by a grant for so long as the property were used for residential purposes. A grant in fee, but subject to the condition that if the property were ever to be used for other than residential purposes, the grantor or his heirs could re-enter and take possession, would create a fee simple subject to a condition subsequent. Finally, a grant for so long as the property were used for residential purposes, but stipulating that if the property were ever used for other than residential purposes it would pass to a third party other than the grantor or grantee, would create a fee simple subject to an executory limitation. In each instance, the grant of a defeasible fee would create a future interest. The future interests that correspond to the three defeasible estates are: the possibility of reverter, the power of termination (or right of re-entry), and the executory interest. The Restatement's classification of these three categories of defeasible fees is more or less in line with other modern sources, and on the whole consistent with the distinctions generally recognized by authorities in the nineteenth century.

These distinctions were of little practical importance to the drafters of deed restrictions in the late nineteenth and early twentieth centuries or to the courts interpreting those restrictions. The fee simple subject to executory limitation was not commonly used for deed restrictions. Though this type of defeasible fee could, in theory, have been used to transfer the responsibility of enforcement of restrictions from developers to neighbors or neighborhood associations who could have been granted the executory interest, the author discovered no examples of this kind of grant. This paucity of fees subject to executory limitation is no doubt attributable to the fact that these interests were subject to the Rule Against Perpetuities, and thus avoided by drafters who feared the many hazards of that Rule.

* * *

More common were deeds expressly stipulating that breaches of conditions would cause the property to "revert to the grantor" or "work forfeiture of the estate," or cause the deed of conveyance to be void, or some combination of these terms. Though these terms seemed to contemplate the automatic reversion, a characteristic of determinable fees, the courts generally interpreted them as creating fees subject to condition subsequent rather than determinable fees. Occasionally, courts interpreted these terms as creating covenants, or described them by hybrid terms such as "conditional estate in the nature of a negative easement" or "right of reverter." A few courts stated that such language created a possibility of reverter, though exhibiting no awareness that the possibility of reverter was distinguishable from the right of entry.

* * *

The defeasible fee differs dramatically from the other forms of restrictions in its remedy. Violation of one of the other forms of restrictions renders the violator liable for damages or injunctive relief. There is necessarily some relationship between the seriousness of the breach and the penalty, if any, imposed. Violation of a restriction imposed by the grant of a defeasible fee results, at least in theory, in forfeiture, a remedy that bears no necessary relationship to the nature of the breach, and that is, in fact, in most instances inappropriately draconian.

Undoubtedly, many developers and their attorneys turned to the defeasible fee as a tool for restricting subdivisions because of the common use of conditions for restricting the use of property in other contexts. However, it must have seemed, at the time, a propitious choice. First, restriction of a subdivision through uniform conditional deeds appeared to offer substantial protection to purchasers of subdivision lots. The threat of forfeiture impressed the legally unsophisticated purchaser of a lot worried about the enforceability of deed restrictions. The purchaser to whom the defeasible deed restriction was touted no doubt believed that if a neighbor built a slaughterhouse or a bay window projecting out beyond the setback line the neighbor's property would revert to the developer. Forfeiture appeared on its face a much more effective deterrent than the threat of a damage suit. Moreover, conditional restrictions enforced by forfeiture clearly ran with the land to bind future purchasers. A purchaser of land in a development did not have to worry that the burden of restrictions might be lifted once its lots began to change hands.

The defeasible fee also met the needs of the developer. Indeed, it yielded benefits not accessible through other forms of deed restrictions. The law was relatively clear that, in theory, restrictions applied through defeasible estates could exist in gross; therefore the power to enforce the restrictions could be held by a developer even though that developer did not retain any other property in the development. This was not clearly true with equitable servitudes or real covenants. Further, the use of defeasible fees appeared to allow the developer to market a subdivision at a premium as a restricted community without really limiting options for future development. Where the developer imposed a restriction through an equitable servitude contained in a deed to a purchaser in a subdivision, and the purchaser believed that the servitude would be imposed throughout the development as part of a common scheme, the developer might be obligated to include such a restriction in all future deeds in the development. The defeasible fee was more clearly a one way device. Technically, the developer who granted the defeasible fee retained an estate or a power, but was not in any way limited as to the development of other properties. If the development sold poorly, the developer could, without apparent liability, change the layout or even sell lots for commercial development. Further, the defeasible fee was well adapted for developers who retained property for themselves within the development or who felt strongly enough about some issues, such as the sale of alcohol or race restrictions, to desire continued control over the development even after their last lots had been sold. This control could be retained more effectively through defeasible fee restrictions than through alternative restrictive devices. Finally, some developers may have desired the gambler's chance of actually recovering property for resale if a condition was breached or the potential for future profit by sale of releases.

* * *

VI. Uses of Defeasible Fee Restrictions

* * *

Excessive use of alcohol was a serious social problem in the early nineteenth century. * * * By the end of the nineteenth century, the neighborhood bar represented the urban, South European Catholic immigrant influence from which many of those buying suburban property were escaping. * * * During the * * * pervasive temperance movement of the 1870's through the 1920's, * * * restrictions [against the sale or manufacture of alcohol] became nearly universal in some areas.

A broader use of conditional fee restrictions was to forbid uses regarded as nuisances in a residential district. * * * [Eventually] deeds appeared forbidding all nonresidential uses.

* * *

A final conditional restriction, the racial exclusion, became common, indeed in some areas ubiquitous, in the 1890's and early 1900's. A great many deeds written during this period provided that if the property were sold or leased to or occupied by members of excluded racial groups, it would revert to the grantor. Blacks (referred to as Negroes, Africans, or Ethiopians) were the racial group most commonly excluded, but many deeds excluded all non-Caucasians, and others, particularly in the West, excluded Orientals (Mongolians).

Race restrictions were regarded at the time by some as essential for planned, restricted developments. They allowed developers to achieve through private restrictions what could not be done through zoning.[211] * * *

Courts uniformly enforced racial restrictions on occupancy (though not necessarily on sale) until the 1950's, finding them to violate neither the Constitution nor public policy. Indeed, the defeasible fee formed one of the last barricades of proponents of legal residential racial segregation. In 1948, the Supreme Court, in *Shelley v. Kraemer,*[215] swept the records clear of all other forms of racially exclusive deed restrictions by holding that the fourteenth amendment forbade their enforcement through the state courts. Seven years later, the North Carolina Supreme Court, in *Charlotte Park and Recreation Commission v. Barringer,*[216] held that *Shelley v. Kraemer* did not apply to determinable fees limited by racial restrictions, since the determinable interest terminated automatically without state involvement if the racial limitation was violated. The Supreme Court denied certiorari. This decision provoked extensive commentary, most of it negative, but is of doubtful continuing effect. Developments in civil rights law and, it is hoped, in public morality have precluded a resurgence of defeasible fee limitations to enforce racial segregation.

* * *

VII. Deficiencies of the Defeasible Fee as a Land Use Planning Device

The popularity of the defeasible fee as a land use planning device was relatively brief. It is not difficult to understand its demise. From the start, the courts were hostile to the use of forfeiture as a tool for land use planning. Traditional abhorrence of forfeitures disposed the courts against enforcing deed restrictions written in conditional language through defeasance. Judges found numerous ways of avoiding forfeiture. The simplest approach was to construe a condition strictly to avoid finding a violation. Other approaches attacked the use of defeasible fees more directly.

Courts frequently permitted defendants to interpose equitable defenses to avoid forfeiture. The most frequently sustained equitable defenses were estoppel, waiver and laches (or, closely related, failure to claim forfeiture within the statute of limitations). * * * Others held that grantors could only enforce conditions if they retained property to which the restricted property was appurtenant, effectively creating a new rule that conditions could not exist in gross. Finally, some courts construed conditional restrictions as enforceable only for a reasonable period of time.

* * *

Even when courts did not expressly refuse to enforce conditions or limitations through forfeiture, they frequently achieved the same result by construing conditional language to create covenants or equitable servitudes. The restrictions would then be enforced through injunctive relief rather than forfeiture. Courts were especially likely to interpret conditional language to create an equitable servitude or covenant rather than a defeasible fee if a deed contained no reversion or re-entry clause—if the remedy of forfeiture was not explicitly reserved. Courts also frequently granted injunctions to enforce conditions in suits brought by neighbors of the violator. Such neighbors were, of course, interested in the equitable relief rather than forfeiture, and seldom held a right of entry or possibility of reverter. Neighbors could equitably enforce conditions reserved by a grantor under the theory that, by accepting a conditional deed, the grantee made a promise to abide by the conditions independently enforceable at equity.

Courts not only interpreted conditions as equitable servitudes, but some jurisdictions applied the changed conditions defense to enforcement of equitable servitudes to avoid enforcing conditions at all. The tendency of the courts to treat conditional restrictions as equitable interests, enforceable, if at all, only through injunctive relief, undoubtedly played a significant role in the development and education of the bar in the lore of equitable servitudes.

The reluctance of the judiciary to enforce conditions as such was not the only cause of the demise of the defeasible fee, which soon exhibited serious deficiencies as a land use planning device. First, it became clear that the defeasible fee was in fact of

---

211 * * * Even before Village of Euclid v. Ambler Realty Co., 272 U.S. 365 (1926), the Supreme Court had held that zoning could not be used to enforce racial segregation. Buchanan v. Warley, 245 U.S. 60 (1917).

215 334 U.S. 1 (1948).

216 242 N.C. 311, 88 S.E.2d 114 (1955) * * *.

little value to purchasers in a subdivision. Forfeiture was not a remedy available to adjoining landowners, who in most instances had the only real interest in enforcing deed restrictions. The right to enforce a conditional restriction by forfeiture could not, in many jurisdictions, be transferred from the developer to interested residents in the subdivision or to a property owners' association. Even where transfer was permitted, difficulties with transfer to many parties of the essentially indivisible right of enforcement made this solution impractical. Further, the owner of the reversionary interest could at any time release it, rendering the residents of the subdivision without protection.

If violation of a restriction was enforced through forfeiture, further problems resulted. Once the property was forfeited to the developer for violation of a condition, the restriction ceased to exist, and the developer could resell or use the property for any other purpose. Moreover, rights upon forfeiture were unclear. Established doctrine, for example, did not clearly decide who should get the value of improvements if property was forfeited.

* * *

Because conditional restrictions in theory made title depend on the manner in which the property was in fact used or developed, the defeasible fee made security of the title of an owner, potential purchaser, or mortgage depend on facts extraneous to the title record. Indeed, some conditions such as alcohol or cost of improvement restrictions could be breached by activity not readily discovered by visual inspection or survey. This, of course, made subsequent purchasers who discovered a condition during a title search nervous and may have discouraged improvement by current owners. A much more important problem, however, was the impact of defeasible fees on lending institutions, which were understandably reluctant to finance the purchase of property subject to the potential of forfeiture for conduct over which they had little control. Indeed, laws regulating financial institutions in some states forbade loans on such insecure collateral. Some developers attempted to deal with this problem by expressly allowing mortgagees to cure violations of conditions prior to forfeiture. A more acceptable solution was to change to restrictions that did not threaten forfeiture.

Abandonment of the use of defeasible fee subdivision restrictions was counseled by more sophisticated planners and developers, who early recognized the limitations of conditions. Some aspirations of developers, like establishing permanent property owners' associations to manage maintenance fees collected under deed restrictions, could be accomplished only with difficulty through conditions. Because most jurisdictions at the time did not permit rights of entry or possibilities of reverter to be transferred, the developer could not transfer the rights to the property owners' association. The interest could have initially been created as an executory limitation in the property owners' association, but then would have been subject to the Rule Against Perpetuities. A well-advised developer could have created an executory limitation in a property owners' association with a duration of less than 21 years, but the author found no examples of this. Developers saddled with rights of entry chafed under the responsibility of enforcing deed restrictions. Other developers found they could restrict property more easily by placing restrictions in the original plat or in a declaration of restrictions, an approach possible with equitable servitudes but not with defeasible fees.

Ultimately, the defeasible fee gave way to the equitable servitude as the restrictive device of choice. For a host of reasons, conditions enforced by forfeiture were inferior to servitudes enforced by injunction for assuring compliance with deed restrictions. Perhaps the most important development contributing to the ascendancy of the equitable servitude was the maturation by the end of the nineteenth century of the doctrine of the equitable servitude common scheme, which permitted developers to impose restrictions on all properties in a subdivision for the benefit of all others. In the end, deed restrictions generally became less important because of the rise of public land use control.

* * *

IX. The Clean Up of the Debris

By 1920, a substantial number of subdivision lots in many states were subject to forfeiture restrictions appearing somewhere in the chain of title. The possibility of forfeiture under most of these provisions was very remote. First, a court presented with the issue would almost always find a reason for not permitting a forfeiture. More to the point, the issue was seldom raised as developers, who technically held the power to enforce forfeitures, rarely had any interest in doing so. Few developers maintained much interest in their subdivisions once the lots were sold. Nevertheless, forfeiture provisions lurked insidiously in the background of many properties, perpetually clouding the title. The construction of a bay window or porch beyond the setback line, the opening of a professional office in the basement, the sale of the property to a black family, could raise the long dormant specter of forfeiture.

* * *

The most obvious solution to these problems was legislation eliminating stale or useless defeasible fee restrictions. Such legislation existed in a few states from the nineteenth century, but did not really become popular until the 1940's. In the 1940's and 1950's, a number of states passed legislation limiting in various ways rights of entry and possibilities of reverter. This legislation took several basic forms. First, several statutes, following the lead of the early Michigan statute, purported to eliminate merely nominal conditions. Second, a number of statutes imposed specific time limits on the duration of defeasible fee limitations or for assertion of defeasance. One statute changed defeasible fee restrictions into covenants after a set period of time. Another subjected actions for enforcing conditions or limitations to defenses available against the enforcement or other forms of restriction.

* * *

X. Conclusion

Though the defeasible fee emerged early as the legal tool for restricting residential development, its career was brief and far from glorious. * * * By the conclusion of our period, the flexible and easily enforced equitable servitude triumphed everywhere over the defeasible fee as the land use planning tool of choice. Even the real covenant, plagued though it was with labyrinthine legal complexities, and the negative easement, despite its fictive character, gained ascendancy over the defeasible fee. In the end, zoning, subdivision controls, and other public land use planning tools overshadowed private restrictions in shaping residential development.

* * *

Wherever the defeasible fee was used as a land use planning device, generations of lawyers have struggled with the title problems left behind. In many jurisdictions, however, old forfeiture restrictions now have been rendered ineffective by reverter and marketable title legislation. Many other restrictions have receded beyond the horizons of interest of title insurance companies and opinion writers. The unfortunate defeasible fee chapter of the history of private land use planning in the United States is by and large closed.

Note

Jost is surely correct in arguing that use of defeasible fees for standard real estate developments is unwieldy at best. Are there ways, however, in which such property interests might productively be used? Consider *Charlotte Park and Recreation Commission v. Barringer*, 242 N.C. 311, 88 S.E.2d 114 (1955), discussed by Jost. Putting aside the racial content of the gift in the case, did Barringer make a wise decision to use a defeasible fee to set up Revolution Park in Charlotte? This was in essence a gift "in gross," that is a gift where the conditions on the donation did not benefit or burden any other land. In such cases, do defeasible fees work better than covenants? Are there other devices, such as trusts, which are even easier to use than defeasible fees?

Garrett Power, *Apartheid Baltimore Style: The Residential Segregation Ordinances of 1910–1913*, 42 Md. L. Rev. 289-325 (1982)*

On May 15, 1911, Baltimore Mayor J. Barry Mahool, who was known as an earnest advocate of good government, women's suffrage, and social justice, signed into law "[a]n ordinance for preserving peace, preventing conflict and ill feeling between the white and colored races in Baltimore city, and promoting the general welfare of the city by providing, so far as practicable, for the use of separate blocks by white and colored people for residences, churches and schools." Baltimore's segregation law was the first such law to be aimed at blacks in the United States, but it was not the last. Various southern cities in Georgia, South Carolina, Virginia, North Carolina, and Kentucky enacted similar laws.[2]

The legal significance of housing segregation laws in the United States was shortlived. In 1917 the United States Supreme Court struck down the Louisville, Kentucky ordinance[3] and thereby constitutionally eviscerated the ordinances of other cities as well. But the historical significance of Baltimore's segregation ordinances remains.

History remembers the Mahool administration for having placed Baltimore in the forefront of municipal reform. The story of how the Mahool government earnestly proposed and enacted an apartheid statute as a progressive social reform has a contemporary message: It cautions us to discount the righteous rhetoric of reform; it reminds us of the racist propensities of democratic rule; and it sets the stage for understanding the development of a covert conspiracy to enforce housing segregation, the vestiges of which persist in Baltimore yet today.

Throughout the early nineteenth century Baltimore housing was not racially segregated, and even following the Civil War, blacks lived in all of Baltimore's twenty wards. Although the majority of blacks resided in the city's central, southern, and eastern sections, there was no Negro quarter or ghetto. Blacks were scattered throughout the northern reaches of the town, clustering together in narrow, two-story alley houses and working nearby in domestic service while more affluent whites lived on the main thoroughfares.

Urbanization was to modify this fluid mixture. * * * Between 1880 and 1900 Baltimore's black population increased 47% from 54,000 to 79,000. * * *

Negro newcomers with little money and limited job opportunities sought out the cheapest housing in town. They rented shanties and doubled up in small houses, resulting in Baltimore's first sizable slums. The first slum to reach maturity was "Pigtown" in Southwest Baltimore. A contemporaneous account from 1892 describes it as follows:

> Open drains, great lots filled with high weeds, ashes and garbage accumulated in the alleyways, cellars filled with filthy black water, houses that are total strangers to the touch of whitewash or scrubbing brush, human bodies that have been strangers for months to soap and water, villainous looking negroes who loiter and sleep around the street corners and never work; vile and vicious women, with but a smock to cover their black nakedness, lounging in the doorways or squatting upon the steps, hurling foul epithets at every passerby; foul streets, foul people, in foul tenements filled with foul air; that's "Pigtown."[7]

As neighbors who could afford to do so moved away from this squalor, Pigtown ripened into a ghetto. Whites were not the only residents to take flight. In this time of relative permissiveness in race relations, blacks also were free to buy houses elsewhere in the city. Baltimore's black bourgeoisie, then perhaps 250 in number, sought to remove themselves from the "disreputable and vicious neighborhoods of

---

[2] C. Johnson, Patterns of Negro Segregation 173–75 (1943); Rice, *Residential Segregation by Law*, 1910–1917, 34 J.S. Hist. 179, 181–82 (1968). The cities were: Atlanta, Ga.; Greenville, S.C.; Ashland, Roanoke, Richmond, Norfolk, and Portsmouth, Va.; Winston-Salem, N.C.; and Louisville, Ky.

[3] Buchanan v. Warley, 245 U.S. 60 (1917).

[7] Baltimore News, September 20, 1892, quoted in J. Crooks, Politics & Progress: The Rise of Urban Progressivism in Baltimore 1895 TO 1911, at 20 (1968).

their own race."[9] Thus a first wave of blacks relocated in the northwestern part of the city as those blacks that could afford to do so purchased second-hand housing around St. Mary's Orchard and Biddle Streets, in what was to become the 17th Ward. * * * Their neighborhood began in the alleys and then moved out to the wider streets, displacing Bohemians and Germans.

The Negro migration to Northwest Baltimore accelerated as whites abandoned their homes there and fled to newly opened suburban tracts. * * * By 1903 the Negro population was perhaps the majority in the 17th Ward; the slum that had developed in the Biddle Alley neighborhood in the lower portions of the ward had replaced Pigtown as the worst in the city.

* * *

These slums were but a symptom of the social chaos in turn-of-the-century Baltimore. Between 1870 and 1900, the city's population grew from 250,000 to 500,000, as ex-Confederates, Negroes, and European refugees crowded into the city. The year 1890 was the beginning of a severe slump in the economy. Families could not afford even the cheapest housing so they doubled and tripled up. Unemployment was rampant; women and children worked for minuscule wages under horrendous conditions in an effort to make ends meet. Services proved inadequate or nonexistent—police, fire protection, water supply, and schools were deficient and the city had not yet constructed a sanitary sewer system. Urbanization, industrialization, and depression had concentrated in Baltimore a growing population of the poor, the sick, and the ignorant.

The crisis in Baltimore and other cities produced a movement for social reform. Social reformers joined the already established Progressive Movement in opposing political machines such as the Rasin-Gorman Ring in Baltimore, and in advocating civil service reform, the merit system, streamlined government, home rule, and corrupt-practices legislation. But the social reformers who came from the universities and churches had greater ambitions. They advocated initiatives designed to remedy the fundamental ills of society—illiteracy, pestilence, crime, and poverty.

The first leader of the organized Social Reform Movement in Baltimore was Daniel Coit Gilman, President of the Johns Hopkins University. In 1881, he founded the Charity Organization Society and modeled it after similar groups in London, Buffalo, Boston, and New York. It provided the poor with gifts of food, clothing, and coal, along with "friendly visitors" who volunteered to help on a one-to-one basis. In addition, Jane Addams's pioneer settlement house in Chicago was soon copied by Baltimore clergyman Edward H. Lawrence. Further, Baltimore philanthropists Robert Garrett and Henry Walters copied projects undertaken elsewhere in sponsoring playgrounds and public baths.

* * *

Not surprisingly, these first efforts at social reform proved unequal to the task. Self-help, friendly visiting, volunteerism, and timid government initiatives failed to abolish poverty, to prevent crime, and to cure tuberculosis and other infectious diseases. Among the reformers' greatest shortcomings was their failure to do more for blacks. The half-dozen privately financed settlement houses reached at most several hundred Baltimoreans; Negroes never saw a settlement. As initially established, public baths and playgrounds designed to humanize the urban environment were for whites only. These facilities were not available to blacks until 1905 and 1908, and then only to a limited extent. Fledgling public health efforts had made no discernible impact on the black communities—the Negro death rate from both smallpox and tuberculosis was twice that of the white average.

Notwithstanding their failures, social reformers remained undaunted. Unable to treat or to cure the fundamental ills from which the urbanizing, industrializing society suffered—illiteracy, morbidity, crime, and poverty—their response was to focus on a symptom rather than the disease. Slum housing came to the forefront of the reformers' concerns; environmentalism came to be an article of faith.

* * *

Gilman's Charity Organization Society commissioned an investigation entitled Housing Conditions in Baltimore.[30]

* * *

The *Housing Conditions in Baltimore* report, interrupted by the Baltimore Fire of 1904, was finished in 1907, under the direction of Janet E. Kemp. Its statistics and photographs vividly display the horrors of the slums and the plight of the slum-dwellers * * *. * * *

The report suggested legislative requirements that differed for tenements and alley houses. The report

[9] Haynes, *Conditions Among Negroes in the Cities*, 49 ANNALS 105, 111 (1913).

[30] J. KEMP, HOUSING CONDITIONS IN BALTIMORE (1907).

proposed an inexpensive "market" solution for tenement districts. It sought to force landlords to improve existing tenements, and to require builders to construct model tenements, by proposing regulations setting height limits, requirements of separate toilets for each apartment, and annual inspections. The proposal was plausible. In the early twentieth century, tenements were profitable ventures. Commercial developers were building new flats for the "dollar-a-day" man. Together, housing codes and building restrictions might eliminate all substandard tenements by forcing entrepreneurs to pay the cost of improving them. The solution also was consistent with the classic concept of the state's police power. The report proposed regulations protecting health, safety, and morals which businessmen might not transgress in the pursuit of profit, but otherwise did not interfere with the economic order.

The report's recommendations for alley districts differed. It proposed to reduce the density in existing alley houses, to condemn those that were uninhabitable, to ban sleeping in basements, and to prohibit erection of additional alley houses. Although these measures would improve the quality of housing, they necessarily would reduce the quantity. Thus the report's recommendations would work a particular hardship on blacks, who lived in the alleys, for whom no new houses were being built, and who encountered resistance when attempting to move into white neighborhoods. In effect, the report relegated the growing Negro population to a shrinking number of houses.

The report also distinguished between the inhabitants of tenements and alley-houses. Negroes were singled out for criticism: "This is not a study of social conditions, but it is impossible to observe these gregarious, light-hearted, shiftless, irresponsible alley dwellers without wondering to what extent their failings are a result of their surroundings, and to what extent the inhabitants, in turn, react for evil upon their environment." The "low standards and absence of ideals" among Negroes was "held to some degree accountable for the squalor and wretchedness" which characterized the alley neighborhoods.[44]

Despite the plausibility of its proposals and the prestige of its sponsors, the city took no action on the *Housing Conditions in Baltimore* report. In the northwest the Negro district continued to grow both in population and size. By 1910, 12,738 blacks had crowded into the 17th Ward, constituting over fifteen percent of the city's overall Negro population and sixty-one percent of the ward's overall population. The few remaining whites were rapidly leaving. It was the worst slum in the city.

Not surprisingly, those in the black community who could afford to do so also sought to move away from the squalor and disease. Middle-class blacks began to look covetously at quiet residential houses to the west and north. Between 1903 and 1910, the western boundary of the Negro district moved six or seven blocks from Argyle Avenue to Gilmore Street in the 15th and 16th Wards. To the north, the black population in the 14th Ward continued to grow. By 1910, 8,392 Negroes resided there, the second highest number. Negroes were distributed fairly evenly over the remainder of the city, excepting five wards where their numbers were negligible.

Expansion of the Negro district to the west and north was not without incident. White residents struggled against the "black sea" for years. For example, a protest convinced the School Board to reverse a decision converting a white school to a black one. Windows were broken and black tar was smeared on white marble steps. And when a black family moved into a house on Stricker Street they were attacked and the house was stoned. But white terrorism was no match for the combined purchasing power of housing-hungry blacks. Money talked.

In their effort to move eastward, on the other hand, blacks had been unsuccessful. Druid Hill Avenue had remained the eastern boundary of the Negro district. In its 1600 block, residences of the "best" Negro families were directly across the street from Western High School, the "best" public girl's school—which was for whites only. This barrier was reinforced by the affluence of the white neighborhood to the east. Eutaw Place was a broad, landscaped boulevard which had been designed to encourage residential development and to enhance property values in the vicinity. The plan was a success and the Eutaw Place neighborhood had become one of the most fashionable residential sections of Baltimore. It had spread three blocks west of the boulevard itself with Druid Hill Avenue serving as its western boundary.

In the summer of 1910, George W.F. McMechen purchased a house at 1834 McCulloh Street. McMechen, a Yale law graduate and a practicing attorney, moved with his wife and children from his former

[44] Id. at 16–18.

house on Prestman Street, ten blocks to the west. McMechen was celebrating his professional success by moving into one of the most fashionable neighborhoods in Baltimore. The move is memorable only because McMechen and his family were black. He had crossed the eastern boundary of the Negro district and purchased a house in the Eutaw Place neighborhood.

This violation of the color line provoked considerable agitation. Police were necessary to protect the McMechen house from young ruffians. A mass meeting was held on July 5, 1910 and a petition prepared requesting that the Mayor and City Council: "take some measures to restrain the colored people from locating in a white community, and proscribe a limit beyond which it shall be unlawful for them to go . . . ." The petitioners were concerned that Negroes intended to "plant themselves on Madison Street and Eutaw Place" as well.

Milton Dashiell was George W.F. McMechen's brother at the Maryland Bar. Dashiell had been born in Dorchester County, Maryland in 1859; he attended St. John's College in Annapolis, read law, and was admitted to practice in 1882. For a time, he practiced in Kentucky before he returned to his home state. According to all reports, his career was undistinguished; he was a "briefless lawyer."

Dashiell resided on the southern fringe of the 11th Ward at 1110 McCulloh Street. The neighborhood was all white, but it was located just a block away from the Biddle Alley district, the infamous "lung block." The "Negro invasion" of Eutaw Place inspired Dashiell to draft a law designed to prevent blacks from further encroaching on white neighborhoods. The bill was introduced into the City Council by Councilman Samuel L. West.

The bill took a long and tedious course. Public hearings were held at which the primary spokesmen against the ordinance were Negroes. Both branches of the City Council finally passed the ordinance, by a strict party vote—all Democrats voted in favor and all Republicans voted against.

The Baltimore Sun summarized the ordinance's provisions as follows:

> That no negro can move into a block in which more than half of the residents are white.
>
> That no white person can move into a block in which more than half of the residents are colored.
>
> That a violator of the law is punishable by a fine of not more than $100 or imprisonment of from 30 days to 1 year, or both.
>
> That existing conditions shall not be disturbed. No white person will be compelled to move away from his house because the block in which he lives has more negroes than whites, and no negro can be forced to move from his house if his block has more whites than negroes.
>
> That no section of the city is exempted from the conditions of the ordinance. It applies to every house.

In addition, the ordinance prohibited negroes from using residences on white blocks as a place of public assembly and vice versa.

* * *

Mayor J. Barry Mahool signed the ordinance into law on December 20, 1910. The occasion was a ceremonial one. Two pens were used in the signing—one was given to Dashiell and one to Councilman West. The pen was a "favor" which Dashiell announced he would "treasure . . . from every point of view." West got into the spirit of the occasion by announcing that he would have a copy of the ordinance framed and hung in his home.

It is easy to understand racist Dashiell's pride of authorship, but from today's perspective, Mayor Mahool's support is enigmatic. This experiment in apartheid was at best a sell-out to Baltimore plutocracy, and at worst an invidious denial of housing to Baltimore's blacks. Yet Mahool, who is remembered as a champion of social justice, eagerly signed the ordinance without apology.

At first it seems anomalous that a member in good standing of the Progressive Movement—which advocated the elimination of slums as the breeding ground for crime, disease, and poverty—would enthusiastically support a law designed to worsen Negro housing conditions. But in a broader historic context it makes sense. Progressive reformers like Mahool found themselves faced with social chaos. Their efforts had failed to cure the fundamental ills—illiteracy, morbidity, crime, and poverty—from which the urbanizing, industrializing society suffered. Thus defeated, they resolved to treat two of the most bothersome and visible symptoms of society's ailments: riots and epidemic disease.

Because the riots were often racial in nature, and because the black slums were viewed as the source of contagion, the reformers focused on the black neighborhoods. The ultimate goals of the Progressives, however, were not directed to improving the living conditions of black slum families. Progressive reformers were not concerned with the plight of Negroes; as C. Van Woodward observed: "The blind spot in the . . . progressive record . . . was the Negro . . . ." "Victim blaming" was much less costly than attempting to solve the underlying social problems.

Social Darwinism provided the ideological basis for this view, and some reformers used it to posit a basic inferiority of black people.[74] For example, the campaign rhetoric of the Disenfranchisement Movement (a nationwide effort to deny Negroes their right to vote) depicted blacks as slovenly and corrupt brutes. Turn-of-the-century census data supported the view that Negroes were a dying race: blacks showed a higher mortality rate and a lower birth rate than whites.

* * *

Many Progressives thus agreed that poor blacks should be quarantined in isolated slums in order to reduce the incidents of civil disturbance, to prevent the spread of communicable disease into the nearby white neighborhoods, and to protect property values among the white majority.

* * *

The first segregation ordinance proved to be politically and legally deficient. It was a foregone conclusion that the ordinance would be vehemently opposed by the Negro community. But blacks were not alone in opposing the ordinance: they were joined in opposition by real estate brokers and white owners of property located in mixed neighborhoods. * * * [T]he ordinance was politically flawed in that it worked at cross purposes to the economic well-being of a significant white constituency.

* * *

A legal challenge to the ordinance was not long in coming. In less than a month, twenty-six criminal cases were sent to court. In the first one to go to trial, Judges Harland and Duffy of the Supreme Bench of Baltimore, without going into the merits of the legislation, declared the ordinance ineffective and void because it was "inaccurately drawn." * * * The title of the first segregation ordinance was nondescriptive; it grandly declared that the provision was "[a]n ordinance for preserving order, securing property values and promoting the great interests and insuring the good government of Baltimore City," without mentioning racial segregation of housing.

Partisans of the segregation ordinance were undaunted. Indeed, they viewed the court's decision as an encouragement "to push further their war into Africa." Councilman West decided to drop lawyer Dashiell, however, and to seek the assistance of more eminent counsel. He turned to William L. Marbury, whose credentials as a segregationist were well established by his role in the Disenfranchisement Movement.

The second segregation ordinance corrected the legal flaws of the first. Further, in a major substantive change, Marbury drafted the ordinance to be inapplicable to "mixed" blocks. All black blocks were to remain all black, all white blocks were to remain all white, and integrated blocks were left to pursue their market destiny. Marbury designed this change to quiet opposition from white landowners and real estate professionals. * * *

Not everyone was pleased with the second segregation ordinance. A delegation of black property owners urged its veto, and some brokers reiterated their concern that the ordinance would depress real estate values in mixed neighborhoods. * * * These objections notwithstanding, Mahool signed the ordinance on April 7, 1911.

* * *

A challenge to Baltimore's * * * segregation ordinance was two years in coming. A criminal indictment was filed against John E. Gurry, "a colored person," charging that he had unlawfully moved into a residence on an all-white block. Gurry was defended in the Criminal Court of Baltimore City by W. Ashbie Hawkins, a Negro, who was to play an active role in legally attacking the segregation ordinances.

At trial the court dismissed the indictment against Gurry, finding the ordinance nonsensical. * * * The Maryland Court of Appeals * * * [also] had a substantive quarrel with the ordinance * * *. It found the ordinance unconstitutional because it took away the vested rights of the owner of a dwelling to move into it if he happened to be white and the block was all black, or vice versa.

There was no lapse in coverage, however: a week before the Maryland Court of Appeals struck down the * * * segregation ordinance, the Baltimore City Council had enacted [another] * * *. The * * * ordinance cured the constitutional infirmity of its predecessor by making its application prospective only; it provided "that nothing herein contained shall be construed or operate to prevent any person, who at the date of the passage of this ordinance, shall have acquired a legal right to occupy, as a residence any building or portion thereof . . . from exercising such legal right . . . ."

In the short run the segregation ordinances served the goal of their proponents—the protection of Eutaw

---

[74] Schmidt, *Principle and Prejudice: The Supreme Court and Race in the Progressive Era. Part 1: The Heyday of Jim Crow,* 82 COLUM. L. REV. 444, 453–54 (1982).

Place from a "Negro Invasion"—while presenting blacks with few problems. To the contrary, blacks at first were able to buy or to rent at distress prices as whites fled mixed blocks. The ordinances failed to accomplish the more long term goals of the white majority, however, and eventually worked a positive hardship on blacks, the effects of which are apparent even today.

* * *

The ordinances * * * were disastrous for Baltimore's black community because their effect was to limit further the overall housing supply available to an increasing black population. An economist asked to guess the likely impact of a law which limited the supply of housing for which there was an increasing demand would make two prophecies—the price of Negro housing would increase, and the quality of Negro housing would decline. Both came to pass. Although the ordinances at first made some housing available to blacks as whites abandoned their homes on mixed blocks, only a limited number of mixed blocks existed and the pressure for additional Negro housing was unrelenting. The Negro population in Baltimore was 85,000 in 1910. It had been increasing by approximately 600 per year during the previous decade, yet the additional housing available to blacks was being exhausted. A growing population was "bottled-up" into a limited number of houses.

* * *

The "Baltimore idea" for promoting residential segregation was quickly adopted in other southern and border cities. In 1912 Mooresville and Winston-Salem, North Carolina enacted segregation ordinances. One year later Asheville, North Carolina; Richmond, Norfolk, and Roanoke, Virginia; Atlanta, Georgia; Madisonville, Kentucky; and Greenville, South Carolina passed similar legislation. And in 1914 Louisville, Kentucky; Birmingham, Alabama; and St. Louis, Missouri followed suit.[125]

Indeed the success of residential segregation ordinances was the catalyst for the emergence of the National Association for the Advancement of Colored People as an effective counterforce to segregation. The NAACP had been founded in 1909. But its membership and political power grew as it established local branches to press court challenges to the segregation ordinances. * * *

* * * [T]he Baltimore branch of the NAACP, under the leadership of W. Ashbie Hawkins, * * * challenged * * * the constitutionality of Thomas S. Jackson's criminal conviction for violation of Baltimore's * * * segregation ordinance.

* * *

The Maryland Court of Appeals postponed its decision in the case pending a decision by the United States Supreme Court in a closely related case.[135] In 1914, the City of Louisville, Kentucky had passed a segregation ordinance of its own. The text of the Louisville ordinance closely resembled the text of the first segregation ordinance which Milton Dashiell had drafted for Baltimore. The ordinance made it unlawful for blacks to reside in residential blocks more than fifty percent white and vice versa.

The Supreme Court case was a product of the efforts of the NAACP's national headquarters. The NAACP had formed a Louisville branch and had recruited prominent local counsel, but orchestrated the litigation from its New York office. With the assistance of the local black leaders and white members of the Louisville Real Estate Exchange, it created a test case in the context least favorable to the ordinance's constitutionality.

The scenario had William Warley, president of the Louisville branch of the NAACP, contract to buy a corner lot from Charles Buchanan, a white real estate agent. The lot in question was in a "white block" but was surrounded by black residences. The contract provided that Warley was not required to perform "unless I have the right under the laws of the State of Kentucky and the City of Louisville to occupy said property as a residence." Buchanan sought specific performance of the contract in the state courts and Warley set up the ordinance as his excuse for not performing. The state courts held the Louisville ordinance constitutional and therefore a complete defense to Warley.

Hence the case of *Buchanan v. Warley* had been staged to work a role reversal. Buchanan, the plaintiff challenging the constitutionality of the ordinance, was a white real estate agent. Warley, the defendant defending the ordinance, was the black president of the Louisville branch of the NAACP. The explanation of this litigation strategy is straightforward. At the turn of the twentieth century the U. S. Supreme Court had come to accept Jim Crow laws: in *Plessy v. Ferguson*,[139] decided in 1896, the Court found state law requiring racial segregation on railroads consistent with the fourteenth amendment; and in *Berea College v. Kentucky*,[140] decided in 1908, it found that the state of Kentucky had the power to require racial

---

[125] Schmidt, supra note 74, at 499–500.

[135] Buchanan v. Warley, 245 U.S. 60 (1917).

[139] 163 U.S. 537 (1896).

[140] 211 U.S. 45 (1908).

segregation in a private college. But during this same era the Court had actively embraced the credo of "economic laissez-faire." In 1905, in *Lochner v. New York*,[141] the Court constitutionally protected freedom of contract in the baking business from maximum-hour legislation. In *Buchanan*, the NAACP hoped to convince the Court to protect Buchanan's constitutional right to engage in the real estate business without meddlesome interference from the City of Louisville (and thereby incidentally to protect blacks from residential housing segregation).

Buchanan v. Warley was first argued before the Supreme Court in April of 1916 before seven justices. The Court then ordered reargument before a full bench. The significance of the case was well recognized; twelve amicus briefs were filed on both sides. From Baltimore, City Solicitor Field filed a brief defending the ordinance, while W. Ashbie Hawkins (who had hoped himself to argue a case challenging the Baltimore ordinance before the Supreme Court) filed a brief on behalf of the Baltimore NAACP. The case was reargued and the Court finally rendered a decision in November of 1917.

The NAACP's litigation strategy almost backfired. Justice Holmes prepared a dissent in which he argued that the case should be dismissed because of its collusive nature. Holmes said: "The contract sounds so very like a wager upon the constitutionality of the ordinance that I cannot but feel a doubt whether the suit should be entertained without some evidence that this is not a manufactured case." But Holmes decided not to deliver his dissent and a unanimous Court held the Louisville housing segregation ordinance unconstitutional.

The NAACP's tactic had worked. Justice Day's opinion emphasized Buchanan's property right to dispose of his lot as he saw fit. Also in the opinion, however, were expressions of concern for the rights of Negroes. Day found "the difficult problem arising from a feeling of race hostility" an insufficient basis for depriving citizens of their constitutional rights to acquire and to use property without state legislation discriminating against them on the sole basis of color. From today's perspective the opinion seems analytically imprecise. The Court intertwined Buchanan's right to substantive due process with Warley's right to equal protection. But the opinion served perfectly the NAACP's purpose. The Supreme Court was afforded a mechanism through which it could squelch residential segregation laws without overruling recent precedents that had sustained racial segregation in transportation and schools.

* * *

Black Baltimoreans seized the opportunity to renew their movement into white neighborhoods. Two black families moved into the 1100 block of Bolton Street, one of the oldest middle-class residential sections of the city; another family moved into the 1200 block of McCulloh Street. White Baltimoreans responded with petulance and frustration. Miss Alice J. Reilley asked, "What is the use of trying to beautify a city or put in any civic improvements if Negroes are to acquire all of the property?"

Mayor Preston was undaunted. He sought the advice of Dr. A.K. Warner of Chicago, where plans for keeping Negroes out of white territory were in effect. In addition to pursuing the Chicago Plan, Mayor Preston conceived of another "radical measure" to complement his plan for segregation. He proposed "the elimination of certain congested sections, populated by Negroes, in which has been noted a very high percentage of deaths from . . . communicable diseases."

It is doubtful that Preston appreciated the irony of his requesting advice from Dr. Warner. Chicago was then undergoing widespread rioting in response to Negro movement into white neighborhoods. Before it was over there would be fifty-eight bomb explosions, two Negroes dead, many people of both races injured, and property damage in excess of $100,000. Chicago was a peculiar place to seek advice for one whose avowed purpose was improving race relations.

Nevertheless, Preston determined to implement the Chicago Plan. It was a simple one. The plan was "to forc[e] out the blacks already residing in [white] neighborhoods and [to ensure] that no others entered. The activities of [the white property owners' association] consisted both of mass meetings to arouse the neighborhood residents against the blacks and the publication in white journals of scathing denunciations of the race." The auspices of the Real Estate Board of Baltimore, the City Building Inspector, and the Health Department also would be employed to discourage "block busting." In essence, Preston proposed to replace de jure segregation with de facto segregation, enforced by a conspiracy in restraint of rental or sale to Negroes.

* * *

The first public slum clearance project provided for "the parking of St. Paul and Courtland Streets"

---

[141] 198 U.S. 45 (1905).

between Lexington and Centre Streets. The city began in 1914 to buy up properties that were used as third-rate rooming houses and cheap flats. Eventually, in 1917, proceeds from a harbor loan were used to hire landscape architect Thomas Hastings, who replaced Courtland Street with a sunken garden and widened St. Paul Street. The project was intended to improve the traffic flow, as well as to eliminate a downtown slum. When completed in 1919, some Baltimoreans called it Preston's Folly, others called it Preston Gardens.

Hence, in the aftermath of *Buchanan v. Warley*, the Baltimore plan for segregation had come to consist of two discrete strategies—clearance and containment. Clearance was used to remove Negro slums from areas where they were not wanted; containment was used to prevent the spread of black residential districts.

* * *

[T]he city undertook to clear "pest holes." One such effort was the construction of a Negro school on one-half of the Biddle Alley district—the old "lung block." The black community objected that because substitute housing was not provided, such projects merely removed poor blacks from one slum to another.

Although improved public health continued to be used as a justification for slum clearance projects, this justification was not taken too seriously. Knowledgeable observers recognized that clearance projects merely crowded the displaced population into other blighted areas. A 1934 study prepared for Mayor Howard W. Jackson provided a more candid rationalization: blighted black areas close to the downtown commercial district and white neighborhoods yield declining tax reserves and are a nuisance. Therefore, the public interest would be served by their replacement with white housing or industry.

* * *

Containment was the other strategy. We have already discussed how, when de jure segregation failed, de facto segregation was implemented through a conspiracy which restrained residential sales or rentals to Negroes in white neighborhoods. Once the conspiracy was in place it grew and formalized. Originally it was enforced through peer pressure from neighbors, administrative harassment by housing and health inspectors, and by the suasion of the Baltimore Real Estate Board. Later this conspiracy came to be institutionalized.

In 1922 the National Association of Real Estate Brokers (NAREB), of which the Baltimore Board was a member, published a textbook entitled Principles of Real Estate Practice. The textbook emphasized that "the purchase of property by certain racial types is very likely to diminish the value of other property." It was deemed unethical to sell blacks property that was located in white neighborhoods. As recently as 1950 the NAREB's code of ethics provided:

> The realtor should not be instrumental in introducing into a neighborhood a character of property or occupancy, members of any race or nationality or any individual whose presence will clearly be detrimental to property values in the neighborhood.

* * * Some builders perpetuated this restriction by placing restrictive covenants in the deeds prohibiting resale to blacks. The Maryland Court of Appeals upheld the enforcement of racial restrictions under the fourteenth amendment, because the discrimination was private rather than public.[186]

Mortgage lenders joined in the conspiracy. Traditionally in Baltimore, most house purchases were financed by mutual savings and loan associations, which discriminated against blacks. Credit unions for ethnic and white church groups, and for work organizations (e.g., B&O), also excluded blacks from participating. And when general banking institutions began to extend mortgage credit they "redlined" black and integrated neighborhoods as unstable and risky. Later, in the 1930's when the federal government became active in housing fields, it denied Federal Housing Administration support in neighborhoods with "inharmonious racial groups."[188]

In Baltimore in 1934 the 3,800 middle-class black families who could afford to own a house were those most immediately affected by the conspiracy of containment. If they already owned a home it was likely to be in the upper Druid Hill Avenue district, which still was the best that Negroes could get in the city proper. Yet the neighborhood was in some respects unsatisfactory: it was noisy as a result of street cars, lacked recreational facilities, was removed from shopping facilities, and had areas of improper sanitation. Moreover, it was undergoing change. The neighborhood had been encroached upon by brothels and saloons. Landlords were outbidding individuals for some of its large houses with a view toward creation of tenements. Black homeowners

---

[186] Meade v. Dennistone, 173 Md. 295, 301, 196 A. 330, 333 (1938).

[188] U.S. COMM'N ON CIVIL RIGHTS, UNDERSTANDING FAIR HOUSING 4–5 (Clearinghouse Pub. No. 42, 1973).

attempting to escape these problems had no place to go.

* * *

Baltimore's housing market was to retain most of these characteristics for the next 30 years. But one inexorable force for change remained: between 1930 and 1960 Baltimore's black population grew from 142,000 to 326,000. The market described above made no allowance for increasing the number of black housing units. This gap was widened by actions of the city government. Between 1930 and 1960 programs of school building, slum clearance, urban renewal, and expressway construction displaced large numbers of households. Between 1951 and 1971 alone, 75,000 people were removed, and eighty to ninety percent of them were Negroes. During this same period the city had various public housing programs, but by 1976 only 15,000 public housing units were available. Hence, the city exaggerated the shortage by demolishing many more houses than it created.

"Blockbusting" was the answer. Economists have commented upon the difficulty of enforcing multiparty agreements in restraint of trade. The problem is simple: "The temptation of members to cheat is strong . . . because the returns from cheating are substantial . . . ."[198] This certainly proved to be true in Baltimore's housing industry. The treaty between white homeowners, the real estate industry, financiers, and the Federal Housing Administration had left unmet the demand for black housing. A house could be sold at a premium to a black buyer by a seller willing to violate the treaty. Moreover, this premium could be multiplied by real estate speculators who capitalized on the panic in white neighborhoods that had begun to change in racial make-up. Brokers bought whole blocks at a distress price from nervous white sellers, and sold at a premium to housing-hungry black buyers.

Later, speculators broadened their market. They used their credit to borrow money from financial institutions. Turned-over houses were then sold on easy terms to low-income, high-risk black buyers pursuant to "buy-like-rent" contracts. The sales were often illusory; foreclosure was the rule rather than the exception. The speculator would sell and resell the same house to a series of buyers. By this technique the blockbusters took a profit from the under-class as well as the middle-class Negroes. Blockbusting transferred tens of thousands of houses from the white market to the black market.

Blockbusting poses an ethical enigma. Its practitioners were outlaws, violating the real estate industry's code of ethics and cheating on the cartel between white homeowners, real estate dealers, mortgage lenders, city government, and the FHA, which restrained the sale or rental of housing to blacks in white neighborhoods. Speculators employed a psychology designed to scare white homeowners out of their accumulated equities. They sold to black purchasers for whatever the market would bear, sometimes exacting exorbitant profits. Conversely, its practitioners were providing housing opportunities otherwise unavailable to Negroes. And the "ethical" precept which they violated was part of a racist conspiracy. Speculators provided financing and housing when mortgage lenders and "ethical" real estate brokers refused to do so. The unsavory blockbuster or the respectable conspirators: Who is to blame?

Although apartheid, Baltimore style, was doomed to failure, the white body politic refused to accept defeat gracefully. It fought for the city's territory district-by-district, neighborhood-by-neighborhood, and block-by-block. In an effort to maintain de facto segregation in housing, it used the whole bag of tricks: Negro removal through slum clearance, public works projects, and urban renewal; restrictive covenants denying blacks access to "exclusive" white neighborhoods; refusal of financing for black or integrated housing; and professional sanctions against real estate brokers dealing with blacks in white neighborhoods. But unrelenting demographic forces were increasing the black population of Baltimore from fifteen to seventy percent. Over the long term the dwindling white majority lacked both the political and economic power to keep a restrictive cordon around the black community.

Once again it was the United States Supreme Court that cut the knot. In 1948 the Court took the first step in *Shelley v. Kraemer*.[201] It ruled that the legal enforcement of private, racially restrictive covenants was unconstitutional under the equal protection clause of the fourteenth amendment. The Court conceded that the amendment was directed only against state action and not private conduct, but found that state judicial enforcement of private agreements brought them within the amendment's purview.

---

[198] R. Posner, Economic Analysis of Law 115 (1972).
[201] 334 U.S. 1 (1948).

Shelley was a setback for segregated housing, but for twenty years the conspirators fought on, using the other tools of de facto segregation—peer pressure, "redlining" of mortgages, and professional sanctions. Finally, in 1968, the Supreme Court decided in *Jones v. Mayer*[202] that the 1866 Civil Rights law passed pursuant to the thirteenth amendment bars all housing discrimination, private as well as public. This decision, taken along with the 1968 Federal Housing Law which prohibited discriminatory practices by real estate brokers, builders, and lenders dismantled the dual housing market. In Baltimore and in the other urban areas that share much of this housing history, the white market and the black market merged into one housing market.

Disappearance of the dual housing market does not mean that housing is desegregated, that racial discrimination has been eliminated, or that good housing is available for the poor. Residential housing in Baltimore remains by-and-large segregated. In part this segregation is a result of preference: Blacks and whites alike may prefer to live in their old neighborhoods that developed in the days of de facto segregation. Segregation also results from economics: The median black family income is lower than that of whites, creating an economic barrier to entry into more affluent areas. But the notion that blacks need only a larger income to gain an equal choice of housing is inaccurate. Old practices die hard; muted voices of discrimination persist in the real estate and financing fields. Black buyers are steered to black neighborhoods, and mortgage money is more readily available to whites. Studies show that black families have less access to suburban housing than do white families of equivalent income.

Moreover, the power of local governments to select the site for public projects may be used to perpetuate racial segregation. In the 1960's, expressways in Baltimore sought out the routes of least resistance—black ghettos. When the roads were built, displaced residents lacked reasonable relocation opportunities; when the roads were not built, whole neighborhoods, such as Rosemont, were left desolate and abandoned. In one instance the city took the houses in what had been a working-class black neighborhood, condemned them for a highway which was never built, and then created the fashionable Otterbein district for the affluent professionals returning to reside in the gentrified city. Class distinction, if not racial discrimination, influences the location of public projects.

Finally, elimination of the dual housing market has done little to improve the quality of housing available to low-income blacks. When Baltimore's plan for segregation was first conceived, the building industry was providing low-income housing. Commercial builders catered to the dollar-a-day man. Tenements and flats were profitable speculative ventures. Negroes were excluded from these buildings on racial grounds. Today the free market no longer produces low- and moderate-income housing. Increased costs of energy, financing, and construction price housing beyond the reach of the poor and near-poor. Public and federally subsidized housing partially fill the void. But Baltimore's 15,000 public units, along with the various federally subsidized units, fall far short of meeting the demand. And it is impossible to locate a new subsidized low-income housing project without encountering outraged community opposition. Thus most of Baltimore's poor (both black and white) continue to live under slum conditions.

* * *

[T]he details of the Baltimore story provide insight and lessons with broader implications. * * * First, the facts and descriptions in this history call into question free-market economic analysis of the causes of racial segregation. Much of Baltimore's housing history follows the economist's script. Economic theory would have predicted the development of slums as a market response to the demand for inexpensive housing by a growing population of low-income city dwellers. Moreover, fear of crime and contagion predictably provided economic incentives for self-segregation by middle- and upper-income residents who responded with a willingness to pay a premium to locate in neighborhoods remote from slums. Finally, separation by income level naturally will tend to result in separation by race because blacks have lower average incomes than whites and spend less on housing.[207]

But some analyses go a step further and attempt to explain all residential segregation by race as individually motivated. For example, economist Richard Muth argues that segregation is the natural result of whites having a greater preference for segregation than blacks have for integration. To make his model work, Muth must assume that middle-class blacks are less averse to living in

---

[202] 392 U.S. 409 (1968).

[207] *See* R. MUTH, URBAN ECONOMIC PROBLEMS 86–110 (1975).

proximity to slums than middle-class whites; otherwise one would expect to find middle-class black families sprinkled throughout neighborhoods remote from slums. The details of this study belie his assumption. We have documented the efforts of the black bourgeoisie (e.g., George W.F. McMechen, the Morgan College faculty, the Baltimore Colored Law and Order League), to remove themselves from the vicinity of slums. In Baltimore, the aversion to crime and contagion knew no color line.

Muth also rejects the possibility that a conspiracy between home owners, real estate agents, mortgage lenders, and local government officials limited the availability of housing to blacks. The conspiracy argument cannot be taken "very seriously" he says, because each individual in the urban housing market would have a profit incentive not to join it: "[b]y not doing so he avoids his share of the costs of the conspiracy, but, having a negligible effect on the outcome, shares in its benefits." Notwithstanding Muth's rejection, our study shows that a dual housing market in fact was created. The white majority, first through the segregation ordinances and then through a publicly sponsored conspiracy, enforced racial segregation in the city. The shared incentives of the white majority (isolation of crime, quarantining of disease, and maintenance of property values at black-white boundaries) proved collectively powerful enough to support a loose treaty which stifled sales to blacks. This treaty was violated from time to time by outcast blockbusters willing to buy from white sellers and to sell to black buyers, but ironically these blockbusters became political partisans of the dual housing market because it afforded them an opportunity for profit-taking. Blockbusting vented the pressure and permitted the treaty to endure.

In rejecting the possibility of a conspiracy, Muth errs by assuming that behavior in the aggregate is nothing more than a summation of individual behaviors. Political economist Thomas C. Schelling provides a more sophisticated view in his book *Micromotives and Macrobehavior.*[210] Therein he opines that housing segregation is at once individually motivated, collectively enforced, and economically induced. Baltimore's history of residential segregation supports Schelling's thesis.

* * *

[210] T. SCHELLING, MICROMOTIVES AND MACROBEHAVIOR 137–66 (1978).

Note

The United States Supreme Court began the slow process of removing overt racism from American property law with its decision in *Shelley v. Kraemer*, 334 U.S. 1, in 1948. Can you articulate why it took another twenty-three years before the Court began a similar process with respect to gender? *See Reed v. Reed,* 404 U.S. 71 (1971), holding unconstitutional a preference for male executors of estates; *Kirchberg v. Feenstra*, 450 U.S. 455 (1981), invalidating the ability of a husband to unilaterally encumber community property when a wife lacks the same power. *Compare Goessart v. Cleary*, 335 U.S. 464 (1948), validating a Michigan preference for male bartenders, the same year *Shelley* was decided.

Richard H. Chused, *Background to* Village of Euclid v. Ambler Realty Co., *adapted and revised from* CASES, MATERIALS AND PROBLEMS IN PROPERTY 1156–1163, 1173–1174 (1988)*

The Supreme Court's opinion in *Village of Euclid v. Ambler Realty Company* was eagerly awaited by important federal government officials, Progressive Era reformers, real estate developers and local government officials across the country. It was widely viewed as a crucial test of the validity of the Standard Zoning Enabling Act, adopted by 1925 in just under half of the states and under consideration in many others.

The adoption of zoning legislation was part of a much broader effort to reform national housing policies in the early twentieth century. Muckraking books such as Lincoln Steffens' SHAME OF THE CITIES (1904) and Upton Sinclair's THE JUNGLE (1906) mirrored widespread concern about the state of urban America. Tenement house regulations first appeared in New York City in 1901 and, along with building codes, spread gradually to many urban areas by the 1920's. Shortly after Warren G. Harding assumed the Presidency in 1921, his Secretary of Commerce, Herbert Hoover, appointed an Advisory Committee on Zoning in the Department of Commerce. In 1924, the year following Harding's death and Calvin Coolidge's move to the White House, the Advisory Committee issued the Standard State Zoning Enabling Act and recommended its adoption by the states.[1] By the end of the following year, nineteen states, including Ohio, had followed the Committee's advice. By the end of the decade, some or all localities in every state had been granted the power to zone.[2]

The Advisory Committee also reviewed the status of subdivision regulations in the various states. Some control of subdivisions had existed in many places well back into the nineteenth century. They were designed to assure that plat maps were correctly drawn and filed, and that engineering studies were appropriately completed. Other functions were gradually added, such as requiring that new streets tie into old ones and that utility lines be correctly laid. Shortly after *Euclid* was decided the Advisory Committee published a Standard City Planning Enabling Act, making subdivision regulation a tool of comprehensive planning, placing administration of subdivision controls in the hands of local planning boards, and establishing certain guarantees that improvements planned in subdivisions were actually carried out. The Standard Act, or some other similar regulatory scheme, was eventually adopted by most states. The two Standard Acts drafted by the Commerce Department are still the basic statutory structures used in many jurisdictions.

The Village of Euclid actually adopted its first zoning ordinance in 1922, two years before the Commerce Department published its final draft of the Standard Zoning Enabling Act.[3] Euclid followed in the footsteps of New York City which adopted its first zoning ordinance in 1916, two years after the New York state legislature adopted the nation's first zoning enabling statute.[4] When Euclid adopted its zoning ordinance, the town's sixteen square miles of territory contained less than 4,000 people. It was mostly agricultural. While some land speculators,

[1] Virtually all persons favoring adoption of zoning argued that each municipality had separate and distinct problems and that actual implementation of zoning had to come at a local level. But most cities were then and are now legal creatures of state legislatures, limited in their authority to the powers granted in state legislation. It was therefore necessary for states to adopt legislation enabling city governments to adopt their own zoning schemes.

[2] NATIONAL COMMISSION ON URBAN PROBLEMS, BUILDING THE AMERICAN CITY, H.R. Doc. No. 34, 91st Cong., 1st Sess., 201 (1968).

[3] Fluck, *Euclid v. Ambler: A Retrospective*, 52 J. AMER. PLANNING ASSOCIATION 326, 328 (1986). Fluck's article is a nice history of the case. *See also*, S. I. TOLL, ZONED AMERICA 213–253 (1969). Euclid may have been ahead of the general trend because Alfred Bettman, who drafted the Standard Act for President Hoover, was from Ohio and deeply involved in development of land use legislation in the state.

[4] The most prominent entity seeking adoption of zoning enabling legislation in New York was the Fifth Avenue Commission established in 1913 by the Manhattan Borough President. The Commission was concerned about the growth of tall buildings in lower Manhattan and the negative effects of the garment industry. *See* TOLL, ZONED AMERICA 143–171 (1969).

including Ambler Realty, had bought up parcels of land in the town anticipating future industrial development, there were no factories in the Village of Euclid. Indeed, during the decade before Euclid adopted its zoning plan, Ambler sold off some tracts east of the 68 acre site that became the subject of litigation in *Euclid* and imposed covenants prohibiting commercial and industrial development.[5]

Aptly named Euclid Avenue was the major thoroughfare running through the town. Ambler's 68 acres sat between Euclid Avenue on the southeast and the Nickel Plate Railroad tracks and the Cleveland city limits on the northwest. Under the first version of Euclid's plan, Ambler's land was zoned industrial (U-6) for a distance of 500 to the southeast of the railroad tracks and two family residential (U-2) over the rest of the site. Ambler's protests led Euclid to modify the plan so that a two family residential zone covered the area 620 feet to the northwest of Euclid Avenue, apartment use (U-3) was permitted on the next 130 feet, and industrial use on the remainder.

Despite the modifications creating a significantly larger industrial zone, Ambler filed suit seeking to enjoin enforcement of the zoning scheme. The Village sought to have the case dismissed, arguing that Ambler was required to pursue available administrative remedies to its claimed deprivation of property before seeking judicial relief. The motion to dismiss was denied by Judge David Westenhaver, who was appointed to the federal bench by President Wilson in 1917. Westenhaver was appointed in large part because of the influence of Ambler's attorney, Newton Baker. Baker served as Wilson's Secretary of War and was a close friend of Westenhaver's.[6] A short time later, Westenhaver rendered his decision finding Euclid's ordinance unconstitutional.[7]

Even though Westenhaver had close ties to Baker, it is virtually impossible to contend that his decision distorted prior Supreme Court jurisprudence in Ambler's favor. Within the two years before Westenhaver's January, 1924, opinion appeared, the Court decided three cases in a manner quite adverse to the notion that states had broad authority to regulate land or the economy. And in prior terms, the Court had made known its general hostility to property regulation in any number of opinions.

In his opinion, Westenhaver noted that many of the older cases involved statutes designed to prevent activities commonly viewed as nuisances, such as livery stables and brick manufacturing plants, near residences. It was easy for him to view the sorts of land use restrictions imposed by Euclid's ordinance as quite different from the typical regulatory fare that had previously come before the Supreme Court. Though there were certainly some examples that were hard for Westenhaver to deal with,[8] most of the cases gave significant support for his general thesis that mediation of nuisance was not the primary objective of Euclid's zoning plan.

He relied heavily, for example, on *Buchanan v. Warley*, decided in 1918.[9] Westenhaver argued that if, as *Buchanan* held, racial zoning was invalid, then certainly Euclid's plan had to fall. It was so obvious to Westenhaver that "colored" people and certain groups of immigrants were nuisances, that the Court's refusal to approve racial zoning removed all doubts about the invalidity of zoning for other purposes. Comparing the *Buchanan* and *Euclid* ordinances, he wrote:

> It seems to me that no candid mind can deny that more and stronger reasons exist, having a real and substantial relation to the public peace, supporting * * * [the *Buchanan*] ordinance than can be urged under any aspect of the police power to support the present ordinance as applied to plaintiff's property. And no gift of second sight is required to foresee that if this Kentucky statute had been sustained, its provisions would have spread from city to city throughout the length and breadth of the land. And it is equally apparent that the next step in the exercise of this police power would be to apply similar restrictions for the purpose of segregating in like manner various groups of newly arrived immigrants. The blighting of property values and the congesting of the population, whenever the colored or certain foreign races invade a residential

---

[5] Fluck, *supra* note 3, at 327–328.

[6] *Id.*

[7] Ambler Realty Co. v. Village of Euclid, 297 F. 307 (N.D.Ohio 1924).

[8] *See,* for example, Welch v. Swasey, 214 U.S. 91, 29 S.Ct. 567, 53 L.Ed. 923 (1909), which involved limitations on building height. Even recognizing that tall buildings and the light they block were a major concern of the New York legislature when they first adopted zoning statutes, Westenhaver could say little more than the case involved "merely a reasonable regulation of the height of buildings." 297 F. at 315.

[9] 245 U.S. 60 (1918).

section, are so well known as to be within the judicial cognizance.

Cases decided by the Supreme Court during the two terms before *Euclid* came before Westenhaver provided him with additional significant support. The most important of the cases was *Pennsylvania Coal v. Mahon,*[10] the 1922 decision finding that Pennsylvania's attempt to control subsidence of the surface from mining activities was a taking. Two other cases appeared in 1923, *Adkins v. Children's Hospital,*[11] invalidating a Washington, D.C., minimum wage statute, and *Wolff Co. v. Industrial Court,*[12] striking down a Kansas compulsory labor arbitration law. Westenhaver relied upon all three. The tenor of this segment of his opinions is revealed in the following excerpt:

> [C]onfusion of thought appears to exist touching the nature and extent of the police power. * * * [C]ounsel [for Euclid] deduce * * * that since the ordinance in question does not take away plaintiff's title or oust it from physical possession, the power of eminent domain has not been exercised, but that the police power has been. This conception recognizes no distinction between police power and sovereign power. The power asserted is not merely sovereign, but is power unshackled by any constitutional limitation protecting life, liberty, and property from its despotic exercise. In defendant's view, the only difference between the police power and eminent domain is that the taking under the former may be done without compensation and under the latter a taking must be paid for. It seems to be the further view that whether one power or the other is exercised depends wholly on what the legislative department may see fit to recite on that subject. Such, however, is not the law. If police power meant what is claimed, all private property is now held subject to temporary and passing phases of public opinion, dominant for a day, in legislative or municipal assemblies.[13]

It was a major surprise when the Supreme Court reversed Judge Westenhaver and upheld Euclid's zoning ordinance. The reasons for this result have not become entirely clear, although suggestions have been made by those writing about the case. The Court may have been influenced by the recommendations emerging from successive, increasingly conservative, Republican administrations that zoning statutes be adopted. These endorsements of land use controls reflected a widespread feeling that urbanization problems were getting a bit out of hand, that skyscraper technology threatened the fabric of large cities, and that middle and upper income single family residential areas needed protection from high density apartment and industrial development.

A sense of the scope of change overtaking the United States may be gleaned by a quick glance at some demographic trends. The table below shows that the decade of the 1920's was the first era when more than half of the population of the United States lived in urban areas and more than 10,000,000 cars were registered with local authorities. In addition, the major eastern cities were swamped with the millions of immigrants that had crowded these shores before World War I. If ever there was a propitious time for city planners to have an impact on policies of urban America, the 1920's was that time.

---

[10] 260 U.S. 393 (1922).
[11] 261 U.S. 525 (1923).
[12] 262 U.S. 522 (1923).
[13] *Id.* at 313 314.

DEMOGRAPHIC TRENDS[14]

Year	Percent Population Urban	Auto Registrations	Decade Immigration Rate
1830	9%	—	2.4%
1840	11%	—	4.2%
1850	15%	—	12.4%
1860	20%	—	5.3%
1870	26%	—	8.1%
1880	29%	—	7.6%
1890	35%	—	7.3%
1900	40%	—	6.0%
1910	46%	8,000	11.0%
1920	51%	465,000	3.7%
1930	56%	9,239,100	1.7%
1970	73%	108,407,300	1.0%

The *Euclid* Court was evidently troubled by these land use issues. After oral arguments were first heard during January of 1926, the case was set down for reargument that fall. Reargument is a rare event. Since the Court never states reasons why a case is set down for further discussion, historians may only speculate about why it happened in *Euclid*. Several intriguing facts are known about the case which may help explain the situation. James Metzenbaum, Euclid's village counsel, requested and was granted the right to file a reply brief after the oral arguments; the other side was granted the same right. The month after these briefs were filed, the court announced it had set the case for reargument.[16] In addition, the National Conference on City Planning wished to file an amicus curiae brief in the case, but inadvertently missed the original filing deadline. Their counsel, Alfred Bettman, was a long time advocate of city planning, the draftsman of much of Ohio's zoning legislation and secretary to the Advisory Committee on Housing and Zoning of the Commerce Department that drafted the Standard Zoning Enabling Act. He wrote to Chief Justice Taft[17] the month after the oral arguments in *Euclid* explaining the importance of the case to city planners and asking if he could file an amicus brief. Taft replied that he had brought the matter up in conference with the Court and invited Bettman to submit the brief. Finally, a law clerk to Justice Harlan Fiske Stone at this time has claimed that Justice Sutherland, while writing an opinion striking down Euclid's zoning ordinance, was shaken in his convictions about the case after talks with those who would have dissented from his opinion.[18] Justice Sutherland was also absent from the first oral arguments in *Euclid*, making it somewhat easier for him to justify rehearing the case. It may be of some importance that Justice Sutherland's three well known conservative colleagues—Justices Van Devanter, McReynolds and Butler—dissented from Sutherland's majority opinion when the *Euclid* case was finally decided. Perhaps Sutherland and another justice switched sides. The dissenters' failure to publish an opinion may indicate they were unwilling to squabble publicly with their conservative colleague. In any case, Sutherland's authorship of the opinion has been declared a "jurisprudential miracle."[19]

In hindsight, Justice Sutherland, like Judge Westenhaver, may also have been influenced by the enormous racial controversy of the World War I era. As Garrett Power's essay, excerpted just above, on Baltimore's segregation ordinances, real estate agent

---

[14] Data is taken from BUREAU OF THE CENSUS, DEPARTMENT OF COMMERCE, STATISTICAL HISTORY OF THE UNITED STATES FROM COLONIAL TIMES TO THE PRESENT at 8, 11-12, 105-106, 716 (1976). The immigration rate listed is the number of immigrants entering the United States as a percentage of total population for a ten year period beginning five years before the listed year and ending five years after the listed year. The number in the table is the sum of ten years of data, with each year representing Total Immigration/Total Population for that year.

[16] Fluck, note 59 *supra* note 3, at 331.

[17] Bettman was an old friend of Taft's and a fellow Cincinnatian. *Id.*

[18] *Id.*

[19] *Id.* at 333.

cabals, and racial covenants suggests, devices to overcome *Buchanan*'s limitations on apartheid rules were in widespread use during the first half of this century. Attempts to establish separate zones for single family houses and apartments were surely part of that process. At a minimum, it is fair to say that keeping tenement houses and other structures likely to be occupied by disfavored people separate from middle and upper class residential areas was perfectly compatible with racial segregation. Perhaps Sutherland, more than his conservative colleagues on the Court, recognized that superficially neutral zoning ordinances could be used quietly for the very same purposes *Buchanan* banned from explicit use.

Notes

1. Is *Village of Euclid v. Ambler Realty Co.*, 272 U.S. 365 (1926), an embodiment of Realist jurisprudence?

2. What can the Takings Clause in the Constitution mean to a Realist? If property is once endorsed by the state and therefore given "realist" reality, may it be taken back later by the state only with payment of compensation? If so, are historic notions of wealth, once sanctioned by the state, forever frozen into our national charter?

D. Property as Protection From Large Enterprises and the Government: Individualism and the Welfare State in the 1960s

1. Liberty and Property in the Vietnam War Era

The Realist reconstruction of property as a set of relational rights between people endorsed by the state effectively merged the notion of property into a system of government organization. The significant increase in the scope of economic regulation accomplished by the New Deal, the dramatic regulatory apparatus accompanying World War II, and the systematic anti-Communist ordering of the McCarthy era created great concern about the status of individuals or unprotected groups in the developing welfare state. The civil rights movement, a new wave of feminist activity, welfare recipient organizations, tenant groups and anti-Vietnam War actions all brought the status of individuals to public notice in passionate ways.

Charles Reich's article on *The New Property* hit the legal world like a bombshell. Reich's argument that both accretion and loss of wealth were so dominated by state controlled systems of largess that individual liberty was threatened turned lights on for a generation of lawyers. For conservatives it was a clarion call to rethink the underpinnings of the welfare state; for liberals it provided justifications for controls over the more arbitrary features of the modern state. For all it produced a vibrant dialog about the meaning of property.

Thinking of property, as Reich did, as a barrier between the individual and the corporate state is quite different from the early Republican use of property ownership to define civic responsibility. Rather than setting a norm for merger of public and private functions, property for Reich established a boundary between public power and private needs. As a result, process became a major focus of attention. Bringing disputes into the public eye, providing a forum for evaluation of arbitrary actions, and establishing settings for individuals to dispute openly the legality of actions by government or other large organizations in society was an important method for giving property-like powers to those receiving government largess. Even the Supreme Court paid heed, holding in *Goldberg v. Kelly,* 357 U.S. 254 (1970), that welfare benefits could not be terminated without a hearing. Though the scope of procedural rights that attach to government largess has diminished with the decisions of later Supreme Courts, Reich's thesis had an important, and perhaps ongoing, moment in the sun. For his own retrospective views on *The New Property*, *see* Charles A. Reich, *Beyond the New Property: An Ecological View of Due Process*, 56 BROOKLYN L. REV. 731 (1990). For a critique see Jennifer Nedelsby's *Law, Boundaries and the Bounded Self*, in part II(A) of this anthology.

The same basic reasoning structure produced a second famous article, by Christopher Stone, claiming that inanimate objects in the environment ought be deemed holders of property rights subject to protection in American courts. If property is a right of exclusion endorsed by the state, then why not remove the requirement of a human relationship from the definition of property and permit protection of the ecology so that both human and ecological relationships may flourish?

But the articles of Reich and Stone, like those of the Realists before them, ultimately contained no clear guidance for defining property. To argue that property is both the creature of government, and the safeguard of individual liberty and environmental well being is to place liberty and well being constantly at risk. It in fact conflates public and private realms even as it proclaims the need for their separation.

The rest of this anthology contains a variety of materials selected to allow you to attempt your own reconstruction of the idea of property as a meaningful cultural category. Basic legal commentary is mixed with a variety of works using non-legal disciplines to structure analysis.

Charles A. Reich, *The New Property*, 73 YALE L. J. 733, 756–760, 762–764, 768–774, 777–779, 781–787 (1964)*

III. THE PUBLIC INTEREST STATE

What are the consequences of the rise of government largess and its attendant legal system? What is the impact on the recipient, on constitutional guaranties of liberty, on the structure of power in the nation? It is important to try to picture the society that is emerging, and to seek its underlying philosophy. The dominant theme * * * is "the public interest," and out of it there grows the "public interest state."

A. *The Erosion of Independence*

The recipient of largess, whether an organization or an individual, feels the government's power. The company that is heavily subsidized or dependent on government contracts is subjected to an added amount of regulation and inspection, sometimes to the point of having resident government officials in its plant. And it is subject to added government pressures. The well known episode when the large steel companies were forced to rescind a price rise, partly by the threat of loss of government contracts, illustrates this. Perhaps the most elaborate and onerous regulation of businesses with government contracts is the industrial security system, which places all employees in defense industries under government scrutiny, and subjects them, even high executives, to dismissal if they fail to win government approval.

Universities also feel the power of government largess. Research and development grants to universities tend to influence the direction of university activities, and in addition inhibit the university from pursuing activities it might otherwise undertake. In order to qualify for government contracts, Harvard University was required, despite extreme reluctance, to report the number of Negroes employed in each department. The University kept no such information, and contended that gathering it would emphasize the very racial distinctions that the government was trying to minimize. Nevertheless, the University was forced to yield to the Government demand.

Individuals are also subject to great pressures. Dr. Edward K. Barsky, a New York physician and surgeon since 1919, was for a time chairman of the Joint Anti-Fascist Refugee Committee. In 1946 he was summoned before the House Committee on Un-American Activities. In the course of his examination he refused, on constitutional grounds, to produce records of the organization's contributions and expenditures. For this refusal he served six months in jail for contempt of Congress. Thereafter the New York State Education Department filed a complaint against him, under a provision of law making any doctor convicted of a crime subject to discipline. Although there was no evidence in any way touching Dr. Barsky's activities as a physician, The Department's Medical Grievance Committee suspended his medical license for six months. The New York courts upheld the suspension * * *, [as did] the United States Supreme Court.[124] * * *

If the businessman, the teacher, and the professional man find themselves subject to the power of government largess, the man on public assistance is even more dependent. Welfare officials, often with the best of motivations, impose conditions intended to better a client, which sometimes are a deep invasion of his freedom of action. In a memorable case in New York, an old man was denied welfare because he insisted on living under unsanitary conditions, sleeping in a barn in a pile of rags. The court's opinion expresses a characteristic philosophy:

> * * * One would admire his independence if he were not so dependent, but he has no right to defy the standards and conventions of civilized society while being supported at public expense. This is true even though some of those conventions may be somewhat artificial. One is impressed with appellants argument that he enjoys the life he leads in his humble "home" as he calls it. It may possibly be true, as he says, that his health is not threatened by the way he lives. After all he should not demand that the public at its expense, allow him to experiment with a manner of living which is likely to endanger his health so that he will become a still greater expense to the public.
>
> It is true, as appellant argues, that the hardy pioneers of our country slept in beds no better than the one he has chosen. But, unlike the appellant, they did it from necessity, and unlike the appellant, they did not call upon the public to support them while doing it.[128]

* * *

The pressures on the individual are greatly increased by the interrelatedness of society and the pervasiveness of regulation. The individual with a black mark against him, merited or unmerited, finds that it dogs him everywhere, from locality to locality, and from one kind of work to another. Even a mountain guide in the west must now be a "person of good moral character" in order to be licensed. And licensing control can reach the point achieved by New York, where all entertainers and cabaret employees must be fingerprinted. As Judge J. Skelly Wright has pointed out, a man's "innermost secrets . . . long buried and known only to himself" may pursue him wherever he tries to find work.[139] Indeed, the consequences of a criminal conviction, no matter how innocuous the circumstances, are so serious and the structure of regulation is so rigid that a bill was introduced in the New York City Council to nullify the effect of criminal convictions growing out of participation in civil rights demonstrations. Caught in a vast network of regulations, the individual has no hiding place.

B. *Pressures Against the Bill of Rights*

The chief legal bulwark of the individual against oppressive government power is the Bill of Rights. But government largess may impair the individual's enjoyment of those rights.

* * *

Largess * * * brings pressure against first amendment rights. The Pacifica Foundation was for a long period in danger of losing its three radio licenses because of "controversial" broadcasts, including "extreme" political views. For an extended period the FCC delayed action on the Foundation's application for renewals. The FCC demanded that the Foundation's directors, officers, and managers give answers disclosing whether they were or had been members of

[124] Barsky v. Board of Regents, 347 U.S. 442 (1954).

[128] Wilkie v. O'Conner, 261 App. Div. 373, 25 N.Y.S.2d 617 (1941).

[139] Dew v. Halaby, 317 F.2d 582, 590 (D.C. Cir. 1963) * * *.

the Communist Party or of any groups advocating or teaching the overthrow of government by force. The Foundation refused to answer. Eventually the FCC renewed the licenses.

It takes a brave man to stand firm against the power that can be exerted through government largess. This is nowhere better shown than by the case of George Anastaplo. In the fall of 1950, Anastaplo passed the Illinois bar examination, and applied to the Committee on Character and Fitness, which in Illinois has the duty "to examine applicants who appear before them for moral character, general fitness to practice law and good citizenship." Anastaplo came from a small town in Illinois, served honorably in the Air Force during World War II, and graduated from the University of Chicago. * * * When Anastaplo appeared before a subcommittee of the Character Committee * * * one member asked him whether he was a member of any organization on the Attorney General's list, or of the Communist Party. Anastaplo refused to answer these questions on the ground * * * he was privileged not to answer under the first amendment. * * * [H]e was [later] notified * * * that * * * he had failed to prove such qualifications as to character and general fitness as would justify his admission to the bar of Illinois.

The United States Supreme Court upheld the denial of admission * * *.[153] * * *

The foregoing * * * suggest[s] that the growth of largess had made it possible for government to "purchase" the abandonment of constitutional rights. * * * Recipients of largess remain free to exercise their rights, of course. But the price of free exercise is the risk of economic loss, or even loss of livelihood.

* * *

D. *The New Federalism*

The characteristics of the public interest state are varied, but there is an underlying philosophy that unites them. This is the doctrine that the wealth that flows from government is held by its recipients conditionally, subject to confiscation in the interest of the paramount state. This philosophy is epitomized in the most important of all judicial decisions concerning government largess, the case of *Flemming v. Nestor.*[175]

Ephram Nestor, an alien, came to this country in 1913, and after a long working life became eligible in 1955 for old-age benefits under the Social Security Act. * * * From 1933 to 1939 Nestor was a member of the Communist Party. Long after his membership ceased, Congress passed a law retroactively making such membership cause for deportation, and a second law, also retroactive, making such deportation * * * grounds for loss of retirement benefits. In 1956 Nestor was deported, leaving his wife here. Soon after his deportation, payment of benefits to Nestor's wife was terminated.

In a five to four decision, the Supreme Court held that cutting off Nestor's retirement insurance, although based on conduct completely lawful at the time, was not unconstitutional. Specifically, it was not a taking of property without due process of law: Nestor's benefits were not an "accrued property right." * * * The Court stated further that, in any case where Congress "modified" social security rights, the Court should interfere only if the action is "utterly lacking in rational justification." * * *

The implications of *Flemming v. Nestor* are profound. No form of government largess is more personal or individual than an old age pension. No form is more clearly earned by the recipient, who, together with his employer, contributes to the Social Security fund during the years of employment. No form is more obviously a compulsory substitute for private property; the tax on wage earner and employer might readily have gone to higher pay and higher private savings instead. No form is more relied on, and more often thought of as property. No form is more vital to the independence and dignity of the individual. Yet under the philosophy of Congress and the Court, a man or woman, after a lifetime of work, has no rights which may not be taken away to serve some public policy. * * *

The philosophy of *Flemming v. Nestor* * * * resembles the philosophy of feudal tenure. Wealth is not "owned," or "vested" in the holders. Instead, it is held conditionally, the conditions being ones which seek to ensure the fulfillment of obligations imposed by the state. Just as the feudal system linked lord and vassal through a system of mutual dependence, obligation, and loyalty, so government largess binds man to the state.

* * *

The public interest state is not with us yet. But we are left with large questions. If the day comes when most private property ownership is supplanted by government largess, how then will governmental power over individuals be contained? What will

---

[153] In re Anastaplo, 366 U.S. 82 (1961).
[175] 363 U.S. 603 (1960).

dependence do to the American character? What will happen to the Constitution, and particularly the Bill of Rights, if their limits may be bypassed by purchase, and if people lack an independent base from which to assert their individuality and claim their rights? Without the security of the person which individual wealth provides and which largess fails to provide, what, indeed, will we become?

IV. Property and the Public Interest: An Old Debate Revisited

The public interest state, as visualized above, represents in one sense the triumph of society over private property. This triumph is the end point of a great and necessary movement for reform. But somehow the result is different from what the reformers wanted. Somehow the idealistic concept of the public interest has summoned up a doctrine monstrous and oppressive. It is time to take another look at private property, and at the "public interest" philosophy that dominates its modern substitute, the largess of government.

A. *Property and Liberty*

Property is a legal institution the essence of which is the creation and protection of certain private rights in wealth of any kind. The institution performs many different functions. One of these functions is to draw a boundary between public and private power. Property draws a circle around the activities of each private individual or organization. Within that circle, the owner has a greater degree of freedom than without. Outside, he must justify or explain his actions, and show his authority. Within, he is master, and the state must explain and justify any interference. * * *

Thus, property performs the function of maintaining independence, dignity and pluralism in society by creating zones within which the majority has to yield to the owner. Whim, caprice, irrationality and "antisocial" activities are given the protection of law; the owner may do what all or most of his neighbors decry. The Bill of Rights also serves this function, but while the Bill of Rights comes into play only at extraordinary moments of conflict or crisis, property affords day-to-day protection in the ordinary affairs of life. Indeed, in the final analysis the Bill of Rights depends upon the existence of private property. Political rights presuppose that individuals and private groups have the will and the means to act independently. But so long as individuals are motivated largely by self-interest, their well-being must first be independent. Civil liberties must have a basis in property, or bills of rights will not preserve them.

Property is not a natural right but a deliberate construction by society. If such an institution did not exist, it would be necessary to create it, in order to have the kind of society we wish. The majority cannot be expected, on specific issues, to yield its power to a minority. Only if the minority's will is established as a general principle can it keep the majority at bay in a given instance. Like the Bill of Rights, property represents a general, long range protection of individual and private interests, created by the majority for the ultimate good of all.

Today, however, it is widely thought that property and liberty are separable things; that there may, in fact, be conflicts between "property rights" and "personal rights." Why has this view been accepted? The explanation is found at least partly in the transformations which have taken place in property.

During the industrial revolution, when property was liberated from feudal restraints, philosophers hailed property as the basis of liberty, and argued that it must be free from the demands of government or society. But as private property grew, so did abuses resulting from its use. In a crowded world, a man's use of his property increasingly affected his neighbor, and one man's exercise of a right might seriously impair the rights of others. Property became power over others; the farm landowner, the city landlord, and the working man's boss were able to oppress their tenants or employees. Great aggregations of property resulted in private control of entire industries and basic services capable of affecting a whole area or even a nation. At the same time, much private property lost its individuality and in effect became socialized. Multiple ownership of corporations helped to separate personality from property, and property from power. When the corporations began to stop competing, to merge, agree, and make mutual plans, they became private governments. Finally, they sought the aid and partnership of the state, and thus by their own volition became part of public government.

These changes led to a movement for reform, which sought to limit arbitrary private power and protect the common man. Property rights were considered more the enemy than the friend of liberty. The reformers argued that property must be separated from personality. * * * During the first half of the twentieth century, the reformers enacted into law their conviction that private power was a chief enemy of society and of individual liberty. Property was subjected to "reasonable" limitations in the interests of society. The regulatory agencies, federal and state, were born of the reform. In sustaining these major inroads on private property, the Supreme Court rejected the older idea that property and liberty were one, and wrote a series of classic opinions upholding the power of the people to regulate and limit private rights.

* * *

The reform took away some of the power of the corporations and transferred it to government. In this transfer there was much good, for power was made responsible to the majority rather than to the arbitrary and selfish few. But the reform did not restore the individual to his domain. What the corporation had taken from him, the reform simply handed on to government. And government carried further the powers formerly exercised by the corporation. Government as an employer, or as a dispenser of wealth, has used the theory that it was handing out gratuities to claim a managerial power as great as that which the capitalists claimed. Moreover, the corporations allied themselves with, or actually took over, part of government's system of power. Today it is the combined power of government and the corporations that presses against the individual.

From the individual's point of view, it is not any particular kind of power, but all kinds of power, that are to be feared. This is the lesson of the public interest state. The mere fact that power is derived from the majority does not necessarily make it less oppressive. Liberty is more than the right to do what the majority wants, or to do what is "reasonable." Liberty is the right to defy the majority, and to do what is unreasonable. The great error of the public interest state is that it assumes an identity between the public interest and the interest of the majority.

B. *Largess and the Public Interest*

The fact that reform tended to make much private wealth subject to "the public interest" has great significance, but it does not adequately explain the dependent position of the individual and the weakening of civil liberties in the public interest state. The reformers intended to enhance the values of democracy and liberty; their basic concern was the preservation of a free democracy and liberty; that basic concern was the preservation of a free society. But after they established the primacy of "the public interest," what meaning was given to that phrase? In particular, what value does it embody as it has been employed to regulate government largess?

Reduced to simplest terms, "the public interest" has usually meant this: government largess may be denied or taken away if this will serve some legitimate public policy. * * * A contract may be denied if this will promote fair labor standards. A television license may be refused if this will promote the policies of the antitrust laws. Veterans benefits may be taken away to promote loyalty to the United States. A liquor license may be revoked to promote civil rights. A franchise for a barber's college may not be given out if it will hurt the local economy, nor a taxi franchise if it will seriously injure the earning capacity of other taxis.

Most of these objectives are laudable, and all are within the power of government. The great difficulty is that they are all simplistic. Concentration on a single policy or value obscures other values that may be at stake. Some of these competing values are other public policies * * *. In the regulation of government largess, achievement of specific policy goals may undermine the independence of the individual. Where such conflicts exist, a simplistic notion of the public interest may unwittingly destroy some values.

* * *

It is not the reformers who must bear the blame for the harmful consequences of the public interest state, but those who are responsible for giving "the public interest" its present meaning. If "the public interest" distorts the reformers' high purposes, this is so because the concept has been so gravely misstated. Government largess, like all wealth, must necessarily be regulated in the public interest. But regulation must take account of the dangers of dependence, and the need for a property base for civil liberties. Rightly conceived, the public interest is no justification for the erosion of freedom that has resulted from the present system of government largess.

V. Toward Individual Stakes in the Commonwealth

Ahead there stretches—to the farther horizon—the joyless landscape of the public interest state. The life it promises will be comfortable and comforting. It will be well planned—with suitable areas for work and play. But there will be no precincts sacred to the spirit of the individual man.

There can be no retreat from the public interest state. It is the inevitable outgrowth of an interdependent world. An effort to return to an earlier economic order would merely transfer power to giant private governments which would rule not in the public interest, but in their own interest. If individualism and pluralism are to be preserved, this must be done not by marching backwards, but by building these values into today's society. If public and private are now blurred, it will be necessary to draw a new zone of privacy. If private property can no longer perform its protective functions, it will be necessary to establish institutions to carry on the work that private property once did but can no longer do.

In these efforts government largess must play a major role. As we move toward a welfare state, largess will be an ever more important form of wealth. And largess is a vital link in the relationship between the government and private sides of society. It is necessary, then, that largess begin to do the work of property.

The chief obstacle to the creation of private rights in largess has been the fact that it is originally public property, comes from the state, and may be withheld completely. But this need not be an obstacle. Traditional property also comes from the state, and in much the same way. Land, for example, traces back to grants from the sovereign. In the United States, some was the gift of the King of England, some that of the King of Spain. The sovereign extinguished Indian title by conquest, became the new owner, and then granted title to a private individual or group. Some land was the gift of the sovereign under laws such as the Homestead and Preemption Acts. Many other natural resources—water, minerals and timber, passed into private ownership under similar grants. In America, land and resources all were originally government largess. In a less obvious sense, personal property also stems from government. Personal property is created by law; it owes its origins and continuance to laws supported by the people as a whole. These laws "give" the property to one who performs certain actions. Even the man who catches a wild animal "owns" the animal only as a gift from the sovereign, having fulfilled the terms of an offer to transfer ownership.

Like largess, real and personal property were also originally distributed under conditions, and were subject to forfeiture if the conditions failed. The conditions in the sovereign grants, such as colonization, were generally made explicit, and so was the forfeiture resulting from failure to fulfill them. In the case of the Preemption and Homestead Acts, there were also specific conditions. Even now land is subject to forfeiture for neglect; if it is unused it may be deemed abandoned to the state or forfeited to an adverse possessor. In a very similar way, personal property may be forfeited by abandonment or loss. Hence, all property might be described as government largess, given on condition and subject to loss.

If all property is government largess, why is it not regulated to the same degree as present-day largess? Regulation of property has been limited, not because society had no interest in property, but because it was in the interest of society that property be free. Once property is seen not as a natural right but as a construction designed to serve certain functions, then its origin ceases to be decisive in determining how much regulation should be imposed. The conditions that can be attached to receipt, ownership, and use depend not on where property came from, but on what job it should be expected to perform. Thus in the case of government largess, nothing turns on the fact that it originated in government. The real issue is how it functions and how it should function.

To create an institution, or to make an existing institution function in a new way, is an undertaking far too ambitious for the present article. But it is possible to begin a search for guiding principles. Such principles must grow out of what we know about how government largess has functioned up to the present time. And while principles must remain at the level of generality, it should be kept in mind that not every principle is equally applicable to all forms of largess. Our primary focus must be those forms of largess which chiefly control the rights and status of the individual.

A. *Constitutional Limits*

The most clearly defined problem posed by government largess is the way it can be used to apply pressure against the exercise of constitutional rights. A first principle should be that government must have no power to "buy up" rights guaranteed by the Constitution. It should not be able to impose any condition on largess that would be invalid if imposed on something other than a "gratuity." Thus, for example, government should not be able to deny largess because of invocation of the privilege against self-incrimination.

* * *

The problem becomes more complicated when a court attempts * * * to "balance" the deterrence of constitutional rights against some opposing interest. In any balancing process, no weight should be given to the contention that what is at stake is a mere gratuity. It should be recognized that pressure against constitutional rights from denial of a "gratuity" may be as great or greater than pressure from criminal punishment. And the concept of the public interest should be given a meaning broad enough to include general injury to independence and constitutional rights. It is not possible to consider detailed problems here. It is enough to say that government should gain no power, as against constitutional limitations, by reason of its role as dispenser of wealth.

* * *

C. *Procedural Safeguards*

Because it is hard to confine [legislative grants of authority by imposing standards of] relevance and [limited bureaucratic] discretion, procedure offers a valuable means for restraining arbitrary action. This was recognized in the strong procedural emphasis of the Bill of Rights, and it is now being recognized in the increasingly procedural emphasis of administrative law. The law of government largess has developed with little regard for procedure. Reversal of that trend is long overdue.

The grant, denial, revocation, and administration of all types of government largess should be subject to scrupulous observance of fair procedures. Action should be open to hearing and contest, and based upon a record subject to judicial review. The denial of any form of privilege or benefit on the basis of undisclosed reasons should no longer be tolerated. Nor should the same person sit as legislator, prosecutor, judge and jury, combining all the functions of government in such a way as to make fairness virtually impossible. There is no justification for the survival of arbitrary methods where valuable rights are at stake.

* * *

D. *From Largess to Right*

The proposals discussed above, however salutary, are by themselves far from adequate to assure the status of individual man with respect to largess. The problems go deeper. First, the growth of government power based on the dispensing of wealth must be kept within bounds. Second, there must be a zone of privacy for each individual beyond which neither government nor private power can push—a hiding place from the all-pervasive system of regulation and control. Finally, it must be recognized that we are becoming a society based upon relationship and status—status deriving primarily from source of livelihood. Status is so closely linked to personality that destruction of one may well destroy the other. Status must therefore be surrounded with the kind of safeguards once reserved for personality.

Eventually those forms of largess which are closely linked to status must be deemed to be held as of right. Like property, such largess could be governed by a system of regulation plus civil or criminal sanctions, rather than a system based upon denial, suspension and revocation. As things now stand, violations lead to forfeitures—outright confiscation of wealth and status. But there is surely no need for these drastic results. Confiscation, if used at all, should be the ultimate, not the most common and convenient penalty. The presumption should be that the professional man will keep his license, and the welfare recipient his pension. These interests should be "vested." If revocation is necessary, not by reason of the fault of the individual holder, but by reason of overriding demands of public policy, perhaps payment of just compensation would be appropriate. The individual should not bear the entire loss for a remedy primarily intended to benefit the community.

The concept of right is most urgently needed with respect to benefits like unemployment compensation, public assistance, and old age insurance. These benefits are based upon a recognition that misfortune and deprivation are often caused by forces far beyond the control of the individual, such as technological change, variations in demand for goods, depressions, or wars. The aim of these benefits is to preserve the self-sufficiency of the individual, to rehabilitate him where necessary, and to allow him to be a valuable member of a family and a community; in theory they represent parts of the individual's rightful share in the commonwealth. Only by making such benefits into rights can the welfare state achieve its goal of providing a secure minimum basis for individual well-being and dignity in a society where each man cannot be wholly the master of his own destiny.

CONCLUSION

The highly organized, scientifically planned society of the future, governed for the good of its inhabitants, promises the best life that men have ever known. In place of misery and injustice of the past there can be prosperity, leisure, knowledge, and rich opportunity open to all. In the rush of accomplishment, however, not all values receive equal attention; some are temporarily forgotten while others are pushed ahead. We have made provisions for nearly everything, but we have made no adequate provision for individual man.

This article is an attempt to offer perspective on the transformation of society as it bears on the economic basis of individualism. The effort has been to show relationships; to bring together drivers' licenses, unemployment insurance, membership in the bar, permits for using school auditoriums, and second class mail privileges, in order to see what we are becoming.

Government largess is only one small corner of a far vaster problem. There are many other new forms of wealth; franchises in private businesses, equities in corporations, the right to receive privately furnished utilities and services, status in private organizations. These too may need added safeguards in the future. Similarly, there are many sources of expanded governmental power aside from largess. By themselves, proposals concerning government largess would be far from accomplishing any fundamental reforms. But, somehow, we must begin.

At the very least, it is time to reconsider the theories under which new forms of wealth are regulated, and by which governmental power over them is measured. It is time to recognize that "the public interest" is all too often a reassuring platitude that covers up sharp clashes of conflicting values, and hides fundamental choices. It is time to see that the "privilege" or "gratuity" concept, as applied to wealth dispensed by government, is not much different from the absolute right of ownership that private capital once invoked to justify arbitrary power over employees and the public.

Above all, the time has come for us to remember what the framers of the Constitution knew so well—that "a power over a man's subsistence amounts to a power over his will." We cannot safely trust our livelihoods and our rights to the discretion of authorities, examiners, boards of control, character committees, regents, or license commissioners. We cannot permit any official or agency to pretend to sole knowledge of the public good. We cannot put the independence of any man * * * wholly in the power of other men.

If the individual is to survive in a collective society, he must have protection against its ruthless pressures. There must be sanctuaries or enclaves where no majority can reach. To shelter the solitary human spirit does not merely make possible the fulfillment of individuals; it also gives society the power to change, to grow, and to regenerate, and hence to endure. These were the objects which property sought to achieve, and can no longer achieve. The challenge of the future will be to construct, for the society that is coming, institutions and laws to carry on this work. Just as the Homestead Act was a deliberate effort to foster individual values at an earlier time, so we must try to build an economic basis for liberty today—a Homestead Act for rootless twentieth century man. We must create a new property.

Note

How would Reich resolve *International News Service v. Associated Press*, 248 U.S. 215 (1918)?

Christopher D. Stone, *Should Trees Have Standing?—Toward Legal Rights for Natural Objects,* 45 S. Cal. L. Rev. 450–464, 471–479, 489–490, 495–499 (1972)*

Introduction: The Unthinkable

In *Descent of Man*, Darwin observes that the history of man's moral development has been a continual extension in the objects of his "social instincts and sympathies." Originally each man had regard only for himself and those of a very narrow circle about him; later, he came to regard more and more "not only the welfare, but the happiness of all his fellow men"; then "his sympathies became more tender and widely diffused, extending to men of all races, to the imbecile, maimed, and other useless members of society, and finally to the lower animals. . . ."[1]

The history of the law suggests a parallel development. Perhaps there never was a pure Hobbesian state of nature, in which no "rights" existed except in the vacant sense of each man's "right to self-defense." But it is not unlikely that so far as the

[1] C. Darwin, Descent of Man, 119, 120–21 (2d ed. 1874). * * *

earliest "families" (including extended kinship groups and clans) were concerned, everyone outside the family was suspect, alien, rightless. And even within the family, persons we presently regard as the natural holders of at least some rights had none. Take, for example, children. We know something of the early rights-status of children from the widespread practice of infanticide—especially of the deformed and female. (Senicide, as among the North American Indians, was the corresponding rightlessness of the aged.) Maine tells us that as late as the Patria Potestas of the Romans, the father had *jus vitae necisque* —the power of life and death over his children. *A fortiori*, Maine writes, he had power of "uncontrolled corporal chastisement; he can modify their personal condition at pleasure; he can give a wife to his son; he can give his daughter in marriage; he can divorce his children of either sex; he can transfer them to another family by adoption; and he can sell them." The child was less than a person: an object, a thing.[6]

The legal rights of children have long since been recognized in principle, and are still expanding in practice. * * * We have been making persons of children although they were not, in law, always so. And we have done the same, albeit imperfectly some would say, with prisoners, aliens, women (especially of the married variety), the insane, Blacks, foetuses, and Indians.

Nor is it only matter in human form that has come to be recognized as the possessor of rights. The world of the lawyer is peopled with inanimate right-holders: trusts, corporations, joint ventures, municipalities, Subchapter R partnerships, and nation states, to mention just a few. Ships, still referred to by courts in the feminine gender, have long had an independent jural life * * *. We have become so accustomed to the idea of a corporation having "its" own rights, and being a "person" and "citizen" for so many statutory and constitutional purposes, that we forget how jarring the notion was to early jurists. "That invisible, intangible and artificial being, that mere legal entity" Chief Justice Marshall wrote of the corporation in *Bank of the United States v. Deveaux*[14]—could a suit be brought in its name? Ten years later, in the *Dartmouth College* case,[15] he was still refusing to let pass unnoticed the wonder of an entity "existing only in contemplation of law." Yet, long before Marshall worried over the personifying of the modern corporation, the best medieval legal scholars had spent hundreds of years struggling with the notion of the legal nature of those great public "corporate bodies," the Church and the State. How could they exist in law, as entities transcending the living Pope and King? It was clear how a king could bind *himself* —on his honor—by a treaty. But when the king died, what was it that was burdened with the obligations of, and claimed the rights under, the treaty his tangible hand had signed? The medieval mind saw (what we have lost our capacity to see) how *unthinkable* it was, and worked out the most elaborate conceits and fallacies to serve as anthropomorphics flesh for the Universal Church and the Universal Empire.

It is this note of the *unthinkable* that I want to dwell upon for a moment. Throughout legal history, each successive extension of rights to some new entity has been, therefore, a bit unthinkable. We are inclined to suppose the rightlessness of rightless "things" to be a decree of Nature, not a legal convention acting in support of some status quo. It is thus that we defer considering the choices involved in all their moral, social, and economic dimensions. And so the United States Supreme Court could straight-facedly tell us in *Dred Scott* that Blacks had been denied the rights of citizenship "as a subordinate and inferior class of beings, who had been subjugated by the dominant race. . . ."[19] In the nineteenth century, the highest court in California explained that Chinese had not the right to testify against white men in criminal matters because they were "a race of people whom nature has marked as inferior, and who are incapable of progress or intellectual development beyond a certain point . . . between whom and ourselves nature has placed an impassable difference.[20] The popular conception of the Jew in the 13th Century contributed to a law which treated them as "men *ferae naturae*, protected by a quasi forest law. Like the roe and the deer, they

[6] H. MAINE, ANCIENT LAW 153 (Pollock ed. 1930). * * *

[14] 9 U.S. (5 Cranch) 61, 86 (1809).

[15] Trustees of Dartmouth College v. Woodward, 17 U.S. (4 Wheat.) 518 (1819).

[19] Dred Scott v. Sandford, 60 U.S. (19 How.) 396, 404–05 (1856).

[20] People v. Hall, 4 Cal. 399, 405 (1854). The statute there under interpretation provided that "no Black or Mulatto person, or Indian shall be allowed to give evidence in favor of, or against a white man," but was silent as to Chinese. The "policy" analysis by which the court brings Chinese under "Black . . . or Indian" is a fascinating illustration of the relationship between a "policy" decision and a "just" decision * * *.

form an order apart."[21] * * * The first woman in Wisconsin who thought she might have a right to practice law was told that she did not, in the following terms:

> The law of nature destines and qualifies the female sex for the bearing and nurture of the children of our race and for the custody of the homes of the world . . . . [A]ll life-long callings of women, inconsistent with these radical and sacred duties of their sex, as is the profession of the law, are departures from the order of nature; and when voluntary, treason against it . . . . The peculiar qualities of womanhood, its gentle graces, its quick sensibility, its tender susceptibility, its purity, its delicacy, its emotional impulse, its subordination of hard reason to sympathetic feeling, are surely not qualification for forensic strife. Nature has tempered woman as little for the juridical conflict of the courtroom, as for the physical conflicts of the battle field . . .[23]

The fact is, that each time there is a movement to confer right onto some new "entity," the proposal is bound to sound odd or frightening or laughable.[23a] This is partly because until the rightless thing receives its rights, we cannot see it as anything but a thing for the use of "us"—those who are holding rights at the time. In this vein, what is striking about the Wisconsin case above is that the court, for all its talk about women, so clearly was never able to see women as they are (and might become). All it could see was the popular "idealized" version of *an object it needed.* Such is the way the slave South looked upon the Black.[25] There is something of a seamless web involved: there will be resistance to giving the thing "rights" until it can be seen and valued for itself; yet, it is hard to see it and value it for itself until we can bring ourselves to give it "rights"—which is almost inevitably going to sound inconceivable to a large group of people.

The reason for this little discourse on the unthinkable, the reader must know by now, if only from the title of the paper. I am quite seriously proposing that we give legal rights to forests, oceans, rivers and other so-called "natural objects" in the environment—indeed, to the natural environment as a whole.

* * *

Toward Rights for the Environment

Now, to say that the natural environment should have rights is not to say anything as silly as that no one should be allowed to cut down a tree. We say human beings have rights, but—at least as of the time of this writing—they can be executed. Corporations have rights, but they cannot plead the fifth amendment; *In re Gault* gave 15-year-olds certain rights in juvenile proceedings, but it did not give them the right to vote. Thus, to say that the environment should have rights is not to say that it should have every right we can imagine, or even the same body of rights as human beings have. Nor is it to say that everything in the environment should have the same rights as every other thing in the environment.

What the granting of rights does involve has two sides to it. The first involves what might be called the legal-operational aspects; the second, the psychic and socio-psychic aspects. I shall deal with these aspects in turn.

The Legal-Operational Aspects

What it Means to be a Holder of Legal Rights

There is, so far as I know, no generally accepted standard for how one ought to use the term "legal

---

[21] Schechter, *The Rightlessness of Mediaeval English Jewry*, 45 JEWISH Q. REV. 121, 135 (1954) quoting from M. BATESON, MEDIEVAL ENGLAND 139 (1904). * * *

[23] *In re* Goddell, 39 Wisc. 232, 245 (1875).* * *

[23a] Recently, a group of prison inmates in Suffolk County tamed a mouse that they discovered, giving him the name Morris. Discovering Morris, a jailer flushed him down the toilet. The prisoners brought a proceeding against the Warden complaining, *inter alia*, that Morris was subjected to discriminatory discharge and was otherwise unequally treated. The action was unsuccessful, on grounds that the inmates themselves were "guilty of imprisoning Morris without a charge, without a trial, and without bail," and that other mice at the prison were not treated more favorably. * * *

The whole matter seems humorous, of course. But what we need to know more of is the function of humor in the unfolding of a culture, and the ways in which it is involved with the social growing pains to which it is testimony. Why do people make jokes about the Women's Liberation Movement? Is it not on account of—rather than in spite of—the underlying validity of the protests, and the uneasy awareness that a recognition of them is inevitable? * * * Query too: what is the relationship between the conferring of proper *names, e.g.*, Morris, and the conferring of social and legal *rights*?

[25] "The second thought streaming from . . . the older South [is] the sincere and passionate belief that somewhere between men and cattle, God created a *tertium quid*, and called it a Negro—a clownish, simple creature, at times even lovable within its limitations, but straitly foreordained to walk within the Veil." W.E.B. DUBOIS, THE SOULS OF BLACK FOLK 89 (1924).

rights." Let me indicate how I shall be using it in this piece.

First and most obviously, if the term is to have any content at all, an entity cannot be said to hold a legal right unless and until some public authoritative body is prepared to give *some amount of review* to actions that are colorably inconsistent with that "right." * * *

But for a thing to be a *holder of legal rights*, something more is needed than that some authoritative body will review the actions and processes of those who threaten it. As I shall use the term, "holder of legal rights," each of three additional criteria must be satisfied. All three, one will observe, go towards making a thing count jurally—to have a legally recognized worth and dignity in its own right, and not merely to serve as a means to benefit "us" (whoever the contemporary group of rights-holders may be). They are, first, that the thing can institute legal actions *at its behest*; second, that in determining the granting of legal relief, the court must take injury to it into account; and, third, that relief must run to the *benefit of it*.

* * *

When I say, then, that at common law "natural objects" are not holders of legal rights, I am not simply remarking what we would all accept as obvious. I mean to emphasize three specific legal-operational advantages that the environment lacks, leaving it in the position of the slave * * *.

The Rightlessness of Natural Objects at Common Law

Consider, for example, the common law's posture toward the pollution of a stream. True, courts have always been able, in some circumstances, to issue orders that will stop the pollution * * *. But the stream itself is fundamentally rightless, with implications that deserve careful reconsideration.

The first sense in which the stream is not a rights-holder has to do with standing. The stream itself has none. So far as the common law is concerned, there is in general no way to challenge the polluter's actions save at the behest of a lower riparian—another human being—able to show an invasion of his rights. This conception of the riparian as the holder of the right to bring suit has more than theoretical interest. The lower riparians may simply not care about the pollution. They themselves may be polluting, and not wish to stir up legal waters. They may be economically dependent on their polluting neighbor. And, of course, when they discount the value of winning by the costs of bringing suit and the chances of success, the action may not seem worth undertaking. * * *

The second sense in which the common law denies "rights" to natural objects has to do with the way in which the merits are decided in those cases in which someone is competent and willing to establish standing. At its more primitive levels, the system protected the "rights" of the property owning human with minimal weighing of any values: "*Cujus est solum, ejus est usque ad coelum et ad infernos.*"[34] Today we have come more and more to make balances—but only such as will adjust the economic best interests of identifiable humans. For example, continuing with the case of streams, * * * what the courts are balancing, with varying degrees of directness, are the economic hardships on the upper riparian (or dependent community) of abating the pollution vis-a-vis the economic hardships of continued pollution on the lower riparians. What does not weigh in the balance is the damage to the stream, its fish and turtles and "lower" life. So long as the natural environment itself is rightless, these are not matters for judicial cognizance. * * * The stream itself is lost sight of * * *.

The third way in which the common law makes natural objects rightless has to do with who is regarded as the beneficiary of a favorable judgment. Here, too, it makes a considerable difference that it is not the natural object that counts in its own right. To illustrate this point, let me begin by observing that it makes perfectly good sense to speak of, and ascertain, the legal damage to a natural object, if only in the sense of "making it whole" with respect to the most obvious factors. The costs of making a forest whole, for example, would include the costs of reseeding, repairing watersheds, restocking wildlife—the sorts of costs the Forest Service undergoes after a fire. Making a polluted stream whole would include the costs of restocking with fish, water-fowl, and other animal and vegetable life, dredging, washing out impurities, establishing natural and/or artificial aerating agents, and so forth. Now, what is important to note is that, under our present system, even if a plaintiff riparian wins a water pollution suit for damages, no money goes to the benefit of the stream itself to repair its damages.[41] This omission has the

[34] To whomsoever the soil belongs, he owns also to the sky and to the depths. *See* W. BLACKSTONE, 2 COMMENTARIES *18.

[41] Here again, an analogy to corporation law might be profitable. Suppose that in the instance of negligent corporate management by the directors, there were no

further effect that, at most, the law confronts a polluter with what it takes to make the plaintiff riparians whole; this may be far less than the damages to the stream, but not so much as to force the polluter to desist. * * * Similarly, even if the jurisdiction issues an injunction at the plaintiffs' behest (rather than to order payment of damages), there is nothing to stop the plaintiffs from "selling out" the stream, i.e., agreeing to dissolve or not enforce the injunction at some price (in the example above, somewhere between plaintiffs' damages * * * and defendant's next best economic alternative). * * *

* * *

Toward Having Standing in its Own Right

It is not inevitable, nor is it wise, that natural objects should have no rights to seek redress in their own behalf. It is no answer to say that streams and forests cannot have standing because streams and forests cannot speak. Corporations cannot speak either; nor can states, estates, infants, incompetents, municipalities or universities. Lawyers speak for them, as they customarily do for the ordinary citizens with legal problems. One ought, I think, to handle the legal problems of natural objects as one does the problems of legal incompetents—human beings who have become vegetable. If a human being shows signs of becoming senile and has affairs that he is de jure incompetent to manage, those concerned with his well being make such a showing to the court, and someone is designated by the court with the authority to manage the incompetent's affairs. The guardian (or "conservator" or "committee"—the terminology varies) then represents the incompetent in his legal affairs. Courts make similar appointments when a corporation has become "incompetent"—they appoint a trustee in bankruptcy or reorganization to oversee its affairs and speak for it in court when that becomes necessary.

On a parity of reasoning, we should have a system in which, when a friend of a natural object perceives it to be endangered, he can apply to a court for the creation of a guardianship. * * *

The guardianship approach * * * is apt to raise * * * objections. * * * The first is that a committee or guardian could not judge the needs of the river or forest in its charge; indeed, the very concept of "needs," it might be said, could be used here only in the most metaphorical way. The second objection is that such a system would not be much different from what we now have: is not the Department of Interior already such a guardian for public lands, and do not most states have legislation empowering their attorneys general to seek relief—in a sort of *parens patriae* way—for such injuries as a guardian might concern himself with?

As for the first objection, natural objects can communicate their wants (needs) to us, and in ways that are not terribly ambiguous. I am sure I can judge with more certainty and meaningfulness whether and when my lawn wants (needs) water, than the Attorney General can judge whether and when the United States wants (needs) to take an appeal from an adverse judgment by a lower court. The lawn tells me that it wants water by a certain dryness of the blades and soil—immediately obvious to the touch—the appearance of bald spots, yellowing, and a lack of springiness after being walked on; how does "the United States" communicate to the Attorney General? For similar reasons, the guardian-attorney for a smog-endangered stand of pines could venture with more confidence that his client wants the smog stopped, than the directors of a corporation can assert that "the corporation" wants dividends declared. We make decisions on behalf of, and in the purported interests of, others every day; these "others" are often creatures whose wants are far less verifiable, and even far more metaphysical in conception, than the wants of rivers, trees, and land.

As for the second objection, one can indeed find evidence that the Department of Interior was conceived as a sort of guardian of the public lands. But there are two points to keep in mind. First, insofar as the Department already is an adequate guardian it is only with respect to the federal lands as per Article IV, section 3 of the Constitution. Its guardianship includes neither local public lands nor private lands. Second, to judge from the environmentalist literature and from the cases environmental action groups have been bringing, the Department is itself one of the bogeys of the environmental movement. (One thinks of the uneasy peace between the Indians and the Bureau of Indian Affairs.) Whether the various charges be right or wrong, one cannot help but observe that the Department has been charged with several institutional goals (never an easy burden),

---

institution of the stockholder derivative suit to force the directors to make *the corporation* whole, and the only actions provided for were direct actions by stockholders to collect for damages *to themselves qua* stockholders. Theoretically and practically, the damages might come out differently in the two cases, and not merely because the creditors losses are not aggregated in the stockholders' direct actions.

and is currently looked to for action by quite a variety of interest groups, only one of which is environmentalists. In this context, a guardian outside the institution becomes especially valuable. Besides, what a person wants, fully to secure his rights, is the ability to retain independent counsel even when, and perhaps especially when, the government is acting "for him" in a beneficent way. I have no reason to doubt, for example, that the Social Security System is being managed "for me"; but I would not want to abdicate my right to challenge its actions as they affect me, should the need arise. I would not ask more trust of national forests, vis-a-vis the Department of Interior. The same considerations apply in the instance of local agencies, such as regional water pollution boards, whose members' expertise in pollution matters is often all too credible.[77]

* * *

Toward Recognition of its Own Injuries

As far as adjudicating the merits of a controversy is concerned, there is also a good case to be made for taking into account harm to the environment in its own right. As indicated above, the traditional way of deciding whether to issue injunctions in law suits affecting the environment, at least where communal property is involved, has been to strike some sort of balance regarding the economic hardships on *human beings*. Even recently, Mr. Justice Douglas, our jurist most closely associated with conservation sympathies in his private life, was deciding the propriety of a new dam on the basis of, among other things, anticipated lost profits from fish catches, some $12,000,000 annually.[81] Although he decided to delay the project pending further findings, the reasoning seems unnecessarily incomplete and compromising. Why should the environment be of importance only indirectly, as lost profits to someone else? Why not throw into the balance the cost *to the environment?*

The argument for "personifying" the environment, from the point of damage calculations, can best be demonstrated from the welfare economics position. Every well-working legal-economic system should be so constructed as to confront each of us with the full costs that our activities are imposing on society. Ideally, a paper-mill, in deciding what to produce—and where, and by what methods—ought to be forced to take into account not only the lumber, acid and labor that its production "takes" from other uses in the society, but also what costs alternative production plans will impose on society through pollution. The legal system, through the law of contracts and the criminal law, for example, makes the mill confront the costs of the first group of demands. When, for example, the company's purchasing agent orders 1000 drums of acid from the Z Company, the Z Company can bind the mill to pay for them, and thereby reimburse the society for what the mill is removing from alternative uses.

Unfortunately, so far as the pollution costs are concerned, the allocative ideal begins to break down, because the traditional legal institutions have a more difficult time "catching" and confronting us with the full social costs of our activities. In the * * * mill example, * * * many * * * interests—and I am speaking for the moment of recognized homocentric interests—are too fragmented and perhaps "too remote" causally to warrant securing representation and pressing for recovery: the people who own summer homes and motels, the man who sells fishing tackle and bait; the man who rents rowboats. There is no reason not to allow the lake to prove damages to them as prima facie measure of damages to it. *By doing so, we in effect make the natural object, through its guardian, a jural entity competent to gather up these fragmented and otherwise unrepresented damage claims, and press them before the court even where, for legal or practical reasons, they are not going to be pressed by traditional class action plaintiffs.* Indeed, one way—the homocentric way—to view what I am proposing so far, is to view the guardian of the natural object as the guardian of unborn generations, as well as of the otherwise unrepresented, but distantly injured, contemporary humans. By making the lake itself the focus of these damages, and "incorporating" it so to speak, the legal system can effectively take proof upon, and confront the mill with, a larger and more representative measure of the damages its pollution causes.

So far, I do not suppose that my economist friends (unremittent human chauvinists, every one of them!) will have any large quarrel in principle with the concept. Many will view it as a *trompe l'oeil* that

[77] *See* the L. A. Times editorial *Water: Public vs. Polluters* criticizing:

> . . . the ridiculous built-in conflict of interests on Regional Water Quality Control Board. By law, five of the seven seats are given to spokesmen for industrial, governmental, agricultural or utility users. Only one representative of the public at large is authorized, along with a delegate from fish and game interest.

Feb. 12, 1969, Part II, at 8, cols. 1–2.

[81] Udall v. FPC, 387 U.S. 428, 437 n.6 (1967).

comes down, at best, to effectuate the goals of the paragon class action, or the paragon water pollution control district. Where we are apt to part company is here—I propose going beyond gathering up the loose ends of what most people would presently recognize as economically valid damages. The guardian would urge before the court injuries not presently cognizable—the death of eagles and inedible crabs, the suffering of sea lions, the loss from the face of the earth of species of commercially valueless birds, the disappearance of a wilderness area. One might, of course, speak of the damages involved as "damages" to us humans, and indeed, the widespread growth of environmental groups shows that human beings do feel these losses. But they are not, at present, economically measurable losses: how can they have a monetary value for the guardian to prove in court?

The answer for me is simple. Where it carves out "property" rights, the legal system is engaged in the process of *creating* monetary worth. One's literary works would have minimal monetary value if anyone could copy them at will. Their economic value to the author is a product of the law of copyright; the person who copies a copyrighted book has to bear a cost to the copyright-holder because the law says he must. * * * I am proposing we do the same with eagles and wilderness areas as we do with copyrighted works * * *: *make* the violation of rights in them to be a cost by declaring the "pirating" of them to be the invasion of a property interest. If we do so, the net social costs the polluter would be confronted with would include not only the extended homocentric costs of his pollution * * * but also costs to the environment *per se*.

How, though, would these costs be calculated? * * *

Decisions of this sort are always hard, but not impossible. We have increasingly taken (human) pain and suffering into account in reckoning damages, not because we think we can ascertain them as objective "facts" about the universe, but because, even in view of all the room for disagreement, we come up with a better society by making rude estimates of them than by ignoring them. We can make such estimates in regard to environmental losses fully aware that what we are really doing is making implicit normative judgments (as with pain and suffering)—laying down rules as to what the society is going to "value" rather than reporting market evaluations. In making such normative estimates decision-makers would not be wrong if they estimated on the "high side," putting the burden of trimming the figure down on the immediate human interests present. All burdens of proof should reflect common experience; our experience in environmental matters has been a continual discovery that our acts have caused more long-range damage than we were able to appreciate at the outset.

* * *

THE PSYCHIC AND SOCIO-PSYCHIC ASPECTS

There are * * * a number of developments in the law that may reflect a shift from the view that nature exists *for men*. These range from increasingly favorable procedural rulings for environmental action groups * * * to the enactment of comprehensive legislation such as the National Environmental Policy Act * * *. Of such developments one may say, however, that it is not the environment *per se* that we are prepared to take into account, but that man's increased awareness of possible long range effects on himself militate in the direction of stopping environmental harm in its incipiency. * * * Even the far-reaching National Environmental Policy Act, in its preambulatory "Declaration of National Environmental Policy," comes out both for "restoring and maintaining environmental quality *to the overall welfare and development of man*" as well as for creating and maintaining "conditions under which *men and nature can exist in productive harmony.*" * * *

But the time is already upon us when we may have to consider subordinating some human claims to those of the environment *per se*. * * *

A radical new conception of man's relationship to the rest of nature would not only be a step towards solving the material planetary problems; there are strong reasons for such a changed consciousness from the point of making us far better humans. If we only stop for a moment and look at the underlying human qualities that our present attitudes toward property and nature draw upon and reinforce, we have to be struck by how stultifying of our own personal growth and satisfaction they can become when they take rein of us. * * *

What is it within us that gives us [a] * * * need not just to satisfy basic biological wants, but to extend our wills over things, to objectify them, to make them ours, to manipulate them, to keep them at a psychic distance? Can it all be explained on "rational" bases? Should we not be suspect of such needs within us, cautious as to why we wish to gratify them? * * * [Think] of the passage in Carson McCullers' *A Tree, A Rock, A Cloud*, in which an old derelict has collared a twelve year old boy in a streetcar cafe. The old man asks whether the boy knows "how love should be begun?"

The old man leaned closer and whispered:
"A tree. A rock. A cloud."

. . .

"The weather was like this in Portland," he said. "At the time my science was begun. I meditated and I started very cautious. I would pick up something from the street and take it home with me. I bought a goldfish and I concentrated on the goldfish and I loved it. I graduated from one thing to another. Day by day I was getting this technique. . . .

. . .

. . . "For six years now I have gone around by myself and built up my science. And now I am a master. Son. I can love anything. No longer do I have to think about it even. I see a street full of people and a beautiful light comes in me. I watch a bird in the sky. Or I meet a traveler on the road. Everything. Son. And anybody. All stranger and all loved! Do you realize what a science like mine can mean?"

To be able to get away from the view that Nature is a collection of useful senseless objects is, as McCullers' "madman" suggests, deeply involved in the development of our abilities to love—or, if that is putting it too strongly, to be able to reach a heightened awareness of our own, and others' capacities in their mutual interplay. To do so, we have to give up some psychic investment in our sense of separateness and specialness in the universe. And this, in turn, is hard giving indeed, because it involves us in a flight backwards, into earlier stages of civilization and childhood in which we had to trust (and perhaps fear) our environment, for we had not then the power to master it. Yet, in doing so, we—as persons—gradually free ourselves of needs for supportive illusions. Is not this one of the triumphs for "us" of our giving legal rights to (or acknowledging the legal rights of) the Blacks and women?

Changes in this sort of consciousness are already developing, for the betterment of the planet and us. * * * The Vietnam war has contributed to this movement, as it has to others. Five years ago a Los Angeles mother turned out a poster which read "War is not Healthy for children and other living things." It caught on tremendously—at first, I suspect, because it sounded like another clever protest against the war * * *. But as people say such things, and think about them, the possibilities of what they have stumbled upon become manifest—in its suit against the Secretary of Agriculture to cancel the registration of D.D.T., Environmental Defense Fund alleged "biological injury to man and other living things." * * * This heightened awareness enlarges our sense of the dangers to us. But it also enlarges our empathy. We are not only developing the scientific capacity, but we are cultivating the personal capacities *within us* to recognize more and more the ways in which nature—like the woman, the Black, the Indian and the Alien—is like us * * *.

The time may be on hand when these sentiments, and the early stirrings of the law, can be coalesced into a radical new theory or myth—felt as well as intellectualized—of man's relationships to the rest of nature. I do not mean "myth" in a demeaning sense of the term, but in the sense in which, at different times in history, our social "facts" and relationships have been comprehended and integrated by reference to the "myths" that we are co-signers of a social contract, that the Pope is God's agent, and that all men are created equal. Pantheism, Shinto and Tao all have myths to offer. But they are all, each in its own fashion, quaint, primitive and archaic. What is needed is a myth that can fit our growing body of knowledge of geophysics, biology and the cosmos. In this vein, I do not think it too remote that we may come to regard the Earth, as some have suggested, as one organism, of which Mankind is a functional part—the mind, perhaps: different from the rest of nature, but different as a man's brain is from his lungs.

Note

How would Stone have resolved the nuisance problems posed by *Boomer v. Atlantic Cement Co.*, 26 N.Y.2d 219, 257 N.E.2d 870 (1970), and *Spur Industries, Inc. v. Del E. Webb Development Co.*, 108 Ariz. 178, 494 P.2d 700 (1972)?

2. Two Major Property Developments of the Vietnam War Era: Reform of Landlord-Tenant Law and the Arrival of Federal "Open Housing" Controls

a. Landlord-Tenant Reform

One of the most remarkable transformations in the history of American property law occurred between 1965 and 1980 in landlord-tenant law. The development of the implied warranty of habitability is now a staple of first year property courses. The era in which habitability became an accepted part of legal dialog obviously was full of change, discord and agitation. The arrival of legal services for the poor had much to do with the timing of *Javins v. First National Realty* and the other well-known cases. But segments of the public at large were also strongly committed to changing the legal structure of leases. Piven and Cloward's *Rent Strike* is one sample of the rhetoric of the time. Their image of a large unresponsive government against which tenants must struggle to attain their liberty echoes much of the language of Reich's *New Property*. Three other excerpts follow. Mary Ann Glendon, in *The Transformation of American Landlord-Tenant Law*, argues that the 1960's reforms in landlord-tenant law, while quite extensive, were closely related to a series of changes that had previously occurred in many other areas of law, including consumer transactions, torts, and civil procedure. Edward Rabin's *Revolution in Residential Landlord-Tenant Law* discusses some of the causes for the legal reforms. Finally, Duncan Kennedy, taking on the (for him) unusual pose of an economist in *The Effect of the Warranty of Habitability on Low Income Housing: "Milking" and Class Violence*, contends that the traditional economic argument that strong enforcement of the implied warranty will increase rents and reduce the supply of housing for low income tenants, is wrong. He also discusses a number of the major articles on the economic impact of the implied warranty. For additional reading, *see* Olin L. Browder, *The Taming of the Duty—The Tort Liability of Landlords*, 81 MICH. L. REV. 99 (1982); Roger A. Cunningham, *The New Implied and Statutory Warranties of Habitability in Residential Leases: From Contract to Status*, 16 URBAN L. ANNUAL 3 (1979); Hirsch, Hirsch & Margolis, *Regression Analysis of the Effects of Habitability Laws Upon Rent: An Empirical Observation on the Ackerman-Komesar Debate*, 63 CAL. L. REV. 1098 (1975).

Frances Fox Piven & Richard A. Cloward, *Rent Strike: Disrupting the System*, THE NEW REPUBLIC (December 2, 1967)*

For a few feverish months during the winter of 1963–64, rent strikes broke out in New York's ghettos. Activists of various persuasions moved in to canvass the tenements, blending the language of the building codes with language of direct action. In a short time, some 500 buildings were on strike. Then almost as quickly as it had erupted, the movement subsided. By late spring, there were few traces to be seen.

The rent strike of 1963–64 was not the first. In the 1890's, after a half-century of turbulence among the urban poor, rent strikes were common in New York. They occurred again after World War I and during the early years of the depression. Accused of bolshevism and threatened with reprisals, tenants nonetheless compelled government to limit rent increases and curtail evictions. These earlier strikes usually began spontaneously, often leading to massive street violence. Radicals tried to capitalize upon these uprisings to build permanent "peoples' organizations," hoping by education and exhortation to turn the seemingly incoherent energy of the mob into consistent pressure for continuing reform through the electoral process. And this is ironic, for the reforms produced by rent strikes resulted from the disruptions themselves, not from the influence of tenant organizations which, if they emerged at all, were small and unstable. In retrospect, the rent strike of 1963–64 was probably the least disruptive in history; it was also the least successful in producing any important reforms. Its failure suggests some lessons for the future.

By the early 1960's, New York City had been plagued with a housing shortage for at least two decades. Then, as now, the shortage took its severest toll from blacks and Puerto Ricans, who occupied the 550,000 units classified by the census as "deteriorated, dilapidated, or lacking essential facilities" and the 100,000 other units classified as "overcrowded." The hardships created by inadequate and insufficient housing were intensified by the destruction and dislocation caused by urban renewal and public works programs, which had set the city's low-income neighborhoods on edge. And by the late summer of 1963, after the March on Washington, activists were beginning to turn to the ghettos of New York and other Northern cities to stimulate blacks to act on political and economic issues.

In this climate of discontent and protest, a maverick named Jessie Gray announced a Harlem rent strike. On November 1 Gray took out 16 buildings. A month later, the number had risen to 50. Volunteers from the Northern Student Movement then joined forces with Gray, and another 50 Harlem buildings went on strike. A CORE chapter on the Lower East Side took six buildings out on strike in the fall, and later its efforts were augmented when Mobilization for Youth, an antipoverty project sponsored by the federal and city governments, helped a variety of community groups to form "The Lower East Side Rent Strike," bringing about 50 more buildings into that movement. Meanwhile, an especially effective CORE group in Brooklyn organized 200 buildings. In East Harlem, 50 buildings struck, some organized by the East Harlem Tenants Council and others by two local CORE chapters. A union of low-paid blacks and Puerto Ricans, Local 1199 of the Drug and Hospital Workers, helped put 30 more buildings on strike by working with tenants who were union members. With Gray at its head, a massive protest seemed about to burst forth from the black slum. The civil rights movement had indeed come north.

But day-to-day organizing had little drama. After the first flush of enthusiasm, young and experienced organizers began to accept the guidance of the Metropolitan Council on Housing, an organization of older radicals which had formed during the earlier struggles against urban renewal and whose leaders urged cautious tactics consistent with the complex statutes governing rent withholding. The law prescribed an elaborate bureaucratic course, and the courts interpreted the law rigidly. Judges admitted only the inspection records of the Department of Buildings as evidence of hazardous violations. To obtain those records, organizers had to fill out forms and arrange and follow up appointments for inspections; check agency files to make sure that hazardous violations had been posted; and meanwhile see that rents withheld by tenants were being collected and deposited in a private escrow account. (If the tenants lost in court, these funds were turned over to the landlord; if they won, the money was turned over to the clerk of the court, to be given to the landlord after repairs were made). Finally, organizers had to shepherd tenants through the courts. And all of this turned out to require enormous effort and expertise.

At the outset, rent-strike cadres were not dismayed by these elaborate proceedings. Indeed, they defined them as a means of educating tenants and building tenant associations. Canvassing door-to-door to discover housing violations was a way of making contact with tenants; filing "multiple form" complaints was a way of stimulating building meetings; assigning tenants the responsibility for collecting rents and managing escrow accounts was a way of strengthening building committees and developing leadership. And through these tenant groups, organizers believed the poor could be educated to the large political issues underlying slum housing. Such "radicalizing" of tenants was presumably to produce mass associations capable of exerting regular influence on government; each arduous bureaucratic task would contribute to the creation of a permanent "people's organization." That public agencies were thereby dictating the tactics of the movement struck no one as anomalous.

The emphasis on bureaucratic rules and procedures was also dictated by fear that tenants would be evicted if other tactics were followed. A few evictions did occur, and they sometimes evoked frenzied but haphazard resistance. Early in February, Gray and 10 of his aides were arrested for attempting to prevent an eviction by "strong-arming" city marshals. Sometimes, when marshals appeared, organizers sat on the furniture while one of their number hurried to file a stay of eviction with the court. When furniture was already piled on the street, organizers occasionally moved it back to gain time to get the tenants into court. But while such "holding" tactics usually worked, they were not employed regularly, for the organizers concentrated on using legal safeguards. When CORE organizers failed to resist the eviction of a family on the Lower East Side, other striking tenants, fearing that they also would be turned out, hysterically demanded the money from their escrow accounts. That event broke the strike in the CORE stronghold on Eldridge Street. Such experiences seemed to affirm the importance of adhering all the more to elaborate bureaucratic procedures. Organizers became clerks, and political action was reduced to bookkeeping.

The test of these tactics was to come in the courts. The first two cases were heard during a barrage of publicity and were won by the tenants. But public interest quickly faded, and in subsequent decisions judges reaffirmed traditional property rights. When, sometimes mysteriously and sometimes because of slip-ups, records subpoenaed from the Department of Buildings failed to show hazardous violations, judges rejected the testimony of tenants or photographs of building conditions and ordered the rents to be paid, often berating the organizers for trouble making. Landlords frequently asked for adjournments, since they knew that many tenants would prefer to pay the rent rather than spend another day in court. Such failures led organizers to adhere even more rigidly to procedure, to focus more and more energy on fewer and fewer buildings.

But the bureaucratic rites by which repairs were to be exacted, and tenants educated, exhausted organizers and bewildered tenants. To cope with agency procedures required precisely those resources of money, expertise and forbearance which are scarcest among the poor. Meanwhile, landlords exploited bureaucratic intricacies and corruptibility to evade or overcome the challenge. Even occasional tenant victories in the courts yielded only minor and temporary repairs. Unable to produce repairs quickly and to multiply them widely, tenant affiliation did not expand, and the strike developed little political force. Thus the movement began to subside a few months after it formed.

At first blush, rent strike appears to be a simple and powerful strategy to bring about housing reform. It can be just that, but only if it acquires the momentum to compel government action. In the strike of 1963–64, the landlord was the target, and that was the first mistake. Slum landlords generally do not have the resources to rehabilitate their buildings—not, at least, unless rents are substantially increased. The slum is the underbelly of the real-estate market: tenants who cannot compete for housing elsewhere are preyed on by entrepreneurs who lack the capital or competence to compete for profit elsewhere. More prosperous and stable real-estate investors put their capital in the regular market, where money can be made in less demeaning ways, leaving the slum to be exploited by men who seek to gain on dubious speculative exchange or who, restrained by rent-control laws from levying large increases, shore up their declining profits by skimping on repairs and services. The result is inflated prices and deteriorated buildings—a situation that can be remedied only by public action.

Public programs exist on the books, but are unused. In New York City, for example, low-cost municipal loans can be made to landlords to reduce the burden of undertaking rehabilitation; by 1963, however, only one such loan had been made, because the city was reluctant to become implicated in the shadowy finances of slum housing. The receivership program empowers the city to take over and repair hazardous buildings; after a year of operation, only 16 buildings had been acquired and, at that, the Commissioner of Real Estate reported indignantly that the city was finding the venture unprofitable! Thus, despite a wide variety of programs and powers available to municipalities, the bulk of slum housing remains and worsens—the rent strikers of 1963–64 lived in some of the same tenements which inspired the protests of such 19th-century reformers as Jacob Reis and Lillian Wald.

Political leaders and public agencies never became the target of the 1963–64 strike. On the surface, municipal agencies were conciliatory. The Department of Buildings put an inspector at Gray's disposal, and similar concessions were made to leaders elsewhere. Meanwhile, the mayor and his aides spoke out publicly against the slums, bewailing housing conditions and invoking the villain landlord of ancient myth. They called for more housing inspectors as well as legislation authorizing higher fines and jail sentences. These responses were predictable, if not perennial: the law already permitted considerably higher fines than were being levied by the courts, and housing agencies, we have noted, already had substantial powers and programs they were not employing. In the end, government escaped unscathed, having made only a few meaningless concessions.

How can government be forced to act? One thing is certain: the tactics used in 1963–64 won't do. Organizers reasoned that with the promise of repairs as the initial inducement to participate, stable organizations of the poor would eventually be formed, and that these would influence government. But the continuing emphasis on building permanent associations rests on a mistaken premise: that public decisions are made only in response to organized voting numbers. This view overlooks the impact of crisis as a way of compelling public action. When crisis occurs, many groups are aroused; they view disorder as a failure of governmental responsibility and demand measures (whether concessions or repression) to restore order. Crisis thus has a potential political force far greater than the number of citizens, organized or not, who participate in the disruptive action itself. The legalistic tactics of 1963–64 did not generate a public crisis, but other, more disruptive rent strike tactics would.

The key to a disruptive rent strike is for tenants to pocket the rent, not place it in escrow. Widespread action of this kind would throw the slum housing economy into chaos, for many landlords would have to abandon their property, leaving thousands of tenants in buildings without services or even minimal maintenance. As health hazards multiplied and the breakdown of landlord-tenant relations threatened to spread, the clamor would mount for governmental action to solve the crisis.

Pocketing the rent money would mean an immediate gain for tenants—a far more compelling incentive to participate than the vague hope of getting minor repairs. The main job of organizers would be to expand the strike by exciting indignation and urging tenants to spend their rent money for other needs. Such activity is much more compatible with the skills and temperament of organizers than canvassing for violations, filing forms, searching records, maintaining escrow accounts, and sitting endlessly in courtrooms. Relieved of these wearisome chores, they should be able to reach far more people than in 1963–64.

What of the dangers? It will be argued that the city can retaliate—at the very least, evictions might result. To minimize this risk, organizers need to mobilize at least a few hundred buildings to launch the strike, adding more buildings during the two- or three-month period it takes landlords to process evictions. It is unlikely that thousands, or even hundreds, of families would be put out on the streets, especially on the streets of ghettos whose growing and turbulent populations politicians can no longer afford to antagonize flagrantly. Furthermore, mass evictions would be viewed by many in the wider public as an even greater disorder than the breakdown of slum property relations.

It is important to understand that political leaders can prevent evictions, for the decision to evict is as much political as judicial. City governments, for example, have the legal right to initiate court proceedings against landlords who fail to correct violations. New York City has, in addition, the power to undercut legal actions taken against tenants by such landlords, simply by reducing rents to a dollar a month in buildings with multiple violations. Nor would housing courts in most cities, typically run by politically appointed judges, be so lenient with landlords when pressed by political leaders. Finally, to obtain time to wash out dispossess actions, mayors in most cities can simply order city marshals to delay all evictions, as a New York City mayor did during the violent rent strike of 1933. The legalistic tactics employed by the tenants in 1963–64 enabled political leaders to leave the strikers at the mercy of the agencies and the courts. But faced with tactics which ignore bureaucratic procedures and court proceedings, public officials would have to use their powers to forestall mass evictions or risk a major threat to political stability. Except in the face of a crisis, however, chief executives will not use these powers. Even if they did act, organizers would have to develop cadres to resist isolated evictions, defending the lone tenant by pitting the ghetto against the city's marshals and thus raising the specter of large-scale violence. Street action is far easier to mobilize than stable organizations of tenants. In 1963–64, however, organizers did not encourage street action, having pinned hope on the bureaucracies and courts.

By now it should be abundantly clear that the strategy we advocate is in no way limited to those few cities with statutes authorizing rent withholding. These laws are irrelevant, if not diversionary. Our analysis shows the futility of efforts to help masses of tenants make individual use of cumbersome procedures of legal redress. Disruptive tactics have a different purpose: to shift the burden of action against slum landlords from tenant to city governments.

There are measurable gains to be made by a disruptive rent strike. At the very least, this tactic should impel cities to use such programs as exist, whether offering low-cost loans to landlords who are willing to make repairs or making extensive emergency repairs and billing landlords for the cost. Most important, under the cumulative impact of disruptive actions, thousands of buildings would be abandoned—left to the government to take over. It is crucial to understand why this result would follow.

Slum housing is rampantly illegal, yet public agencies have never made much effort to enforce housing codes in New York. Even in those few cases where landlords were taken to court, the fines levied per violation averaged only $22 in 1963. By 1966 they had fallen to $14. Code-enforcement machinery is not allowed to work for good reason: a crackdown would produce massive dislocation of landlords and tenants. Repairs are extremely expensive, and building income is limited by the poverty of the captive tenant market as well as by rent-control laws. Just a modest step-up in enforcement activity under a new administration in New York City recently resulted in an upsurge in the number of foreclosures, tax delinquencies and vacate orders. If slumlords were pushed out, government would have to house the minority poor. So the enforcement agencies use their powers gingerly and selectively, usually paying heed only when tenants have the tenacity or the "pull" to compel enforcement.

In other words, slum profits have depended on collusion between city agencies and landlords: in return for nonenforcement of the codes, the slumlord takes the blame for the slum and enables the city to evade the political ire of the ghetto. But once municipal agencies are compelled to act on the codes, many owners of deteriorated buildings will be forced out of business, unable or unwilling to make the required repairs. Considering the highly marginal character of the slum market, the rent-strike tactics we propose could precipitate change no less fundamental than large-scale public takeover of land and buildings.

What would a city government do with slum buildings? Very likely, it would divest itself as quickly as possible of responsibility for them. To maintain the slums could only be expensive and politically onerous. City officials would run the risk of angering tenants dissatisfied with repairs and services, as well as tax-payers disgruntled by new investments in housing for the black and poor. Under such circumstances, municipalities might well move to sell or lease slum lands and buildings to private redevelopers. New governmental schemes are now in the making to stimulate investments in ghettos by national corporations, with federal subsidies to guarantee profits (e.g., tax benefits, low-cost loans and insurance, and rent supplements). These schemes, if implemented, would provide a way out for municipalities thrust by disruptive rent strikes into the role of slum landlords.

Federally subsidized corporate redevelopment will result in better housing and facilities; it will also bring the ghetto under the hegemony of an alliance of national corporations and federal bureaucracies. Now that blacks are coming into power in many large cities, the ghettos would be much better off with the municipality acting as redeveloper and landlord. Nevertheless, corporate ownership appears to be the wave of the future, and the leverage of the vote will have limited effect on corporate policies regarding location and design, tenant selection, or rents.

To deal with corporations on these policies, tenants will need to develop modes of influence beyond the vote. In this connection, corporate ownership might provide a favorable context for organizing mass-based tenant unions. As we noted earlier, most tenants now live in buildings owned by small entrepreneurs who themselves have limited financial resources; with nothing much to gain, tenants cannot easily be organized. Furthermore, ownership is so fragmented that efficient negotiating is virtually impossible. Under a system of national corporate ownership, however, tenants would confront large-scale landlords with ample resources to be conceded at the bargaining table. Tenant organization would then be comparable to the organization of workers in the factory system or in that sector of agriculture controlled by large corporations. Thus rent strikes could be mobilized to demand partial control of management policies and lower rents (so it would fall to large corporations, not the poor, to fight with Congress for higher rent subsidies). Most important, strikers might hold out for concessions which would nurture stable tenant unions—especially collective bargaining contracts and a dues check-off from rent payments. In Chicago, a few tenant groups have used rent strikes as leverage against several large landlords, forcing through contracts which include check-offs. But whether the object is to compel housing improvements in a system of fragmented slum ownership or to create tenant unions in a system of large-scale ownership, disruptive tactics are the key.

There are only certain periods when a disruptive force can be mobilized, for the poor are ordinarily passive, obeisant to the rules prescribed by dominant institutions. But from time to time normative control weakens and unrest mounts, as in 1963–64. Now such a time is upon us again; there is greater turbulence in the ghetto than ever before. Young and aggressive leaders are emerging who are unencumbered by ties to white institutions. Whatever else might be said about the rhetoric of black power, it serves to undermine the legitimacy of established arrangements, freeing people for militant action.

This is also a time when disruption might have unique force in moving government. The black masses are swelling in many cities, and more than a few white municipal leaders remain in office merely because blacks are not yet sufficiently mobilized, or antagonized, to unseat them. Under the impact of disruptive tactics, white politicians wishing to retain control of municipal government, would have to make concessions. In New York, for example, Mayor Lindsay, a Republican, was assured of election in 1965 because blacks, ordinarily Democratic, gave him an unprecedented 42 percent of their vote. Were he to permit mass evictions, his subsequent defeat would seem a foregone conclusion. Elsewhere, the potential for black reprisals against white politicians is far greater; blacks compose a mere 15 percent of New York's population, but they are approaching (or have already reached) a majority in many cities.

Of course, a disruptive strategy is always uncertain because it is not guided by legal and political conventions. But if in violating these conventions the poor are exposed to risk, they are worse off on what may seem less treacherous ground. For in playing by institutional rules, they take on the full complement of inhibiting requirements imposed by powerful groups who make the rules. Unable to meet these requirements, they can only lose.

Mary Ann Glendon, *The Transformation of American Landlord-Tenant Law*, 23 B.C. L. REV. 503–505, 509–511, 521–523, 536–540, 542–557 (1982)*

It is generally acknowledged that the 1960's and 1970's saw a revolution of sorts in American landlord-tenant law,[1] but the nature of that revolution is disputed. To many, the essence of the change has seemed to be a shift of the basis of lease law from principles of property to principles of contract. This view is particularly noticeable in the opinions of judges who have been instrumental in bringing about fundamental alterations in the common law of landlord-tenant,[2] and it also seems to have been central to the thinking of the draftsmen of the Uniform Residential Landlord and Tenant Act (URLTA). In fact, however, landlord-tenant case law was already deeply pervaded by contract notions by the end of the nineteenth century.[4] * * *

This article proposes to show that what has been called a revolution appears, in historical perspective, to have been no more or less than the culmination, in one area of the law, of certain long-standing trends that have transformed not only landlord-tenant law, but private law generally over the past century. Lease law was never pure property law. By the turn of the century, and up to the 1960's, it was an amalgam of real and personal property principles and of property and contract notions. It consisted mostly of case law, but even in the nineteenth century it had acquired an overlay of statutory regulation. Over the twentieth century, the elimination of certain anomalies within lease law brought it into closer harmony with modern principles of contract, tort, civil procedure and commercial law.

What is new, if not revolutionary, in the past twenty years, is that residential and commercial landlord-tenant law have gradually diverged, the

[1] Abbott, *Housing Policy, Housing Codes and Tenant Remedies: An Integration*, 56 B.U.L. REV. 1,2 (1976) [hereinafter cited as Abbott]; Cunningham, *The New Implied and Statutory Warranties of Habitability in Residential Leases: From Contract to Status*, 16 URB. L. ANN. 3,6 (1979) [hereinafter cited as Cunningham].

[2] E.g., Javins v. First Nat'l Realty Corp., 428 F.2d 1071, 1074, 1075 (D.C. Cir.), cert. denied, 400 U.S. 925 (1970) * * *.

[4] *See* * * * Hicks, *The Contractual Nature of Real Property Leases*, 24 BAYLOR L. REV. 443 (1972); Siegel, *Is the Modern Lease a Contract or a Conveyance? — A Historical Inquiry*, 52 J. URB. L. 649 (1975) * * *.

former more influenced by developments in consumer law, the latter by commercial law. The decisive element in the transformation of the residential landlord tenant relationship has been its subjection to pervasive, mostly statutory, regulation of its incidents. Contrary to a widespread belief among jurists, this process has been less the product of highly publicized court decisions establishing implied warranties of habitability in residential leases, than of steadily proliferating legislation. Together, legislative and judicial treatment of leases of dwellings now make it plain that the movement in residential lease law has been not from one area of private law to another, but from private ordering to public regulation. In this process of transition from private to public law, the habitability issue, which has dominated residential landlord-tenant law for the past two decades, is now yielding center stage to developments even more far-reaching in their implication: rent regulation, security of tenure for the tenant, and the qualification of the landlord's traditional rights to alienate the freehold or to convert it to another use.

The present article examines these fundamental shifts in the technical foundations of commercial and residential landlord-tenant law, and traces the accompanying alteration in conceptions of the respective proprietary rights of residential landlord and tenant. Underlying these latter changes is the idea that shelter is a basic human necessity, and that public regulation of the terms and conditions on which it is offered and held is therefore appropriate. Increasing acceptance of this implicit premise has made legislative and judicial regulation of the residential rent contract as inevitable as it was of the employment contract. Yet the relation of regulatory landlord-tenant law to the supply and quality of rented housing is problematic, raising serious questions for future housing policy.

* * *

II. Classical Landlord-Tenant Law

A. The Basic System

American commercial and residential landlord-tenant law assumed the form that it had on the eve of the landlord-tenant "revolution" over the course of the nineteenth century in an era when property was losing, and contract was gaining, predominance in private law.[41] Notions of freedom of contract and laissez-faire were at their zenith. Three leading ideas, one from property and two from contract, met and intertwined in the fundamental rules which governed the landlord-tenant relationship. The first notion was the conception of the lease as a sale of possession for rent. The second was the idea that contracts should be held sacred: *pacta sunt servanda*. This second idea was contained within the third, which is the broad notion of freedom of contract, which meant that, subject to narrow limits, the legal system would enforce the bargain of private parties as written in the same way that it would enforce legislation. Courts rarely disturbed contractual clauses of the type which today would be called onerous.

There was very little public control over the quality, type and location of housing, rented or otherwise, in the nineteenth century, except in certain of the nation's largest cities where conditions in the tenements that had appeared with industrial expansion and immigrations were believed to be a menace to public health. The activity of the federal government in the housing area was sporadic and small-scale until the Depression years of the 1930's, and, with few exceptions, that of state governments was practically nil until the 1960's.

The contours of classical landlord-tenant law can be delineated by describing a few of its basic rules. Most of these rules, from their inception, were subject to qualifications, exceptions, and to judicial avoidance through characterization of the facts of individual cases. But until the late 1960's, they still constituted the starting points for any legal analysis of landlord-tenant relations. A gradual process of erosion culminated in the demise of many of these rules in the 1960's and 1970's and in the substitution of new and often opposite starting points, especially where residential tenancies are concerned. The legal treatment of leases of dwellings has become differentiated from that of business tenancies where there is more apt to be bargaining between the parties, and from farming or mineral leases where structures are either not involved or are incidental to the main purpose of the transaction. Before discussing such developments, however, it is necessary to outline the classical landlord-tenant relationship.

In the classical scheme, the landlord's principal obligations related to possession and the tenant's to rent. Thus, the landlord was obliged to give the tenant at least good title and a clear right to

---

[41] J. W. Hurst, Law and the Conditions of Freedom in the Nineteenth Century United States 12 (1956).

possession at the commencement of the term. During the term, the tenant had the right to expect that his possession would not be materially disturbed by the landlord, anyone acting under the landlord's authority, or anyone with a title paramount to that of the landlord. This right, inherent in the tenant's estate, came to be expressed as the implied covenant for quiet enjoyment. The landlord had no obligation to deliver the premises in any particular physical condition or state of repair, and, *a fortiori*, no duty to maintain or repair them during the term. The lessee was expected to examine the premises and decide for himself whether they were fit for his purposes. After the lease was entered, as after a sale, the risk of loss of deterioration belonged to the lessee. Thus, even if the premises were destroyed or rendered unfit for the tenant's purposes during the lease term, the tenant's obligations to pay rent in principle continued unaffected. The tenant's obligations towards the landlord with respect to the premises were defined by the law of waste, that is, by the same body of rules that governed a life tenant's duties towards remaindermen or reversioners. Hence, the tenant was obliged to make such ordinary repairs as were necessary to prevent waste and deterioration, but not to make substantial, lasting and general repairs.

The tenant's obligation to pay rent was grounded both in the property law notion that the rent "issued from the land" as a tenurial service of the tenant's estate, and (where the tenant had expressly covenanted to pay rent) in the idea of absolute contractual obligation. This made it doubly difficult for a tenant to defend a rent action. Furthermore, the contract doctrine of mutual dependence of promises, developed by Lord Mansfield in the late eighteenth century, was not imported into the law of lease. Thus, even a breach by the landlord of an express covenant, such as a covenant to repair, did not relieve the tenant of any part of his obligation to pay rent, and the breach by the tenant of his rent covenant did not give the landlord the right to retake possession. The aggrieved party was limited to suing for contractual relief (plus, in the case of the landlord, to seizing and holding chattels on the land as security for rent) unless a statute or the lease itself gave him additional rights.

* * *

III. The Demise of Classical Landlord-Tenant Law in Residential Leases

* * *

A trilogy of District of Columbia Circuit Court of Appeals cases, decided between 1960 and 1970, in which housing codes played an important role, symbolized the decisive stages in the disintegration of classical landlord-tenant law * * *. In *Whetzel v. Jess Fisher Management Co.,*[120] the court allowed a tenant's tort suit to be based on a landlord's code violation. In *Edwards v. Habib,*[122] a tenant was permitted to defend an eviction action on the grounds that the landlord had terminated her month-to-month tenancy in retaliation against the tenant for having reported code violations. Finally, in *Javins v. First National Realty Corp.,*[124] the court discarded several common law rules at once: the landlord's lack of duties with respect to the physical condition of the premises; the independence of the tenant's obligation to pay rent from the landlord's obligations with respect to the premises; and the constructive eviction requirement that a tenant must vacate the leased premises before asserting defenses to rent based on the condition of the premises.

The crumbling of the classical rules in the case law of the late 1960's is traceable in no small part to the fact that, under the Johnson administration's "Great Society" programs, legal assistance was made much more accessible to indigent persons than it had been in the past. In the atmosphere of that time, expanding legal services bureaus began to attract lawyers who were interested not only in aiding individual poor clients, but in bringing about change in the legal and social systems. Thus "ordinary" residential landlord-tenant cases often became test cases which could be financed, staffed and appealed, even though the amounts actually in controversy might be quite small.

Legal aid bureaus all over the country were active in landlord-tenant matters in the 1960's, but it is probably not a mere accident that the most far reaching judicial changes were initially accomplished in the District of Columbia. In the first place, housing conditions in Washington, D.C., were such as to arouse public concern. But unlike several other jurisdictions, such as California and New York, with

---

[120] 282 F.2d 943 (D.C. Cir. 1960).

[122] 397 F.2d 687 (D.C. Cir. 1968).

[124] 428 F.2d 1071 (D.C. Cir. 1970). One might also mention here Brown v. Southall Realty Co. 237 A.2d 834 (D.C. 1968), where the District of Columbia Court of Appeals, using contract principles, held void a lease entered into in violation of the housing code. Unlike the decisions of the United States Court of Appeals for the District of Columbia Circuit, this case and its novel approach have had little influence outside the District of Columbia. * * *

similar problems in their metropolitan areas, the District had not responded with legislation affording private remedies. The circumstances thus favored a judicial response of some sort. It is also significant that a federal court * * * then sat as, in effect, the Supreme Court of the District. The judges on this court were immersed on a day-to-day basis in public and administrative law, and turned naturally to it for analogies. They also were ready to see a public law dimension in seemingly private litigation. Furthermore, two of the judges on that bench, Bazelon and Wright, were already well known for their willingness to innovate in other areas. The stage was thus set for a judicial overthrow of classical landlord-tenant law in its application to residential leases.

In retrospect, it can be seen that the District of Columbia cases were only the flagships of a movement that had been long building. The way for change had been prepared by the gradual proliferation of exceptions to the classical rules. As the current of change began to accelerate in the social climate of the 1960's, it was swelled by a case-law stream building on the housing codes adopted to obtain federal aid, and by a less remarked, but in the end stronger, statutory stream, until at last the classical law was submerged and relegated to an undertow, tempering and qualifying the new doctrines of residential landlord-tenant law.

* * *

4. Reforms of Summary Process

The possessory remedy of summary dispossess, or forcible entry and detainer, as it is called in some states, has also undergone profound changes in the process. To the extent that material breach of the landlord's obligations with respect to the condition of leased premises has been made available as a defense in eviction actions, the very basis of traditional summary process law has been undermined. Just as landlord-tenant tort law had become an anomaly within the body of modern tort law, so nineteenth century summary proceedings were islands of anachronism within streamlined modern civil procedure law. They were constitutional, however, as the United States Supreme Court made clear in its 1972 decision, *Lindsey v. Normet.*[224] The court there upheld Oregon's traditional summary procedure law, even though the statute limited the issues that could be litigated in a possession action to whether the tenant had paid the rent, had held over wrongfully or had honored his covenants. According to the majority opinion, a state can validly single out possessory actions by landlords against tenants for especially expedited judicial settlement because of the "unique factual and legal characteristics of the landlord-tenant relationship" [requiring speedy adjudication.] * * * The practical effect of *Lindsey* in an implied warranty state which has not modernized its summary process law would be that a tenant in default in his rental obligation could be permitted to raise a habitability defense in an action for rent but denied this opportunity in an action for possession only. Landlords of low-income tenants could be expected to forego bringing actions for probably uncollectable past-due rent, and to content themselves with regaining possession. Thus, there would be few occasions for litigating habitability issues.

That a state is not constitutionally *required* to permit a tenant to raise habitability issues in an eviction action for nonpayment of rent, however, has not prevented most implied warranty states, including Oregon one year after the *Lindsey* case, from electing to furnish tenants with this opportunity. * * *

The increased willingness of courts and legislatures to permit the habitability defense in possession actions has focused attention on the need to strike a proper balance between the tenant's legitimate desire to resolve rent-related disputes before losing possession of his home, and the landlord's legitimate desire to continue to receive the rental income from which debt service, operating expenses and repairs would ordinarily be paid. * * *

Modernizing the procedure in eviction cases is not * * * an entirely simple matter * * *. The hearing of the tenant's defenses may prolong litigation for a considerable period of time during which the landlord may receive no rent while his expenses continue to accrue. At the end of the lawsuit, the court may find that the tenant owes the entire rent, but the landlord may be unable to collect if it has not been deposited in court.

* * * [One suggestion] is that tenants today, in keeping with modern practice, should be allowed routinely to plead a wide variety of defenses and counterclaims in possession actions, but that they should be allowed to delay eviction only when they can make the kind of showing of irreparable harm and likelihood of success that a litigant ordinarily has to make in order to obtain a preliminary injunc-

---

[224] 405 U. S. 56 (1972).

tion.[234] * * * If the court concluded that the eviction should be delayed, it could require the tenant to post security for the delay * * *.

While [this] * * * proposal may indicate a way to harmonize procedure in eviction cases with civil procedure law and the new framework of landlord-tenant law, another problem raised by the habitability defense is not so easily resolved. Although defenses relating to the condition of leased premises are raised in only a minority of all eviction cases, they quickly put a considerable strain on the over-burdened judicial system. One response to this burden has been the creation of special courts for dealing with housing or landlord-tenant matters. But the nature of landlord-tenant litigation, with its high volume, each case typically involving a small amount of money, has suggested to some observers that alternatives to the judicial method of dispute resolution should be explored in this area.

* * *

5. Security of Tenure

Traditionally, continuity of tenure has been a characteristic that set freehold ownership apart from mere leasing. In the classical scheme, it was unquestioned that the landlord had the right to possession of the leased premises upon the expiration of a term for years or upon the proper termination of a tenancy at will or a periodic tenancy. The right was absolute in principle because the landlord could * * * terminate or refuse to renew a leasehold estate for any reason or for no reason; evidence concerning his motives was inadmissible.

* * *

Many of the new rights acquired by tenants as landlord-tenant law was transformed in the 1960's and 1970's could have been virtually nullified if landlords could terminate or refuse to renew the leases of tenants who exercised them. Month-to-month tenants, who tend to be found mainly in low-rental units, were especially vulnerable, since their leases in principle can be ended upon 30 days' notice for any or no reason. So, largely as a byproduct of the development of the implied warranty, statutory and case law began to inhibit landlords from using their prerogatives to terminate tenancies, or to raise rents, or to refuse to renew leases, in reprisal for the exercise of the tenant's right to participate in tenants' unions or to assert defenses based on the landlord's failure to maintain the premises. In the leading case of *Edwards v. Habib*,[248] Judge Wright held unlawful a landlord's termination of a month-to-month tenancy in retaliation for a tenant's reporting code violations on the premises.

* * *

Recently, in several states and municipalities, further limitations have been placed on evictions. Reacting to the loss of rental units caused by their conversion into cooperatives or condominiums, a number of legislatures have severely curtailed the ability of landlords to terminate or refuse to renew existing tenancies for this purpose. Even without legislation, the case law developments could go quite far in the direction of limiting the landlord's ability to terminate tenancies. The increasing disposition of courts to carry new and old principles of contract law over into residential lease law * * * might well result in holding landlords to a standard of good faith that would be much broader in scope than the retaliatory eviction concept.

* * * [T]he foregoing exceptions to the common law lease termination rules have involved an increase in security of tenure arising from the prohibition of evictions, or refusals to renew, for forbidden reasons. * * * [O]ther developments, * * * at present rather limited in scope, would prevent landlords from terminating or refusing to renew leases unless they affirmatively can show "good cause" for so doing. "Good cause" eviction is not an *exception* to the landlord's common law right to repossess at the end of the term. It constitutes rather the introduction of an opposite principle, that of the tenant's presumptive right to continue in possession.

A "good cause" requirement for eviction exists already where the dwellings involved are in public housing programs, in most rent-controlled tenancies, and applies to virtually all rental housing in two jurisdictions. Tenants in conventional public housing or federally subsidized rental housing are protected against eviction by administrative rules and regulations affording them the right, not only to security of tenure, but to a hearing on the reasons for eviction before they are deprived of possession. * * * In the private, but rent-controlled sector, local regulations typically provide that a landlord can terminate a controlled tenancy only for "just cause," that is for one of the statutorily enumerated reasons.

* * *

These developments reflect a certain incorporation into the law of the notions that the tenant's

---

[234] Chused, *Contemporary Dilemmas of the* Javin *Defense: A Note on the Need for Procedural Reform in Landlord-Tenant Law,* 67 GEO. L.J. 1385 (1979).

[248] 397 F.2d 687 (D.C. Cir. 1968).

interest in his home and the public's interest in maintaining the supply of rental units are more important than the landlord's investment. This was made explicit by Judge Wright in *Robinson v. Diamond Housing,*[263] a retaliatory eviction case: "The right to a decent home is far too vital for us to assume that government has taken away with one hand [with summary process] what it purports to grant with the other [tenants' rights]."

Some courts, like the Supreme Court in *Lindsey v. Normet*, may still refer to the landlord as the "owner" and to the leased dwelling as the landlord's "property." But in conventional property law terms, a leasehold estate always involved at least two proprietary interests: the present possessory estate of the tenant and the reversion of the landlord. What seems to be happening at present is that the traditional emphasis on what the landlord owns is now giving way to an increased emphasis on what the tenant owns. That these developments can go quite far in a common law country is shown by the experience of England where broad legislative schemes of rent regulation and eviction control have been in operation since the post-war period. Although most English texts treat the "statutory tenancies" created by these laws as consisting of merely personal, not proprietary, rights, the tenant's continuing right to possession is considered by some commentators to be a new kind of property right. In the United States, it is already clear that with respect to lease termination, as with other areas * * *, technical change in landlord-tenant law has been accompanied by subtle ideological change. * * *

IV. The Rise of Regulatory Landlord-Tenant Law

The differences between the legal norms that presently govern a transformed residential landlord-tenant relationship in most American states and those of the classical law are striking. But the essence of the transformation of lease law is not revealed merely by comparing classical and current law or by tracing the evolution and decline of various substantive and procedural rules. From one angle, the twentieth century evolution of landlord-tenant law has involved the absorption into lease law of new principles of contract, sales, tort and civil procedure law as those fields themselves have been modernized. From this point of view, landmark cases removing such anomalies as the independence of covenants, the landlord's tort immunity and the limitation on rent-related defenses and counterclaims in eviction actions have simply made lease law more consistent with other fields of private law. As new doctrines within contract, tort and commercial law began to accord consumers different legal treatment in many respects from that given to merchants, residential landlord-tenant law has diverged from commercial landlord-tenant law to become a kind of "consumer law."

* * *

As the new residential landlord-tenant law matures, the analogy between a lease and a sale of goods, so influential in the early development of the implied warranty, has begun to break down. The appearance, establishment, elaboration, and eventual transmutation of the implied warranty could furnish a series of textbook illustrations for Edward Levi's discussion of how new concepts enter the legal system, change the prior law, and are themselves changed. Levi called attention to the importance of finding a "ready word" or phrase for a new legal concept.[276] He notes that, looking back over a line of cases, one can often discern a period when the courts were fumbling for a phrase. In landlord-tenant law, a new characterization, in part, explains why the Minnesota Supreme Court's recognition in 1931 of a landlord's "implied covenant that the premises [in modern apartment buildings] will be habitable"[279] attracted little attention at the time. Eventually, when circumstances had changed sufficiently to make a thorough restructuring of landlord-tenant law possible, Judge Wright found the phrase that would thereafter be repeatedly invoked to trigger influential, though imperfect, analogies to a changing sales law. The subject matter of the lease was no longer to be called "premises"; it was, rather, a "well known package of goods and services." Implied in the transfer of this package was not a "covenant," the conveyancing word used in *Delameter*, but a "warranty," a word evoking the UCC warranties of merchantability and fitness for a particular purpose.

As Levi noted, legal categories typically undergo change in the course of being applied in the "moving classification system" of the law. This can be illustrated by the transformation of the meaning of "warranty" in the residential lease context. It is clear

263 463 F.2d 853 (D.C. Cir. 1972).

276 E. Levi, An Introduction to Legal Reasoning 8 (1949).

279 Delameter v. Foreman, 239 N.W.148, 149 (Minn. 1931).

even from *Javins* that the implied warranty of habitability in residential leases has small resemblance to implied warranties in the sale of goods. The implied warranty of habitability applies even to patent defects obvious to the "buyer" at the time of the "sale," and it obliges the "seller" to maintain the premises during the term of the lease. Under the UCC, the buyer has no warranty protection against defects which he ought to have discovered by inspection, nor is there any continuing duty on the part of the seller to keep goods in repair. Furthermore, the UCC expressly recognized that sales can be made on an "as is" basis and that implied warranties can be excluded or modified in other ways, while the implied warranty of habitability generally either cannot be contracted out at all, or can be affected by contract only in strictly limited ways. When the implied warranty is materially breached, the tenant may be allowed to remain in possession and yet be excused from all or part of his rental obligation. Under the Uniform Commercial Code, however, a buyer of defective goods generally has to choose between rejecting the goods, or keeping them and suing for damages.

In this last respect, the difference between the lease of real property and an ordinary sale of goods appears crucial. A sale, even on credit, is meant eventually to sever the seller's connection with the goods and to make the buyer the owner. A lease establishes an ongoing relationship between lessor and lessee, which, whether characterized as a property or contractual relation, is meant to be temporary, with all rights to be reunited in the lessor at some future time. The landlord retains an interest in the leased real estate in a way that a seller of tomatoes, sewing machines, or tools, does not. Indeed, it is unclear to what extent, if at all, the UCC warranty provisions are applicable to leases of personal property. This is why the Supreme Court in *Lindsey v. Normet*[292] would not hold that the state of Oregon had acted unconstitutionally in singling out the landlord's possessory action for more expedited treatment than other civil actions. As Levi has noted, however, the misuse or misunderstanding of a concept need not impede its progress in the law.

Thus *Javins*, not *Delameter*, marked the point in the case law where the implied warranty idea was accepted, given definition, and connected to other ideas. But characteristically, as reasoning by analogy proceeded, and cases were classified as within or without its reach, the concept of implied warranty itself changed. As a term implied in nearly every residential lease, regardless of the will of the parties, it does not belong to the domain of contract but to that of regulation. This was made especially clear in *Foisy v. Wyman*,[297] where the tenant of a single-family house with an option to buy was permitted to assert breach of implied warranty as a defense to an unlawful detainer action even though the rent had been fixed at a low rate because of obvious defects on the premises. The Washington Supreme Court swept aside the landlord's contention that bargaining had in fact occurred, saying, "[w]e believe this type of bargaining by the landlord with the tenant is contrary to public policy and the purpose of the doctrine of implied warranty of habitability."

The implied warranty was soon joined by a growing list of other lease terms that are either required or forbidden, or strictly controlled, by court decision or statute. The landlord cannot be exculpated from liability for his own negligence. The lease may not include a confession of judgment by the tenant, an agreement to pay attorney's fees, or a waiver of any of his rights and remedies under the Act. The taking and use of the tenant's security deposit is carefully regulated. For public housing, the list is different, but even more extensive.

As the list of required and forbidden terms expands, it begins to resemble a lease implied-in-law. At the same time, a great deal of judicial discretion in dealing with landlord-tenant disputes is authorized by the doctrines of good faith and unconscionability that emerged in contract law, were consolidated in commercial law by the Uniform Commercial Code, and are now included in the URLTA. These innovations might at first appear to be a long-needed response to the problem of the standardized lease. Llewellyn long ago recognized that traditional contract law was not suited to deal with standardized form contracts and proposed that they should be handled within a private law framework by enforcing only those terms "which a sane man might reasonably expect to find" on the form.[306] * * *

Current American residential landlord-tenant law, however, has replaced the standard form lease, not with terms based on the reasonable expectations of the parties, or even of one them, but with terms usually justified by reference to the public interest. This need not exclude the idea of protecting expectations. But as Charles Reich pointed out in a now

[292] 405 U.S. 56 (1972).
[297] 83 Wash. 2d 22, 515 P.2d 160 (1973).
[306] Llewellyn, Book Review, 52 HARV. L. REV. 700, 704 (1939).

famous article, "'the public interest' is all too often a reassuring platitude that covers up sharp clashes of conflicting values, and hides fundamental choices."[309] In fact, regulatory landlord-tenant law seems to be less concerned with reliance and expectations than are traditional contract law and commercial law. It tends, rather, to reflect ever-changing compromises among, and fluctuating perceptions of, the interests involved, as well as diverse views about the relationship of law to economic and social reality. It is therefore susceptible to more frequent, abrupt and unpredictable changes than are the private law remnants of property and contract. Thus, research in landlord-tenant law no longer involves study of the gradual judicial elaboration and qualification of rules, standards, and principles, so much as it does consultation of the annual legislative deposit in the pocket parts of each state's statute books.

In this respect, the judge-made component of lease law has become similar to its counterparts in the law governing employment contracts, franchise agreements, and other relational contracts that are considered to be of great social importance. From this point of view, the forces that have been at work in landlord-tenant law are merely elements of a more general transition in attitudes about the role of the judge in developing private law. At least since Cardozo, it has been accepted that judges have a creative law-making role in the private law areas. However, until the 1960's it was widely believed that such judicial activity should proceed through a process of reasoned elaboration and that it should rest on some rule, principle or standard. Today, as the former private law fields become more public and administrative, judges express these attitudes less frequently, and engage more openly in speech and activities that would once have been considered legislative.

* * *

[I]t would be a mistake to interpret these recent case-law developments as themselves constituting the dawn of the era of regulatory landlord-tenant law. They represent only a judicial recognition of the largely accomplished fact of the transition of residential lease law from the private law fields of property and contract to an area in which public regulatory law predominates. The basic rules of residential landlord-tenant law are now, overwhelmingly, to be found in an extensive network of statutes, codes and ordinances. And, although the phrase, "implied warranty of habitability" may evoke the names of certain landmark cases to most lawyers, those cases, as we have seen, were themselves dependent on legislation, either by elaborating policy contained in, or by deriving private rights from, anterior housing codes or other safety laws. Furthermore, these cases were often followed by legislation codifying or qualifying their results. As we have seen, contrary to what many believe, the implied warranty in most states was established by legislation, not judicial action. At least nineteen states have comprehensive, systematic landlord-tenant legislation, while in many other states, especially the most urbanized ones, the landlord-tenant laws are more varied and voluminous than the Uniform Residential Landlord-Tenant Act. Indeed, the very mass, complexity and changeability of landlord-tenant law in a state like Massachusetts, for example, constitute obstacles to rational codification.

* * *

Besides URLTA and similar legislation establishing new relationships between landlord and tenant, there are in various states and localities other forms of regulation of leasing which are more far-reaching and more explicitly directed to public goals: condominium-cooperative conversion control, rent regulation, eviction control, and consumer protection laws applicable to residential leasing by persons in the rental housing business. About half of the states, and over half of the central cities in the thirty-seven largest metropolitan areas in the United States, have adopted some form of regulation protecting tenants in buildings about to undergo conversion into condominiums or cooperatives. It has been estimated that as many as one-eighth of all rental units in the United States may be subject to some form of rent regulation. Like conversion control laws, rent regulation typically includes a complex scheme of eviction controls. Two jurisdictions have general eviction controls. Finally, statewide consumer protection legislation forbidding unfair or deceptive trade practices has been made applicable to leases in a number of states.

Most remarkable among these laws are the 1974 New Jersey statute, and two District of Columbia statutes. The New Jersey law, statewide in application, simultaneously regulates evictions and condominium-cooperative conversions, and initiates a form of general rent regulation by providing that a tenant cannot be removed after a valid notice to quit and

---

[309] Reich, *The New Property*, 73 YALE L.J. 733, 787 (1964).

notice of increase in rent, unless the proposed increase in rent is "not unconscionable." The District of Columbia Rent Control Law imposes eviction controls on all rental units within the District and establishes a system of rent control applicable to all multifamily rental housing, with the exception of most newly constructed buildings. The District of Columbia Rental Housing Conversion and Sale Act of 1980 regulates both the sale and conversion of all rental housing within the District. In the case of sales, it requires the landlord to afford individual tenants or tenants' organizations (depending on the type of property) an opportunity to purchase the property before it can be sold. It also provides that occupied rental property may not be converted to condominiums or cooperative unless a majority of the tenants vote in favor of such a change. Even when a landlord receives authorization to convert, the Act provides that he may not evict for this reason any tenants age sixty-two or over whose household incomes are less than $30,000 a year. Since the statute expires by its own terms in September, 1983, it is uncertain whether these extended interests of elderly tenants can endure until they die, move away or give cause for eviction, or whether they can exist no longer than the effective duration of the Act.

With rent and eviction control, regulation moves from the collateral to the core terms of the lease or rental agreement. Typically the only provisions in residential leases that are "bargained for" are the rent and the duration of the lease. When these provisions are regulated by law, the role of the will of the parties tends to be confined to the decision of whether to enter the relationship or not. The landlord is treated as controlling a resource of such central importance in society that it must be regulated, and the courts start borrowing analogies, not from sales law, but from public utility law.

Landlords, now coming under similar kinds of regulation to those long imposed on employers, have fewer options with respect to their increased costs of doing business. In particular, the option of passing all or part of such costs on to the consumer is more problematic since the consumer is the tenant. Furthermore, a rent increase, like an eviction, may be treated as retaliatory, or may be limited by rent control laws. To the extent the landlords have to absorb such increased costs, it has been feared that the effects on the supply of low-income rental housing will be adverse, because some landlords will abandon their buildings and others will convert them to more profitable uses. Predictably, landlords who have sought to change the form of their investment have begun to encounter obstacles to the exercise of their rights to alienate or alter their interest, just as employers have in connection with moving or closing down plants.

The ongoing transformation of the technical foundations of landlord-tenant law is obviously related to well-known and advanced changes in certain basic assumptions of classical property and contract law. The notions of freedom of contract and private property that once dominated legal thought have given way, as various forms of regulation have become relatively permanent features of the legal landscape. There is more regulation of the landlord-tenant relationship, however, than there is of other consumer-supplier relationships. Although much of the statewide landlord-tenant legislation and the evolving landlord-tenant case law is recognizable as an aspect of the development of "consumer law," rent control and condominium-cooperative conversion controls tend to be established by local ordinances and have no analogies in the law governing the purchase or lease of their goods and services.

* * *

With increased regulation, the landlord-tenant relationship takes on some characteristics of a status, with its terms and conditions fixed by law. The movement in residential landlord-tenant law turns out not to have been a movement from one field of private law to another, but a movement from private law to public law. * * * [I]n the vast majority of residential leases, important terms and conditions are framed by courts and legislatures rather than by "landlords or their advisors," and * * * appellate courts have tended to incline toward the residential tenant, rather than the landlord on doubtful points. Power has shifted mainly, however, not to the tenant, but to the state.

Note

How far has security of tenure for tenants gone? Should a tenant be allowed to move a new member of her "family" into "her" apartment? Consider *Hudson View Properties v. Weiss*, 109 Misc.2d 589, 442 N.Y.S.2d 367 (Sup. Ct. 1981), where a tenant lost her lease after allowing her male companion to move in. The lease permitted additional tenants only after marriage. What of family members surviving a deceased tenant? Should they have the "right" to remain in "their" apartment? Consider *Braschi v. Stahl Associates Company,* 74 N.Y.2d 201, 543 N.E.2d 49, 544 N.Y.S.2d 784 (1989), in which the male companion of a deceased man was allowed to stay in the latter's rent controlled apartment under a statute allowing "family" members to take over leases of deceased tenants.

Edward H. Rabin, *The Revolution in Residential Landlord-Tenant Law: Causes and Consequences*, 69 CORNELL L. REV. 517–520, 540–549, 558–562, 577–578 (1984)*

INTRODUCTION

In the last two decades we have experienced a revolution in residential landlord-tenant law. The residential tenant, long the stepchild of the law, has now become its ward and darling. Tenants' rights have increased dramatically; landlords' rights have decreased dramatically. * * *

This article draws several conclusions. First, the structure of the residential landlord-tenant relation has radically changed. A large number of doctrines have been fundamentally revised. Second, most of the changes were caused not by a deepening crisis in rental housing, but rather by social, political, and intellectual currents that emerged in the sixties. One change, however, most rent control legislation, was enacted in response to an economic force—inflation—rather than to social or intellectual developments. Third, the detrimental impact of rent control on tenant welfare predominantly affects future tenants and those persons unable to vote. This explains why over 200 communities have adopted rent control despite its generally adverse effect on housing. Fourth, despite their widespread use, vacancy rates are worthless as indicators of housing shortages. Judges and analysts who have relied on them have been led astray. Finally, each individual change in the law must be judged independently with respect to its effect on the availability and cost of housing. For example, although the warranty of habitability applied to latent defects promotes the efficient provision of housing, the same warranty applied to patent defects retards it. The key question is, Does the law reflect what the parties would have bargained for with full knowledge and experience? To the extent that it does, the law promotes the efficient provision of housing.

* * *

II

CAUSES OF THE REVOLUTION

* * *

A. Housing Conditions and Trends in the Sixties

1. The Physical Reality

By any measure, the American people were better housed in 1968 than they had ever been before. Rich and poor, tenants and homeowners, had shared in the benefits of the substantial improvements that had occurred over the previous decades. Table I shows that between 1950 and 1970 the proportion of the nation's housing stock that was "dilapidated" decreased by more than fifty percent; the proportion lacking complete plumbing decreased by more than eighty percent; and the proportion that was overcrowded decreased by almost fifty percent. The proportion that was over thirty years old decreased from 45.7% in 1950 to 40.6% in 1970.[122]

[122] U.S. DEP'T OF HOUS. AND URBAN DEV., NATIONAL HOUSING POLICY REVIEW, HOUSING IN THE SEVENTIES 166 (1974) [hereinafter cited as HOUSING IN THE SEVENTIES].

A significant improvement in housing conditions occurred even in central city slums:

> Overall, the changes in the 50 low-income neighborhoods indicate some surprising results. The neighborhoods were selected with an expectation of neighborhood decline, yet it was found that of virtually all neighborhoods studied, housing conditions and real incomes actually improved. All indices, however, still revealed relatively poor housing conditions.

TABLE I
MEASURES OF HOUSING INADEQUACY

	1940	1950	1960	1970	1974	1977
Percent of all units lacking some or all plumbing	45.2	35.4	16.8	6.5	4.0	3.1
Percent of all units dilapidated or needing major repairs	17.8	9.8	6.9	4.6	NA	NA
Percent of all units substandard: dilapidated, or lacking plumbing	49.2	36.9	18.2	9.0	NA	NA
Percent of occupied units with 1.51 or more per room	9.0	6.2	3.6	2.0	NA	NA
Percent of occupied units with 1.01 or more persons per room	20.2	15.8	11.5	8.0	5.3	4.4
Percent of occupied units with one or more subfamilies	NA	NA	NA	NA	1.5	1.4

Between 1960 and 1970 housing had also become more affordable. Although the rent-to-income ratios for each income class had risen from 1960 to 1970, this rise is misleading. If one adjusts for inflation and for changes in the quality of rental housing, income ratios fell from 1960 to 1970. For example, someone earning about $3,500 in 1960 had the same real income as someone earning $4,500 in 1970. That individual's rent-to-income ratio was 22.3% in 1960 and had risen to 26.7% in 1970. However, he or she was eight times more likely to have airconditioning, one-third less likely to be overcrowded, and half as likely to lack plumbing. Thus, in constant dollars and in terms of comparable quality, rental housing rent-to-income ratios had become more favorable for tenants in 1970 than they were in 1960.

I do not suggest that in 1968 there were no renters living in poor housing, for millions were. I merely argue that any suggestion of a growing crisis was mistaken. Housing conditions had improved steadily and substantially over the decade. The general perception of housing conditions, however, was very different.

2. As Perceived at the Time

a. The Douglas Commission. In March 1965, President Johnson called for a commission to study the causes of slums and urban blight, and to make appropriate recommendations.[129] Congress subse-

---

[129] U.S. NAT'L COMM'N ON URBAN PROBLEMS, BUILDING THE AMERICAN CITY, H.R. DOC. NO. 34, 91st Cong., 1st Sess. VII (1978) [hereinafter cited as BUILDING THE AMERICAN CITY].

quently authorized such a study, to be completed by December 31, 1968. Although the Commission report made passing pro forma reference to the "great gains in our housing stock," the dominant message of the report concerned the existence of a housing crisis of great proportions. The report stated that the complex problem of racial segregation in housing remained "critical." The accomplishments of subsidized housing were "extremely inadequate" and a "squeeze on low-income families seeking decent housing" existed. The Commission recognized a "need [for] a new generation of housing codes embracing higher standards and tied in with environmental standards." There was also a "need for a real political commitment to solve our problems," which constituted an "urban crisis." Indeed, the Commission stated in its summary: "The solutions we call for are a tall order, but they are in proportion to the enormity of the problems of our urban areas."

The Commission recommended a startling increase in housing construction. It recommended annual housing production of from 2.0 to 2.25 million housing units per year; 500,000 of those units to be designed specifically for low and moderate income families (exclusive of the elderly). Because the Commission's own statistics indicated that in the 1960s only 15.3 million units were built (1.53 million per year on average), the Commission's recommendation would have meant an annual average increase of 33% in the number of units constructed over the previous comparable period. It is impossible to sum up a report of 500 pages in a few sentences. Yet the general perception of the Douglas Commission can be summarized by the following quotation:

> At the present levels of family income and at present rentals and mortgage rates, about a third of the families in the Nation cannot buy or rent decent housing at market rates by paying a reasonable proportion of their income for shelter (no more than 20 to 25 percent at most).

b. The Kaiser Committee.[142] The Kaiser Committee submitted its report to the President only one day before the Douglas Commission submitted its report. The Committee first received its charge in June 1967 and participated in the development of the Housing and Urban Development Act of 1968 (passed in August of 1968). The Kaiser Report, like the Douglas Report, generally saw a crisis in housing:

> [T]his Committee reached a fundamental conclusion: . . . There is an immediate and critical social need for millions of decent dwellings to shelter the nation's lower-income families. Overlying this need is one raising an unprecedented and challenging production problem. The nation is heading toward a serious shortage of housing for the total population, unless production is sharply increased.

To meet the need described above, the Kaiser Committee recommended producing twenty-six million new and rehabilitated units by 1978, including between six and eight million subsidized units. The report acknowledged the enormity of this goal, calculating that it required 70% more housing production in the next decade than the total production of the 1950s. A staff study appended to the Kaiser Committee Report acknowledged that housing conditions had improved in the previous few decades, but concluded that "without a major National effort, there is little prospect for any substantial net gains in the condition of substandard metropolitan area housing in the decade ahead." In President Johnson's June 2, 1967, statement, forming appendix A to the Kaiser Committee Report, he described the problem as follows: "No domestic task facing this Nation today is more demanding or more urgent than reclaiming the corroded core of the American city. A substantial part of that task is the rebuilding of the slums—with their 7 million dilapidated dwellings—which shame this Nation and its cities."

Just as the Douglas and Kaiser Reports perceived a housing problem requiring heroic solutions, so too did judges see a need for brave new theories and approaches. In the landmark *Javins* case Judge Wright referred to the "increasingly severe shortage of adequate housing" to justify his new approach."[153] In support of this reference to an "increasingly severe shortage," he cited the Kaiser Committee Report, and on related issues cited the Douglas Commission Report. Other leading cases simply assumed that the growing housing shortage was so self-evident as not to warrant extended discussion or citation.[155]

---

[142] President's Comm. on Urban Hous., A Decent Home (1968) [hereinafter cited as A Decent Home].

[153] Javins v. First National Realty, 428 F.2d 1071, 1079 (D.C. Cir. 1970).

[155] *See, e.g.,* Green v. Superior Court, 10 Cal.3d 616, 517 P.2d 1168, 111 Cal.Rptr. 704 (1974) * * *; Marini v. Ireland, 56 N.J. 130, 265 A.2d 526 (1970) * * *.

3. Reconciling the Perception and the Reality

The substantial improvement in the quantity, quality, and affordability of housing in the fifties and sixties is not inconsistent with the view that heroic measures were urgently needed to improve housing conditions. The 1968 House Report that accompanied the historic Housing and Urban Development Act of 1968 implicitly took this position when it recognized prior achievements, but simultaneously deprecated them:

> While we can take pride in these accomplishments, they have fallen far short of today's needs. . . . A basic factor in the magnitude and urgency of our present housing problems has been the failure to include all parts of our population in the general rise in incomes and wealth. . . . Because of this contrast and the unrest it has created, the task of our housing and urban development programs is more critical than ever.

It is not possible, however, to reconcile completely the reality of steadily improving housing conditions with the perception of an increasingly severe shortage of housing. In 1968, the public consensus seemed to hold that housing conditions were actually getting worse, whereas in fact, they were getting better. Smaller shortcomings loomed larger in the eyes of the observer in 1968 than larger shortcomings had loomed in the eyes of earlier observers. We had developed an increased sensitivity to the gap between the reality and the ideal; a reduced tolerance for imperfections.

4. The Practical Effect of the Decreased Tolerance for Shortcomings in the Nation's Housing

In enacting the landmark Housing and Urban Development Act of 1968, Congress explicitly adopted as a national goal the Kaiser Committee's recommendation to produce or rehabilitate 26 million housing units over the next ten years. Although the goal was not fully achieved, Congress vastly increased housing expenditures, and housing programs proliferated in the years following the 1968 Act. Similarly, the general perception of a housing crisis contributed to the development of new judicial doctrines and to the drafting of the Model Code of 1969. The Model Code served as the basis for URLTA [Uniform Residential Landlord Tenant Act], which in turn became an important force for change in the seventies.

B. What Made Formerly Tolerable Housing Conditions Now Intolerable?

1. The Civil Rights Movement

A major thesis of this article is that the civil rights movement of the sixties was the dominant force behind the changes in landlord-tenant law in the late sixties and early seventies.[160] It created a climate of activism that demanded prompt, dramatic changes. Judges and legislators responded accordingly.

Although the post World War II civil rights struggle started as a movement against segregation and blatant racism in the South, by the early 1960s, it had assumed a more national character. The national character of the movement perhaps had its symbolic beginning on January 1, 1963, when Martin Luther King, Jr., made his immortal "I have a dream" speech to commemorate the centennial of the Emancipation Proclamation. On August 28, 1963, some 200,000 people, black and white, from the North and South, marched on Washington to demonstrate their support for racial justice. In March 1964, President Johnson declared a "national war on poverty" and in July 1964, he signed the Civil Rights Act of 1964 into law. These efforts, however, did not succeed in halting the militant phase of the civil rights movement, which had already begun. There were riots in black sections of New York and Philadelphia that summer.

Violent civil rights protests escalated dramatically in the summer of 1965. The riots in the Watts section of Los Angeles left thirty-four persons dead and $40 million in property destroyed. In the summer of 1967, there were race riots in Cleveland, Chicago, and Atlanta. In the summer of 1967, there were riots in 127 American cities, killing at least 77 and injuring at least 4,000 people. In Detroit the disturbances were so severe that federal troops were called in—the first use of federal troops to maintain order since 1942. Significantly, in view of the leading role the courts in Washington, D.C. were to play in landlord-

---

160 * * * Although * * * change in landlord-tenant law would have occurred in the United States even without these two social forces, I still would argue that the catalyst for change in the United States was the civil rights movement and the Vietnam War. I freely concede, however, that if these two events had not occurred other events probably would have precipitated these changes in landlord-tenant law. The anachronistic law of landlord-tenant was a tinderbox waiting to be ignited by a spark that could originate from any number of sources.

tenant law, there was also an episode of arson and rock throwing in that city.

No judge sitting in Washington in 1968 could fail to have been affected by the civil rights movement unfolding before him—least of all Judge J. Skelly Wright. James Skelly Wright was born and raised in New Orleans and received his college and law school education at Loyola University in that city. After practicing law first as an assistant U.S. Attorney and then as a U.S. Attorney, he was appointed a United States District Judge in 1949. In his work in the federal courts in New Orleans, he was intimately involved in desegregation law, and from his earliest days on the bench had shown a sensitivity to the demands of black citizens for equal treatment.

Even before *Brown v. Board of Education*[173] was decided in 1954, Judge Wright twice ordered Louisiana State University to admit black students to its programs. In 1960, he became known in New Orleans as the "integration judge" when he became the first judge in the deep South to order desegregation of the public schools.

By the end of 1960, Skelly Wright had become the most hated man in New Orleans. Pairs of federal marshals alternated in eight-hour shifts at his home to ensure his physical safety, and they escorted him to and from work. With few exceptions, old friends would step across the street to avoid speaking to him.

Judge Wright was elevated to the United States Court of Appeals for the District of Columbia by President Kennedy and began sitting there in 1962. The court during that period heard, among other matters, appeals involving landlord-tenant disputes that arose in the District of Columbia. Only six years after his appointment, Judge Wright wrote his important opinion barring retaliatory evictions.[178] And only two years later, he wrote his landmark *Javins* opinion. During the years immediately preceding these opinions many significant events had occurred including the march on Washington, the race riots throughout the country, the passage of the Civil Rights Acts of 1964 and 1968, and the assassination of Martin Luther King, Jr. In a candid letter to me, Judge Wright acknowledged that his opinions in the landlord-tenant area were influenced by sympathy for the black struggle of those years. It is reasonable to assume that other judges were similarly influenced.

UNITED STATES COURT OF APPEALS
WASHINGTON, D.C. 20001-2867

J. Skelly Wright
United States Circuit Judge

October 14, 1982

Professor Edward H. Rabin
School of Law
University of California, Davis
Davis, California 95616

Dear Professor Rabin:
Why the revolution in landlord-tenant law is largely traceable to the 1960's rather than decades before I really cannot say with any degree of certainty. Unquestionably the Vietnam War and the civil rights movement of the 1960's did cause people to question existing institutions and authorities. And perhaps this inquisition reached the judiciary itself. Obviously, judges cannot be unaware of what all people know and feel.

With reference to your specific question, I was indeed influenced by the fact that, during the nationwide racial turmoil of the sixties and the unrest caused by the injustice of racially selective service in Vietnam, most of the tenants in Washington, D.C. slums were poor and black and most of the landlords were rich and white. There is no doubt in my mind that these conditions played a subconscious role in influencing my landlord and tenant decisions.

I came to Washington in April 1962 after being born and raised in New Orleans, Louisiana for 51 years. I had never been exposed, either as a judge or as a lawyer, to the local practice of law which, of course, included landlord and tenant cases. I was Assistant U.S. Attorney, U.S. Attorney, and then U.S. District Court judge in New Orleans before I joined the U.S. Court of Appeals in Washington. It was my first exposure to landlord and tenant cases, the U.S. Court of Appeals here being a writ court to the local court system at the time. I didn't like what I saw, and I did what I could to ameliorate, if not eliminate, the injustice involved in the way many of the poor were required to live in the nation's capital.

---

[173] 347 U.S. 483 (1954).
[178] Edwards v. Habib, 397 F.2d 687 (D.C. Cir. 1968).

I offer no apology for not following more closely the legal precedents which had cooperated in creating the conditions that I found unjust.

Sincerely,
s/J. Skelly Wright

* * *

III

Effect of the Revolution in Landlord-Tenant Law on Housing Conditions

The revolution in landlord-tenant law was one in which courts and legislatures attempted to improve housing conditions for tenants. Many critics of the revolution argued that regardless of intent, the revolution would hurt tenants more than it would help them. This Part examines this proposition.

A. The Literature

1. Theoretical Studies and Predictions

a. Mainstream Analyses. It is arguable that each increased tenant protection and landlord duty must ultimately be paid for by the consumers of rental housing, the tenants. Those least able to pay increased rents will lose more than they gain from additional protections. Illustrative of this view is an influential article by Charles Meyers.[221] Professor Meyers addressed the following fact pattern, adapted from one posed by the Restatement (Second) of Property:

> Landlord leases an apartment to Tenant on a month-to-month basis for $30 per month. The apartment is located in a slum and does not comply with the housing code in several important respects. Both Landlord and Tenant are aware of the violations but agree to enter into the lease anyway.

Under the *Restatement Second* rule, as ultimately adopted, the landlord would still have a duty of providing habitable premises. If the landlord breaches this duty, the tenant would be entitled to the usual contract remedies resulting from an agreement that is "unconscionable or significantly against public policy." Professor Meyers summarized his objections to the Restatement Second's position as follows:

> In summary, the economic consequences of the Restatement rules on habitability are likely to be the following:
>
> 1) Some proportion of the substandard rental housing stock would be upgraded and rents would be raised to cover the added costs. Tenants formerly occupying the housing would either be forced out or be required to pay a higher proportion of their income for rent. Those tenants who are unable or unwilling to pay for the upgraded housing will move out, creating an increased demand for lower-priced, lower-quality housing.
>
> 2) For some proportion of the substandard rental housing stock, rents could not be raised, but landlords could still upgrade the housing without incurring a deficit. In these cases the tenants would enjoy a short-term wealth transfer, for they would enjoy better housing at no increase in rent. But low-income tenants as a class would not benefit in the long run, for the covenant of habitability will retire this component of the housing stock sooner than would otherwise be the case and will discourage new investment in low-rent housing.
>
> 3) The third portion of the substandard housing stock will be abandoned as soon as the owner determines that income will not cover the expenses of Restatement repairs and concludes that this deficit is likely to persist.

Other commentators have held similar views.[226]

b. Dissident Theories. Perhaps the most ambitious attempt to demonstrate that under certain conditions code enforcement could improve housing conditions without leading to increased rents was an article by Professor Bruce Ackerman.[227] The Ackerman article was the subject of an extremely critical review by Professor Komesar.[228] It is unnecessary to repeat here the substance of the criticism. It is sufficient to note that even Professor Ackerman recognized that poor tenants would benefit from housing code enforcement only given certain assumptions. Among the more questionable of these is the assumption that non-slum-dwellers will refrain from moving into former slum buildings after they are brought up to code standards. This assumption is crucial because if

---

[221] Meyers, *The Covenant of Habitability and the American Law Institute,* 27 STAN. L. REV. 879 (1975).

[226] *See, e.g.,* * * * Berger, *The New Residental Tenancy Law—Are Landlords Public Utilities?,* 60 NEB. L. REV. 707 (1981) * * *.

[227] Ackerman, *Regulating Slum Housing Markets on Behalf of the Poor: Of Housing Codes, Housing Subsidies and Income Redistribution Policy,* 80 YALE L.J. 1093 (1971).

[228] Komesar, *Return to Slumville: A Critique of the Ackerman Analysis of Housing Code Enforcement and the Poor,* 82 YALE L.J. 1175 (1973).

upgrading a slum building attracted persons who would not otherwise live in the building, rents would rise and the original slum-dwellers might be harmed rather than helped by the upgrading. Even if Professor Ackerman's assumption is valid in some cases, he ignores the possibility that existing residents of a slum area, who might otherwise choose to leave when their income permits, would be more likely to stay if the area or building were brought up to code. If this latter possibility occurred—as it surely has in some cases—rents in the slum area would rise due to increased demand, and the poorer slum-dwellers still might be injured rather than helped by the code enforcement program.

Another article, written by Professor Markovitz, also defends housing codes.[231] Markovitz argued that a code enforcement program would normally benefit tenants more than it would hurt them. Markovitz's analysis, however, is fatally flawed. At most, he proves only that certain tenants will be helped by a code enforcement program more than certain other tenants will be injured. His model measures the magnitude of the benefit by the dollars that benefited tenants would have paid for the improvement had payment been required. The model measures the magnitude of the detriment by the dollars that would be necessary to compensate the injured tenants for the detrimental effects of code enforcement. Assuming that Markovitz's analysis is correct and that the dollar amount of the former is greater than the dollar amount of the latter, this still leaves the injured tenants worse off than before code enforcement because code enforcement programs do not provide a mechanism by which benefited tenants compensate injured tenants. In Markovitz's model, the injured tenants are the poorest tenants, and the benefited tenants are the wealthier tenants. In fact, the poorer the tenant, the more he will be injured by the code enforcement program. Code enforcement programs presumably attempt to ameliorate the housing deficiencies faced by the poorest members of society. Because Markovitz's analysis implicitly recognizes that the poorest tenants are hurt rather than helped by such programs, his article hardly provides powerful support for code enforcement programs. Although Professor Markovitz would surely argue to the contrary, his article tends to support the mainstream position that code enforcement policies will hurt more than help poor tenants.

B. An Alternative Analysis

The mainstream analysis was undoubtedly correct in predicting that vigorous code enforcement would tend to discourage the preservation or production of housing and thus tend to create a scarcity of rental housing. This tendency, however, was outweighed by other factors that improved rental housing conditions. During the seventies all income classes of tenants enjoyed more spacious accommodations with better facilities and lower rents, after adjusting for inflation and differences in quality. Rental housing improved because during the seventies housing consumers developed a heightened preference for ownership status over rental status. This benefited those consumers who remained as tenants because less competition existed for rental housing. Conversely, the change in consumer preferences discouraged landlords from building new unsubsidized housing units, and tended to depress rents and profits of landlords.

Regardless of any change in consumer preferences, the long-term trend toward improved housing conditions and living standards continued. Also, during the seventies there was a massive increase in housing subsidies for the poor. If the revolution in landlord-tenant law affected the supply of rental housing detrimentally, the countervailing combination of generally improving living standards, increased housing subsidies, and changes in consumer preferences provided a more significant beneficial effect.

On the other hand, four facts seem to support the prediction of mainstream analysts that increased tenants' rights would tend to cause a shortage of rental housing, with a concomitant increase in average rents. During the seventies: (1) tenants' average rent-to-income ratios increased significantly; (2) the rental housing business became less profitable; (3) construction of unsubsidized rental housing units fell, relative to construction of other housing; (4) vacancy rates decreased. If interpreted properly, however, none of these facts indicates a growing shortage of rental housing. The rise in rent-to-income ratios and the fall in profitability and construction of rental housing were primarily the result of a reduced demand for rental housing by the more affluent segment of housing consumers. Similarly, the decrease in vacancy rates during the seventies is not a positive indicator of a growing housing shortage.

* * *

---

[231] Markovitz, *The Distributive Impact, Allocative Efficiency, and Overall Desirability of Ideal Housing Codes: Some Theoretical Clarifications,* 89 HARV. L. REV. 1815 (1976).

The legal developments of the seventies reduced the growth in supply of rental housing less than the inflation of that period reduced the growth in demand; supply grew faster than demand despite legal developments that discouraged some construction. Reduced demand, not changes in legal doctrine, caused reduced profits.

The declining rental vacancy rate in the seventies requires a different explanation. Vacancy rates do not indicate the degree of tightness in the housing market. The decline in vacancy rates indicates that landlords moderated their asking prices in relation to market equilibrium prices. This moderation was caused, at least in part, by the deteriorating legal position of landlords. Thus, it appears that through a unique concatenation of historical events, the major statistically measurable effect of the previous decade's legal developments has been a lowering of the vacancy rate. This reflects an increased landlord predisposition to favor existing tenants whom landlords deem desirable over new tenants who might have characteristics that landlords deem undesirable. It is doubtful that the legal reformers of the seventies would have welcomed this bittersweet result.

In short, although certain statistics appear to suggest that changes in housing conditions resulted from changes in legal doctrine, they in fact offer little support for this proposition. The highly plausible theory that increased tenant protections, other things remaining equal, would reduce the supply of rental housing has been neither proved nor disproved by the evidence discussed in this article. Other things did not remain equal.

Note

Do either Glendon or Rabin have explanations for these decisions:

Sommer v. Kridel, 74 N.J. 446, 378 A.2d 767 (1977) and like cases, requiring landlords to mitigate their losses by making reasonable attempts to find a new tenant before suing a defaulting tenant for unpaid rent?

Kendall v. Ernest Pestana, Inc., 40 Cal.3d 488, 709 P.2d 837, 220 Cal. Rptr 818 (1985), and like cases, forbidding landlords from unreasonably withholding their consent to the sublease or assignment of leases.

Duncan Kennedy, *The Effect of the Warranty of Habitability on Low Income Housing: "Milking" and Class Violence*, 15 FLA. ST. U.L. REV. 485–494, 496–497, 502–506, 512–514, 518–519 (1987)*

In this article I argue that enforcement of a nondisclaimable warranty of habitability in leases of low income urban housing might, under particular market and institutional circumstances, benefit low income tenants at the expense of their landlords. This thesis is controversial. As Edward Rabin[1] recently put it, the "mainstream" view among writers on housing law is that the enforcement of a warranty of habitability will hurt tenants as a class, including low income tenants. I believe that the mainstream view is wrong, at least as far as one can tell on the basis of plausible assumptions and generally accepted analyses of the low income market.

---

[1] Rabin, *The Revolution in Residential Landlord-Tenant Law: Causes and Consequences*, 69 CORNELL L. REV. 517, 558 (1984).

The "dissident" view, according to Rabin, is that of Bruce Ackerman[3] and Richard Markovitz.[4] I start from different assumptions and reach somewhat different conclusions, but my analysis is based on their work, which I see as the most important contribution to the field to date.

My argument is as follows: According to the "filtering model" of low income housing supply, poor people are likely to live in neighborhoods where building values are declining, even when housing conditions are improving. Under conventional neoclassical microeconomic assumptions, we would expect landlords to undermaintain, or "milk," buildings in declining slum neighborhoods. The degree of undermaintenance is theoretically indeterminate. Enforcing a code or warranty should prevent it, prolong building life, and increase housing supply. Contrary to the conclusions of "mainstream" analysis, the effect of comprehensive code or warranty enforcement on the price and quantity of slum housing is therefore indeterminate. Selective enforcement could increase supply more than it decreases it, and depress rent levels for the poor. Institutional conditions make it likely that slum landlords will sometimes seriously rather than trivially undermaintain, and that neighborhood effects will amplify individual landlord decisions into large scale trends. Selective warranty enforcement against "milkers" is at least worth experiment, in neighborhoods where the model suggests it is likely to work.

I. The Filtering Model

No new housing, or very little, is currently built for poor people in urban areas. It has long been the case that new housing becomes available to the poor through trickle down, otherwise known as the filtering process. As higher income people build new housing for themselves in the suburbs, lower income people "filter up" through the existing stock, so that today's poor often live in housing built for an earlier middle class.

The filtering process involves steady decline in the value of existing housing, as new housing is built and lower income people move upward through the neighborhood chain. The reason for this, within the model, is that the new occupant of a given unit has lower income than the departing occupant, and should therefore offer less for that unit at any given amenity level. Because the unit commands less rent at a given level of maintenance expenditure, it generates less cash flow, and therefore has a lower capital value.

Maintenance also declines, because new residents will not pay as many dollars as older residents, out of their smaller incomes, for a given level of amenity. But, the new residents should still be getting more amenity for those dollars than they did in the older and less desirable structures they lived in before. Otherwise, they would not move.

If filtering is working right, the number of functioning units should grow no faster than the population (assuming constant preferences about household composition), but the composition of the stock should improve. There should be abandonment and conversion to nonresidential uses, corresponding to new construction, but only of housing that is so bad that, given the alternatives filtering down, no one can be found to rent it. (Much of the housing already abandoned through filtering lacked indoor plumbing, electricity, running water, central heating, and so forth.)

If the middle and upper classes build themselves new housing faster than old housing is abandoned or converted, the model suggests that the rent for buildings at the very end of the chain will eventually decline to a level that reflects only the price of ongoing maintenance (plus taxes) and premiums for good location. In other words, the Ricardian quasi-rent[8] for the structures themselves should decline to zero. Unmaintained housing, albeit the least desirable then in the stock, should be a free good, and its quality should increase steadily over time.

The reason for this is that landlords at the end of the chain have no bargaining power with tenants, other than for the provision of maintenance and location. A landlord who tried to charge rents that reflected more than maintenance (and location) would lose his tenants to the competition from the new units filtering down. As between similarly situated units available at the bottom, tenants should choose those that deliver the greatest amenity for the least maintenance cost.

---

[3] Ackerman, *Regulating Slum Housing Markets On Behalf of the Poor: Of Housing Codes, Housing Subsidies and Income Redistribution Policy*, 80 YALE L.J. 1093 (1971).

[4] Markovitz, *The Distributive Impact, Allocative Efficiency, and Overall Desirability of Ideal Housing Codes: Some Theoretical Clarifications*, 89 HARV. L. REV. 1815 (1976).

[8] A quasi-rent is a return to a factor that is in temporarily fixed supply but whose quantity can be increased over the long run. A true rent, by contrast, is a return to a factor like location or natural soil fertility whose quantity is just given.

Lower rents and cheaper home ownership opportunities in the neighborhoods into which the poor are moving should, according to the model, be at the expense of those long time owners in the area who decide to stay put. There are, however, strategies by which landlords caught in the downward chain reaction can minimize the losses allocated to them by filtering, and these involve shifting the losses to incoming and older tenants, and to banks.

If the rate of abandonment and conversion at the end of the chain is equal to or greater than the rate of new construction at the top of the chain (minus units absorbed by increased demand of the middle and lower middle class before they reach the bottom), then the stock of units available to the poor will remain constant or decrease. Landlords at the bottom will be able to charge rents that reflect the scarcity of units (quasi-rents) as well as location and maintenance costs.

Where that is the case, the poor receive the level of amenity they can afford, but only after they have subtracted from their incomes the part of their rent which reflects the scarcity of buildings. (This is the basic Henry George point.)[11] As a matter of fact, low income rents generally reflect substantial scarcity payments, as is evident from the fact that dilapidated buildings in slums have positive market value. One of the factors that counteracts the growth in supply of housing at the bottom of the chain is the landlord behavior known as milking to abandonment.

What follows is a model of landlord maintenance decisions in a declining neighborhood. The idea is to show that the behavior of a rational landlord facing decline may be socially undesirable, in a way that we might be able to cure by enforcing the warranty of habitability.

II. Definition of Milking

The specific landlord behavior involved I call "milking." I mean by milking the decision to reduce maintenance below the level necessary to keep a building in existence as a residential unit. In other words, the milking landlord treats his property as a wasting rather than a renewable asset. He adopts a strategy of renting for what the market will bear as the building deteriorates, fully understanding that within some relatively short period of time he will be out of business. Either tenants will no longer pay him anything, or the authorities will close the building. At that point, he expects the building to have no market value. He will walk away from it, give it away, or lose it to tax foreclosure.

Take the longtime owner with no mortgage debt and small holdings in the area. Suppose he is taken by surprise when decline sets in, and does not sell until the value of his property has fallen sharply, reflecting the common expectation that rents have begun an irreversible decline. The new tenants moving in (and old ones as well) are willing and able to pay rents that would maintain the area at a marginally lower level than when the departing affluent were there, but it does not follow that it is rational for the landlord to provide this service.

He faces a trade-off. Cutting back maintenance will lead to a shorter life for the asset and reduce the rent he can charge, but it will also reduce current outlays. What is the right solution for him? It depends on how rapidly rental income will decline if he continues to maintain at the old level, on how sensitive rents will be to declines in amenity if he decides to cut back maintenance, and on how fast the building will deteriorate for a given reduction in maintenance.

Suppose the landlord expects rents to decline very quickly no matter what he does, that they will not decline much faster if he reduces amenity, and that he can keep going at low or zero maintenance for a long time before he loses the building. Under these conditions, it may be a rational investment strategy to stop or reduce maintenance and let the building gradually deteriorate toward abandonment. This is milking, a maintenance strategy that treats the building as a wasting asset rather than an indefinitely renewable long-term investment.

III. When Is Milking Rational?

The case that I am going to deal with is that of the landlord who wants to reduce maintenance below the renewable level before rent falls so low that he has no other choice. In other words, I am going to argue that it will sometimes be rational for a landlord to begin to milk a building before the rent roll has fallen so far that rent will not cover maintenance (plus taxes, insurance, and a normal profit). And I am going to argue that it would be a good idea to enforce the warranty of habitability to prevent this behavior.

It is easy to see why a slum landlord milks a building when the exodus of more affluent tenants filtering up and out has driven rent down so far that

[11] H. George, Progress and Poverty (1879).

keeping the building viable would put him in the red. Likewise, it is easy to see that a stable low income neighborhood might be abandoned through milking if the income of long-term tenants declined far enough (due to a reduction in welfare payments, for example). But where rent will cover maintenance (plus taxes, insurance, and a normal profit), it would seem the landlord is hurting his own interests if he in effect destroys his property by undermaintenance.

Imagine that we know how much a tenant will pay for the unit kept in renewable shape, and how much a tenant will pay for it if the landlord stops maintenance and the unit begins to deteriorate. So long as this rent premium for amenity is greater than the cost of providing it, we assume that profit-maximizing landlords will not milk. They will go on maintaining in order to maximize their income from the building. But now suppose that as the neighborhood deteriorates there comes a time when tenants will not pay a premium for the maintained premises equal to the cost to the landlord of keeping them that way. The landlord will at least consider stopping maintenance payments since those payments no longer generate a concomitant increase in rent.

But if he stops maintaining, he will lose his investment when the building becomes uninhabitable or is condemned by the city. Moreover, each monthly rent payment will be smaller for the unmaintained premises, though the decrease will not be as great as the savings on maintenance. In other words, maintenance does not increase monthly income by as much as it costs, but it does prevent loss of a future income stream and earns back a part of its cost. The landlord will have to offset the gains from milking (generated by the suspension of maintenance payments) against these losses (reduction of the monthly payments for now less desirable premises, and reduction in the longevity of the income stream).

The income lost through milking should, under conventional economic assumptions, become less and less as the neighborhood declines. First, the difference between rent payments for the building maintained and for the building unmaintained should become smaller and smaller. This follows from the conventional assumption that poorer and poorer tenants will offer a smaller and smaller premium for any given quantity of amenity. In other words, imagine that a family with a $15,000 per year income will offer $400 per month for the landlord's premises if they are deteriorating toward abandonment, and an additional $100 per month if the landlord is maintaining at the renewable level.

If family income falls to $10,000, the family could only offer, say, $300 per month for deteriorating premises, and a premium of $75 for the same apartment maintained. This means that as the neighborhood declines, the landlord foregoes less and less monthly income when he decides on a given cutback of maintenance.

Second, as the neighborhood deteriorates, the value of the income stream the landlord will have to forego if he abandons becomes smaller and smaller. Imagine that if the landlord maintained at the renewable level, he would have eleven years of (declining) income before rent payments became so small they would not cover maintenance (plus taxes, insurance, and normal profit). Let us say that at that point (eleven years) it would make sense for him to stop maintenance altogether, and just collect marginal rent until he lost the building, after, say, another four years. Under the best of circumstances, the life of the building is only fifteen years from the start of neighborhood decline.

Now imagine that he starts milking as soon as neighborhood decline confronts him with falling rent, and as a result, he loses the building after four years. He has foregone eleven years of (declining) rent payments. But for each year he delays the start of milking, the foregone income stream is one year shorter. Thus if he starts milking after six years of declining rent, and it still takes four years for the building to leave the stock (at the ten year mark), he foregoes only five years of rental income, years in which the unit would have commanded relatively little anyway.

As the neighborhood deteriorates and the building approaches the eleven-year mark (at which the landlord is sure to stop maintaining, we suppose, because rent payments have gone through the floor), the savings from eliminating maintenance decline. The landlord who milks prematurely in year ten saves only a year's expense. But the gains from maintaining become smaller faster, as the tenant premium for amenity declines, and the foregone income stream becomes shorter and shorter, approaching zero. At some point before year eleven, the gains from milking must exceed the gains from maintaining, and at that point a rational landlord will let the building go down.

IV. Graphical Illustration of the Rationality of Milking

In this section, I will illustrate graphically the conclusion that, under the assumptions I have been making, there must come a time, before rent falls below maintenance cost (plus taxes, insurance, and profit), when a rational landlord will decide to milk his building. If you do not like graphs, and are satisfied with the statement in the text above, I suggest you skip to the next section. If you would prefer a more elegant and more definitive mathematical statement of the conclusion, I can only apologize for my inability to provide one.

As always, we need heroic assumptions in order to reduce the problem to graphic form. As always, the claim is that though artificial, they do not obviate the interest of the result. The first assumption is that the landlord operates either at a renewable level, or at zero maintenance. Second, whenever he stops maintaining, the rent he can charge falls instantly from the renewable to the "deteriorating" level, and remains there for four years, at which point the building leaves the stock. Making both rent and building life continuous functions of variable maintenance expenditure would greatly complicate the analysis without changing the outcome.

In Figure 1, line AB represents the declining rent offers through time for the premises maintained at the renewable level (this is not a demand curve: it shows the dollar rent for a given unit in succeeding years, rather than dollar rent for more and more units). Line CB shows the rent for the premises if the landlord is spending no money at all on maintenance. AB and CB slope downward through time because tenants are getting poorer and poorer and can offer less and less for the premises, whether maintained or deteriorating. They converge because as tenants become poorer the rent premium for amenity declines.

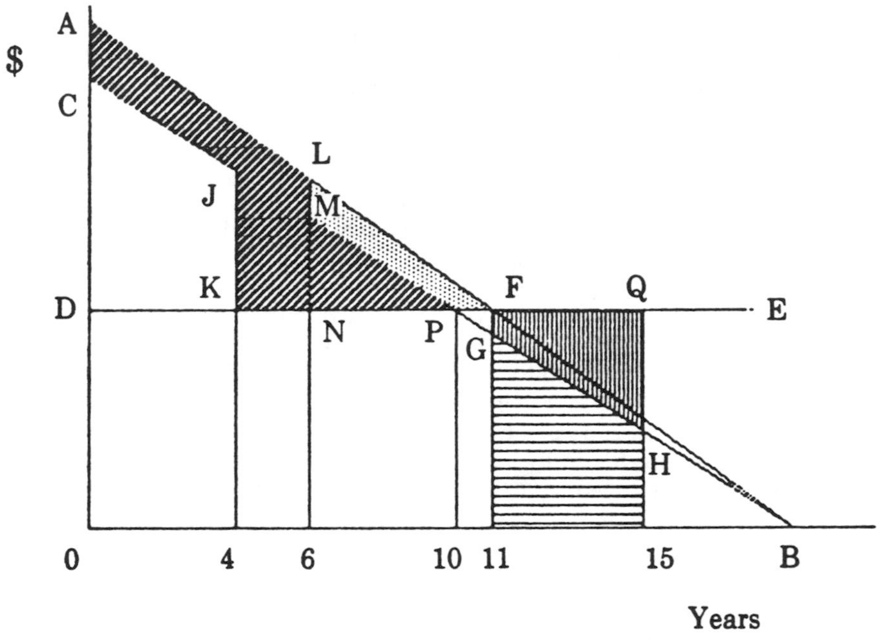

Figure 1:
Comparison of Revenues from Milking and Maintaining

Line OD is the amount of maintenance needed to keep the unit in the stock (the renewable level), and it remains the same through time, as shown in line DE. Distance OD is greater than distance CA because during the period that interests us tenants are unwilling to pay a rent premium for amenity equal to the cost of maintenance at the renewable level. At point F (year eleven) the rent offer for the premises maintained falls below the cost of maintenance, as line AB intersects line DE. My goal is to show that a rational landlord will begin to milk at a point to the left of (earlier than) F, that is, at a time when tenants are still offering enough rent to keep the building in the stock.

Suppose that at time O, the landlord considers the possibility of beginning to milk, and compares it with a policy of continuing to maintain until, at point F, it becomes an obviously losing course. Maintaining will yield, first, an income represented by the area ADF (total revenue of OAF[11], less maintenance cost of ODF[11]). At year eleven, the landlord will stop maintaining, and earn a milker's terminal income of [11]GH[15] during the four years the building remains in the stock in deteriorating condition.

Now suppose he begins to milk at time O. Rent falls immediately to OC, and continues to decline for the four years the unit remains in the stock. Total income is OCJ[4], with no deduction for maintenance, because none is done. This course is less remunerative than the alternative, because the net revenue lost through milking, area ACJKF plus area [11]GH[15], is patently greater than the net revenue gained, area ODK[4].

But now suppose that the landlord waits until year six, and then reconsiders a milking course. Rent will fall from [6]L to [6]M. He will lose the premium for amenity for the five years remaining to year eleven and point F, represented by area LMPF. He will also lose the terminal milking profits represented by area [11]GH[15]. He will gain four years of suspended maintenance payments, represented by area [6]NP[10].

Milking is more profitable than maintaining as of year six, because area [6]NP[10] is greater than area LMPF plus area [11]GH[15]. The visual test of this is as follows:

[6]NP[10] = [11]FQ[15] (both equal four years of maintenance costs).

[6]NP[10] minus [11]GH[15] therefore = Area FGHQ.

Area LMPF is, by visual inspection, less than area FGHQ.

Therefore, the saving from milking, area [6]NP[10] is greater than the lost revenue, area LMPF plus [11]GH[15], from maintaining to point F.

* * *

V. The Significance of Milking

There are three important points about this conclusion. First, it means that if we permit milking, the actual life of the building (under the assumptions) will always be shorter than the fifteen-year life span it would have if we selectively enforced the warranty of habitability. Assume that we can enforce the warranty just enough to compel the landlord to maintain the building at the renewable level. In our hypothetical, it would be eleven years until the rent did not cover this cost (plus taxes, insurance, and normal profit). At that point, if we continue to enforce the warranty, the landlord will walk away. But if we then relax enforcement, she will milk for four years, to the end of the building's fifteen-year life span. In other words, if real world circumstances corresponded to the model, selectively enforcing the warranty could extend the lives of buildings in declining neighborhoods.

Second, and equally important, the length of the extension is indeterminate unless we have a great deal of specific data about the building and the market. It might be the case that milking made sense from the very beginning of neighborhood decline. And it might also be the case that it only made sense in the very last part of the cycle. The life extension brought about by enforcing the warranty might be very substantial, or trivial, or anything in between.

Third, extending the life of buildings in the stock adds to the supply of housing. Thus if the warranty extends building life, it should also depress rents, an outcome not contemplated by the dominant view. Of course, the amount of the supply-increasing, rent decreasing effect is indeterminate, and we have to assess it in the context of the general impact of the warranty on the price and quantity of low income housing.

* * *

VIII. Critiques of the Supply Effect

It seems to be a common intuition among people with law and economics training that this result just has to be wrong: it should not be possible to help the poor by enforcing the warranty. I will respond here to two different lines of attack.

First, the withdrawal of the milking option reduces the profitability of low income housing by increasing its cost to landlords, and should therefore reduce supply, not just through abandonment but also by reducing new construction and slowing the filtering process. Second, even if life extension through an antimilking warranty drove prices down, any benefit to the poor would be wiped out either by the choking off of filtering (this time by lower prices rather than by higher costs), or by an influx of middle income tenants bidding for upgraded units.

With respect to the first, there are really two arguments. There is the question of the impact on upper income construction of loss of the milking option if and when the building filters down. In other words, a perfectly foresighted builder would calculate into the expected income stream of a new unit some discounted sum reflecting the advantage of milking over maintaining in the final stages of decline. Ackerman argues convincingly that uncertainty as to which neighborhoods will decline and when makes it unlikely that upper income builders' reactions to code enforcement in the slums will have an impact on new construction.[25]

But enforcing the warranty (or code) might affect landlord decisions, and therefore supply, at the point when neighborhood decline begins. Landlords who know they will be forced to keep maintaining, at least until rents have fallen below maintenance costs (plus taxes, insurance, and normal profit), will take a less sanguine view of the future of their investment than they would if they knew they could start to milk whenever it appeared to be the profit-maximizing strategy.

Under the simplest kind of filtering model, this reduction of landlord expectations of gain will not affect the filtering process. The simplest models assume either a chain of single houses of declining quality, or that each neighborhood is homogeneous and filters down as a unit. If this is the case, the effect of new construction at the top of the chain is that each successive owner further down simply loses his earlier tenants who move up.

In this situation owners have no choice but to rent to the people moving in from below, at whatever price will clear the market. The full impact of the prohibition on premature milking falls on low income landlords. Because they are "locked in," meaning that they no longer have higher income tenants, they have to let their units filter. Once they have done this, it is in their interest to go on operating until rent no longer covers whatever maintenance is compelled through the warranty. Even though they could make more money if they were allowed to milk, they will not, as the previous analysis showed, prematurely withdraw their units by abandonment.

Now suppose that new construction for the rich allows more middle income people to move out of their old neighborhood. But instead of imagining that these units go automatically to the poor, imagine that some longtime middle income residents will increase their consumption of space, say turning three-family into two-family houses, if prices are low enough. In this model, the ultimate disposition of the vacancies created by new construction depends on the point of equilibrium between the price middle income people will pay for more space and the price poor people will pay to filter up into a new neighborhood.

Even in this more complicated model, the warranty does not slow filtering. Landlords have no reason to discriminate as between middle income and low income tenants. The whole neighborhood will eventually decline as new construction elsewhere further softens demand. The loss of the option of premature milking means that landlords will have fewer options, regardless of who they rent to.

But now suppose that filtering is occurring in the context of residential segregation by income class, brought about by the willingness of middle income renters to pay a premium to live in an entirely middle income neighborhood. Further suppose a border area or transition zone that is less attractive to the middle class than their core neighborhood, and more attractive to the poor than theirs. Border landlords can decide which class of tenants to rent to, and their decisions determine the equilibrium position of the dividing line between zones.

Suppose landlords assume that the choice to move a border unit from middle to low income occupancy will likely be irreversible, and that the course of events over the period of decline will be different in the two areas. In the shrinking middle income area prices will decline, but more slowly than in the low income area, as the middle class departs and the better off among the poor move in behind them. Abandonment occurs only in the core of the low income area.

Under these assumptions, the milking option is likely to be more attractive to low income than middle income landlords. A border landlord who loses the milking option because of the warranty will find low income tenants marginally less attractive, compared to middle income tenants, than he did before. It follows that enforcing the warranty might slow the rate of filtering. Softening demand has to drive prices down further in the middle income area before it makes sense for a border landlord to switch a unit from middle to low income occupancy. (On the other hand, it is easy to imagine that neighborhood effects, in this case group expectations about what is going to happen to the border zone as a whole, will be

---

[25] Ackerman, *Regulating Slum Housing Markets on Behalf of the Poor: Of Housing Codes, Housing Subsidies and Income Redistribution Policy,* 80 YALE L.J. 1093, 1117 (1971). *Compare* Komesar, *Return to Slumville: A Critique of the Ackerman Analysis of Housing Code Enforcement and the Poor,* 82 YALE L.J. 1175, 1188–91 (1973) (arguing that the costs of a code enforcement program would have a significant effect on new housing construction) *with* Ackerman, *More On Slum Housing and Redistribution Policy: A Reply to Professor Komesar,* 82 YALE L.J. 1194, 1204–06 (1973) (arguing that uncertainties as to the future effects of code enforcement make it unlikely that builders would consider those future costs in new construction planning).

so strong that a unit will filter or not on that basis, without much sensitivity to changes in the profitability of individual buildings.)

What this means is that in estimating the overall impact of enforcing the warranty, we have to take account of the possible slowing of the filtering process, along with abandonment and rent increases through upgrading. This is an effect we cannot evade even by highly selective enforcement.

When we turn to the impact of a fall in rents, the situation is less complex. First, it is correct that if the warranty increases supply and decreases rents, there will be a slowing of the filtering process. But this is not a coherent objection to the claim that the warranty will help the poor at the expense of their landlords. The reduction in filtering occurs because the poor are unwilling to bid as much for housing filtering down as they were before life extension increased the low income stock. As a result, middle income renters will acquire a greater share of the space made available by new construction for the rich. The warranty therefore benefits them as well as those below them in the chain.

Second, the filtering model presupposes that the poorest households rent at the bottom of the chain. If enforcing the warranty were to increase supply by extending the lives of buildings that were about to be prematurely milked, and drive down the prices for units at the end of the chain, it is possible that there would be an influx of middle income people who would bid these now cheap units up and away from the poor.

The model we have been discussing is one of neighborhood decline. Within the standard filtering analysis, incomes do not increase and their distribution does not change. New construction by the rich is the motor that drives the system. The reason for premature milking is failure of demand for maintained low income housing.

In this model, there will indeed be some influx of middle income tenants to the low income neighborhood in response to a fall in rent there. But this effect, like the slowing of filtering, occurs because the poor are no longer willing to pay enough for now more plentiful housing to keep all of it in their hands. If the warranty depresses rents, some middle income families will bid against existing residents, and the border between neighborhoods may move. Middle income people will thus benefit. They will filter backwards to the extent that the slackening of low income demand makes it cheaper for them to convert in the slums than to move up the chain in response to new construction by the rich.

This is not to deny even for a moment the reality of the phenomenon of gentrification, in which increased and redirected middle class demand displaces and impoverishes low income tenants. When this happens, it is typically driven by market forces that dwarf the conceivable impact of a warranty that merely requires maintenance at the renewable level. It would be silly to blame it on the warranty, or as I will argue later on, to expect the warranty to do more than a little to stop it. We need other ways to deal with it (rent control, eviction for cause laws, condo conversion restrictions, removal permits, and so forth).

But it is wrong to conclude from the fact that gentrification occurs that it is occurring or will occur everywhere. In many neighborhoods and indeed whole regions of the country there is little or no danger from this direction. The argument for the warranty is addressed to those situations where the reality is neighborhood decline and the goal is to stop displacement through abandonment rather than through middle class buy out.

I conclude that it is perfectly possible that an enforcement campaign that attacked all substandard conditions could slow down premature milking so much that, even with substantial upgrading and abandonment, rents would end up lower and quantities greater than they were to begin with. But the campaign could end up with just the opposite result, or it could improve quality while leaving price and quantity unchanged. Which it will be is a question that can be settled only by an appeal to the facts of particular cases. Microeconomic theory at this level of abstraction cannot tell us what to expect.

It is an important corollary that a policymaker working with this model does not have to choose between comprehensive enforcement and no enforcement at all. In this respect, the model is strikingly different from Ackerman's. If we can identify with confidence a single unit that is about to be prematurely milked, it makes sense to enforce the warranty against it to extend its life in the stock. This will increase supply, however marginally, and put downward pressure on rents.

* * *

XII. Neighborhood Effects and Unstable Equilibrium

In this section, I will argue that premature milking plays a more important role in the dynamics of neighborhood decline than appears from the analysis of individual buildings. Because the decision of one landlord influences that of his neighbors, there may be external effects, downward vicious cycles, and prisoner's dilemmas that lead to far more milking than suits anyone's interests. Where this is the case, warranty or code enforcement may work to bring about results that look good in efficiency terms, and * * * redistribute favorably to low income tenants.

People's decisions about how to treat the housing they own are affected by the decisions of their neighbors. For example, the value of rental property is a function not only of structure and upkeep, but of the structure and upkeep and occupancy of nearby buildings. Indeed, it is often the case that the market perception of the desirability of a neighborhood has a strong enough effect on the value of any given house to dwarf the impact on value of individual owner decisions about maintenance.

Because of these interconnections or externalities, it is possible for all the landlords in a neighborhood to find themselves "forced" to make investment decisions that all agree are worse for them than those that would occur if it were possible for them to act in concert. For example, every landlord might be able to invest more in maintenance of existing structures, hoping thereby to get higher rents and increase property values, were it not for the fact that each believes that others are and will continue disinvesting, so that the neighborhood is in an inevitable state of decline.

The most important implication of neighborhood effects is the possibility of an "unstable equilibrium" or "downward vicious cycle" in those neighborhoods that are at the end of the filtering chain. Remember that in its own terms the filtering model requires a process of declining housing values leading ultimately to abandonment or conversion. If neighborhood effects come into play, this process may not be "orderly": it may not lead to gradual declines with abandonment only of those units that have become unrentable because there is better housing now available to their former tenants.

Rather, the softening of values in a lower income neighborhood, along with the gradual influx of poorer tenants who are "filtering up" as old residents themselves move up and out, may cause a chain reaction. In particular, the milking of a building may destroy the viability of its neighbor so that it too has its highest valued use as a wasting asset. This is "blight." "A bad apple spoils the barrel." One shooting gallery spoils the neighborhood.

A milking outcome for the whole neighborhood may be the result of a prisoner's dilemma in which no owner can afford to invest in maintenance because so long as all other owners are milking, the investment is overwhelmingly likely to be lost. If it were possible to make and enforce an agreement to maintain without cost, such an agreement might be the most profitable strategy for all.

Once the downward chain reaction gets going, it may lead to far more abandonment in the neighborhoods where it began than the filtering model requires. Conversely, other neighborhoods that might, in an "orderly" process, undergo moderate decline may escape unscathed. Because of neighborhood effects and unstable equilibria, the market process of adjustment to new upper income housing construction in the suburbs may be a random but dramatic pattern of low income neighborhood destruction, combined with an equally random pattern of low income neighborhood stability or even upgrading.

XIII. Racism in the Filtering Process

Racism pervades the low income housing market, affecting the housing conditions of the poor in many different ways. Here we are concerned with classic housing discrimination. Housing discrimination constricts the black population of a city to a limited number of neighborhoods, whether by the use of force against black pioneers in white neighborhoods or through nonviolent refusals to sell or rent. It slows the filtering of units to poor blacks by preventing them from moving into white neighborhoods where values are softening due to the movement to the suburbs. The limiting of the possible supply of housing for the black poor will drive up the price even of unmaintained shelter in the ghetto, thereby squeezing low incomes. The squeeze means that poor black families will have less disposable income available to bid for amenity through maintenance at the renewable level.

The smaller the income available to bid for amenity, beyond what is necessary to buy the worst shelter, the more likely it becomes that the best course for the landlord is to milk the building. (As we saw earlier, milking becomes more profitable relative to maintaining as the premium for amenity gets smaller.) Milking ghetto buildings to abandonment means a permanent reduction in the low income housing supply, since incomes are too low to sustain new construction and discrimination prevents moving into neighboring areas (except in tipping cases). The result will be to raise the price of unmaintained shelter still higher, further reducing the desirability of maintaining vis-a-vis milking, and so on.

This might be called the self-feeding effect of racial discrimination on milking: Discrimination constricts the supply of bad housing by raising its price, which sops up the income available to bid for amenity through maintenance, making milking more attractive, and through milking further reducing the supply of housing while raising its price.

* * *

XVII. Conclusion

The problems of defining guidelines for identifying buildings that are viable, of framing rules so that they are administrable, and of choosing between public and private enforcement, or a combination of the two, are all difficult. An experimental attempt at serious code or warranty enforcement would have to face these problems, but I have nothing to say about them here. My argument has been that the "mainstream" analysis that would advise against such an experiment is incomplete because it leaves out potential supply-increasing effects of the warranty. Welfare economics does not, contrary to the mainstream view, suggest that the warranty will hurt the poor. Rather, the impact of comprehensive enforcement is indeterminate without detailed contextual analysis, and there is no reason in principle why selective enforcement should not reduce the price and increase the quantity of low income housing.

Note

Does the economic theory used by Duncan Kennedy in his *Milking* article also justify the use of rent control?

b. Federal "Open Housing" Controls

Housing discrimination was the last major area of public life to be dealt with by federal civil rights statutes and Supreme Court decisions. While many other areas of law dealing with race and poverty underwent dramatic transformations in the 1960's, racial housing patterns were left largely untouched by federal regulation. Years of civil rights demonstrations, Congressional debates, and public discussion, did not produce any results until the spring of 1968, just after the assassination of Martin Luther King. Both Congress and the Supreme Court then quickly took stabs at grappling with segregation in housing. Congress enacted Title VIII of the Civil Rights Act of 1968 immediately after King's death. A short time later, the Supreme Court rendered its opinion in *Jones v. Alfred Mayer Co.*, 392 U.S. 409 (1968), holding that Section 2 of the Thirteenth Amendment granted Congress broad power to remedy the lingering effects of slavery, even if the legislation moved beyond constraining the actions of states to control the actions of private persons, and that 42 U.S.C. §1982, originally adopted as part of the Civil Rights Act of 1866, prohibited racial discrimination in the sale of real property. The decision reinvigorated civil rights legislation that had gone virtually unused for a century and effectively lifted any lingering notion that Congress' ability to legislate on civil rights was limited to control of government activity by the state action provision of the Fourteenth Amendment.

Excerpts from two articles are reprinted below. The first, from Charles Lamb's *Congress, The Courts, and Civil Rights: The Fair Housing Act of 1968 Revisited*, recounts some of the difficulties in getting Congressional action on housing legislation. As you read it, recall that Dr. Martin Luther King, Jr. made a significant shift in tactics during the two years prior to his assassination, organizing marches against discrimination in housing in Chicago beginning in 1966, developing plans for a poor people's campaign, and supporting a strike by sanitation workers in Memphis just before his death. Perhaps the shifting politics of the Senate in the winter of 1968, particularly the change of heart by Senator Dirksen of Illinois, was related to these developments. The other excerpt, from John Calmore's *Fair Housing vs. Fair Housing: The Problems with Providing Increased Housing Opportunities Through Spatial Deconcentration*, was part of an ongoing debate on the wisdom of devoting large amounts of energy attempting to disperse African Americans in largely white communities. Additional segments of that debate may be found in Bittker, *The Case of the Checker-Board Ordinance: An Experiment in Race Relations*, 71 YALE L. J. 1387 (1962); Note, *The Integration Ordinance: Honi Soit Qui Mal Y Pense*, 17 STAN. L. REV. 280 (1965), and in the enormous literature on New Jersey's *Mt. Laurel* litigation.*

Continuing patterns of racial segregation in all major urban areas suggest that the issues surrounding race and housing are still largely unresolved. The literature reflects that ongoing concern. *See*, for example, Michael Potter, *Racial Diversity in Residential Communities: Societal Housing Patterns and a Proposal for a "Racial Inclusionary Ordinance,"* 63 S. CAL. L. REV. 1151 (1990); Rodney A. Smolla, *In Pursuit of Racial Utopias: Fair Housing, Quotas, and Goals in the 1980's*, 58 S. CAL. L. REV. 947 (1985); J. Gregory Richards, *Zoning for Direct Social Control*, 1982 DUKE L. J. 761.

*[Editor's Note: *Southern Burlington County N.A.A.C.P. v. Township of Mt. Laurel*, 67 N. J. 151, 336 A.2d 713 (1975); *Southern Burlington County N.A.A.C.P. v. Township of Mt. Laurel*, 92 N. J. 158, 456 A.2d 390 (1983)].

Charles M. Lamb, *Congress, The Courts, and Civil Rights: The Fair Housing Act of 1968 Revisited*, 27 VILL. L. REV. 1115, 1116-1126 (1982)*

II. THE LEGISLATIVE HISTORY OF TITLE VIII: PRESIDENTIAL LEADERSHIP AND CONGRESSIONAL INDIFFERENCE

Since the late 1950's, the United States Congress has had too few liberal critics of its role in promoting civil rights. For example, Gary Orfield, a well-known authority on both civil rights and Congress, acknowledges that Congress was a "graveyard for civil rights during the eight decades between 1875 and 1957."[16] However, he maintains that the congressional initiative in passing the Civil Rights Acts of 1957 and 1964 was instrumental to those enactments, and that Congress even went significantly beyond President John F. Kennedy's proposals to strengthen the 1964 Act.

Some commentators disagree with Orfield's view that Congress has exercised a leadership role in promoting civil rights.[20] More troubling, however, is Orfield's argument that Congress has been a proponent of laws to guarantee fair housing. For example, Orfield asserts that, two years prior to the passage of the Fair Housing Act of 1968, "there was a majority in each house in favor of fair-housing legislation" even though open housing was "an idea still considered suspect by much of the public."[22]

* * *

This portrayal of congressional leadership in fair housing is misleading. To be sure, many liberal congressmen from both political parties have periodically voiced substantial concern over housing discrimination. Nonetheless, Congress, as an institution, is a highly unlikely body to provide the type of leadership and direction necessary to overcome discriminatory housing practices and residential segregation. Congress lacks the centralized nature of the executive branch. Its diverse membership prevents it

[16] GARY ORFIELD, CONGRESSIONAL POWER: CONGRESS AND SOCIAL CHANGE 63 (1975).

[20] *See* Comment, *Title VI of the Civil Rights Act of 1964—-Implementation and Impact,* 36 GEO. WASH. L. REV. 824, 829-831 (1968). Contrary to Orfield, Rodgers and Bullock argue that instead of taking the initiative, Congress usually passes civil rights legislation only in a crisis situation. *See* H. RODGERS & C. BULLOCK, LAW AND SOCIAL CHANGE: CIVIL RIGHTS LAWS AND THEIR CONSEQUENCES 212-213 (1972). * * *

[22] ORFIELD, *supra* note 16, at 67-68.

from speaking with one voice on any issue, and its size slows the decision-making process considerably. The potential for congressional leadership in the area of housing desegregation is further undermined by the susceptibility of representatives and senators to pressures from constituents and special interest groups opposed to open housing. Such pressures resulted in the congressional failure to pass the Fair Housing Amendment Acts of 1979 and 1980, and in the patent inadequacies in the Home Mortgage Disclosure Act of 1975 and the Housing and Community Development Act of 1974.

Until an anxious President Johnson and a largely reluctant Congress joined forces to pass Title VIII of the Civil Rights Act of 1968, the federal government had rarely taken noteworthy steps toward the goal of achieving equal housing opportunity. Because of congressional resistance, however, Title VIII was substantially weakened before it ever reached President Johnson's desk for signing. Title VIII was "the result of political compromise, a product more of the desire for passage than the desire for a rational scheme for uprooting discrimination."[29] * * * The congressional bargaining of 1968 crippled the enforcement of Title VIII by providing HUD with only powers of conference, conciliation, and persuasion in resolving housing discrimination complaints.

Comprehensive legislation to fight housing discrimination was not introduced in Congress until 1966, and it was President Johnson who assumed the leadership role that resulted in the law's enactment. Indeed, Johnson was the first president to urge a national fair housing statute during the twentieth century. In his State of the Union message of January 8, 1964, Johnson pledged his administration to the goal of eliminating housing discrimination and asked Congress to pass related legislation. On January 27, 1964, Johnson once more spoke out publicly in favor of fair housing. This was long before a congressional majority had ever seriously considered the idea, for no hearings had yet been scheduled or convened on the subject.

Congress did not budge, but the President was persistent. In his January 12, 1966, State of the Union message, he recommended that Congress "take additional steps to insure equal justice for all of our people . . . by outlawing discrimination in the sale and rental of housing." Two weeks later, in his message to Congress on a program for cities and metropolitan areas, Johnson said:

> * * *
>
> Where housing is poor, schools are generally poor. Unemployment is widespread. Family life is threatened. The community's welfare burden is steadily magnified. These are the links in the chain of racial discrimination.
>
> This administration is working to break that chain—through aid to education, medical care, community action programs, job retraining, and the maintenance of a vigorous economy.
>
> The time has come when we should break one of its strongest links—the often subtle, but always effective force of housing discrimination. The impacted racial ghetto will become a thing of the past only when the Negro American can move his family wherever he can afford to do so.
>
> I shall, therefore, present to the Congress at an early date legislation to bar racial discrimination in the sale or rental of housing.

On April 28, 1966, in a special civil rights message to Congress, the President also emphasized that the legislative branch should "declare a national policy against racial discrimination in the sale or rental of housing, and . . . create effective remedies against discrimination in every part of America." When the House finally passed a weak version of the fair housing law on August 9, 1966, President Johnson issued a statement approving the House's action. But Johnson was disappointed. "This provision is not," he stressed, "as comprehensive as that we had sought." He added: "Our expectation turns now to the Senate, and we join in the hope and expectation that final action on the Civil Rights Act of 1966 will follow without unnecessary delay."

However, in 1966, fair housing legislation could scarcely get off the ground in the Senate. The vast majority of senators apparently subscribed to the view that the federal government should not interfere with property rights and that every individual has the right to do whatever he pleases with his private property.[45] The Senate failed to pass the proposed

---

[29] Note, *Discrimination in Employment and Housing: Private Enforcement of the Civil Rights Acts of 1964 and 1968*, 82 HARV. L. REV. 834–835 (1969).

[45] * * * Indeed, this idea is still in vogue with many congressmen. For example, in 1979, Senator Orrin G. Hatch, a Republican from Utah, stated that legislation updating Title VIII would lead to further "federal oppression," and "inordinate controls" by the federal government, "interfering with property rights" and "abrogating the rights of our society." * * * Similarly, Senator Alan K. Simpson, a

1966 legislation. The following year, congressional advocates of fair housing, led by Congressman Emanuel Celler, a Democrat from New York, were willing to settle for any statute that was "politically feasible."

Johnson was clearly upset with the Senate's refusal to pass the 1966 fair housing proposal. On February 15, 1967, the President presented, in detail, an outline of his legislative proposal to Congress, and urged once more that the majority overcome its entrenched opposition to housing desegregation. The proposed Civil Rights Act of 1967 contained a watered-down, "politically feasible" fair housing provision. Once more it passed in the House of Representatives, primarily because it was so weak that opponents of housing desegregation viewed it as meaningless. Debate on the Senate floor, however, was prolonged for over a month by southern Democrats, who condemned fair housing as "forced housing." Senator Everett Dirksen, a Republican from Illinois, and the Senate minority leader, joined the southern Democrats in their opposition. The bill ultimately died a slow death in the Senate, as its predecessor had in 1966, without ever being voted on.

In his civil rights message to Congress of January 24, 1968, President Johnson pressed once more for legislation aimed at fair housing.

* * *

This time the Senate responded positively. Senator Dirksen's role was especially critical in increasing the gradual momentum in the Senate in favor of fair housing legislation. In February, 1968, Dirksen switched his opposition to open housing and bargained a compromise proposal with the Democratic leadership. This compromise bill was ultimately what became known as the Civil Rights Act of 1968. Despite the continued opposition of several southern senators, the bill contained a fair housing provision that was substantially stronger than anything that Congress had seriously considered in prior decades. Normal hearings on Title VIII were avoided in 1968 since it was an amendment added during the Senate floor debate over a committee-reported bill to provide federal penalties for violence or intimidation in the South against those attempting to secure the legal rights already guaranteed, at least on paper, by the Civil Rights Act of 1964 and the Voting Rights Act of 1965. Now, with the support of the Senate Democratic and Republican leadership, a successful cloture vote cut short what surely would have been a prolonged and bitter southern filibuster. While forty-three amendments were proposed to dilute Title VIII further, most of them were voted down in regular order. Floor debate ended on March 11, 1968, with an unpredicted wide vote of 71 to 26 in favor of the entire Civil Rights Act of 1968.

The Act was then forwarded to the House, where a great ground swell of conservative hostility, led by Gerald R. Ford, had been growing as the Senate's measure proceeded through floor debate. Yet the murder of Dr. Martin Luther King, Jr. on April 4, 1968 turned the tide against the resistance. As President John F. Kennedy's assassination had spurred the passage of the Civil Rights Act of 1964, so did Dr. King's death spur the passage of the Civil Rights Act of 1968. On the day of King's funeral, the House Rules Committee reported the 1968 Act out for floor passage, adding credibility to the notion that only crisis can normally greatly speed the incremental process of Congress' passage of far-reaching civil rights legislation. The Rules Committee limited House debate on the proposal to only one hour and dictated that the House either accept or reject the Dirksen compromise with no floor amendments. Speaker John McCormack, a Democrat from Massachusetts, scurried through the House chamber pressing for approval of the Senate bill, while Congressman Celler urged approval in the major speech given favoring the bill. The final vote, 250 to 172, was not as close as many had expected. Congressional liberals, responding to Johnson's leadership, had won a surprising victory.

Republican from Wyoming, expressed concern over narrowing the exemptions allowed under Title VIII, stating that "with such 'conformity,' I think we are heading into some real problems with regard to private ownership of private property." * * * The point is that these notions persist despite the fact that because of discrimination in the rental and sale of housing, many minorities are forced to live in housing characterized by overcrowded, disproportionately expensive, deteriorating, substandard conditions, in neighborhoods that have high crime rates and poor public services. * * *

John Calmore, *Fair Housing vs. Fair Housing: The Problems with Providing Increased Housing Opportunities Through Spatial Deconcentration*, 14 CLEARINGHOUSE REV. 7–12 (1980)*

Like the irony of the fire boat burning and sinking, now, as the attraction of suburban living pales daily and the phenomenon of urban reinvestment becomes large-scale reality, the nation's commitment to fair housing is significantly linked with a policy to disperse its urban poor and non-whites to the growingly disfavored suburbs while attracting the more affluent suburbanites to the revitalized inner cities. While pursuing a dispersal policy of integrating neighborhoods, the policy of providing federally assisted housing in impacted areas, *i.e.*, those areas with concentrations of poor or nonwhite households, is being substantially obstructed if not foreclosed. This policy of spatial deconcentration has produced more frustration than housing opportunities, and as a consequence, the national effort toward "fair housing" means little of benefit to our client community. Just as the Holy Roman Empire was reputed to be neither holy nor Roman, this fair housing is neither fair nor housing.

The underlying theme of this article is that our national housing policy's present emphasis on dispersal tactics to achieve racial and economic integration is too often curtailing the provision of housing opportunities and community enrichment for those most in need. In the name of expanding housing opportunities, the government has actually restricted housing for poor inner-city residents and has adversely affected the social and political integrity of their communities. Because fair housing efforts, particularly on behalf of the nonwhite poor, have been and continue to be futile in other than tokenistic terms, the provision of low-income housing and community enrichment is being sacrificed without creating viable alternatives. Moreover, the occurrence of spatial deconcentration is too often merely a reconcentration of people in a different space. Finally, in light of extensive urban reinvestment, many so-called impacted areas are really transitional areas; absent more low-income housing in these areas, many poor will suffer displacement, being replaced by the return of the middle-class to the inner city. In this regard, the concern for the poor and the nonwhites appears to be subsidiary to the objectives of attracting the more affluent back to the city, improving the city tax base, and removing a drain on municipal services.

The right to equal housing opportunities ought to be interpreted to mean not only a right not to be discriminated against and excluded from areas where low-income housing can be built, but also a right to have such housing built in the neighborhood of one's residence.

As an introductory caveat, it is noted that some will misread this article as a call for the abandonment of efforts to achieve racial and economic integration in housing and neighborhoods. This article raises no such hue and cry. The call is not to abandon such integration, but rather to pursue it more thoughtfully and carefully. The position articulated here fully supports good faith, productive efforts directed at providing an open choice of housing opportunities for the urban nonwhite and poor. At the same time, housing opportunities furthering the choice of the urban nonwhite and poor to live *under improved circumstances* in their own neighborhoods must receive far greater emphasis and support in order for fair housing to be truly that.

* * *

THE PROBLEM IN PERSPECTIVE: QUESTIONS PRESENTED

In Washington, D.C., during September 19–21, 1979, the author attended a joint meeting with members of the Legal Services Community Development Block Grant Task Force, the Working Group for Community Development Reform, and the National Citizens Monitoring Project on CDBG. The monitoring experiences of these groups confirm that in many cities, large and small, the object of expanding housing opportunities through the spatial deconcentration of the nonwhite and urban poor, accompanied by the broad prohibitions related to building and rehabilitating federally-assisted low-income housing in impacted areas, is causing severe problems in meeting the housing and community development needs of low-income residents in such areas.

One blatant local horror story involved the loss of 85 units of large family rental housing on the fringe of an urban renewal zone in Connecticut because HUD refused to approve a rehabilitation proposal on the ground that the building was too near other assisted housing. Eighty-five predominantly Spanish-speaking families lost their housing in a city with a near-zero vacancy rate, a four to eight year wait for public housing and a high condominium and commercial conversion rate. Everyone in the city, including the mayor, objected to HUD's decision. The building was demolished after the usual fires.

* * *

While the present dispersal policies were originally motivated to further integration, primarily of the nonwhite poor, truly bad things are happening in the name of integration. Any attempt to resolve the issues is immediately placed on the defensive since people misperceive or mischaracterize it as an attack against integration itself rather than against integration's dysfunctional consequences. As Derrick Bell has stated,

> . . . racial justice in America has always been measured less by the harm done Blacks, than by the quantum of relief Whites felt they could afford. Racial recompense is usually so diluted to ensure White dominance and minimize White inconvenience that policies designated "relief" inflict further "injury."[5]

* * *

Both in terms of national policy formulation and implementation at the local community level, the policy of dispersal raises many questions: (1) Should neighborhood integration through dispersal strategies be the paramount goal when its pursuit conflicts with other national housing goals to provide affordable, decent, safe and sanitary housing to those most in need? (2) Is dispersal practical as an approach to satisfy the housing needs of low-income nonwhites when it is generally token or merely transitional, leading either to minimal benefits or reconcentration of nonwhites? (3) Is spatial deconcentration desired by low-income nonwhites, and, if so, is it more desired than affordable, decent, safe and sanitary housing within existing nonwhite neighborhoods and communities? (4) Does spatial deconcentration at the expense of providing low-income housing within existing nonwhite neighborhoods and communities encourage blight and housing abandonment as a prelude to urban reinvestment and the middle class replacement of low-income residents through gentrification and displacement? (5) Does spatial deconcentration at the expense of the provision of low-income housing within impacted areas destroy nonwhite ties and sense of community, culture and political power? (6) Is spatial deconcentration a realistic objective in light of suburban resistance to housing nonwhite families generally and nonwhite poor families particularly? (7) Does placing subsidized housing in the suburbs really attract inner-city nonwhites or does it merely divert needed benefits away from them? (8) In pushing dispersal, are fair housing agencies responding to the needs and desires of an upwardly mobile middle-class constituency at the expense of low-income nonwhites? (9) Given the government's history of civil rights nonenforcement and active support of segregation, what hidden agenda may lurk behind dispersal's justifying rhetoric of "freedom of choice," "increased housing opportunities" and "fair housing"?

THE BACKGROUND OF DISPERSAL

The present dispersal strategy is but the latest variation of an out-of-tune theme. Under the first Nixon administration, central city programs were deemphasized. The provision of subsidized housing has not recovered from the Presidential moratorium imposed in January of 1973. At the same time, revenue sharing and block grants have grown increasingly important in allocating governmental largesse to all areas of the nation, with little regard to need, diluting funds once targeted for the cities. Socioeconomic theory supporting a suburban strategy was provided by many of the nation's intellectual community which practically wrote off central cities as beyond saving. Also, the suburban strategy was supported by groups such as the NAACP which made housing integration its top priority for the 1970's. Until the recent case of *King v. Harris*,[10] however, the NAACP had never actually gone to court to *oppose* the development of low-income housing designed to benefit nonwhites.

For low-income urban nonwhites, the final injurious insult was expressed by HUD's site selection criteria, which were designed to force housing subsidy allocations into suburban areas, at the expense of inner cities. Section 8 regulations presently provide

[5] Bell, Book Review, 92 HARV. L. REV. 1826, 1832 (1979).
[10] 464 F.Supp. 827, 830 (E.D.N.Y. 1979).

that a site shall not be located in an area of nonwhite concentration unless sufficient, comparable opportunities exist for housing low-income nonwhite families outside areas of nonwhite concentration or unless the project is necessary to meet overriding housing needs which cannot otherwise feasibly be met in that housing market area. Note, however, that the regulations do not permit an "overriding need" to serve as a basis for determining that a site in an impacted area is acceptable if the only reason the need cannot otherwise feasibly be met is due to discrimination rendering outside sites unavailable. Additionally, a site may not even be located in a "racially mixed" area if the project will cause a "significant" increase in the proportion of nonwhite to white residents in the area. Finally, the site must avoid undue concentration of assisted persons in areas containing a high proportion of low-income persons. Significantly, Section 8 substantial rehabilitation contains only the latter limitation.

* * *

THE IMPRACTICALITY OF DISPERSAL

Creating a rule which imposes a substantial duty on HUD and its agents to employ federal housing programs to decrease racial concentration necessarily depends upon the ability of HUD, local agencies, and private landlords to employ site selection and tenant selection mechanism to achieve the intended result. True, controls over such factors as site selection, tenant selection and assignment may maximize integration in low-income housing. Also true, however, dangerous social engineering becomes a larger factor. * * *

Notwithstanding the effectiveness of site selection and tenant assignment as furthering integration, a rigid policy forcing HUD to approve projects only when they decrease racial concentration conflicts with other important national housing policies. Aside from the national policy to provide integrated housing, it is also national policy to produce sufficient housing to keep up with demonstrated housing need. Because local agencies or private sponsors initiate new construction, the constraints of review at the local political level may well create conflicts between a policy of building housing that is needed and a policy of integrating neighborhoods. * * *

Section 8, the nation's current primary federally assisted housing program, is also the primary vehicle for achieving the Housing and Community Development Act of 1974's goal of reducing the isolation of income groups within communities and promoting neighborhood diversity and vitality through the spatial deconcentration of housing opportunities for persons of lower income and the attraction of persons of higher income. When the fact that nonimpacted areas are likely to resist the building of Section 8 new construction is combined with the site selection prohibitions against building in impacted areas, there is a real possibility that new construction will remain undeveloped and those most in need will continue to be shut out.

* * *

In *Subsidizing Tolerance for Open Communities*,[33] Silverman, while not questioning the wisdom of the dispersion goal, traces the many obstacles associated with its implementation, citing the legislative and administrative failure to promote dispersion effectively, the growing judicial reluctance to support dispersion, and the suburban governments' resistance to dispersion. Thus, Silverman is led as a last resort to propose that America's closed communities be opened up through subsidizing tolerance. While Silverman's proposal may be quixotic, his article provides an excellent overview.

The bottom line remains that we can expect the suburbs to continue their resistance to subsidized housing. While many upwardly mobile blacks are now residing in and working in integrated suburbs, the majority of blacks leaving the inner cities have relocated in predominantly black areas, close to the inner city. Moreover, suburban subsidized housing production has primarily served the needs of the elderly and of the white working-class homeowners. * * *

NONSEGREGATION AS REAL FREEDOM OF CHOICE

It is unclear whether spatial deconcentration bestows on poor nonwhites substantive economic or sociological benefits. Rather, it may well help to destroy nonwhite political power, sense of community, culture, and neighborhood-based support systems.

* * *

The goal of expanding housing opportunities should not necessarily be limited to integration * * *, but rather should include "nonsegregation" which would enable nonwhites to locate wherever in the city they feel would best meet their needs. HUD's present policy unduly focuses on desegregation. * * *

---

[33] 1977 Wisc. L. Rev. 375.

Part III
The Present State of Property Law

This part of the anthology contains recent commentary on an array of property law issues typically covered in a first year course. The articles include surveys of many basic legal rules, historical reviews of some classic cases and legal structures, and critical commentaries of property regimes. Many of these authors are searching for new property paradigms to replace those scrapped since the days of the Realists. Some use the structure of other fields—such as economics or philosophy—to explicate new property norms. Others seek new forms of community, at times with modern echoes of republican notions citizenship so prevalent during the country's founding decades.

A. Estates in Land, Inheritance and Family Wealth

Three related sets of problems are taken up here. First, many of the common law chestnuts that dominated the law of estates in land have passed into the mists. David Fishman's fantasy piece, *The History of a Maryland Title: A Conveyancer's Romance Renewed*, describes many of them. Further commentary on such questions may be found in Dukeminier, *Cleansing the Stables of Property: A River Found at Last,* 65 IOWA L. REV. 151 (1979). Second, other types of estates, such as fee simples determinable, fee simples subject to condition subsequent and fee simples subject to executory limitation, have surprisingly rich (and recent) histories. Timothy Jost's article, *The Defeasible Fee and the Birth of the Modern Residential Subdivision*, excerpted in Part II(C), describes some of that lore. Despite the rich history, pressure now exists to rid our world of many of the remaining estates. One such critique, Gerald Korngold's *For Unifying Servitudes and Defeasible Fees: Property Law's Functional Equivalents*, is excerpted after Fishman's article. Additional commentary is provided in *Contingent Remainders and Executory Interests: A Requiem for a Distinction*, 43 MINN. L. REV. 13 (1958), by Jesse Dukeminier, who takes the position that the label "executory interest" ought be pronounced deceased, and in *Perpetuities: Three Essays in Honor of my Father*, by Susan French, who reviews the ongoing debates over reform of the Rule Against Perpetuities. Finally, the law of estates is most relevant to the passage of family wealth from generation to generation. The nature of such wealth has changed dramatically over the years. The last article in this section, *The Twentieth-Century Revolution in Family Wealth Transmission,* by John Langbein, describes some features of this history.

1. The Old Estate Chestnuts

Uriel H. Crocker, as Retold by David H. Fishman, *The History of a Maryland Title: A Conveyancer's Romance Renewed*, 42 MD. L. REV. 496–507 (1983)*

We live in a time of law reform. Many who cherish the old and the traditional believe that the law of real property should be a bastion of the older approach and of the "old learning." Some say that reform of the law of real property is "a Herculean task, beyond the power of contemporary mortals," and that "no person, no force strong enough" is competent to tackle the job.[1] In Maryland, however, there has been much change in the body of property law in recent years; over the past century, many areas of the law of real property have changed beyond recognition. The change has been gradual, but persistent. Even without conscious broad-scale reform on the English model of the early 1920's, Maryland has, bit by bit, altered the original mass of land law as received in this state. It is only rarely that the old learning jumps up to bite the unsuspecting citizen (and his lawyer!).

In 1875, Uriel H. Crocker, a member of the Boston Bar, published an article entitled "The History of a Title: A Conveyancer's Romance"[3] in the *American Law Review*. The article is a fictional account of the title to a parcel of property in Boston and the operation of various obscure principles of real property law which resulted in multiple and unexpected changes of ownership of the property over a very few years. I first happened upon this article through a citation in Casner and Leach's casebook on real property. I read it again while preparing a chapter on title insurance for a book on Maryland residential real property transactions, and thought it would be useful in an analysis of the evolution of Maryland real property law over the last century. Accordingly, I here retell the history of this title, only moving the locale from Boston to Baltimore, setting it in the period from 1865 to 1881, rather than 1860 to 1875, replacing references to Massachusetts law with citations to appropriate Maryland statutes, texts, and decisions, and making minor changes in the tale to accommodate differences between Massachusetts and Maryland law. The story, as relocated and updated, is set forth as a narrative *interrupted by passages* detailing the evolution of the principles of Maryland real property law that are pertinent to the story. Here, then, begins the tale:

Of the locality of the parcel of real estate, the history of the title of which it is proposed to relate, it may be sufficient to say that it lies in the city of Baltimore within the limits of the territory ravaged by the great Clay Street fire on July 25, 1873.[7] In 1865, this parcel of land was in the undisturbed possession of Mr. William Ingalls, who referred his title to it to the will of his father, Mr. Henry Ingalls, who died in 1835. Mr. Ingalls, the elder, had been a very wealthy citizen of Baltimore; and when he made his will a few years before his death, he owned this parcel of real estate, worth about $50,000, and possessed, in addition, personal property and some small parcels of real property to the amount of between $200,000 and $300,000. By his will he specifically devised this parcel of land to his wife, for life, and upon her death to his only child, the William Ingalls before mentioned, in fee. His will further directed his executor to pay to two nephews, William and Arthur Jones, the sum of $25,000 each to be charged against the residue of the estate, both real and personal. He also gave the large residue of

---

[1] Dukeminier, *Cleansing the Stables of Property: A River Found at Last*, 65 IOWA L. REV. 151 (1979); * * *.

[3] Crocker, *The History of a Title: A Conveyancer's Romance*, 10 AM. L. REV. 60 (1875).

[7] The Clay Street fire was the largest conflagration in Baltimore prior to the Great Fire of 1904. * * *

his property to his son, William. After the date of his will, however, Mr. Henry Ingalls engaged in some unfortunate speculations and lost most of his land holdings; and upon the settlement of his estate the residue of his real and personal property proved to be barely sufficient for the payment of his debts, and the nephews got no portion of their legacies. The large parcel of real estate we are concerned with, however, afforded to the widow a comfortable income, which enabled her during her life to support herself in a respectable manner.

Upon her death, in 1850, the son entered into possession of the estate, which had gradually increased in value; and he had been enjoying for fifteen years a handsome income derived therefrom, when he was one day surprised to hear that the two cousins, whom his father had benevolently remembered in his will, had advanced a claim that this real estate should be sold by his father's executor, and the proceeds applied to the payment of their legacies. This claim, now first made thirty years after the death of his father, was of course a great surprise to Mr. Ingalls. He had entertained the popular idea that twenty years' possession effectually cut off all claims. Here, however, were parties, after thirty years' undisputed possession by his mother and himself, setting up in 1865 a claim arising out of the will of his father, that will having been probated in 1835. Nor had Mr. Ingalls ever dreamed that the legacies given to his cousins could in any way have precedence over the specific devise of the parcel of real estate to himself. It was, as a matter of common sense, so clear that his father had intended by his will first to provide for his wife and son, and then to make a generous gift out of the residue of his estate to his nephews, that during the thirty years that had elapsed since his death it had never occurred to anyone to suggest any other disposal of the property than that which had been actually made. Upon consulting with counsel, however, Mr. Ingalls learned that although the time within which most actions might be brought was limited to a specified number of years, there was no such limitation affecting the bringing of an action to recover a legacy.

This advice of Mr. Ingalls' counsel was confirmed as correct by the Court of Appeals only a few years later in Ogle v. Tayloe,[9] *which held that "legacies are not barred by the statute of limitations," and refused to apply laches on the facts. The law in Maryland continued to be such for a while. As to actions against administrators directly, a statute of limitations applied. Now, however, both personal representatives and heirs are protected by a statute of limitations.*

Mr. Ingalls also learned that as he was an only child, and as his father's will gave him, after his mother's death, the same estate that he would have taken by inheritance had there been no will, the law looked upon the devise to him as void, and deemed him to have taken the estate by descent. What he had supposed to be a specific devise of the estate to him was then a void devise, or no devise at all; and his parcel of real estate, being in the eye of the law simply a part of an undevised residue, was of course liable to be sold for the payment of those legacies contained in his father's will which were expressly made charges on the residuary real estate! It was an asset which the executor was bound to apply to that purpose. This exact point had been determined in the then recent case of *Mitchell v. Mitchell.*[14]

This is but one manifestation of the "Doctrine of Worthier Title" which is presumably still in force in Maryland when the testator leaves one heir.

Thus, Mr. Ingalls was finally compelled to see the estate, the undisputed possession of which he had enjoyed for so many years, sold at auction by the executor of his father's will for $135,000, not quite enough to pay the legacies to his cousins, which legacies, with interest from the expiration of one year after the testator's death, amounted at the time of the sale in 1866 to $143,000. The Messrs. Jones themselves purchased the estate at the sale, deeming the purchase a good investment of the amount of their legacies, and Mr. Ingalls instituted a system of stricter economy in his domestic expenses, and pondered much on the uncertainty of the law and the mutability of human affairs.

By one of those curious coincidences that so often occur, Messrs. William and Arthur Jones had scarcely begun to enjoy the increased supply of pocket money afforded them by the rents of their newly acquired property, when they each received one morning a summons to appear before the Superior Court of Baltimore City, "to answer unto John Bolton in an action of ejectment," the premises described in the writ being their newly acquired estate.

The Messrs. Jones were at first rather startled by this unexpected proceeding; but as they had, when they received their deed from Mr. Ingalls' executor, taken the precaution to have the title to their estate

[9] 49 Md. 158, 176 (1878).
[14] 21 Md. 244, 253–54 (1864).

examined by a conveyancer, who had reported that he had carried his examination as far back as the beginning of the century, and had found the title perfectly clear and correct, they took courage, and waited for further developments. It was not long, however, before the facts upon which the action of ejectment had been founded were made known. It appeared that for some time prior to 1750 the estate had belonged to one John Buttolph, who died in that year, leaving a will in which he devised the estate "to my brother Thomas, and, if he shall die without issue, then I give the same to my brother William." Thomas Buttolph had held the estate until 1775, when he died, leaving an only daughter, Mary, at that time the wife of Timothy Bolton. Mrs. Bolton held the estate until 1786, when she died, leaving two sons and a daughter. This estate she devised to her daughter, who subsequently, in 1810, conveyed it to Mr. Henry Ingalls, before mentioned. Peter Bolton, the oldest son of Mrs. Bolton, was a non-compos mentis, but lived until the year 1859, when he died at the age of 75. He left no children, having never been married.

John Bolton, the plaintiff in the action of ejectment, was the oldest son of John Bolton, the second son of Mrs. Mary Buttolph Bolton, and the basis of the title set up by him was substantially as follows. He claimed that under the decision in *Dallam v. Dallam's Lessee*,[16] the will of John Buttolph had given to Thomas Buttolph an estate tail, the law construing the intention of the testator to have been that the estate should belong to Thomas Buttolph and to his issue as long as such issue should exist, but that upon the failure of such issue, whenever such failure might occur, whether at the death of Thomas or at any subsequent time, the estate should go to William Buttolph.

In 1750, the date of John Buttolph's death, the words "die without issue" were construed to mean indefinite failure of issue at any time in the future, and thus equivalent to the words "heirs of his body," thus creating a fee tail general estate. In 1862, the General Assembly provided that such words in a will should be construed to mean definite failure, at the death of the first taker. The same provision as to deeds was later enacted. Thus, after 1862, Thomas would have taken a fee simple estate under the wording of John Buttolph's will. Thomas' fee simple, however, would have been subject to a gift over to his brother William if Thomas had died without issue. Because he did not die without issue, this gift over, called an "executory interest," failed, and a fee simple absolute would have vested in Thomas' daughter, Mary, by his will. This apparently was the construction placed on the will of John Buttolph by the lawyer who examined the title for Henry Ingalls when he purchased the land from the daughter of Mary Bolton in 1810.

It had also been decided in *Chelton v. Henderson*,[21] and *Smith v. Smith*,[22] that prior to the Act to Direct Descents of 1786 an estate tail did not descend in Maryland, like other real estate, to all the children of the deceased owner in equal shares, but, according to the old English rule of primogeniture, exclusively to the oldest son, if any, and to the daughters only in default of any son; and it had been further recognized in the landmark case of *Newton v. Griffith*[25] that prior to the Act to Direct Descents, an estate tail could not be devised or in any way affected by the will of a tenant in tail.

The Act to Direct Descents of 1786 virtually abolished estates tail general (i.e., a grant to A and the heirs of his body). Any remaining doubt as to this result was removed by the General Assembly in 1820. Estates tail special (i.e., a grant to A and the heirs of his body borne by Mrs. A), however, continued to be possible in Maryland until 1916. In that year, estates tail special were converted by statute into estates in fee simple.

Mr. John Bolton claimed then that the estate tail given by the will of John Buttolph to Thomas Buttolph had descended at the death of Thomas to his only child, Mary Bolton; that at her death in 1786, instead of passing, as had been supposed at the time by virtue of her will, to her daughter, that will had been wholly without effect upon the estate, which had, in fact, descended to her oldest son, Peter Bolton. Peter Bolton had indeed been disseized in 1810, if not before, by the acts of his sister in taking possession of and conveying away the estate; but, as he was a non-compos mentis during the whole of his long life, the Statute of Limitations did not begin to run against him. His heir in tail, namely, John Bolton, the oldest son of his then deceased brother, John, was allowed by the Statute of 21 James I, ch. 16, § II (1623), in force in Maryland, to bring his action within ten years after his uncle Peter's death. As these ten years did not expire until 1869, this action, brought in 1868, was seasonably commenced;

[16] 7 H. & J. 220, 236 (Md. 1826).
[21] 9 Gill 432, 437 (Md. 1850).
[22] 2 H. & J. 314, 318 (Md. 1806).
[25] 1 H. & G. 111, 130-32 (Md. 1827); * * *.

and it was prosecuted with success, judgment in his favor having been recovered by John Bolton in 1869.

The correctness of this decision and analysis was recognized by the Court of Appeals only a few years later in Wickes v. Wickes.[31] *The British statute has since been repealed in Maryland, and the ten year period after removal of the disability is now usually three years.*

The case of *Bolton v. Jones* was naturally a subject of remark among the legal profession; and it happened to occur to one of the younger members of that profession that it would be well to improve some of his idle moments by studying up the facts of this case in the Baltimore City Land Record Office. Curiosity promoted this gentleman to extend his investigation beyond the facts directly involved in the case, and to trace the title of Mr. John Buttolph back to an earlier date. He found that Mr. Buttolph had purchased the estate in 1730 of one Hosea Johnson, to whom it had been conveyed in 1710 by Benjamin Parsons. The deed from Parsons to Johnson, however, conveyed the land to Johnson simply, without any mention of his "heirs"; and the young lawyer, having only recently completed his reading in the area of real property law preparatory to being called to the Bar, was familiar with the statute enacted in Maryland in 1856 which for the first time eliminated the common-law requirement that a fee simple estate could be created only by use of the word "heirs." He thus perceived that Johnson took under this deed only a life estate in the granted premises, and that at his death the premises reverted to Parsons or to his heirs.

Prior to 1856, a deed which omitted the word "heirs" in the granting clause created only a life estate.

The young lawyer, being of an enterprising spirit, thought it would be well to follow out the investigation suggested by his discovery. He found, to his surprise, that while Hosea Johnson had conveyed the property to John Buttolph in 1730, he did not die until 1786, the estate having, in fact, been purchased by him for a residence when he was twenty-one years of age, and about to be married. He had lived upon it for twenty years, but had then moved his residence to another part of Baltimore County, and sold the estate, as we have seen, to Mr. Buttolph. When Mr. Johnson died, in 1786, at the age of ninety-seven, it chanced that the sole party entitled to the reversion, as heir of Benjamin Parsons, was a young woman, his granddaughter, aged eighteen, and just married. This young lady and her husband lived, as sometimes happens, to celebrate their diamond wedding anniversary in 1861, but died during that year. As she had been under the legal disability of coverture from the time when her right of entry upon the estate, as heir of Benjamin Parsons, first accrued in 1786, at the termination of Johnson's life estate, the provision of the Statute of Limitations, before cited, gave her heirs ten years after her death within which to bring their action.

"Coverture," i.e., marriage, was a disability which tolled the period of limitations prior to 1894.

These heirs of Benjamin Parsons' granddaughter proved to be three or four people of small means, residing in remote parts of the United States. What arrangements the young lawyer made with these parties and also with a Mr. John Sharpe, a speculating moneyed man of Baltimore, who was supposed to have furnished certain necessary funds, he was wise enough to keep carefully to himself. Suffice it to say that in 1870 an action was brought by the heirs of Benjamin Parsons to recover from Bolton the land which he had just recovered from William and Arthur Jones. In this action the plaintiffs were successful, and they had no sooner been put in formal possession of the estate than they conveyed it, now worth a couple of hundred thousand dollars, to the aforesaid Mr. John Sharpe, who was popularly supposed to have obtained in this case, as he usually did in all financial operations in which he was concerned, the lion's share of the plunder. The Parsons heirs, probably, realized very little from the results of the suit; but the young lawyer obtained sufficient remuneration to establish him as a brilliant speculator in suburban lands, second mortgages, and land patent rights. Mr. Sharpe had been but a short time in possession of his new estate when the great fire of July, 1873, swept over it. He was, however, a most energetic citizen, and the ruins were not cold before he was at work rebuilding. He bought an adjoining lot in order to increase the size of his estate, the whole of which was by early in 1875 covered by an elegant building, conspicuous on the front of which could be seen his initials, "J.S.," cut in the stone.

While the estate which had once belonged to Mr. William Ingalls, was passing from one person to another in the bewildering manner we have endeavored to describe, Mr. Ingalls had himself, for a time, looked on in amazement. It finally occurred to him,

---

[31] 98 Md. 307, 326, 56 A. 1017, 1025 (1904). * * *

however, that he would go to the root of this matter of the title. He employed a skillful conveyancer to trace that title back, if possible, to Lord Baltimore. The result of this investigation was that it appeared that the parcel which he had himself owned, together with the additional parcel bought and added to it by Sharpe, had, in 1690 constituted one parcel, which was then the "possession" of one "Maudid Engle," who subsequently, in 1695, under the name of "Mauditt Engles," conveyed it to John Carroll, on the express condition that no building should ever be erected on a certain portion of the rear of the premises conveyed. Now it had so happened that this portion of these premises had never been built upon before the great fire, but Mr. Sharpe's new building had covered the whole of the forbidden ground. It was evident, then, that the condition had been broken; that the breach had occurred so recently that the right to enforce a forfeiture was not barred by the statute, and could not be deemed to have been waived by any neglect or delay; and that consequently, under the decision in *Dolan v. Mayor & City Council of Baltimore*,[39] a forfeiture of the estate for breach of this condition could now be enforced if the true parties entitled by descent and by residuary devises under the original "Engle" or "Engles" could only be found. It occurred to Mr. Ingalls, however, that this name, "Engles," bore a certain similarity in sound to his own; and as he had heard that during the early years after the settlement of this country, great changes in the spelling of names had been brought about, he instituted an inquiry into his own genealogy, the result of which was, in brief, that he found he could prove himself to be the identical person entitled, as a remote heir of Maudid Engle, to enforce, for breach of the condition in the old deed of 1695, the forfeiture of the estate now in the possession of John Sharpe.

The correctness of Mr. Ingalls' theory was confirmed only shortly thereafter by the Court of Appeals in Reed v. Stouffer.[40] *The forfeiture of an estate upon breach of a condition in the grant creating the estate was long recognized in Maryland, until the legislature required the periodic reregistration of restrictions and conditions in order to keep them alive. This statute is in keeping with a general trend of reform in this area of the law all over the country.*[43]

When Mr. Sharpe heard of these facts, he felt that a retributive Nemesis was pursuing him. He lost the usual pluck and bulldog determination with which he had been accustomed to fight at the law all claims against him, whether just or unjust. He consulted the spirits; and they rapped out the answer that he must make the best settlement he could with Mr. Ingalls, or he would infallibly lose all his fine estate—not only that part which Mr. Ingalls had originally held, and which he had obtained for almost nothing from the heirs of Benjamin Parsons—but also the adjoining parcel for which he had paid its full value, together with the elegant building which he had erected at a cost exceeding the whole value of the land. Mr. Sharpe believed in the spirits; they had made a lucky guess once in answering an inquiry from him; he was getting old; he had worked like a steam-engine during a long and busy life, but now his health and his digestion were giving out; and when the news of Mr. Ingalls' claim reached his ears, he became, in a word, demoralized. He instructed his lawyer to make the best settlement of the matter that he could, and a settlement was soon effected by which the whole of Mr. Sharpe's parcel of land in the burnt district was conveyed to Mr. Ingalls, who gave back to Mr. Sharpe a mortgage for the whole amount which the latter had expended in the erection of his building, together with what he had paid for the parcel added by him to the original lot. Mr. Sharpe, not liking to have any thing to remind him of his one unfortunate speculation, soon sold and assigned this mortgage to the Maryland Life Insurance Company; and as the well-known counsel of that institution has now examined and passed the title, we may presume that there are in it no more flaws remaining to be discovered.

In conclusion, we may say that Mr. William Ingalls, after having been for some ten years a reviler of the law, especially of that portion of it which relates to the title to real estate, is now inclined to look more complacently upon it, being again in undisturbed and undisputed possession of his old estate, now worth much more than before, and in the receipt therefrom of an ample income which will enable him to pass the remainder of his days in comfort, if not in luxury. But, though Mr. Ingalls is content with the final result of the history of his title, those lawyers who are known as "conveyancers" are by no means happy when they contemplate that history, for it has tended to impress upon them how full of pitfalls is the ground upon which they are

---

[39] 4 Gill 395, 404-06 (Md. 1846).

[40] 56 Md. 236, 253-55 (1881) * * *.

[43] See Chaffin, *Reverters, Rights of Entry and Executory Interests: Semantic Confusion and the Tying Up of Land*, 31 FORDHAM L. REV. 303, 321 n.71 (1962).

accustomed to tread, and how extensive is the knowledge and how great the care required of all who travel over it; and they now look more disgusted than ever, when, as so often happens, they are requested to "just step over" to the Record Office and "run down" a title; and are informed that the title is a very simple one, and will take only a few minutes; and that So-and-so, "a very careful man," did it in less than half an hour last year, and found it all right, and that his charge was five dollars.

2. The Disappearing Estates: Defeasible Fees and Executory Interests

---

Gerald Korngold, *For Unifying Servitudes and Defeasible Fees: Property Law's Functional Equivalents*, 66 TEX. L. REV. 533-548, 559-562 (1988)*

I. Introduction

Real property law has developed many distinct interests designed to allocate to their holders a nonpossessory right in land—covenants, equitable servitudes, easements, rights of entry, possibilities of reverter, and executory interests. Although these interests are functional equivalents evoking similar policy concerns, classical legal theory gives each a separate label and a distinct set of doctrinal rules. In this fragmented legal universe, the label is often the key to results. Arcane rules divert decision makers' attention from underlying policy issues and the larger fabric of private land use rights. History, doctrinal mystique, and separate jurisprudential origins help to perpetuate the disunity.

Commentators in recent years have articulated convincing arguments for the abolition of classical distinctions between the fee simple subject to a condition subsequent and the fee simple determinable.[2] Consistent with those views, this Article treats the two estates as a single interest—*a fee on condition.* Commentators also have criticized the false distinctions between fees on condition and fees simple subject to executory limitation. In this Article, *defeasible fee* refers collectively to fees on condition and fees on executory limitation and *condition* refers to the limiting conditions in both interests. In addition, a number of commentators recently have urged the integration of covenants at law, equitable servitudes, and easements into a single interest known as a servitude.[6]

This Article argues for a further unification of private land use allocation devices. Specifically, the law should integrate defeasible fees involving land use controls and servitudes. These interests serve the same purpose: they create rights and corresponding restrictions related to the use of land. The tensions between freedom of contract rights and the policy disfavoring restrictions on land inhere in both interests. The confusion in cases involving recently creat-

---

[2] *See, e.g.,* Chaffin, *Reverters, Rights of Entry, and Executory Interests: Semantic Confusion and the Tying Up of Land,* 31 FORDHAM L. REV. 303, 320-22 (1962) * * *; Dunham, *Possibility of Reverter and Powers of Termination—Fraternal or Identical Twins?,* 20 U. CHI. L. REV. 215, 234 (1953); * * *.

[6] *See, e.g.,* C. Berger, *Some Reflections on a Unified Law of Servitudes,* 55 S. CAL. L. REV. 1323, 1337 (1982) [hereinafter Berger, *Reflections*]; Browder, *Running Covenants and Public Policy,* 77 MICH. L. REV. 12, 12-13 (1978); Epstein, *Notice and Freedom of Contract in the Law of Servitudes,* 55 S. CAL. L. REV. 1353, 1358-68 (1982); French, *Toward a Modern Law of Servitudes: Reweaving the Ancient Strands,* 55 S. CAL. L. REV. 1261, 1304-19 (1982); * * * Reichman, *Toward a Unified Concept of Servitudes,* 55 S. CAL. L. REV. 1177, 1227-60 (1982); Rose, *Servitudes, Security, and Assent: Some Comments on Professors French and Reichman,* 55 S. CAL. L. REV. 1403, 1409-16 (1982); * * *. *But see* * * * Sterk, *Freedom from Freedom of Contract: The Enduring Value of Servitude Restrictions,* 70 IOWA L. REV. 615, 660-61 (1985) * * * The American Law Institute currently is exploring an integration of these interests. *See* RESTATEMENT (THIRD) OF PROPERTY (SERVITUDES) (Prelim. Draft No. 3, 1987).

ed defeasible fees, the forthcoming *Restatement (Third) of Property (Servitudes)*, and current scholarship examining the relationship between economic efficiency and rules governing consensual agreements[11] underscore the need for integration. Logic, fairness, and the need to further land use policy goals compel an integration.

* * *

II. The Foundation for Unification

A. Servitudes and Conditions as Functional Equivalents

A condition imposed in a defeasible estate and a servitude limiting a fee are methods for transferring from the fee owner to another person a nonpossessory ownership interest in the land burdened by the servitude or condition. This ownership interest can be a negative restriction controlling activities on the burdened parcel, or an affirmative right requiring the servient owner to perform an act or tolerate an intrusion on her fee. Numerous nonpossessory ownership rights have substantively equivalent prohibitions or entitlements, and they differ only in the form chosen to memorialize the transaction. Landowners employ both conditions and servitudes to create negative restrictions on permissible uses of property, type and quality of construction,[14] manufacture or sale of alcohol, and competing business activities, as well as to improve affirmative obligations such as a requirement to seek approval from an architectural committee before building or to maintain or build certain structures on the land. The remedies available for breach of condition and servitude differ theoretically, but the two vehicles are simply alternative ways to accomplish the same allocation of rights in land. That a third party holds the enforcement right with a fee simple subject to an executory limitation does not distinguish the interest from other land rights allocation devices; rather, it is similar to a servitude enforced, under third-party beneficiary theory, by a party other than the covenantee. The condition and the servitude are essentially functional equivalents.

Traditionally, classification as a defeasible fee or a servitude depends on the language chosen by the parties. Defeasible estates arise when words of conveyance limit the fee and provide for automatic expiration in favor of the grantor on the occurrence of a stated condition, for a power of termination or right of entry in the grantor upon breach of a condition, or for an executory limitation in a third party upon occurrence of a stated event. Real covenants, in contrast, are created by language of promise and usually appear in bilateral agreements rather than grants.

Recognizing different rules and results for servitudes and defeasible fees, however, is illogical when the only true distinction between them is language—the imperfect signs chosen to express the parties' intent—and the parties' underlying understandings are essentially the same. Even if such a distinction were viable theoretically, it would be difficult to apply. One court demonstrated the confusion by stating that "this covenant grants a conditional estate, in the nature of a negative easement."[27] Technical differences in language should not prevent a merger of easements and real covenants, treatment of all fees on condition as functional equivalents, or a rationalization of classical distinctions between fees on condition and fees on executory limitation; similarly, these differences should not bar an integration of the law of servitudes and defeasible estates. With technical arguments eliminated, the policies that underlie both servitudes and conditions may be analyzed to determine whether their similarity justifies such an integration. Identifying and exploring the common policy concerns in conditions and servitudes also will indicate the issues that a unified law must accommodate.

B. The Contract and Antirestrictions Dichotomy

Servitudes and defeasible fees are treated as distinct areas of the law, even though the interests share the same policy conflict. Two major, conflicting themes—freedom of contract and a policy disfavoring restrictions on land—underlie both the law of servitudes and the law of defeasible fees and make case resolution difficult.

1. Freedom of Contract.—One major strain running through real covenant cases is the idea that freedom of contract validates these interests. Real covenants are enforced like other consensual arrangements between private parties. Treating real covenants as contracts supports values of moral obligation, efficiency, and freedom of choice. Similar freedom of contract values are inherent in defeasible fees,

---

[11] *See, e.g.*, Ellickson, *Alternatives to Zoning: Covenants, Nuisance Rules, and Fines as Land Use Controls*, 40 U. CHI. L. REV. 681, 711-19 (1973).

[14] *See, e.g.*, * * * Snow v. Van Dam, 291 Mass. 477, 197 N.E.2d 224 (1935) (real covenant; single-family dwelling and minimum value).

[27] Duester v. Alvin, 74 Or. 544, 552, 145 P. 660, 663 (1915) * * *.

although they are obscured by various factors. A major obstacle to recognition of contract values is that defeasible fees are created by deed, a unilateral instrument, rather than by contract, a document of bilateral promises. Classical theory shows that an owner of a defeasible fee is not bound by a promise made respecting the land; rather, the law limits her ownership rights because she was granted less than a fee simple absolute. A restricting agreement is unnecessary because the 'bundle of sticks' that the grantee received did not include the right in question. For the purpose of analyzing freedom of contract values, however, this Article will treat defeasible fees as two-party contracts. Indeed, underlying any such unilateral grant is a bilateral agreement between the grantor and grantee in which the grantee accepts (and presumably pays for) a lesser estate. Viewed in this manner, a defeasible fee is functionally indistinguishable from a grant of a fee simple absolute with a corresponding promise by the grantee to the grantor in the form of a real covenant. Some courts are not distracted by the classic distinction and recognize that a fee on condition involves a bilateral exchange and a contracting process. Easements, like defeasible fees, are memorialized in unilateral deeds, but it is clear that courts interpret easements as bilateral agreements governed by the intent of the parties.

(a) Moral obligation.—Courts imply that conditions and servitudes should be enforced against successors to the original grantee or covenantor because of a moral obligation rooted in the notion of contract. Some courts are concerned about the injustice of allowing a successor purchaser with notice of a condition to ignore the condition and contest its enforcement. Decisions also reflect disapproval of a grantee's attempts to 'enlarge his estate' and recover greater consideration by reselling the land free of a condition. Although these decisions use the traditional terminology of unilateral conveyance and limited estates, one court, perhaps unconsciously, underscored the common link between conditions and servitudes by quoting *Tulk v. Moxhay*,[40] the leading equitable servitude case, on the issue of moral blameworthiness.

(b) Efficiency.—Private agreements allocating nonpossessory land use rights help to achieve an efficient use of limited land resources. A party seeking a negative or affirmative right over a parcel of land need not acquire full title, but can purchase the limited entitlement from the fee owner. The purchaser does not have to devote the additional resources necessary to acquire a greater interest than she desires. Additionally, the fee owner can convert a portion of his ownership rights without having to sell more of the property than he wishes. Both the parties and society benefit by avoiding a wasteful allocation of resources. Such efficiency-maximizing transactions are only possible when the law validates and enforces them without exacting inordinate transaction costs.

Servitudes are justified because they encourage the efficient allocation of land resources. Conditions often achieve the same goal. Courts hesitate to disturb the economic arrangement of a fee on condition because of the potential windfall to the fee owner if the condition holder's interest is not enforced. Courts, unfortunately, do not express similar concern with the possible inefficiencies of the forfeiture remedy, which is granted for violations of conditions.

(c) Freedom of choice.—Land use allocation agreements allow parties to achieve their individual choices and to exert control over a small part of a large world. Freedom of contract encourages personal preferences, which become part of the arrangement whether cast as a condition or servitude. Courts find that the intention of the parties controls, even though one may disagree with their point of view. Other courts express this deference as the right of property owners to annex conditions onto property they are conveying. While this phrasing obscures the bilateral nature of defeasible fee conveyances, it makes clear the regard for individual choice.

2. *The Antirestrictions Policy.*—Real covenants doctrine, while lauding freedom of contract values, expresses the concern running throughout real property law over burdensome restrictions on land. Some defeasible fee cases also declare the importance of a public policy favoring free alienability of land or a free and untrammeled use of property. Yet courts give little explanation to the meaning of these concepts and fail to indicate their relevance to conditions. This lack of guidance is worsened by the inconsistency that results from applying the Rule Against Perpetuities to executory limitations but not to fees on condition. Courts must recognize that an antirestrictions policy essentially concerns marketability of land and limitation of the dead hand.

(a) Marketability.—Courts and commentators have criticized defeasible fees and real covenants for hindering the marketability of realty. The presence of

---

[40] 41 Eng. Rep. 1143 (Ch. 1848).

a condition should not have this effect. Theoretically, the market in lesser estates should function as smoothly as the market in fees simple absolute. A buyer, relying on the title system, could ascertain the ownership interests and discount her offer accordingly. She furthermore might choose to purchase not only the defeasible fee, but also the right created by the condition; she would thus obtain a fee simple absolute. Defeasible fees, however, have certain characteristics that create either excessive transaction costs (at the minimum) or an imperfect market (at the extreme).

Because defeasible fees typically are held in gross, significant problems may develop in tracing the many successors in interest who own fragments of the possibility of reverter, right of entry, or executory interest. Even if one is willing to buy out these condition holders, locating them may be inordinately expensive or even impossible. The excessive transaction costs that result from this search do not exist with appurtenant servitudes because the interest holder must own land contiguous to the burdened property.

Because many buyers refuse to purchase a defeasible fee, a defeasible fee owner is left to sell in a limited market or to acquire the holder's right in order to obtain the fee simple absolute for eventual sale. The second alternative may create a distorted market with the opportunity for a future interest holder to extract exorbitant payments. A seller of a fee subject to a servitude, in contrast, has access to an active market. Financing difficulties also may hinder transferability. The grantee may have difficulty in obtaining financing because lenders might avoid transactions in which potential borrowers offer defeasible estates as security.

Defeasible fees also create marketability problems because of the uncertainty that results from the need to rely on unrecorded facts to determine whether a breach of the condition has occurred. This difficulty arises with real covenants as well, but the gravity of the forfeiture remedy heightens the problem for conditions. Even after a breach has been determined, deciding when the statute of limitations begins to run creates further difficulties. This issue requires a clear resolution by the legislatures and courts.

(b) The dead hand.—The antirestrictions policy focuses on dead hand control of land. Servitudes and fees on condition allow perpetual burdens on land, which have potential negative effects on the burdened landowner and society. In contrast, the Rule Against Perpetuities, which does not apply to rights of entry, possibilities of reverter, or servitudes, voids executory interests that might vest remotely and thus prevents an executory limitation from creating an endless tie.

Land restrictions imposed by a prior owner limit the autonomy of the current landholder. Even though the Rule Against Perpetuities does not apply to fees on condition and servitudes, its underlying purpose of preventing perpetual burdens on land, which frustrate the aspirations of current owners, cannot be ignored. Some courts recognize the perpetuity danger with fees on condition. One court stated that a "whimsical obsession [and] an expression of testator's vanity" do not control the grantee.[67] Another court, in an action to quiet title by a successor to an original grantee, refused to void a condition limiting subdivision development to residential purposes. Although the court speculated on whether such conditions violated public policy, it felt constrained by stare decisis:

> There may be strong grounds in public policy against arbitrarily limiting and restricting the manner of use of real property for indefinite periods, which may extend far beyond the existing conditions which make such limitations reasonable and justifiable when created; but our courts have held that such limitations are not void, as against public policy . . ..[68]

Dead hand control also negatively affects society because land subject to historical ties cannot readily meet society's current needs. Moreover, unbending enforcement of restrictions on land leads to frustration of other important policies, such as encouraging private subdivision arrangements, democratic self-determination, and flexibility in private land use controls.

3. Striking a Balance.—Express references to the antirestrictions policy appear less frequently in cases involving fees on condition than in those involving real covenants. The reason for this difference is unclear. Perhaps the more intractable historical roots of fees on condition make them less subject to challenge. Yet the courts' decisions do acknowledge the importance of the antirestrictions policy for fees on condition. Although judicial concern over forfeiture and emphasis on strict construction focuses on

---

[67] Cast v. National Bank of Commerce Trust & Sav. Ass'n, 186 Neb. 385, 391, 183 N.W.2d 485, 489 (1971).

[68] Strong v. Shatto, 45 Cal. App. 29, 36, 187 P. 159, 162 (1919). * * *

remedies, it may also demonstrate an unease with the desirability of the restriction itself.

Regardless of most courts' failure to focus on the issues, the antirestrictions policy is relevant and important for both conditions and servitudes. Free alienability considerations must be balanced against freedom of contract values when crafting rules of law. Public policy must at times prevail over consensual agreements.

The Rule Against Perpetuities, employed by courts to void executory limitations, fails to provide an adequate response to the freedom of contract and antirestrictions dichotomy. The Rule does provide a rough accommodation by limiting the duration of executory limitations. This helps to minimize the number of potential transferees of such rights, which reduces the transaction costs of tracing them. Moreover, the Rule limits dead hand control to a fixed time period. * * * [H]owever, the Rule is ultimately an unsatisfactory solution because on the one hand, it does not adequately address some important antirestrictions issues, and on the other hand, it undermines freedom of contract values by unnecessarily frustrating the parties' intent.

Accommodating both values and striking a balance between the conflicting policies are most difficult when enforcement of the land use restriction is sought against a successor to the original grantee (as in the case of conditions) or covenantor (as in the case of real covenants). Unlike the original burdened party, successors have made no express promise nor accepted the condition. Moreover, the passage of time often exacerbates the difficulties with ties on land. Much of the law of real covenants developed to leap the theoretical hurdle of enforcing an agreement against a person who never made a promise. Similarly, courts dealing with defeasible fees justify binding a successor owner on the basis that she has notice and accepts the condition when she acquires the lesser estate.

C. Common Issues

Servitudes and defeasible fees, in addition to sharing the freedom of contract and antirestrictions conflict, raise similar issues as to the permissible extent of private land use agreements. These issues include remedies, 'in gross' interests, the subject matter of land restrictions and rights, and termination and modification doctrines. The wooden categories separating the law of servitudes and conditions, however, often translate into different resolutions for the same problem. Moreover, courts rarely address these issues when dealing with executory limitations. Perhaps this is due to the comparatively few executory limitation cases involving land use controls; more likely, it is because of an unarticulated and incorrect belief that the Rule Against Perpetuities adequately resolves these problems.

* * *

III. The Unification Choice

Because servitudes and conditions share the same policy dynamic and face similar issues of creation and enforcement, the legal rules controlling them should be unified. The benefits, disadvantages, and means of achieving an integration must be assessed. Moreover, because traditional treatment of defeasible fees and servitudes is only one example of the fragmented state of real property law,[141] this examination can be instructive in other problem areas.

A. Why Unify?

1. The Case for Merger.—Several considerations support unification. First, fairness and reason require that situations with similar facts and policy concerns receive equal treatment by the law. To achieve this goal, one must develop a consistent conceptual framework. Similar disposition of functionally equivalent land use allocation devices cannot occur when distinct labels and legal doctrines for servitudes and conditions prevail. Such distinctions have led to a preoccupation with classifications that bear little relation to the substance of the transfer and the policy dynamics. While the common law over time developed these separate doctrinal boxes, ironically, some early American judges viewed fees on condition and servitudes as functional equivalents and stated that results should not depend on subtle and artificial distinctions. They sought decisions grounded in good sense and sound equity to the object and spirit of the contract in the given case.

Second, unifying and clarifying the law of defeasible fees and servitudes benefit parties engaging in land use allocation transfers. The current disparate treatment of allocation devices creates confusion for those wishing to engage in such transactions. Courts treat fees on condition with great suspicion, sometimes straining to prevent enforcement by resorting

---

[141] Examples of other interests that are functionally equivalent yet treated differently include an installment sales contract and a conveyance with a purchase money mortgage, licenses and leases, and a vested remainder subject to divestment and a contingent remainder with a condition precedent.

to various interpretive devices and savings doctrines, and preferring whenever possible to construe a provision as a real covenant rather than a fee on condition, even when the parties apparently intended a fee on condition. Executory limitations fare no better when courts apply the Rule Against Perpetuities to trump the parties' intentions and void interests that would be upheld if interpreted as fees on condition or servitudes. Because of the unpredictable shell game of labeling interests, parties can have little confidence that a court will not attach an unintended label to an interest and trigger an unwanted set of rules and an unexpected result. An integrated law of servitudes and defeasible fees would allow parties to transact more securely. While legitimate and articulated public policy considerations might provide limitations on any agreement, eliminating the current system of judicial labeling would end the frustration of drafters' and planners' goals. Integration would maximize the efficiency of land use allocation devices and could reduce transaction costs in the process.

Moreover, when functional equivalents have distinct labels and rules, the skilled drafter may grasp an opportunity to avoid application of a desirable public policy. For example, courts have denied recent attempts to enforce real covenants limiting use of a residence to related persons against group homes for the mentally ill, because real covenants in violation of public policy traditionally are unenforceable. Could a court enforce a fee on condition of similar substance, given that there is no clear parallel body of law in the jurisprudence of conditions? Should the validity of such a restriction cast as an executory limitation be tested only by the Rule Against Perpetuities? A court applying a functional equivalents analysis would not answer these questions affirmatively, but under current law, that is a possible outcome. To decide private land use device cases, whether servitude or defeasible fee, by express reference to the policy concerns and rules of law developed to accommodate them is superior to legal rules that allow landowners to manipulate the labels in order to avoid these policy decisions.

2. Concerns About Integration.—Although some arguments against a merger of servitudes and defeasible fees have merit, they ultimately prove unsatisfactory and should not prevail. Providing parties with a number of legally valid alternatives so that they may choose the structure that best achieves their goals is beneficial, but servitudes and conditions are functional equivalents and actually do not present different options for allocating land rights. Forfeiture, a critical distinguishing feature, may be desirable in special circumstances, but it does not require a separate legal interest. Moreover, if third-party beneficiary theory is available, someone other than the original grantor will not need a separate device, such as the executory limitation, to allow them to enforce a land use right.

Additionally, the defeasible estate's origin and strong historical tradition should not prevent unification. Although generations of lawyers have been schooled that there is a valid distinction between conditions and servitudes, and players in the legal system are invested in the existing structure, these considerations, like historical tradition, do not make the present structure any more valid or conceptually sound. The inevitable uncertainty in defining the limits of merger cannot justify the current state of the law. Because no arguments opposing unification are convincing, careful and sensitive unification of the law of conditions and servitudes, like the proposed merger of covenants, equitable servitudes, and easements into a single law of servitudes, is possible.

* * *

Note

In *Mahrenholz v. County Board of School Trustees*, 93 Ill.App.3d 366, 417 N.E.2d 138 (1981), land was conveyed to a school district on the condition it be "used for school purpose only." When it was construed to have created a fee simple determinable rather than a fee simple on a condition subsequent, rights in the property fell to the heir of the original grantor rather than to the successor in interest of the grantor's reversion by way of purchase. Even though the original grantor had conveyed all of his rights in the reversion, Illinois' prohibition on sales of non-possessory reversions meant that the grantor's successors gained the land when school use ended. How would Korngold decide this case?

Jesse Dukeminier, *Contingent Remainders and Executory Interests: A Requiem for a Distinction*, 43 MINN. L. REV. 13–14, 23–25, 31–33, 37–39, 41, 51–55 (1958)*

A few years ago James Thurber spun a whimsical yarn about a Duke who "limped because his legs were of different lengths. The right one had outgrown the left because, when he was young, he had spent his mornings place kicking pups and punting kittens. He would say to a suitor, 'What is the difference in the length of my legs?' and if the youth replied, 'Why, one is shorter than the other,' the Duke would run him through with the sword he carried in his swordcane and feed him to the geese. The suitor was supposed to say, 'Why, one is longer than the other.' Many a prince had been run through for naming the wrong difference."[1]

Many a student in future interests has been run through by his instructor for an error of equal magnitude: calling a contingent remainder an executory interest (or vice versa). We who pretend to some knowledge of future interests are wont to stress the importance of precise labeling, of carefully classifying the interest by the rigid and artificial criteria of the common law. But if the legal consequences which flow from the label "executory interest" are the same as the consequences which flow from "contingent remainder" then the student is likely to believe he is being impaled by a crotchet. Either label should do. And would, were it not for our professional love of being able to speak well the language of the dead.

The question is, is a contingent remainder an interest that differs in important ways from an executory interest? This must be answered "no" before we can dismiss proper labeling as a mere matter of good form. In order to answer it we * * * have to look into the criteria for applying the labels and then examine the situations where it has been suggested the label matters. These situations are:

A. *Creation*

(1) Application of the Rule in Shelley's Case
(2) Application of the Rule Against Perpetuities
(3) Invalidity of gift over where first taker has power to alienate

B. *Termination of Possessory Estate*

C. *Rights Against Owner of Possessory Estate*

(1) Waste
(2) Security for personal property

D. *Alienation Inter Vivos*

There are many, many other problems that may arise concerning contingent future interests, such as: may the holder partition, sue a third party in tort, recover a portion of condemnation proceeds? What rights has he against a possessory owner who fails to pay taxes or interest on the mortgage? In these problems there is no evidence that the two interests might be treated substantially differently. Hence they are excluded from discussion.

If we conclude that executory interests and contingent remainders are treated alike in the seven situations discussed, the question then arises whether it is wise to preserve the two concepts in seemingly unchanged historic form or whether it would be better to revamp them to account for factors modern cases reveal to be important. If the concepts are too stubborn to change, they may have to be discarded altogether. I shall take up this question at the end of the article.

* * *

[Editor's Note: Discussion of most of the potential differences between contingent remainders and executory interests have been omitted. Those interested in them should check the original.]

Application of the Rule Against Perpetuities

The Rule Against Perpetuities, as formulated by John Chipman Gray, provides that "no interest is good unless it must vest, if at all, not later than twenty-one years after some life in being at the creation of the interest."[28] To satisfy the rule it is not necessary that an interest vest in possession (become possessory) within the period; it is satisfied if the interest "vests in interest." If both contingent remainders and executory interests can vest in inter-

[1] Thurber, THE 13 CLOCKS 20 (1950).

[28] GRAY, THE RULE AGAINST PERPETUITIES §201 (4th ed. 1942).

est there is no difference in the application of the rule to them.

* * *

It is obvious that a contingent remainder can turn into a vested remainder and thereby "vest in interest." So can an executory interest. Take this case: "to A for life, than to B and his heirs, but if B does not survive A, to C and his heirs." Under orthodox classification C has an executory interest, but if B dies within the lifetime of A, C's executory interest will change into a vested remainder. This capacity of an executory interest to change into a vested remainder was recognized by Gray when he said executory interests are "not vested interests until they take effect in possession or are turned into vested remainders." The statement is equally true of contingent remainders. * * *

Both contingent remainders and executory interests can be saved under the Rule Against Perpetuities if it is certain that the labels will change (to vested remainders) or the interests will fail within the period. * * * [I]n the recent Tennessee case of *Sands v. Fly,*[33] * * * an executory interest was saved. There was a devise which may for our purposes be stated as follows: to A for life, then to A's surviving children for their lives, remainder in fee to B, "provided she should be then living, and if not then" to C in fee. The court classified the remainder to B as a vested remainder and thus the gift to C must be an executory interest. The court held both gifts valid. The executory interest is valid because either one of two events must happen within B's life: (1) A and A's children all die, leaving B surviving, in which case C's interest fails altogether, or (2) B dies before A and A's children all die, in which case C's interest turns into a vested remainder.[34] If the second event happens, C's interest may vest in possession long after the death of all persons in being at T's death, but his interest is nevertheless valid. Hence, the statement that "the Rule Against Perpetuities requires that executory interests become possessory within the lives in being and twenty-one years"—a statement that has received wide currency in the cases as dictum—must be qualified by adding "or turn into a vested remainder." Precisely the same requirement is made of a contingent remainder.

* * *

Termination of Possessory Estate (Herein of destructibility of contingent remainders)

The medieval mind was obsessed with the idea that there could be no gap in seisin. A remainder had to follow hard on the heels of a possessory estate. If there was a moment of time between the termination of the possessory estate and the time when the remainderman had the right to possession by the terms of the instrument there was a gap in seisin. And it was fatal. The remainder was destroyed. Since a vested remainder by definition was ready to take whenever and however the preceding estate ended, a vested remainder was not subject to destruction. Not so the contingent remainder. If perchance the contingent remainder was not ready to take when the life estate ended, because he was unborn or unascertained or some prescribed event had not happened, he could never take. This was known as the doctrine of destructibility of contingent remainders.

The destructibility doctrine did not apply to executory interests which were by definition indestructible by a gap in seisin. That is, to say A has a springing executory interest is to say he has an interest which will follow a gap in seisin. If the gap destroyed the interest, it would be impossible to create a springing executory interest. The same is true of a shifting executory interest, which shifts seisin out of a preceding vested estate. By definition, no gap is possible between the preceding estate and the shifting executory interest. Thus if executory interests are recognized they must be indestructible by a gap in seisin.

The destructibility of contingent remainders was the great historic difference between executory interests and contingent remainders. It was the tap root of a poisonous crop of verbalisms, but fortunately it has been extirpated, root and branch, almost everywhere. * * * In twenty-five states plus the District of Columbia and Hawaii the doctrine of destructibility has been abolished in its entirety by statute or judicial decision. As remainders are unknown to the civil law, the doctrine is not in force in Louisiana. In four states by statute contingent remainders cannot be destroyed by premature termination of the life estate, and in at least two of them the doctrine has probably been wholly eliminated. It also seems reasonably certain the doctrine does not prevail in * * * [six other states.]

[33] 292 S.W.2d 706 (Tenn. 1956) * * *.

[34] The interests in B and C could have been construed as alternative contingent remainders, but they both still would be valid. Each one was bound to become a vested remainder, or fail altogether, at or before B's death. * * *

* * *

In [three other states] * * * there are some old cases applying destructibility, but its present vitality is very doubtful.

* * *

[O]nly in Florida is it clear that the destructibility doctrine prevails.

* * *

Even if it is assumed, however, that destructibility is still a spectre at a few bars, the area in which it can operate is fairly limited. It does not apply to equitable remainders or to remainders in personal property, and today the chief form of wealth is personalty. This partly explains why modern cases on destructibility are so scarce. Destructibility is limited to legal contingent remainders in land, and they can be destroyed only in two ways, (a) by the death of the life tenant before the remainder vests, and (b) by merger of the life estate into the reversion.

* * *

Executory interests can be divided into two groups: (1) those that are in an ascertained person on an event certain to happen, and (2) those that are given to unascertained persons or on an uncertain event. Executory interests of the first type are rare. Examples are "to A thirty years from date," "to A after my death." The first is analogous to a vested remainder after a term of years, the second to a vested remainder after a life estate. These executory interests are treated like vested remainders under the Rule Against Perpetuities, and, although the cases are scarce, it is believed that they would also be treated as "vested" for other purposes as well. If they do not differ in consequences from vested remainders, they may as well be called vested future interests or vested remainders. And by a number of courts they have been. In this Article they have not been included within the term "executory interests" * * *. * * *

Executory interests of the second type are analogous to contingent remainders. It is with these executory interests that we have been primarily concerned. The foregoing analysis indicates there is no difference between them and contingent remainders except where the issue is destructibility * * *. That relic of feudalism exists in Florida and, viewed in the friendliest fashion, possibly, although certainly not probably, in less than a dozen other states. In three-quarters of the states destructibility has been wholly done away with. Thus, in at least three-quarters of the states, there is no discernible difference between executory interests and contingent remainders. Only in Florida are we sure of any difference between them.

Is there any reason for retaining two concepts that produce the same consequences? Of what value are the hours after hours spent teaching students to use labels properly, when they are functional equivalents? It is clear the concepts cannot be revamped in any useful way. The alternatives are keeping the two concepts separate and merging them under one label. I shall deal briefly with each of them.

The arguments for retaining the two concepts are both, in a sense, pedagogical. The first is that students must be taught to distinguish between the two interests because the different labels are currently used by judges and lawyers. The second suggests that while the distinction may be unimportant for contemporary purposes all the history wrapped up in it ("gaps in seisin," "destructibility" and so forth) is of educational value. The first seems fallacious in that it assumes that the labels are meaningfully used today by courts. There is no need to cite again the many cases wherein the labels are treated with utmost indifference, where the wrong label is applied or where the labels are used interchangeably.

The second has merit, and I am sure it could be stated with much greater effect by one who believes in it more strongly than I do. The great trouble I have with it is that it proves both too much and too little. All history has many insights to offer, but it cannot all be taught. When the emphasis shifts from the reasons for, and methods of, change and growth to technicalities, the value sharply diminishes. In this field all too often has the mind's eye skipped over the greatness of the common law as a process constantly adapting forms to changing circumstances and fixed uncritically on the technicalities: on * * * destructibility, on contingent interests as "mere possibilities," on form rather than substance. What is justified as history becomes only training in the worst sort of artificial reasoning.

The first argument for abandoning the distinction is doctrinal simplification. Even John Chipman Gray, ruled though he was by a passion for rigid adherence to theorems, saw the need of paring off useless, artificial distinctions beyond the comprehension of the ordinary lawyer. * * * Gray's genius was achieving insight within apparent complexity by discovering a simpler doctrinal order. His energy was fired by an *elan* to understand multiplicity in terms of a few basic ideas. If he was wrong in thinking that clear and rational doctrines could be built on such words as "vest," "condition precedent," "divest," he was right in thinking that, in order to be useful in advocacy and decisions, words have to have some meaning for the ordinary lawyer and judge.

Society, and by reflection the lawyer's practice, has become far more complex than in Gray's time. Lawyers are even less likely to "have at their fingers' ends the fundamental distinctions" between such things as contingent remainders and executory interests. If we are truthful we must admit that not too many students master the distinction and most of these forget about it in their first years of practice. If they think very, very hard they may remember that executory interests are "divesting" or "springing" or "shifting" interests, but that is about as far as their memory and understanding go. More often than not their "knowledge" of executory interests simply clutters up their minds with ambiguous verbalisms and half-understood maxims, such as "there can be no remainder after a fee." (That particular maxim has led astray a good many lawyers and judges who did not realize all it means is that we call the gift over by another name.)

As a result of this surfeit of vaguely understood words, arguments in future interests cases are often remarkable for their vacuity and for their failure to come to grips with the fundamental problem. Many of the cases cannot be read without writhing.[145] Here, more than in any other field, there is a tendency to collect familiar quotations, glue them together and by sheer humbug make them applicable to the problem. It is hard for the lawyer to know why he has won and even harder for losing counsel to understand why he has lost. Thus the more profane practitioner comes to regard future interests as not a divine madness at all, but, like William James' algebra, a peculiarly low sort of cunning.

It is a reasonable assumption that two labels stand for two different things; and when they do not, when we have two labels for equivalent future interests, confusion is the natural result. Abandoning the distinction between contingent remainders and executory interests would not be a giant step toward improving his situation, but it would be a much larger step than some might imagine. For understanding the distinction requires at least a speaking acquaintance with "gaps in seisin" and "destructibility"—an acquaintance not likely to be quickly made. If the distinction goes, "gaps in seisin" and "destructibility," which make up a large part of the history of real property law, can go with it.

The second argument for abandonment is that emphasizing labels leads to an unfortunate type of reasoning. It makes form important and substance unimportant. It moves from words to label to result. Numerous examples of this type of reasoning have been exhibited in this Article * * *. * * * [I]n terms of results in the cases, the distinctions were illusory. The right inference from this is that the labels had better be dispensed with in analysis of these problems; they are not an adequate substitute for analysis of the many factors that move decisions. The same thing may be said of other problems as well, for there is no proof that labels affect results except in one case (destructibility) in one state (Florida).

It is enchantment with labels that is the hidden cause of most of the law's failures in the field of future interests. So long as we concern ourselves with labels and purely verbal distinctions, we can have no doctrinal structure that is more than a play with words, no doctrines that can justify themselves in terms of policy, no doctrines that can recognize the important factors, that can give predictability. All in all, the way to a useful, critical analysis of future interests seems to lead, not through gaps in seisin, but around them.

---

[145] A leading contender for honors is *Sands v. Fly*, 292 S.W.2d 706 (Tenn. 1956) * * *. Testatrix devised land to her only son Howard for his life, then to his children for their lives, and at the death of the last child of Howard in fee to named nieces and nephews, the issue of any deceased niece or nephew to take his or her share per stirpes, and if any niece or nephew be then dead without issue, his share to the surviving nieces and nephews or their issue. The court held the remainder in fee vested immediately and was entirely valid even though an event to happen later was said to be a "condition precedent" to the remainder's vesting. Counsel quoted Gray §108, to the effect that a remainder is contingent where the conditional element is incorporated into the gift to the remaindermen. The court agreed that here "the conditional element was incorporated in the gift to the remaindermen," but, said the court, "it definitely and conclusively appears that this condition was satisfied at the time of the testatrix's death, all children of Howard J. Sands being alive at that time." Having survived living persons is undoubtedly a neat trick, but even more marvelous is having survived the unborn (for the court later conceded that some children of Howard "might be born after the death of the testatrix"). The best argument for invalidity—that the remainder in fee was a gift to a class which would not close until the death of Howards' children—was not mentioned by the court.

Other features of this bizarre case include an argument by Howard that the remainder in his children for life and the remainder in fee were alternative contingent remainders; a contention by the guardian *ad litem* of the children that his wards' remainder was void; and a finding of an alternative remainder after a vested remainder in fee. The court cited numerous cases as authority, not one of which was in point. The case is annotated in 57 A.L.R.2d 188 (1958) by an inapposite note entitled "Character of remainder limited surviving children of life tenant."

Note

An example of the demise of the common law rules on the destructibility of contingent remainders is *Abo Petroleum Corp. v. Amstutz*, 93 N.M. 332, 600 P.2d 278 (1979).

Susan F. French, *Perpetuities: Three Essays in Honor of My Father*, 65 Wash. L. Rev. 323, 332–335, 348–353 (1990)*

* * *

II. ENDING THE PERPETUITIES WARS OF THE LATE TWENTIETH CENTURY: A BETTER REFORM PACKAGE

When Professor James Casner persuaded the American Law Institute to adopt the "wait and see principle" in 1979, he touched off a new and ferocious round[22] in the Perpetuities War begun in 1952 by his former colleague, Professor Barton Leach. The war was begun over the question how and not whether the common law Rule Against Perpetuities should be modified. Although some have quarreled with Professor Leach over the extent of the problem caused by the Rule in its traditional form, no one disagrees with his basic premise that the common law Rule goes too far in striking down reasonable dispositions because of remote and fantastical possibilities.

In the first War, the major battlefield was the "wait and see" principle, named by Professor Leach, and carefully expounded and refined by Professor Dukeminier. Opponents of wait and see claimed that the doctrine is unnecessary, and that in most of its forms it is incoherent because there is no principled way to determine the length of the waiting period within the framework of the common law Rule Against Perpetuities. Instead of wait and see, opponents led by Professor Lewis Simes proposed adoption of limited, specific statutory reforms tailored to eliminate particular violations of the Rule.[27] Some also advocated statutory grants of cy pres powers to permit judicial reformation of instruments that violate the Rule.

In drafting the *Restatement Second of Property, Donative Transfers*, Professor Casner incorporated an expanded version of wait and see into his statement of the common law Rule. When his position carried the day at the American Law Institute, wait and see received a tremendous boost. The Uniform Law Commissioners undertook preparation of a Uniform Statutory Rule Against Perpetuities based on the principle of wait and see. Under the leadership of the Reporter, Professor Waggoner, the Uniform Act expanded wait and see again, and finally converted it from a doctrine based on "measuring lives" to a simple 90-year time period.

When the Uniform Act was approved in 1986, it appeared that wait and see had won the war. However, the expansion and conversion of the wait and see doctrine worked by Professors Casner and Wag-

---

[22] After the adoption of wait and see by the Institute, Professor Lawrence Waggoner of Michigan and Professor Jesse Dukeminier of UCLA joined the fray. They have since become the principal protagonists. Professor Waggoner published *Perpetuity Reform*, 81 Mich. L. Rev. 1718 (1983) * * *, and then Professor Dukeminier published *Perpetuities: The Measuring Lives*, 85 Colum. L. Rev. 1648 (1985) * * *. The two continued with Waggoner, *Perpetuities: A Perspective on Wait-and-See*, 85 Colum. L. Rev. 1714 (1985); Dukeminier, *A Response by Professor Dukeminier*, 85 Colum. L. Rev. 1730 (1985); Waggoner, *A Rejoinder by Professor Waggoner*, 85 Colum. L. Rev. 1739 (1985); and Dukeminier, *A Final Comment by Professor Dukeminier*, 85 Colum. L. Rev. 1742 (1985). The exchange grew even more heated with Dukeminier, *The Uniform Statutory Rule Against Perpetuities: Ninety Years in Limbo*, 34 UCLA L. Rev. 1023 (1987), and Waggoner, *The Uniform Statutory Rule Against Perpetuities: The Rationale of the 90-Year Waiting Period*, 73 Cornell L. Rev. 157 (1988) * * *. Their struggle continues in state law revision commissions and state legislatures considering adoption of the Uniform Act.

[27] L. Simes, Public Policy and the Dead Hand 78–79 (1955).

goner provoked sharp dissension in the ranks of wait and see proponents. Professor Dukeminier has staunchly maintained that the measuring lives can be determined within the logic of the common law Rule. Professor Waggoner has been equally vehement in contending that there is no principled method of selecting measuring lives this way. The ferocity of this round in the Perpetuities Wars has given new hope to those who would reform the Rule without wait and see, and has spurred me to search for an alternative reform package that might prove acceptable to both sides.

Opposition to the Uniform Act centers on its use of an alternate 90-year period, which can either be used by a drafter as a period in gross, or by the intended beneficiaries of an interest that violates the common law Rule as the wait and see period. The primary objection to the 90-year period is that it is likely to encourage the use of long-term trusts, which will lead to increased dead hand control of property in the United States. Proponents of the Uniform Act respond that use of some arbitrary time period is necessary in an effective wait and see regime, and claim that reducing the perpetuities violations in trust instruments drafted for ordinary people will not lead to an increase in dead hand control in any event. Neither side has taken the position that an extension of dead hand control would be desirable, a possibility I raise in my third essay.

* * *

III. WHY NOT A 90-YEAR TRUST? WHAT'S SO BAD ABOUT DEAD HAND CONTROL, ANYWAY?

Everyone involved in the current Perpetuities Wars embraces the idea that the common law Rule Against Perpetuities strikes the right balance between permitting people to tie up their own property into the future and preventing them from doing it for too long. A major subject of contention between professors Dukeminier and Waggoner in the current Perpetuities Wars, however, is the question whether the Uniform Act changes the balance struck by the common law Rule. Professor Dukeminier takes the position that the Uniform Act's adoption will radically extend the amount of property subject to dead hand control in America. Professor Waggoner as emphatically denies that the extension is significant.

Professor Dukeminier strongly opposes the Uniform Act on two different, but related grounds. He believes that very few trusts drafted under existing law will last for 90 years. He predicts that adoption of the Uniform Act will encourage the use of 90-year trusts, and trigger widespread marketing of 90-year trusts by financial services vendors. As a result, the amount of property held in trust will be greatly increased, which he believes is socially undesirable because trust property is subject to dead hand control.

He also opposes the Act because it will permit continuation of trusts containing perpetuities violations for up to 90 years, and perhaps longer. This is undesirable both from a societal point of view because it extends the period of dead hand control, and from the family's point of view. An instrument that violates the Rule was probably drawn by an unskilled lawyer, who probably also failed to include the powers necessary to incorporate flexibility into a long-term trust. Validating the contingent interests permits the defective trust to continue to the detriment of the family, which will be caught up in the trust's straitjacket. He also suggests that 90-year tax saving trusts marketed by the financial services industry will be similarly unsuited to the task.

Professor Waggoner has completely opposing views. He predicts that the effect of the Uniform Act will simply be to rescue beneficiaries from the mistakes of their donors' lawyers. In his view, the Uniform Act makes available to all the benefits that heretofore have been reserved for those rich enough and lucky enough to find a lawyer who could create long-term trusts without violating the Rule. The Act creates social benefits by effectuating donor intent, even if the result is to tie up property within the outer limits of the common law Rule. In addition, he disagrees that the American public will be attracted to use of 90-year trusts.

While I am inclined to agree with Professor Dukeminier's assessment of the probability that instruments creating Rule violations are also badly drafted in other respects, and with the likely attractiveness of a 90-year tax saving trust, I am also inclined to think that there are other solutions to those problems. Recent statutory revisions in California provide courts with the ability to modify trust provisions that become counterproductive, whether those provisions govern management of the assets or disposition of the income and principal. Similar provisions could be enacted in conjunction with enactment of the Uniform Statutory Rule Against Perpetuities. In states which adopt the Uniform Act without such additional statutes, judges could look to statutes in other jurisdictions as additional bases on which they might extend their traditional equitable powers to modify trust provisions to adapt to unforeseen circumstances. If courts or legislatures are willing to remedy poor drafting by providing flexibility, the egalitarian ideal of making the benefits of long-term trusts available beyond the group of the super rich or sophisticated could be furthered with the 90-year trust of the Uniform Act.

That brings us to the more difficult questions: are long-term trusts good or harmful for society or for families? If they are good, are they good only for a certain period of time? If there is a limit beyond which they become undesirable, does "lives in being plus 21 years" capture that limit? Should long term trusts be made available to everyone whose assets will justify the expense of trust management? All of the participants in the current Perpetuities Wars seem to accept, almost without discussion, the ideas that dead hand control is bad and that lives in being plus 21 years imposes a suitable limit on its reach.

While I am inclined to agree, the question might be worth some further exploration. In particular, I think a readily available 90-year trust might have some benefits. If you believe that Americans do not save enough, and we are therefore in the process of losing our dominant position in the world's economy, you might also believe that we should be actively looking for ways to encourage ourselves and our fellow citizens to save. Increasing the availability of IRA's is recurrently suggested as a way to promote more savings, but 90-year trusts could do much more. A well drafted trust can provide a stable but flexible financial base for a family, as well as a source of forced savings for the economy. Since the size and terms of the trusts can be tailored to family needs, they are likely to attract more funds than IRA's. If Americans can be encouraged to save more by readily available 90-year trusts, the Uniform Statutory Rule Against Perpetuities may promote sound public policy, rather than the reverse.

Those who argue that encouraging long-term trusts is bad social policy raise a number of points. Some say that assets in trust harm the economy rather than helping it because they must be conservatively invested. I am not convinced. It seems to me that some portion of a society's assets should be placed in conservative investments, and that portion might as well include the assets held in private trusts. The question we need to ask is whether we have too many assets restricted to conservative investments, and if this is a problem, whether the assets held in private trust contribute significantly to the problem. Personally, I doubt that they do.

Others argue that the property of the world should be controlled by the living rather than the dead. While this argument has intuitive appeal, the premise is subject to some question. When property is held in trust, management of the assets is not controlled by the dead, but by a trustee who is a living person, within the confines of trust investment law which is controlled by legislatures and courts with living members. Under the prudent investor standard which controls most trust investments, permissible investments are determined entirely by practices of living investors. Even when the donor has specified a different investment policy, courts can modify it if the policy produces unacceptable levels of risk or return.

The arguments over the costs and benefits of dead hand control are no easier to assess in trying to determine whether long-term trusts are good or bad for families. The primary effect of the Rule Against Perpetuities is to limit the extent to which the dead hand can control future ownership of property. The Rule requires that ultimate ownership be knowable within 21 years after lives in being. The harm controlled is that of uncertainty. Whether uncertainty is really bad for families is another hard question to answer.

Certainty of ownership is good both for the person who ends up owning the property and for the person who loses it, because it permits both to plan their lives accordingly. On the other hand, certainty of receiving gift property may reduce the incentive to productive labor for the recipient. Certainty of loss may produce a sense of unfairness, and demoralization or worse in the loser, which may lead to unproductivity or even unsocial conduct. Having property tied up in a trust providing a steady stream of economic benefits to a family may provide a solid base from which family members can pursue productive lives without the insecurity and compromises on education and culture that lack of money may bring. Alternatively, it may induce them to arrogance and sloth. If more members of our society had a secure financial base, we might have a healthier, better educated and more creative society. We might end up, however, with a more complacent, boring, and less productive society. Who knows?

In sum, I find it very difficult to feel certain either that more dead hand control is a bad thing or that it is a good thing. I envy those who are confident that we will be better or worse off if we permit 90-year trusts—I am not at all sure. Of one thing, however, I am sure: enactment of the Uniform Statutory Rule Against Perpetuities would not be the end of the world. Whatever problems would be created by bad drafting of long-term trusts could be ameliorated by increasing the discretionary powers of trustees, and increasing the ability of courts and beneficiaries to modify and terminate trusts. The law does not need to leave beneficiaries of poorly drafted 90-year trusts tied up in straitjackets.

3. Wealth Transmission Between Generations

John H. Langbein, *The Twentieth-Century Revolution in Family Wealth Transmission*, 86 MICH. L. REV. 722–730, 732–734, 736, 739–751 (1988)*

The ancient field of trust-and-estate law has entered upon a period of serious decline. * * * Although it has been fashionable to attribute this decline to the dramatic 1981 revision of the federal transfer taxes, which effectively relieved the middle classes from entanglement with the estate tax, the theme of this article is that the phenomenon has causes far more profound. The decline of the probate bar reflects the decline of probate. The decline of probate has two quite different dimensions. One is the much-remarked rise of the nonprobate system. Financial intermediaries operate a noncourt system for transferring account balances and other property on death with little or no lawyerly participation. * * *

The decline of probate has another dimension that has not been well understood. Fundamental changes in the very nature of wealth have radically altered traditional patterns of family wealth transmission, increasing the importance of lifetime transfers and decreasing the importance of wealth transfer on death.

In this article I shall be concerned with private-sector wealth.[3] Into the eighteenth century, land was the dominant form of wealth. The technological forces that broke up older family-centered modes of economic organization called forth two new forms of private-sector wealth. One category is what we today call financial assets—that is, stocks, bonds, bank deposits, mutual fund shares, insurance contracts, and the like—which now comprise the dominant form of wealth. The other great form of modern wealth is what the economists call human capital. It is the skills and knowledge that lie at the root of advanced technological life.

The main purpose of this article is to sound a pair of themes about the ways in which these great changes in the nature of wealth have become associated with changes of perhaps comparable magnitude in the timing and in the character of family wealth transmission. My first theme * * * concerns human capital. Whereas of old, wealth transmission from parents to children tended to center upon major items of patrimony such as the family farm or the family firm, today for the broad middle classes, wealth transmission centers on a radically different kind of asset: the investment in skills. In consequence, intergenerational wealth transmission no longer occurs primarily upon the death of the parents, but rather, when the children are growing up, hence, during the parents' lifetimes.

My other main theme, * * * arises from the awesome demographic transformation of modern life. For reasons that I shall explore, those same parents who now make their main wealth transfer to their children inter vivos are also living much longer. The need to provide for the parents in their lengthy old age has put a huge new claim on family wealth, a claim that necessarily reduces the residuum that would otherwise have passed to survivors. A new institution has arisen to help channel the process of saving and dissaving for old age: the pension fund. The wealth of the private pension system consists almost entirely of financial assets. I shall emphasize a distinctive attribute of pension wealth, namely, the

[3] More than twenty years ago in a notable law review article, Charles Reich called attention to one species of 'new property'—claims to government largess, especially those we have come to call entitlement programs, such as Social Security and Medicare. Reich, *The New Property*, 73 YALE L.J. 733 (1964). Reich's "new property" lies largely outside the scope of this article, because the entitlements he identified lie mostly outside family dominion. You can neither give nor sell nor bequeath your Social Security claims.

bias toward annuitization. When wealth is annuitized, virtually nothing is left for transfer on death.

* * *

At the outset, I must emphasize a pair of exclusions from the trends being described in this article. I shall be talking about the patterns of wealth transmission that characterize the broad generality of American wealth-holders roughly, the upper third to upper half of the populace. I mean, in short, the middle and especially the upper-middle classes, which is to say, the mostly white-collar, technical, managerial, and professional cohort. These people propel the knowledge-based economy of our post-industrial age, and they command much of its wealth. The trends I shall be discussing have had less influence upon the wealth transmission practices at the extremes of our society—among the very rich and among the poor.

* * *

I. Prologue: Family Wealth Then and Now

It is often the case that the best way to broach the subject of the new is to identify the important characteristics of the old. In this instance, I begin by flipping the calendar backward a century and more, to the days when Abraham Lincoln lived on the American prairie and when his contemporaries were building the cities of the Atlantic seaboard, the Great Lakes, and the Ohio and Mississippi Valleys. We want to remind ourselves of some central traits of wealth holding and wealth transmission in this period.

A. Family Property Relations in the Last Century

The family was prototypically a unit of production. Nineteenth-century America was overwhelmingly a nation of small farms. In the towns and cities, the predominant economic entities were small-firm producers and small shops. Farmers, artisans, and shopkeepers had in common the tradition that the entire family worked in the enterprise. In those circumstances, contemporaries had little occasion to distinguish between what we think of as earned income (income from one's labor) and investment income (the return to property). The two income streams were merged in a single endeavor. Both the generation of the parents and the generation of the children looked to the farm or the firm for their livelihood, with scant attention to idle accounting questions about how much of their income to apportion to labor and how much to property.

In emphasizing that the returns to labor and capital were composite, I do not mean that the property component was unimportant. Property was desperately important. Ownership of a farm or a firm rescued you from a mean life of stoop labor in someone else's field, mill, or household. In former times, it was vastly harder to live by your skills alone, without patrimony. Accordingly, people of means aspired to nothing so much as to leave their children similarly advantaged. You hoped to transmit the farm or the firm, and thus in the quaint phrase of the time, to make for your children 'a provision in life.'

There was relatively little formal education. This was a low-tech age, and the transmission of skills, like so much else, could still occur within the family. You learned your trade alongside your parents and your relations, in the fields, in the firm, or at the hearth. Put differently, the family was not only the primary unit of production, it was the primary educational entity as well. Only a few crafts and learned professions required external education; and even in those pursuits, education was frequently assimilated to a domestic model through the apprenticeship system of training.

Succession to ownership rights in this multigenerational enterprise occurred upon death—that is, upon the death of the parents, typically of the father. Various familiar arrangements were made for the widow, not only the common-law life estate known as dower, but also life interests in fee or in trust that could provide a larger fraction than dower and that could extend beyond realty. But the tendency both in intestacy and for testate estates was to limit the widow to a life interest, in order to assure continuity of the enterprise in the hands of the next generation, whose members had already been long employed in the enterprise.

Notice in this connection that widowhood was materially less common than today. * * * [O]ver the century [prior to 1965], female survivorship expanded from a modest probability to a probability that is better than two-to-one. The reasons, of course, are not hard to discern. There has been a precipitous decline in the rate of mortality associated with childbearing. Furthermore, while both sexes have benefited from huge increases in longevity across the century, the advantage in favor of women has consistently expanded. Whereas spousal succession today is overwhelmingly a widow's business, in earlier times the wife was materially less likely to survive her husband than she is today; and when she did survive him, it was not likely to be for very long.

Accordingly, succession to the family farm or family firm typically occurred on the father's death. There was no reason for him to surrender dominion over the family patrimony inter vivos. Ownership until death reinforced parental control over the extended family and over its collective enterprise. Remember that although wealth transmission occurred on death, death occurred very much earlier than it does today. That is to say, succession on death occurred when both the parents and the children were younger than we now expect. This difference is, of course, no mystery. It results from the awesome change in life expectancy over the past century * * *. Thus, even though wealth transfer in the previous century tended to occur on death rather than inter vivos, decedents were less often elderly. The successors were typically young adults, as compared to the middle-aged children who typically succeed when parents die in modern circumstances.

Finally, to complete this snapshot of important traits of nineteenth-century wealth transmission patterns, I wish to say something about the diminished expectations of daughters. Perhaps the easy way to make this point is to remind you how often you have come across some family firm from earlier times in which the father associated the son or sons in the firm's name—for example, Steinway & Sons; but you have not seen firms called Steinway & Daughters. Although there were many exceptions, the wealth transmission process tended to favor the male line. The firm or the farm had to be worked. Except when a family had only a daughter or daughters, continuity within the patrimony emphasized the son.

B. Family Property Relations in Modern Times

In the late twentieth century, the family has in general ceased to be an important unit of production. To be sure, you can still find dribbles of cottage industry in America, and there is still a fair amount of Mom-and-Pop retailing, but in the main the production and sale of goods and services has forever left the home. The technological sophistication and marketing complexity of modern modes of production and distribution impose enormous capital requirements. Village blacksmiths cannot manufacture automobiles, airplanes, and oil rigs. The village entrepreneur can still sell a screwdriver or make a hamburger, but the evidence is overwhelming that the customer mostly prefers to patronize K-Mart or McDonald's. Thus, the characteristic unit of production in our age is corporate rather than domestic, it is the share company.

These trends extend to farming as well. American agriculture is ever more technology driven and capital intensive. It has become a byword that we live in an era of corporate agriculture. Family farms still exist in America, indeed, in some farming areas it would be fair to say that family farms remain characteristic. But a large fraction of them are hobby farms, secondary enterprises conducted by people whose main livelihood derives from employment outside the home. As farms have grown in size and productivity, an astonishing agricultural depopulation has occurred. In what used to be a nation of farmers, we are now fed by a mere 5% of the population, down from 44% in 1880, and it should be remembered that these people are not only feeding the rest of us, they are running our largest export industry as well.

Thus, in the main, we neither farm nor manufacture at home. The family has undergone a specialization of function. In economic terms, the family remains a unit of consumption but no longer a unit of production. Enterprise is organized outside the home, and the worker now leaves the home for his employment. Such a worker contributes his labor to his employment, but he no longer supplies the plant and equipment as he did in the bygone day of the family enterprise. The reason that most workers use external capital is, of course, closely connected to the technological and marketing forces that have magnified the size and complexity of the productive processes, the forces that drove the worker out of the home in the first place. Modern modes of enterprise are capital intensive. The blacksmith could afford his anvil, but we cannot expect the autoworker to supply his factory or the airplane pilot to bring along his own Boeing 747.

The ever-larger capital requirements of technologically advanced enterprise required modes of financing that exceeded the capabilities of the family. Ownership of a small firm or a small farm could lie within the scope of family-based capital accumulation and capital transmission, but we understand why IBM, General Electric, and AT&T cannot be family firms. The corporate form arose to facilitate the pooling and allocation of capital, as did the specialized institutions of finance. In the late twentieth century we recognize three dominant modes of financial intermediation: first, the corporation, and with it, the securities industry that makes the market in corporate shares and corporate debt; second, banking—commercial, investment, and savings and loan; and third, the insurance industry. All three were primitive in antebellum America. Not only have these financial intermediaries now displaced the family's role as the unit of capital accumulation, they have also created the new forms of wealth in financial assets—the various securities, depository claims, and other contract rights.

These instruments of financial intermediation now absorb the savings that the family previously devoted to the family enterprise. Because family wealth is no longer retained but rather invested externally, it now takes the form of claims on outside enterprises. These financial assets have become the characteristic form of transmissible wealth. It is the stuff of the financial pages. * * *

II. WEALTH TRANSFERS THROUGH HUMAN CAPITAL

The same underlying technological and economic forces that caused the dissolution of family-based enterprise have also stripped the family of much of its role as an educational institution. This development, which is in a sense quite obvious to us all, has had enormous implications for family wealth transmission, implications that have not been adequately appreciated.

It is a truism that a technological age requires a technologically proficient workforce. The awesome expansion of human knowledge over the past century and more has made the family obsolete as a repository and transfer agent for this huge range of knowledge. In olden times, I have said, you learned your trade at home and hearth, or else in apprenticeship to a neighbor. Only a handful of callings required training beyond these domestic patterns. Today, by contrast, we have gone so far in the opposite direction—toward externalizing education—that we even send people outside the home to prepare for life in the home. (I refer not simply to the study of what is called home economics, but to our ever-greater reliance upon the schools for basic acculturation.)

A. Educational Expenditure

The educational demands of modern economic life have become immense, and so has the cost of providing children with this educational endowment. A central thesis of this article is that paying for education has become the characteristic mode of intergenerational wealth transmission for most American families.

Look at the statistics in order to get a sense of the underlying magnitudes. Total expenditures for formal education in the United States in 1840 have been calculated at $9.2 million.[18] This sum increased over the nineteenth century, a period of relatively low inflation, to stand at $289.6 million in 1900. By 1959 the figure had reached $23.9 billion, which amounted to 4.8% of gross national product. Less than thirty years later, in the 1986–1987 academic year, the total expenditure on formal education stood at $282.1 billion, a figure that represented 7% of gross national product. Of these amounts, 60% went to fund primary and secondary education, 40% went to higher education.

* * *

Human capital, being literally embodied in mortals, is distinguished from physical capital by the frailty of the human condition. Human capital dies with the holder and thus needs to be created afresh in each generation. Of course, the highly transitory quality of human capital is really more a difference of degree than of kind. Machines and structures also fall apart or become obsolete, which is why we systematically account for the artifacts of physical capital by means of depreciation schedules.

* * *

There is no mystery about who has been paying the bill for this vast expansion of education. Even allowing for some scholarships, loans, and student labor, the main burden falls upon the parents. Indeed, even childless people pay substantial sums in taxes to support the public educational establishment. But for present purposes, the focus is upon propertied families who are raising children.

My thesis is quite simple, and, I hope, quite intuitive. I believe that, in striking contrast to the patterns of last century and before, in modern times the business of educating children has become the main occasion for intergenerational wealth transfer. Of old, parents were mainly concerned to transmit the patrimony—prototypically the farm or the firm, but more generally, that "provision in life" that rescued children from the harsh fate of being a mere laborer. In today's economic order, it is education more than property, the new human capital rather than the old physical capital, that similarly advantages a child.

* * *

Now it is quite obvious that very few families can afford to pay [for college and university expenses] on what we would call—in an accounting sense—a current basis. That is especially true when the family has more than one child in the educational mill at the same time. For most families, therefore, these education expenses represent capital transfers in a quite literal sense: The money comes from savings, that is, from the family's capital; or debt is assumed,

[18] Fishlow, *Levels of Nineteenth-Century American Investment in Education*, 26 J. ECON. HIST. 418, 420 (1966).

meaning that the money is borrowed from the family's future capital.

* * *

From the proposition that the main parental wealth transfer to children now takes place inter vivos, there follows a corollary: Children of propertied parents are much less likely to expect an inheritance. Whereas of old, children did expect the transfer of the farm or firm, today's children expect help with educational expenses, but they do not depend upon parental wealth transfer at death. Lengthened life expectancies mean that the life-spans of the parents overlap the life-spans of their adult children for much longer than used to be. Parents now live to see their children reaching peak earnings potential, and those earnings often exceed what the parents were able to earn. Today, children are typically middle-aged when the survivor of their two parents dies, and middle-aged children are far less likely to be financially needy. It is still the common practice within middle- and upper-middle-class families for parents to leave to their children (or grandchildren) most or all of any property that happens to remain when the parents die, but there is no longer a widespread sense of parental responsibility to abstain from consumption in order to transmit an inheritance.

* * *

III. The Pension Revolution

The other great chapter in the saga of fundamental change in family wealth transmission being told in this article concerns the phenomenon of retirement and the rise of the private pension system. Pension funds are another artifact of the new forms of wealth that arose in consequence of the breakup of older, family-centered modes of production. Neither on the prairie nor in the cities of Abraham Lincoln's day had anybody ever heard of a pension fund. Your life expectancy was such that you were unlikely to need much in the way of retirement income. If you did chance to outlive your period of productive labor, you were in general cared for within the family.

Not only is the need for a retirement income stream relatively recent, but so too is the mode of wealth that now supplies it. Pension funds are composed almost entirely of financial assets—the instruments of financial intermediation—that distinctively modern form of property that was still of peripheral importance in the last century.

* * *

A. The Enhancement of Life Expectancy

The way to begin thinking about the pension revolution is to grasp the magnitude of the underlying demographic phenomena that brought it about. Life expectancy a hundred years ago was about forty-five years. Today, it is seventy-five years and climbing.

Behind the awesome spurt in life expectancy over the last century or so is a phenomenon that has been called "the elimination of premature disease."[49] In a nutshell, the insight is that diseases belong in two categories—the infectious or acute diseases that we have now largely banished from the mortality tables; and those diseases of old age that appear to set intrinsic limits on human longevity. Some researchers think that they see age eighty-five as the approximate eventual norm of the human life span. In 1980 white females were living to within seven years of that ideal. Three of those seven years of what is called 'average premature death' are accounted for by violent death—automobile accidents, bathtub falls, and so forth. Thus, from the medical viewpoint, it is being said that the "task of eliminating premature death . . . has been largely accomplished."

* * *

Part of what makes the AIDS epidemic so haunting is that it has happened against this background of utter triumph over earlier forms of infectious disease. What we cannot yet know is whether AIDS will remain an exception in a world where other infectious diseases remain insignificant; or whether the elimination of the ancient infectious diseases has set the stage for the development of new ones that, like AIDS, are resistant to the environmental measures and to the antibiotics that vanquished the old ones.

* * *

The pension fund is a direct response to the new demographics, in the setting of the new property. That point is best made if we return for a moment to our baseline in antebellum America, in order to see how the phenomenon of aging transpired when family wealth relations centered on the common patrimony in farm or firm.

Why were there no pension funds? The most important explanation is that, on account of the lower life expectancy of the times, far fewer people

---

[49] Fries & Crapo, *The Elimination of Premature Disease*, in Wellness and Health Promotion for the Elderly, at 19 (K. Dychtwald ed. 1986).

outlived their period of productive employment. You were, so to speak, much more likely to die with your boots on. I do not want to exaggerate this point. The forty-five-year life expectancy that prevailed a century ago is a composite figure, greatly distorted by infant mortality. Your chances of surviving to a reasonable age were much enhanced in the last century once you had navigated the shoals of infancy. * * * [But] even after we correct for infant mortality, the diminished life expectancy of the last century was marked enough to explain why contemporaries so seldom had occasion to talk about what we call the retirement income problem. If you chanced to outlive your productive years, you did not in general do it for very long.

But what of the relative handful who did need retirement support? The well-known pattern was one of reverse transfer. Within the family, the children, now mature, would support superannuated parents. For propertied persons, however, this image of reverse transfer conceals an important point. In the age of family-centered economic organization, the parents still owned the farm or the firm. In a sense that defies accounting precision but that is nevertheless worth emphasizing, when the elders received support from the children, they were living from their capital in the family enterprise—that enterprise to which the children would succeed when the elders died.

Now return to the late twentieth century to see what has changed. Not only have the demographics altered so that the elders are routinely surviving for long intervals beyond their years of employment, but in consequence of the transformation in the nature of wealth, their property has taken on a radically altered character. That family farm or family firm that was the source of intrafamilial support in former times has become ever more exceptional. Most parental wealth (apart from the parents' own human capital) now takes the form of financial assets, which embody claims upon those large-scale enterprises that have replaced family enterprise.

B. Pension Wealth

In propertied families, today's elderly no longer expect much financial support from their children. The shared patrimony in farm or firm that underlay that reverse transfer system in olden times has now largely vanished. Instead, people of means are expected to foresee the need for retirement income while they are still in the workforce, and to conduct a program of saving for their retirement. Typically, these people have already undertaken one great cycle of saving and dissaving in their lives—that program by which they effected the investment in human capital for their children. Just as that former program of saving was oriented toward a distinctively modern form of wealth, human capital, so this second program centers on the other characteristic form of twentieth-century wealth, financial assets.

A priori, we might expect that individuals would be left to save for retirement without government guidance, much as they are left alone to save and spend for other purposes, but that has not been the case. Instead, the federal government has intervened by creating irresistible tax incentives to encourage people to conduct much or most of their retirement saving in a special mode, the tax-qualified pension plan.

There are * * * crucial advantages to conducting retirement saving through a tax-qualified pension plan. First, most contributions to the plan are tax-deferred. When my employer contributes to a qualified pension or profit-sharing plan on my behalf, or when I contribute to a defined contribution plan such as a 401(k) or, in the case of academic personnel, a 403(b), I am saving with pretax dollars. If I am in the 25-percent bracket, the Treasury is contributing to my pension savings plan 25 cents in foregone taxation for my 75 cents in foregone consumption.

The second great tax advantage is that the earnings on qualified plan investments accrue and compound on a tax-deferred basis. It is not until the employee retires and begins to receive distributions of his pension savings that he pays income tax on the sums distributed. * * *

* * *

C. Annuitization Eliminates Succession

From the standpoint of our interest in the patterns of family wealth transmission, what is especially important about the pension system is that it has been deliberately designed to promote lifetime exhaustion of the accumulated capital. The same body of federal law that encourages pension saving also tries to ensure that pension wealth will be consumed over the lives of the worker and his spouse. I do not mean to say that the federal policy in favor of lifetime consumption of retirement savings cannot be defeated for particular clients using appropriately designed plans; indeed, that is one of the major avenues of tax and estate planning for the carriage trade that has arisen with the pension system. My point is simply that, in the main, the federal policy achieves its goal, and only a negligible fraction of pension wealth finds its way into intergenerational transfer.

The mechanism by which pension wealth is consumed is annuitization. Just as life insurance is insurance against dying too soon, annuitization insures against living too long. Annuitization allows people to consume their capital safely, that is, without fear of running out of capital while still alive. Annuitization requires a large pool of lives, which is achieved by various methods of aggregating the pension savings of many workers. * * * Annuitization is wonderfully effective in allowing a person to consume capital without fear of outliving his capital, but the corollary is also manifest: Accounts that have been annuitized disappear on the deaths of the annuitants. Not so much as a farthing remains for the heirs.[67]

From this brief tour of the private pension system, I hope it will be clear why I place this topic alongside my other main topic, wealth transfer by means of investment in human capital, as the two central chapters in what I have been calling the twentieth-century revolution in family wealth transmission. Both are developments of enormous magnitude, and both lead away from traditional wealth transfer on death. Propertied parents used to live from their patrimony in farm or firm and then transmit the patrimony at death. Modern parents tend to possess nontransmissible human capital more than older forms of property. Using their human capital to create lifetime income streams, modern parents now undertake two cycles of saving and dissaving, one for the children's education, the other for retirement. The investment in the children necessarily occurs in the parents' lifetimes. And especially when the retirement saving program is channeled through the enticing format of the qualified pension plan, the pressures for annuitization cause this enormous component of modern family wealth to be largely exhausted upon the parents' deaths. Transfer on death, the fundamental pattern of former times, is, therefore, ceasing to characterize the dominant wealth transmission practices of the broad middle classes.

IV. Wealth Transfer on Death

A. The Carriage Trade

Decline is not extinction. The trust-and-estate bar survives, and the main reason is the carriage trade. * * * [T]he revolution in family wealth transmission stops short of really substantial accumulations of wealth. The carriage trade is hugely important. * * * The top sliver of wealth holders is indeed very affluent, and among them the need for estate planning services will continue unabated.

To be sure, the transformation in the nature of property has affected great wealth holders as well as small. The family enterprise is less common, the portfolio of financial assets more prevalent. But the changes in the patterns of wealth transfer that I have been describing for the middle and upper-middle classes are much less important for the very well-to-do. * * * [T]he educational expenditures that loom so large for conventionally propertied families constitute for dynastic wealth holders a much smaller drain on family wealth.

Likewise, the qualified pension-plan account is not an acceptable vehicle for great fortunes. * * * The simple truth is that dynastic wealth cannot be stuffed into a pension account.

B. The Middle Market

Turning to the middle and upper-middle classes, we can identify a variety of factors that explain why the trust-and-estate lawyer survives even where he can no longer thrive. The personal circumstances of some propertied decedents fall outside the prototype that I have described—for example, people who are childless, or whose employers did not offer much opportunity for pension saving. But even people who fully experience the two cycles of saving and dissaving that I have described will have additional property outside the pension accounts. This wealth is likely to comprise both financial assets and real estate, especially residential real estate, although much of that real estate is held in probate-avoiding forms of concurrent ownership.

* * *

[M]uch of the nonpension wealth that survives for transfer on death in middle- and upper-middle-class families is deeply affected by another great trend that has fundamentally diminished the lawyerly role in wealth transfer on death. I refer to the explosive growth in the use of nonprobate modes of transfer. Residential real estate is widely held in joint tenancy, under which a death certificate suffices to clear title without probate or other court proceedings. The more interesting phenomenon is the rise of the mass

[67] Unless the plan offers and the participant elects a mode of annuitization that provides a guaranteed income stream (typically 10 or 20 years); in such cases, successors take the remainder of the stream if the annuitants die within the period.

will substitutes that employ noncourt transfer systems—life insurance, pension accumulations prior to annuitization, POD accounts, joint accounts, and so forth.

* * *

Apace with the decline in demand for lawyer-assisted planning services has been the diminution of demand for lawyer-assisted transfer services even when probate or administration of an estate must occur. The probate reform movement of the 1960s, epitomized in the Uniform Probate Code's provisions for simplified probate and for nonadministration of very small estates, has further limited the scope for court-operated transfer services.

A comprehensive account of the patterns by which inter vivos wealth transfers now displace transfers that in former times occurred on death would also embrace the huge twentieth-century increase in the divorce rate. Dissolution upon divorce has replaced dissolution upon death as the predominant mode of terminating a marriage. The property transfers that divorce precipitates, both transfers to spouses and transfers to children, supplant in some measure a wealth transfer process that used to occur through succession.

V. Conclusion

Increasingly, estate planning services for the middle and upper-middle classes have the quality of contingency planning. The client is motivated largely by concern to make arrangements for his family in the unlikely event that he should die prematurely. He does not expect property actually to pass under the instrument he executes. In this sense, he views his estate plan somewhat like his term life insurance policy. It is catastrophe insurance, worth having even though it is unlikely to be needed.

The modern expectation is that for middle-class wealth, the main intergenerational transfer will occur in mid-life, in the form of educational expenditures. The characteristic wealth of later years, the income streams from the public and private pension systems, do not give rise to heirship. Thus, wealth transfer on death is ever less important to the middle classes; and when it does occur, it is ever more likely to be channeled through the nonprobate system. These are the great forces that underlie the decline of the trust-and-estate bar.

So long as the carriage trade abides, the trust-and-estate bar will not go the way of the blacksmith, but the precipitous decline of the middle-class market is likely to continue. From the revolutionary changes that have affected the family property relations of the middle and upper-middle classes, only table scraps remain for the trust-and-estate lawyer. The days of routine, lawyer-guided wealth-transfer-on-death for the middle classes have largely passed.

B. Concurrent, Marital and "New Family" Ownership

The standard common law concurrent estates have remained virtually unchanged for quite some time. The tenancy in common and joint tenancy with rights of survivorship have not been a recent source of controversy. Marital estates and the status of non-traditional families, however, have been the source of both change and debate. The adoption of marital property statutes for the division of property at divorce in the common law states has dramatically altered the contours of family property law. Some of the consequences of that change in legal regime are discussed by Joan Williams in her article, *Women and Property*. She also quarrels with some of the conclusions John Langbein makes in his article, *Twentieth-Century Revolution in Family Wealth Transmission*, excerpted in the prior section. Carol Rose adds another layer of issues to the distribution of wealth within families and society, arguing in her article *Women and Property: Gaining and Losing Ground*, that cultural attitudes about women systematically undermine their ability to accumulate wealth.

Dramatic changes have also occurred in the composition of "families." Since the decision in the now classic case of *Marvin v. Marvin*, 18 Cal.3d 660, 557 P.2d 106 (1976), vast amounts of commentary have been published on the development of new rules for governing the property transactions by and the dissolution of non-marital intimate relationships. William A. Reppy's article, *Property and Support Rights of Unmarried Cohabitants: A Proposal for Creating a New Legal Status*, is excerpted here. After reading it, you might ask if a feminist like Joan Williams would come to the same conclusions as Reppy. For additional reading, consult an earlier, but still insightful, piece by Grace Ganz Blumberg, *Cohabitation Without Marriage: A Different Perspective*, 28 UCLA L. REV. 1126 (1981).

Further material on the history of concurrent and family estates may be found in Ray August, *The Spread of Community Property Law to the Far West*, 3 WESTERN LEG. HIST. 35 (1990); Richard H. Chused, *Married Women's Property Law: 1800–1850*, 71 GEO. L. J. 1359 (1983).

1. Marital Property

Joan C. Williams, *Women and Property* 1-13, 17-20 (1992) (Unpublished Manuscript)*

* * *

The feminization of poverty is not new, but it is dramatic. Sixty percent of all people in poverty and two-thirds of the elderly poor are women. Female-headed families are five times more likely to be poor and up to ten times more likely to stay poor than families with a male present. Single mothers and their children have become the paradigm poor at a time when their numbers are increasing: 19% of all families, and fully fifty percent of black families are headed by women.[1]

Children are even poorer than women. They are, in fact, the poorest group in the United States. Nearly one-fourth of all children, one-half of black children, and two-thirds of children living in female-headed households are poor.

Thus statistics suggest that our property system enriches men at the expense of women and children, a view in sharp variance with the official story about the relationship of women and property. That the property system used to block women from property ownership is uncontroversial. Before the nineteenth century, the common law system of coverture was an integral part of a gender system that viewed women as intellectually, spiritually and morally weaker than men, in need not only of men's physical protection, but of their practical and spiritual guidance as well. For the wife's "own protection" she had to obey and submit to her husband. The law expressed this view through the doctrine of marital unity, paraphrased in Blackstone's famous statement that "the husband and wife are one, and that one is the husband." Married women "covered" by their husbands (hence "coverture") lost control over property brought into the marriage, and never gained control over property acquired during it. Wives' personal property was owned by the husband in fee simple; husbands were entitled to possession, use and income from wives' real estate; a husband's interest could be mortgaged by him and seized by his creditors.[18] In unsettled economic times—common in the 19th century—wives' property often was seized for husbands'

---

*Copyright Joan C. Williams, 1993. Reprinted with the permission of the author. Another version of this article is soon to be published under the title *Privatization as a Gender Issue*, in GREGORY S. ALEXANDER & GRAZYNA SKAPSKA (EDS.), A FOURTH WAY?: PROPERTY, PRIVATIZATION AND THE NEW DEMOCRACIES (RUTLEDGE, CHAPMAN & HALL, INC. 1993).

[1] [Editor's Note: Citations for these and other statistics, edited out to conserve space, are included in the version of this article soon to be published. *See* note * *supra*.]

[18] Husbands received an "estate jure uxoris," which left legal title with the wife, but gave the husband the right to possession, rents and profits to all lands of which the wife was seized either before or during the marriage for the duration of the marriage or the joint lives of the couple. The husband could sell and mortgage his estate in the land, and it could be seized by his creditors. * * * In other words, the wife could regain access to her real property if she outlived her husband. Husbands could not alienate wives' land outright without their "free" consent through the practice of "private examination." *See* MARYLYNN SALMON, WOMEN AND THE LAW OF PROPERTY IN EARLY AMERICA 15 (1986).

debts.[19] "Although a man was morally obligated to cherish and support his wife, the common law permitted him to squander her property with impunity, to deprive her at will of creature comforts, and if she complained to 'chastise her roundly,'"[20] (but with a stick no thicker than his thumb).[21]

Husbands' rights over real estate were particularly important because real estate was the chief form both of on-going self-support and of wealth. Yet for wives—particularly abandoned wives—who sought to support themselves through wage labor or small businesses, coverture's enforcement of dependence meant that their contracts were legally unenforceable and their wages were the property of their husbands.

Coverture was an integral part of a gender system built around the ideology of female inferiority and designed for an agrarian economy. Between 1780 and 1830, this system gave way to a new gender system in which males gradually entered the market as wage laborers for work that was, for the first time, temporally and geographically isolated from the home. In theory, anyway, they earned a "family wage" that allowed mothers to eschew wage labor in favor of domestic work.[27] This economic shift accompanied ideological shifts in the conceptualization of children's needs and mothers' roles. Under the agrarian/inequality model, mothers had to fit childrearing in around household production: if mothers did not make clothes, food, candles and keep fires burning, everyone would quite literally starve in the dark. Older siblings and servant girls helped with care of younger children, and fathers were charged with the training of older boys.

In the nineteenth century, all this changed. With fathers now out of the house, child care was reconceptualized as requiring full-time attention from mothers who were, the new ideology of domesticity asserted, uniquely suited to that role by their natural bent towards nurture and self-sacrifice. In the words of historian Nancy Cott, "childrearing became the exclusive province of mothers and the province of mothers alone."[30] Only 2.5% of married white women worked outside the home as of 1890.

The traditional story told by legal historians is that the Married Women's Property Acts ended women's blocked access to property by abolishing coverture in favor of a more enlightened embrace of equality for women. Recent work by historians of women has substantially undermined this interpretation. Many Married Women's Property Acts, passed simultaneously with other debtor relief statutes, were designed not to achieve gender equality but to protect family property from husbands' creditors in uncertain economic times. Equality for women was not an invariable—or perhaps even a frequent—goal or effect of Married Women's Property Acts.[34] Instead, supporters called upon imagery, drawn from domesticity, of virtuous wives victimized by unscrupulous fortune-seeking-husbands, and often focused on mothers' need for control over property so they could protect and nurture in their characteristically domestic sphere. Once Married Women's Property Acts are viewed as expression more of domesticity than of equality, it also becomes easier to explain their slow-as-molasses progress in granting women anything approaching full relief from the strictures of coverture. Many of the acts only allowed women to continue ownership of property they brought into marriages, but not, for example, the right to contract or to their wages. In Georgia, for example, wives gained ownership of their wages only in 1943.

The revisionist interpretation of the Married Women's Property Acts generally only defers, for a period, the triumphal vision of equality for women. If equality in fact was achieved, how do we explain the statistics with which we began?

The contemporary impoverishment of women and children is rarely recognized for what it is: an integral part of the sex/gender system that has succeeded domesticity. The most overt characteristic of this system is the shift from domestic ideology to the

---

[19] *See* Richard H. Chused, *Married Women's Property Law: 1800–1850*, 71 GEO. L.J. 1359, 1400–1404 (1983).

[20] MAX BLOOMFIELD, AMERICAN LAWYERS IN A CHANGING SOCIETY, 1776–1876, 95 (1976), *quoted in* Isabel Marcus, *Locked In and Locked Out: Reflections on The History of Divorce Law Reform in New York State*, 37 BUFF. L. REV. 375, 396 (1988/89) [hereinafter Marcus, *Locked Out*] * * *.

[21] This is the origin of the phrase "rule of thumb." The historical common law rule defined the width of the switch with which a husband could legally beat his wife in this way. *See* Caitlin Borgmann, Note, *Battered Women's Substantive Due Process Rights: Can Orders of Protection Deflect Deshaney?*, 65 N.Y.U.L. REV. 1280, n.3 (1990).

[27] *See* Maurine Weiner Greenwald, *Working-Class Feminism and the Family Wage Ideal*, 76 J. AM. HIST. 118 (1989) for a recent contribution to the literature on the family wage ideal.

[30] NANCY F. COTT, THE BONDS OF WOMANHOOD 46 (1977).

[34] *See* Suzanne Lebsock, *Radical Reconstruction and the Property Rights of Southern Women*, 53 J. SOUTHERN HIST. 195 (1977); * * * Richard Chused, *Married Women's Property Law: 1800–1850*, 71 GEO. L. J. 1359 (1983); * * * Norma Basch, *The Emerging Legal History of Women in the United States*, 12 SIGNS 99 (1986) * * *.

ideology of gender equality. This shift was accompanied by key changes in the institution of marriage. Marriage traditionally involved an irreversible commitment; yet as emotional gratification and personal fulfillment "became the sine qua non of marriage, divorce became an indispensable element in the institution of matrimony."[40] The divorce rate skyrocketed: only 8% of marriages ended in divorce in 1870; today nearly 50% do.

The divorce rate and the ideology of gender-equality are widely recognized as important phenomena; less well understood is that they are integral parts of a larger family ecology. A central tension in that ecology is that the ideology of equality coexists with sharply differentiated gender patterns within marriage. In the contemporary United States, wives ordinarily subordinate their careers to their husbands' even in the absence of children—perhaps the single most open continuation of wives' traditional subordinate status.[42] Moreover, once children are born, wives do 80% of the housework[43] and a highly disproportionate share of the child care: one study estimated that fathers spend an average of only twelve minutes a day on solo child care.[44] Fathers' lack of family contributions means that employed mothers bear a "double burden" of market and domestic labor, which translates into less sleep,[45] less leisure,[46] less time at meals,[47] and much longer hours than either their husbands[48] or traditional housewives.[49] Wives' "second shift" works in combination with sex discrimination, sex segregation and the pattern of subordinated careers to bar women disproportionately from desirable jobs: the result is that labor market participation differs dramatically between men and women. Fully 40% of mothers with children under six do not work outside the home; roughly one-third of employed women work part-time. The contemporary sex/gender system, therefore, combines three basic elements: the ideology of equality, marital instability, and sharply differentiated gender patterns within marriage. The key gender shift between the domesticity/wage labor gender system and the contemporary system is not—as is often believed—a shift from dependent to independent wives. Instead, the key shift is from wives totally cut off from market resources to wives who are secondary workers with careers subordinated to both their husbands' and their children's (socially constructed) needs. Wives' "double burden" means that men's market participation is relatively unaffected by fatherhood: most men of all classes feel entitled to perform as ideal workers, which in practice means workers without daytime child care responsibilities.

The final element of the contemporary sex-gender system is the least well-recognized of all: a shift in the nature of wealth. In an insightful article, John Langbein has documented a key shift in the nature of wealth in the twentieth century.[53] Whereas, as of the beginning of the nineteenth century, wealth was held primarily in the form of real estate, by the end of the twentieth century a key form of wealth was human capital. Langbein notes that, although traditionally "wealth transmission from parents to children tended to center upon major items of patrimony such as

---

[40] Frank Furstenberg, *Divorce and the American Family*, 16 ANN. REV. SOC. 379, 380 (1990) * * *.

[42] *See* Norma Heckman, Rebecca Bryson & Jeff Bryson, *Problems of Professional Couples: A Content Analysis*, 39 J. MARRIAGE & FAM. 323 (1977) (finding women willing to place their careers secondary to the needs of their families and the needs of their husband's careers); Jeylan Mortimer, Richard Hall & Reuben Hill, *Husbands' Occupational Attributes as Constraints on Wives' Employment*, 5 SOC. WORK & OCCUPATIONS 285 (1978) (suggesting that attributes of husband's work limit sharing of family work and put pressure on wife to support husband's career to the detriment of her own work participation and attainment).

[43] *See* Donna H. Berardo, et al., *A Residue of Tradition: Jobs, Careers and Spouses' Time in Housework*, 49 J. MAR. & FAM. 391, 388 (1987). Another study showed that husbands barely contribute enough domestic labor to make up for the additional work their presence in the household creates. See Judith A. Heath & David H. Cicel, *Patriarchy, Family Structure, and the Exploitation of Women's Labor*, 22 J. ECON. ISSUES 781, 788 (1988).

[44] *See* Graeme Russell & Norma Radin, *Increased Paternal Participation: The Fathers Perspective*, in FATHERHOOD AND FAMILY POLICY 139, 142 (Michael Lamb & Abraham Sagi eds. 1983) (reporting on studies that found fathers in typical families average 12 to 24 minutes a day in solo child care). For other studies that report fathers spending more time on child care, *see* Nijole Benokraitis, *Fathers in the Dual Earner Family*, in DIMENSIONS OF FATHERHOOD 254 (Shirley Hanson & Frederick Borett eds. 1985); Frances Grossman, William Pollack & Ellen Golding, *Fathers and Children: Predicting the Quality and Quantity of Fathering*, 24 DEV. PSYCHOLOGY 82, 84 (1988), quoted in Woodhouse, *supra* note 40, at 284.

[45] *See* ARLIE HOCHSCHILD, THE SECOND SHIFT 3, 279, n.2 (1989), *quoting* Shelley Coverman, *Gender, Domestic Labor Time, and Wage Inequality*, 48 AM. SOC. REV. 626 (1983).

[46] *See* A. HOCHSCHILD, *supra* note 45, at 271-73 ("leisure gap" of 11 to 19 hours/week).

[47] *Id.* at 279.

[48] *Id.* at 3 (employed mothers work roughly 15 hours longer than employed fathers each week).

[49] *See* Heath & Cicel, *supra* note 43, at 787 (employed wives work 144% of total time of traditional homemaker).

[53] John Langbein, *The Twentieth-Century Revolution in Family Wealth Transmission*, 86 MICH. L. REV. 722 (1988).

the family farm or the family firm, today for the broad middle classes, wealth transmission centers on a radically different kind of asset: the investment in skills."

In former times, low wage levels meant "it was vastly harder to live by your skills alone, without patrimony." During the period when ownership of physical assets was the key to economic power, women could not own physical assets. Now that they have gained the legal right to own physical assets, such assets no longer constitute the crucial component of economic power. In most families, human capital is the major form of family wealth. Just how unimportant physical assets have become is suggested by data on divorcing couples. Study after study has documented that most divorcing couples own little or no property apart from household possessions. * * *

Family law scholars have long recognized that the primary asset of most American families is not physical property but the human capital of individual family members. Langbein's focus on intergenerational transfers means he misses the single most important mechanism for family wealth transmission: the gender roles that systematically diminish wives', and enhance husbands', human capital.

Feminists have long noted that marriage generally hurts women's, and helps men's careers. The key mechanism here is men's sense of entitlement to performing as a "responsible worker," related to the linkage of virility to employability. Because the "ideal" worker is one without daytime child care responsibilities, even men who believe in gender equality end up tapping a flow of domestic services from their wives: to meet their employers' expectations—and their own.

Although men in general feel entitled to be ideal workers, significant class differences emerge in the mechanisms of disinvestment in women. In the middle and upper classes, where the ideology of gender equality is strong, gender tends less to determine career choice. Instead, disinvestment occurs within marriage. After the birth of children, the wife becomes "more realistic" and "chooses" career marginalization so that her children receive care according to middle class standards without affecting her husband's ability to perform as an ideal worker: the chief mechanism of disinvestment is the "mommy track." Among the working class, where the ideology of gender equality has less strong a hold, gender tends to influence initial career choice: thus the chief mechanism of disinvestment is the "choice" of a career.

Together, these two mechanisms are remarkably effective in concentrating human capital ownership upon men. Yet women, upon divorce, remain responsible for not only the care but for the lion's share of the financial support of children. Studies document that treating fathers' human capital as their personal property not only impoverishes women, but also results in systematic disinvestment in children. Children of divorce, unlike children in intact families, are less likely to equal or surpass their parents' social and economic status or obtain a college education. One study showed that well over half of the children studied were downwardly mobile: they were less likely to go to college, more likely to drop out of college because of financial difficulties, and only about half as likely to enter professions as their fathers. Thus the legal rules defining fathers' human capital as their personal property cuts not only women, but also children, off from human capital accumulation.

To summarize: three systems of property law have been integral parts of three gender systems in different eras of American history. Coverture expressed the pre-nineteenth century view that women's inferiority required their welfare (and their assets) to be entrusted to men. In the nineteenth century, the predominant thrust behind the Married Women's Property Acts was the view that men belonged in the competitive market sphere, while women needed enough—but no more—control over family property than was necessary to protect their separate, domestic sphere. Today, the ideology of equality ensures that women have the formal right to own property, but the law steps in to define property in a way that excludes human capital—leaving women with disproportionately little property to own. Property law thus plays a central role in the contemporary as well as the historical impoverishment of women and the children dependent upon them.

The key legal mechanism that updates coverture is the sense—expressed both in popular legal consciousness and in the laws of divorce—that "he who earns it, owns it." A central irony is that this mechanism is not even considered a part of property law. Consequently, the chief mechanisms for allocating entitlement to human capital—the chief form of societal wealth—are not studied in first-year law school, nor are they recognized as property rights allocations thereafter. Coverture at least was open in debarring wives from economic resources, and arguments for or against coverture rested on substantive reasons for allocating entitlement between men and women. In sharp contrast, the contemporary allocation of human capital rights to men is decided in the context of divorce, through a system that focuses not on the relative merits of different systems of entitlement, but on a particular marital failure and a series of three boxes: child support, alimony and asset division. Both the boxes and the context disadvantage women in significant ways.

The divorce context means that wives' claims to human capital are not decided in the context of a general system of social entitlement, but in the context of a particular marital failure, where the key issue from the husband's viewpoint is whether his freedom is going to be significantly eroded by obligations to his former family. This means that wives' claims to human capital are decided by predominantly male courts and legislatures in a framework where husbands' and wives' interests sharply diverge. Moreover, husbands' interests are easy to frame in the most forceful and persuasive rhetorics available in contemporary American life: the language of entitlement to liberty and personal self-fulfillment. In sharp contrast, the wife making a claim on the family wage has to contend with powerful societal messages about the undesirability of dependence. Americans' distrust of dependence, fed by feminists, dates back much earlier, to the association of dependence and corruption in the republican tradition.[72] While powerful American rhetorics enhance the husbands' position in the divorce context, therefore, equally powerful rhetorics undermine the position of the wife.

Family law's three little boxes disadvantage women in many ways. An obvious one is that the key box for granting post-divorce income to wives is the dismally titled box of alimony. Under the traditional fault system, alimony was awarded only when the husband had defaulted on his marital obligations in an era that took such defaults very seriously. Nonetheless, it became associated with stereotypes traditionally used to control, discredit and disempower women. "Alimony drones" were (and continue to be) associated in the popular imagination with scheming, manipulative women hoodwinking men out of the fruits of their hard work. Alimony, in other words, is a concept improbabilized by misogyny, yet we inherit it as the only family law box available in which to place wives' claims for access to the family wage.

Alimony's off-putting emotional tone means that alimony starts off as a disempowered concept. Hence very few women have ever been awarded alimony.[74] Moreover, alimony's off-putting tone—combined, one suspects, with the self-interest of predominantly male legislatures—led to an evisceration of wives' common law claims during the no-fault "divorce revolution." Common legislative changes both restricted alimony to situations where the wife could not support herself and, even then, to limited time periods for rehabilitation"—as if raising children were some unmentionable disease. The latter shift fundamentally changed property rights by eliminating wives' traditional entitlement to the family wage even for women who had not worked for decades. The former was perfectly designed to eliminate even the possibility of temporary entitlement for a majority of women in a system where the paradigm couple consisted of an idea-worker husband and a secondary-worker wife.

* * *

The entrenched assumptions of family law have affected the scholarship on post-divorce obligations in several ways. At the most basic level, family law has influenced many commentators to translate the problem of post-divorce impoverishment into a call for a new theory of alimony. This formulation greatly understates the importance of what is at issue.

What's at stake is not merely a new rationale for an unattractive concept—alimony—that has never helped the overwhelming majority of women. The issue, instead, is whether property rights will be allocated so that women and children are not cut off from the chief form of societal wealth upon divorce. This new formulation, in my view, spins the issue in a way much more favorable to the interests of women and children than does the formulation within a traditional alimony framework.

A second drawback of the traditional family law formulation is its "divide and conquer" effect of splitting up two issues that should not be separated: entitlements of children, and of their caretakers, to "fathers'" income. The literature on divorce awards at times ignores a central, inescapable fact: divorced mothers' needs stem from the needs of their depen-

---

[72] *See* Stanley N. Katz, *Thomas Jefferson and the Right to Property in Revolutionary America*, 19 J.L. & ECON. 467 (1976) * * *.

[74] Mary C. O'Connell, *Alimony After No-Fault: A Practice in Search of a Theory*, 23 N. ENG. L. REV. 437 (1988) * * *.

dent children. This oversight at times leads commentators to reify an eternal-sounding dichotomy between men's and women's needs, or between a "masculine" and a "feminine" lifestyle. The issue is not one of inherent differences between men and women, but the impact of an historically specific childrearing system in which children's inevitable dependency is translated into economic vulnerability for the vast bulk of their mothers.

The alimony-versus-child support dynamic also means that commentators fail to address the problem of post-divorce obligations in a comprehensive way. For example, commentators focused on alimony do not note that child support, too, systematically excludes on-going family claims to fathers' human capital. The economic studies underlying child support guidelines rigorously preclude any needs beyond day-to-day requirements: the portion of mortgage payments allocable to rent are covered, for example, but not the portion allocated to repayment of capital. The child support system thus cuts children of divorced fathers off from their fathers' ability to accumulate wealth, for college or any other purpose, in a way that is integral to any consideration of fathers' post-divorce obligations.

The first point, then, is that commentators need to substitute a broader inquiry into how to allocate property rights in place of a narrower one into how to structure and justify alimony. Property concepts offer a potentially useful resource in framing that inquiry: the historical notion of the family wage. In the nineteenth century, men mobilized the ideology of domesticity—the notion that women "ought naturally" to be in the home—to support their claims to wages high enough to support a family. While husbands made this argument to their employers, one suspects they less often made it to their wives. And yet the phrase did reflect popular notions of intrafamily property ownership quite different from those prevalent today. Many husbands in working class communities handed over their paychecks to their wives, and received in return only an allowance for their personal discretionary spending. Post-divorce claims to income should be seen in this light. Recent family law scholars, obsessed with fault or its absence, sometimes lose sight of the fact that traditional alimony expressed a different notion of family entitlements than what exists today. The underlying message was that wives have permanent entitlement to the family wage. The question is how to return to that prior understanding.

A threshold issue is whether the "family wage" concept is applicable in contemporary life, given the truism that today wives as well as husbands work. The description of family ecology offered above is helpful in this context. The truism that "most mothers work" * * * veils the fact that 40% of mothers with children under six do not, and that one-third of employed women usually work part-time. Our family ecology, then, is one in which wives marginalize their market participation so their children can have parental care while their husbands perform as ideal workers, earning the bulk of the family income.

This description allows us to reframe the basic unfairness of the current system: at divorce, the family wage is abruptly redefined as the personal property of the husband. This process strikes not only divorced women and their children, but also an extraordinary range of political forces on both the right and the left, as outrageous. The question is how to tap that sense of outrage.

* * *

Note

Marital and community property rules only divide the capital assets of a married couple at divorce. If Williams is correct that use of marital and community property rules systematically underpay divorcing women for "voluntarily" marginalizing themselves in the workplace for the benefit of their husbands and children, should the rules be changed to divide the couples capital assets in inverse proportion to their earnings during the marriage? What about property allocations at death? Should a surviving spouse control that amount of the couple's property which is inversely proportional to the surviving spouse's share of earnings while the marriage existed?

Carol M. Rose, *Women and Property: Gaining and Losing Ground*, 78 VA. L. REV. 421–433, 437–447, 449–459 (1992)*

A quite common perception about women and property is that women do not have much, at least by comparison to men. Even if women do have property formally in their names, men seem to be the ones who initially acquired it and actually control it. Though there are exceptions—even whole societies that are exceptional—they have a rather exotic air. In the ordinary course of things, we are surprised to find women of great wealth, just as we are surprised to find women who lead Fortune 500 companies. On the other hand, it is hardly news that women are disproportionately represented as heads of household among the poor. Between these extremes of wealth and poverty, women just do not seem to be as "propertied" as men, except insofar as they happen to be located in families headed by men. Indeed, even within the household, the serious money often seems to be at the disposal of the husband, not the wife.

Why might this be? Why might women be systematically worse off than men when it comes to acquiring and owning property? There are many possible explanations, including theories of exploitation, sociobiology, and historical circumstance. I will take an approach somewhat different from those, although some of the ideas from those other approaches will appear here, too.

My plan is to take a few simple ideas from game theory and explore how women might systematically do worse than men with respect to acquiring property, if one makes either of two related assumptions. The first assumption is that women have a greater "taste for cooperation" than men. The second, somewhat weaker assumption is that women are merely perceived to have a greater taste for cooperation than men, even though that perception may be erroneous. Following the lead of much of the modern law-and-economics literature, my analysis will draw examples from both market and nonmarket "economies." Though these examples are largely hypothetical, I expect some will seem quite familiar. Indeed, that is precisely the goal: to see if these assumptions can explain a wide range of familiar examples.

* * *

I. THE GAME-THEORY APPROACH

To set the stage, I will discuss two analytical "games" that are now familiar in legal academic circles. The first is the "prisoners' dilemma" ("PD"), named for its most famous illustrative story in which two prisoners are induced to "rat" on each other even though jointly they would be better off if both remained silent. The second, which has no conventional name except perhaps the descriptive "zero-sum game," is a noncooperative game in which the parties vie to win the most of a fixed total payoff.

A. PD Games

PD games ought to be positive-sum games—that is, games that result in gains from working together—but they have an unfortunate propensity to fail. In such games, two (or more) parties are collectively better off if they cooperate than if one or another of them "cheats" or "defects," but both (or all) have an incentive to cheat rather than to cooperate. I will not run through the traditional PD story here because it is so familiar but instead will use an agrarian version: Suppose two people, Sam and Louise (and perhaps a number of others) graze cattle on common grounds. They would be collectively better off if each would cooperate and restrain the number of their cattle or the intensity of their grazing, so that the field's grasses could replenish themselves. But Sam may fear that Louise will cheat while he restrains his cows—that he will be a patsy while she benefits from his self-restraint. On the other hand, even if he thinks she will cooperate, he may calculate that he himself can gain while she goes along with the program and restrains her cows. Thus, whether or not Sam thinks Louise is going to cheat, his immediate wealth-maximizing strategy is to cheat and, by parallel reasoning, so is hers. As a result of these calculations, of course, they wind up with an overgrazed desert—they have reenacted the dilemma, or the "tragedy of the commons," as multiple-person PD games are often called.[12]

[12] The main difference between the PD and the tragedy of the commons is that the former involves only two players whereas the latter potentially involves large numbers of

1. Overcoming PD Problems: Watching and Mimicking

Luckily, there are some ways around the dilemma or tragedy. One such escape route opens up when Sam and Louise can observe each other. Sam will start by restraining his own cows, but he will keep an eye on Louise. If Louise does not restrain her cows, too, he will let his just go ahead and munch. If Louise knows that Sam can detect her noncompliance and will untether his cows when she does not control her own, then she will have a good reason to cooperate. But Louise can watch Sam, too, so he will have the same reason to cooperate. Their cooperative arrangement is enforced by their mutual threat of retaliation—the ability of each to call off the deal and cancel the gains that both might have made.

It has been noted in game-theory literature that there are some major roadblocks to this escape from the PD. One such roadblock is the fact that someone has to start by cooperating, presumably at a point when the players have no prior history of dealing and no reason to trust each other. Beyond that roadblock is another: the escape works only where there is a sequence of moves and where the iteration of the players' respective moves raises the threat of retaliation if one should cheat. But the iterated game has a problem in the so-called "endgame" stage. Unless Sam and Louise anticipate an infinite sequence of cooperative steps, there is going to be a last move in their little minuet. As they approach that point, they realize that there are no further opportunities for retaliation, so each has an incentive to cheat just before the last move. Unfortunately, this endgame incentive infects the second-to-last move, too, where each thinks, "Hmm, I will cheat before he or she does." Then the cheating infects the third-to-last move and so on, all the way back to the first move.

With all these problems, one might suppose that cooperation would be rather rare. Even where cooperation could make all players better off, the tendency to act as self-interested utility-maximizers runs counter to the collective best interest and makes the players more likely to cheat and lose the advantages of cooperation. Prudence dictates that each player let others take the first step toward cooperation even though, if all are prudent, none will take that step.

2. Attitudinal Solutions: A Taste for Cooperation

If we shift gears and move to the real world, however, we realize that cooperation is not rare at all. In fact, we see an enormous amount of cooperative behavior in everyday life. Feminist psychologists such as Carol Gilligan point out that many people are willing to put the common good ahead of their own self-interest.[17] Moreover, many of our legal institutions certainly notice and promote cooperative and altruistic behavior. But we should note that from the perspective of individual utility maximization, this kind of behavior is not rational. At the very least, the willingness to take that trusting, risky first move—the move that makes further cooperative gains possible—depends on one or both parties' behaving imprudently, acting on something like a "taste for cooperation" that is not explained by the pure logic of self-interest.

By "taste for cooperation" I mean one or another of those nonrational attitudinal factors that enable cooperation to begin. By using the word "taste," of course, I do not mean to suggest only mild preferences; I also include deeply felt emotions or convictions. For example, the taste might derive from an enjoyment of the process of working with others. Alternatively, the taste might stem from a personal identification with a team or other group that shares a common goal. Quite commonly, the taste might come from an altruistic enjoyment of, or a sense of responsibility for, the well-being of other individuals. Any of these motivations might lead one to act in the furtherance of a common good or the good of another, even at some risk to one's purely personal self-interest.

Noncooperative attitudes—the converse of the taste for cooperation—also may take several different forms. Most common, no doubt, is a merely "rational" indifference to others or to common interests, or a merely prudent unwillingness to risk personal loss in taking the first steps toward forming or maintaining associations. An intermediate form of noncooperation involves a limited range or scope for cooperation. For example, the noncooperator may be willing to cooperate only on a limited basis, or with some classes of persons but not with others. The most extreme form of noncooperation is malice or hostility—a willingness to take actions that alienate or hurt others, such as punishment or cruelty. This type of noncooperator is the reverse altruist because he does

players—that is, it can be mapped as an "n-person" prisoners' dilemma. * * *

[17] See Carol Gilligan, In a Different Voice (1982)* * *; see also Carol M. Rose, Property as Storytelling: Perspectives from Game Theory, Narrative Theory, Feminist Theory, 2 Yale J.L. & Human. 37, 46 (1990) * * *.

indeed care about the well-being of others, albeit negatively.

In real life, we do find considerable taste for cooperation, though we also see the noncooperative attitudinal factors. Although the former facilitates utility-maximizing cooperation, the latter may hinder such cooperation, particularly at the outset, when a trusting move has to be made. If we make the conventional supposition that rationality means indifference to others, however, the helpful attitudes are irrational (nonindifferent/helping), whereas the unhelpful ones may be either rational (indifferent) or irrational (nonindifferent/hostile).

B. The Zero-Sum Game

All this discussion about cooperative moves, and their difficulties and solutions, brings me to a brief mention of the second game—the zero-sum game. This game is not about making gains through cooperation, but rather about divvying up a fixed sum. At the same time, however, this game does have a bearing on potentially positive-sum games, such as PD games, in which there are gains from acting in concert.

Suppose that our two parties, Sam and Louise, do agree in principle to cooperate on restraining their cows' use of the grazing field. Collectively, the two of them are better off by some amount, which I will call X. They now have a self-renewing grassy field that is worth X dollars more than it would have been had they rushed in to fatten up their cows and left a wasteland behind.

But how are Sam and Louise going to split that gain of X dollars? The point here is that even if Sam and Louise do see the advantage of a cooperative deal, they still have to decide how to split those X proceeds. Every part of X that Sam gets is at Louise's expense, and vice versa. They are faced, in short, with a zero-sum game inside the bigger positive-sum game; indeed, unless someone "gives" on the zero-sum game, they may be unable to solve the larger positive-sum game.

II. The Two Games Applied

How can these two games—the PD game and the zero-sum game—explain the relative property acquisitions of Sam and Louise? One way to think about this is to focus on the taste for cooperation. In the discussion that follows, I will suppose that the taste for cooperation is distributed unevenly between the genders and that women have this taste more strongly than men do. I will not try to prove that such a gender difference actually exists, though the idea might find support from a variety of quarters.[26]

* * * Moreover, my hypothetical assumption does not suggest that all women are cooperators and no men are. Even though I will continue to talk about Sam and Louise in a generic sense, the assumption can coexist with lots of wonderfully cooperative Sams and stubbornly uncooperative Louises. The only assumption is that women, taken as a group, are more likely to make cooperative moves than men, taken as a group.

All the same, even this generic mode is quite a strong assumption, and at certain points I will relax it considerably. At those points, I will ask instead how things would look if women were merely thought to have a more highly developed taste for cooperation. Because it makes the whole picture easier to understand, however, my plan is to begin with the stronger assumption and to explore the ramifications of a hypothetical gender difference in the taste for cooperation.

A. Losing Ground Relatively

1. Sam and Louise Strike a Deal

If we suppose that Louise has a greater taste for cooperation than Sam, we can predict that it will be easier for Sam and Louise to arrive at a cooperative use of the grazing field than it would have been for, say, Sam and Tom. This means that Louise's taste for cooperation aids in the creation of the agreement that produces collective gains. We also can predict that Louise will be better off than she was before she and Sam decided to cooperate. But, alas, we also can predict that she will not be as much better off as Sam. She will wind up with the smaller share of the proceeds.

Why is this so?

At the outset, Louise has to offer Sam more to induce him to cooperate. He may not even notice so readily that cooperative arrangements are beneficial. In any event, he puts his own interests before a cooperative deal and certainly will not take any risky first steps to get things started. Because a cooperative deal does not rank as high in Sam's priorities as

---

[26] The idea is also stated—and vigorously debated—in feminist literature, where some argue that women are more concerned with relationships than men. See generally, Deborah L. Rhode, The "Woman's Point of View," 38 J. Legal Educ. 39, 42–44 (1988)* * *; Robin West, Jurisprudence and Gender, 55 U. Chi. L. Rev. 1, 14–15 (1988).

in Louise's, he can insist that he take a disproportionate amount of the proceeds, so that, in the now-familiar example, he gets to run more cows than Louise.

* * *

Notice that Louise is not losing absolutely here; she, too, is getting some portion of the X amount that they are jointly gaining from their arrangement. She is losing ground only relative to Sam, because she contributes more to the deal. Sam, on the other hand, can contribute less to the deal and walk away with the larger portion of the gains from dealing.

Now let us leave the arena of cow-field negotiation and examine how the world of entitlements reflects the Sam-Louise negotiating pattern.

2. *The Nonmarket "Economy" of Domestic Relations*

We may assume that, insofar as material goods are concerned, Sam and Louise are better off married (or at least living together) than they would be if they each maintained a separate residence. The theory here is that two may live more cheaply than one, or, more accurately, than two "ones," so that there are gains to be made from living in a common household.

But from Sam and Louise's bargaining pattern, we can predict that Louise is going to have to do more to keep the household together. In particular, she (like wives generally) will be stuck doing the bulk of the housework. She is the one with the taste for commonality, whereas he can bide his time until he gets a favorable offer on the household work front. Moreover, he can make a more credible threat of withdrawing from the household unless she cooks the meals and keeps his shirts ironed. We may think he is a lout for doing so—indeed, he probably is a lout—but that is not the point. The point is that, because her desire or sense of responsibility for cooperative arrangements is stronger than his, he can cut a deal in which he gets the lion's share of their joint gains.

One might well think that Louise would rather share the household with someone other than Sam, or find a more cooperative Sam; no doubt many Louises do feel this way. Can Louise do anything about it—say, find a different domestic partner or organize her domestic affairs differently? Well, yes, but it is tricky to do so within conventional notions about sexuality and family. Quite aside from any difficulties associated with single-sex relationships, monogamous marriage itself has a bearing on Louise's problem. Whatever the attractions of monogamy (and they are no doubt many), the institution does mean that each monogamous domestic unit places one Louise with one Sam. If enough such units are formed, and if the taste for cooperation is indeed distributed unevenly between the genders, then at least some cooperative Louises will be stuck with loutish Sams. Indeed, even though they phrased it somewhat differently, some nineteenth-century Mormons thought that the Sams' greater propensity for loutishness was a pretty good reason for plural marriage, where the more cooperative Sams got lots of wives and the less cooperative ones presumably got none.

Short of divorce, then—that is, giving up on a common household—there is little Louise can do to extricate herself from this regrettable state of affairs, at least within traditional notions of domestic relations. Besides, divorce negotiations themselves may only replicate the bargaining disadvantage that Louise has in marriage.

* * *

4. *Tastes and Deals in the Bigger Picture*

It is important to notice that Louise's taste for cooperation is not a bad taste, from the point of view of the world at large. In fact, we are much better off if at least some people have such a taste; otherwise, it would be much harder to start and to sustain cooperative arrangements. Indeed, the taste for cooperation is not a bad taste even for those individuals who have it, so long as they are dealing with other individuals who share the taste. Nor, finally, is a taste for cooperation entirely a bad thing for those who have it even if they have to deal with others who do not share it equally. Even in this circumstance the cooperators do get something out of the deals they make. They just do not get as much as their bargaining partners, who are less eager to work collectively.

Louise's situation suggests a very important point: successful cooperative ventures, taken over a broad mix of partners, require both cooperative and noncooperative traits or tastes. The success of the "tit-for-tat" strategy has become almost a cliche in the game-theory literature, and this strategy entails both a willingness to cooperate, in order to get things under way, and a willingness to exit or even retaliate to protect against noncooperation. The characteristic flaw of those with a taste for cooperating, but not for retaliating, may be vulnerability to exploitation by noncooperators; this may explain some of Louise's travails in the examples above. On the other hand, the noncooperators have a characteristic flaw, too, and, in a way, it is a good deal more serious. The noncooperator's flaw is the inability to get things going in the first place, or perhaps even to imagine how a cooperative solution might occur. This is not a trivial matter: a systematic failure of this sort could dramatically constrict the social gains available through cooperative ventures.

I will return to the importance of making cooperation safe for cooperators. Before doing so, we should examine why, if we weaken the assumption that women actually have a greater taste for cooperation, we may find more or less the same relationship between Sam and Louise. We need to assume instead a certain set of norms or cultural beliefs about men and women.

B. Losing Ground Relatively, Reconsidered: The Culture Version

It may not matter very much that any difference actually exists between Sam's and Louise's respective tastes for cooperation. What may matter is that people think such a difference exists. [Consider] * * *, for example, [an] * * * employer who offer[s Louise] * * * a low percentage of their mutual gains from the employment relationship [in the belief that her taste will induce her to give up more to be in such a relationship]. * * *

Suppose, however, that she has no such taste and refuses to take such a low cut. Given a sufficiently widespread cultural presumption that women have a greater taste for cooperation than men, the employer will continue to make low bids for women for some time before he changes his mind. Moreover, he may never change his mind at all because at least some Louises will take his low offer, and this will make him think he was right about Louises all along.[53]

Indeed, in a sense the employer may be right, because Louise may be unable to challenge this set of beliefs. If she thinks that she will only face another low bid from Employer B, she may well just accept Employer A's offer. The Louise who insists on something better may well not get a job at all, given a widespread set of beliefs about what her wage demands should be. In other words, it costs her something to try to break the stereotype that affects all the Louises in the labor market. Why, then, should she be the first to stick her neck out to break the pattern, particularly when the effort looks hopeless? This set of beliefs, in short, presents Louise with a collective action problem; her failure to solve that problem only reinforces the belief system.

The employer's offer to Sam, on the other hand, will be higher, on the assumption that Sam will demand a higher percentage of the gains from the employment relationship. This assumption can be quite false for any given Sam: a particular Sam might well have accepted a job at lower pay. But, given the employer's beliefs about Sam, and given that dickering over wages costs time and money, the employer will not think it worth the effort to challenge or "test" Sam with a low offer. Hence, here, too, the actions the employer takes, on the basis of even weakly held cultural beliefs, may reinforce those very beliefs.

A similar tale can be told of physical threats to women. Suppose that people believe women are weaker than men. A particular woman in fact may be very strong, but she will have to prove it constantly if she goes to places where others think women are vulnerable. A man in the same situations actually may be weaker than she, but he will not be challenged, or not challenged so constantly, because it is assumed that he can retaliate, even if he cannot. Hence, a man is more likely to feel that he can roam where he wishes, whenever he chooses. A woman, on the other hand—even a physically strong woman—may grow weary of the constant challenges and simply stay at home. By doing so, of course, she reinforces the very stereotype that disadvantages her.

One also can think of domestic examples of this belief-reinforcing phenomenon. Husband Sam may assume that wife Louise will cook and do the dishes, too, but when he is out with his hunting buddies he will split the campground chores. Louise faces the prospect of a scene if she refuses, whereas Sam's hunting buddies do not even encounter a request. Sam simply assumes that they will "play the game" only on even terms. As between Louise, who has to face a scene, and Sam's friends, who face no such scene, Louise is doubtless more likely to give in and do a disproportionate amount of the housekeeping. Here, too, her acquiescence only reinforces Sam's belief that he can shirk with Louise in a way that he cannot with his hunting pals.

C. Cumulative Effects

The effect of all this is that Louise falls relatively behind Sam, whether she actually has a taste for cooperation or is just thought to have it. Note the

---

[53] Cf. Ian Ayres, Fair Driving: Gender and Race Discrimination in Retail Car Negotiations, 104 Harv. L. Rev. 817, 827-836, 850-851 (1991), reporting auto sellers' disparate price offers and bargaining tactics based on the race or sex of the potential purchaser and that sellers' bargaining assumptions may be a self-fulfilling prophecy.

snowball effect of this pattern, too, because this is where things can get really serious.

Let us now make a quick move to the world of finance. Louise does get something from her various cooperative relationships with Sam, but not as much as Sam. This means that, by comparison to Sam, Louise acquires relatively few assets, and this makes her a riskier investment prospect. As a consequence, she has to pay higher interest or otherwise bear relatively unfavorable credit terms. Not only might a bank look to Louise's relatively low assets in setting these terms, but it also might assume that she will be insufficiently quick to retaliate against the uncooperative Sams of the business world and hence may risk business losses that Sam would not. From the bank's point of view, she is a riskier proposition than Sam, so she is going to have to pay more to obtain capital. This means, of course, that it is more difficult for Louise to be financially independent.

* * *

As with conventional business investments, Louise also may fall behind with respect to * * * human capital investments. Potential investors (such as parents) may be reluctant to pay for her education, for example, because they think that she is going to get suckered too often in dealing with the Sams and that an investment in her will just not pay off. The investors will think it better to put their money on Sam's education; they think he will protect himself (and, by extension, their investment in him) by ready retaliation. In fact, the general belief in Sam's readiness to retaliate means that he may never even be faced with that unpleasant prospect. By contrast, Louise will be challenged at every step, and she is bound to slip sometimes. At every turn, it seems that the better bet is to invest in Sam—in his business, in his education, in his health and nutrition, too, and in whatever other projects for which he needs capital, whether financial or "human."

In these investment decisions, Louise's second-fiddle status starts to hurt her exponentially. This is where her taste for cooperation—or the mere belief in her cooperative taste—really begins to limit her possibilities. And this is where we might begin to suspect that her apparent taste for cooperation really derives from her relative lack of alternatives. Investment could have made her more independent, but she is competing for scarce investment resources against the Sams, who look like a better bet. Hence Louise is looking more and more stuck: her willingness to take the short end of the stick—or, more accurately, the belief in her willingness to do so—ultimately puts up a barrier to her independence and further limits her alternatives. The belief that she will stand back and make sacrifices for others finally may mean that she has little choice but to do so, whatever her real taste may be.

Now, this is a rather bleak place to shift to a new story, but things are going to get bleaker, at least for a time.

III. Losing Ground Absolutely

The problem of falling behind absolutely—that is, not just a tale of Louise getting fewer of the gains from trade than Sam, but rather of losing the assets she had before the "game" started—initially made me think that game theory might have some application in the analysis of Louise's cooperative moves. In particular, the problem that set me thinking was that of battered women, and of their battered or murdered children, whose plight appears all too often in horrifying stories of women who appear to have bargained away all assets, literal and figurative. That such ghastly scenarios could happen all of a sudden hardly seemed plausible. Rather, each seemed much more likely to have been played out in a kind of dreadful sequence, where the woman adopted some losing strategy and each move left her worse off than she had been before.

Do women get into such scenarios in disproportionate numbers? And if they do, can one analyze these scenarios on the assumption of an unevenly distributed taste for cooperation? I think one can, but once again, there is a version with a strong assumption, and a version with a weaker assumption. The strong version postulates that women do indeed have a greater taste for cooperation than men. The weaker version is cultural—that women are thought to have such a taste—but though in a sense "weaker," this version is, if anything, even more devastating to Louise's prospects and aspirations.

A. Disinvesting in Assets, Literal and Figurative

Let us begin by picking up the subject we just left, namely, investment. With conventional assets, if you do not continue to invest in a given asset, you may find it losing ground compared to the assets of others—for instance, your manufacturing plant may decline, relatively speaking, if owners of other plants are plowing more funds back into retooling. But there is more to the story than that: whether your asset is a farm or a factory, you may need to make continuing investments just to keep the asset in good working condition. If you never reinvest even in maintenance, your farm or factory eventually will become less productive than it once was, and you are simply treating it as a wasting asset. This is a sensible decision, of course, when repair costs are too high relative to expected future gains. Sensible or not, if you decide to consume your assets by failing to keep them in good repair, you may have a higher initial income from them, but the cost will be paid later: over time, your farm or factory will decline, relative both to other farms or factories and to what your own farm or factory used to earn. This is one result from having a high "discount rate"—you consume lots now, but you have less to work with later.

One can say much the same about "human capital." Suppose your only assets are your body and mind, and their ability to labor. Even here you need to "invest" over a very short run, for example, in food, so that you can work later in the day. Over a longer period, you need to invest in your health so that you can continue to work, and in your education and training so that you can keep up with changing needs for labor. If you do not make these investments—if your discount rate is too high, and you spend too much on other things right now—you are effectively disinvesting, albeit gradually. You are treating your abilities as wasting assets, and your greater consumption today comes at the cost of lesser wealth tomorrow.

Now, how does a taste for cooperation relate to this sort of disinvestment? To start with something already discussed, we know that noncooperation can bring about disinvestment, especially in a jointly held asset. This disinvestment, of course, is what the "tragedy of the commons" is all about. The "tragedy" involves assets that are available to a number of persons who need to cooperate by investing positively (e.g., by buying fertilizer) or by restraining practices that disinvest through overuse (e.g., overgrazing). If the partners do not cooperate in investing or restraining disinvestment, the common asset effectively wastes away.

In the case of the tragedy, lack of cooperation wastes a commonly held asset. In some cases, too much cooperation—as in the adage about "too many cooks"—also may waste common goods. But usually the disinvestment that comes from too much cooperation has a different structure. Louise's problem is the disinvestment that comes from asymmetrical cooperation; here, the disinvestment is likely to be in the assets of only one of the partners, namely, hers. If Louise cooperates too much, she might get into a pattern of decisions whereby, step by step, she loses the assets with which she started.

B. Losing Ground Absolutely: The Strong Version

One major reason why our friend Louise may have such a seemingly self-destructive inclination is that her cooperative tastes create "hostages"—persons or things that Sam can use as leverage in bargaining with Louise because she values them more than he does. These hostages put her at risk. One type of hostage is a relationship itself, which may matter more to Louise than it does to Sam, perhaps because Louise is one of those "women who love too much" and becomes "overinvested" (as we sometimes say) in sticking to some nogoodnik. Another reason why Louise might care more about her relationship with Sam is that, trusting soul that she is, she has given up more for the relationship at the outset than Sam has, and thus she has more to lose from its collapse.[65] For Louise, this means that something that matters very much to her is controlled by another.

Then, too, the hostages in question may be children, or other people that Louise worries about—elderly parents or other relatives, or an ailing friend. Louise is disproportionately burdened by such hostages, of course, if she does have a greater taste for commonality and its attendant responsibilities. Because she cares about other persons, or at least feels responsible for them, she cannot make a threat as credible as Sam's that she will abandon existing relationships. Conversely, she has to believe the feckless Sam when he says he will not take care of Mom or the kids, leaving only her to undertake these efforts.

Children (or other hostages for whom Louise feels responsible) are a negative factor in Louise's ability to make rational investment choices. The needs of hostages may make her even more anxious to have current income, even if this means a job with low wages and killing hours. Their needs also may induce her to bargain away personal relationships or her own

---

[65] See Lloyd Cohen, Marriage, Divorce, and Quasi Rents; or, "I Gave Him the Best Years of My Life," 16 J. Legal Stud. 267, 287-89 (1987), analogizing marriage to a contractual relationship in which one party, the wife, performs first, creating "quasi rents" that, like hostages, may be exploited by the other party. See also June Carbone, Economics, Feminism, and the Reinvention of Alimony: A Reply to Ira Ellman, 43 Vand.L.Rev. 1463, 1491-94 (1990), exploring restitution as a remedy to compensate divorced women who sacrificed career opportunities for their families during the marriage, and Frances E. Olsen, The Family and the Market: A Study of Ideology and Legal Reform, 96 Harv.L.Rev. 1497, 1537 (1983), pointing out that easy divorce may create greater risk to one who has sacrificed more for a relationship.

aspirations, sometimes in order to persuade Sam, her higher wage spouse, to help her support the kids. Thus, Louise's sense of responsibility to others translates into a higher discount rate: she has to use up more of her current resources to take care of others, even if the cost is long-term disinvestment in her own abilities, personal well-being, or even the respect of the community. For her, the price of losing the kids or seeing them suffer is even greater than the price she will pay later in life for being poor, ill-trained, and perhaps sick and friendless.

Louise might be a better bargainer and might make better investment decisions if she did not have the kids, but she cannot make a credible threat to give them up or stop caring for them. Her high discount rate is obvious to all; thus, her bargaining position is weakened vis-a-vis those who might wish to take advantage of her.[68] And she gives in, takes the job, and maybe moonlights, too. She may even "spend" more of her assets than she takes in—that is, she spends the assets she has in her bodily health and social contacts, and does nothing to retool her skills. She is treating what she has as a wasting asset. She is losing ground.

It is this sense that Louise's hostages can do her in: they make her vulnerable to third parties. In the larger bargaining world of commerce and employment, the relevant third parties have no direct control over the hostages Louise gives up; hostages are simply a factor that others can use, more or less abstractly, for greater bargaining leverage with Louise. Even if such parties do exploit their bargaining advantage, they may not know or care that Louise is treating herself as a wasting asset.

Domestically, however, the story may be very different. At home, the hostages Louise gives up may be in the direct control of Sam and may make her an object of purposeful abuse—a steady assault on the assets that could enable her to act independently. Through threats to her hostages, most notably to her children and to her own body, Louise can be punished radically for noncooperation. Though she may cooperate to stave off threats and protect the hostages, she herself loses ground each time she does so. Renewed threats of violence may lead her, step by step, to bargain away her own sources of income, her contacts with friends and family, and ultimately the independent judgment that such contacts would provide. Now she no longer is bargaining to get some part—even a relatively small part—of a positive joint good; instead, in the face of each new threat, she is bargaining to keep from losing more of what she has and cares about, and losing that even faster. In short, because Louise's hostages make her subject to the control of a third party, they eventually may make her lose grip on whatever assets she had at the outset.

* * *

This is an extremely grim scenario. It presumes not only that Louise is burdened by her concern for some form of hostage, but also that Sam has a taste for domination that is not frequently encountered—or at least not noticed—in everyday experience. All the same, it is not an entirely unrecognizable scenario. Quite to the contrary, it is all too recognizable, not only in the worst and most extortionist relationships between men and women, but in the worst and most extortionist relationships between anybody and anybody else—relationships that we think of in the context of kidnaping, enslavement, and the most lawless forms of imprisonment.

C. Losing Ground: The Weaker Version of Culture and Politics

So far I have been speaking of Louise's disinvestment as a result of her greater taste for cooperation. I have been supposing that this taste reinforces, and is reinforced by, her concern for hostages—a concern that may induce her, step by step, to sacrifice her assets, including the various forms of her human capital. Another way to look at her disinvestment is to make only a weak assumption—not that Louise has a taste for cooperation, from which she derives a concern about hostages, but rather that many people share a cultural belief that she has or should have this taste. Perhaps Louise has no use for cooperation and feels no responsibility for others, perhaps she does not have children, perhaps she acquires nothing else that could be treated as a hostage, perhaps she is, in general, a very cool and calculating character.

All the same, because of the cultural expectations that she will or should cooperate, third parties may punish her if she does not. How do they do so? The easy forms of punishment are gossip about her or charges that she is unpleasant or peculiar. More importantly, she may face social isolation and refusals to deal with her on an equal basis (or perhaps on

68 As an example, in divorce negotiations, husbands sometimes enhance their bargaining position for family assets by strategically threatening to seek child custody. See, e.g., Martha A. Fineman, The Illusion of Equality 164 (1991); Lenore J. Weitzman, The Divorce Revolution 310–13 (1985); Richard Neely, The Primary Caretaker Parent Rule: Child Custody and the Dynamics of Greed, 3 Yale L. & Pol'y Rev. 168, 171–72, 178–79 (1984).

any basis at all), and those third parties who do deal with her may face similar punishment.

A more formal way in which these cultural expectations may result in her disinvestment once again has to do with a kind of investment, namely, political investment. * * * If Louise does not have the assets to make substantial investments in influencing either culture or politics, then in the political arena cultural expectations about her may turn into legal demands that she cooperate. These legal demands may take the form of denying her the ability to live independently or to make alliances with others who might cooperate with her on a more equal basis. The law, for example, may deny her the capacity to own her own property, to be employed outside the home, to contract on her own, to obtain an education, or to form associations outside her father's or her husband's family. By the same token, such laws may give her no recourse against her father's or her husband's discipline.

* * * Hence, no matter how much she may hate cooperation, particularly with husband Sam, her lack of alternatives means that she cannot make a credible threat of noncooperation. Moreover, she cannot convince anyone to assist her to escape: It is dangerous for another party to help her or to deal with her, and no one believes she can make it on her own, anyway. In short, if she is not playing the game, she is dead-dead because there is no other game for her to play. Of course, even if she is playing this game, she may be dead too, over a slightly longer run.

In a sense, Louise has become a hostage herself. She has no control over her own efforts and cannot turn them into assets independent of Sam; she has no alternatives to his control. Given a sufficiently domineering Sam, she may be faced with the downhill moves of the losing game in which she can only cut her losses at each step, preferring the temporarily lesser losses that come from giving Sam what he wants to the immediate drastic punishments that he and others will inflict on her for defiance.

Obviously, a woman in this position is in a situation comparable to slavery. In slavery, too, defiance is punished and made even less palatable than cooperation. In slavery, too, there may be no game superior to cooperating with an owner's demands, even though cooperating with a master's wishes may be self-disinvesting for the slave. And in slavery, too, potential helpers of slaves also may be policed, so that, for example, none of the enslaved class members may be emancipated, because the presence of the emancipated could make it more difficult to control those still enslaved.

In slavery, of course, a potent way to enforce cooperation is to deny the slave the ability to own property and to contract on his or her own. Not all slavery systems have had these disabilities; where slaves have been entitled to own property, however difficult their position, at least some have been able to purchase their freedom. But where the slave—like the subordinated wife—cannot acquire or own property, he or she cannot exit even a losing game with the master, because the property-less or entitlement-less person has no alternative game to play. One who cannot acquire and own property can have no assets, and the person who has no assets has nothing to bargain with, except perhaps bodily integrity, attachments to friends and family, and, ultimately, independence of spirit.

It often has been noted that the slave's status is that of a person who is also an object of property. Perhaps less remarked is the status of the slave as a person who can own no property and have no assets. As John Locke noted, however, these persons are one and the same.

IV. Some Lessons for Louise (and Sam, Too)

At the outset of this Article, I noted that women are better off with the ability to own property than they would be without that ability. The inability to own property is a guarantor of some version of enslavement, however benevolent it may be in any particular instance. Property and assets generally are the means through which one may make choices about one's interactions with the world, and property at least gives Louise an opportunity to make some gains, even if, relatively speaking, she may fall behind Sam in her dealings with him.

A part of this Article has argued that one can see how women fall behind if one assumes a greater "taste for cooperation" on the part of women, but in working through the arguments it seems that a weaker assumption—that women are merely thought to have such a taste—is, if anything, an even more powerful determinant of their relative lack of assets. That weaker assumption has to do with culture, and that is both bad news and good. It is bad news because cultural presumptions are hard to change; they present collective action problems to those who would try to break with them. The good news is that cultural change does happen sometimes, through education and conscious effort.

If culture may be changed, what can Louise do about her relatively short shrift on the property front? One encouraging point is that there are others from whom Louise can learn. First, there are other groups, like new immigrants, who also have been in a position in which their needs have required them to accept, at least for a time, lesser gains from their cooperation with more powerful persons. The escape of at least some immigrant groups from this situation should give women some cues.

One cue is that even the short end of the deal is better than no deal at all. Those who get something, even if it is the short end, can save and invest that sum and turn it into something larger so that in their future dealings they may not have to accept bad terms from a situation of need. Another cue is that gains can be made by cooperation among others in a like station. Again, get-ahead immigrants have notoriously helped their own; in so doing, they have dramatically illustrated the way in which cooperation may increase a group's wealth: One can look to one's allies for help in dealing with nonallies. When Louise starts to deal with Sam, then, she may do well to make certain that her alliances with other Louises are intact so that they can give her advice, assistance, and, if necessary, an escape route.

Another group from which Louise can learn may be the participants in some of the traditional women's crafts practices—those oft-demeaned quilting bees and cookoffs, or, a distinctly modern version of them, the "story trees" that some women science-fiction writers have jointly created. Modern feminism has interested the art world in the aesthetic merit of such crafts, suggesting that such cooperative forms of creativity may attain very high levels, despite the often strained circumstances of their creation and the disdain with which our legal institutions have treated them. Aside from artistic merit, however, these group activities also might be studied for what we might call their "politics": if women do have a more capacious taste for cooperation, or even if they are just assumed to have such a taste, they ought to be able to turn that real or purported taste to their own mutual advantage in their joint pursuits. After all, it should be cheaper for such groups to maintain cohesion for common projects than it is for groups with a lesser taste for cooperation.

I wonder particularly whether these groups might be able to turn their own limited opportunities, and, most particularly, the classic "hostage" problem, into a kind of advantage. The theory of cartels suggests that collusive groups—such as the Organization of Petroleum Exporting Countries or the old railroad cartels—begin to fall apart after the membership rises to what is really a rather low number, perhaps eight at most. This occurs because the members cannot police one another in larger numbers, so that, in larger groups, any given member can safely cheat. When several do, the cartel collapses.

One way to assure adherence to the cartel—or to some more benevolent cooperative group—is to use "precommitment devices." For example, the members may post bond, or, as the practice has actually been dubbed, they may exchange "hostages." Precommitment devices work only if they are credible, however, and this is where women's concern for hostages becomes an advantage. If women are thought to be concerned about others in ways that put them at some risk, especially if their outside opportunities are limited—that is, if each knows of her own and her compatriots' vulnerability and need for the group's support—one might expect such groups to attain a higher level of solidarity (at lower "policing costs") than groups having more outside opportunities and no hostages to exchange. Hence, if Louise does have a taste for cooperation, or even if people merely think she does, she should be able to turn the real or purported taste to advantage and not just be victimized by it. The taste for cooperation could be an asset itself, insofar as it helps Louise to make alliances with others and stick with them, and insofar as it helps others to recognize her as someone who will hold by her deals.

The issue that may be most difficult for Louise is selective noncooperation: she and the other Louises are going to have to learn to enforce their collective deals and collective interests by occasional threats of noncooperation with nonparticipants. In a world that mixes "testers" with the cooperators, cooperation alone is not enough. One also must be able to police one's deals and to enforce them by exit or even by retaliation. Louises have to learn not to permit, or even give the impression that they will permit, shirking by those with whom they deal. They have to learn as well to punish slanderers, politicians, or others who systematically would cut down on their opportunities to gain "assets," whether financial, educational, or psychological. Even in this unpleasant task of punishment, however, Louise's alliances with other Louises may help. Together they may be able to reinforce each other to do these unpalatable retaliatory tasks collectively, even if they have a difficult time with them individually.

A rather different point is that Louise might well pay attention to alliances that she can make with sympathetic Sams, or even with Sams who are simply indifferent to the local customs that might otherwise short-shrift women. Such indifferent Sams—perhaps newly arrived employers or entrepreneurs—at least are not hostile. Because they do not necessarily share any local expectation that

Louise might accept particularly low wages, they might help Louise get a better break than she would have had under established customs.

Moreover, Louise should not despair of educating the Sams of the world and then making alliances with them. The long history of philanthropy, and indeed the modern civil rights movement and antidiscrimination laws, suggest that some elements of a taste for cooperation are, in fact, fairly widely distributed. These historical examples indicate that, whatever the gender differences may be, it would be a great error to think that all Sams are completely indifferent to anything but their own immediate well-being; or that they are all impervious to what used to be called "self-interest rightly understood," that is, an understanding that one's own welfare is tied up in a common enterprise with others; or that they are all morons empathically, unmoved by the narrations and metaphors of those who are differently situated. We may not think that our own substantial legal changes have resulted in perfect justice, but they are strong evidence of the possibility of cultural learning and change. The married women's property acts, the franchise, the legislation restraining discrimination in employment and education, the laws attempting to enforce child support—all give evidence of cultural learning, no matter how much is left to teach.

Even the "strong" assumption of an uneven gender distribution in cooperative tastes is compatible with the fact that some Sams, or even most Sams, share some cooperative capacities, and that some are not indifferent to the plight in which women may be caught. Women, in turn, should not be indifferent to this fact and should be encouraged by the very substantial gains that they have made through alliances, at least in the modern West.

Some of the behavior and relationships I have been describing are deplored by most civilized people, and, at least to some degree, are proscribed by our laws, however imperfectly and incompletely. Where the law restrains the exploitation of cooperative moves, it does so, at least in part, because all of us need cooperative activities. All of us, even the Sams, are worse off when the incentives to cooperate are reduced by the punishment and disparagement of cooperators. This is, of course, a generalized problem with letting the cooperative Louises lose out systematically to the uncooperative Sams: such scenarios teach a lesson, too, and tend to drive down the overall level of cooperation in any given social group. If Louise's cooperative or seemingly cooperative traits routinely result in advantage-taking at her expense, we may expect lots of people to get the message that cooperation is personally problematic, and we may expect that many potential gains from wider cooperation will be lost to the fear of exploitation.

It has sometimes been noted that more developed societies tend to be characterized by a greater equality for women; my point is that the correlation is not simply coincidental. From a larger perspective, we must consider the incentive effects of norms and practices that let jerks win systematically and nice people finish last, also systematically. These norms and practices may have ramifications for a larger social well-being in that they discourage the "niceness" that lets cooperative ventures occur. And that, of course, is one of the major reasons why not just the Louises, but the Sams, too, should be interested in figuring out why women do not have much property—and in doing something about it.

Note

In her article, Rose is careful to note that the notion of women as more cooperative than men is a caricature which may, at best, be only partially true. Could she have written a very similar article making a somewhat different, but non-gendered, set of assumptions? For example, assume that those with lots of money will tend to obtain more money more quickly than those without much money. If women have been denied access to wealth over time, they will then tend to accumulate money at a slower rate than men. They may also feel some of the same need to cooperate with those who have money in order to survive at an "acceptable" level. Does this all mean that Rose's "weaker" assumption that men think women are more cooperative is actually the more important—in the sense of describing a major cultural consequence of gross inequalities in the distribution of wealth?

2. New Family "Estates"

William A. Reppy, Jr., *Property and Support Rights of Unmarried Cohabitants: A Proposal for Creating a New Legal Status*, 44 LA. L. REV. 1678–1679, 1683–1685, 1694, 1696–1697, 1705–1708, 1712–1721 (1984)*

INTRODUCTION

In the United States in the mid-1980's millions of couples, consisting of a man and a woman involved in a sexual relationship, live together although unmarried to each other. At the termination of the cohabitation relationship—either by death or by simply the parting ways—the courts are asked to declare what, if any, support, property, or contract rights one cohabitant has against the other (or the estate of a deceased cohabitant).

The problem of how cohabitants fit into the legal framework can also arise at a time when the relationship is ongoing and stable, not through claims of the cohabitants inter se but usually through disputes with third parties. For example, one of the cohabitants may seek recovery for loss of consortium from a tortfeasor who injured the other cohabitant. A creditor of one of the pair may seek to recover from earnings of the other cohabitant during their relationship on the theory that it is the legal equivalent of community property.

This article reviews critically American law's initial treatment of the cohabiting couple, the recognition of what can be called a negative status which, rather than create rights and obligations between the cohabitants, disabled them from making contracts with each other and in some jurisdictions barred certain types of donations by one to the other.

A majority of jurisdictions seem to have abandoned the negative status approach and have employed contract law to determine the property-related rights of cohabitants. This article notes the uncertainties of this contract-law approach and the difficulty of meshing into federal law of taxation and bankruptcy the position of domestic partners who lack a status relationship.

The article concludes that the negative-status approach must be rejected as based on outdated social mores and inaccurate notions as to the power of domestic relations law to alter contemporary lifestyles. While cohabitants certainly ought to be free to make express contracts with each other concerning property and support rights and obligations, contract law cannot provide adequate solutions to the problems raised by the large number of cohabiting couples.

It is recommended that these problems be approached primarily through status law. The common-law marriage doctrine should be revived in states that once recognized it but abolished it. * * * [T]he major thrust of the article is the somewhat novel suggestion that legislation be enacted to create a new status—lawful cohabitation—with rules concerning support, property and associated rights and obligations corresponding to the expectations of typical cohabitants. It is proposed that cohabitants be able to formally enter this status by official recordation (or even a ceremony) but that, in addition, a doctrine which can be called common-law cohabitation be recognized where the acts of the couple in entering into the relationship can cause the status to attach.

* * *

I. COHABITATION AS CREATING A NEGATIVE STATUS

American law initially responded to cohabitation by creating a status for the cohabitants. * * * [I]n the great majority of jurisdictions this status was the

---

product of common law, judge-made rules. Given various names—concubinage, meretricious relationship, illicit cohabitation—the status was unique in law. It initially conferred no rights at all on the parties (whom we shall refer to hereafter as CM for cohabiting man and CW for cohabiting woman). Rather, the rules of law attaching because of the status were negative, the primary one being an incapacity to make contracts with each other, contracts that in many states would have been permissible for persons living together in a nonsexual relationship.

* * *

[I]t is highly unlikely that judicial decisions (and a few statutes) adopting the negative-status approach to cohabitation have any significant impact on the decision of a couple to begin cohabiting. With respect to those who are aware of this legal approach in the state where they live, chances are as good that such a legal approach encourages rather than discourages the practice.

It is urged that, wholly apart from deterrence, the law's permitting mere cohabitants to obtain any of the benefits associated with legal marriage—such as a contractual arrangement similar to a community of acquets and gains—will demean and denigrate marriage. This argument is sound only if, as Justice Clark feared in his *Marvin* dissent,[32] the rejection of the negative-status approach is accompanied by adoption of such a large bundle of remedies for cohabitants that comparison of marriage and cohabitation from the viewpoint of a domestic relations legal scholar reveals cohabitation to be the preferable mode of sexual union from a practical standpoint. (As noted above, the writer does not think conclusions drawn from such a technical examination will have measurable effect on the numbers of people who elect cohabitation over marriage, although it could over time as more persons learn about the actual governing law and as "moral" pressure to marry diminishes.)

The answer to this "denigration" argument is simply that the law must heed Justice Clark's warning and not confect rules that make cohabitation preferable to marriage. It should be noted that to adhere to this goal, changes can be made on both sides of the balance. As legal remedies are accorded to cohabitants, the law can, and should, remove some of the strictures historically placed on married couples (such as the incapacity to contract in advance of a falling out how property and support claims will be handled in the event of divorce).

Note too, that even if one fears that recognition of the numerous contractually-based remedies for cohabitants mentioned in *Marvin* will denigrate marriage, that reservation probably cannot fairly be said about the recognition of a new status of lawful cohabitation as recommended in this article. The reciprocal rights and obligations arising out of this status will be narrower than those attached to marital status.

The proposed new status for most cohabiting couples will fill a different function than does marriage. It will provide a legally sanctioned mode of sexual union for those who have doubts about the life-long and greater commitment of persons who elect to marry.

Moreover, is not marriage more demeaned (than it would be by recognition of an additional and alternative status) by the law's attempting to force into it with a life-long commitment persons who desire a heterosexual, monogamous lifestyle yet are uncertain about making the life-long commitment? If, as the writer believes, the divorce rate would substantially drop were the law to create a new status of lawful cohabitation, surely the institution of marriage would be strengthened. Will not the question "will you marry me?" be more meaningful to a loved-one under a system of law where "Let's be lawful cohabitants" is a sanctioned alternative?

Finally, the negative-status approach may be breeding contempt in general for the law by former cohabitants harmed by application of this theory. Almost every case of a cohabiting couple who agree to pool gains in ignorance of the illegality of the contract is a prime candidate for engendering such contempt. The pain of dashed expectations that the law would provide some relief also attends the breakup of a couple who assumed (erroneously) that something like a common-law marriage doctrine attached to at least a long-term cohabitation.

Where the law has little hope of advancing perceived morality by altering conduct, its best posture is to respond to typical expectations concerning the impact of law in a particular situation. The writer does not think the negative-status theory reflects such expectations.

---

[32] Marvin v. Marvin, 18 Cal.3d 660, 685, 557 P.2d 106, 123, 134 Cal. Rptr. 815, 832 (1976). * * *

II. Abandonment of Negative-Status in Favor of a Contract-Law Approach

* * *

Marvin authorizes an express agreement for a sharing of gains similar to that under a community property regime, based on a pooling of efforts in the classic noncommercial situation where one of the pair (CW in *Marvin*, as in most such cases) was expected to give up work and be a stay-at-home wife-equivalent. A kind of severance is required. It is not fatal to such contracts that they are made after cohabitation begins; they are enforceable "unless they rest on an unlawful meretricious consideration." An express agreement for support that would create contractual obligation similar to alimony would be similarly enforceable under the *Marvin* theory, as would a contract giving the surviving cohabitant upon termination of the arrangement by death a claim against the other's property similar to a nonbarrable share under common law statutory succession schemes * * *.

Subject to the same required severance from illicit taint, an implied contract—at least for sharing of gains—would be recognized in jurisdictions adhering to *Marvin*, and a *quantum meruit* claim for services rendered nongratuitously could be asserted. As a remedial device under this contract approach, equitable remedies such as the resulting or constructive trust have been employed.

A number of jurisdictions have fully accepted *Marvin*, while others allow suit on an express but not an implied-in-law contract. In some states the implied-in-law (*quantum meruit*) contract remedy is recognized while other aspects of *Marvin* remain undecided.

A. Criticism of the Marvin Approach

[Editor's Note: Reppy argues here that *Marvin* is an inadequate approach because parties in intimate relationships cannot use it to predict how the law will treat them. Express written contracts are rare. Even when present they are vulnerable to claims that sexual services were part of the consideration. Allegations of oral contracts are subject to truth telling contests. Implied contracts to pool assets are hard to prove. Behavior is likely to create a variety of inferences. *Quantum meruit* claims are available only if the service provider reasonably expected payment, another hard to prove proposition. Implied-in-law trusts are always subject to the counter that the "donor" intended to make a gift.]

* * *

B. Interaction With Federal Law

1. Federal Taxation

* * *

Even though the cohabitants may reside in a community property state and contract for a sharing of gains under provisions identical to the local community property law, splitting of income on tax returns will not be allowed. For this purpose, it is irrelevant whether the contract is self-executing so that CW is the immediate owner of half of CM's earnings without his having to do anything by way of assignment, delivery, or transfer of title, in order to implement the pooling contract.

* * *

[There are] *detriments* of a fifty-fifty pooling contract between cohabitants * * *. In the situation of a stay-at-home CW, at least part of the consideration for the sharing of CM's gains will often be CW's rendition of services of a type for which remuneration is paid. Examples are cooking, house-cleaning, and caring for CM during illness. * * * [T]he Internal Revenue Service can fairly assert that CM is taxable on one-hundred percent of his gain and CW is taxable on fifty percent of it, which passes to her by assignment because she earned it by performing services. * * *

If both CW and CM have income-producing jobs or investments, the pooling agreement will have less disastrous results. With respect to earned income, no contract between the cohabitants can create a marital status; thus they are not in danger of incurring the marriage penalty of federal income tax law which * * * burdens the lawfully married when both have substantial incomes from labor. * * *

* * *

III. Creating a Positive Status

A. Common-Law Marriage Should Be Adopted in States Not Recognizing This Institution

Fourteen American jurisdictions continue to recognize common-law marriage. This doctrine makes a lawful marriage (with all of the rights and obligations attached to a marriage created by formal and licensed ceremony) out of cohabitation if the parties agree between themselves to be married, hold themselves out to the community as married, and live together some substantial period of time. It is generally held that the agreement between the couple to marry can be inferred from their conduct.

Although now recognized in a minority of jurisdictions, common-law marriage formerly had widespread acceptance. The move toward legislative abolition of common-law marriage in the early part of this century reflected two primary considerations. First, the doctrine was thought to generate litigation and encourage perjured testimony about an agreement to marry by a cohabitant seeking the benefits of lawful marriage at the termination (either by death of the other cohabitant or by the couple's parting) of the relationship. Secondly, it was urged that the need for the doctrine had disappeared. Its purpose was to legitimate cohabitation by a couple seeking to marry lawfully who lived so far from the county seat that travel by horseback to the courthouse to obtain a license would be long and difficult and perhaps at some times of year even impossible due to road and weather conditions.

The contemporary need for recognizing common-law marriage is quite different. It has been shown that a contract by cohabitants to establish between themselves property and support rights and obligations similar to those of married persons either is void (under the negative-status approach to cohabitation) or fails to achieve the benefits accorded the lawfully married under federal taxation, bankruptcy, and welfare law. Nevertheless, there will be some couples who are unaware of the invalidity of the contract or of the unfavorable treatment given to contractual cohabitants by federal law. Their expectations would be realized if the common-law marriage doctrine were recognized.

Fear that revival of the common-law marriage doctrine will encourage litigation and even perjury is a pertinent policy consideration only in states using the negative-status approach, for in other states the cohabitant who would assert common-law marriage can and will assert the same agreement upon which common-law marriage is founded as a *Marvin*-style claim. Actually, the enticement to give perjured testimony would be decreased in most *Marvin* states by the recognition of common-law marriage, since under that doctrine the cohabitant does not have to try to convince the trier of fact that sharing of sexual favors was not part of the consideration for the contract. Under common-law marriage sex is supposed to be at the heart of the consideration.

* * *

Of course, common-law marriage is under federal law of taxation, bankruptcy, and entitlements the equivalent of formal, ceremonial marriage. Thus revival of the doctrine will create benefits that contract law cannot now achieve. In sum, there is good reason to revive common-law marriage, and only in states presently employing the negative-status approach to cohabitation—an unacceptable alternative in this writer's view—will doing so increase litigation and invite perjured claims.

* * *

C. Total Assimilation Should Be Rejected

* * * [The] total assimilation approach goes far beyond the common-law marriage doctrine, for it recognizes the marriage status without a contract to be married and, apparently, without the holding out of the couple to the public as being married. The writer finds this total assimilation approach unacceptable from a public policy standpoint.

When the cohabitants have taken care not to represent to each other or to the public that they have the status of the lawfully married, their expectations concerning the benefits and burdens arising out of the relationship should be different from those attached to the lawful marriage status. Most likely one or both of the parties who are cohabiting without a holding out of marital status declines to assume the primary burden of marriage—a life-long support obligation. Probably, too, one or both of such cohabitants is purposefully avoiding a legal status that can be terminated only through adversary legal proceedings (divorce) that are often quite costly (with the husband often ending up having to pay not only his own attorney's fees but those of his wife as well).

When only one of the cohabitants has such objections, the other must be aware at least in general that her mate is declining to accept the status of marriage. She has no reasonable expectations to be dashed when the law in response does not fix the status of lawfully married on the couple.

The law could take the position that those who want a sexual relationship have to pay for it, and that the cost is a life-long support obligation plus entanglement in costly divorce proceedings. But what is to be gained? The writer cannot see how morality is advanced by the law's telling a couple that it will treat them as married even though they do not want to be. The fact remains that this type of cohabiting couple is known in the community to have a sexual relationship while deliberately refusing to marry. Whatever affront to marriage results surely cannot be even substantially eliminated by a rule of law that treats them as married anyway. To foist on the couple the status of marriage as a punishment for their lifestyle is itself a greater affront to formal marriage.

The total assimilation approach is thus unacceptable. It is as wrong to impose the status of lawfully married on a couple seeking to avoid marriage as to imply in such a case a contract under which the pair agree to all of the benefits and burdens of lawful marriage.

D. Ad Hoc Extension of Particular Benefits and Burdens of Marriage Is an Insufficient Remedy

A number of jurisdictions have judicially or legislatively picked out certain aspects of the status of lawful marriage and affixed them as a matter of status, not contract law, to certain types of cohabitants. * * * By using status rather than contract law, this *ad hoc* assimilation approach has the benefit of more certainty. If a long-term cohabitation can be shown, the benefits and burdens attach automatically without concern about a taint of sexual consideration or what inferences concerning intention of the parties are to be drawn from their conduct. Presumably, only an express contract between the pair to avoid the aspect of lawful marriage which the jurisdiction attaches to cohabitants would be effective to avoid that result.

* * *

[However, one] problem with the *ad hoc* assimilation approach is that it may take decades for the courts of a jurisdiction (with or without help from the legislature) to provide the answer with respect to each of scores of legal issues that may arise (such as availability of the marital privilege of evidence law, applicability of the "necessaries" doctrine of contract law, and method for determining the domicile of CW). Meanwhile, as the jurisdiction attaches to cohabitants more and more of the benefits and burdens of lawful marriage, the cohabitants' posture under federal law of taxation, bankruptcy and welfare will become murky. Much litigation will be necessary to determine whether a sufficient number of rules of lawful marriage have been affixed to cohabitation so that federal law should view the couple as married.

E. The Legislature Should Enact a Comprehensive Bill Creating a New Status of Lawful Cohabitation

1. The New Status Should Be Denominated a Form of Marriage

If contract law, total assimilation, and ad hoc assimilation are ineffective remedies for dealing with the rights and obligations of cohabitants, only one course appears to remain: recognition of a new status. Avoidance of the *ad hoc* approach requires that this result be achieved legislatively. What is needed is a thorough study culminating in a bill that covers all, or at least all significant, legal issues that can arise with respect to the rights of the cohabitants *inter se* and in interaction with third parties. With each issue the legislature has three choices: (1) create no rights; (2) borrow fully from the law applicable to the lawfully married; and (3) create a new rule tailored for the new status (usually imposing a lesser obligation than that arising under the status of lawfully married).

It is important that the legislation specifically declare the new status to be a form of marriage, since so much of the federal law conditions the granting of benefits on the existence of such a status. Of course, the mere declaration by the legislature that the new status is a form of marriage will not be binding on the federal government in administering tax, bankruptcy and welfare laws; however, the state law reform will extend a considerable amount of the law applicable to the lawfully married to cohabitants, and the writer believes the intention of the legislature that the new law be treated as matter of marriage law reform would carry weight with federal courts and agencies.

* * *

It may be of interest that the most difficult problem the writer has faced * * * is what to call this new status. He has opted for "lawful cohabitation" as a temporary measure and hopes that someone else will succeed where he has failed in the matter of nomenclature.

Although the reform bill must for federal law purposes declare the new status to be an aspect of marriage law, use of a term including the word marriage (the writer had considered demi-marriage) probably has to be rejected if the legislation has accepted the proposal to revive or enact common-law marriage. The cohabitants must not call each other husband and wife nor refer to themselves as married, or else they will probably end up being married under this scheme.

The ideal nomenclature would accommodate formal invitations to attend a ceremony creating the status and society page announcements as well as introductions ("I'd like you to meet Joe, my lawful cohabitant") simply will not do.*

2. Both Formalized and Common-Law Forms of the New Status Should be Recognized

A couple who wish to enter into the new status should be able to do so immediately by filing a formal document of union that would be recorded like a certificate of lawful marriage. * * *

No matter how easy the law makes it formally to enter the new status, many couples will simply begin living together and, at some point, should be gov-

* [Editor's Note: Does the more modern "domestic partner" work any better?]

erned by the new status law. Thus the reform legislation should include a "common-law" form of lawful cohabitation under which the status automatically attaches. This status could attach in a brief period of time if the couple contracted to be lawful cohabitants and held themselves out publicly as such. In other situations, the relationship could be converted from a non-status sexual sharing to lawful cohabitation after a period of time—six months, one year, two years—specified in the statute and applicable to relationships where no contract was made and/or no holding out occurred.

The cohabitants should be free to avoid entering into the status and to continue a non-status living arrangement beyond the specified period. Since one of the main reasons for moving from the reliance on contract-based remedies under *Marvin* to status law is avoidance of uncertainty, only an express contract to avoid lawful cohabitation status should be effective; i.e., if the statutory period was one year and the sexual cohabitation extended beyond a year, a party to the union should not be able to avoid the obligations of the status by urging a contrary implied-in-fact agreement between the couple.

* * *

3. Dissolution of the Status Should Be Quick and Should Avoid Costly Procedures.

The writer has noted that one of the main reasons that persons choose to cohabit rather than marry is that one or both of the couple objects to the costs in money, time, and emotions of divorce proceedings necessary to dissolve a lawful marriage. The new status of lawful cohabitation will not satisfy a contemporary need unless the status can be terminated efficiently. No more should be required than filing of a certificate of dissolution signed by both spouses, indicating that their cohabitation has ended and that they have agreed on terms for division of property and for support payments. (Birth of a child to lawful cohabitants should convert their union to a lawful marriage, since concern for a child's welfare after dissolution warrants supervision by a court over the termination of the status.)

If the couple filed such a document without making agreements concerning property and support, the law should supply a contract for them. The writer would recommend the waiver of support (alimony) rights and a confirmation of property under which the form of title controls. Ownership of assets having no title should go to the ex-cohabitant peaceably taking possession, and in all other instances the couple should remain coowners until they work out an exchange or are forced to resort to partition actions.

* * *

4. In Community Property States Lawful Cohabitants Should Be Subject to a Community of Gains

It is more probable than not that a couple that comes under the status of lawful cohabitants would want to share ownership of gains by both during their union. Thus the law should make a community of gains an aspect of this new status. An express contract to the contrary—e.g., to live separate in property—should be necessary to avoid this benefit-burden of lawful cohabitation. * * *

5. The Support Obligation of a Lawful Cohabitant Should Be Strictly Limited

Since the life-long support obligation is probably the burden of lawful marriage most likely to cause a cohabitant to reject marriage for an alternative living arrangement, the new status of lawful cohabitation should handle the support obligation differently. Certainly the cohabitants should be free to contract expressly against any support obligation, even though the statute might impose a limited duty. A legislative determination that the basic rule would be no support obligation at all (unless agreed to by contract) should not be faulted, but there will be situations of such sacrifice of career opportunities by a cohabitant assuming the role of the stay-at-home domestic that placing a limited support obligation on the other cohabitant could be an acceptable compromise between the no-support and the life-long-support positions.

A substantial case of equities should exist before any support obligation is engrafted on the new status. For example, the law might provide that no cohabitant is entitled to support unless he can show at least five years of career sacrifice because of the role played as cohabitant. Since under this proposal the birth of a child should convert the lawful cohabitation into a lawful marriage, the occasion for CW to assume a stay-at-home domestic role as a cohabitant will not often arise.

Under no circumstances should the support obligation exceed a short, fixed period of time such as two years. The policy here is not to make lawful cohabitation so similar to marriage as to discourage marriage as an institution. A further restriction, such as one based on a percentage of net income of the obligor cohabitant, should be considered as well.

Note

Compare Reppy's arguments with the concerns articulated by Joan Williams earlier in this section of the anthology. Would Williams favor establishment of a new status of "lawful cohabitation," or would she view it as a structure likely to further impede the ability of women to improve their economic position in society? Might Williams favor automatic integration of all cohabiting couples into a reformed community property system?

Reppy, concerned about diluting the status of marriage, argues that the law must not "confect rules that make cohabitation preferable to marriage." Would he therefore be unwilling to permit homosexual marriage? Might he, however, be amenable to giving same-sex couples access to the status of lawful cohabitation?

C. Land Sale Transactions

The traditional rule that specific performance is usually available to enforce a land sale contract has been under great stress in recent decades. The Uniform Land Transactions Act, as well as recent case law, provides that sellers usually must mitigate and pursue normal damage remedies against recalcitrant buyers rather than sue for performance by payment of the price, while the buyers may sue the sellers for performance. The standard rational is that sellers are normally in a better position than buyers to resell real property after a contract breach; requiring them to do so by making suits for performance unavailable saves transaction costs. At least one author, however, takes the position that specific performance, rather than damages, ought to be the standard remedy in all contract cases, including those for the sale of land. That piece, *The Efficiency of Specific Performance: Toward a Unified Theory of Contract Remedies*, by Thomas Ulen, is briefly excerpted below. Other areas that have undergone recent change include the treatment of installment land sale contracts as mortgages and the imposition of implied warranties on some sellers of improved real estate. Title system reforms have also been the subject of recent discussion. Carol Rose, in *Crystals and Mud in Property Law*, uses the controversy surrounding warranties, mortgages and recording systems to say some intriguing things about the meaning of change in the institution that is property law.

Despite recent reforms in many areas of land sales, settlement of a standard residential transaction is still a cumbersome and costly event. Discussion of serious reform has gone on for years, usually with little, if any effect. C. Dent Bostick, in *Land Title Registration: An English Solution to an American Problem*, suggests in a recent article that we ought to take a close look at the revolution in land sale systems that occurred in Britain in 1925. His work concludes this section.

Thomas S. Ulen, *The Efficiency of Specific Performance: Toward a Unified Theory of Contract Remedies,* 83 MICH. L. REV. 341–346, 364–366, 401–402 (1984)*

INTRODUCTION

By invoking the notion of economic efficiency, economists and legal scholars have recently made great headway in developing a new and unified theory of contractual relationships.[1] The key advance was the economists' recognition that there are circumstances in which at least one party can be made better off, without making anyone worse off, by one party's breaching rather than performing a contractual promise. This insight suggested that long-established rules for forming and enforcing contracts should be reexamined to see to what extent they fostered or hindered the efficient exchange of reciprocal promises.

The law, it has been urged, should not hinder the breaching of contracts where the breach offers a Pareto-superior outcome.[3] This view suggests that a contract should not be enforced at law solely because to break it is morally repugnant, a repudiation of one's solemn oath. Justice Holmes made the same point without the aid of economic analysis, viz., that the common law should move away from a moral interpretation of contract:

> The duty to keep a contract at common law means a prediction that you must pay damages if you do not keep it, and nothing else. If you commit a tort, you are liable to pay a compensatory sum. If you commit a contract, you are liable to pay a compensatory sum unless the promised event comes to pass, and that is all the difference. But such a mode of looking at the matter stinks in the nostrils of those who think it advantageous to get as much ethics into the law as they can.[4]

If we agree with Holmes and accept for the time being that contractual relations and breach of contract should be evaluated on efficiency grounds, we are led to consider, inter alia, the efficiency characteristics of various remedies for breach. We should invoke those remedies that encourage breach when breach is Pareto-superior to performance and discourage it otherwise. There is a long distance, however, between simply stating this goal with regard to remedies and deciding which among the numerous remedies is the most efficient.

The bulk of the scholarship on efficient remedies has concerned the award of money damages, and a consensus has been reached on the form of damages that is most likely to promote economic efficiency. Alternatives to money damages have not received the same attention from lawyers and economists who have written on the efficiency aspects of contract law. For example, specific performance, the most notable alternative form of court-imposed remedy for breach of contract, has only rarely been subjected to the same sort of scrutiny under the efficiency criterion as has money damages. Nor has there been sufficient attention paid to what might be called party-designed or self-help means of achieving enforcement of value-maximizing reciprocal promises through, for example, liquidated damage clauses, arbitration, and bonding. Nor has there been enough written on the role that market forces, such as a regard for one's future business reputation, might play in mitigating inefficient breach of contract.

The purpose of this essay is to begin the development of an integrated theory of contract remedies by delineating the circumstances under which courts should simply enforce a stipulated remedy clause or grant relief to the innocent party in the form of

[1] The best attempt to integrate economic efficiency into the fundamentals of contract law is Eisenberg, *The Bargain Principle and Its Limits*, 95 HARV. L. REV. 741 (1982); *see also* R. POSNER, ECONOMIC ANALYSIS OF LAW 65–98 (2d ed. 1977); Goetz & Scott, *Enforcing Promises: An Examination of the Basis of Contract*, 89 YALE L.J. 1261 (1980). * * *

[3] A Pareto-superior outcome is one in which, by comparison to some original position, no one is, in his own estimation, worse off and at least one person is, in his own estimation, better off. * * *

[4] Holmes, *The Path of the Law,* 10 HARV. L. REV. 457, 462 (1897). * * *

damages or specific performance. The conclusion, in brief, is that in the absence of stipulated remedies in the contract that survive scrutiny on the usual formation defenses, specific performance is more likely than any form of money damages to achieve efficiency in the exchange and breach of reciprocal promises. If specific performance is the routine remedy for breach, there are strong reasons for believing, first, that more mutually beneficial exchanges of promises will be concluded in the future and that they will be exchanged at a lower cost than under any other contract remedy, and, second, that under specific performance postbreach adjustments to all contracts will be resolved in a manner most likely to lead to the promise being concluded in favor of the party who puts the highest value on the completed performance and at a lower cost than under any alternative.

The argument [focuses on] * * * the relationship between different contract remedies and the costs imposed on contracting parties and on society at the time that promises are exchanged and during negotiations, if any, after the breach. A central tenet of the argument is that the transaction costs facing parties who have already concluded a contract are less, even if there has been a breach, than the costs of a court's resolving the dispute.

* * *

I. Efficient Breach

There are circumstances in which performance of an otherwise legitimate contractual promise would be inefficient. Suppose, for example, that A promises to sell B a house for $100,000. Let us assume that B values the house at $115,000. Thus, at A's asking price, B realizes a consumer surplus of $15,000. Before the sale is completed, C offers A $125,000 for the same house. Should the law compel A to deliver on his promise to B, or should it allow, indeed encourage, him to breach his promise to B in order to sell to C?

From an economic standpoint the answer is clear. Economic efficiency will be served if resources are allocated to their highest-valued uses while minimizing the cost of reallocation. Thus, if, as previously assumed, efficiency is our goal, contract law should specify a remedy for breach that will lead to ownership of the house by the person who values it the most, and should attempt to reach this result at the lowest possible resource cost. In this case, the house apparently has the greatest value to C: we know that he places a value of at least $125,000 on the house; B, by assumption, values it at $115,000; and A values it at something less than $100,000.

It might be objected that contract law in general and remedies for breach of contract in particular need not serve the goal of economic efficiency. There are, it is true, other worthy goals to guide us in designing rules of contract law. * * *

* * * I shall use the efficiency criterion to evaluate various remedies for breach of contract. However, that statement should not be taken to mean that I necessarily believe that those who urge different standards for the law are incorrect. At least with regard to remedies in contract law, I believe it to be the case that widely held notions of fairness and morality argue for the same sort of conclusions as emerge from an efficiency analysis. To the extent that this is true, there is no conflict between efficiency and the other norms often urged in the fashioning of contractual remedies.

* * *

The argument of this paper is normative: the courts should make specific performance the routine remedy and, by extension, any stipulated remedy that was not inserted because of fraud, duress, or coercion should be enforced. Those readers who desire more positivism should consider what follows as being the elaboration of a hypothesis, which, before being accepted or rejected, must be confronted with the relevant data.

* * *

IV. The Efficiency of Specific Performance

Damage payments are the legal remedy for contract breach; specific performance is the equitable remedy. Specific performance is a judicial order requiring the promisor to perform his contractual promise or forbidding him from performing the promise with any other party. If, for example, A has promised to sell a house to B for $100,000 but breaches in order to sell to C for $125,000, B might seek relief in the form of a court order requiring A to sell to B. Alternatively, B might ask the court for an injunction forbidding A to sell to anyone but B. As a general rule, the court invokes equitable remedies only when it thinks that legal remedies are likely to offer inadequate relief, that is, to be under-compensatory. The granting of equitable relief is at the discretion of the court upon a demonstration by the plaintiff that damages will not adequately compensate him. The typical cases in which this undercompensation is said to arise are in the sale of "unique goods," the sale of land (considered by the law, largely for historical reasons, to be a unique good),[85] and long-term input contracts. When an otherwise innocent party asks for specific performance, the breacher is permitted to mount defenses that are not usually available against a damage award: insufficient certainty of terms, inadequate security for the innocent party's performance, the breacher's unilateral mistake, and the high level of supervisory costs that the court might incur in enforcing performance.

The economic efficiency of this state of affairs is open to question. In particular, it is not obvious that the efficient exchange of reciprocal promises or the enforcement of valid contractual promises is best served where specific performance is reserved for the circumstances noted above. * * * I [believe] * * * that specific performance should be, on efficiency grounds, the routine contract remedy. The reasons for this conclusion may be * * * summarized here. First, if contractual parties are on notice that valid promises will be specifically enforced, they will more efficiently exchange reciprocal promises at formation time. In particular, they will have a stronger incentive than currently exists under the dominant legal remedy to allocate efficiently the risks of loss from breach rather than leaving that task, in whole or in part, to the court or to post-breach negotiations conducted under the threat of a potentially inefficient legal remedy. Second, and perhaps most importantly, specific performance offers the most efficient mechanism for protecting subjective values attached to performance. Thus, it promotes contract breach only if it is efficient, that is, if someone will be better off and no one will be worse off because of the breach. In this regard, specific performance and an expansive enforcement of stipulated remedies constitute integral and inseparable parts of a unified theory of efficient contract remedies. Third, if specific performance were the routine remedy, the post-breach costs of adjusting a contract in order to move the promise to the highest-valuing user would be lower than under the most efficient legal remedy. The central reason for this is that under specific performance the costs of determining various parties' valuation of performance are borne by those parties in voluntary negotiations. This means that the costs of determining willingness-to-pay are borne by those most efficiently placed to determine that amount. Finally, because the costs of ascertaining any subjective values of the innocent party through evidence presented to a court are so high and because, therefore, the possibility of under compensating the innocent party through a damage remedy is high, specific performance is far less likely to be under compensatory and far more likely to protect the breachee's subjective valuation than is any other judicially imposed contract remedy.

* * *

[R]emedies for breach of contract are not now entirely consistent with the goal of economic efficiency. The routine remedy is the awarding of money damages, whereas economic efficiency considerations urge specific performance as the routine remedy. Following Calabresi and Melamed's analysis of legal and equitable remedies in nuisance law, I propose that the efficient exchange of mutually beneficial promises would be better served by using the level of transaction costs as the guide for choosing a contract remedy: if transaction costs are low between the defaulter and the innocent party, then an award of specific performance will encourage the parties to exchange the right to performance voluntarily and efficiently; if, however, those costs are so high that no voluntary exchange can take place, then the court should intervene and compel an exchange at a collectively determined price; that is, the court should award money damages. Since it is most likely to be the case that parties to a contract have low transaction costs in that they, unlike, say, tortfeasors and their victims, have already established a relationship, courts should presume that specific performance is to be awarded, with money damages being the exceptional award. This is precisely the opposite of current practice.

The contention that specific performance will greatly increase administration costs or post-breach negotiations costs [is] * * * inaccurate. By comparison to the award of expectation damages, the court costs of specific performance are much less and much more accurate in protecting the breachee's expectancy. There is no less an incentive to mitigate the innocent party's losses under specific performance than there is under efficient money damages. Nor will consequential damages be inefficiently captured under specific performance where they are efficiently excluded under legal relief. Lastly, there are two valid defenses to an action for specific performance: impossibility of performance and high supervision costs. * * * [H]owever, * * * even high supervision costs are not a necessary or sufficient condition for not award-

---

[85] * * * *But cf.* UNIF. LAND TRANSACTIONS ACT § 2-506(b) * * *, rejecting the notion that a seller of real property is automatically entitled to specific performance.

ing specific performance. This is because there are factors that lessen the inefficiencies of equitable relief in cases where supervision costs are most likely to be high: viz., the breacher's regard for his reputation and the possibility that it may be more efficient for the parties to bargain out of performance of the contract than to risk high supervision costs, even if those are to be paid out of the public fisc. Additionally, specific performance should be imposed in instances of high supervision costs if, through the use of special masters, the cost of supervision can be shifted to the litigants and away from the public.

* * *

Note

Would Ulen grant the seller specific performance in *Centex Homes Corp. v. Boag*, 128 N.J. Super. 385, 320 A.2d 194 (1974). In thinking about this question, note that the Boags failed to perform simply because they changed their mind, not because (as implied in the opinion) Mr. Boag's job was suddenly shifted to Chicago. For more information on the facts of *Centex*, *see*, CHUSED, CASES, MATERIALS AND PROBLEMS IN PROPERTY 822–823, 827 (1988).

Carol M. Rose, *Crystals and Mud in Property Law*, 40 STAN. L. REV. 577–610 (1988)*

Property law, and especially the common law of property, has always been heavily laden with hard-edged doctrines that tell everyone exactly where they stand. Default on paying your loan installments? Too bad, you lose the thing you bought and your past payments as well. Forget to record your deed? Sorry, the next buyer can purchase free of your claim, and you are out on the street. Sell that house with the leak in the basement? Lucky you, you can unload the place without having to tell the buyer about such things at all.

In a sense, hard-edged rules like these—rules that I call 'crystals'—are what property is all about. If, as Jeremy Bentham said long ago, property is "nothing but a basis of expectation,"[1] then crystal rules are the very stuff of property: their great advantage, or so it is commonly thought, is that they signal to all of us, in a clear and distinct language, precisely what our obligations are and how we may take care of our interests. Thus, I should inspect the property, record my deed, and make my payments if I don't want to lose my home to unexpected physical, legal, or financial impairments. I know where I stand and so does everyone else, and we can all strike bargains with each other if we want to stand somewhere else.

Economic thinkers have been telling us for at least two centuries that the more important a given kind of thing becomes for us, the more likely we are to have these hard-edged rules to manage it. We draw these ever-sharper lines around our entitlements so that we know who has what, and so that we can trade instead of getting into the confusions and disputes that would only escalate as the goods in question became scarcer and more highly valued.

At the root of these economic analyses lies the perception that it costs something to establish clear entitlements to things, and we won't bother to undertake the task of removing goods from an ownerless 'commons' unless it is worth it to us to do so. What makes it worth it? Increasing scarcity of the

[1] J. BENTHAM, THEORY OF LEGISLATION, PRINCIPLES OF THE CIVIL CODE pt. 1, ch. 8, at 68 (Baxi ed., Hildreth trans., 1975).

resource, and the attendant conflicts over it. To use the example given by Harold Demsetz, one of the most notable of the modern economists telling this story, when the European demand for fur hats increased demand for (and scarcity of) fur-bearing animals among Indian hunters, the Indians developed a system of property entitlements to the animal habitat.[6] Economic historians of the American West tell a similar story about the development of property rights in various minerals and natural resources. Easy-going, anything-goes patterns of appropriation at the outset came under pressure as competition for resources increased, and were finally superseded by much more sharply defined systems of entitlement. In effect, as our competition for a resource raises the costs of conflict about it, those conflict costs begin to outweigh the costs of taking it out of the commons and establishing clear property entitlements. We establish a system of clear entitlements so that we can barter and trade for what we want instead of fighting.

The trouble with this 'scarcity story' is that things don't seem to work this way, or at least not all the time. Sometimes we seem to substitute fuzzy, ambiguous rules of decision for what seem to be perfectly clear, open and shut, demarcations of entitlements. I call this occurrence the substitution of 'mud' rules for 'crystal' ones.

Thus, in the examples with which I began, we find that, over time, the straightforward common law crystalline rules have been muddied repeatedly by exceptions and equitable second-guessing, to the point that the various claimants under real estate contracts, mortgages, or recorded deeds don't know quite what their rights and obligations really are. And the same pattern has occurred in other areas too. In Wisconsin's *Prah v. Maretti*,[9] for example, what seemed to be a workable crystalline rule about sunlight rights—that your neighbor has no right to the sunlight that crosses your lot unless your neighbor has gotten an easement from you[10]—has been transformed into a mud doctrine. Now, if you block the light, your neighbor may have a nuisance action against you—at least in Wisconsin.

Now, nuisance is one of those extraordinarily shapeless doctrinal areas in the law of property. In *Prah*, the nuisance question hinged on a typically vague formulation: "all the underlying facts and circumstances." Does it matter that you built first? Could you or your neighbor have adjusted your respective buildings to avoid the problem? How valuable was the sunlight to you, and how valuable to your neighbor? You don't know in advance how to answer these questions and how to weigh the answers against each other; that is to say, you don't know whether your building will be found a nuisance or not, and you won't really know until you go through the pain and trouble of getting a court to decide the issue after you have built it or have had plans drawn up.

Quite aside from the wealth transfer that may accompany a change in the rules, then, the change may sharply alter the clarity of the relationship between the parties. But a move to the uncertainty of mud seems disruptive to the very practice of a private property/contractual exchange society. Thus, it is hardly surprising that we individually and collectively attempt to clear up the mud with new crystal rules—as when private parties contract out of ambiguous warranties, or when legislatures pass new versions of crystalline record systems—only to be overruled later, when courts once again reinstate mud in a different form.

These odd permutations on the scarcity story must give us pause. Why should we shift back and forth instead of opting for crystal when we have greater scarcity? Is there some advantage to mud rules that the courts are paying attention to? And if so, why do we not opt for mud rules instead?

This paper is about the blurring of clear and distinct property rules with the muddy doctrines of "maybe or maybe not," and about the reverse tendency to try to clear up the blur with new crystalline rules. * * *

I. From Crystal to Mud and Back: Three Examples

From all appearances, and despite the obvious advantages of crystalline property rules for the smooth flow of trade and commerce, we seem to be caught in an era of intractable and perhaps even increasing muddiness.[18] One could choose any num-

---

[6] Demsetz, *Toward a Theory of Property Rights*, 79 AM. ECON. REV. PROC. 347-349 (1967).

[9] 108 Wis. 2d 223, 321 N.W.2d 182 (1982).

[10] For this position, *see* Parker v. Foote, 19 Wend. 308 (N.Y. Sup. Ct. 1838); Fontainebleau Hotel Corp. v. Forty-Five Twenty-Five, Inc., 114 So. 2d 357 (Fla. Dist. Ct. App. 1959), *cert. denied*, 117 So. 2d 842 (Fla. 1960). Both cases rejected a British doctrine of "ancient lights" whereby a right to sunlight could be acquired by prescription.

[18] *Cf.* Cribbet, *Concepts in Transition: The Search for a New Definition of Property*, 1986 U. ILL. L. REV. 1 * * *.

ber of areas to see this, and I will briefly discuss only a few, namely the examples with which I began. The first is the example of the law of caveat emptor in real estate transactions, which in recent years has shown a strikingly generalized pattern of the slide towards mud.

A. *The Demise of Caveat Emptor*

For several hundred years, and right up to the last few decades, caveat emptor was the staple fare of the law of real estate purchases, at least for buildings already constructed. The purchaser was deemed perfectly capable of inspecting the property and deciding for himself whether he wanted it, and if anyone were foolish enough to buy a pig in a poke, he deserved what he got. Short of outright fraud that would mislead the buyer, the seller had no duties to disclose anything at all.

One chink in this otherwise smooth wall was the doctrine of "latent defects," which, like the exception for fraud, suggested that perhaps the buyer really can't figure things out entirely. For some time now, in at least some states, a seller has had to tell a buyer about material problems with the property known to the seller but undiscoverable by the purchaser upon reasonable inspection. The doctrine began to raise a few problems of muddiness: What defects are "material"? What does the seller "know"? To what extent should the buyer "reasonably" have to inspect for herself?

Within the last few decades, the movement to mud in this area has become even more pronounced as some courts and legal commentators maintain that builder/vendors implicitly warrant a new house "habitable." But what does habitability mean? Is the house's habitability coterminous with the local housing code, or does "habitability" connote some less definite standard? What if the defects were obvious, and just what does "obvious" mean, anyway? We don't know until we litigate the issues.

Even if builder/vendors' warranties do muddy up property rights, there are some plausible reasons for them. After all, the builder/vendors are professionals, and they should know more about their own construction; they even might have avoided the problems in the first place by building more carefully.[26] It is somewhat more difficult to extend those arguments to sellers who are themselves merely homeowners instead of builder/vendors, yet we find that even these nonprofessional sellers have increasing obligations to anticipate the buyers' desires, and to inform buyers about disagreeable factors that might make the buyers think twice. A California court, for example, has ruled that the sellers had to inform the buyer that a mass murder had taken place a decade previously in a particular house.[28] The courts now seem to presume a buyer who can't figure out much at all, and to protect that buyer they have adopted a mud standard: like good neighbors, sellers must tell buyers about any "material" defects—whatever those may be.

The increasingly mushy relationship between buyers and sellers of real estate has parallels in the law of consumer sales generally, and the real estate cases borrow much of their language from other cases about such items as cars, hairdryers, and water heaters. These developments might suggest that the scarcity story is exactly backwards, and that the normal movement of property law is not towards ever harder edged rules, but towards the fluidity and imprecision of mud.

But there is a countermove as well: Even if the legal rules have moved toward mud, private bargainers often try to install their own little crystalline systems through contractual waivers of warranties or disclosure duties (for example, the "as is" or "no warranty" sale). These private efforts in effect move things into the pattern of a circle, from crystal to mud and back to crystal. And the circle turns once again when the courts ban such waivers, as they sometimes do, and firmly re-establish a rule of mud—only to be followed by even more artful waivers.

The back-and-forth pattern of crystal and mud is even more evident in the next example, the loan secured by landed property—a form of real estate transaction whose history * * * resembl[es] * * * a seesaw.

B. *Of Mortgages and Mud*

Early common law mortgages were very crystalline indeed. They had the look of pawnshop transactions and were at least sometimes structured as conveyances: I borrow money from you, and at the same time I convey my land to you as security for my loan. If all goes well, I pay back my debt on the agreed "law

---

26 *See, e.g.*, Humber v. Morton, 426 S.W.2d 554, 562 (Tex. 1968) * * *. If the cost to the builder of "warranty" work is higher than expected damages, however, builders may not build better but may rather accept losses from occasional damage suits.

28 Reed v. King, 145 Cal. App. 3d 261, 193 Cal. Rptr. 130 (1983).

day," and you reconvey my land back to me. But if all does not go well and I cannot pay on the appointed day, then, no matter how heartrending my excuse, I lose my land to you and, presumably, any of the previous payments I might have made. As the fifteenth century commentator Littleton airily explained, the name "mortgage" derived from the rule that, if the debtor "doth not pay, then the land which he puts in pledge . . . is gone from him for ever, and so dead."[35]

This system had the advantage of great clarity, but it sometimes must have seemed very hard on mortgage debtors to the advantage of scoundrelly creditors. Littleton's advice about the importance of specifying the precise place and time for repayment, for example, conjures up images of a wily creditor hiding in the woods on the repayment day to frustrate repayment; presumably, the unfound creditor could keep the property. But by the seventeenth century, the intervention of courts of equity had changed things. By the eighteenth and nineteenth centuries, the equity courts were regularly giving debtors as many as three or four "enlargements" of the time in which they might pay and redeem the property before the final "foreclosure," even when the excuse was lame. * * *

The muddiness of this emerging judicial remedy argued against its attractiveness. * * * Instead of a precise and clear allocation of entitlements between the parties, the "equity of redemption" and its unpredictable foreclosure opened up vexing questions and uncertainties: How much time should the debtor have for repayment before the equitable arguments shifted to favor the creditor? What sort of excuses did the debtor need? Did it matter that the property, instead of dropping in the lap of the creditor, was sold at a foreclosure sale?

But as the courts moved towards muddiness, private parties attempted to bargain their way out of these costly uncertainties and to reinstate a crystalline pattern whereby lenders could get the property immediately upon default without the costs of foreclosure. How about a separate deal with the borrower, for example, whereby he agrees to convey an equitable interest to the lender in case of default? Nothing doing, said the courts, including the United States Supreme Court, which in 1878 stated flatly that a mortgagor could not initially bargain away his "equity of redemption."[45] Well, then, how about an arrangement whereby it looks as if the lender already owns the land, and the "borrower" only gets title if he lives up to his agreement to pay for it by a certain time? This seemed more promising: In the 1890s California courts thought it perfectly correct to hold the buyer to his word in such an arrangement, and to give him neither an extension nor a refund of past payments. By the 1960s, however, they were changing their minds about these "installment land contracts." After all, these deals really had exactly the same effect as the old-style mortgages—the defaulting buyer could lose everything if he missed a payment, even the very last payment. Human vice and error seemed to put the crystal rule in jeopardy: In a series of cases culminating with a default by a "willful but repentant" little old lady who had stopped paying when she mistakenly thought that she was being cheated, the California Supreme Court decided to treat these land contracts as mortgages in disguise.[48] It gave the borrower "relief from forfeiture"—a time to reinstate the installment contract or get back her past payments.

With mortgages first and mortgage substitutes later, we see a back-and-forth pattern: crisp definition of entitlements, made fuzzy by accretions of judicial decisions, crisped up again by the parties' contractual arrangements, and once again made fuzzy by the courts. Here we see private parties apparently following the "scarcity story" in their private law arrangements: when things matter, the parties define their respective entitlements with ever sharper precision. Yet the courts seem at times unwilling to follow this story or to permit these crystalline definitions, most particularly when the rules hurt one party very badly. The cycle thus alternates between crystal and mud.

But the subject matter that has truly defied the scarcity story, often to the despair of property professors, has not been mortgages or mortgage substitutes. It has been the recording system, to which I now turn.

C. *Broken Records*

In establishing recording systems, legislatures have lent support to private parties' efforts to sharpen the definition of their entitlements. The raison d'etre of such systems is to clarify and perfectly specify landed property rights for the sake of easy and smooth transfers of land.

---

[35] LITTLETON'S TENURES § 332 (E. Wambaugh ed. 1903).

[45] Peugh v. Davis, 96 U.S. 332, 337 (1878).

[48] MacFadden v. Walker, 5 Cal. 3d 809, 488 P.2d 1353, 97 Cal. Rptr. 537 (1971) * * *.

But the Anglo-American recording system in fact has been a saga of frustrated efforts to make clear who has what in land transfers. Common law transfers of land required a certain set of formalities between the parties, but thereafter, conflicting claims were settled by the age-old principle, "first in time, first in right." Thus, on Tuesday I might sell my farm to you, and on Wednesday I might wrongfully purport to sell it once again to innocent Farmer Brown. Poor Farmer Brown remains landless even though he knew nothing about the prior sale to you and indeed had no way of knowing about it. This outcome was hardly satisfactory from a property rights perspective. "First in time, first in right" may work well enough in a community where everyone knows all about everyone else's transactions, but outside that context, the doctrine does little to put people on notice of who owns what, and the opportunities for conflicting claims are endless.

But the efforts to remedy this flaw have gone through new cycles of certainty and uncertainty. Henry VIII attempted—without great success—to establish public registration of land claims through the Statute of Enrollments in 1536. Versions of the Statute resurfaced in Massachusetts' 1640 recording act and in other seventeenth and eighteenth century colonial recording acts, all of which were much more widely (though still somewhat irregularly) applied than their Henrician model had been.

Henry's Statute and its original American counterparts reflected an emphatically crystalline view of property. Their literal language suggests that they were versions of what has come to be called a "race" statute the first purchaser to record (the winner of the "race" to the registry) can hold his title against all other claimants, whether or not he was in fact the first to purchase. In such a system, the official records become an unimpeachable source of information about the status of land ownership; the law counts the record owner, and only the record owner, as the true owner. The purchaser can buy in reliance on the records without fear of divestment by some unknown interloper, and without the need to make some cumbersome extra-record search for such potential interlopers.

This system was too crystalline to last. The characters to muck up this crystalline system by now should be sounding familiar: ninnies, hard-luck cases, and the occasional scoundrels who take advantage of them. What are we to do, for example, with the silly fellow who buys an interest in property but simply forgets to record? Or with the more conscientious one who does attempt to record his interest, but whose records wind up in the wrong book? Or with the lost soul whose impeccably correct filing is dropped behind the radiator by the neglectful clerk? Some courts take a hard line, perhaps concluding that the first owner was in a better position than our innocent outsider—that is, the next purchaser—to detect and correct the flaws in the records. But our sympathies for the luckless unrecorded owner put pressure on the recording system that would divest him in favor of the later-arriving outsider.

Our sympathies are all the greater when the outsider is not so innocent after all. What shall we do, say, when the unrecorded first buyer is snookered out of his claim by a later purchaser who knows perfectly well that the land had already been sold? Shall we allow this nasty second buyer to perfect a claim simply because he carefully follows the official recording rules? This thought was too much for the courts of equity, and too much for American legislatures as well. By the early nineteenth century, the British equity courts had imported an element of non-record "notice" into what had initially been a "race" system. Under these doctrines, the later purchaser could take free of the prior claims only if he did not know about those prior claims, either from the records or from non-record facts that should put him "on notice." American legislatures followed this move to such a degree that, at present, only a handful of states maintain a race system with any rigor. The other states deny the subsequent claim of the person who had or should have had notice of the earlier claim.

This development means mud: What "should" a purchaser know about, anyway? To be sure, if someone is living on the land, perhaps the potential purchaser should make a few inquiries about the occupant's status. But what if the "occupant's" acts are more ambiguous, consisting of, say, shoveling some manure onto the contested land? Well, said one court, a buyer should have asked about the source of all that manure—and since he didn't, and thus did not find out about the manure shoveler's prior but unrecorded claim, the later buyer did not count as an innocent; his title was a nullity.[63]

With the emergence of this judicial outlook, the crystalline idea of the recording system has come full cycle back to mud. To be sure, the recording system

[63] Miller v. Green, 264 Wis. 159, 58 N.W.2d 704 (1953).

can give one a fair guess about the legal status of any given property. But by the end of the last century, * * * the test of a title's "marketability" became a question of whether the title was subject to "reasonable" doubt—a matter, of course, for the discretion of the court. In the meantime, a whole title insurance industry sprang up to calm the fears of would-be purchasers who wanted to avoid questions about which doubts were reasonable and which were not. It is this industry, in a sense, that once again makes crystals out of the recording system's mud; and according to the reformers, it is this industry that now stands in the way of a more rational method of cleaning up the mess once and for all.[67]

Yet one must wonder whether cleaning up the mess might not just repeat the cycle of mud/crystal/mud. One of the most popular suggestions for reform is the so-called "Torrens" system, named for someone who thought that shipping registry methods could be used beneficially in real estate. In this system, all claims on a given property—sales, liens, easements, etc.—are first registered and then incorporated in a certificate. Torrens registration echoes eerily the colonial "race" statutes: No unregistered claim counts, and the owner's certificate for a given property acts as the complete record of everything that anyone might claim.

Well, perhaps not everything: Government liens, fraudulent transactions, and, according to some courts, even simple errors or neglect in registration can produce unregistered claims that count. Hence this neo-race system provides no complete relief from the recording system's mud. Even after we look at the Torrens certificate, we still have to be on the lookout for the G-men, the forgers, and the ninnies who neglected to register their claims properly. Not a lot of mud, to be sure, but just wait. In some jurisdictions with a long history of Torrens registration, courts have in effect reestablished a "notice" system, defeating the interest of one who registers his claim when he knows about a prior unregistered one—or merely when he should have known about the prior claim. This practice, of course, means that the registry and certificate no longer count as the complete source of information about a property's title status.

The most striking aspect of these developments is that first the title recording acts, and later the registration systems, represented deliberate choices to establish crystalline rules for the sake of simplicity and ease of land sales and purchases. People who failed to use the records or registries were supposed to lose their claims, no matter how innocent they might have been, and no matter how nastily their opponents might have behaved. Yet these very crystalline systems have drifted back into mud through the importation of equitable ideas of notice—only to be replaced by new crystalline systems in the form of private contract or public legislation.

All these examples put the scarcity story to the test: What has happened to that story, according to which our rules should become more crystalline as resources become more scarce and more valuable? Why instead do we shift back and forth between hard-edged, yes-or-no crystalline rules and discretion-laden, post hoc muddy rules? Why do we have, over time, both mud and crystal rules with respect to the very same things, without any notable relation to their scarcity or plenty? The following section runs through a few theories that might help to explain this mystery.

II. Some Tentative Explanations

A. *Taking Sides*

One way to cope with the mud/crystal dilemma is to choose one type of rule over the other. Perhaps in keeping with the market-conscious spirit of the 80s, legal academics seem to favor crystals.

* * *

Frank Easterbrook recently applauded what he describes as the ex ante perspective of recent court decisions. Instead of trying to adjudge situations ex post, doing fairness to the parties from the perspective of what we know about their positions after things fall apart, the courts should try to consider matters from the perspective of persons similar to the parties at the outset of their relationship, and then figure out how we want them to think and act before all contingencies become realities.[79] How do we want them to act? We want them to be careful planners so that things don't fall apart so easily.

To put it baldly, the ex ante perspective generally means sticking it to those who fail to protect themselves in advance against contingencies that, as it happens, work out badly for them. No muddiness here. All parties are presumed to be clear-sighted overseers of their own best interests; it is up to them

---

[67] *See* Lobel, *A Proposal for a Title Registration System for Realty*, 11 U. RICH. L. REV. 501 (1977).

[79] Easterbrook, *The Supreme Court 1983-Term—Foreword: The Court and the Economic System*, 98 HARV. L. REV. 4, 10-11, 19-21 (1984).

to tie up all the loose ends that they can, and the courts should let the advantages and disadvantages fall where they may. Why? Because this will encourage people to plan and to act carefully, knowing that no judicial cavalry will ride to their rescue later. It will also allow the people that John Locke once called "the Industrious and Rational" to reap the fruits of their industry and rationality, and thus encourage productivity generally.

But this approach means that the legal consequences of rules ought to be clear in advance, in other words, crystals rather than mud. The industrious and rational need to know that the consequences of their dealings are fixed, at least legally; no shifts of responsibility after the fact. Judicial punctiliousness about establishing and following clear rules, one would suppose, can influence behavior in the direction of greater productivity or carefulness.

Things would be easier if one could say that crystals are the uniform choice among the modern scholars knowledgeable about these matters. But that is not the case. Several scholars in recent years, particularly those associated with the Critical Legal Studies movement, have decried what we might call the excessively crystalline character of our legal system, which they associate with a kind of alienated individualism.[82] Instead, they plump for more attention to mud, or, as the phrase has it, to "standards" instead of "rules." Duncan Kennedy, who popularized the current distinction between rules and standards, argues that hard-edged, crystal doctrines systematically abandon people to the wiles of the bad and the mean-spirited. As Kennedy reminds us, Holmes even framed these doctrines in terms of the "bad man." They are designed to tell the bad man the limits within which he can get away with his badness. Standards, on the other hand, are aimed at protecting goodness and altruism—whatever internal contradictions may lurk in the notion of enforcing goodness by a legal order.

* * *

The difficulty with adopting either position is that to do so suggests that we in some way have a choice between crystal and mud, whereas the history of property law tells us that we seem to be stuck with both. Even when we choose one (such as a hard-and-fast recording system), the choice seems to dissolve, and instead of really choosing, we seem to oscillate between them. Because this pattern recurs so often in so many areas, it is difficult to believe that it is due to abnormal foolishness or turpitude, or that it can be permanently overcome by a more thoughtful or more virtuous choice of one side or the other.

B. *Refinements on the Economic Perspective*

Some economic theory relates the crystal/mud problem to the different characteristics of the objects we consider to be "property." One theory looks to what are called "transaction costs" to explain why we sometimes have crystals and sometimes mud. Thomas Merrill has argued that where transaction costs are low—where it is easy to make a deal—we tend to have clear, hard-edged, yes-or-no rules.[92] Thus, in trespass law, any invasion of my property, no matter how trivial, is an actionable wrong. * * *

On the other hand, the argument goes on, we find "discretionary" (or muddy) rules where the costs of transacting are high, as, for example, in the area of nuisance doctrine. Here the conflicts typically involve numerous parties, such as the victims of noxious odors that spread through a neighborhood. It is not easy for all affected parties to find each other, to agree on a common strategy, and to negotiate a deal whereby the sufferers pay to have the fumes stopped, or alternatively, where the fume-producing plant pays some agreed-upon price to make up for the sufferings it causes. Since the parties cannot easily arrive at a negotiated agreement, a court must solve the mess itself, deciding whether the costs of the fumes outweigh the benefits. Thus, where transaction costs are high, we have no nice clear deals that put a price on costs and benefits, and a court has to muddle through with conjectures. These are the scenarios in which we need judicial discretion—as well as the ambiguous, muddy doctrines that allow for judicial guesswork.

The difficulty with this explanation is that we sometimes fall back on muddy doctrines even where transaction costs are low. Wisconsin's new "nuisance" treatment of sunlight rights, for example, flies in the face of what would seem to be a relatively easy negotiation between neighbors. The other examples given earlier suggest the same pattern. The all but universal abandonment of the caveat emptor rule for house purchases also seems to have occurred against a backdrop of low transaction costs (one buyer, one seller), as does the movement to introduce equitable mushiness into the hard-edged contractual relations

---

[82] *See* Kennedy, *Form and Substance in Private Law Adjudication*, 89 HARV. L. REV. 1685, 1745, 1774 (1976) * * *.

[92] Merrill, *Trespass, Nuisance, and the Costs of Determining Property Rights*, 14 J. LEGAL STUD. 13–14 (1985).

of mortgages and installment land contracts, or the repeated muddying of land record systems even when the systems are relatively easy to use. Thus something in the back-and-forth between crystals and mud seems to elude straight transaction costs.

* * *

III. Forfeiture as Overload: The Problem and the Players

A strong element of moral judgment runs through the cases in which mud supersedes crystal. These cases are often rife with human failings—sloth and forgetfulness on the one hand, greed and self-dealing on the other. These vices put pressure on our efforts to elaborate clear and distinct property specifications, and make judges and others second guess the deals that call for a pound of flesh.

Perhaps we can get at this human element by thinking not about the moral qualities that are at issue, but rather about the pound of flesh. We have already seen that in the decisions about mortgages and installment land contracts, there lurks a deep antipathy to what is explicitly called the debtor's "forfeiture." The same antipathy to "forfeiture"—a loss disproportionate to the lapse—also appears in our other examples. Thus, the non-recording (or improperly recording, or negligently recording) owner would lose the very property itself; thus, the non-inspecting (or imperfectly inspecting, or negligently inspecting) buyer would get stuck with a house that may be flooded twice a week with the neighbor's sewage.

* * *

[W]hy should we find a distaste for forfeiture in people's contractual agreements about their property * * *? After all, contracting parties presumably know about the potential for forfeiture and agreed to it anyway. Why complicate their relations by asking elaborate ex post questions comparable to "last clear chance"—that is, who could have avoided the redistributive event that both apparently contemplated as a possibility? Are there reasons to make this post hoc inquiry, regardless of how firmly the parties seem to have agreed to possible forfeitures ab initio?

Forfeiture might be seen as a symptom of the overloading of crystal rules. Crystalline property doctrines yield fixed consequences, and their predictability makes these doctrines attractive; but for that very reason they may be overused or overloaded in contexts that make them unpredictable and counterproductive.

Consider the way that the enforcement of a penalty affects the incentives of persons on either side of a property entitlement. If we were to enforce penalties against defaulters or violators, the persons involved undoubtedly would be especially careful about avoiding violations. But perhaps they would be too careful, and try to live up to their obligations even when circumstances changed radically, and when everyone would really be better off if someone defaulted and paid normal damages for whatever harm their default caused another. Penalties might also affect the behavior of the non-defaulting parties. Because they would gain much more than damages if penalties were enforced, unscrupulous dealers might expend efforts to find trading partners who would fail rather than succeed, or take measures to make them trip up, in order to take the penalty proceeds and run. These victims are the people that petty con artists in my hometown of Chicago might call "mopes," a term that undoubtedly could include the unsuspecting house purchasers who overestimate their ability to live up to the loan payments, or who never suspect that there might be rats in the basement, or who don't have a clue that they have to record their titles.

Fools on the one side and sharp dealers on the other, then, are central players in the crystal-to-mud story, because they are the characters most likely to have a leading role in the systematic overloading of crystalline rules. From this perspective, as indeed the more sophisticated economic analyses tell us, crystalline rules seem less the king of the efficiency mountain than we may normally assume. One can argue that elaborate ex post allocations of responsibilities might be efficient too, even if they make people's entitlements fuzzier ex ante. The very knowledge that one cannot gull someone else, and get away with it, makes it less likely that anyone will dissipate time and effort in trying to find the gullible. This knowledge will also reassure those of us who fear we may be made fools; we can go about our business and take part in the world of trade without cowering at home because we think we need to hire a lawyer and an accountant every time we leave the car at a commercial parking lot.

* * *

IV. The Context of Forfeiture: Crystals and Mud as Institutional Responses to Estrangement

What can be said to generalize the context of forfeiture, where crystal rules are overloaded? Where is it in our commercial life, for example, that we find the invocation of those crystalline rules at the cost of great forfeiture to another? * * *

[Editor's Note: Professor Rose argues that contract and property law developed historically as a substitute for trading communities. By enforcing deals, clear rules of property and contract could recreate the trust that had previously rested on traders' common membership in close-knit groups, and thus these legal rules made commercial dealings possible among strangers.]

* * *

[W]hat is easily overlooked is that mud rules, too, attempt to recreate an underlying non-legal trading community in which confidence is possible. In those communities, the members tend to readjust for future complications, rather than drive hard bargains. Mud rules mimic a pattern of post hoc readjustments that people would make if they were in an ongoing relationship with each other. People in such relationships would hardly dupe their trading partners out of their titles, sell them defective goods, or fail to make minor readjustments on debts. If they did such things, they would lose a trading partner (or suffer denunciation in church, or become black sheep), and everyone would know it.

Now we can see why crystal and mud are a matched pair. Both are distilled from a kind of non-legal commercial context where people already in some relationship arrive at more or less imperfect understandings at the outset and expect post hoc readjustments when circumstances require. Just as the parties call on courts to enforce promises and protect entitlements that would otherwise be enforced by the threat of informal sanctions, so too do they call on the courts to figure out the post hoc readjustments that would otherwise have been made by the parties themselves.

In our one-time dealings with strangers a wedge appears that splits a trading relationship into ex ante and ex post, crystals and mud. These dealings are the situations in which it seems most important to have clear definitions of obligations, but in which it is also important to have some substitute for the pattern of ongoing cooperation that would protect us against sudden and unexpected loss.

* * *

Given this condition, judges, who see everything ex post, really cannot help but be influenced by their ex post perspectives. They lean ever so slightly to mud, in order to save the fools from forfeiture at the hands of scoundrels. Indeed, if judges have even an occasional preference for post hoc readjustments, to avoid forfeiture, this preference will gradually place an accretion of mud rules over people's crystalline arrangements. These considerations suggest a modification of claims about the efficiency of common law adjudication. We are more likely to find that judicial solutions veer towards mud rules, while it is legislatures that are more apt to join with private parties as "rulemakers" with a tilt towards crystal.

Here, then, the circular pattern emerges: If things matter to us, we try to place clear bounds around them when we make up rules for our dealings with strangers so that we can invest in the things or trade them. The overloading of clear systems, however, may lead to forfeitures—dramatic losses that we can only see post hoc, and whose post hoc avoidance makes us (as judges) muddy the boundaries we have drawn. Then, at some point we may become so stymied by muddiness that as rulemakers we will start over with new boundaries, followed by new muddiness, and so on.

V. Does it Matter? "Mere" Rhetoric in the Opposition of Crystals and Mud

* * *

A dominating strand of our inherited social theory posits a world of individuals whose dealings with each other are based on entitlement and self-interest rather than fellow-feeling. Thus, it matters how we talk about our dealings with strangers because that is the way that we deal with everyone. I am going to suggest, however, that neither crystal rhetoric nor mud rhetoric can sustain the image of a world of strangers.

The rhetoric of crystals suggests that our safety with strangers is derived from an ability to define and bound off every entitlement with a kind of perfect language, a language that reflects in the present all future contingencies. This rhetoric suggests that, regardless of context, background, or culture, everyone understands the content of each entitlement, so that in trade, each party understands what he is giving up and what he is gaining—or can at least "discount" any risks into a present value. And because of this perfect language, this perfect present understanding of the future and its contingencies, it is only fair to enforce promises and property entitlements to the limit.[149]

---

[149] It is not coincidental, I believe, that Richard Epstein, a well-known proponent of the crystal position, argues that the meaning of legal doctrine is stable over time. *Compare* Epstein, *Possession as the Root of Title*, 13 Ga. L. Rev. 1221, 1241 (1979) * * * *with* Rose, *Possession as Origin of Property*, 52 U. Chi. L. Rev. 73, 84–85 (1985) * * * . * * *

* * *

What is wrong with this idea? The chief accusation leveled at crystal rhetoric, chiefly by scholars associated with Critical Legal Studies, is that crystalline rules are hardhearted and mean-spirited, that they glorify the attitude of self-centeredness and "me first," and that they act as a kind of coverup for the domination of the weak by the strong through the vehicle of unbridled capitalism. A related and in some ways more profound objection is that the notion of fixed entitlements, known or "discounted" perfectly in the present and traded around in their discounted form, is a kind of false understanding of the importance of time in human affairs. It is a notion that equates knowledge of human action with knowledge about the objects of nature. It supposes that human beings have no memories or new ideas that influence later choices, no ability to persuade each other—in short, no changes of consciousness over time that will cause them to redefine their views about "entitlements," just as they redefine other aspects of their thought.

But if time does matter in human consciousness, then the paths we take and the things we think we are "entitled to" may be explained completely only by ex post narrative and cannot be foreseen in advance or predicted from what falsely appears to be a set of identical conditions in the past. To adopt the rhetoric of crystal rules, then, seems to be a way of denying the necessarily dialogic character of human interactions and acting as if we can compel human behavior by a perfect specification of unchanging rights and obligations.

But it is often forgotten that there is a much softer, more sociable and dialogic side to crystal rules and to the commerce that accompanied their development. At least some Enlightenment thinkers thought about commerce in a way that now seems novel: They hoped that commerce would enlarge sociability and would, in a sense, be a constituitive force in ever larger communities of "interest." They argued that "gentle commerce"—and presumably also the fixed entitlements that commerce seems to require—would not harden manners but rather soften them and make its practitioners more attentive to the needs of others, precisely because everyone could count on a reliable return in meeting those needs. Thus, commerce and fixed entitlements would create communities—at the very least, communities of interest—and the ongoing dialogue that is a part of such communities.

Lest this view be too rapidly written off as Enlightenment Panglossianism, we should note that recent historians have attributed the development of eighteenth and early nineteenth century philanthropy to the legal rhetoric of fixed entitlements and promise-keeping. It seems that confidence in firm rules did indeed instill a sense that one could deal with strangers; and when commercial traders dealt with strangers, they came to feel sympathy for the plight of those strangers, as well as confidence in their own ability to help. Indeed, it is hard to imagine the historical development of anything like altruism—in the sense of selfless attention to the needs of strangers—in the absence of the far-flung commercial ties that seemed to overcome the casual savagery towards outsiders so characteristic of earlier times.

Moreover, the language of crystal rules sometimes conveys a kind of sturdiness that, at least in our culture, suggests a very important social virtue: namely, courage. The rhetoric of firmly delineated entitlements supports that courage. One can envision almost in romantic terms the pioneer woman who, armed and ready, turns away the intruders at the threshold of her homestead cottage, or the tavern owners who refuse all offers to give up their little establishment and instead force the giant office building to be built around them and their happy customers. Even the child psychologists tell us that uncertainty about rules is not always good for us and that it does not improve our temperaments, our character, or our ability to get along with others.

Thus, crystal rules not only depend upon shared social understandings, they at least arguably enhance sociability and facilitate ongoing social interactions. In this respect, crystal rules turn out to mirror mud rules.

It is indeed the element of ongoing social interactions that mud rules focus upon. They attempt to introduce an element of continuing dialogue among persons who acted as if they were ordering their affairs as strangers. When a court introduces ambiguity into the fixed rules that the parties initially adopted, it in effect reinstates the kind of weighing, balancing, and reconsidering that the parties might have undertaken if they had been in some longer term relationship with each other. Thus, if the mortgage can't be paid on time, the lender's expectation of prompt payment has to be weighed against the borrower's loss of the deal; if the house buyer discovers a leaky sewage line, perhaps he should get some concession from the seller to make up for this unexpected damage. But these judicial interventions are a crude substitute for dialogue, for talking things over and adjusting entitlements, as one would be likely to do in an ongoing trading relationship, or as one would in a family or religious community.

The chief criticism leveled against mud—particularly by scholars associated with law and economics—is that, all other things being equal, mud is inefficient: Mud rules make entitlements uncertain and thus increase the costs of trading and of resolving disputes at the same time that they discourage careful planning. But this complaint overstates the case: At least in some instances, there is a great deal more clarity and certainty about a mud rule than a crystal one. This view is reflected in the Uniform Commercial Code, where a muddy term like "commercial reasonableness" is regarded as a standard that is more predictable to business people than such arcana as the mailbox rule of offer and acceptance. Perhaps we could dream up some formulation that would more clearly express our understanding than "commercial reasonableness" does, and commercial traders indeed often do so. But language is always imperfect, and much of the time it is not worth the effort to specify everything. It is easier and cheaper to rely on a set of socially understood conventions. Mud rules, then, can take on a greater clarity in a social setting among persons with some common understanding—who know, for example, that a "baker's dozen" numbers thirteen.

Just as there is a version of sociability and dialogue in crystal rules, there is a version of certainty and predictability in mud rules. These reversals occur just where crystals or mud move into a genuine social context, and it is no wonder that this is the locus of the reversal. Crystals and mud are rhetorical extractions from the practices of ongoing trading relationships where the participants are likely to enjoy both upstream security as well as downstream readjustment. In our dealings with strangers, it seems as if we can only have the one or the other—hence crystals on the one hand, for upstream security, and mud on the other, for downstream readjustment. But in fact, most of our interactions are much more sociable than the one-shot deal; we are repeat customers, we care about our reputations, and we hope that our clients will come back. And it is at this juncture, where we establish some longterm tie, that crystals and mud dissolve into each other.

To be sure, from time to time we do deal with strangers on a one-shot basis, so that they stay strangers. Those are the points where we are faced with a choice of crystals and mud and where, over time, we seem to shift back and forth between these two jurisprudential modes. It is an illusion to think that either of these rhetorical modes are paradigms for normal living or even normal commercial dealings. Instead, they are our metaphors for the lapses of community.

But it is precisely as metaphor or rhetoric that the choice between crystal and mud matters. The lapse of community may occur only infrequently in our everyday lives, but this world of estrangement has had a robust life in our highly individualistic talk about politics and economics since the seventeenth century.[165] In the context of that talk of universal individualism, the metaphoric or rhetorical character of crystals and mud has a certain independent significance. However much crystal rules may have a dialogic side like mud, and however much mud rules may lend the certainty of crystal, as rhetoric, crystals and mud bear sharply divergent didactic messages. They suggest quite different ways that each self-contained individual should behave and converse with all those other self-contained individuals. Thus, crystal rhetoric suggests that we view friends, family, and fellow citizens from the same cool distance as those we don't know at all,[168] while mud rhetoric suggests that we treat even those to whom we have no real connection with the kind of engagement that we normally reserve for friends and partners. And for this reason—for the sake of the different social didactics, the different modes of conversation and interaction implicit in the two rhetorical styles—we debate endlessly the respective merits of crystals and mud.

---

[165] For a well-known recent example, *see* J. RAWLS, A THEORY OF JUSTICE 11 (1971), [for whom] * * * principles of justice in a society are those that would be chosen by "free and rational persons concerned to further their own interests" * * *.

[168] *See* Radin, *Market-Inalienability*, 100 HARV. L. REV. 1849, 1877–81, 1884 (1987), [discussing how] * * * rhetoric of commodification * * * treating human values as commodities, distorts perceptions and alters attitudes about human relationships, particularly those of an intimate character * * *.

NOTE

Is the decision in *Messersmith v. Smith*, 60 N.W.2d 276 (N. Dak. 1953) muddy or crystalline? The rule applied—that deeds which are recorded but lack an adequate acknowledgment convey no title—seems crystalline. The outcome—that a party who failed to record his deed at all prevails over a taker of title in the recorded but flawed line—seems muddy. Does the outcome in *Messersmith* really depend on a moral evaluation of whether the original holder of title who started both lines of ownership intended to commit a fraud upon either side?

C. Dent Bostick, *Land Title Registration: An English Solution to an American Problem*, 63 IND. L.J. 55–56, 58–64, 67–75, 77–87, 90–97, 100–103, 105–111 (1988)*

INTRODUCTION

Some fifty years ago, respected American legal scholars engaged in an extended debate on the virtues and the feasibility of land title registration.[1] The subject was not one that might be expected to rivet the attention of the academic legal community, let alone that of the profession at large. Beyond the legal profession, there was probably no awareness of this scholarly debate among the American public. Yet this professorial exchange centered on a subject of substantial national importance. It is not an overstatement to suggest that problems relating to matters of title assurance have affected directly the pocketbook of every American who has bought or sold land in this century. Any practitioner who has had to explain to a client the astonishingly high "closing costs" related to title search and title insurance, and any client who has had to pay these costs, is painfully aware of the shortcomings of title assurance under the existing American practice.

* * *

It is surely one of the curiosities of the late twentieth century that broad segments of English law, developed from the middle ages to the nineteenth century, survive in the United States more or less intact while the nation in which this law principally evolved long since has abandoned its most archaic and non-functional features. One has only to see the smile of puzzled bemusement on the face of a British professor at the suggestion that the Rule in Shelley's Case may well be operative in half a dozen American states to gauge the contemporary gap between our law and the British structure from which it was derived. Add to this oddity some attempt to explain the workings of the American recordation system with its amazing cost and duplication and the English lawyer's disbelief grows, especially since few English lawyers today recall their own archaic practices before the enactments of the modern legislation. How can it be, they may well ask, that a society whose science has conquered the moon is preoccupied with such irrelevances in an important sector of its jurisprudence? How indeed? Yet these cobwebs continue to plague our realty practice. These enduring anachronisms, ever more expensive to indulge, may gratify the ghosts of those ancient conveyancers who devised them, and their survival may warm the heart of the dedicated teacher of future

---

[1] Prompted by the failure of three of the four title insurance companies operating in New York City, the Real Estate Board of New York procured a grant from the Carnegie Corporation to the New York Law Society which engaged Professor Richard R. Powell of Columbia University to conduct a study of title registration. The publication of his results was the starting point of the approximately four-year debate. *See* R. POWELL, REGISTRATION OF THE TITLE TO LAND IN THE STATE OF NEW YORK (1938).

* * *

interests. It is less likely, however, that anyone else will be persuaded as to the merits of this practice.

* * *

By 1925, [English] reform reached full flower in the final enactment of the four property statutes considered by this Article. This extraordinary legislation, which swept away much of the flotsam that had so long clogged the law of property, has reached mature years from which its effectiveness can be measured. The legislation is far from a perfect answer to all contemporary needs, yet by any standard, it has been a remarkable advance over the old English practice. Surprisingly little litigation and, indeed, widespread acceptance of the basic principles of the legislation have resulted. From time to time Parliamentary Reform Commissions have convened to consider change, but most of their recommendations have amounted to little more than tinkering or fine tuning of the basics. The structure remains solidly rooted in the original legislation.

Despite this acceptance, flaws exist, and some of them are quite serious. Furthermore, some flaws are growing more serious due to modern societal concerns. These defects are clearly visible through the prism of sixty years experience and will receive special attention here. This Article proposes that despite the deficiencies in the English title assurance system, the present American title assurance system can be improved by adopting some of the successful features of the British system, especially features of the Land Registration Act of 1925.

I. The Goal of Title Assurance Systems

Before moving to a review of current American practice, it is appropriate to consider what an ideal title assurance plan should involve. The philosophy of an ideal system is that it provides, as conclusive title binding all the world, a state-guaranteed registration evidenced by a certificate which reflects the exact state of the title at any moment in time. The ideal system substitutes registration for any inquiry into actual or constructive notice of facts about ownership. Presently, inquiry is concerned with evidence of title obtained through recordations, actual notice, or possession. Under the ideal system, however, inquiry is solely a matter of whether there is a registration and what that registration contains.

The registration scheme must be so comprehensive as to provide procedures for handling every kind of interest possible: legal estates, marital rights, bankruptcy claims of every kind, and all equitable interests. It must be possible to register any legitimate interest or claim, so that the moving question is whether the claim is or is not registered. If the claim is properly registered, it is effective; if it is not registered, it is ineffective. The compensation fund, mentioned below, must resolve matters of fraud, error, and mistake.

The ideal plan should reduce drastically the number and complexity of interests that concern the person undertaking to establish title. At present, the myriad of possible legal estates and the details of all equitable interests bearing on the land are of primary importance to the conveyancer and his purchaser because they all bear directly on a successful assurance of title. The methods by which the English reduced the number of possible legal estates, converted the rest to equitable estates, provided for overriding many equitable estates so that they need not burden the purchaser, and limited concurrent estates are discussed below. These features are an essential corollary to a successful registration scheme.

Once the number of relevant interests is reduced, the registration system will function so that one registration card, clearly and simply arranged, will mirror exactly the state of a title at any given moment. In addition, the card must be consistent and totally accessible, quickly and inexpensively amendable to reflect current change, and absolutely binding on all parties. Administrative procedures, not a full scale judicial hearing, should accomplish the initial registration. Ideally, public revenues should support registration costs. The title should be state-guaranteed and backed by sufficient financial resources to compensate adequately those who are innocent, yet suffer losses because of fraud, error, or the mistakes of others. The process should rest on a system of tract identification, rather than on the ambiguities and vagaries of a name index. Those administering the system should be highly trained, competent professionals. Registration procedures, once established, should prove relatively cheap to maintain and administer.

The successful system is one that is simple, accessible, inexpensive to administer once in place, and above all reliable. It is the premise of this Article that the current American system is none of these.

II. Current American Practice

A rural Georgia lawyer who began his practice during the depression once told the author, "Son, I never began searching a title unless I was starving to death, and I never finished one without wishing I had." That remark is understandable when one considers the modern American methods of title assurance, unchanged in their basics since before the 1930's.

Each of the American jurisdictions has a somewhat different system, often with significant variations. Although the theme is fundamentally the same and centers inevitably on a system of recordation of the evidence of title, as opposed to a recordation of the title itself how, where, and by whom these records are kept varies considerably among the states. The practice of examiners in reviewing either the original records, or an abstract of them prepared by someone else, also varies. Nevertheless, all methods have the goal of producing a certificate of opinion prepared by a competent professional, ordinarily an attorney, accurately assessing the state of the title at the moment of transfer. The evidence of the records and of certain extrinsic matters, such as actual possession, serve as the basis for the certificate in most cases.

Because such a certificate hinges on the professional competence of the certifier, and therefore on the ability of the examiner to make good any deficiencies in certification, a supplementary assurance for the purchaser has developed in the form of title insurance. Title insurance undertakes to insure the purchaser against those defects enumerated in the policy and supposedly provides a back-up compensation for certification errors. For this transfer of risk, the insurer charges a substantial premium ordinarily linked to the purchase price of the property.

As an additional back-up, many deeds contain warranties. Warranties are contractual guarantees by the transferor about the state of the title. This technique is the oldest of the types of protection offered today and is certainly the least effective because of the drastic limitations on the amounts recoverable, limitations on the identity of those who can be pursued, and the lack of standard meaning for the phrases used to construct the warranties.[20]

Finally, in some states a system of registration based on the "Torrens system" exists alongside the recordation system. This system seemed to hold bright promise in the early days of this century, but has failed to take hold in any American jurisdiction for reasons particularly pertinent to this Article's proposals.

The American title assurance plan is, then, one of patchwork. Various elements of it evolved centuries ago. Some features of it arose only in this century. Due to various reasons—the problems of multiple jurisdictions, lawyers' vested interests in the current system and their resistance to change, perceived constitutional problems, title insurance company opposition, and the peculiar sanctity always accorded to land ownership and the law surrounding it—a systematic, pervasive scheme of reform has never evolved in the United States.

* * *

B. The Recordation System

The recordation system is the center of modern American title assurance. It is the link on which all else depends. The system has ancient roots on this side of the Atlantic, existing in some form since long before the Revolution. Interestingly, no comparable system evolved in England. Various reasons have been advanced for its absence there and its development here. The vast stretches of available land, less likely to be visibly occupied by the owner, must have played a part in the perceived need for an alternative method of putting purchasers on notice of claims. The statutes were by no means uniform in their development and have resulted in four recognized forms.[35]

---

[20] Different jurisdictions attach various interpretations to the covenants of title. For example, in a majority of American jurisdictions, the covenant of seisin indicates ownership of the land, but in a few states this covenant attests only to the grantor's possession of the conveyed land. * * * *See, e.g.*, Simpson v. Johnson, 100 Idaho 357, 361-62, 597 P.2d 600, 604-05 (1979) (finding that grantees were entitled to relief when grantors did not have legal title to all of the property described in a warranty deed containing a covenant of seisin); Brown v. Lober, 75 Ill.2d 547, 550-51, 389 N.E.2d 1188, 1190-91 (1979) (citing the Illinois statute which states that a grantor covenants to a grantee that he is "lawfully seized of an indefeasible estate in fee simple" when he makes and delivers the deed to the grantee, and emphasizing that a covenant of seisin "assure[s] the grantee that the grantor is ... lawfully seized and has the power to convey . . . [that] which he professes to convey"). * * *

The covenant of warranty can be either all-inclusive or specifically restricted in its scope. * * * An all-inclusive, or general warranty, usually indicates that a grantor, his heirs, and his personal representatives warrant the property against any future claims or demands made by anyone on the grantee, his heirs, personal representatives and assigns. * * * In contrast, special warranty covenants restrict a grantor's warrant to claims and demands of the grantor or those claiming through or under him. * * *

[35] The four types of recording statutes are the following:

a. Race—The grantee who records first prevails over any other grantees from a common grantor. Even if the grantee who records first took the property with notice of a conveyance to a prior grantee who did not record, the statute protects the first grantee to record.

b. Period of grace—The first grantee receives protection under the statute for a set period of time. If he does not record by the end of that time, he is no longer protected, and

The extent to which the records bind, the modes of record keeping, and the overall quality of the system vary widely from jurisdiction to jurisdiction. As to the latter, even within the states themselves, variation occurs, especially from rural to urban areas. The systems, however, are similar in the following respects: most records are indexed on a name basis rather than a tract basis; all anticipate their use as the vehicle for establishing a "chain of title" over some period of time; all purport to contain "evidence" of title rather than title itself; and all in theory should contain within their bounds most of the "evidence" of title needed to make a basic judgment as to the validity of the title. If one cannot find the appropriate chain of title and the related transactions, the title is of course defective. Remember, however, that not every fact bearing on title is recordable. Nor must every factor bearing on title be recorded to have effect against purchasers. Typically an instrument does not require recordation to be effective between the parties to it.

The records that constitute notice under the recording system are themselves widely scattered. Usually they are county-based. If the land is spread over several counties, a search of the records of each county is required. Pertinent records may be found in a county clerk's office, in a Federal Building, in a City Hall, in a zoning office, in state and federal environmental offices, and throughout the records of courts of all jurisdictions. The possibilities are extraordinary. The level of competence and accuracy in record keeping is wide ranging as well, with presentation running from handwriting to computer cards. Officials and their staffs vary from incompetent to highly trained and motivated professionals. Regrettably, the custodial office is often political, with no prescribed qualifications, and the result is an officeholder whose personal popularity may exceed professional competence.

Against this backdrop of myriad complexity and uncertainty, two additional problems confound the effort to provide a proper title assurance, and both contribute to the overburdening of the recording system. The first problem concerns substantive American property law. The intricate nature of the various means by which and by whom title to realty may be held aggravates and complicates any effort to improve the existing creaky system. The second problem involves the vastly complicated procedures which must be followed to identify and evaluate the substantive property law interests.

The first problem results from substantive American property law allowing for the creation of too many legal interests. The British had the same problem before 1925, and they realized that any successful new approach had to deal with this aspect of the law as an integral part of the reform. Legal estates creatable in most American states include at least: fee simple absolutes, determinable fees, fees on condition, the life estates, the term of years, various lesser tenancies, and a full range of traditional future interests. Even fee tail still can be created in a few states. In addition to these legal estates, various legal interests such as easements, licenses and restrictive covenants can be created.

The problem of concurrent legal estates also remains. Not every state recognizes all the traditional forms possible, but most have some form of joint tenancy and tenancy in common. Many states recognize the marital estate of tenancy by the entirety as well.

A title search must also move through a maze of equitable interests of all kinds. Many of these are recordable; some are not and yet may be effective against a purchaser. The system requires meticulous confirmation that fiduciaries have carried out details of their responsibilities regarding retention or disposition of land. A searcher must confirm that necessary court orders were obtained and establish evidence that sales conformed to requirements of documents or statutes. Confirmation of appropriate dispersal of any resulting proceeds is also necessary. Proper inquiry does not end with the recording system but extends to investigation of conditions on the land which may constitute notice even though not recorded.

The second problem of effective title assurance is evidenced by the searcher who sorts through the records and discovers a procedural nightmare. Working through indexes that most often are name based, the searcher must first construct a chain of title. More often than not, deeds fail to contain references

---

a subsequent grantee who records will prevail in a contest over ownership of the land. The use of this type of recording statute has declined over time.

c. Race-notice—A subsequent purchaser who takes without notice and records first is protected by the statute.

d. Notice—This type of recording statute protects a subsequent purchaser who takes the property without notice. The statute covers a later grantee even if a prior grantee records after the conveyance to the subsequent purchaser and before the subsequent purchaser records, if he records at all. J. CRIBBET, PRINCIPLES OF THE LAW OF PROPERTY 220–21 (1962).

to former owners or to earlier deeds in which the same property may have been differently described. The searcher, therefore, is left to rely on evidence ranging from modern tax records to memories of those who might recall the details of long past owners' lives and relationships. The possibility for error in establishing the chain for the requisite period and for examining the acts of each owner for the time required is thus very high.

Other problems include unadministered estates or improperly administered estates; name changes through marriage, adoption, error and otherwise; possibilities of large numbers of tenants in common, especially in cases of large families with several generations of intestate deaths and unadministered estates; marital rights flowing from either common law or statute; incompetency of owners; and vague or difficult to manage conditions in wills that may shift estates on virtually as many contingencies as the mind can devise. The list of potential pitfalls continues with such matters as modern constitutional doubts about spousal prerogatives in dealing with realty held by husband and wife as tenants by the entirety. There is as well the entire range of claims by third parties against owners. These claims include taxes, judgments and marital separation claims. To add to the title examiner's difficulties, the information to be gleaned requires the laborious search of many different sources often housed in different offices or even different cities, as described above.

A second fundamentally unacceptable feature of recordation is that this tedious, expensive and often inaccurate process must be conducted more than once to establish title. It is incomprehensible that the process is repeated de novo on each occasion of transfer. Since the end product is a certificate expressing a professional opinion as to the state of the title, the certifier cannot afford to risk that opinion based on an earlier examination by another person. Hence, each person making a certificate must form a judgment. It is true, of course, that practice varies among the states. For example, lawyers in some states search the records at the source itself and base their opinions on this search, while in other states lawyers examine an "abstract" of the records prepared by someone else, and carefully hedge their opinions regarding the accuracy of the abstract. Another variation is to rely on the title insurer to "certify the title" and to virtually eliminate the attorney, a practice that has led to much dispute.

In each instance, therefore, an "expert" personally examines some record for the period of time covered by the certificate. As a result, the hapless client must pay for the endless duplication of effort. However, the necessity to pay does not end with the examiner's certificate. In contemporary practice, yet another expensive backstop in the patchwork of security has evolved: title insurance.

C. Title Insurance

The certificate of title is worth only as much as the examiner's own pocketbook (and perhaps as much as the professional liability insurer) can bear in the event of error in the search. For this reason, the custom of "insuring" titles to land has developed. At first there was a rather modest start of hiring an "approved" attorney to examine title to property and issuing, or not issuing, a policy based on that attorney's opinion. Subsequently, title insurance companies moved aggressively into the entire fabric of conveyancing. In some cities it is common for those companies to have their own title "factories" containing information, gleaned from official records and various other sources, on many titles. The advantage for the company lies in the fact that its records are more efficiently organized and collated than those of the official agencies. Each policy issued is a separate matter with each individual. If the same title, for example, should change hands once each day for a week, seven different policies, each carrying a full premium, may be required. This is true even though each policy was based on essentially identical information available on the first day of the week.

Beyond the expense, another fundamental objection to title insurance is that policies are often quite limited in their scope of coverage. This practice leads to substantial difficulties because the exceptions in policies often relate to those problems most likely to be encountered. The variety of exceptions, coupled with policy limitations on the amount of liability, often not reflecting the value of the property at the time of the loss, can lead to understandable disillusionment in the insured. These inherent defects make questionable the actual efficiency of this lucrative business in affording a proper measure of protection.

* * *

III. The English Experience

Old habits die hard in England. A probably apocryphal story tells of the distinguished solicitor who was taken up on a high hill overlooking the gorgeous farms of an English countryside. He stood for a moment and said: "The sight of all that registered land makes me sick." Colleagues at a British university are fond of telling another story involving the elderly professor at a fine university who until the mid-1970's always referred to the 1925 Land Acts as "the recent land legislation." These comments demonstrate that England is a land much given to the values of tradition, and provide one all the more reason to marvel at the Act's excellent success.

* * *

B. The Legislation of 1925

1. The Grand Design

* * * Parliament was concerned with four broad legislative purposes. One purpose of the acts was to reduce the number of legal estates in land to a manageable number so that the purchaser would have to deal with a minimal number of estates and parties in securing good legal title. A further very important benefit from the drastic reduction in the number of legal estates was to make possible a simpler land registration system.

A second purpose of the acts was to provide a system of registration which would mirror exactly, at any point in time, the status of title to real estate. The title so appearing would have been judicially determined and guaranteed by the state.

The third purpose of the acts, achieved through the use of the trust device, was to sweep equitable estates and interests off the legal title and into the fund created by a sale of the land. By such process the purchaser only had to know that equitable arrangements existed in order to pay the purchase money over to the appropriate trustees. Upon making payment, the purchaser was totally relieved of the details and consequences of the trust arrangements. Finally, the acts were meant to provide appropriate protection for "commercial" type encumbrances, as opposed to "family" type encumbrances.

To achieve all these purposes, the acts did two things. First, they reduced the number of legal estates to two: the fee simple absolute and the legal term of years. All other legal estates formerly possible still could be created, but only as some form of equitable interest. The equitable mandate exempted the term of years because it was seen most often as a business arrangement, and as such, often an inappropriate candidate for use behind a trust arrangement. In addition to reducing the number of possible legal estates, the acts provided for certain legal "interests" other than "estates" to be created. Examples of such interests are easements and profits which are of the same duration as the legal estates. An easement for life, therefore, can be created only as an equitable interest, but an easement for a term of twenty-one years can be created as a legal interest.

The second way in which the acts achieved Parliament's purposes was to divide equitable estates and interests into two basic categories: those that can be overreached, and those that cannot be overreached. In the first category are all of the so called family arrangements. Family arrangements, such as strict settlements, involve either direct grants to family members in succession, or a similar conveyance to trustees on comparable uses. These arrangements are overreached when the property is sold so that the interests of the equitable owners have no relation to the land and need not be the concern of the purchasers. The concept of overreaching is that the equitable interests of beneficiaries are detached from the land and attached instead to the purchase money paid to the trustees for the land. In this sense, overreaching means "being detached from the land." The equitable owners' interests are attached instead to the fund created by the purchase price and are protected in that manner.

The second basic category involves the equitable interests that cannot be overreached. Into this category fall restrictive covenants, estate contracts, and certain equitable interests in the land of another, such as an equitable easement. These are regarded as "commercial" equitable interests as opposed to "family" equitable interests and as such cannot be overridden. Some of the legislation defines and governs only family settlements, and different statutory arrangements often define and govern commercial interests. Both types of equitable interests are contemplated and dealt with by the Land Registration Act of 1925, as will be seen below.

2. The Implementing Acts

All of the changes discussed above were the product of some six pieces of legislation enacted by Parliament in 1925. Two of these acts, the Administration of Estates Act and the Trustee Act, are beyond the purview of this Article and will not be considered here. The acts discussed are: the Law of Property Act, the Settled Land Act, the Land Charges Act, and the Land Registration Act.[89]

---

[89] Law of Property Act, 1925, 15 & 16 Geo. 5, ch. 20. Settled Land Act, 1925, 15 & 16 Geo. 5, ch. 18. Land Charges Act, 1925, 15 & 16 Geo. 5, ch. 22, amended by Land Charges Act 1972, ch. 61. Land Registration Act, 1925, 15 & 16 Geo. 5, ch. 21.

* * *

To ensure a mechanism for handling affairs under the Settled Land Act and the Law of Property Act, interim arrangements were provided. These arrangements still prevail where the land is not yet within a registered land jurisdiction (perhaps twenty percent of England and Wales at this writing), or where the land is within a registered land area, but no statutorily defined event has occurred to require the registration of the particular tract of land in question.

For unregistered land, the general scheme of the 1925 legislation provides that:

(a) Legal title need not be registered, but continues to be validated by ancient title deeds and possession concepts;

(b) Family economic arrangements such as strict settlements are governed by either the Settled Land Act or the "trust for sale" provisions of the Law of Property Act, which provide for notice of any equitable interests of this kind; and

(c) Commercial claims and interests such as "estate contracts" are protected by registration under the Land Charges Act. That Act deals almost exclusively with specified equitable interests of the commercial variety. Because the Land Registration Act provides for the equitable commercial interests fully, it was believed in 1925 that as the registered land system spread, the Land Charges Act, all purposes of which are subsumed into that broader Act, would pass into oblivion.

In summary, the reform acts made interim provisions for protection of all the possibilities pending the arrival of the Registered Land Act: legal estates and interests in the way they existed prior to 1925; family type overreachable interests through the Settled Land Act or the trust for sale; and commercial, non-overreachable arrangements by the Land Charges Act. The substance of those acts, as a background to how they influence the registration scheme, will be examined in the next section.

a. The Settled Land Act of 1925

The Settled Land Act is designed to define and manage private economic arrangements relating to land, primarily family settlements, by forcing all future interests behind a trust. The details of the trust are of no interest or concern to a purchaser who has bought from the person entitled to convey the legal fee simple absolute title. The Act, though ingenious in concept, is marred by unnecessary complexity. This is especially so because it requires two instruments to achieve a proper settlement: the "vesting deed" and the trust instrument itself. In addition, there are taxation disadvantages attached to the use of a settlement under the Act. These problems have led the legal profession to virtually abandon the Act, especially since all of its purposes can be accomplished through the simpler trust for sale device without the major tax problems. A settlement under the Settled Land Act is most likely to be encountered today when a careless conveyancer fails to properly create a trust for sale, because the Settled Land Act by its terms applies to any settlement that is not a part of a trust for sale.

Despite its relegation to little more than a snare for the uninformed or the careless, the Settled Land Act does contain some features that should be of interest to an American audience considering reform. The Act builds on the Law of Property Act's provisions, reducing the number of possible legal estates to two and forcing all other interests under a settlement into equitable interests behind a trust. Consequently, the critical feature of this Act is the role of the person designated as the "tenant for life." This person may in fact be a life tenant under the terms of the settlement, but the individual also may be one who holds any present estate, even one other than a traditional life tenancy. The significance of the position is that the tenant for life, in virtually all cases, holds the legal title to the fee simple absolute. That position carries the right to convey the legal title and to deal effectively as full owner in other respects for both the benefit of the tenant for life, in whatever present possessory equitable interest that person holds under the settlement, and for the benefit of all other equitable owners. All equitable interests in the land are thereby overreached and attached to the fund created by the action in lieu of the interest in the land.

* * *

b. The Law of Property Act of 1925

The Law of Property Act of 1925 is a remarkable piece of legislation, both for its innovations and for the fact that it managed to pass through Parliament. Virtually overnight, this Act swept away the practice of centuries. It is difficult to imagine an American jurisdiction acting quite so broadly or boldly as this, at least in regard to land.[117] Hopefully, an assess-

[117] *See* Comment, *The Torrens System of Title Registration: A New Proposal for Effective Implementation*, 29 UCLA L. REV. 661, 668–71 (1982) (addressing the reasons for opposition to land law reform, especially that of the title

ment of the success of the British legislation might encourage some to try. The resistance in Parliament was formidable, and final passage took place only after appeasing some in the House of Lords by incorporating such measures as retaining the fee tail estate, which survives even today as a rather curious relic among such advanced provisions.

As stated, the Act's provisions are wide ranging. For purposes here, two segments are of special interest: the sections defining the new legal and equitable interests possible, and the provisions relating to the trust for sale.

It is certainly one of the most valuable aspects of the "estates" system in Anglo-American law that the concept of ownership, measured on a plane of time, permits extraordinary flexibility in the quality of possible arrangements. Consequently, when the decision was taken to reduce the number of possible legal estates to two, it was vital that the former legal estates survive in the form of equitable estates. There was no conceptual or practical objection to the existence of these estates, because the estates were essential to flexible arrangements. The objection was that the equitable estates attached to land in such a way that the identity of an owner, who was always able to convey the total fee simple estate, could be lost for long periods of time. The solution was to permit the creation of the former legal estates but now only in equity, where they had long been creatable in any event. Then, at least in the case of family settlements, the provisions of the settlement attached to the proceeds of a sale when overreached by the sale of the legal title. Rights of the commercial type were, of course, not overreached and were protected by notice to the purchaser, first through the vehicle of the Land Charges Act, and ultimately through the Land Registration Act.

A second major variance of the Law of Property Act was its treatment of concurrent estates. Those who developed the legislation recognized that one of the principal factors that would overwork a registration system was the old practice of permitting the creation of unlimited numbers of legal tenancies in common. If undivided shares could be created in vast numbers of owners at law, the volume of matters necessary to be registered relating to that ownership might either overwhelm the system or make it so cumbersome as to compromise the basic need for simplicity. This situation was perceived as a fundamental difficulty in establishing title. Provisions that treated any named concurrent tenants as joint tenants holding the property on implied trust for sale for themselves, and perhaps for others as well, resolved the matter. In England, it is no longer possible to own legal title to land concurrently except on trust for sale as joint tenants. The number of joint tenants holding legal title on trust for sale is limited to four. Whether the equitable interests behind the trust are also joint interests, or whether those interests are treated as equitable tenancies in common, depends on the circumstances of the basic transactions. Either result is possible. With the number of legal title holders limited to four, and with the survivorship features of joint tenancy further simplifying matters, the registration procedures and conveyancing concerns remain relatively uncluttered.

The third principal innovation of the Law of Property Act important to this Article was that the Act introduced the trust for sale. This device proved so successful and popular in its relative simplicity of operation that it soon drove the more cumbersome machinery of the Settled Land Act out of business.

The fundamental premise of the trust for sale is that when land is transferred on a settlement, that is, on successive interests, and when there is a mandatory direction to the trustees to sell the property to implement the trust, a trust for sale arises under the Law of Property Act, rather than a settlement under the Settled Land Act. Legal title rests in the trustees for sale, and the trustees, two of whom are required in most instances, must manage the property and act in accordance with the mandate of the trust. While the creation of a trust for sale requires that the property be sold, and does not give merely a power or entitlement to sell it, it is a curiosity of the operation of the trust for sale that immediate sale is not necessary. Indeed, the device is often used to implement a long term family settlement when the expectation is that the property will not be sold for a very long period of time, if ever. Such a course may, however, require the consent of the beneficiaries. The interests of the beneficiaries are in effect converted to personalty since the property is required to be sold and "equity looks on that as done which ought to be done." For purposes of devolution, for instance, the assets are treated as personalty. Elaborate provisions govern the responsibilities of the trustees in taking into account the views of the equitable owners in making their decisions. Unlike the trustees of the settlement in Settled Land matters, the trust for sale

---

industry which derives its livelihood from the current system). * * *

trustees perform as active, responsible fiduciaries in the management, general decisionmaking and sale of the trust property. Theirs is not a supervisory role; it is an active, decision-making role.

The trust for sale may arise in ways other than direct, express provision. For example, it is implied when title holders convey to grantees as concurrent owners. As stated above, irrespective of what was said or intended, the grantees are deemed to be joint tenants to the legal title and they are deemed to hold the ownership of the equitable interests for themselves and others in whatever form is appropriate. Trust for sale is also implied in circumstances in which legal title is in fact held by one person, but under conditions where the legal title holder should be deemed as trustee for one or more persons, perhaps including the trustee.

An implied trust may arise most often in the case of the marital home. Without doubt, marital home ownership and the problem of the protection of that home for both spouses, has emerged as a major concern for the entire field of land law, especially as it relates to the Land Registration Act. When both spouses contribute to the purchase price of a marital home, and the legal title is taken in the name of one only, usually the husband, the courts, without a clear legislative mandate, now imply a trust. Moreover, the trust implied is a trust for sale, with the spouse in whose name the legal title is held taking that title as trustee for sale for both spouses. The difficulty posed for a purchaser in discovering this implied trust has posed a serious problem when the legal titleholder acts without authority and outside the parameters of the Act in dealing with the realty.

* * *

In summary, the Law of Property Act dramatically reformed the substantive law of property by reducing the number of legal estates to two. In the trustee for sale concept, this act provides a convenient vehicle for conveying title. These two developments make possible the operation of the efficient, simple registration system established by the Land Registration Act.

* * *

d. The Land Registration Act of 1925

The last of the English acts to be considered, and the one of most immediate concern for purposes of this Article, is the Land Registration Act of 1925. This Act, together with the Law of Property Act, is the most important of the 1925 property legislation. The expense of its implementation coupled with the notable problems of the British nation since 1925 have delayed, even until the present day, the full advantages that the Act promises. The Act's provisions are compulsory in those areas to which it has spread and eventually will be compulsory throughout England and Wales. It is now estimated that something over eighty per cent of the land in England and Wales has been drawn within the network of registered land. It is also estimated that the rest of the country will soon be covered by its provisions. Of course, not all land within the areas subject to registration is now registered since in many instances no event has yet occurred that requires an original registration.

The Land Registration Act is ambitious because it purports to deal with every conceivable estate or interest in land. Also, the Act seeks to exemplify, in its fullest sense, the "mirror principle," that is, an exact display of the state of the title at any given moment. The Act also undertakes to provide both a state-guaranteed title for proprietors and a proper scheme of compensation for those improvidently harmed by the existence of that title. The Act has failed to achieve totally any of these goals, in part because of unnecessarily restrictive interpretations, and most importantly because it contains within its provisions an Achilles heel known as "overriding interests."

i. Purposes of the Land Registration Act

Technically, the Land Registration Act of 1925 is structured to meet the requirements of an effective system. The Act's stated purpose is that a transferee for valuable consideration takes the legal title to an estate subject to entries on the register and subject to overriding interests, but free from all other estates and interests. But for the ominous "overriding interests" gap, the stated purpose would seem to confer on the register that absolute "mirror" quality that any successful system must have to function as the sole source of title status.

* * *

ii. Registration procedures

The workings of the registration and recordation structure are admirably simple: one register is located in London and thirteen are in District Registries. Each proprietorship register is based on an index card system. Each registration is placed on an index card that is divided into three parts. The first part designates the tract of land with reference to a plan or map showing the land parcel. The second part describes the features of the title in terms of quality, that is, absolute, good leasehold, qualified, or possessory. This subdivision also lists the name and address of the registered proprietor and sets out limitations. These limitations are known as cautions, inhibitions, notices and the restrictions on proprietorship. The third portion of the card provides for entry of notice of rights adverse to the land, such as easements, restrictive covenants and mortgages, as well as all other rights defining and protecting rights over the land.

Since it is the land registration itself that is the title, not the title deeds as was formerly the case, a copy of the "land certificate," or the registration document, is given to each registered proprietor. No transfer of the title occurs until the registration actually takes place at the Register Office. Because deeds in the American sense are no longer used to effect the transfer of title, all the infirmities surrounding the use of deeds, such as improper delivery, are avoided. This illustrates how the Act, which was designed and intended to improve the conveyancing mechanism, has in fact had a much wider impact in altering the basic law of property. The Act not only has altered the time and manner in which title passes, it has changed other fundamental concepts as well, such as the extent to which one can pass to a purchaser a better title than one has.

Because it is the act of registration that effectively passes title, it follows that when registration is compulsory the registerable transaction is ineffective to convey legal title until the registration occurs. In the case of a first registration, such a transaction is void as to the legal estate unless the registration occurs within two months. The Register office may extend this time for "sufficient cause." In the case of land already registered, the grantor is said to hold the title on trust for the grantee until the registration occurs. In this situation, the two-month limitation seemingly does not apply.

iii. Interests which must be registered

The Land Registration Act provides that three classes of interests—"Registered Interests," "Overriding Interests," and "Minor Interests"—must be registered. The first of these classes, the "Registered Interests," are the legal estates only, and in England this indicates either a legal fee simple absolute or a term of years. The Act is much too complex and obfuscated regarding the registration of leasehold estates and has been widely criticized for this deficiency.

The second class, "Overriding Interests," deals with rights which bind the purchaser even though they do not appear on the register. Thus, these rights override the register. This category includes legal easements, rights relating to adverse possession, and most difficult and significant of all, "rights of every person in actual occupation of the land or in receipt of the rents and profits thereof, save where enquiry is made of such person and the rights are not disclosed." This provision has undercut dramatically the philosophical underpinning of the 1925 legislation. The problem is so potentially serious that, if left unattended, given the present drift of the House of Lords on the matter, it may threaten the progress of the 1925 legislation towards title security. The reason is obvious. To the extent that one can prevail on the basis of rights outside the register, the seeker of good title must return to the dreary business of establishing who is or is not in possession of the property, and who knows or should have known about those claimed rights.[211]

* * *

One of the most difficult situations is that of spouses occupying property as tenants in common. Because this sort of tenancy now cannot exist at law, it can take effect only behind a trust. * * * [T]his situation often arises in the case of a wife who has in fact made a contribution to the purchase of the family home, but the title to the property has been taken in the name of the husband only. Here, the Law of Property Act has been interpreted to imply a trust for sale with the husband deemed a trustee for the benefit of both himself and his wife. Despite the fact that under the doctrine of conversion the wife's interest is regarded as personalty for many purposes, it is nonetheless regarded as "an interest subsisting in reference to land" to bring it within the overriding interests category of the Land Registration Act.

In 1983, Parliament enacted the Matrimonial Homes Act, providing for a statutory "right of occupation" in a spouse in certain situations. The Land Registration Act of 1925, however, refuses to

---

[211] The largest single reason for the failure of the Torrens system in the United States is that judges could not bring themselves to uphold the title registration system in favor of one who used the system against innocent people. Thus, courts went outside the registration system to provide relief to those whose claims were not covered by the system. * * * This same attitude now threatens to diminish the effectiveness of the English registration system. This author advocates adhering strictly to the registration system and compensating innocent victims from the insurance fund.

grant an overriding interest to a spouse who acquired rights under the Matrimonial Homes Act. Nevertheless, she may still be a person in occupation and own an overriding interest by reason of her status as an equitable tenant in common. The matrimonial right of occupation can be registered as a minor interest by an appropriate entry of notice, but even if it is not so registered, the wife may still prevail. If she is in occupation and has an equitable property right by reason of a contribution to the property, this right has status as an overriding interest that saves the wife's claim. This variety of claim particularly is a trap for the conveyancer because nothing visible suggests that the reason for the wife's occupation is anything other than the spousal relationship.

* * *

The array of rights protectable under this category includes restrictive covenants (enforceable only in equity in England), estate contracts and, very importantly, rights such as family and other interests which fall either behind a trust under the Settled Land Act, or behind a trust for sale under the Law of Property Act. These rights are protected by putting a purchaser on notice that the prescribed procedures in the Settled Land Act or the trust for sale sections must be observed if there is to be an overreaching of the private arrangements under their provisions.

* * *

vi. Absoluteness versus the right to rectification

Any evaluation of the English acts must consider the costs and benefits of the provisions for amending the land title register. It can be said that if the goals of a title registration act are met, the registered title owner has, as nearly as possible for any system, a title that is absolute and guaranteed as such by the state. In fact, this concept of guaranteed absolute title is considerably watered down in the English version when one considers the amendability aspects of the register. The English call this procedure for amendment "rectification." Any American adaptation should weigh carefully a system as broadly subject to amendment as that in England, and should consider a more restrictive approach.

* * *

C. Assessing King George's 1925 Legislation

From the long English experience, valuable conclusions are possible about what has worked and what has not worked in the area of title assurance. Unquestionably, the acts have been a huge overall success in achieving most of what they were intended to achieve. It is equally certain, however, that they need revision. The American advantage is that of the blank page. A jurisdiction considering reform is free to consider either a fresh start, or perhaps a modification of the system presently in place. Which should it be?

* * *

The existing system can be improved, and impressive on-going efforts are underway to do so. Statutory forms of deed warranties, with generally predictable consequences in their use, somewhat enhance this old safeguard. The recording system itself is being made measurably more efficient in many areas by the establishment of tract indexes. Other improvements are emerging. For instance, sometimes more elaborate mapping of counties takes place to assure more standardized descriptions of property,[273] and a better consensus of the time frame required for an adequate title search is emerging. To effect improvements, several developments still must occur. For instance, it is essential that the pertinent records are housed centrally and more efficiently, just as title factories have done. Also, widespread adoption of some of the proposed uniform laws on marketable title and simplified land transfer may be a proper response to many problems.[275] Abolishing a great many county governments with the consequent centralization of record-keeping authority and efficiency would be an excellent step, but this is probably beyond the political realities of today.

In the end, all of these steps would produce a better system, yet one still fundamentally inept and inadequate to handle the needs of modern life. Conservative measures are not enough. What is needed is surgery. If, then, the move is to be towards comprehensive, major reform, American jurisdictions

---

[273] Many scholars regard tract indexing as superior to the use of a grantor-grantee index system. Use of a tract index system simplifies a title search because it not only describes the particular property but also provides information about all transactions affecting the parcel of land. One advantage of a tract index over a grantor-grantee index is that instruments outside the chain of title are easily discoverable on the tract index, whereas such instruments are not apparent on the face of the grantor-grantee index. Another reason to prefer the use of a tract index is to decrease problems associated with the misspelling of a grantor's or grantee's name on the index. * * *

In spite of the enumerated advantages of a tract index system, a majority of jurisdictions employ a grantor-grantee index system or use the two systems in combination. * * *

[275] *See, e.g.*, UNIF. LAND TRANSACTIONS ACT, 13 U.L.A. 469 (1986); UNIF. SIMPLIFICATION OF LAND TRANSFERS ACT, 14 U.L.A. 209 (1980 & Supp. 1987).

must be highly selective in what they take from the modern English legislation. The models are available, and for the most part, they work. The case law is adequate, and in general, it addresses sensibly the gaps in legislation that have become apparent in the decades since the basic enactments. From the models themselves and an examination of how they have worked, one may conclude specifics about the acts.
* * *

IV. Construction of a New American System of Title Assurance

Clearly, an American scheme of title assurance reform can benefit in major ways by adopting both philosophies and procedures worked out and tested in Britain. No wholesale, or "as is," adoption is desirable. If starting again, the British themselves might do it somewhat differently. What is suggested as appropriate is to incorporate into an American reform effort the broad strengths and themes of the best of the English acts. The principal theme is simplicity and certainty. The broad strengths of the legislation following on those basics are (i.) comprehensive legislation "clearing the decks" for a truly workable and reliable assurance system, and (ii.) the creation, made possible by (i.), of a secure registration system which meets within its parameters all of the title assurance needs of any transferee.

A. Designing a Workable System in the United States

To meet the requirements of creating a workable and reliable assurance scheme, a matter of first priority is that the substantive property law must be reformed to assure that the number of permissible legal estates is drastically reduced. The English have been successful in reducing the number to two such estates with recognition of comparable legal "interests." No discernable policy or practical reason exists why the same reform could not be effective here. Similarly, the English abolished the concurrent legal estates in property, other than joint tenancy, and this has been singularly effective in simplifying the substantive law. The several concurrent legal estates that are possible in most American jurisdictions complicate considerably and unnecessarily the search for secure title. A reduction to a single permitted form of concurrent legal ownership would have the same beneficial effect here that it has had in England.

Finally, the provision of a much restricted arrangement for the holding of legal title to land held on successive estates and for land owned concurrently is essential to the goal of title security. In an earlier age in which land ownership signified uniqueness and was near sanctity because of its importance as a form of wealth ownership, these changes would have been unthinkable. Today is a time when wealth most often takes a form other than legal ownership of land. Therefore, when the money flowing from the land's sale can be at least as valuable an item as the land in its original form, no reason exists for restricting land ownership to advance other goals, such as easy conveyancing and easy title security. Once the preliminary work of substantive reform has been achieved, the benefits of that reform can be woven into a successful registration program.

The general outline of the English registration act should serve well as the basis for American legislation. Those provisions that enhance the theme of sanctity of registered title should be adopted and enhanced. Those provisions, such as the "overriding interests" categories, that cut the other way should be evaluated skeptically and avoided when this can be done reasonably. The emphasis on a "just" result in hard cases should be on the use of the compensatory fund, not on a dilution of the mirror quality of registered title. * * *

A second modification of the English act should deal with the provisions for registering leases. British conveyancers have long utilized what seem to be extraordinarily long leases to achieve various purposes. Most likely, the preservation of the term of years as one of the two retained legal estates possible is a recognition of both the importance of the lease and the inappropriateness of its use within the trust structure in many commercial settings. This is understandable as a measure of the importance placed on the lease in a society in which fee simple ownership was so long regarded as the basis of enduring wealth, and the long-term lease served that purpose. At the same time, the long-term lease permitted the owner to benefit from the income from the property. The Land Registration Act makes intricate and obtuse distinctions in leasehold registrations, usually based on the duration of the lease. Hence, some leases must be registered, some cannot be registered, and others may be registered optionally. The result is more snare than utility and these provisions have proven to be an unpopular feature of the legislation.
* * *

B. Will the English System Work in the United States?

One of Professor John Chipman Gray's fundamental propositions on the Rule Against Perpetuities is that one first decides whether the Rule applies, and if it does apply, then "the rule is to be remorselessly applied."[301] That is, the application is without regard to what may be wrought among the interests affected. This principle of "remorseless application" has proven difficult for American courts in perpetuities matters. The reason is understandable. Such a rule results in some very hard cases indeed. The reluctance to give effect to Gray's directive has spawned many reform efforts in the field of perpetuities. Yet each has its own cost. Gray's solution had the indisputable advantage of early resolution of perpetuities problems. The "Wait and See" reform may save some otherwise void dispositions, but it requires that one "wait to see" what happens, and sometimes for a long period of time. "Cy Pres" reforms require the grant to tribunals of wide powers to rewrite wills and deeds, sometimes to the point of unrecognizability.

Problems of title security present an obvious analogy to problems of perpetuities. No doubt the reluctance, indeed refusal, of some American courts to abandon old equity notice rules in favor of a highly credible registration system contributed much to the failure of early Torrens system efforts in this country. The English too have had difficulties in abandoning these long held equity notice principles. Especially in regard to the Law of Property Act and the Land Registration Act, the dilemma of how much to dilute the register by introducing notice concerns has become more intense as recent changes in societal views on the status of women has crept into policy debates on registered land. The question of rights in the matrimonial home, and especially the right of one spouse to dispose of or mortgage a home without the consent or knowledge of the other spouse, has become a matter of national importance.

Distinguished British scholars have dealt at length with the emerging problem of the marital home as it relates to registration. The debate seems to be a part of a broader national concern. Currently, political leaders in Britain often speak of the "caring society." The question is asked whether a given law, politician, or political party is "caring" in its approach to social issues. Some who treat the subject of the matrimonial, or even "cohabitational," home in the context of registered land, frame their positions in terms of this inquiry. Those who push for a more secure title system are portrayed as representing both selfish "commercial" property interests and the conveyancer's obsessive preoccupation with certainty at the expense of the higher societal goals. The secure title advocates are presented as "uncaring" in their narrow protective concerns. Little regard is expressed for the notion that whatever the merits of spousal rights, it would seem that spouses have at least as much interest in secure title as anyone else.

Better means exist to address this valid concern than tampering with and substantially weakening the registration system. Interestingly, one proposal as an alternative to the overriding rights in registered land approach is a suggestion that matrimonial homes be treated always in substantive law as some form of community property. The property would be regarded as owned by both spouses so that any purchaser is always bound to consider the claims of the spouse as a matter of course. This route seems to suggest a return to something looking like tenancy by the entirety, long abolished in England. Despite our headlong rush from some of their efforts, not all of our ancestors were fools, and perhaps we can still learn from them.

C. Overcoming Obstacles to the New System

One of the major obstacles to the new system will be the expense of putting it into place. This is especially true if the initial registration must take place in the form of a full scale judicial procedure. To this concern the author submits several responses.

First, much of the expense of a registration procedure is duplicated by any title search, and although the burden will fall on different parties in the chain, the ultimate expense relating to any single title will be much reduced because of the ease of subsequent transfers. An argument can thus be mounted that the ultimate governmental savings in extravagant recordation arrangements can justify a shift of all or a proportion of the burden on public expense. Second, if the proposed registration alternative were combined with concurrent reform of the substantive property law of legal and concurrent estates in the English fashion, a far smaller volume of transactions would occur with which a register would have to cope. Finally, contemporary constitutional law may well allow for a registration procedure of an administrative nature rather than a full blown judicial proceeding. This seems especially likely if provisions are made for adequate and full financial compensation to those injured by the process.

---

[301] J. GRAY, THE RULE AGAINST PERPETUITIES § 629 (4th ed. 1942).

One of the most important lessons to be learned from the English experience is that overly-generous exemption of interests from registration, or a progressive dilution of a good system to meet current related social issues, can be the undoing of the entire effort. * * * Fairness must concentrate on the compensation scheme, not on rectification or dilution of the register through "overriding interests." Such a frailty killed the earlier "Torrens" efforts. The American reform effort must not be taken over by the kind of response made towards spouses who lacked knowledge about their right to register, nor by the fear that if this group were to have that knowledge and were to exercise their right to register, it would overwhelm the system. A financial arrangement must be provided to properly compensate those who, in hard cases, are denied the realty through operation of the register. To modify the register to meet these cases is to deny it that remorseless character it must have to function efficiently.

Conclusion

Radical change in law is never easy. This is a factor for stability. But when the procedures, techniques, and substance of an important portion of the law come to serve the needs of those who administer it at the expense of those for whom it is designed to serve, it is time for a change. Americans are fortunate to have a comprehensive, well thought out and well-tried scheme for a better way in the English land law legislation. Granted, Americans are in a vastly different situation. The whole of England and Wales are scarcely bigger than the state of Georgia, our twenty-first state in size, yet together, England and Wales are peopled with some fifty million. We are a nation close to 240 million inhabiting a continent. For centuries, the English have relied on the services of a small, highly proficient group of solicitors who are experts in the field of conveyancing. They enjoy a high level of professional competence along with those skilled bureaucrats who run the register and who are in fact creating a kind of informal common law about how the register should be conducted. Finally, the English have a long tradition of acquiescence to central authority in London.

This very European trait of centralism, in contrast to the American federal system, permits a high level of concentration of resources and methods without particular regard to local political sensibilities which are especially evident when realty is involved. Nevertheless, the English system is one from which we can learn much in the long overdue reform of our land law.

D. Easements, Covenants and Equitable Servitudes: The Merger of Three Common Law Concepts of Private Land Use Controls

Virtually all modern commentary on easements, covenants and equitable servitudes argues that these three concepts serve similar purposes and ought to be merged. The history of their use during the latter part of the nineteenth and early part of the twentieth century is told by Timothy Jost in *The Defeasible Fee and the Birth of the Modern Residential Subdivision*, excerpted in Part II(C) of this anthology. This part begins with the classic article urging merger of easements, covenants and equitable servitudes, Uriel Reichman's *Toward a Unified Concept of Servitudes*. Reichman's article was the first important attempt to merge easements and covenants into a single structure. His work is now being taken quite seriously by the American Law Institute as it drafts the Restatement of the Law, Property (Servitudes) to reflect a unification of easements, covenants and equitable servitudes. Stewart Sterk's *Neighbors in American Land Law* follows. It is a discussion of the ways in which the need for neighborliness is reflected in a variety of legal concepts, including easements and covenants. The article is part of a growing literature on the communitarian, as opposed to individualistic, characteristics of American property law. One of the most controversial areas in servitude law involves the circumstances in which private land use controls ought to be terminated. The doctrines of abandonment in easement law and changed circumstances in covenant law have spawned a lively literature, much of which is summarized and elaborated upon in an article by Glen Robinson, *Explaining Contingent Rights: The Puzzle of "Obsolete" Covenants*. One of the authors he takes to task, Gregory Alexander, is then allowed to speak for himself in an excerpt from *Freedom, Coercion and the Law of Servitudes.*

For additional reading, *see* Robert C. Ellickson, *Alternatives to Zoning: Covenants, Nuisance Rules and Fines as Land Use Controls*, 40 U. CHI. L. REV. 681 (1973); Uriel Reichman, *Residential Private Governments: An Introductory Survey*, 43 U. CHI. L. REV. 253 (1976); Richard Epstein, *Covenants and Constitutions*, 73 CORNELL L. REV. 906 (1988); Susan F. French, *Servitudes Reform and the New Restatement of Property: Creation Doctrines and Structural Simplification*, 73 CORNELL L. REV. 928 (1988); Stewart E. Sterk, *Foresight and the Law of Servitudes*, 73 CORNELL L. REV. 956 (1988); James L. Winokur, *The Mixed Blessing of Promissory Servitudes: Toward Optimizing Economic Utility, Individual Liberty, and Personal Identity*, 1989 WIS. L. REV. 1.

Uriel Reichman, *Toward a Unified Concept of Servitudes*, 55 S. CAL. L. REV. 1179–1182, 1231–1245, 1247–1250, 1252–1260 (1982)*

* * *

Servitudes provide the legal foundation of many of today's comprehensive private planning schemes that determine the physical layout, regulation, and operation of large residential and commercial developments. The market's sophistication is not matched, however, by an adequate analytical process in the courts. The American law of servitudes remains a murky subject burdened with obsolete forms and rules that have caused confusion and uncertainty.

Students of property law are initially confronted with three concepts: easements, real covenants, and equitable servitudes, all of which fit into the generic group of servitudes. Different rules apply to each of these forms. The following examples are illustrative.

"Privity of estate" is necessary for the "running" of covenant obligations, but is inapplicable to the other two classes. No servitudes, other than easements, can be acquired by prescription or held "in gross." Rights acquired according to a "general scheme," however, can usually only be enforced under a theory of equitable servitudes. Once created, covenants "run" with the promisor's estate (vertical privity), whereas easements and equitable servitudes are "attached to land" and seem to be enforceable even against a person who acquired title by adverse possession. Only equitable servitudes are enforceable against a subsequent owner who had no notice of the restriction, provided that no value was given for the land. In some cases, an action for breach of covenant can be maintained by the original promisee against the original promisor, notwithstanding the fact that the land was transferred prior to the violation. No such remedy is available to the owner of an easement or an equitable servitude. The doctrine of "change in circumstances" applies to equitable servitudes, and perhaps to covenants, but not to easements. Other defenses, like laches, hardship, and unclean hands, are traditionally only associated with equitable servitudes.

The above rules reflect what seems to be the majority view, but the subject is so marred with disagreement that contradictory authority can be found to refute almost all of the above propositions. In some jurisdictions, differences also exist as to the effect of eminent domain procedures and tax sales on existing servitudes.

Since different rules seemingly apply to each form of servitude, distinguishing between the servitudes is important. According to the Restatement of Property, easements are "executed transactions" which convey "property rights"; covenants are "promises respecting the use of land" which create "property interests"; and equitable servitudes result "solely from the enforceability in equity of a promise respecting the use of land." Unfortunately, very little substance lies behind these phrases and using such definitions to distinguish between the forms is virtually impossible.

The only sensible way to distinguish between the three rights would be to identify each of them with a particular type of land use regulation. In American law however, unlike the English system, the forms of servitudes historically were never entirely identified with subject matter distinctions. The most widely used servitudes are those aimed at restricting land uses. In this country such burdens have been simultaneously classified as "negative easements," covenants, and equitable servitudes. When examining restrictive servitudes, then, the courts were able to use the forms as interchangeable concepts. Free to frame each right as belonging to one category or another, the desired result often dictated the classification. Much the same was true of affirmative obligations, i.e., the duties of one owner to perform some activity on his own land to benefit his neighbor. These duties were generally regarded as covenants, but some older decisions analyzed such obligations as "spurious easements," and modern case law tends to treat them as equitable servitudes.

Choosing between the forms enabled the courts in some cases to avoid application of cumbersome rules. That attitude caused fusion of the forms. Employing several concepts where one concept is sufficient has practical shortcomings. Arbitrary categorization of servitudes enables the courts to reach intuitively desired results by resorting to dated technical rules. Judicial discretion might therefore be distorted because of a failure to openly analyze policy considerations. More worrisome is the possibility that a court will be trapped in a categorization that will lead to a bad decision. The fictional distinctions reduce predictability, encourage litigation, and unduly complicate the drafting of private planning documents. The complexities of the subject make it the domain of experts. This is particularly unfortunate at a time when many Americans live in horizontal or vertical developments and are directly affected by servitudes.

The thesis of this Article is that the three forms of servitudes should be considered as one concept. The normative distinctions indicated above would therefore almost entirely disappear. It is unimportant whether the unified concept is entitled a servitude, a land obligation, or any other term. The importance is in understanding that only a single concept is necessary—a concept which primarily partakes the qualities of what is presently described as an easement. In fact, the proposed approach accords with today's practices. All servitudes appear in the same documents and substantially serve the same function. By clarifying the subject, the problems mentioned above will be alleviated and private land use planning will gain greater flexibility. In most jurisdictions the reform called for could be implemented by the judiciary without the need to resort to legislation. The proposed model would dispense with empty labels without affecting the bulk of the rules governing servitudes.

* * *

II. UNIFYING THE SERVITUDES RULES

The fusion of the three forms of servitudes will not only allow easier application of the law, it will clarify the law's underlying policy considerations. Of course, one might argue that merging the three forms would only serve to create more confusion. That is, one might contend that whatever analytical mistakes, misreading of legal history, or undesired absorption of foreign law occurred in the past, there exists today an established body of law and unless remedied by legislation, it is better to leave the matter as it is rather than to resort to judicial change. Such apprehension is unwarranted. Dealing with servitudes as a unified concept merely acknowledges a development that has already occurred. Thus, no essentially radical changes are here advocated. Indeed, only accurate description and elimination of a few obsolete and rarely applied rules is needed.

This Article deals with conceptual housecleaning; full formulation of the principles of servitudes is beyond its scope. The following discussion comments on the definition of servitudes and shows that the fusion of the forms could easily be accomplished by the judiciary.

A. Surveying the Domain of Servitudes

1. *A Functional Analysis of Servitudes*

The phenomenon of servitudes can be best explained by a functional analysis: The common denominator of most servitudes is the promotion of the efficient utilization of land resources. From the dogmatic perspective, ownership is defined as the freedom to do with a piece of land whatever the owner pleases. That freedom, although restricted by specific rules believed to serve the public interest, manifests itself through a corresponding duty of noninterference imposed on the public at large. However, protection of owners' freedom is essential, but insufficient by itself, to promote the efficient use of land resources; unless voluntary transfers are possible, property could not shift to its best use.

Effective accommodation of sellers' and buyers' utilities requires flexibility in molding transactions. For that reason, not only is title transferable in its entirety, but separate elements are transferable as well. Possession, sometimes without title, can be segmented and sold by reference to physical criteria (e.g., condominium units, air space, and subsurface minerals) or by reference to time (e.g., lease duration, future interests, and time sharing).

Situations arise, however, where even partial possession is not the desired object of a transaction. Servitudes are used to transfer owners' entitlements, other than possession, for the efficient utilization of land. "Transfer," as here used, is meant to imply that certain rights, which a person has as an owner of land, could be permanently replaced by a corresponding obligation to do, or not to do, certain specified actions. It follows that the grantor of a servitude cannot defeat it by transferring his title or a conflicting interest. "Owners' entitlements" is used here in a broad sense, namely whatever an owner can do or refrain from doing respecting his land. Finally, "possession" is used in contradistinction to a servitude itself, although the line between the two is not always easily drawn. The distinction is nevertheless important since possession has other functions, and is differently regulated. Exclusivity of use distinguishes possession from servitudes in most cases, but there are varying degrees of exclusivity.

There are three characteristics of servitudes, each of which is important to land use planning: limited scope (not amounting to possession), permanency, and flexibility in structuring the right. Without the ability to purchase nonpossessory segments of ownership entitlements, some beneficial transactions will not be concluded and other transactions will result in waste. The theoretically perpetual duration of servitudes encourages reliance and capital investment. Promoting the efficient utilization of land is more than a common characteristic of servitudes, it is the overriding policy governing these rights and carries normative implications. A review of the judicial role in creating and terminating servitudes substantiates this assertion. * * *

In situations where a promise has no bearing on land use regulation, the courts treat the arrangement as a contract between the original parties and exempt the promisor's transferees from liability. In such cases, it is irrelevant whether or not the transacting parties clearly expressed their written intention that the promise would "run with the land," or that the promisor's transferee had actual or constructive notice of the obligation. As a matter of positive law, where land use efficiency gains could not conceivably be accomplished, servitudes are not recognized. By applying the "touch and concern" test, the courts are actually exercising their power to fix the boundaries of servitudes.

This somewhat unusual interventionist theory is justified because the permanent attachment to land of merely personal obligations is likely to frustrate the objectives of a private land holding system.

* * *

There is another reason for the "touch and concern" rule. Private property is sanctioned by society not only to promote efficiency, but also to safeguard individual freedom. Servitudes are a kind of private legislation affecting a line of future owners. Limiting such "legislative powers" to an objective purpose of land planning eliminates the possibility of creating modern variations of feudal serfdom. There might be nothing objectionable in personal agreements concerning personal labor, adherence to ideologically prescribed modes of behavior, or promises to buy from a certain supplier. When such obligations, however, become permanently enforced against an ever-changing group of owners, the matter acquires different dimensions. One point needs emphasis: The courts are not involved in measuring efficiency gains; this is clearly the prerogative of the parties. The courts only deny the permanency of agreements clearly unrelated to land use.

Judicial termination of obsolete servitudes also helps to achieve efficiency. An obsolete servitude is of no value to the beneficiary; it could be of great value to the owner of the encumbered land, however, since it prevents the best use of the property. A consensual termination may not be reached if excessive "blackmail" money is demanded or if transaction costs are too high. Instead of waiting for such an agreement to be reached, the courts simply pronounce the death of the servitude. Thus, when the positive utility of the servitudes has ended, the courts do not allow it to become a bare device to collect money.

2. The Content of Servitudes

Having discussed the elements and general function of servitudes, the content of these rights can now be considered. Servitudes are employed in two major contexts. One category of servitudes deals with accommodating land uses among neighbors. The other category of servitudes deals with situations where the possessor and another person share benefits derived from the same piece of land.

a. *Accommodations among neighbors:* Most servitudes fall into this category. Through individual bargaining or initial private planning the combined use of several separate units is made more efficient.

In short, servitudes are often used to implement the Coase theorem.[283]

Servitudes are not limited to certain patterns of legal relations. All four types of Hohfeld's fundamental jural relations[284] can be the subject matter of servitudes. The right-duty relationship is manifested by positive and negative promises. Thus, a duty to maintain the front lawn or not to build more than two stories in height could qualify as a land obligation. To the extent the purchase of such rights serve the utilities of the owners involved, a more efficient land use pattern is established. In other words, the right-duty relationship coordinates uses between the benefited and encumbered estates. The same applies to the privilege-no right relationship. That relationship is manifested by an active right to enter a neighbor's land and conduct some activity that is beneficial to the use of another's land. Examples of such activities are laying sewage pipelines on a neighbor's land or driving through his land to a main road. The immunity-disability class is demonstrated by servitudes to cause nuisance. Such rights provide immunity from nuisance actions, regardless of whether the remedy sought is damages or injunction. Thus, servitudes to cause a nuisance generally provide more extensive protection from private nuisance actions than public planning. Finally, some servitudes perpetuate power-liability relations. Minimum lot size restrictions can restrict, or even eliminate, an owner's power to subdivide. Another example is the power often vested in homeowners' associations to unilaterally impose new servitudes on units within their "jurisdiction."

Essentially, transacting parties are free to mold whatever types of servitudes they desire, constrained only by the "touch and concern" doctrine. To determine if the arrangement is a "nonrunning" personal obligation or a land use related promise, the transaction must be reviewed as a whole, including its effect on both "dominant" and "servient" estates. For example, where the elimination of a spillover is not the reason for the imposition of a negative duty, a land use function was probably not contemplated. Similarly, where a positive duty is to be performed outside the burdened estate, it is most likely that the intention was a purchase of labor rather than accommodation of the owners' relations. Finally, a servitude providing immunity from civil actions can be acquired only where liability could arise from a continuous activity that is carried out in one unit and affects the use of another unit. As these examples show, in cases of doubt the inquiry must concentrate on both the nature of the benefit (better use of the land) and the nature of the burden (limiting ownership privileges).

It has been noted that servitudes can be structured in different ways. Servitudes resembling "duties" are often described in contractual terms, but this does not mean that they create contractual rights. All servitudes impose a duty of some kind on possessors or owners of land. It is possible, therefore, to describe all these rights as obligations. Indeed, this Article uses "land obligations" * * * as a synonym for servitudes. But terminology will not resolve the controversy over whether to conceptualize servitudes as contractual or property rights. Servitudes have certain characteristics that contractual rights do not. All land obligations perform substantially the same function, and are only supervised to serve that function. Furthermore, they are all nonpossessory rights that "run with land." Most importantly, servitudes are uniformly treated by the courts as interests in land.

"Interests in land" is a fundamental concept in real estate law, denoting a multitude of legal consequences. It prescribes the usual requirements for the creation of such rights, and it explains both their duration and why they are most often specifically enforced. Furthermore, the treatment of servitudes as interests in land allows servitudes to survive even in situations where the land is taken or coercively sold. In sum, treating servitudes as interests in land implies that servitudes are, in fact, property rights and should be dealt with as one concept, in accordance with the "property premise." The dated theories viewing servitudes as merely a branch of contract law should be disregarded.

b. *Sharing the benefits of one piece of land:* The second category, that of sharing the benefits of a single piece of land by the possessor and another person, is marked by far less flexibility. The benefit of these servitudes, by definition, inures only to a given person and does not benefit or attach to land. After a few generations a single beneficiary might be

283 Coase, *The Problem of Social Cost,* 3 J. L. & ECON. 1 (1960). The Coase Theorem states that if there are no transaction costs and if the parties possess perfect information, market transactions between two parties will lead to the same results independent of the initial legal position of the two parties.

284 Hohfeld, *Fundamental Legal Conceptions as Applied in Judicial Reasoning,* 26 YALE L.J. 710, 710–33 (1917). Hohfeld's jural relations are: right-duty, privilege-no right, power-liability, and immunity-disability. * * *

replaced by many heirs. Even where such a servitude is greatly diminished in utility, it is difficult to reach a termination transaction. Transaction costs might be substantial; more troubling is the possibility that not all the beneficiaries could be located. Attempts to judicially terminate the right would be hampered by procedural problems.

Experience has made the law of servitudes sensitive to possible land use impediments and many impediments are avoided at the outset by withholding recognition of such rights. The problem, however, has not caused the rejection of all servitudes in gross. It has only made the judiciary more cautious in sanctioning personal benefits. Generally, only those "land obligations" that provide active user rights are recognized by the courts. Several reasons can be given for this judicial attitude. First, the difficulties associated with these rights are balanced by the utility of having such sharing arrangements. Important servitudes, such as the right to drill for water or oil, to construct railroads, or to cut timber, clearly should not be banned. Second, active user rights give the privilege of using the servitude to the beneficiary. To do some positive act requires expense or inconvenience. The beneficiary would rarely bother to exercise his right if the servitude were of no value. Accordingly, in some cases the courts hold the right abandoned, and therefore declare it expired. Where the duty is placed on the owner of the burdened land, however, a finding of abandonment is more rare. The application of the "change in circumstances" doctrine also is troublesome where a benefit is derived only personally; the inclination of the courts has been to postpone any determination for at least the full period of limitation of action. Finally, in situations where the beneficiary has neither access to the land nor possession of benefited property, negative or positive obligations are usually obtained for purposes unrelated to land use. Such personal rights might therefore prevent the efficient utilization of land.

If the agreement *in toto*, rather than only the attributes of the burden, is considered, nonprivilege servitudes in gross rarely deserve recognition. A duty to grow only strawberries and sell them to the beneficiary at a fixed price, or to use only materials produced by the beneficiary for fencing, relates to the use of land, insofar as the owner of the encumbered property is concerned. But the primary objects of these agreements are, respectively, the sale of agricultural products and the forced acquisition of certain building materials. The harmful effects of enforcing such promises against a line of owners are clearly evident.

The above discussion indicates that judicial supervision of servitudes in gross is largely justified. This supervision, however, should not take the form of mere adherence to rigid patterns. Accordingly, in addition to active privileges, other "land obligations" could qualify to "run with land." The public's right to view a landmark house or a forest, even from outside a fenced estate, is, in essence, a sharing of land. Negative servitudes purchased for such purposes should therefore be held to be valid servitudes in gross.

3. Use of the Functional Test To Define Content

The three forms of servitudes provide very little guidance regarding the permissible content of the rights. The needed guidance, however, can come from the functional test described above: servitudes are transfers of owners' entitlements, other than possession, for the efficient utilization of land. The test corresponds to the prevailing judicial attitude and permits discretion in borderline cases by its reliance upon the overriding policy that governs servitude creation. Though the functional test is somewhat imprecise, it nonetheless enables the courts to be responsive to changing circumstances and needs. For example, certain promises that were considered in the past to indicate hypersensitivity, and were therefore considered personal, have since become both market commodities and recognized servitudes. Similarly, social changes might broaden the definition of land use in the future. Security-related activities in communal living arrangements could provide an example of such a change.

The functional test also accommodates the flexibility required for modern private planning. Developers aspire to preserve discretion regarding large projects, especially in unpredictable markets. Homeowners' associations, which have become more popular with the decline in municipal services, require discretion in enforcing and amending existing servitudes. As a result, there has been a marked increase in the use of conditional and discretionary[299] servitudes, as well as servitudes that are of limited duration or that can be amended or terminated by a predetermined body or person. There has also been an increase in "floating servitudes." Floating servitudes are common in horizontal and vertical developments where a set of land use regulations will become

---

[299] * * * *See* * * * Reichman, *Residential Private Governments: An Introductory Survey*, 43 U. CHI. L. REV. 253 (1976) * * *.

effective upon the enlargement of an existing project to include adjacent land.

Various types of servitudes can often be framed to accomplish effectively identical objectives. Consider for example, a negative duty not to build certain structures and a positive promise to paint a building. Both covenants can be enforced by affirmative privileges; one enabling the beneficiary to demolish the prohibited structure, and the other enabling the beneficiary to carry out the painting job at the expense of the owner. Many modern servitudes therefore tend to provide substantial discretion; they are imposed as cross-servitudes on many units and are enforced by a corporate body acting as the agent or trustee of the beneficiaries. The growing importance and complexity of servitudes demonstrates the need to clarify basic policies and to eliminate conceptual hindrances to those policies.

Using the functional definition of servitudes requires a reevaluation of accepted legal classifications. Conditional estates, for example, are legitimately used to enforce dedications or family arrangements. But conditional estates are also employed to enforce land use regulations intended to benefit another's land. In the latter case, the arrangement should be treated as a servitude with a supplementary, agreed upon remedy. This analysis is superior to highly artificial analyses which construe conditions as covenants.[302] Under a functional analysis, the courts would be free to apply the "change in circumstances" rule and other rules, in determining the validity of the claimed right. Whether to apply the remedies for servitudes or to order forfeiture would thus be left to judicial discretion. Since forfeiture is an overly harsh remedy, its use would not be likely. Where the violated condition can be corrected, specific performance can, in most cases, adequately serve the beneficiary's interest. In other cases, compensation is more appropriate than partial confiscation. Forfeiture should be considered a viable remedy only in those rare situations where court-ordered compliance with land use regulations is disregarded.

On the other hand, certain rights which are currently treated as servitudes should be excluded. One such class of rights includes continuing monetary obligations. Currently, an obligation to pay "for a benefit received in the use of the [promisor's] land" is considered a servitude. Admittedly, "running" promises to pay money are important. They enable community residents to privately satisfy the community's needs. Also, security interests are aimed at collection, and depend on the existence of an obligation. Unless the fiction is introduced that the original owner promised to forever pay assessments without personal recourse, mortgages and liens cannot provide continuous financing. "Land obligations" solve the problem because they impose a duty on whoever is the owner when the payment is due. Once the perpetual obligation is established, it can become the object of a security interest. But "running" monetary promises have nothing to do with land-use regulation and therefore have been traditionally treated as rent charges or ground-rents. Their conversion into servitudes might have been the result of judicial disfavor of the archaic ground-rent, and the concept of covenants was used to sanction the transformation. The result, however, is unsatisfactory. As a servitude, the "touch and concern" rule requires that the money collected be earmarked for land use purposes that benefit the payor's land. Thus, such funds cannot be used to pay for a Fourth-of-July community party, for football uniforms for the local school's team, for books for the community library, or for any number of legitimate community purposes. Such an outcome is of doubtful wisdom. In today's developments, adequate safeguards against mishandling of funds are found in the homeowner's associations' by-laws, the fiduciary duties of its directors, and supervision by public authorities. The "touch and concern" rule is inappropriate here, and instead produces only undue restrictions. In general, ground-rents disappeared because of their disutility in a market that does not enjoy monetary stability for long periods. They are not likely to reappear in the future. The "communal services charge," however, is alive and should be treated as such and not as a servitude. Conceptual deficiencies behind such service charges are best addressed through legislative reform.

Finally, a widespread misconception concerning the "running" of benefits should be corrected. The "running" of benefits per se has nothing to do with servitudes. Unless the burden is capable of "running with the land," i.e., capable of binding a transferee of the encumbered land, only a personal obligation is involved. The benefit of a personal obligation can inure to a group of people, identified by their ownership of land, as third party beneficiaries or assignees by implication. Not being interests in land, however, the running of such benefits to transferees should not depend on the land use qualities of the

---

[302] *See* Goldstein, *Rights of Entry and Possibilities of Reverter as Devices to Restrict the Use of Land*, 54 Harv. L. Rev. 248 (1948).

benefit. Accordingly, the running of the benefit should require neither a writing nor recordation.

B. Creation

1. *Explicit Creation*

Every recorded obligation which is intended to "run with the land" and which satisfies the judicial criteria discussed in the previous section, is a valid servitude. This statement reflects the current state of the law, in the event the horizontal privity rule is finally laid to rest. Both the legal and practical reasons for the horizontal privity rule disappeared long ago and there are very few modern cases applying the rule to invalidate a servitude. Those cases which used horizontal privity involved peculiar servitudes, and instead of applying the "touch and concern" test, the courts invoked the privity rule as an unjustified short cut. Although cases applying horizontal privity have had a negligible impact, cautious lawyers have no choice but to abide by this pernicious rule. Formal judicial abolition of the horizontal privity rule is clearly desirable and once achieved, will extinguish the only remaining difference between the forms regarding the explicit creation of servitudes.

2. *Informal Creation*

There are situations in which the courts will recognize the existence of a servitude although the owner of the burdened land never agreed in writing to grant such a right. Five theories support that result: implication, necessity, implied reciprocity, estoppel in rem, and prescription. This Article will not discuss these partially overlapping theories, but it will show that the forms servitudes may take are not vital to the functioning of these rules.

a. *Basic tensions:* The rules governing judicial involvement in the creation of servitudes are essentially structured in a way that reaches a compromise between two sets of opposing considerations. The first set of considerations is the expectations of the parties. Cases often arise when one owner of land maintains justifiable expectations that ownership entitlements of his neighbor will be curtailed to enhance the utility of his own property. Courts will generally enforce the servitude when the owner, against whom the servitude is claimed, caused the expectation to arise by his representations or, in some instances, by his inaction. Courts are more likely to recognize informal servitudes if there is actual reliance, such as investment of money or labor, and failure to stop such reliance, especially where legal action could be commenced.

Fairness to the one claiming the servitude has to be balanced against fairness to a third party who purchases the land on which the servitude is claimed to exist. Such a third party purchaser has justifiable expectations of his own that may conflict with those of the party claiming the servitude. If the claimed right was a contract instead of a servitude, the right would automatically terminate upon transfer of land. The nature of servitudes, however, requires courts to take into account third party expectations.

The second set of considerations is the degree of direct judicial involvement desired in creating servitudes. There are situations where owners fail to enter into an agreement regarding use of the land even though a servitude would increase the value of the "dominant estate" several times more than the resulting decrease in value of the "servient estate." Under such circumstances, should the court impose a servitude (with or without compensation)? It could be persuasively argued that the purpose of efficient land utilization could be served by judicial intervention. Admittedly, permanent damages issued in nuisance cases create rights similar to servitudes,[312] but extending the nuisance approach to permit judicial creation of servitudes creates problems. Taking from one owner to benefit another not only raises constitutional questions but also ignores the choices of the parties, substituting coercion for bargained accommodations. Although attention focuses on the litigants before the court in nuisance cases, community-wide standards are established. Judicial creation of servitudes, however, usually would only correct a specific failure of a transaction, without the broader implications of reallocating entitlements.

The conflicts between expectations of the parties and judicial intervention are not satisfactorily resolved. Courts do not impose servitudes outright, but will hold that they have been implicitly created. The utility or necessity of the right involved plays a key role in the judicial willingness to recognize the right's informal creation. Actual expectations and the utility of the right are therefore the most important elements considered in passing upon the validity of servitudes that were not explicitly granted.

---

[312] In Boomer v. Atlantic Cement Co., 26 N.Y.2d 219, 228, 257 N.E.2d 870, 875, 309 N.Y.S.2d 312, 319 (1970), the court recognized that the granting of permanent damages in nuisance amounted to a judicially created servitude on the plaintiff's land.

b. *Theories of informal creation:* The theories which informally create servitudes can now be examined. The traditionally separate discussion of easements conveys the wrong impression that only "privilege-type" rights can be created by "implication" or "necessity." Both implication and necessity deal with situations where land owned by one is divided and a part of it conveyed to another. The courts may conclude in such cases that the seller has implicitly granted to the purchaser a servitude, burdening the parcel he retained. In more exceptional situations, the court may determine that the seller reserved a servitude on the parcel transferred to benefit the rest of his property. Because the title was transferred, the courts can avoid some troubling questions. Since the parties were involved in a transfer, the courts only have to interpret the intent of the parties to determine the range of interests conveyed. The intention to create the right is ascribed to the parties and the courts cannot be alleged to have created a servitude. The fine line between implied-in-fact and implied-in-law cannot always be clearly drawn. Not surprisingly, therefore, the greater the utility of the servitude, the more willing the courts will be to impute intentions which were not expressed at the time of the transaction.

Absent those cases where the parties merely neglected to state what they understood among themselves, the implication theory is used as an enforced duty of conscionability. Instead of finding a violation of the duty of conscionability and granting a remedy for its breach, the court assumes the parties have met the required standards and have agreed to the reservation or grant of the appropriate servitude. The question of writing is resolved in the same fictitious manner. Since the transfer of title involves a writing, that document is considered to be merely interpreted or supplemented with the norms of law that were not contractually eliminated.

Positive easements are usually implied from apparent and continuous uses of the land before part of it was transferred. The courts deem that both vendor and purchaser expected that uses which are beneficial to the enjoyment of their units (e.g., roads and pipelines) will continue following the transfer. Even without evidence of previous use an easement can be implied by "necessity." The doctrine of necessity applies to situations in which, in the absence of a servitude, a parcel of land can be used with only "disproportionate effort and expense." In these instances, typically involving a right of way in favor of a landlocked unit, it is assumed that the servitude was implicitly granted or reserved.

* * *

Servitudes can also be informally created without a transfer of title. According to the *Restatement*, the same principles of estoppel relate to both rights in the nature of easements[324] and "promises respecting the use of land."[325] In certain circumstances, the estoppel extends beyond the "parties to the representation" by the doctrine of estoppel in rem. The application of this theory, as well as the theory of unjust enrichment, depends on the circumstances of each case and the kind of activity involved. Acquiescence, for example, might be sufficient to warrant enforcement of the estoppel where the rights of others are involved. In such a case, the failure to issue a warning or to promptly enforce one's rights could make estoppel an appropriate remedy, even though no active representation was made. On the other hand, there is no general obligation to correct self-induced mistakes. Accordingly, no estoppel is recognized where one owner makes investments upon the mistaken belief that the current use of his neighbor's land will continue.

The distinction between acquiescence and mistake is of particular importance where a party claims to have acquired the benefits of a servitude by prescription. Prescription is based on adverse use, a continuous and apparent violation of the owner's rights by another. Failure to contest a known adverse claim to an entitlement for a period of several years may result in legal transfer of the entitlement. Where there is no violation of a right, not only is the entitlement unchallenged, but there is nothing against which the owner can act. It is therefore reasonable to allow the acquisition by prescription of "privilege" and "immunity"-type servitudes but not "duty"-type servitudes. In the latter instance, no adverse use can be established, and any misallocation of entitlements must be corrected, if at all, by nuisance law. Although only certain types of servitudes can be acquired by prescription and estoppel based on acquiescence, that result is dictated by the function of the rules themselves. The forms of servitudes are therefore unnecessary to explain the operation of the norms, and unification of the forms would not affect the application of the rules.

---

[324] *See* RESTATEMENT OF PROPERTY §§ 514, 519(4), comments e-g (1944).

[325] *Id.* § 524 & comment b.

C. Enforcement

1. *Parties Against Whom a Servitude Can Be Enforced*

This section considers two issues: first, against whom can a servitude be enforced and, second, what remedies are available to the beneficiary? The purpose of this section is to indicate the changes needed to unify the servitudes' forms.

The issue of "parties to the servitudes" has [several] * * * aspects: (1) the equitable characteristics of equitable servitudes, (2) the vertical privity rule, [and] (3) the enforceability of benefits * * *.

a. *Equitable characteristics of equitable servitudes:* It has been argued that since equitable servitudes are equitable interests they may sometimes provide greater protection than other servitudes. For example, a bona fide donee may be bound by an equitable servitude but not by an easement or real covenant. * * * [T]he concept of equitable servitudes changed from a purely equitable right to a legal right resembling an easement. In the United States the ability to record such rights has rendered them indistinguishable from other servitudes. Equitable servitudes therefore should be treated as legal interests. Equitable theories still have a place in the American law of servitudes, however. Specifically, since servitudes are conceptualized as interests in land, a promise to grant such a right will implicate equitable rules. Equitable servitudes should therefore provide no more and no less protection than other land obligations. The provisions of the recording acts define the position of a grantee who paid no consideration for the land and had no actual or constructive notice of a previously created right. The type of servitude involved is immaterial.

b. *The vertical privity rule:* One of the major deficiencies of real covenants is the vertical privity rule. According to this rule a covenant is enforceable only against a successor to exactly the same interest, or one of corresponding duration, "held by the promisor at the time the promise was made." The Restatement explains vertical privity as a measure of "formal identification," justified by the policy of keeping the running of burdens within "narrow formal limits." The Restatement's rationale for the vertical privity rule is unpersuasive, however. Historically, the rule emerged as an unwarranted extension of lease theories to agreements among neighbors. Yet the threat that the lease might be terminated should alone be sufficient to deter even a sublessee, who owes no duty to the landlord for want of privity, from disregarding the lessee's obligations. No such remedy is available to the beneficiary of a real covenant.

* * *

Fortunately, the vertical privity rule is not often applied. By calling the land obligation an equitable servitude or negative easement, the rule is simply avoided. Easements and equitable servitudes are considered attached to land and every possessor, regardless of how he obtained the possession, must comply with the servitudes' obligations. Why then should not the contract-privity analysis be eliminated altogether? Proponents of the rule point out that in certain cases it would be unfair to place substantial liabilities on one who possesses the land for only a short time (as in the case of a lease for a few months). Most examples offered by proponents of the rule relate to monetary obligations, such as community assessments or payments for repair and maintenance of party walls. As previously explained, these obligations should not have been conceptualized as servitudes. Since they are servitudes under current American law, however, the issue cannot be avoided.

The best solution to the problem of monetary obligations is a unified approach entailing a presumption that servitudes apply to all possessors of encumbered land. The defendant-possessor would have the burden of proving that the servitude was not meant to impose a specific obligation upon him. The presumption clearly could not be rebutted where servitudes such as residential restrictions or a duty to keep up a lawn are involved; but, unduly burdensome monetary obligations may cause different results.

* * *

c. *The enforceability of benefits:* There are no substantial differences between real covenants, easements, and equitable servitudes regarding the right of enforcement. Where a servitude benefits another's land, a purchaser without notice of the benefit may logically enforce the right. The Restatement recognizes that no horizontal privity is required as a condition to the "running of benefits." Furthermore, instead of strict vertical privity, only succession to "some interest" of the promisee is needed. As a general rule every lawful possessor of the dominant estate is entitled to demand compliance with a servitude.

Because servitudes are intended to supplement possessory rights, their benefits naturally inure to the possessor. Owners are likewise permitted to enforce servitudes to protect their reversionary interests, and in cases where monetary obligations are involved, one might logically conclude that owners alone are provided with the right of enforcement. But *Neponsit Property Owners' Association v. Emigrant*

Industrial Savings Bank,[346] a case which applies to all types of servitudes, permitted a homeowners' association to enforce the benefit as an "agent or representative" of the owners. The effect of the fusion of the forms on the "running of benefits" is therefore minimal.

* * *

2. *Remedies Available to the Beneficiary*

Notwithstanding theoretical differences, all servitudes are enforced in substantially the same way. The *Restatement* maintains that easements are protected as property rights under the law of torts, whereas real covenants are enforced as contractual obligations. Accordingly, injunctions are considered the natural remedy in the former case and damages in the latter. This description only compounds analytical mistakes. Since covenants can be treated as equitable servitudes, their violation would be prevented by an injunction unless the remedy at law is appropriate. If one combines the rules for enforcing covenants and equitable servitudes as the same "promise respecting the use of land," it is apparent that this "property interest" is enforced like an easement. The very act of separating covenants from equitable servitudes led to the conclusion that the enforcement of each of them varied from the rules governing the enforcement of easements. By refusing to admit that "equitable servitudes" were full-fledged property rights, the *Restatement* was forced to carefully detail the defenses of laches, acquiescence, and relative hardship. When dealing with easements, however, a reference to the principles of the law of torts was deemed sufficient. Of course, the defenses of laches, acquiescence, and relative hardship do apply to easements by virtue of the "general principles of the law of torts" which govern that subject.

In practice, all servitudes receive substantially the same legal protection. Theoretically, however, the outlined approach can reach odd results. When a court refuses to provide an equitable remedy to protect an easement, a judgment for damages will usually be granted. A decision that a "promise" does not qualify for injunctive relief is actually tantamount to a declaration that the "equitable servitude" is terminated. On such an occasion, according to the conventional explanation, the "separate" category of covenant would immediately assume the leading role and the "contractual" right would be enforced by providing damages.

Without pretending to exhaust the topic of remedies for servitude violations, this Article suggests a few modifications which could provide the judiciary with greater flexibility. Servitudes tend to be efficient upon creation. Absent significant changes, the right should be specifically enforced. This attitude promotes the expectations of the parties and encourages utilization of private planning. Problems arise, however, as the utility of the servitude fluctuates over time. Changes in patterns of land uses and technological developments often necessitate judicial ingenuity in structuring remedies. Where the utility of the servitude is reduced, the courts have traditionally resorted to one of the two following measures: (1) damages in lieu of specific performance or (2) a declaration that the right is totally extinguished. These attitudes are particularly justified where several owners of burdened lots are involved. Prohibitive transaction costs, including freeloader problems, may prevent the conclusion of a termination transaction. By decreeing damages the courts are actually forcing resale of entitlements. In more extreme cases, where the servitude has lost almost all of its original benefits, the right is judicially abolished to solve the transactions costs and freeloader problems.

* * *

D. Extinguishment

Substantially similar factors cause the termination of easements, covenants, and equitable servitudes. The principles of merger, release, abandonment, and estoppel govern all servitudes. As previously suggested, the grounds for eliminating equitable servitudes also apply to easements.

* * *

Servitudes are intended to enhance utilization of land resources. Where they no longer contribute to any "use or enjoyment" of the dominant estate they are not allowed to become bare instruments for collection of heavy extinguishment fees. Probably due to judicial reluctance to admit such an active role in abolishing interests in land, the courts have provided other explanations for reaching the same result. Typically the rhetoric surrounding easement cases is not identical to that used in covenant cases. The theory of abandonment, although having a legitimate role in other contexts, is usually used as a means to extinguish obsolete easements. The usefulness of a positive right can be reasonably deter-

---

[346] 278 N.Y. 248, 15 N.E.2d 793 (1938).

mined by scrutinizing the beneficiary's behavior. Accordingly, the courts routinely find an intention to abandon the easement in two instances: (1) the servient estate has not been utilized for a long time (even when shorter than the prescription period), or (2) the dominant estate has been used in a manner which indicates that the right would never be utilized. However, it is unlikely that a person would willingly give up such rights when they could be sold to the owner of the servient estate.

Where negative or affirmative burdens are concerned it is more difficult to accept the owner's actions as an indicator of the obsolescence of the rights. In such cases, objective standards have to be employed. The application of the "change in circumstances" rule is therefore justified to the extent that no benefit could be derived from the restriction. The explanations of such holdings are just as fictitious as the ones offered in easement cases. The courts simply impute to the original parties the intention that the promise is to expire when rendered valueless. One easily can imagine that the abandonment and "change of circumstances" explanations of the extinguishment rules could lead to diverging results, but the actual resolution of most cases is substantially the same. Therefore, the "change in circumstance" rule should be applied to easements directly.

* * *

Stewart Sterk, *Neighbors in American Land Law*, 87 COLUM. L. REV. 55–56, 88–90, 93–104 (1987)*

Most allocation of land in this country started with division of surface area into discrete parcels separated by rigid boundary lines. Doctrinal rules embodying the familiar maxim that whoever owns the soil owns from the heavens to the depths of the earth have extended these discrete parcels into three dimensions. Whoever is allocated an ownership right to one of these discrete parcels is largely free to do with it as he sees fit, to use it to pursue his private preferences, either through personal use or through market exchange.

Rules that reduce uncertainty to a minimum, like this rigid, "geometric-box" allocation of rights, have been championed as an ideal mechanism for facilitating market exchange.[3] Rules that promote certainty assure that when more than one individual values a particular right, all will know who has the right to sell it. The individual who values it most, at least so long as we equate value with willingness to pay, is likely to emerge with the right.

In a number of instances American land law departs from the geometric-box allocation. * * * Many of these instances involve externalities, where the transaction costs of accounting for all those with interests in promoting or preventing a particular land use are high. In these instances, the market is an unreliable guide to the value, measured in willingness to pay, that all interested parties collectively attach to a particular land use. Thus, for instance, nuisance rules, zoning controls, and even rules governing removal of servitudes depart from the geometric-box allocation and substitute some form of public intervention.

* * *

These departures from the geometric-box allocation require exploration.

* * *

IV. LAND LAW AS A REFLECTION OF SOCIAL NORMS: THE DOCTRINAL CONCEPTION OF NEIGHBORS.

A. *The Interdependence of Legal Doctrine and Social Norms*

With what values do members of our society approach transactions in land? That question is of interest to economic analysts who cannot evaluate the efficiency of land law rules without either answer-

[3] See, e.g., Epstein, *Notice and Freedom of Contract in the Law of Servitudes*, 55 S. CAL. L. REV. 1353 (1982); * * *.

ing it or assuming it away.[114] But the question is also of more general interest to anyone who seeks insight about our society. A variety of social science disciplines examine value structures and, more particularly, the patterns of interaction that individuals follow in implementing their value structures. The study of legal doctrine also provides data about the ways in which people interrelate within the society.

To some extent, legal doctrine shapes the ways in which people interrelate. Judges, legislators, and academics frequently justify particular rules as likely to produce reactions (presumably desirable) among the populace. Thus, a court or legislature may impose a particular form of tort or criminal liability in order to deter some species of behavior and to encourage others. But legal doctrine also reflects social norms as it reinforces them. A judge who imposes rules designed to deter particular activity must have formulated somehow the belief that the activity ought to be deterred.

In fact, as Robert Gordon has put it, "it is just about impossible to describe any set of 'basic' social practices without describing the legal relations among the people involved."[118] Law and social values are interdependent; neither can be explored without reference to the other. As a result, the study of legal doctrine inevitably provides insight into the social value structure, because legal doctrine itself is one of the pillars of that structure.

Legal rules do not perfectly shape or perfectly reflect social norms. If they did, the rules themselves would become superfluous. And to a considerable extent, social practice does proceed without conscious regard for legal rules.[119] In a system with firmly established and widely shared social norms, legal rules may be of little consequence, because the costs of enforcing legal rights are high compared to alternative methods of dispute resolution that bypass legal processes. But even the most firmly established norms break down on occasion. When breakdowns occur, when nonlegal mechanisms fail, disputing parties sometimes turn to the legal system for dispute resolution.

Land law doctrine may be too narrow a corner of law to warrant sweeping generalizations about social value structures. Nevertheless, the doctrinal choice to adhere to or depart from the geometric-box allocation does illuminate our society's conception of at least one common social and sometimes economic relation: the relation between neighbors. The geometric-box allocation generally permits landowners to avoid interaction with others, including neighbors, unless both the landowner and the other provide for interaction by explicit agreement. Like the doctrinal structure in many other areas, then, the geometric-box allocation is generally well adapted to a society whose members highly value individualism and autonomy. To the extent, however, that * * * various easement, boundary dispute, and spite fence doctrines depart from the geometric-box allocation, they reverse the societal preference for individualism and autonomy by mandating (and perhaps assuming) a pattern of interaction between neighbors, absent explicit agreement to the contrary. These departures, then, suggest a society whose members do not treat relations with neighbors in the same way they treat relations with strangers.

* * *

C. *The Geometric-Box Allocation: Autonomy, Individualism and Market Exchange*

Measured against alternative allocations—communal ownership, for instance, or division of surface rights from air or underground rights—an allocation based on discrete geometric boxes facilitates private exchange and promotes individual autonomy. It facilitates private exchange by defining rights crisply so that the background for negotiations is unmistakable. It promotes individual autonomy by combining rights in a way that empowers individual owners to make many land use decisions unilaterally. Thus, a landowner who wanted to build a ham radio antenna or a two-story basement need not obtain consent from someone who separately has been allocated air rights or underground rights.

The desirability of private exchange and personal autonomy are not, however, beyond dispute. An allocation decision that promotes private exchange and unilateral decision making excludes virtually all of society from participation in any single decision. That exclusion is both its greatest advantage and its heaviest cost. Exclusion is an advantage because the cost of obtaining consent can be enormous, especially as the number of people whose consent is necessary increases. As Kennedy and Michelman have demonstrated, however, whether the cost is large or small

---

[114] Kennedy & Michelman, *Are Property and Contract Efficient?*, 8 HOFSTRA L. REV. 711 (1980).

[118] Gordon, *Critical Legal Histories*, 36 STAN. L. REV. 57, 103 (1984).

[119] Ellickson, *Of Coase and Cattle: Dispute Resolution Among Neighbors in Shasta County*, 38 STAN. L. REV. 623 (1986); * * *.

depends not on immutable economic principles, but on contingent social norms.[131] At the same time that limiting participation in the decision making process reduces the cost of obtaining consent, exclusion can also produce psychic costs and inefficient substantive decisions that a communal decision making process could avoid.

One need only look to the varying forms of political organization to recognize that the cost-benefit calculus of communal decision making is not a universal one. Take a New England town's decision to eschew representative government in favor of frequent town meetings. For the townspeople, the decision might, despite increased expenditure of time and energy, increase the overall efficiency of decision making in two ways. First, the participatory process may produce psychic pleasures—citizens may enjoy the participatory process, or they may enjoy the feelings of virtue that accompany participation. Second, direct participation may internalize costs that representative government would leave external, thus leading to more efficient substantive policies. A town meeting form of government, then, would be more or less efficient in different communities with different attitudes towards the decision making process. The same factors suggest that no particular system for allocating land use rights need be universally efficient. A system that permits a broad array of unilateral decisions about land use would be silly in a society where exclusion from the decision making process is itself painful and where a larger community can rapidly reach agreement, either unanimously or by unanimously accepted processes, on uses of land. No system of unilateral decision making can internalize the positive externality attached by individuals in such a society to the process of communal decision making. Similarly, in a society where communal decision making is harmonious and quick, the advantages of free exchange evaporate. The opportunity for private exchange is important only if individuals mistrust the communal decision making process.

Moreover, even if communal decision making produces no positive externalities, free exchange may be an inferior allocation system if transacting parties may not cheaply acquire information relevant to their potential exchanges. Information costs may be high for a variety of reasons. For instance, transacting parties may have no mechanism for ascertaining their own future preferences as consumers of goods they purchase, or the difficulties of eliminating free-riders may lead potential suppliers of information to supply less than the optimal level of information. Further, to the extent that transacting parties are altruistic rather than self-regarding, their preferences may not be independent, but may instead be intertwined with the preferences of others. If the preferences of relevant others are similarly dependent, obtaining information about preferences becomes more complicated, and free exchange might well promote coordination failure and consequent frustration.

The point is that if American landowners could painlessly make communal decisions about land use, or if they faced serious information difficulties, a geometric-box allocation, or any other allocation that provided great opportunity for unilateral decision making and free exchange, would be a curious mechanism for solving the society's coordination problems. By the same token, an allocation that did promote unilateral decision making and free exchange could hardly avoid inclining the society toward a more individualistically oriented social structure. Regardless of whether either factor—social structure or legal framework—can be given precedence, the prevalence of the geometric-box allocation suggests a society that places a premium on individualism and autonomy.

D. *Cross-Boundary Allocations: Relations Between Neighbors*

1. *Of Norms and Neighbors.*—Entitlements that cross record boundaries foster neither private exchange nor individual autonomy. Instead, they promote and indeed require limited cooperation between neighboring landowners. To the extent that these cross-boundary allocations reflect social norms, they suggest the inadequacy of a social and legal model that depicts landowners simply as economic actors seeking, through discrete transactions, to maximize personal material advantage and personal autonomy. Instead, these cross-boundary entitlements capture a somewhat different vision of landowner as neighbor. In imposing on landowners a limited duty to cooperate, the doctrinal framework suggests a conception of neighbors that includes continuing mutual dependence rather than a pattern of discrete and unrelated transactions.

Robert Ellickson's recent study of dispute resolution between ranchers and farmers in Shasta County,

[131] *See* Kennedy & Michelman, *supra* note 114, at 728–729.

California, illustrates this conception of mutually dependent neighbors.[135] Ellickson discovered a strong norm of cooperation among the farmers and ranchers he interviewed. Even cattlemen, Ellickson noted, believe that they should keep their cattle from eating the crops of neighboring farmers. This belief, Ellickson found, was independent of the legal rule governing intrusions, and violation of the norm triggered a set of informal adjustments by farmers and ranchers that involved no assertion of legal claims. The seeming indifference of landowners to their legal rights provides, in Ellickson's view, evidence that legal rules are largely irrelevant constraints upon landowner behavior. Nevertheless, as Ellickson notes, the litigation, albeit infrequent, that has arisen out of Shasta County cattle intrusions has produced decisions consistent with the norm shared by area landowners. My suggestion here is that a large body of land law doctrine incorporates similar norms of neighborliness.

* * *

Legal doctrine never imposes on a landowner an inescapable duty to cooperate with his neighbors. First, a landowner who chooses not to cooperate may, of course, escape his obligation by selling his land. More fundamentally, in most cases, a landowner who takes appropriate steps to apprise his neighbor of his intent not to cooperate can escape an obligation that might otherwise arise. In one sense, then, the duty to cooperate can be viewed simply as a duty to communicate, a duty to warn. Of course, communication is in its own right one of the most basic forms of cooperation. But in a broader sense, imposing on a neighbor the obligation to be explicit if he chooses not to cooperate assumes a norm of cooperation beyond communication alone, a background duty to cooperate that can be limited or shed only if the landowner makes the appropriate communications. And the scope of the landowner's background duty to cooperate with his neighbor itself varies both with the nature of the relationship between the neighboring landowners and with the magnitude of the neighbor's predicament.

2. *Relations That Give Rise to Neighborly Obligations.*—Neighbors exist everywhere. Yet the geometric-box allocation accords to landowners the right to decide, unilaterally, questions relating to use of the landowner's geometric box. Mere ownership of neighboring land, then, does not generally create obligations to cooperate different from the general obligations a landowner might owe to anyone. Instead, a landowner's obligation to share decision making power over his own geometric box appears, for the most part, to arise after a course of dealing between landowner and neighbor, or after a neighbor's own assertions of decision making power have continued without objection over a period of time.

First, consider the effect of a course of dealing. A stranger who seeks access to a roadway across land he does not own generally has no right to access without the landowner's consent. The situation is the same if the "stranger" is a neighbor, or even a landlocked neighbor. But if the landlocked parcel and the neighboring parcel were once held in common ownership, the landlocked owner, at severance, acquired an easement by necessity. The fact of negotiations for sale of the landlocked parcel (or the access parcel) imposes on the owner of the neighboring parcel a choice of obligations. Either he must warn the landlocked owner of his predicament, or else he must cooperate with the landlocked owners by providing access. When the parties have engaged in negotiations, when they have dealt with one another, their failure expressly to resolve the landlocked owner's access rights results in acquisition by the landlocked owner of a right to access over his neighbor's parcel.

Similarly, if a landowner lays gravel over a roadway on his neighbor's land without the neighbor's permission, the neighbor may generally remove the gravel and forbid the landowner to use the roadway. Suppose, however, the two neighbors have had a conversation, however vague, that one landowner construes as a grant of permission to use the roadway. The oral permission does not itself transfer an irrevocable right to use the roadway. Nevertheless, if the landowner lays the gravel, he acquires a right to continue using the roadway unless his neighbor promptly warns him that his action—laying the gravel—will not make the oral permission irrevocable. Once a landowner has dealt with his neighbor, he is obliged to resolve any ambiguities in their dealings that might put the neighbor in a serious predicament.

This treatment of easements by necessity, implication, and estoppel as reflections of neighborly norms does not undermine traditional justifications of these doctrines as contract-like, intent-enforcing devices. Instead, the norms provide a background against which one can justify these cross-boundary

[135] Ellickson, *supra* note 119.

allocations in intent-enforcing terms. * * * [They are] reasonable * * * given the set of cooperative norms I have outlined; it would not necessarily be reasonable against a different set of behavioral norms.

* * *

Compare, now, the obligations of neighbors who have not engaged in a course of dealing. Consider again the landowner who lays gravel over a roadway on his neighbor's land. While the neighbor generally has a right to exclude both the gravel and the landowner who laid it, his right to exclude is lost if not exercised within some period of time. In doctrinal terms, the landowner will have acquired an easement by prescription, or perhaps title to the strip by acquiescence or adverse possession. The neighbor need not be as quick to protect his right as if there had been a prior course of dealing, but even anonymous neighbors owe each other some obligation, albeit more limited, when problems arise.

Note, however, that the improving neighbor does not acquire an immediate right to maintain his encroaching improvements. In those cases where the encroaching improvements are more valuable than gravel on a driveway, the improver might hope to limit the record owner to a remedy of money damages rather than an injunction, but absent either a course of dealing or the passage of time, the improver will remain liable.[153]

Finally, there are some neighborly obligations a landowner assumes merely by purchasing land. First, succession of unrecorded easement rights sometimes results in imposition of undiscoverable cooperative obligations. Second, the obligation not to produce nuisances is an obligation to cooperate with landowners whatever their past or present relationship. Spite fence prohibitions are an example. One who deliberately avoided dealing with a neighbor may still be prohibited from constructing a spite fence that annoys the neighbor. Thus, legal doctrine sometimes imposes an obligation to cooperate even when the particular landowner greatly values his right to ignore his neighbor's wishes.

The obligation to cooperate with neighbors varies, then, with the relationship between the neighbors. While some obligations exist merely by virtue of proximity, others depend on the passage of time. The most developed obligation to cooperate exists between neighbors who have established a course of dealing.

3. *The Scope of Neighborly Obligations.*—No doctrinal rule of land law embodies the biblical command to "love thy neighbor as thyself." A landowner is not obligated to cooperate with his neighbors merely because the neighbors would find cooperation helpful or convenient. Even when there has been an extensive course of dealing between neighboring landowners, courts adhere to record title and the geometric-box allocation unless the neighbor would otherwise face a serious predicament.

Easements are implied, for instance, only in cases of "necessity," cases where the easement-seeker would not readily be able to find substitutes for the easement. No easement by necessity exists if the landowner has alternative access, even if the alternative is substantially less convenient. And where there has been apparent use of a "quasi-easement" prior to severance, establishing an easement by implication still requires some showing of severe financial hardship, often termed necessity.

Easements by estoppel arise only when the easement seeker has made "substantial expenditures" in reliance on his neighbor's permission—outlays that would be valueless to him if his right to use the easement were not secured. Similarly, several of the boundary dispute doctrines generally protect encroachers only when they have made significant investments in the mistaken belief that they have acted on their own land. Even to acquire prescriptive rights, one must establish actual, continuous use of the neighbor's land for a considerable period. Persistent use for a long period, particularly if combined with the improvements likely to make proof of use persuasive, will often be good evidence that the easement-seeker's predicament would be great if he were denied a prescriptive right.

Finally, in spite fence cases, prohibitions tend to be enforced only when the threat to the neighbor's enjoyment of his land is great. Statutes that presume the acceptability of fences under a stated height and vest discretion in courts to permit even higher structures assure that no fences will be prohibited

---

[153] *See* Radin, *Property and Personhood,* 34 STAN. L. REV. 957, 986-987, 1013-1015 (1982), suggesting that "personal" property rights merit (and receive) greater protection than fungible ones. Thus a landowner who has not, through personal use, bound himself up with his boundary strip might, in Radin's hierarchy of property rights, be limited to a liability rule. Radin also suggests that attachments to things can become more intertwined with "personhood" over time. Hence, a landowner who stands by as he sees his neighbor become attached, through use, to the landowner's land, may even lose his right to recover damages. * * *.

absent at least a credible threat to use and enjoyment.

While a landowner is not obligated to cooperate with his neighbor unless the consequences of noncooperation are serious for the neighbor, the landowner is also not obligated to cooperate if cooperation would, measured by community standards, be onerous to him. In general, the landowner by prompt communication may relieve himself of any obligation to cooperate. Even if he fails to communicate, easements by implication, estoppel, and prescription all ripen from intrusions on the dominant estate that have heretofore existed without complaint. In some cases, of course, the landowner's obligation extends beyond communication. Spite-fence rules obligate landowners to refrain from building structures offensive to neighbors. But even then, if the fence builder can establish a "reasonable use" for his fence, he need not cooperate.

CONCLUSION

The geometric-box allocation of land that characterizes much of American land law is frequently tempered by doctrines that allocate rights across boundary lines. Courts frequently justify these doctrines as intent-enforcing mechanisms. Indeed in many situations, the doctrines undoubtedly operate to effectuate party intent. But in other cases, as courts have recognized, the connection between cross-boundary allocations and party intent is largely fictional. Cross-boundary allocations persist in these cases nevertheless. This Article has suggested that the most plausible efficiency justification for these departures from the geometric-box allocation focuses on the bilateral-monopoly relationship in which neighboring landowners frequently find themselves. The cross-boundary allocations operate to allocate rights to neighbors who would appear to value them most, thereby avoiding the need for the neighbors to engage in what might be a costly bargaining process.

I have argued, however, that neither party intent alone, nor efficiency alone, nor both in combination suffice to explain doctrinal departures from the geometric-box allocation. Both the intent-enforcing justification and the efficiency justification rest on a set of assumptions about behavioral norms, assumptions that need not be universally true. In a society where neighbors relate to each other differently, the existing rules might frustrate intent and promote inefficiency.

Indeed, I have suggested that any attempt to justify legal rules exclusively in efficiency terms is fatally flawed. Any intellectually responsible investigation of the efficiency of legal rules must expose the assumptions about social context that underlie the analysis. The difficulty for the economic analyst of law, however, is that most of the data necessary to verify the assumptions are not accessible. Frequently, legal doctrine is the most accessible evidence of social context available to the economic analyst of law. But an argument that uses existing legal doctrine as a contextual foundation for establishing the efficiency of that doctrine is inherently circular. One could, of course, formulate judgments about social behavior to serve as a basis for efficiency analysis without using legal doctrine as a foundation for those judgments. One might instead look to some combination of intuition and experience as a basis for judgments about social context. But if, based on those judgments, doctrine appears not to be efficient, it is at least as likely that the analyst's judgments about social context are in error as it is that judges consistently follow inefficient rules. The argument that existing doctrinal departures from the geometric-box allocation are efficient, then, casts as much light on the social norms of neighborliness as it does on the efficiency of legal rules. Land law doctrine, I have suggested, both reflects and reinforces nonindividualist behavioral norms in relations between neighbors.

Notes

1. The notion of neighborliness appears in many areas of property law. Consider how Sterk might deal with these two problems:

Gifts *causa mortis*: Two cases commonly used in property texts, *Gruen v. Gruen*, 68 N.Y.2d 48, 496 N.E.2d 869, 505 N.Y.S.2d 849 (1986), and *Foster v. Reiss*, 18 N.J. 41, 112 A.2d 553 (1955), involve contests about alleged gifts made when possession of the property did not shift to the donee until the death of the donor. Both disputes were said by the courts to turn on the existence of an intention to make a gift and the completion of delivery to the donee. Can concepts of neighborliness be used within a family context to help determine the wishes of a donor? In both cases there was evidence of estrangement among various members of the family. Does that negate the power of Sterk's analysis?

Tenant Selection: Landlords are sometimes said to have the "right" to select new tenants. Does this notion conflict with the idea of neighborliness? Presumably it does under various civil rights laws limiting the right of landlords to use certain sorts of reasons to refuse people tenancies. But what of *Hudson View Properties v. Weiss*, 109 Misc.2d 589, 442 N.Y.S.2d 367 (Sup. Ct. 1981), in which a lease provision requiring occupancy only by the named tenant was used to terminate the tenancy of a woman who had allowed her male lover to move in? *Compare Braschi v. Stahl Associates Company,* 74 N.Y.2d 201, 543 N.E.2d 49, 544 N.Y.S.2d 784 (1989), in which the male companion of a deceased man was allowed to take over a rent controlled apartment as a successor family member.

2. Can Sterk's notion that a course of dealing over time creates mutual obligations be used to solve problems about the non-divisibility of easements in gross? Consider, for example, *Miller v. Lutheran Conference & Camp Association*, 331 Pa. 241, 200 A. 646 (1938), in which boating, fishing and bathing rights in a lake were said to be assignable, but non-divisible. The result compelled feuding concurrent owners to agree on use of the lake. Would principles of neighborliness now preclude any effort to partition rights in the lake? Compare *Miller* with *Henley v. Continental Cablevision*, 692 S.W.2d 825 (Mo. 1985), in which the existing owners of rights to hang cables on utility poles were allowed to divide that right and grant pole access to a cable television company even though cable television technology did not exist when the utility easements were first created. Would concepts of neighborliness require a new grant of authority to the cable TV company? Or would the existing owners of the easement have the "right" to be "neighborly" and share access with a new venture?

Glen O. Robinson, *Explaining Contingent Rights: The Puzzle of "Obsolete" Covenants*, 91 COLUM. L. REV. 546–548, 560–580 (1991)*

Property law is famous for mysterious doctrines and classifications that seem to defy contemporary justification, and no area of property law better fits this description than the law of servitudes. Much of the problem in contemporary servitude law is the confusion arising from different legal rules associated with easements, real covenants, and equitable servitudes; while nominally distinct, these rules serve the same basic purposes in defining nonpossessory rights over the use of land possessed by others. There is little dispute that the law needs simplification and unification.[2] It simply cannot make sense to have important legal outcomes turn on arcane classifications and labels that serve no purpose other than to confuse law students. But however desirable it may be to have a consistent, unified body of law to deal with servitudes, it would be mischievous to unify the law around the wrong set of models.

The law dealing with real covenants that become "obsolete" because of changed conditions is only a small part of the sprawling, complex body of servitude law, but it is an important part, both practically

[2] See, e.g., *French, Toward A Modern Law of Servitudes: Reweaving the Ancient Strands*, 55 S. CAL. L. REV. 1261, 1264–66 (1982); Reichman, *Toward a Unified Concept of Servitudes*, 55 S. CALIF. L. REV. 1177, 1227–31 (1982).

and conceptually. The changed conditions doctrine is simple and succinct: when conditions have so changed since the making of the covenant that it is no longer possible to secure in substantial measure the benefits originally contemplated, the covenant is unenforceable. Practically, this doctrine is important because it is a common task of courts to review real covenants claimed to be unenforceable by reason of a change in conditions. Conceptually, the doctrine takes us close to the heart of what covenants are all about, and this in turn invites us to examine basic models of contract and property obligations.

* * * I argue that neither model provides a sound foundation for the doctrine.

Looking * * * to the contract model, [I] * * * examine * * * the changed conditions doctrine as a species of conventional frustration of purpose or commercial impracticability doctrines. Framing the question in terms of contract frustration or impracticability principles offers the benefits of added perspectives from a distinct area of the law, but it does not resolve the puzzle, it merely relabels it: instead of asking why the law relieves servient land owners of covenant obligations because of changed conditions, the question focuses on why the law relieves promisors of ordinary contract obligations because of frustration of purpose or impracticability. In the context of conventional contracts, rules governing frustration and impracticability operate as convenient default rules for allocating the burden of risk. Though the rule of changed conditions might be similarly viewed, in practice it appears not to be, suggesting a different, if unarticulated, conception of the rule.

[I] * * * also examine * * * the changed conditions doctrine as an application of the theory of efficient breach.[4] But efficient breach theory does not explain why, when conditions change in the context of real covenants, we need a judicial finding that circumstances provide the occasion for an "efficient" buy out. It is inherent in the efficient breach theory that the market determines when efficient breach is appropriate, not the courts, since it is only when the market provides a superior alternative to performance that it will be practicable for the promisor to pay breach damages and still be better off. More fundamentally, contract scholars have pointed to serious flaws in the efficient breach theory within the general domain of contract law. Though it is possible that the notion of efficient breach may have some validity in the context of obsolete servitudes, that validity depends on introducing public policies that go beyond the policy of efficient contracting.

* * * I examine the property model and its justifications for the changed conditions doctrine, and argue that the implications of the property model are almost as ambiguous as those of the contract model. Property rights are supposed to be more durable and more robust than contract rights: the former are not contingent on the continuation of exogenous circumstances and are not defeasible by payment of "fair market value" in the form of damages. But property rights, like contract rights, are subject to public policy constraints; the changed conditions rule is essentially an application of the policy that prohibits or disfavors restraints on alienability of land because these restraints impede putting land to its highest valued use. Whether that policy can justify the changed conditions doctrine is another matter. I argue * * * that conventional policy statements concerning alienability and the efficient use of land are too facile in suggesting the need for judicial superintendence of land use restrictions. Properly understood, the role of judicial supervision should be to ensure that market transactions for the adjustment or termination of land use restraints are reasonably practicable. Such a role could not justify termination of covenants or other similar restraints on land use so long as an award of damages for destroying the restraint is a feasible alternative, since a damage remedy would allow parties to surmount prohibitive transactions costs.

If * * * [this is] correct, the contingency of real covenants is not convincingly explained by conventional models of property or contract law. Of course, this leaves for consideration the possibility that those models themselves need to be reexamined. Underlying some of the arguments for terminating covenants when external circumstances have changed is the notion that the promisee no longer has any entitlement that deserves protection. This notion may be simply an articulation of contractual expectations and frustration of purpose, but I interpret the argument to embrace a more general theory of contingent rights. * * * I explore this idea briefly and suggest that it is incompatible with accepted concep-

---

[4] Efficient breach theory attempts to explain the general rule of contract remedies—that promises are secured only by an award of damages, not specific performance—as a means of allowing promisors to buy their way out of obligations in order to pursue more efficient alternatives to performance. See R. POSNER, ECONOMIC ANALYSIS OF LAW § 4.8 (3d ed. 1986).

tions of individual rights and obligations. While those conceptions are not beyond rethinking, this little corner of the common law is not a suitable place to start doing so.

[Editor's Note: The contract analysis has been omitted.]

* * *

III. Covenants as Property

Shifting the inquiry from a contract to a property model does not entail a radical alteration in the explanation of covenant rights and obligations, but it does establish some new baselines. In particular, the idea that rights and obligations are shaped by the limited purposes and circumstances that characterize the standard contract model almost drops out of the picture in relation to property rights and correlative obligations.[52] Of course, property rights are created for particular purposes—for instance, to support a home, a trade, or business—but we do not think of property rights as being generally defined by the particular set of purposes that might have prompted their creation. Only when the grant of the property right contains express limitations on use or purposes is it necessary to consider the particular set of purposes that the parties may have entertained when creating the right.[53]

The following simple scenario will illuminate the general point and suggest its application to restrictive covenants. In 1980, Alice buys a home in rural Wonderland County, surrounded by farmland, privacy, and scenic vistas. In 1990, after a new interstate highway has been constructed through a portion of Wonderland, there is a sudden demand for commercial development. Within a few years the entire area will be transformed from an island of bucolic tranquility into a hub of commerce and industry. A commercial entrepreneur enters the scene, proposes to build a shopping mall, and offers to buy Alice's property at current market value, a price greatly in excess of any value the property could command if left in residential use. Alice's original purposes in buying a home in Wonderland have been defeated, for better and for worse—for better because her property value has greatly increased, for worse because it has increased only through the destruction of the noneconomic values that had induced her to move to Wonderland. The defeat of Alice's original purposes in moving to Wonderland has in no way altered her property rights nor altered the obligations of others in relation to them. Alice need not sell her property even if doing so would be the more efficient course of action. The right to resist forced transfers, regardless of their efficiency, is so fundamental to our conception of property rights as to be almost definitional. If Alice refuses to sell, her reasons for refusal are irrelevant; it does not matter whether she is "irrational" in her valuation of the amenities (which will be destroyed whatever she does), or whether she is merely being "strategic" in holding out for a greater share of the surplus value that the buyer will reap from commercial development.

No one who has even a smattering of legal knowledge would dispute this account as a positive statement of the law, and few who believe in private property would dispute it as a normative statement of what the law ought generally to be. Yet it takes only a slight modification to transform this easy case for protecting Alice's property rights into a case for denying them, in whole or in part. Imagine that in acquiring land Alice also became the successor in interest to a restrictive covenant, appurtenant to the land, that prohibits commercial development of adjacent property. Alice's investment in a bucolic environment is thus tied to her ownership of a freehold estate and a covenant servitude on her neighbor's land. Depending upon whether one accepts the Restatement view[55] or the position of other commentators, such as Powell and Rohan,[56] Alice has either a contingent property right in the covenant servitude—contingent upon payment of damages—or

---

[52] The phrase "correlative obligations" here refers to obligations owed to the owner of property rights, not to the obligations of the property owner. In other words, the obligations refer to what Calabresi & Melamed, *Property Rules, Liability Rules, and Inalienability: One View of the Cathedral,* 85 Harv. L. Rev. 1089, at 1106–10 (1972), call a "property rule" for protecting rights.

[53] In this regard, there is a parallel between the changed conditions doctrine and the doctrine of *cy-pres,* which allows charitable trusts to be modified when changed conditions or other circumstances have made the original intent of the grantor impossible or impractical to carry out. * * * However, *cy-pres* assumes the existence of an original, specific purpose that can no longer be fulfilled. Whether one should assume covenants have, or are limited to, such a specific purpose is precisely the question under discussion here.

[55] According to the Restatement of Property, a change in conditions makes it inappropriate to grant specific performance of a covenant, but does not extinguish the obligation and, hence, does not foreclose an award of damages for breach.

[56] These commentators state that while the earlier cases viewed the changed conditions doctrine as simply remedial, more recent cases have viewed it as extinguishing the obligation altogether.

no property right at all when neighborhood conditions change. In Alice's circumstances, which doubtless prevail in many of the changed conditions cases, it probably does not matter what view of the rule is adopted, for Alice has not suffered any economic loss. However, that would also be true if she were compelled to sell her freehold interest to the developer since we hypothesized that the developer's offer exceeded the residential value of her property.

The question of excuse here comes down to a matter of determining "fair" entitlements. Implicit in the above argument about overcoming holdouts is an assumption that the holdout is a strategy for seeking rents to which the promisee has no reasonable entitlement. Defending judicial termination of "obsolete" covenants, Uriel Reichman describes holdouts as "blackmail"[58] and as a "coercive collection of capital payments [that] defeat[s] the very purpose for which the running of promises is recognized" and "transgresses the boundaries for use established by the system [of servitude law]."[59] Describing the holdout demand as "blackmail" implies a moral condemnation that seems excessively self-righteous; one might as readily decry the "opportunism" of those who invoke changed conditions as a basis for excusing obligations that were freely assumed by the promisor. It is important to emphasize here that the subsequent obligor is bound by the covenant not because the restriction is an efficient regulation of land use. Covenants can be efficient vehicles for regulating land use—for avoiding negative externalities or creating positive externalities. However, the legal force of the obligation derives from its voluntary creation and acceptance by parties competent to pursue their own interests and does not depend on its objective efficiency.[61]

A. *Defining Property Rights*

The difference in legal rights here cannot turn on definitions of what is property. Covenants are conventionally characterized as creating property rights, at least when they run with the land. Admittedly, this characterization is frequently a loose one that is made when nothing important turns on it. Where characterization is crucial, as it is in determining whether official termination of a covenant constitutes a taking of property for purposes of eminent domain, for instance, courts are divided. However, a majority of decisions treat the "taken" covenant as a compensable property interest. But rights should not be determined by labels, and it is partly to avoid the tyranny of labels that commentators have sensibly proposed a reformation of servitude law to align it with underlying functional concepts rather than continuing to rely on the artificial labels that have confusingly given us separate rules for things called covenants and things called easements. Still, eliminating the confusion of artificial labels does not alone solve the problem of identifying the correct legal principle to be applied.

Even if covenants or other servitudes are regarded as creating property interests, they do not enjoy the same dignity or the same degree of protection as possessory interests. It is tempting to explain the difference between the two types of property interest as a matter of different expectations: people do not expect their rights in covenants to be as fully protected as they do their rights in freehold estates. Suppose that when Alice purchased her property in Wonderland she expected her home to retain its bucolic splendor indefinitely; she had no expectation that her property would become more valuable because of the encroaching highway and consequential commercial and industrial development. She is nevertheless entitled to as much of the new surplus value brought on by development as she can obtain through tough bargaining with a buyer. Why? Because this is what people expect when they buy a fee simple interest. But when they acquire an interest in someone else's land, in the form of a real covenant, they do not have comparable expectations for this lesser interest; they treat it more as a contract interest than as a property right.

Unfortunately, this argument is circular. The only basis for determining what people expect here is what they have been told to expect based on their legal rights. Apart from this imputed expectation, Alice probably had no expectations with respect to her fee or covenant interests beyond the most rudimentary conception of property. Would Alice suppose that her covenant interest had a different legal status than her freehold interest? We have no basis for speculation on what she knows about the details (often esoteric) of property law and it is irrelevant that her fee estate is a capital investment. The notion of protecting "investment-backed expectations"[66]—

---

[58] *See* Reichman, *supra* note 2, at 1233.

[59] Reichman, *Judicial Supervision of Servitudes*, 7 J. LEGAL STUDIES 139, 157 (1978).

[61] The voluntariness of servitude obligations is challenged by Alexander, *Freedom, Coercion, and the Law of Servitudes*, 73 CORNELL L. REV. 883, 886–92 (1988). * * *

[66] *See* Michelman, *Property, Utility, and Fairness: Com-*

giving special recognition to those expectations that are supported by tangible commitments—is unexceptionable and quite irrelevant here. In Alice's case, the purchase of a fee estate, together with the restrictive covenant servitude interest in adjoining land, represented the acquisition of a package of property interests that comprise, in effect, a single investment. The future development either would not have been capitalized into the asset value of either property interest because it was unforeseen, or if foreseen it would have been capitalized into both property interests. Had Alice paid for the future value of the estate, she also would have paid for the value of the appurtenant covenant with respect to the neighboring land. Hence the investment-backed expectations are the same for the two types of interest.

If the argument from expectations does not explain the difference between the two types of property interest, neither does the converse argument from ignorance or lack of foresight. Stewart Sterk, among others, has argued that limiting the duration of restrictive covenants recognizes the weakness of human planning over the long term.[67] Parties who make long-term covenants restraining the use of property are poor planners with respect to future contingencies. They tend to discount excessively for future events that might render land-use restraints inefficient even from the vantage point of future successors in interest. They also fail either to foresee possible future changes in their own preferences or to make appropriate provision for accommodating these changes.

This is a provocative challenge to the legal recognition of covenants. Perhaps, contrary to conventional wisdom, Ulysses was wrong to have himself bound to the mast by his crew, thereby interfering with his future desire to follow the sirens to his doom. But then again, probably not. How is such a judgment made; or more to the point, when is such a judgment made? The principle of intervention here potentially reaches very far, certainly beyond the realm of land covenants: the limits of human foresight and the possibility of excessive discounting of future events and changing preferences infect all long-term commitments.

Suppose, for instance, that the land developers typically responsible for creating restrictive covenants and the initial buyers of the covenant-burdened property have short-term perspectives. They do not foresee, or at least they deeply discount, the possibility that future land-use patterns will alter the character of the development and thereby frustrate the purpose of the restrictions. Because mistakes in matters of long-term planning are so common, it is natural to view them sympathetically. But sympathy is a poor foundation for constructing legal rights and obligations. If improvident planning provides an excuse from covenant commitments, what about other long-term contractual or property commitments? Could Alice cancel the mortgage she took out because her investment turns out to be less wonderful than she first imagined?

The argument for excuse when surrounding neighborhoods change is no stronger when linked to the need to accommodate endogenous changes in preferences—the preferences of "future selves." First, since endogenous preference changes are a function of personality changes that alter the utility of the earlier commitments, there is no necessary relationship between the legal rule that relates to changes in external contingencies and the altered preferences problem. Second, even if the legal rule were designed to accommodate endogenous preferences, legal commitments like covenants involve other persons. The altered preferences of covenant obligors scarcely provide a credible reason for discharging their obligations.

Even aside from the concern for protecting the legitimate reliance interest of obligees, it is by no means obvious how the law might usefully help obligors adapt to changing preferences. What would be the appropriate strategy for maximizing individual utility? More precisely, what would be the optimal time horizon over which utility would be measured? Plainly, the object of the law cannot be simply to maximize instant satisfaction at discrete moments in time; that would be self defeating. Any planning for future utility (to satisfy future preferences) entails commitments that bind both present and future selves. The propensity to favor present over future satisfactions, after adjusting for risks that may prevent or impair future satisfactions, has been regarded as irrational.[71] But such a propensity does not necessarily imply excessive commitments binding the future self; the preference for present over future utility seems just as likely to produce an

---

ments on the Ethical Foundations of "Just Compensation" Law, 80 HARV. L. REV. 1165, 1233 (1967).

[67] *See* Sterk, *Foresight and the Law of Servitudes*, 73 CORNELL L. REV. 956, 958 (1988); *see also* Alexander, *supra* note 61, at 898.

[71] *See* * * * J. RAWLS, A THEORY OF JUSTICE 295 (1971). * * *

underinvestment in commitments of any kind, present or future. If so, we should not rush to disrupt those commitments people do make—say, in the form of property investments—merely because they may constrain future preferences.

There is little reason to think that legal intervention to reduce long-term commitments can reliably correct the problem in any case. Preference changes do not occur as discrete events, distinctively defining a succession of personalities. Rather, * * * changes in basic preferences are scalar in character. How can the law deal with such gradual change? Are fine adjustments to be made in obligations and rights commensurate with the subtle shifts in preferences? Alice's rights and obligations presumably would decline gradually as a function of the degree to which her preferences changed. Promissory obligations, for instance, would gradually diminish as the original self that made them faded into a future self, rather like the Cheshire Cat in *Alice in Wonderland*, which "vanished quite slowly, beginning with the end of the tail, and ending with the grin, which remained some time after the rest of it had gone." Needless to say, the precise details of such fading rights and obligations would be difficult to work out. How, precisely, does one enforce half of a promise, or one-fourth, or one-tenth, depending upon the degree to which preferences have changed? * * * Alice's remark on observing the Cheshire Cat fade is equally apt: "It's the most curious thing I ever saw in all my life!"

B. *Alienability Restraints*

While ordinary conceptions of property do not provide any convincing argument for the contingency of real covenants, public policy constraints offer somewhat greater promise. Unfortunately, when these constraints are examined closely, the promise is unfulfilled.

Property rights are limited by the state's power of eminent domain, by its police power, and—most relevant to this inquiry—by common law limitations, such as the policy against restraints on alienation. This latter policy is not confined to the explicit prohibition of alienation as it likewise prohibits use restraints so limiting as to be tantamount to an absolute restraint. The typical restrictive covenant involves neither an explicit restraint on alienation nor a restraint on use so substantial as to prevent alienation in fact, but, like all use restrictions, it will impede transferability of land according to the character and scope of the restriction. By unburdening estates of this impediment to alienability, the changed conditions doctrine arguably serves the general policy of promoting alienability. Accepting the policy of free alienability as an explanation of the changed conditions doctrine, however, begs for further justification of the alienability policy itself: to what extent should the courts intervene to promote such transfers *over the objection of parties who have sought to restrain them?*

* * * I will not review the various arguments in detail since the only arguments that have any persuasive power can be collapsed into a single efficiency argument: alienation is essential to promote efficient use of property—notably, but not exclusively, land. In the absence of transferability, property cannot be put to its highest valued use. In this general form, the efficiency argument for transferability is hard to challenge. Still, the principle does not necessarily justify a legal rule against restraints on alienation. A landowner who wishes to donate her land for a limited purpose—for instance, to serve as a school or a park—may grant a fee simple subject to the condition that the land will be used only for that purpose. The grant of such a limited estate is commonly tolerated even though it necessarily restrains future alienability. This tolerance is eminently sensible, as a contrary result would discourage such grants in the first instance—a result that would itself conflict with the policy of promoting alienability.

Even setting aside such cases as perhaps calling for special treatment by virtue of the social importance attached to these particular donative purposes, the promotion of alienability need not entail legal hostility to alienation or use restraints. The case for legal regulation of such restraints properly turns on the practical effects of the restraint on alienability, which may be quite limited. Suppose Alice conveys a fee simple estate to the Wonderland Bird Society for use as a bird sanctuary subject to the condition that, if the land ceases to be used as a bird sanctuary, it is to revert to Alice or her heirs. The practical effect on alienability is the same as if the deed had flatly prohibited a transfer of property, since it is exceedingly unlikely that anyone other than the Society will want the property with such a restriction. The restriction, therefore, might be vulnerable to challenge. However, the legality of the restraint should turn not on an analysis of whether the restricted use effects a restraint on alienation, but on an assessment of the practical feasibility of buying out both the Society's possessory interest and the heirs' future reversionary interest.

The law has long tolerated divided estates despite the fact that they make alienation more costly by making it necessary to bargain with more than one owner in order to obtain a fee simple absolute.

Ensuring alienability requires solving three problems: identifying the parties with the requisite transferable interests, valuing those interests, and arranging for a transactional setting so that negotiations with all parties can take place efficiently and with a minimum of holdouts. These problems are likely to be exacerbated in the case of remote future interests, particularly when they are contingent, making them more difficult to value for purposes of transfer. The only difference between Alice's grant to a bird society and the creation of a life estate, the alienability of which is burdened by the cost of negotiating with the holder of the life interest and the holder of the remainder or reversionary interest, lies in the unlimited duration of Alice or her heirs' contingent interest. The costs of locating successors in interest at some possibly remote period in time or the difficulty of valuing remote contingent interests may justify voiding the restraint. However, it is only when intergenerational restraints substantially increase the difficulty of securing transferable rights that the question whether the restraining hand is dead or alive is of concern. In all cases the problem of alienability can be reduced to one of transactions costs. As the Coase Theorem states, absent transactions costs, parties will bargain to achieve efficient outcomes.[85] If the policy of promoting alienability rests on efficiency considerations, then the legal rule should be no broader than necessary to correct the transactions costs problem.

This proposition still leaves a potentially broad domain for legal intervention. Transactions costs can take a variety of forms. One form is what is sometimes called "market organization costs," or the costs of identifying relevant parties and structuring an effective exchange relationship among them. A broader definition of transactions costs includes not only market organization costs, but also the more dynamic costs associated with the impediments arising from strategic bargaining behavior. If strategic behavior can be as great a threat to efficient bargains as market organization costs, then any legal rule concerned with the efficient transfer of property presumably needs to address that problem.

One way to address strategic behavior impediments to efficient exchange is to enforce the underlying rights that are the subject of exchange with a mere "liability rule," as distinct from a "property rule." My earlier critique of this "efficiency forcing" approach to contract obligations may have even greater force here given that property rights may be accorded more robust protection by means of injunctions or superdeterrent sanctions against interference, such as punitive damages. The law permits invalidation of formal restraints on alienability, but it will not force efficient alienation by allowing a more efficient user to take property in return for damages assessed at fair market value. The policies of promoting alienability and the efficient transfer of property to its highest valued use are trumped by the social interest in preserving property rights and individual autonomy.

Granted, there are exceptions. If, for example, principles of nuisance law are applied in determining the enforceability of restrictive covenants, ordinary property rights protection might be limited by the protection of injured landowners with a "liability rule," or an award of economic damages instead of an injunction. Nuisance law often protects entitlements by damages only, as the famous *Boomer* case illustrates.[89] In *Boomer* both the plaintiff and the defendant had property rights that interacted in a way that necessarily limited each other's full enjoyment of those rights. The court expressly recognized that in protecting the plaintiff's property interest only through an award of damages, it was allowing the defendant to purchase a servitude on the plaintiff's land. By the same token, however, enjoining the nuisance would have given the plaintiff a servitude on the defendant's land. No matter which rule of protection is chosen in nuisance cases, property rights must be compromised. The nuisance context, then, involves competing claims of property rights and no clearly defined baseline by which to determine that one set of rights dominates another. Another way of putting it is to say that the "nuisance" label merely characterizes the fair and efficient adjustment between competing property rights. This is one of the central insights of Coase's original

---

[85] *See* Coase, *The Problem of Social Cost*, 3 J. L. & ECON. 1-15 (1960).

[89] *See* Boomer v. Atlantic Cement Co., 26 N.Y.2d 219, 257 N.E.2d 870, 309 N.Y.S.2d 312 (1970). In *Boomer* the court refused to enjoin a cement plant from operations that produced dirt, smoke, and vibrations that were found to be a nuisance. Instead, it awarded permanent damages to the adjoining property owners. Limiting the protection of an entitlement to damages also can be applied in the converse case, as illustrated by Spur Indus. v. Del E. Webb Dev. Co., 108 Ariz. 178, 494 P.2d 700 (1972); *accord* Calabresi & Melamed, *supra* note 52, at 1105-06; *see also* Rabin, *Nuisance Law: Rethinking Fundamental Assumptions*, 63 VA. L. REV. 1299, 1323 (1977). It is noteworthy, however, that *Spur Indus.* remains a unique case. * * *

analysis. In cases not involving nuisance, property rights are not so conditioned; Alice and her neighbors are not required to maximize the collective value of their land.

Respect for property rights demands discrimination in the selection of cases in the nonnuisance context for which intervention will be appropriate. Multi-party and two-party cases are initially distinguishable. In the simple two-party case a promisee is in a position to hold out for virtually all of the surplus that can be obtained by terminating the restriction. However, this is not a zero-sum game since there can be no gain to *either* party without an agreement. That fact being transparent to each party, one would generally expect them to reach some agreement on division of the surplus, at least in the absence of highly idiosyncratic valuations. When one shifts from this simple two-person bargaining game to an n-person game, the strategic problems are compounded. Each promisee has a veto power over settlement and a threat value equal to the entire surplus, as in the two-person game. At the same time, equal sharing of surplus becomes increasingly less attractive in proportion to the number of parties that have to share. In other words, the opportunity cost of holding out decreases. Thus, even without taking into account the mechanical coordination costs of multi-party bargaining, this situation might be ripe for intervention. Restrictive covenant cases often involve multiple parties and thus might be prima facie candidates for judicial intervention. However, a survey of the reported cases revealed no obvious correlation between application of changed conditions and the presence of a multi-party bargaining problem, so I remain skeptical that this rationale will support the rule as generally applied.

In sum, a satisfactory explanation for the changed conditions doctrine proves to be as elusive under a property model as under a contract model. The argument from alienability is superficially attractive but overstated to the extent that the policy promoting alienability is itself inadequately defined. No doubt there are social efficiency arguments for removing artificial restraints on alienability, but determining what is an artificial restraint is not simple. The notion that we should correct market impediments to efficient exchange of property is unexceptionable, but this does not entail forcing bargains simply because it is perceived that the property owner is holding out for more than a "fair" value. Courts have no common law police power to rearrange property rights to effect socially preferred land uses—at least not if one adheres to the conventional liberal framework of rights, a qualification that calls for a final comment.

IV. Expanding the Domain of Contingency

A principal burden of the argument thus far has been to show that the doctrine of changed conditions cannot be explained simply by reference to general principles or policies of contract or property rights. Parallels do exist in the contract law doctrines of frustration of purpose and commercial impracticability; and the policy of promoting alienability suggests a property rationale for terminating covenants deemed obsolete by reason of changed conditions. But these doctrines represent exceptions to the principles of obligation that underlie both property and contract law, exceptions too limited to justify the general contingency of restrictive covenants.

Nevertheless, it is reasonable to inquire further into these general principles of contract and property rights to ask whether these principles themselves need to be reconsidered. If the contingent nature of covenant rights and obligations is at odds with the traditional conception of noncontingent property rights, perhaps it is the latter and not the former that needs to be adjusted. If restrictive covenants expire when surrounding neighborhood conditions change, perhaps all contracts should expire in response to changed conditions. So too with property rights: when altered conditions terminate Alice's scenic interests, formerly secured by a restrictive covenant, they could also terminate whatever interests are secured by fee simple ownership as well.

In the realm of contract law greater contingency is certainly conceivable. Some scholars have argued for a liberalization of excuses by reason of frustration or impracticability. One might extend such liberalization, for example, by reducing the burden of proof on promisors seeking excuse—making a prima facie case for excuse turn on a simple showing of changed conditions. Making contract rights more contingent would increase contracting costs as parties would be forced to rely on less efficient alternative measures to secure their reliance interests, but contracting would still continue.

Interjecting greater contingency within the realm of property law would be more radical. Certainly anyone who believes in the institution of private property is likely to resist the idea that general property rights should be terminable whenever there is a material change in the conditions that prevailed when the rights were acquired. Even the more modest idea that such rights should be secured only by a liability rule cuts deeply against the grain of conventional assumptions about property rights. Again, however, it is quite conceivable. Framing the notion in functional terms, one would simply say that a particular "stick"—the "holdout stick"—has been removed from the bundle of sticks that, in the aggregate, constitute property.[96] Contemporary definitions of property might be relevant evidence of a present social consensus as to which rights and powers should be included in the bundle of rights we call property, but ultimately rights must be determined by reference to political principles and social policy.[97]

Why do property owners have the right to resist the transfer of rights or to hold out for above-market value? "Holdout rights" are not unlimited. They are subject to the state's eminent domain and police powers. And, in the case of conflicting property rights in nuisance disputes, a forced exchange of property rights may be effected by permitting one owner to buy out the other on the basis of market value, as in the *Boomer* case. The usual justifications for these limitations are a combination of economic efficiency—minimizing transactions costs to facilitate efficient exchange—and community welfare—allowing private rights to be trumped by social welfare needs. To be sure, these limitations are exceptional. In eminent domain situations the community welfare trump requires an authoritative action by the state, which at least in theory implies a paramount public purpose. In the private nuisance case there is no authoritative state assertion of a paramount public purpose, but the court's choice of a liability rule instead of a property rule may be taken to imply that there is a public purpose in allowing the nuisance to continue. The run-of-the-mill property transaction does not involve any authoritative expression of a paramount social interest. Still, there might be implied social interests. If alienability is such a strong public policy, it might trump holdout rights.
* * *

One might put the point this way: Alice's refusal to sell her estate in Wonderland at market value is a kind of "nuisance": she is not doing anything to cause positive harm to her neighbors, but she is "in the way." The community "wants," that is, it has registered an economic demand for, a new shopping mall and Alice is impeding that demand by holding out. The obvious analogy in nuisance law would be to the *Spur Industries* case,[104] in which the presence of a feedlot interfered with the welfare of Del Webb's adjacent "Sun City," a privately developed community. Because the feedlot antedated the community, the court deemed it to have some entitlements, but refused to allow those entitlements to stand in the way of community "progress." Del Webb was ordered to pay for the costs of moving the feedlot; in effect the developer was given a power of eminent domain.

Perhaps the most noteworthy thing to be said about *Spur Industries'* innovative approach is that, despite nearly two decades of academic publicity, it appears not to have been emulated elsewhere even within the context of a traditionally defined "nuisance." And no one to my knowledge has suggested making it the cornerstone of a new theory of contingent property rights. Had the feedlot not emitted an offensive odor, which served to bring it (just barely) within a traditional nuisance framework, I doubt that it would have occurred to the court to force a transfer of property rights in order to put the property to its more highly valued use.

A robust application of *Spur Industries* would destroy some rather deep-seated notions and social expectations about private property. Not only would such a private eminent domain power encourage individuals to bypass markets, it would also encourage them to ride roughshod over private preferences that are not fully validated by markets. At the very least it would discourage people from investing in property if their personal satisfactions were not congruent with community norms, and hence not fully backed by market valuation. Alice might still buy her estate in Wonderland, but she would not likely indulge any personal eccentricities in doing so or in developing the property, thereby demonstrating the undermining of a central ground for property rights in a liberal society—the recognition of individual preferences.

It is an exaggeration to say that allowing forced exchange legitimates theft. There would still be legal restrictions on the right of a buyer to force an exchange. For instance, a requirement that a buyer must make a "good faith" offer to purchase property at some prescribed premium above the proven market value would limit this private eminent domain

[96] The bundle concept of property rights can be traced back at least as far as Hohfeld, but it was the later legal realists who made this concept the standard framework for modern property theory. *See* Grey, *The Disintegration of Property*, 22 NOMOS: PROPERTY 69, 85 n.40 (1980).

[97] At least this much of the realist perspective seems to be beyond argument, *see, e.g.*, Cohen, *Dialogue on Private Property*, 9 RUTGERS L. REV. 357, 374, 378–79 (1954).

[104] Spur Indus. v. Del E. Webb Dev. Co., 108 Ariz. 178, 494 P.2d 700 (1972).

power to cases in which there is a substantial surplus to be realized from the transfer, and this surplus would be shared with the seller. And the private eminent domain power might be limited to certain kinds of land, for instance nonresidential land that is unlikely to have any idiosyncratic value to its owner. But defining all of the requisite restrictions that would make such a private eminent domain power even remotely acceptable would be a vexing task. That fact, coupled with the fact that forced exchange prompts an analogy to theft, is not without social significance. It suggests that the idea of non-contingent private property has a powerful hold on our moral intuition.

Implicit in the foregoing argument is the premise that market-created rights—and private ordering generally—provide the presumptively correct baseline for legal policy. Within the conventional framework of the common law, this notion is inherent in the jurisprudence of contract and property law: rights and obligations created by consenting adults are treated as legitimate unless there is some special showing of market failure, not in general, but in the specific case.

It is always possible to spot market failures if one both looks hard enough and measures "failure" against some idealistic state. Indeed, it is child's play to show that real-world markets do not work in the way they are depicted in elementary economics textbooks. There are imperfections in the competitiveness of the market: there are externalities, strategic behavior problems, or other inefficiencies. The question that must always be asked after such failures have been found is whether this finding justifies a judicial alteration of market-created rights. Responses naturally vary depending on one's ideological predilection. One type of response is incrementalist and cautious: attempt to deal with the specific flaws with measured reform but only if the flaws create significant mischief to social welfare. For instance, one might deal with the problem of strategic holdouts by property owners by forcing them to sell, but only if holdouts create demonstrable social costs. A different response is provided by the radical critic who sees incrementalism as a timid acquiescence in a flawed system. For these critics, who essentially reflect the perspective of the critical legal studies movement, the problem is not simply a matter of patching up a few holes in an otherwise fair and efficient system, but rather a matter of reforming basic conceptions of private ordering.

Something like this latter view underlies a recent critique of servitude law by Gregory Alexander.[111] While most discussions of servitude reforms start from the premise that servitudes are the product of presumptively correct private choices, Alexander would start from the opposite premise, that servitudes reflect a lack of choices by the owners of the burdened lands, who are "coerced" into accepting obligations by the absence of a satisfactory array of market options. People are "coerced" by the bundling of distinctive units of choice: purchasers of burdened property are forced to accept the burdens that they do not want in order to get the property that they do want. But the fact that the market is not perfectly calibrated to countless individual preferences can be considered "coercive" only in a very special and misleading way. Virtually all goods are sold as an aggregation of physically separable units that some buyers would prefer to have unbundled. Sometimes this bundling is seen as a sign of market failure, and possibly a concern of the antitrust laws, but that concern is rightly reserved for special cases in which monopoly power is suspected and the bundling is not justified by efficiency considerations.

In contrast, Alexander seems to believe that any failure to meet each buyer's preferences is tantamount to coercion. He sees no difference in kind or degree between market constraints and legal coercion (the intervention of the law to overturn or ignore market choices), such as private covenants and public zoning for example. Such a conflation of private and public coercion is surely wrong. It may be that if all the property within, say, a county were subject to a set of use restrictions, then the buyer's choices would be as fully constrained as they would be by a comparable county-wide zoning restriction. But such cases are hard to find. And even assuming that privately imposed controls are no different from public controls, the consequences of such an assumption would not be obvious. Certainly it would not follow that we should rely more on public than private controls; if lack of choice is the problem in the former case, as Alexander suggests, it is no less a problem in the latter.

Alexander also decries the mutually constrained "bilateral monopoly" position in which persons find themselves when they seek to bargain out of restrictive covenants or similar burdens, and suggests that

---

[111] *See* Alexander, *supra* note 61.

if the law intervened it might help both parties to the bargain to achieve their objectives. I am skeptical. Forcing exchanges in the name of efficiency might be appropriate for situations in which there are important social interests in removing the burdens on land, but the idea that the law should routinely intervene to help the parties realize their supposedly true objectives is too facile an excuse for interfering with private autonomy. Granted, parties may defeat their own interests by engaging in self-defeating strategic behavior—"chicken games" and the like—but anyone who thinks it possible to specify legal rules that will prevent such games without seriously compromising private ordering should be required to draft a "Uniform Code of Proper Bargaining" to prove its feasibility. It is not enough to chant the words "bilateral monopoly," as if the phrase possessed some talismanic power to solve a problem that is ubiquitous in private bargaining. Virtually every negotiation over the terms of exchange between two persons holding distinctive property rights could be described as a bilateral monopoly to the extent that each party controls ("monopolizes") the terms upon which she will exchange rights. This seems to me to be an insufficient basis upon which courts should create a bargain for the parties.

The desire to intervene in transactions to further socially efficient results is natural and appealing, but also potentially mischievous. Given reasonably functioning markets, we have no a priori reason to think that making rights less secure would promote efficiency. So, too, with promoting fairness: despite the perceptions of Alexander and others that existing rights are coercive, we have no reason to think that they systematically favor one class or oppress another. The holdout phenomenon that some scholars decry is not inherently a tool of wealthy property owners. Quite to the contrary, it is more likely to aid the ordinary Alices of the world than the Del Webbs; before we take away their rights, we need to consider who we help by doing so.

CONCLUSION

I began this Article with a reference to "mysterious doctrines" that permeate the law of property in general and servitudes in particular. It was perhaps misleading to imply that the changed conditions doctrine presents such a mystery, as if to say that it defied rational explanations. In fact, there are a number of explanations that can be derived from general principles of property and contract law, and it was my intent to suggest not that these explanations are irrational, but merely that they are unsatisfactory.

From a contract model of rights and obligations the changed conditions doctrine is commonly seen as an application of frustration/impracticability doctrine. However, the latter is best understood as a default rule for efficient allocation of risks between parties who have made no explicit provision for such. While one might interpret the changed conditions doctrine as a default rule, it is noteworthy that no one seems to see it that way. Principles of contract remedies likewise do not explain the doctrine. On the Restatement view that changed conditions affect only the remedy, not the underlying covenant obligation, the theory of efficient breach seems relevant, but proves too much in suggesting that a judicial finding of changed conditions is superfluous. A more fundamental objection to applying efficient breach theory is that the theory itself is flawed because it rests on facile assumptions about the adequacy of damages as a measure of the value of contract performance and logically incorrect assumptions about the ability of the law to circumvent strategic bargaining behavior merely by altering the parties' respective entitlements.

Viewing real covenants as property only deepens the puzzle over the contingency of covenant rights and obligations. Other forms of property are not defined according to whether the conditions under which they were created remain unchanged. True, property rights are governed by legal rules and principles designed to promote social welfare, including the principle of free alienability. Covenants can claim no exemption from such general principles, but, by the same token, there is no obvious reason why covenants should be specially burdened. Covenants are not inherently more restrictive of alienability than are limited estates in land. The appropriate inquiry here is a practical one: do the restraints on alienability create excessive cost burdens for market transactions?

Framing the analysis of obsolete covenants in terms of conventional contract or property models presumes that these models provide the legitimate baseline for evaluation. It is always possible to think about rights and obligations in ways quite different from those that underlie conventional models. Specifically, it is possible to imagine greater contingency in all rights and obligations. Although it has been argued that this would accommodate changing personal preferences, it is hard to see how this could be accomplished without also undermining personal commitments. The long-term effect of greater contingency seems clear: private ordering would suffer from the absence of stable expectations. Whether we should be concerned about undermining private ordering is, I suppose, a fair follow-up question, but one that involves a level of political inquiry too large to be accommodated within the limited domain of real covenants.

Note

At the end of his article, Robinson leaves us without a strong suggestion about an appropriate model to use for evaluating termination of servitudes. He does, however, suggest that greater contingency in rights and obligations would "undermine personal commitments" and disturb "stable expectations." Is Robinson here (instinctively perhaps) reverting to contract and property talk, voicing contract law based concerns about using frustration of a servitude's purpose to undermine commitment to a contract and property law based concerns about alterations in wealth allocations destabilizing investment expectations? Are there any other models we might use?

Gregory S. Alexander, *Freedom, Coercion, and the Law of Servitudes,* 73 CORNELL L. REV. 883, 890–902 (1988)*

* * *

III
TWO DEBATES IN SERVITUDE LAW

Two issues in American servitude law have been most controversial in recent years; first, whether to retain the traditional touch and concern rule; and, second, whether to recognize a doctrine for terminating or modifying all types of servitudes on the basis of changed conditions. I critique the free choice/coercion dichotomy by demonstrating that both sides claim that their position enhances freedom of choice on each of these issues. I contend that most legal discourse continues to commit the formalist mistake of attempting to derive determinate solutions from an abstract principle, in this case, the principle of individual freedom of property owners.

A. The Touch and Concern Debate

Suppose that a promisor and promisee created a restrictive covenant, indicating clearly their intent to bind all successors, based on their mutual belief that some negative externality would exist if the land were unbounded and that the harmful externality would be of equal concern to all subsequent owners. It turns out, however, that the promisor's successor does not see things the same way and prefers that the land be unbounded. If the successor nevertheless buys the land, should he be bound by the servitude because he has chosen it? Or is there room in the concept of individual choice for a filtering device like touch and concern?

1. *The Problem of Indeterminacy in Freedom of Choice*

Recent arguments over whether to retain the common-law touch and concern requirement illustrate how the liberal freedom/coercion dichotomy leads to stalemate. On behalf of retaining the rule, Uriel Reichman has argued that the rule enhances individual free choice. He states: "Servitudes are a kind of private legislation affecting a line of future owners. Limiting such legislative powers to an objective purpose of land planning eliminates the possibility of creating modern variations of feudal serfdom."[21] This familiar argument appears in virtually

---

[21] Reichman, *Toward a Unified Concept of Servitudes,* 55 S. CAL. L. REV. 1177, 1233 (1982).

every instance where the question of dead hand control appears. It supposes that the problem of justice between generations can be resolved by enforcing the freedom of choice principle. Unless we have some device like touch and concern, the argument goes, the dead hand of past generations will deny future generations the same freedom enjoyed by their ancestors, just as feudal institutions like the fee tail (at least before the invention of common recovery) made it possible for fathers to lock their sons' ownership interests in servitude.

On the other side of the ledger, Professor Epstein offers another familiar argument. He attacks the libertarian defense of the touch and concern requirement as standing freedom on its head. The touch and concern requirement, like the Rule Against Perpetuities and the doctrine against restraints on alienation, is a collective restriction on the current owner's freedom of choice. Epstein argues:

> To say . . . that particular covenants must be struck down in the name of freedom is to confound the usual understanding on which freedom claims are based. . . . Insistence upon the touch and concern requirement denies the original parties their contractual freedom by subordinating their desires to the interests of future third parties, who by definition have no proprietary claim to the subject property.[24]

Both arguments present plausible interpretations of the notion of securing freedom of choice for land owners. Reichman's interpretation seeks to maximize the liberty interests of all owners, present and future. Epstein's interpretation maximizes the freedom of the only owner at the time the servitude is created.

The choice between these two contradictory interpretations cannot be based on an abstract commitment to freedom of choice itself; both choices are simultaneously freedom-enhancing and coercive. Epstein and Reichman want to sanctify a subjective political choice—the allocation of power between generations of owners—by a linguistic gambit, namely, objectifying their political preference as choice maximizing and therefore more consistent with the general policy of servitude law.

The same problem besets the law-and-economics analysis of the touch and concern requirement. Some legal economists argue that the purpose of running covenants is to effectuate intent by enforcing promises that, absent transactions costs, would have survived successive rounds of bargaining among subsequent generations of owners. The touch and concern requirement function filters out those restrictions that subsequent owners would not have agreed to had there been actual negotiations. This analysis reconciles touch and concern with freedom of choice to the extent that restrictions that would not have survived subsequent negotiations are not chosen.

But one can also see this rationale as choice-denying rather than choice-enforcing. This is, I take it, the thrust of Professor Epstein's attack on the touch and concern rule. If the subsequent owner of a parcel burdened with a servitude bought the land with notice of the term, she has chosen it. Moreover, so long as there was notice, the subsequent owner who takes land subject to an unwanted servitude presumably has been compensated for that term by an appropriate discount in the purchase price. Presumably, the promisor initially received the discount from the promisee and simply passed it on to his successor. This discount must have been equal to the servitude's worth to the promisee or else he would not have agreed to it. Hence, the touch and concern filter is unnecessary because there was no coercion in any of the relationships.

2. *Notice and Consent*

I now examine Professor Epstein's argument deriving consent from notice. Several reasons make notice alone an insufficient guarantee of choice. One immediate reason, the purchaser who acted without actual notice that the land she purchased was affected with an obligation may still be held to have had notice. The legal notion of constructive notice, provided by the land recording system, by the surrounding circumstances, which may place on the purchaser a duty to inquire about the existence of restrictions[28] creates this notice. If we base an inference of consent on this type of notice we greatly diminish the meaning, and the normative power, of consent. Ordinary understandings tell us that consent so inferred looks remarkably similar to the sort of collectively-imposed decision that Professor Epstein and others worry about.

The phenomenon of distortion in the formation of preferences presents a second and more serious

---

[24] Epstein, *Notice and Freedom of Contract in the Law of Servitudes,* 55 S. CAL. L. REV. 1353, 1359–60 (1982). * * *

[28] For an extreme example of binding subsequent land purchasers by inquiry notice, *see* Sanborn v. McLean, 233 Mich. 227, 206 N.W. 496 (1925) (subsequent purchaser bound by inquiry notice despite the fact that the servitude was "implied" from a common plan which itself was not expressed in any of the paperwork).

objection to the equation of consent with notice. Enforcement of servitudes raises familiar questions about when and on what basis it is appropriate for legal regulators to interfere with private preferences. Professor Epstein believes that the legal system should enforce preferences unless they generate harms (externalities) to other people. Because Epstein believes servitudes create few externalities, he concludes that courts should rarely interfere with servitudes. This general attitude towards the preferences expressed in servitudes leads him specifically to oppose the touch and concern requirement, which prevents servitudes from running with the land ab initio, and the changed conditions doctrine, which terminates initially enforceable servitudes some time after their creation. In Epstein's view, so long as purchasers from the original contracting parties had legal notice of the servitude they chose to accept it and courts should therefore not interfere with that expressed preference.

Several serious problems arise with the view that the only valid ground for collective interference with the enforcement of private preferences is to prevent negative externalities. First, the concept of externalities itself notoriously is ambiguous. This objection would hardly be worth mentioning but for Professor Epstein's emphasis on the importance of legal certainty ex ante to facilitate private planning. A legal norm whose operation depends on whether a negative externality exists is unlikely to achieve the certainty that Professor Epstein regards as indispensable to private ordering.

More importantly, externalities do not represent the only justificatory basis for legal interference with private preference. Paradoxically, pathology in the process of preference formation may also justify legal intervention as necessary to protect the autonomy of individual preferences. In other words, the purchaser's expressed preference for the servitude may not be the product of autonomous choice. For example, one of the phenomena that social choice theorists have observed as distorting individual preferences is the adaptation of preferences to what people think (correctly or incorrectly) they can get. Most residential developments today include a variety of restrictions of owner use and behavior. The pervasive inclusion of restrictions in residential developments may reflect not the similarity of preferences held by thousands of purchasers but the purchasers' belief (based on the widespread use of detailed restrictions) that ownership in a residential development without a particular restriction is unavailable. The consequence of this pervasive belief is that one cannot simply assume that restrictions are included in deeds because purchasers want them there. Maximizing the autonomy of purchasers' preferences may therefore require legal interference with their nominal preferences.

The argument that pathological preference formation justifies non-enforcement of preferences, unlike Epstein's argument, recognizes and responds to the possibility that individual preferences as expressed through the act of purchase with legal notice of an encumbrance may be defective. Rather than taking preferences as exogenous givens, this argument recognizes that preferences are social constructs.

Related to the problem of distorted preferences is what Mark Kelman has called the "bundling" problem.[34] The promisor's successor may have bought the land even though she did not want it with the restriction because she was unable to control all of the theoretically available terms. The familiar argument at this point runs that if she was aware (perhaps meaning that she had actual, as opposed to constructive notice) of an unwanted restriction and nevertheless purchased the package offered by the promisor, then she must have been compensated for the unwanted servitude by a discount in the purchase price. But we should not be too quick to make that assumption. In a complex transaction the successor (S) may not have adequately focused on the servitude term. S might have demanded a higher level of compensation for the servitude term, had that term been negotiated individually rather than as part of a package containing many items.

A predictable reaction to this argument is that S's failure adequately to discount the price she pays for the land burdened with the servitude represents irrational behavior. But that is just the point; people do engage in irrational behavior. How can contractarians reconcile shrugging off irrational behavior with the principle of maximizing individual choice? Does not the commitment to maintaining servitude law as a realm of uncoerced activity require that we take such behavior into account? Why is it any less a form of coercion to enforce a restriction against an individual who was inadequately compensated for it, simply because we say his deficient evaluation of the entitlement represented by the servitude was "irrational"?

---

[34] M. KELMAN, A GUIDE TO CRITICAL LEGAL STUDIES 107-09 (1987).

Contractarians might argue that the behavior just described is exceptional and that rules should be based on the typical case rather than on aberrations. But this argument fails to respond to my point. The significance of the bundling problem is not the level of its incidence (although I am prepared to argue that it is not aberrational at all) but its undermining effect on the model of free choice and coercion as located in separate, mutually exclusive spheres of activity. It casts doubt on our ability to make easy distinctions between legal options that are choice-enhancing and those that are coercive.

3. *Objective Tests and Denial of the Self*

Before leaving the touch and concern requirement debate I want to address one additional argument to illustrate how choicelessness intrudes upon the discourse of individual freedom in mainstream legal reasoning. Reichman argues that the touch and concern rule is, and should be, used to enforce those promises that are "objectively intended to promote land utilization." He contrasts this with Charles Clark's subjective test according to which benefits and burdens should run to assignees if the servitude affects the landowner's valuation of his land.[37] To demonstrate the desirability of an objective approach to touch and concern, Reichman contrasts two hypothetical fact situations involving similar restrictions. In one, an owner extracts from his neighbor a promise that the neighbor will not drink alcoholic beverages on the Jewish Sabbath. In the second, a developer imposes in all deeds within a neighborhood a restriction against running a tavern in the neighborhood. Reichman asserts that only in the second case does the servitude touch and concern because the restriction against alcohol in that situation is objectively associated with the owners' use and enjoyment of their land. Conversely, the restriction against alcohol consumption in the first case, according to Reichman, was imposed only for "ideological" reasons. Viewed objectively, such restrictions are not connected with the effective use of land. They do not touch and concern, and therefore should not be considered servitudes.

Professor Epstein has pointed out that Reichman's analysis begs the question of why the first restriction is unrelated to land development. Any objective test for touch and concern, Epstein states, "presupposes that we have some collective vision of what [the private land system] is supposed to do." According to Epstein, then, Reichman transparently has stuffed the proverbial rabbit into the hat.

Here, Epstein is clearly right. Requiring that a restriction be "objectively" intended to promote land utilization creates choicelessness under the guise of respecting private intentions. The objective perspective constructs private intentions from a set of beliefs which are supposedly generally held in the community. This conception of private intention, however, reduces the subjective individual will to the collective will. By supposing that each person has the tastes of everyone else, this conception subordinates individual autonomy to the forces external to the self. It is a particularly insidious form of coercion because it purports to effectuate private intentions rather than acknowledging that private volition is being sacrificed for the sake of some collective good. Here, again, free choice and coercion represent contradictory discourses that are simultaneously deployed in mainstream legal argumentation.

The touch and concern controversy belies the attempt to depict servitudes as a noncollective, nonpolitical (and therefore, in liberal ideology, presumptively more legitimate) instrument by which to resolve social disputes among landholders. The easy availability of the notions of free choice and coercion in the arguments establishes as an impossible dream the vision of a purely private, uncoercive regime of servitude law.

Thus far, I have used the touch and concern controversy to undermine the view that servitude law is, or can be, a realm of private ordering, a legal regime that enables conflicting preferences for the use of land to be made without the intrusion of substantive public norms. With respect to the issue itself, I favor retaining the touch and concern requirement as a discretionary norm, the purpose of which is to protect subsequent purchasers who have behaved foolishly and to prevent promisors and their successors from behaving opportunistically. However, we should resist the temptation to lapse into the familiar imagery that would describe touch and concern as a limited instance of collective regulation that somehow compatibly coexists with a general body of doctrine constructed on the foundation of individual freedom of choice. That account (like its counterparts in contract law depicting the unconscionability and promissory estoppel doctrines as collectivist "exceptions" that coexist with the grundnorm of private ordering) represses the pervasive

[37] C. Clark, Real Covenants and Other Interests Which "Run with Land" 111 (1929).

presence within legal thought and practice of irreducible, irremediable, irresolvable conflict. The standard doctrinal imagery of an individualistic core with collectivistic exceptions lulls us into supposing that only a limited number of doctrines engenders painful and embarrassing conflicts of social visions. However settled the doctrinal practice appears to be, such conflicts only lie beneath the surface. We would be better off acknowledging those conflicts and trying to work them out openly and continuously rather than freezing doctrinal practices that entrench power arrangements. Touch and concern represents, as its critics fear, a destabilizing doctrine, but that is why it should be embraced, not spurned.

While the substance of touch and concern ought to be retained, I find it impossible to justify preserving its metaphysical packaging. The phrase "touch and concern" continues to beguile even astute property specialists into believing that it has some objective meaning. Imagine how many ordinary nonlawyers similarly have been tricked. I favor finding a new bottle for the old wine, preferably a bottle whose label indicates its discretionary and normative character.

B. *The Changed Conditions Debate*

Perhaps the most controversial issue facing the new restatement is whether to recognize a general changed conditions doctrine for terminating servitudes. Professor French supports such a doctrine, but several other scholars, including Professor Epstein, have argued strongly against it. As in the case of the touch and concern rule, the debate has been framed by the free choice/coercion dichotomy.

The changed conditions doctrine responds to the problem of obsolescence in servitude law. The obsolescence problem is not peculiar to servitudes; it is a function of duration, and it exists in all legal arrangements that have extended time horizons, including long-term trusts and relational contracts. The dilemma posed by obsolescence for liberal legal thought is how legal intervention that terminates the obsolete property interest can coexist with the basic commitment to private volition.

In one sense, it seems easier to reconcile with the commitment to individual autonomy legal intervention based on changed conditions than legal interference based on a requirement like touch and concern. Personality, identity, and self are constituted by context. As Professor Sterk points out,[43] the self that is affected by subsequent, unforeseeable events differs in significant respects from the self that made the initial commitment to the servitude. Furthermore, these different selves have different preferences. The point here is not that the legal system should always respond to regret. Rather, the argument is that changed conditions have caused preferences to lose their force. By contrast, the touch and concern requirement, insofar as it permits escape from a servitude obligation even though conditions remain unchanged, allows parties to avoid the consequences of a bad choice.

The theory of imputed intent presents a similar argument by which to reconcile this form of legal intervention with individual preferences. Advocates of the changed conditions doctrine and its analogies in other corners of property law (such as the *cy pres* doctrine in the law of trusts) have argued that we should impute to the original contracting parties an intention that the covenant expire if and when it becomes valueless. Posner's analysis of the dead hand problem is a particularly clear example of this transformation of collective interference into private volition:

> [T]he dilemma whether to enforce the testator's intent or to modify the terms of the will in accordance with changed conditions since his death is often a false one. A policy of rigid adherence to the letter of the donative instrument is likely to frustrate both the donor's purposes and the efficient use of resources.[46]

One can plausibly respond, however, that this argument is disingenuous; it stands the notion of private choice on its head. As in the touch and concern context, the argument constructs a conception of the self on the basis of the will of the group. By identifying individual preference with the aggregate preferences of a group at a later time, it denies the autonomy of the self.

At the same time an element of choicelessness arises when servitudes have become obsolete that makes a changed conditions doctrine, or something like it, attractive. The servitude's obsolescence means that those burdened by the servitude have strong incentives to buy the entitlement from the beneficiary. Even assuming that the transaction costs are otherwise low, the exchange may not occur because of strategic behavior by the beneficiary, who knows the burdened landowner has strong incentives, and by the burdened landowner, who knows that the

---

[43] Sterk, *Foresight and the Law of Servitudes*, 73 CORNELL L. REV. 956, 958 (1988). * * *

[46] R. POSNER, ECONOMIC ANALYSIS OF LAW § 18.3, at 390 (2d ed. 1977). * * *

beneficiary can realize the entitlement's value in an exchange with him. A pathology of choice characterizes this familiar situation of bilateral monopoly. Neither side experiences the liberation of an unconstrained market; both sides feel themselves in servitude to each other. Formally, of course, both sides are unconstrained: they are free to walk away. But they do experience constraint. Intervention from an external source, by way of outright termination or, perhaps, as Professor French suggests, through modification,[47] may enable the parties to do what they lack the power to do themselves.

IV
Coercion in the Private Sphere: The Case of Discretionary Servitudes

One of the most striking things about recent commentary on servitudes is how scholars, in discussing the problem of coercion, tend to focus exclusively on public coercion, while denying or minimizing the phenomenon of private coercion. One familiar objection to the touch and concern doctrine and the changed conditions doctrine, for example, focuses on the fact that they involve judicial discretion. Legal scholars worry that judicial discretion will be a source of coercion of private actors even when the court attempts to act in good faith.[49] Their argument for limiting judicial discretion through abolition of the touch and concern and change conditions doctrines represents yet another instance of the naive version of the free choice/coercion dichotomy. I do not wish to argue that no reason exists to worry about judicial discretion. Rather, I want to suggest that the problem of discretion is no less worrisome when it appears in the form of private, "discretionary" servitudes than when it appears in judicial form.

Developers of planned residential communities commonly reserve to themselves or to homeowners' associations discretion in enforcement of restrictive covenants that are included in all of the deeds to lots in the development.[50] * * * [T]he discretionary power of the developer or the homeowners' association creates a serious risk of coercion.

* * *

[T]he gap between formal and experience assent undermines the vision of unconstrained choice in the private sphere. Residents may have evaluated inadequately the discretionary power term. * * * Moreover, as a practical matter, developers possess considerably more market power than residents.

* * *

If discretion is seen as a threat to individual autonomy, then there is no less reason for us to worry about its dominating effect when exercised in the private sphere than when exercised by courts under the rubrics of touch and concern or changed conditions.

Note

Robinson, in the prior article, criticizes Alexander for seeing "no difference in kind or degree between market constraints and legal coercion (the intervention of the law to overturn or ignore market choices), such as private covenants and public zoning for example. Such a conflation of private and public coercion is surely wrong. * * * Certainly it would not follow that we should rely more on public than private controls; if lack of choice is the problem in the former case, as Alexander suggests, it is no less a problem in the latter." Is Robinson correct? Or is there a difference between "coercion" imposed by a developer on present and future purchasers of a condominium and "coercion" imposed by the state to limit the sort of covenants that may be created or the time period they may survive?

---

[47] French, *Toward a Modern Law of Servitudes: Reweaving the Ancient Strands,* 55 S. Cal. L. Rev. 1261, 1317 (1982). * * *

[49] *E.g.,* Epstein, *supra* note 24, at 1366 * * *.

[50] *See, e.g.,* Rhue v. Cheyenne Homes, 168 Colo. 6, 449 P.2d 361 (1969) (architectural control committee had authority under covenant to reject erection of buildings) * * *. Owners' association architectural review boards, for example, are commonly given discretion over both major changes and matters of aesthetic taste and personal behavior. * * *

E. Nuisance and Trespass Law: The "Right" to Control Use of Land by Outsiders

The focus of the realists, excerpted in Part II(B), on the right to exclude has taken on new meanings in our own time. Pollution has disturbed the understanding many had about not only their right, but also their ability, to control the use of their own resources. At the same time, the atomizing effects of automobiles, shopping centers, mail order catalogs and mass communication methods has made it more difficult for individuals to meet and speak with their fellow citizens. The former concern has heightened our desire to control the ways polluters use their land; the latter has increased the desires of many to enter the land of another to communicate with their peers. As a result both nuisance and trespass norms have become the object of significant attention by academics and judges alike.

1. Nuisance

The use of economics in property law has probably had the greatest influence in the analysis of nuisance problems.* The commentary in this area is vast, but all of it pays homage to the path breaking work of Guido Calabresi and A. Douglas Melamed in *Property Rules, Liability Rules, and Inalienability: One View of the Cathedral. The Cathedral*, excerpted first in this section, has set most of the ground rules for the debate over the nature of and the remedies for nuisances. While Calabresi and Melamed dominate the academic debates, a single case, *Boomer v. Atlantic Cement Co.*, dominates classroom discussion. Daniel Farber has written a fascinating piece which significantly revises our understanding of *Boomer*'s history. He also takes issue with the preference of Calabresi and Melamed, and many other writers in the field, for use of damage rather than injunctive remedies in nuisance cases. The last piece in this section is another nuisance classic, Hardin's *The Tragedy of the Commons*, a discussion of the economics of using resources, like the air, which are freely accessible at low cost to the user.

Other works in this field you might wish to consult include Coase, *The Problem of Social Cost,* 3 J. L. & ECON. 1 (1960); POSNER, ECONOMIC ANALYSIS OF LAW 10–40 (1972); Ellickson, *Alternatives to Zoning: Covenants, Nuisance Rules, and Fines as Land Use Controls,* 40 U. CHI. L. REV. 681 (1973); Rabin, *Rethinking Basic Assumptions,* 63 VA. L. REV. 1299 (1977); Polinsky, *Resolving Nuisance Disputes: The Simple Economics of Injunctive and Damage Remedies*, 32 STAN. L. REV. 1075 (1980); Jeff L. Lewin, *Comparative Nuisance*, 50 U. PITT. L. REV. 1009 (1989). Trespass has also been the subject of economic analysis. *See* Merrill, *Trespass, Nuisance, and the Costs of Determining Property Rights,* 14 J. LEGAL STUD. 13 (1985).

---

* Economics has certainly had an impact on many other areas of property law. That is evident in this anthology. For those interested in reading the law and economics materials contained here in a block, *see*, in addition to the nuisance materials in this section, Duncan Kennedy, *The Effect of the Warranty of Habitability on Low Income Housing: "Milking" and Class Violence* [Part II(D)(2)]; Carol M. Rose, *Women and Property: Gaining and Losing Ground* [Part III(B)(1)]; Thomas Ulen, *The Efficiency of Specific Performance: Toward a Unified Theory of Contract Remedies* [Part III(C)]; Thomas W. Merrill, *The Economics of Public Use* [Part III(G)]; Richard Epstein, *Takings: Private Property and the Power of Eminent Domain* [Part IV(B)]; Robert C. Ellickson, *Alternatives to Zoning: Covenants, Nuisance Rules, and Fines as Land Use Controls* [Part IV(B)].

Guido Calabresi and Douglas Melamed, *Property Rules, Liability Rules, and Inalienability: One View of the Cathedral*, 85 HARV. L. REV. 1089–1090, 1092–1096, 1098–1099, 1102, 1104–1108, 1111–1112, 1114–1121, 1123–1124 (1972)*

I. INTRODUCTION

Only rarely are Property and Torts approached from a unified perspective. Recent writings by lawyers concerned with economics and by economists concerned with law suggest, however, that an attempt at integrating the various legal relationships treated by these subjects would be useful both for the beginning student and sophisticated scholar. By articulating a concept of "entitlements" which are protected by property, liability, or inalienability rules, we present one framework for such an approach. We then analyze aspects of the pollution problem * * * in order to demonstrate how the model enables us to perceive relationships which have been ignored * * *.

The first issue which must be faced by any legal system is one we call the problem of "entitlement." Whenever a state is presented with the conflicting interests of two or more people, or two or more groups of people, it must decide which side to favor. * * * The entitlement to make noise versus the entitlement to have silence, the entitlement to pollute versus the entitlement to breathe clean air, the entitlement to have children versus the entitlement to forbid them—these are the first order of legal decisions. * * *

The state not only has to decide whom to entitle, but it must also simultaneously make a series of equally difficult second order decisions. These decisions go to the manner in which entitlements are protected and to whether an individual is allowed to sell or trade the entitlement. * * * It is with the latter decisions, decisions which shape the subsequent relationship between the winner and loser, that this article is primarily concerned. We shall consider three types of entitlements—entitlements protected by property rules, entitlements protected by liability rules, and inalienable entitlements. * * *

An entitlement is protected by a property rule to the extent that someone who wishes to remove the entitlement from its holder must buy it from him in a voluntary transaction in which the value of the entitlement is agreed upon by the seller. It is the form of entitlement which gives rise to the least amount of state intervention: once the original entitlement is decided upon, the state does not try to decide its value. It lets each of the parties say how much the entitlement is worth to him, and gives the seller a veto if the buyer does not offer enough. * * *

Whenever someone may destroy the initial entitlement if he is willing to pay an objectively determined value for it, an entitlement is protected by a liability rule. This value may be what it is thought the original holder of the entitlement would have sold it for. But the holder's complaint that he would have demanded more will not avail him once the objectively determined value is set. Obviously, liability rules involve an additional stage of state intervention: not only are entitlements protected, but their transfer or destruction is allowed on the basis of a value determined by some organ of the state rather than by the parties themselves.

An entitlement is inalienable to the extent that its transfer is not permitted between a willing buyer and a willing seller. The state intervenes not only to determine who is initially entitled and to determine the compensation that must be paid if the entitlement is taken or destroyed, but also to forbid its sale under some or all circumstances. Inalienability rules are thus quite different from property and liability rules. Unlike those rules, rules of inalienability not only "protect" the entitlement; they may also be viewed as limiting or regulating the grant of the entitlement itself.
* * *

II. THE SETTING OF ENTITLEMENTS

What are the reasons for deciding to entitle people to pollute or to entitle people to forbid pollution, to have children freely or to limit procreation, to own property or to share property? They can be grouped

---

under three headings: economic efficiency, distributional preferences, and other justice considerations.

A. Economic Efficiency

Perhaps the simplest reason for a particular entitlement is to minimize the administrative costs of enforcement. * * * By itself this reason will never justify any result except that of letting the stronger win, for obviously that result minimizes enforcement costs. Nevertheless, administrative efficiency may be relevant to choosing entitlements when other reasons are taken into account. This may occur when the reasons accepted are indifferent between conflicting entitlements and one entitlement is cheaper to enforce than the other. It may also occur when the reasons are not indifferent but lead us only slightly to prefer one over another and the first is considerably more expensive to enforce than the second.

But administrative efficiency is just one aspect of the broader concept of economic efficiency. Economic efficiency asks that we choose the set of entitlements which would lead to that allocation of resources which could not be improved in the sense that a further change would not so improve the condition of those who gained by it that they could compensate those who lost from it and still be better off than before. This is often called Pareto optimality. * * *

Recently it has been argued that on certain assumptions, usually termed the absence of transaction costs, Pareto optimality or economic efficiency will occur regardless of the initial entitlement.[12] For this to hold, "no transaction costs" must be understood extremely broadly as involving both perfect knowledge and the absence of any impediments or costs of negotiating. Negotiation costs include, for example, the cost of excluding would-be freeloaders from the fruits of market bargains. In such a frictionless society, transactions would occur until no one could be made better off as a result of further transactions without making someone else worse off. This, we would suggest, is a necessary, indeed a tautological, result of the definitions of Pareto optimality and of transaction costs which we have given.

Such a result would not mean however, that the *same* allocation of resources would exist regardless of the initial set of entitlements. Taney's willingness to pay for the right to make noise may depend on how rich he is; Marshall's willingness to pay for silence may depend on his wealth. * * * Depending on how Marshall's desire for silence and Taney's for noise vary with their wealth, an entitlement to noise will result in negotiations which will lead to a different quantum of noise than would an entitlement to silence. * * * [W]hat is Pareto optimal, or economically efficient, * * * varies with the starting distribution of wealth. Pareto optimality is optimal *given* a distribution of wealth, but different distributions of wealth imply their own Pareto optimal allocation of resources.

All this suggests why distributions of wealth may affect a society's choice of entitlements. It does not suggest why *economic efficiency* should affect the choice, if we assume an absence of any transaction costs. But no one makes an assumption of no transaction costs in practice. * * * [T]he assumption * * * may be a useful starting point, a device which helps us see how, as different elements which may be termed transaction costs become important, the goal of economic efficiency starts to prefer one allocation of entitlements over another.

* * *

B. Distributional Goals

* * *

Difficult as wealth distribution preferences are to analyze, it should be obvious that they play a crucial role in the setting of entitlements. For the placement of entitlements has a fundamental effect on a society's distribution of wealth. It is not enough, if a society wishes absolute equality, to start everyone off with the same amount of money. A financially egalitarian society which gives individuals the right to make noise immediately makes the would-be noisemaker richer than the silence loving hermit. * * *

The consequence of this is that it is very difficult to imagine a society in which there is complete equality of wealth. * * * If perfect equality is impossible, a society must choose what entitlements it wishes to have on the basis of criteria other than perfect equality. In doing this, a society often has a choice of methods, and the method chosen will have important distributional consequences. * * * Which entitlements a society decides to sell, and which it decides to give away, will likely depend in part on which determination promotes the wealth distribution the society favors.

* * *

---

[12] This proposition was first established in Coase's classic article, *The Problem of Social Cost*, 3 J. LAW & ECON. 1 (1960) * * *.

C. Other Justice Considerations

* * *

[W]e should admit that explaining entitlements solely in terms of efficiency and distribution, in even their broadest terms, does not seem wholly satisfactory. * * * The reason that we have so far explained entitlements simply in terms of efficiency and distribution is ultimately tautological. We defined distribution as covering *all* the reasons, other than efficiency, on the basis of which we might prefer to make Taney *wealthier* than Marshall. So defined, there obviously was no room for any other reasons. Distributional grounds covered broadly accepted ideas like "equality" * * * and highly specific ones like "favoring the silence lover." * * * [This] seems to assume that we cannot say any more about the reasons for some distributional preferences than about others. * * * [T]hat, surely, is a dangerous assumption. To avoid this danger the term "distribution" is often limited to relatively few broad reasons, like equality. And those preferences which cannot be easily explained in terms of these relatively few broadly accepted distributional preferences, or in terms of efficiency, are termed justice reasons.

* * *

III. Rules for Protecting and Regulating Entitlements

Whenever society chooses an initial entitlement it must also determine whether to protect the entitlement by property rules, by liability rules, or by rules of inalienability. In our framework, much of what is generally called private property can be viewed as an entitlement which is protected by a property rule. No one can take the entitlement to private property from the holder unless the holder sells it willingly and at the price at which he subjectively values the property. Yet a nuisance with sufficient public utility to avoid injunction has, in effect, the right to take property with compensation. In such a circumstance the entitlement to the property is protected only by what we call a liability rule: an external, objective standard of value is used to facilitate the transfer of the entitlement from the holder to the nuisance.[24] Finally, in some instances we will not allow the sale of the property at all, that is, we will occasionally make the entitlement inalienable.

* * *

A. Property and Liability Rules

* * * Why * * * cannot society limit itself to the property rule? * * * Why do we need liability rules at all?

In terms of economic efficiency the reason is easy enough to see. Often the cost of establishing the value of an initial entitlement by negotiation is so great that even though a transfer of the entitlement would benefit all concerned, such a transfer will not occur. If a collective determination of the value were available instead, the beneficial transfer would quickly come about.

Eminent domain is a good example. A park where Guidacres, a tract of land owned by 1,000 owners in 1,000 parcels, now sits would, let us assume, benefit a neighboring town enough so that the 100,000 citizens of the town would each be willing to pay an average of \$100 to have it. The park is Pareto desirable if the owners of the tracts of land in Guidacres actually value their entitlements at less than \$10,000,000 or an average of \$10,000 a tract. Let us assume that in fact the parcels are all the same and all the owners value them at \$8,000. On this assumption, the park is, in economic efficiency terms, desirable—in values foregone it costs \$8,000,000 and is worth \$10,000,000 to the buyers. And yet it may well not be established. If enough of the owners hold-out for more than \$10,000 in order to get a share of the \$2,000,000 that they guess the buyers are willing to pay over the value which the sellers in actuality attach, the price demanded will be more than \$10,000,000 and no park will result. The sellers have an incentive to hide their true valuation and the market will not succeed in establishing it.

An equally valid example could be made on the buying side. Suppose the sellers of Guidacres have agreed to a sales price of \$8,000,000 * * *. It does not follow that the buyers can raise that much even though each of 100,000 citizens *in fact* values the park at \$100. Some citizens may try to free-load and say the park is only worth \$50 or even nothing to them, hoping that enough others will admit to a higher desire and make up the \$8,000,000 price. Again there is no reason to believe that a market, a decentralized system of valuing, will cause people to express their true valuations and hence yield results which all would *in fact* agree are desirable.

Whenever this is the case an argument can readily be made for moving from a property rule to a liability

[24] *See, e.g.*, Boomer v. Atlantic Cement Co., 26 N.Y.S.2d 312, 257 N.E.2d 870 (1970) * * *.

rule. If society can remove from the market the valuation of each tract of land, decide the value collectively, and impose it, then the holdout problem is gone. Similarly, if society can value collectively each individual citizen's desire to have a park and charge him a "benefits" tax based upon it, the freeloader problem is gone. If the sum of the taxes is greater than the sum of the compensation awards, the park will result.

* * *

Of course, the problems with liability rules are equally real. We cannot be at all sure that landowner Taney is lying or holding out when he says his land is worth $12,000 to him. * * * As a result, eminent domain may grossly undervalue what Taney would actually sell for, even if it sought to give him his true valuation of his tract. * * * The same is true on the buyer side. "Benefits" taxes rarely attempt, let alone succeed, in gauging the individual citizen's relative desire for the alleged benefit.

* * *

B. Inalienable Entitlements

* * *

While at first glance efficiency objectives may seem undermined by limitations on the ability to engage in transactions, closer analysis suggests that there are instances, perhaps many, in which economic efficiency is more closely approximated by such limitations. This might occur when a transaction would create significant externalities—costs to third parties.

For instance, if Taney were allowed to sell his land to Chase, a polluter, he would injure his neighbor Marshall by lowering the value of Marshall's land. Conceivably, Marshall could pay Taney not to sell his land; but, because there are many injured Marshalls, freeloader and information costs make such transactions practically impossible. The state could protect the Marshalls and yet facilitate the sale of the land by giving the Marshalls an entitlement to prevent Taney's sale to Chase but only protecting the entitlement by a liability rule. It might, for instance, charge an excise tax on all sales of land to polluters equal to its estimate of the external cost to the Marshalls of the sale. But where there are so many injured Marshalls that the price required under the liability rule is likely to be high enough so that no one would be willing to pay it, then setting up the machinery for collective valuation may be wasteful. Barring the sale to polluters will be the most efficient result because it is clear that avoiding pollution is cheaper than paying its costs—including its costs to the Marshalls.

Another instance in which external costs may justify inalienability occurs when external costs do not lend themselves to collective measurement which is acceptably objective and nonarbitrary. This nonmonetizability is characteristic of one category of external costs which, as a practical matter, seems frequently to lead us to rules of inalienability. Such external costs are often called moralisms.

If Taney is allowed to sell himself into slavery, or to take undue risks of becoming penniless, or to sell a kidney, Marshall may be harmed, simply because Marshall is a sensitive man who is made unhappy by seeing slaves, paupers, or persons who die because they have sold a kidney. Again Marshall could pay Taney not to sell his freedom to Chase the slaveowner; but again, because Marshall is not one but many individuals, freeloader and information costs make such transactions practically impossible.

* * *

Finally, just as efficiency goals sometimes dictate the use of rules of inalienability, so, of course, do distributional goals. Whether an entitlement may be sold or not often affects directly who is richer and who is poorer. Prohibiting the sale of babies makes poorer those who can cheaply produce babies and richer those who through some nonmarket device get free an "unwanted" baby. * * * Favoring the specific group that has benefited may or may not have been the reason for the prohibition on bargaining. What is important is that, regardless of the reason for barring a contract, a group did gain from the prohibition.

This should suffice to put us on guard, for it suggests direct distributional motives may lie behind asserted nondistributional grounds for inalienability * * *. This does not mean that giving weight to distributional goals is undesirable. It clearly is desirable where on efficiency grounds society is indifferent between an alienable and an inalienable entitlement and distributional goals favor one approach or the other. It may well be desirable even when distributional goals are achieved at some efficiency costs. The danger may be, however, that what is justified on, for example, paternalism grounds is really a hidden way of accruing distributional benefits for a group whom we would not otherwise wish to benefit. For example, we may use certain types of zoning to preserve open spaces on the grounds that the poor will be happier, though they do not know it now. And open spaces may indeed make the poor happier in the long run. But the zoning that preserves open space also makes housing in the suburbs more expensive and it may be that the whole plan is aimed at securing distributional benefits to the suburban dweller regardless of the poor's happiness.

IV. The Framework and Pollution Control Rules

Nuisance or pollution is one of the most interesting areas where the question of who will be given an entitlement, and how it will be protected, is in frequent issue. Traditionally * * * the nuisance-pollution problem is viewed in terms of three rules. First, Taney may not pollute unless his neighbor * * * Marshall, allows it (Marshall may enjoin Taney's nuisance). Second, Taney may pollute but must compensate Marshall for damages caused (nuisance is found but the remedy is limited to damages). Third, Taney may pollute at will and can only be stopped by Marshall if Marshall pays him off (Taney's pollution is not held to be a nuisance to Marshall). In our terminology rules one and two (nuisance with injunction, and with damages only) are entitlements to Marshall. The first is an entitlement to be free from pollution and is protected by a property rule; the second is also an entitlement to be free from pollution but is protected only by a liability rule. Rule three (no nuisance) is instead an entitlement to Taney protected by a property rule, for only by buying Taney out at Taney's price can Marshall end the pollution.

The very statement of these rules in the context of our framework suggests that something is missing. Missing is the fourth rule representing an entitlement in Taney to pollute, but an entitlement which is protected by a liability rule. The fourth rule, really a kind of partial eminent domain coupled with a benefits tax, can be stated as follows: Marshall may stop Taney from polluting, but if he does he must compensate Taney.

* * * Unlike the first three * * * rule four does not lend itself to judicial imposition for a number of good legal process reasons. For example, even if Taney's injuries could practicably be measured, apportionment of the duty of compensation among many Marshalls would present problems for which courts are not well suited. * * * [T]he courts would be faced with the immensely difficult task of determining who was benefited how much and imposing a benefits tax accordingly, all the while observing procedural limits within which courts are expected to function.

* * * To appreciate the utility of the fourth rule and to compare it with the other three rules, we will examine why we might choose any of the given rules.

We would employ rule one (entitlement to be free from pollution protected by a property rule) from an economic efficiency point of view if we believed that the polluter, Taney, could avoid or reduce the costs of pollution more cheaply than the pollutee, Marshall. Or to put it another way, Taney would be enjoinable if he were in a better position to balance the costs of polluting against the costs of not polluting. We would employ rule three (entitlement to pollute protected by a property rule) again solely from an economic efficiency standpoint, if we made the converse judgment on who could best balance the harm of pollution against its avoidance costs. If we were wrong in our judgments and if transactions between Marshall and Taney were costless or even very cheap, the entitlement under rules one and three would be traded and an economically efficient result would occur in either case. * * * While the entitlement might have important distributional effects, it would not substantially undercut economic efficiency.

The moment we assume, however, that transactions are not cheap, the situation changes dramatically. Assume we enjoin Taney and there are 10,000 injured Marshalls. Now *even if* the right to pollute is worth more to Taney than the right to be free from pollution is to the sum of the Marshalls, the injunction will probably stand. The cost of buying out the Marshalls, given holdout problems, is likely to be too great, and an equivalent of eminent domain in Taney would be needed to alter the initial injunction. Conversely, if we denied a nuisance remedy, the 10,000 Marshalls could only with enormous difficulty, given freeloader problems, get together to buy out even one Taney and prevent pollution. This would be so even if the pollution harm was greater than the value to Taney of the right to pollute.

* * *

Under these circumstances, and they are normal ones in the pollution area—we are likely to turn to liability rules whenever we are uncertain whether the polluter or the pollutees can most cheaply avoid the cost of pollution. We are only likely to use liability rules where we are uncertain because, if we are certain, the costs of liability rules—essentially the costs of collectively valuing the damages to all concerned plus the cost in coercion to those who would not sell at the collectively determined figure—are unnecessary. They are unnecessary because transaction costs and bargaining barriers become irrelevant when we are certain who is the cheapest cost avoider; economic efficiency will be attained without transactions by making the correct initial entitlement.

As a practical matter we often are uncertain who the cheapest cost avoider is. In such cases, traditional legal doctrine tends to find a nuisance but imposes only damages on Taney payable to the Marshalls. This way, if the amount of damages Taney is made to pay is close to the injury caused, economic efficiency will have had its due; if he cannot make a go of it, the nuisance was not worth its costs. The entitlement to the Marshalls to be free from pollution unless compensated, however, will have been given *not* because it was thought that polluting was probably worth less to Taney than freedom from pollution was worth to the Marshalls, nor even because on some distributional basis we preferred to charge the cost to Taney rather than to the Marshalls. It was so placed *simply because we did not know* whether Taney desired to pollute more than the Marshalls desired to be free from pollution, and the only way we thought we could test out the value of the pollution was by the only liability rule we thought we had. This was rule two, the imposition of nuisance damages on Taney. At least this would be the position of a court concerned with economic efficiency which believed itself limited to rules one, two and three.

Rule four gives at least the possibility that the opposite entitlement may also lead to economic efficiency in a situation of uncertainty. Suppose for the moment that a mechanism exists for collectively assessing the damage resulting to Taney from being stopped from polluting by the Marshalls, and a mechanism also exists for collectively assessing the benefit to each of the Marshalls from cessation. Then—assuming the same degree of accuracy in collective valuation as exists in rule two (the nuisance damage rule)—the Marshalls would stop the pollution if it harmed them more than it benefited Taney. If this is possible, then even if we thought it necessary to use a liability rule, we would still be free to give the entitlement to Taney or Marshall for whatever reasons, efficiency or distributional, we desired.

* * *

The introduction of distributional considerations makes the existence of the fourth possibility even more significant. * * * Assume a factory which, by using cheap coal, pollutes a very wealthy section of town and employs many low income workers to produce a product purchased primarily by the poor; assume also a distributional goal that favors equality of wealth. Rule one—enjoin the nuisance—would possibly have desirable economic efficiency results (if the pollution hurt the homeowners more than it saved the factory in coal costs), but it would have disastrous distribution effects. It would also have undesirable efficiency effects if the initial judgment on costs of avoidance had been wrong and transaction costs were high. Rule two—nuisance damages—would allow a testing of the economic efficiency of eliminating the pollution, even in the presence of high transaction costs, but would quite possibly put the factory out of business or diminish output and thus have the same income distribution effects as rule one. Rule three—no nuisance—would have favorable distributional effects since it might protect the income of the workers. But if the pollution harm was greater to the homeowners than the cost of avoiding it by using a better coal, and if transaction costs—holdout problems—were such that homeowners could not unite to pay the factory to use better coal, rule three would have unsatisfactory efficiency effects. Rule four—payment of damages to the factory after allowing the homeowners to compel it to use better coal, and assessment of the cost of these damages to the homeowners—would be the only one which would accomplish both the distributional and efficiency goals.

* * *

Thus far in this section we have ignored the possibility of employing rules of inalienability to solve pollution problems. A general policy of barring pollution does seem unrealistic. But rules of inalienability can appropriately be used to limit the levels of pollution and to control the levels of activities which cause pollution.

One argument for inalienability may be the widespread existence of moralisms against pollution. Thus it may hurt the Marshalls—gentleman farmers—to see Taney, a smoke-choked city dweller, sell his entitlement to be free of pollution. A different kind of externality or moralism may be even more important. The Marshalls may be hurt by the expectation that, while the present generation might withstand present pollution levels with no serious health dangers, future generations may well face a despoiled, hazardous environmental condition which they are powerless to reverse. And this ground for inalienability might be strengthened if a similar conclusion were reached on grounds of self paternalism. Finally, society might restrict alienability on paternalistic grounds. The Marshalls might feel that although Taney himself does not know it, Taney will be better off if he really can see the stars at night, or if he can breathe smogless air.

Whatever the grounds for inalienability, we should reemphasize that distributional effects should be carefully evaluated in making the choice for or against inalienability. Thus the citizens of a town may be granted an entitlement to be free of water pollution caused by the waste discharges of a chemical factory; and the entitlement might be made inalienable on the grounds that the town's citizens really would be better off in the long run to have access to clean beaches. But the entitlement might also be made inalienable to assure the maintenance of a beautiful resort area for the very wealthy, at the same time putting the town's citizens out of work.

Note

The law of waste reflects many of the same notions that are buried in nuisance law. The interest of a life tenant, for example, may conflict with those of the party holding the remainder. Two examples of this problem used in many texts are *Baker v. Weedon*, 262 So. 2d 641 (Miss. 1972) and *Melms v. Pabst Brewing Co.,* 104 Wis. 7, 79 N.W. 738 (1899). Use the reasoning of Calabresi and Melamed to resolve either or both of these cases. Now assume that in *Baker* four years passed (as it did before the case was fully litigated). Does the Calabresi-Melamed outcome change? Or in *Melms*, assume that the building destroyed was a structure of great historical importance to Milwaukee and sentimental value to the surviving members of the Pabst family. Does the Calabresi-Melamed outcome change? Might the outcome change still again if the *Melms* case involved a request for injunctive relief before the house was torn down rather than, as in the actual case, a request for damages after the building was gone?

Daniel A. Farber, *Reassessing* Boomer: *Justice, Efficiency, and Nuisance Law,* in PROPERTY LAW AND LEGAL EDUCATION: ESSAYS IN HONOR OF JOHN E. CRIBBET (Peter Hay & Michael H. Hoeflich, eds.) 7–16, 18 (1988)*

Boomer v. Atlantic Cement Co.,[1] * * * has become one of the great teaching cases in American legal education. It appears in virtually every casebook on the law of property, torts, remedies, environmental regulation, and land use planning. A lucky (or perhaps I should say "unlucky") law student can easily encounter the case three or four times.

The prominence of the case may be partly due to historical accident. *Boomer* happened to be decided just at the beginning of the great wave of environmentalism that swept the country in the seventies. It also coincided with a period of intense scholarly interest in nuisance law.[3] But the staying power of the case is probably due more to the power and simplicity of its facts. On the one hand, we have a multimillion-dollar cement plant, on the other, the neighbors victimized by air pollution. Should the neighbors get an injunction, or only damages to compensate them for the relatively small loss in their property's market value? This simple question, resolved by the New York courts in favor of damages, can be used as a springboard for discussing tradeoffs between economics and environmental values, economic theories of property and tort law, the rule of equitable discretion in remedies law, and the rela-

[1] 26 N.Y.2d 919, 309 N.Y.S.2d 312, 257 N.E.2d 970 (1970).

[3] *See* Ellickson, *Alternatives to Zoning: Covenants, Nuisance Rules and Fines as Land Use Controls,* 40 U. CHI. L. REV. 681 (1973); Calabresi & Melamed, *Property Rules, Liability Rules, and Inalienability: One View of the Cathedral,* 85 HARV. L. REV. 1089 (1972); Michelman, *Pollution as a Tort: A Non-Accidental Perspective on Calabresi's Costs,* 80 YALE L. J. 647 (1971). * * *

tionship between private law and public regulatory schemes.

I began work on this essay with the intention of exploring these issues, but as I looked into the *Boomer* record, my research began to take a different direction. The reality of the *Boomer* litigation was substantially different from the impression given by the Court of Appeals opinion. While the conventional understanding of the facts, drawn from the Court of Appeals opinion, is not exactly false, it is profoundly misleading. Air pollution, in the sense of a widespread decline in air quality, was actually the least of the plaintiffs' problems; they suffered much more from the severe local effects of the defendant's operations. Moreover, while the New York courts did award damages, these damages were only loosely tied to any decline in market value and were four times the amount mentioned in the Court of Appeals opinion. Thus, the case we have all been teaching is a bit mythical.

Boomer did not involve (except secondarily) a conventional air pollution problem, with many victims each suffering comparatively slight damages. Instead, a few victims close to the cement plant suffered drastic impairments of their ability to make normal use of their property * * * because of the blasting used in quarrying operations. The narrow question posed by *Boomer* is what remedies should be available to the victims of such egregious nuisances. * * * I * * * argue that such nuisance victims should be presumptively entitled to an injunction. * * *

I. *The* Boomer *Litigation*

Atlantic Cement began construction of its plant in May of 1961. The area was unzoned at the time. Operations began in September of 1961, after Atlantic had invested more than $40 million in this plant, including the most effective available pollution control. The area was described as follows by a real estate expert:

> Prior to the purchase by the Atlantic Cement Company, this property (about a mile and a half or two miles north of the Village of Ravena) * * * was in a state of transition from rural to suburban living, with individual houses built presently along Route 9W with a smattering of commercial enterprises dotted here and there. When I say commercial, I'm referring principally to gasoline service stations or a motel or a drive-in theatre.

All the plaintiffs had owned and occupied their properties prior to the ground-breaking for the plant.

Atlantic's impact on its neighbors was drastic. For example, Floyd and Barbara Millious lived in an eight-room ranch-style house 900 feet from the cement plant, and even closer to an overhead conveyer used to move rocks from the quarry to the plant. Atlantic's quarry was a half mile to the west. According to the Milliouses, the blasting had caused large cracks in the walls, ceiling, and exterior of their home. Moreover, the fine dust blowing onto their property covered everything with what they described as a "plastic-like" coating, which they found impossible to remove. Similar property damage was reported by Joseph and Carrie Ventura, who owned a Cape Cod house about the same distance from the plant and conveyor.

Kenneth and Delores Livengood lived farther from the cement plant but closer to the quarry. Delores Livengood's testimony vividly describes the effects of the blasting on their daily lives, as in this episode in March of 1967:

> Well, we were sitting on the floor in the living room, playing a game when they had this awful tremble, and to me the house seemed like the whole house was rocking, and I would see the lamp shades vibrating and it just scared the children. That was one of the times that they just got up and started to run for the basement. And I didn't go out the door because I knew what it was. I heard the big blast, but the whole house just rocked and I just wondered if it was going to stop. It was terrible.

At least one dairy farm, owned by Avie Kinley, was near the plant. The 283 acre farm consisted of a house, barns, two silos and three tenant houses.

The area was also used by small businesses such as Oscar and June Boomer's automobile junk yard, which was just north of the main plant. They owned about eight acres, on which the Boomers sold used car parts and did auto body and fender work. Mr. Boomer had apparently hoped that his two sons would carry on the family business, but the viability of the business was threatened by the vibration and heavy dust.

The Coach House Restaurant, owned and operated by Theodore and Miriam Richard, was within seven hundred feet of the cement company's stock pile. Before 1961, the restaurant was surrounded by evergreens, and the Coach House served cocktails and sandwiches to its customers outside on the lawn. According to one expert witness, the Coach House had just completed a lengthy start-up period. With the mortgage paid off, it was just about to become profitable when the cement plant opened.

The record also contains considerable information about the cement company and its operations. The company was formed as the Burwill Realty Company in 1959, presumably to facilitate the acquisition of property by concealing the purchaser's plans. Just before construction of the plant began, the name was changed to the Atlantic Cement Company. Although this was the company's only plant, it had distribution centers from Boston to Florida, served either by rail or barge. The quarry included some 1544 acres. The plant normally employed about four hundred people (though there was a strike at the time of the trial), with annual wages of about $3 million. The assessed value of the plant was about half of the assessed value of the township.

The blasting involved something called the "millisecond delay" procedure. Rather than setting off one large blast, a series of blasts would be used to remove one layer after another, so that one layer of rock would be falling away just as the next blast went off. The dust collection equipment, which had cost over $2 million, was said to be the best in the country.

Based on this record, the trial judge found that the plaintiffs had established the existence of a nuisance. He refused to issue an injunction, however, because of Atlantic's "immense investment in the Hudson River Valley, its contribution to the Capital District's economy and its immediate help to the education of children in the Town of Coeymans through the payment of substantial sums in school and property taxes."[29] He awarded the plaintiffs a total of $535 per month in damages for past losses, but suggested that the parties settle the case for the amount of the permanent loss of market value, which he found to total $185,000.

* * *

[T]he Court of Appeals decided that Atlantic should be allowed to avoid a permanent injunction by paying the plaintiffs "such permanent damages as may be fixed by the court." In return, the plaintiffs would convey a "servitude on the land" to Atlantic.

* * *

The proceedings on remand suggest that the Court of Appeals decision was actually more favorable to the plaintiffs than it might have seemed. The trial judge agreed with the plaintiffs that damages would not be limited to the decrease in fair market value. On the other hand, he also rejected the plaintiffs' theory that damages should be awarded under a "contract price theory," that is, for the amount Atlantic would have had to pay to persuade the plaintiffs themselves to agree to lift a permanent injunction. The trial judge considered this unduly excessive. In setting damages, he considered the special market value established by Atlantic itself in paying apparently inflated prices for other property in the neighborhood, as well as the greatly differing testimony of the parties' expert witnesses as to the conventional market value. "[W]hile the fair market value rule may not be the sole criterion, it does serve as a restraining influence on the possible excessiveness of the so-called 'special' market value, and as a sure check on the subject and speculative nature of the so-called 'contract price'." By the time of the judge's decision, all but one of the cases had settled. In the remaining case, the judge found the decline in market value to be $140,000, and awarded $175,000 in damages.

This concluded the nuisance litigation. For the cement company, however, the litigation did not end until 1984, when the Court of Appeals ruled that its insurance policy covered the damages.[40] We know from the appellate division opinion that Atlantic's total liability, including the settlements, ultimately came to $710,000,[41] some four times the amount mentioned in the Court of Appeals decision denying permanent injunctive relief.

It is probably worth mentioning that later New York cases have rather narrowly construed the "*Boomer* rule" on injunctive relief. The New York courts have issued injunctions as a matter of course where a nuisance was also in violation of a zoning ordinance or pollution permit or where the economic disparity between the parties was not "vast."

As we have seen, the realities of the *Boomer* litigation differ from the impression conveyed by the Court of Appeals decision. First, the interference with the plaintiffs' use of their land was much more severe. Second, the damages ultimately awarded exceeded the decline in the fair market value of the land; a "kicker" was included as part of the compensation for conveying a servitude to the defendant.

Still the conventional account is right about one thing, the denial of permanent injunctive relief. In analyzing the *Boomer* problem, then, we must begin with the issue of injunctive relief.

---

[29] 287 N.Y.S.2d 112, 114.

[40] Atlantic Cement v. Fidelity & Casualty Co., 471 N.E.2d 142, 63 N.Y.2d 798 (1984). It is no tribute to the efficiency of the American judicial system that it took almost twenty years to resolve the various ramifications of the opening of a new cement plant.

[41] Atlantic Cement v. Fidelity & Casualty Co., 459 N.Y.S.2d 425, 427 (1983).

II. *Remedies for Egregious Nuisances*

* * *

Scholars have discussed four major sets of remedies for victims of nuisances:

1. *No legal remedy.* Victims receive no assistance from the courts. Their only possible remedy is to "bribe" the polluter to abate the nuisance.

2. *Compensated injunctions.* Victims may obtain an injunction abating the nuisance, but must compensate the polluter for the losses caused by the injunction. This remedy has strong scholarly support, but apart from one freak case,[45] has never been adopted by any court.

3. *Damages under a "liability rule."* Victims receive compensation for the harm they suffer, but no injunctive relief.

4. *Injunctions under a "property rule."* Victims have the right to abate the nuisance. This time it is the polluter whose only remedy is to "bribe" the other party by settling the lawsuit with a cash payment.

In situations like *Boomer*, in which the victims' normal use of land has been severely impeded, the first two remedies are morally unacceptable, because both of them require the victims to pay for a return to the status quo. People like the Livengoods, having bought a quiet house in the country, should not have to pay their neighbors to stop terrifying their children by blasting.

These two remedies unjustifiably transfer wealth from the victims to the polluter, thereby rewarding the polluter for invading the rights of its neighbors. * * *

The third remedy, an award of damages to the victim, is also morally unsatisfactory. If Mr. Boomer had decided to open his own cement quarry, using the limestone on a neighbor's farm, we would certainly not be inclined to limit the neighbor to compensation for the injury to his farmland, thereby permitting Boomer to continue taking the limestone so long as he paid for it. Similarly, we would not be content with a damage remedy if Atlantic had begun dumping tons of waste on Boomer's land. Limiting the nuisance plaintiff to damages is not much different. One use of a parcel of land is as a buffer zone between activities on other parcels and the outside world—or to put it another way, as a dump for adverse environmental effects. Like a private right of eminent domain, a liability rule allows the polluter to make use of the victim's land for these purposes without his consent, so long as compensation is paid.

Damage awards may compensate for the victim's economic loss, but a liability rule slights the more fundamental injury to the victim's dignity as a member of the community. * * * [N]orms of neighborliness mandate cooperation and mutual respect among members of the community. An egregious nuisance is an offense against this norm of mutual respect; the polluter unilaterally takes over the victim's land as a dumping ground without regard to the normal patterns of use in the community. * * *

In contrast, an injunctive remedy upholds the dignity of the victims as members of the community. Rather than allowing the polluter to invade the rights of its neighbors whenever it is willing to pay for the harm, it gives the neighbors control over the situation. If it wishes to continue its operations, the polluter must go to the neighbors and bargain with them as equals. * * *

* * * [R]ecent economic literature * * * indicates that * * * efficiency argument[s] against injunctions [are] * * * much weaker than it might seem.

* * * [G]iving the victims the right to an injunction need not actually result in closing down the source. Suppose that the victims are suffering $150,000 in damages, while the source makes profits of $500,000. The victims are entitled to an injunction, but might be willing to forego that right for a payment in excess of their $150,000 damages. * * * Somewhere in the range between $150,000 and $500,000, the parties can make a deal that leaves all of them better off than they would be with an injunction.

The potential for a mutually beneficial deal does not mean that such a deal will actually take place. If there are a large number of victims, they may find it difficult to organize in order to negotiate effectively. Even with only one victim, bluffing or other negotiating tactics might backfire, preventing a deal from being made. Recent empirical research indicates, however, that these risks have been overestimated. * * * [G]roups of up to forty "victims" had little difficulty in organizing and negotiating mutually advantageous bargains with "polluters." The * * * conclusion was that injunctive relief would not

[45] Spur Indus., Inc. v. Del E. Webb Dev't. Co., 108 Ariz. 178, 494 P.2d 700 (1972). One of the oddities of this case was that the plaintiff (who had to compensate the defendant) was not the victim, but rather the developer who had sold the property to the victims.

interfere with the achievement of economic efficiency.[63]

* * *

[I]n the normal case we should leave this transaction [to forego the injunction] to the market. Sometimes, however, we may be unwilling to trust the market, either because the results of a failure by the parties to make a deal would be disastrous for the community or because the results of the bargain might seem disproportionate. If, for example, the plaintiffs' loss was $1 million and the defendant's profit was $40 million, a payment of $20 million to the defendant might seem extortionate. If so, we might prefer to have a court set the price. Nevertheless there would be no reason to set the price at the very bottom of the possible range, allocating all of the profit from the deal to the polluter.

* * *

[For b]efore Atlantic built, it had the option of locating its operation elsewhere if the buffer rights were too expensive. * * * This possibility constrains the price which the *Boomer* plaintiffs would have been able to obtain for the right to use their land as an environmental sink. Thus, Atlantic * * * must * * * pay in any event the minimum possible voluntary price, which is the amount of harm to the plaintiff's other property uses (including psychological injury). The measure of damages based on the market for buffer rights is more generous than the traditional diminution-in-value measure.

Note

If Farber is correct that Atlantic Cement behaved in a particularly egregious way, the appellate opinions present in all the major property texts are quite misleading. Obviously it suggests that some care must be taken in using appellate cases as a basic tool for teaching the operation of property. For other stories about the misleading qualities of well known appellate cases, *see* CHUSED, CASES, MATERIALS AND PROBLEMS IN PROPERTY 2–6, 1009, 1041–1043 (1988) (on *International News Service v. Associated Press,* 248 U.S. 215 (1918); *Fontainebleau Hotel Corp. v. Forty-Five Twenty-Five, Inc.,* 114 So.2d 357 (Fla. App. 1959); *Neponsit Property Owners' Ass'n v. Emigrant Industrial Savings Bank*, 278 N.Y. 248, 15 N.E.2d 793 (1938)).

Garrett Hardin, *The Tragedy of the Commons*, 162 SCIENCE 1243, 1244–1246 (Dec. 13, 1968)*

The tragedy of the commons develops in this way. Picture a pasture open to all. It is to be expected that each herdsman will try to keep as many cattle as possible on the commons. Such an arrangement may work reasonably satisfactorily for centuries because tribal wars, poaching, and disease keep the number of both man and beast well below the carrying capacity of the land. Finally, however, comes the day of reckoning, that is the day when the long-desired goal of social stability becomes a reality. At this point, the inherent logic of the commons remorselessly generates tragedy.

As a rational being, each herdsman seeks to maximize his gain. Explicitly or implicitly, more or less consciously, he asks, "What is the utility *to me* of adding one more animal to my herd?" This utility

[63] *See* Hoffman & Spitzer, *Experimental Tests of the Coase Theorem with Large Bargaining Groups,* 15 J. LEGAL STUDIES 149, 163–69 (1986) * * *.

Larger groups of plaintiffs become much more of a problem because of the increasing difficulty of organizing the group. Class action mechanisms offer one possible way of reducing transaction costs and thereby avoiding the "large number" problem.

has one negative and one positive component.

1) The positive component is a function of the increment of one animal. Since the herdsman receives all the proceeds from the sale of the additional animal, the positive utility is nearly +1.

2) The negative component is a function of the additional overgrazing created by one more animal. Since, however, the effects of overgrazing are shared by all the herdsmen, the negative utility for any particular decision-making herdsman is only a fraction of -1.

Adding together the component partial utilities, the rational herdsman concludes that the only sensible course for him to pursue is to add another animal to his herd. And another; and another . . . . But this is the conclusion reached by each and every rational herdsman sharing a commons. Therein is the tragedy. Each man is locked into a system that compels him to increase his herd without limit—in a world that is limited. Ruin is the destination toward which all men rush, each pursuing his own best interest in a society that believes in the freedom of the commons. Freedom in a commons brings ruin to all.

Some would say that this is a platitude. Would that it were! In a sense, it was learned thousands of years ago, but natural selection favors the forces of psychological denial. The individual benefits as an individual from his ability to deny the truth even though society as a whole, of which he is a part, suffers. Education can counteract the natural tendency to do the wrong thing, but the inexorable succession of generations requires that the basis for this knowledge be constantly refreshed.

* * *

Even at this late date, cattlemen leasing national land on the western ranges demonstrate no more than an ambivalent understanding, in constantly pressuring federal authorities to increase the head count to the point where over-grazing produces erosion and weed-dominance. Likewise, the oceans of the world continue to suffer from the survival of the philosophy of the commons. Maritime nations still respond automatically to the shibboleth of the "freedom of the seas." Professing to believe in the "inexhaustible resources of the oceans," they bring species after species of fish and whales closer to extinction.

* * *

What shall we do? We have several options. We might sell the * * * [commons] off as private property. We might keep them as public property, but allocate the right to enter them. The allocation might be on the basis of wealth, by the use of an auction system. It might be on the basis of merit, as defined by some agreed-upon standards. It might be by lottery. Or it might be on a first-come, first-served basis, administered to long queues. There, I think, are all the possibilities. They are all objectionable. But we must choose or acquiesce in the destruction of the commons * * *.

Pollution

In a reverse way, the tragedy of the commons reappears in problems of pollution. Here it is not a question of taking something out of the commons, but of putting something in—sewage, or chemical, radioactive, and heat wastes into water; noxious and dangerous fumes into the air; and distracting and unpleasant advertising signs into the line of sight. The calculations of utility are much the same as before. The rational man finds that his share of the cost of the waste he discharges into the commons is less than the cost of purifying his wastes before releasing them. Since this is true for everyone, we are locked into a system of "fouling our own nest," so long as we behave only as independent, rational, free enterprisers.

The tragedy of the commons as a food basket is averted by private property, or something formally like it. But the air and waters surrounding us cannot readily be fenced, and so the tragedy of the commons as a cesspool must be prevented by different means, by coercive laws or taxing devices that make it cheaper for the polluter to treat his pollutants than to discharge them untreated. We have not progressed as far with the solution of this problem as we have with the first. Indeed, our particular concept of private property, which deters us from exhausting the positive resources of the earth, favors pollution.

* * *

How to Legislate Temperance?

Analysis of the pollution problem * * * uncovers a not generally recognized principle of morality, namely: *the morality of an act is a function of the state of the system at the time it is performed.* Using the commons as a cesspool does not harm the general public under frontier conditions, because there is no public; the same behavior in a metropolis is unbearable.

* * *

That morality is system-sensitive escaped the attention of most codifiers of ethics in the past. * * * The laws of our society follow the pattern of ancient ethics, and therefore are poorly suited to governing a complex, crowded, changeable world. Our epicyclic solution is to augment statutory law with administrative law. * * * [W]e delegate the details to bureaus. The result is administrative law, which is rightly feared—* * * "Who shall watch the watchers themselves?" * * *

* * * The great challenge facing us now is to invent the corrective feedbacks that are needed to keep custodians honest. We must find ways to legitimate the needed authority of both the custodians and the corrective feedbacks.

Note

Farber, in his article on *Boomer v. Atlantic Cement Co.*, argues that, despite its pollution overtones, the case was not really a case about the tragedy of the commons. Farber may be correct as to the plaintiffs actually suing in the case, for Atlantic's operation apparently had dramatic impacts upon them. But what of those further away from the quarry, where the level of dust pollution and vibration was smaller? Was that (unlitigated) part of the case a problem of the commons?

2. Trespass

Shopping centers have become the community centers of our era. Their widespread popularity has also drawn controversy, politics and protest. Those seeking to communicate with their fellow citizens are often asked to leave shopping areas by center personnel or arrested for trespass when they refuse to go. Similar problems have arisen in other areas—such as large apartments, schools, and migrant labor camps—where people congregate or providers of social services seek to find their clients. One case, *State of New Jersey v. Shack*, has become a property classic. After a short essay on the background of that case written by me, there is an excerpt from an article by Curtis Berger, Pruneyard *Revisited: Political Activity on Private Lands,* on the federal constitutional and state trespass law surrounding these sorts of controversies.

Richard H. Chused, *Background to* State of New Jersey v. Shack and Tejeras, CASES, MATERIALS AND PROBLEMS IN PROPERTY 328–330, 335–336 (1988)*

Disputes about many major American institutions were rife in the late 1960's. The status of migrant farm workers was no exception. Most of the highly publicized activity occurred in Florida, Texas and California, where Cesar Chavez's efforts to organize workers became a national cause célèbre. But farm worker issues also arose in some smaller growing areas, such as Cumberland County in southern New Jersey. In fact, New Jersey's legislature, partially in response to the national concern over the issue, adopted legislation in the spring of 1967 to strengthen regulation of migrant labor camps in the state. Shortly after this legislation was adopted the New Jersey Farm Bureau, a private association of growers, sold 4,000 *NO TRESPASSING* signs to its members in an apparent effort to keep anti-poverty workers, union organizers and newspaper reporters off the farms during the coming summer. And in December, 1967, Governor Hughes appointed a task force to investigate and report on migrant worker issues.

Ron Sullivan, a reporter for the *New York Times* and the author of most of the stories on New Jersey migrant workers published in that paper, estimated that in the summer of 1966, about 7,000 black persons migrated from the south to work the New Jersey fields, along with about 5,400 Puerto Ricans. An additional 1,000 persons, mostly from nearby cities like Philadelphia, Camden and Newark, were driven in each day. When the New Jersey Farm Bureau *NO TRESPASSING* signs appeared, the NAACP Legal Defense Fund, deeply interested in the issue because of the large number of black workers, revealed plans to ask federal courts to have the signs removed as a violation of the First Amendment rights of the workers to freely associate with persons of their choice.[6] A short time later the interagency group set up by Governor Hughes to enforce the newly enacted legislation on migrant labor urged that a number of labor camps be closed because of inhumane conditions. Five farmers, including Morris Tedesco who owned the land that was the subject of the *Shack* case, were warned to clean up their camps or face court closure actions. The closure actions were never brought by the state, though migrant workers later confirmed their right to sue the state to demand that migrant camp regulations be enforced.[7]

In 1968, the Governor's task force issued its report on migrant labor, recommending that the state take steps to encourage unionization of the labor force. The notion of constructing state operated housing for migrant laborers was rejected, though such housing had been constructed in the early 1940's by the federal government and seriously considered in New Jersey at about the same time. In any case, the report was never acted upon by the state government. Tensions in the fields grew. By the summer of 1970, guns were being brandished and threats made against anti-poverty workers, lawyers and reporters. Frank Tejeras noted, "We got sick and tired of getting pushed out. Often the farmers would come out with guns. I used to kiss my wife and daughter goodbye everyday because I didn't know if I'd be coming home."

On August 6, 1970, Frank Tejeras, a field worker for the Farm Workers Division of the Southern Citizen Organization for Poverty Elimination (SCOPE), went to Tedesco's farm to pick up Tona Rivera, whose face had been slashed some weeks earlier, and take him to the hospital to remove stitches from the wound. The injury was festering because the stitches had been in too long—three weeks. Tejeras passed the *NO TRESPASSING* signs posted along the roadside of the farm and walked up the dirt road toward the migrant camp. Tedesco, rifle in hand, confronted Tejeras and told Tejeras to leave. He left.

Tejeras called Peter Shack, a staff attorney at the Farm Workers Division of Camden Regional Legal Services. The two of them agreed to return to the farm the next day with Ronald Sullivan of the *Times*. At about nine o'clock the next morning Shack, Tejeras and Sullivan (with camera in hand) entered Morris Tedesco's farm. Once again they passed the *NO TRESPASSING* signs posted along the roadside of the farm and walked up the dirt road toward the migrant labor camp.

Tedesco was not pleased. Though without his rifle this time, he was reported to have cursed Shack and Tejeras, said that not "even President Nixon" would be allowed to see the farm, and, when Sullivan tried to take his picture, struck the camera against Sullivan's face and yelled, "I'll smash you for this; I'm going to get you for this. This is my property. You can't come in here looking around!" Shack, Tejeras and Sullivan decided to stay at the farm. State troopers were called and about two hours later all three were arrested and charged with trespass. Later in the day, Tejeras went back to the farm, picked up Rivera and took him to the hospital. Two days later, Tejeras went back to the farm and picked up another worker, Ramon Cruz, whom Shack had wanted to see at the farm. Cruz had suffered a cut on his hand while working in the fields. He was unable to work and had not received wages for a month.

---

[6] The case was filed, but dismissed on state action grounds. That holding was reversed and remanded, but only for a factual hearing on whether state action was present. *Peper v. Cedarbrook Farms, Inc.*, 437 F.2d 1209 (3d Cir. 1971). The case was then dropped. By that time the New Jersey Supreme Court had agreed to review the *Shack* case and the NAACP Legal Defense Fund correctly assumed their interests would prevail in that setting. *See* Casenote, *State v. Shack*, 46 N.Y.U. L. Rev. 834, 840–845 (1971).

[7] *Colon v. Tedesco*, 125 N.J. Super. 446, 311 A.2d 393 (1973).

The case against Sullivan was severed from the Shack-Tejeras matter by Judge Steven Kleiner. Kleiner may have been influenced to split the cases by the First Amendment overtones of the Sullivan matter or by the fact that the *New York Times* had sued Tedesco in tort for damages caused the paper by the battery of its employee, Sullivan. The charges against Sullivan were eventually dropped and the *Times* agreed to dismiss the tort action. The dispute and the resultant publicity led to another round of calls for action by state and federal officials against poorly run farms in southern New Jersey and for adoption of legislation guaranteeing government workers and certain other persons access to labor camps. Early the next year, the Justice Department sued for the first time, seeking access to a migrant labor camp to investigate potential violations of civil rights.[10]

* * *

[After the decision was rendered] Morris Tedesco reacted strongly * * *. "We now might as well turn the country over to the Russians," he said. The decision, he added, will only create more conflict this summer and force the remaining farmers in New Jersey to "clear out within six months." Access problems have apparently eased somewhat since the decision. People have more confidence going in [to farms], though there is still some resistance. Migrant life itself has not changed a whole lot according to Tejeras. But the composition of the work force has. The vast majority of seasonal workers are Puerto Rican. Black migrants from the South are not appearing in large numbers now.

---

10 * * * *See Folgueras v. Hassle*, 331 F.Supp. 615 (W.D. Mich. 1971).

Curtis J. Berger, Pruneyard *Revisited: Political Activity on Private Lands*, 66 N.Y.U. L. REV. 633-636, 648-657, 659-670, 674-675, 678-679, 681-682, 690-692 (1991)*

INTRODUCTION

More than a decade has passed since the Supreme Court decided *Pruneyard Shopping Center v. Robins*,[1] a case that pitted free-speech rights against those of private-property. In *Pruneyard*, the Court held that the California State Constitution's grant to individuals of the freedom to enter a privately owned shopping mall and gather petitions did not violate the property owner's first and fifth amendment rights under the United States Constitution. In the same opinion, the Court cemented earlier holdings[6] that had denied such an "expressive" right of entry founded exclusively upon the first and fourteenth amendments. No federal constitutional right existed, the *Pruneyard* Court reasoned, because the mall owner's decision to curb political activity upon his premises did not implicate the requisite state action.

The intervening years have seen nearly a dozen state appellate courts wrestle with the *Pruneyard* issue under their respective constitutions. A current scorecard shows that advocates of free expression are losing out to supporters of the private owner's autonomy.[10] But the battle continues. It is being waged with growing sophistication and—viewing

---

1 447 U.S. 74 (1980).

6 See Hudgens v. NLRB, 424 U.S. 507, 523 (1976); Lloyd Corp. v. Tanner, 407 U.S. 551, 570 (1972).

10 Mall owners have prevailed in Arizona, Connecticut, Georgia, Michigan, New York, North Carolina, Pennsylvania, and Wisconsin but have lost in California, Massachusetts, Washington, and Oregon. In Washington, however, a later decision, Southcenter Joint Venture v. National Democratic Policy Comm., 113 Wash. 2d 413, 780 P.2d 1282 (1989), has limited the protection afforded to free speech under the state's constitution to the right to solicit signatures for an initiative.

both the frequency with which courts are narrowly divided and the rhetoric of their division—intense emotion. Moreover, the struggle has spilled over onto other privately held lands, such as university campuses, office parks, and residential communities, all of which are characterized by some degree of public access.

In this post-*Pruneyard* era, two related sets of legal questions continue to vex the courts. The first concerns the potential boundaries of the "public forum" doctrine. Although the Supreme Court has announced that privately owned lands are not first amendment public forums, the analyses in these cases fuel an approach toward an extraconstitutional view of a public forum. They do so in two ways: first, by stressing the forum's importance to the political process; and second, by indicating why certain land is or is not well suited to classification as a public forum.

The second post-*Pruneyard* issue concerns the suitable limits of a state law that permits access onto private land without the owner's consent. Twice in recent years, in *Loretto v. Teleprompter Manhattan CATV Corp.*[16] and *Nollan v. California Coastal Commission,*[17] the Supreme Court has struck down local laws that have permitted the occupancy of private lands without the owner's consent. Although the *Loretto* and *Nollan* Courts took special care to reaffirm *Pruneyard*, its intellectual foundation nevertheless must be reexamined in light of the holdings in these cases.

Pruneyard and its progeny pit two vital themes of a democratic society against each other: free speech and private property. The imperative of an informed, politically conscious electorate requires access to information and opinion, access that should not depend upon a candidate's or an advocate's wealth or financial support. In contrast, the gospel of private ownership regards as fundamental the right to control entry to one's land. As with other pairs of constitutionally protected yet competing interests, some accommodation must be found. Unfortunately, in setting the fulcrum between speech and property, both state and federal courts have given far greater leverage to property than any sensible weighing of the competing interests dictates.

This Article argues that land ownership should not become the legal vehicle for closing off appropriate channels of political expression. Once the private owner has opened its lands to the public generally, it relinquishes some of the autonomy owners otherwise enjoy. Using the modern marketplace—the mall—as a paradigm, this Article asserts that where the land's configuration and the activity it attracts begin to resemble those of a public forum, the owner's autonomy recedes in the face of a heightened need to find alternative channels for grassroots political activity.

* * *

II
Toward an Expanded Definition of "Public Forum"

Access to a public space in which politicians and citizens may air their views lies at the very foundation of American politics. Whether one believes that democracy draws strength from an engaged citizenry or from a robust "marketplace of ideas," participation in politics is essential. Because of the Supreme Court's deference in *Pruneyard* to state "chartered" political activities upon private lands, this Article seeks to develop an innovative means of preserving some private arenas for political discourse under state law. Part II takes the first step toward this goal: defining "public forum" and considering when a state may decide that privately held property should fall within this definition.

A. *The Narrow Strictures of Supreme Court "Public Forum" Doctrine*

Coined in Harry Kalven's seminal 1965 article,[89] the phrase "public forum" began to appear regularly in the Court's opinions by 1974 and had assumed the status of a fundamental principle of First Amendment doctrine by 1984. As a constitutional matter, a forum is "public" only when it is governmentally controlled or, in limited circumstances,[92] when the controlling private body is a quasimunicipality. Title is an essential element; constitutionally there is (almost) no such thing as a privately held "public forum."[93]

Although this constitutional "bright line" limits greatly the term's potential sweep, the litmus test of ownership does not ensure that space that is public

[16] 458 U.S. 419 (1982).

[17] 483 U.S. 825 (1987).

[89] Kalven, The Concept of the Public Forum: Cox v. Louisiana, 1965 Sup. Ct. Rev. 1, 11–12. * * *

[92] See, e.g., Marsh v. Alabama, 326 U.S. 501, 507–08 (1946).

[93] See Hudgens v. NLRB, 424 U.S. 507, 513 (1976) * * *.

will be a protected forum. A military base, a nuclear weapons test area, and a state prison exemplify public property upon which the government may bar any political activity. Although these cases may be regarded as exceptional because of the security needs associated with the sites, municipally owned public utility poles, city bus advertising space, and a high school newspaper also have failed to meet the "public forum" threshold.

* * *

The Court has limited political activity even in the most traditional public forum—the public street. For example, in *Frisby v. Schultz*[102] the Court held a municipal sidewalk to be "off limits" to various forms of common political activity. In that case, Brookfield, Wisconsin had enacted an ordinance making it "unlawful for any person to engage in picketing before or about the residence of any individual." The Court upheld the ordinance against the claims of peaceful antiabortion picketers who wished to assemble in front of a doctor's home. Justice O'Connor, who wrote for the divided Court, acknowledged that public streets and sidewalks are the archetypical public forums and pointedly rejected the city's claim that, because of their physical structure and residential character, the streets and sidewalks should be considered a non-public forum. But having securely cemented the public forum label to these streets and sidewalks, Justice O'Connor refused to protect the type of "focused picketing" that intruded upon an individual resident's quiet enjoyment. * * *

B. A Proposal for Defining the Modern "Public Forum": Balancing Between Private Home and Marketplace

1. The Elements of the Private Home

What is it, then, that makes space a suitable "public forum," without regard to ownership or control? That question might be approached initially by asking what makes some property "so private" that a set of circumstances in which an unwilling owner could be forced to permit the entry of strangers for political activity cannot be imagined.

Consider, for example, the private home—the paradigm of a privileged sanctuary—protected from invasion even in the face of recognized public interests: the news media on the trail of a fast-breaking story; police officers who have not obtained a warrant; and, not surprisingly, private solicitors. Certain characteristics and assumptions, regardless of its ownership, make the home "private."

* * *

These attributes of one's home—privacy, quiet enjoyment, limited access, associational choice, exclusivity, territoriality, and security—do not depend upon the resident's ownership of the premises. The tenant in a rented apartment—except to the extent she has bargained otherwise—thinks of her home similarly. Nor may a state weaken a tenant's freedoms because she is "only" a tenant. Limits on state power are even more pronounced when the state, itself, is the landlord, as in the case of a public housing authority.

2. The Elements of a Marketplace

The public market provides a stark contrast to the traditional private home. Throughout history, in vastly diverse societies, the market has provided a central meeting place, not only for the exchange of goods and services but also for commerce in ideas. The agora, the marketplace of ancient Greece, was one of the earliest public forums. Today, a visit to the Bedouin market in Be'er Sheba, the rug market in Istanbul, the fruit and vegetable market at Covent Garden, or the piers and walkways at Fisherman's Wharf in San Francisco will evoke many of the same sensations. Although these markets began in different centuries and flourish on different continents, they share an organic commonality. * * * [T]he elements intrinsic to the marketplace [are] * * * little expectation of privacy, * * * no expectation of quiet, * * * multiple points of entry, * * * restricted freedom of association, * * * privilege of free entry, * * * lack of territoriality, * * * [and] reduced expectation of security.

C. Comparing Public and Private Spaces

The polarities that divide the home, the paradigm private space, and the market, the paradigm public place, do not rest upon the circumstance of ownership. The public-housing occupant regards her home as private, although the state holds title. The shopping-center occupant feels that she has entered a public space although a limited partnership or insurance company may hold the deed. Where it is important legally to distinguish between private and public space, as must be done in the search for a public forum, one should look beyond the property's title, focusing instead on its physical layout, its

[102] 487 U.S. 474 (1988).

ongoing activity, and the occupants' reasonable expectations.

Political discourse naturally complements the medley of ongoing activity within the marketplace. As the American city evolved, the market expanded into the streets and sidewalks of the central business district. More recently, as suburban America developed, the privately owned mall has transformed the marketplace once again.[131] Each stage of evolution, from a discrete public marketplace to the expanded central business district to the privately owned mall, has embodied attributes that well suit the forum role. Thus, it seems natural to define the modern public forum not in terms of ownership but rather as a gathering place, which joins those who wish to deliver a political message to those who—at the least—do not think it strange to find the forum to be the delivery point.

* * *

There is a broad spectrum of land use lying between the private home and the public market. If the public forum concept is to extend to some privately owned lands, both courts and legislators sometimes will face difficult decisions. Yet occasional uncertainty is far better than the bright line of private title that arbitrarily has limited the area in which persons may participate in political activity. Balancing the nature of the particular forum against any rationales for exclusion is essential to resolving the ambiguity presented by such "middleground" settings.

* * *

III
THE NON-CONSTITUTIONAL "PUBLIC FORUM"

* * *

Absent state intervention, formidable obstacles bar persons who wish to enter shopping malls for any sort of political effort. Many centers flatly forbid all such entry and will restrain those who carry on political activity after entrance. Other owners open their centers to particular groups, causes, or forms of expression but tightly control the mode and content of any political activity within their property. Even where state courts have followed *Pruneyard*, mall owners usually have responded grudgingly, refusing to extend the right of entry beyond the narrow activity that the court has approved and burdening the permitted activity with unreasonable "time, place, and manner" restrictions. One also might infer a general hostility among mall owners toward political use of their properties by their concerted opposition to all legislative moves in that direction. Any step that would weaken a mall owner's autonomous control over its center is understandably threatening, and one needs little imagination to envision a situation that might temporarily disrupt the center's normal business activity. That such disruptions rarely occur, happening with far less frequency than such "normal" disturbances as fires, acts of God, or accidents, might persuade a court or a legislator that owners are unduly concerned. However, it probably will not persuade owners generally to take a more forthcoming attitude. Therefore, the law's choice becomes apparent: it must either allow new forums for political expression despite recalcitrant private ownership or remain silent as the traditional realm for grassroots political activity withers away. State legislatures and state courts can play an active role in shaping public forum doctrine. Free-speech advocates may be dismayed by the *Pruneyard* progeny's hesitance to use state constitutions to expand the public forum to include some privately held lands. However, the state's power to intervene need not depend upon an activist reading of a state's constitution.

A. The Common-Law "Public Forum"

Contemporary lawyers, law professors, and jurists, weaned from the common-law tradition, seem less ready than were their forebears to trust courts to define legal rights and duties. This distrust stems partly from doubts about the courts' institutional competence to effect and monitor systemic change in today's complex world. But the doubts also rest on a belief that courts have no business in overriding majoritarian views, as legislatively expressed, except in the narrow range of instances where a statute has offended the Constitution; and even here, as to most claims of unconstitutional lawmaking, majority def-

[131] At the end of 1990, the United States had more than 36,500 shopping centers, which accounted for 55.5% of all nonautomotive retail sales. O'Neill, Planning Ahead for 1991, Monitor, Nov. 1990, at 27. In some states, shopping centers have a near monopoly on retail sales. In Arizona, for example, 88% of retail sales occur in shopping centers, and in Florida 82% of retail sales take place in such locations. International Council of Shopping Centers, The Scope of the Shopping Center Industry in the U.S. 8, 22 (1990).

In a typical month, 172.4 million adults—94% of the population over the age of 18—visit a shopping center at least once; those shopping at regional malls do so an average of 3.9 times per month. Id. at 1.

erence is expected of the courts. Further, in the property domain, courts' alteration of settled doctrine may affect land titles and economic values.

This generation, nevertheless, has seen an extraordinary display of the common-law method, as courts have refashioned much of the property relationship between landlord and residential tenant. * * * The impetus for reform was the courts' growing conviction that the circumstances that defined the legal status quo had changed, and that the body of common law, which defined the landlord-tenant relationship, no longer fairly mediated the legitimate concerns of the two parties to the lease and often caused tenants great hardship and injustice. As it became clear that legislatures were reluctant to initiate the reforms, the courts stepped in, influencing other non-property realms such as unconscionability, products liability, at-will employment contracts, and corporate law.

Free expression is protected by the federal Constitution but only against state-imposed control. However, the values that such speech promotes—participatory democracy and an informed electorate—are imbedded in American political theory. For speech to flourish, expressionists need settings where they can meet their audiences—today's dispersed and motorized citizenry—cheaply and efficiently. Thus, when presented with evidence that vast urban galleria and suburban multiactivity malls have displaced downtown sidewalks and strip retail stores opening to the sidewalk, a common-law court should stand ready to declare these malls, and other forum-like private lands, to be appropriate, indeed vital, complements to more traditional public space. Rather than awaiting legislative recognition of the need for new public forums, especially when legislatures have shown no disposition toward acting, the courts might create the expressionist right themselves. This section examines in detail two cases that illustrate how courts might effect this change.

The New Jersey Supreme Court's 1971 decision in *State v. Shack*[170] provides a useful model for exploring how common-law courts might extend the public-forum doctrine to private lands. The *Shack* court held that New Jersey common law did not permit the owner of a migrant farm to exclude unreasonably either a lawyer or a medical aide, who wished to meet with migrant workers, from the workers' rented homes. The farm owner had asked the two professionals to leave his property unless they agreed to the owner's presence at the meetings between the lawyer and his clients. Having refused to accept this condition, the lawyer and the medical aide remained on the farm until they were arrested. They subsequently were tried and convicted for criminal trespass.

In overturning the conviction, the New Jersey Supreme Court did not rest its decision on the federal Constitution. Despite the then viability of *Amalgamated Food Employees Union Local 590 v. Logan Valley Plaza, Inc.*,[175] which set forth a first amendment right to picket in a shopping center, the *Shack* court did not hold that a migrant farm was equivalent to a "company town." Alternatively, the court might have agreed with the defendants' argument that the federal supremacy clause prohibited a trespass conviction since criminal liability would have defeated the purpose of the federal antipoverty statutes that funded their activities. But the court eschewed these and other constitutional claims in favor of the defendants' common-law property right to enter the migrant farm free from the owner's restrictive conditions.

The *Shack* court held that under state law the ownership of real property did not include the right to bar access to governmental services available to migrant workers. Hence no trespass had occurred within the meaning of the penal statute.

* * *

Shack illustrates how a court first should decide whether the rights of the specific property holder outweigh the interests of the party seeking entry. The nature of the private property at issue should be an essential part of this analysis. Persons seeking expressive entry to a mall would have to convince a court to regard the property, despite its private ownership, as the equivalent of a public forum—a highly appropriate location for the activity in question. Should expressionists persuade the court to protect the political activity, the court might well conclude that "under our State law the ownership of" this shopping mall "does not include the right to bar access to" persons seeking to enter the mall for enumerated political activities and hence there was no trespass.

Shack is not a remarkable case, except possibly in the breadth and eloquence of its rhetoric. The owner

---

[170] 58 N.J. 297, 277 A.2d 369 (1971).

[175] 391 U.S. 308 (1968). * * * Four years later, after the New Jersey Supreme Court had decided Shack, the Court eviscerated Logan Valley in Lloyd Corp. v. Tanner, 407 U.S. 551, 561–64 (1972). In 1976, the Court expressly overruled Logan Valley in Hudgens v. NLRB, 424 U.S. 507, 517–21 (1976). * * *

of real property has never enjoyed an absolute right to exclude strangers or to regulate activity upon its premises. Instead, the common law historically has shaped and refined the network of relationships between landowners and those seeking entry to or already present upon the land. In fact, the Second Restatement of Torts contains more than twenty sections—exceptions to the law of trespass—enumerating "privileged" entries on land over the owner's objection.[192] These include: entry by a remainderman to view waste or make repairs; entry to abate a private nuisance; entry by a former licensee to remove his possessions; entry by a landlord to demand defaulted rent; entry by a traveler on a public highway that has become impassable to enter neighboring land to continue his journey; and entry because of private necessity. Pursuant to this common-law tradition, there is room for state courts to declare that in the circumstances of a *Pruneyard*-like mall, the private owner—having opened its property to thousands of strangers daily—may not refuse entry to persons seeking to engage in peaceful picketing and political solicitation. One court has done just that.

In *Lloyd Corp. v. Whiffen*,[200] the Oregon Supreme Court held that the defendants were permitted to enter a shopping mall to solicit petition signatures without the plaintiff owner's permission. In ruling for the defendants, the court rested its decision solely on nonconstitutional grounds.

The facts of *Whiffen* were undisputed. The plaintiff owned the Lloyd Center in downtown Portland, which contained stores, professional and business offices, covered walkways, and parking areas. More than sixty-six blocks of publicly owned sidewalks traversed the site. Since the center's opening in 1960, the plaintiff had barred distribution of political leaflets and petitioning within the mall. In 1985, the defendants entered the center to gather signatures for three initiative petitions. When the defendants refused to cease their activity, the plaintiff sued for both injunctive and declaratory relief.

* * *

Starting from the premise that equity will not provide a remedy for every wrong, the court declared that a "very real public interest" was at stake, and if an injunction would cause that interest serious injury, the injunction should not issue unless the owner "would experience a more serious injury." The public interest here, the court continued, was "well defined. . . . The signature-gathering process for political petitions is a form of political speech and no one contests that free speech is one of our society's most precious rights." In this instance, the process of gathering signatures would be substantially impaired—requiring nearly twice the amount of time to gather signatures—if conducted on the nearby public walkways or parks instead of in the mall.

Turning its attention to the other side of the balance, the *Whiffen* court acknowledged that the defendants' activity, "buttonholing" potential customers and setting up card tables in heavily trafficked areas, might cause injury to the plaintiff's commercial enterprise. This "obtrusive" activity could be enjoined to minimize any interference with the center's tenants and their customers. However, a blanket order, entitling the plaintiff to exclude the defendants from entering the center "for any purpose other than shopping," simply went too far.

* * *

B. The Regulatory Public Forum

* * *

Using the regional mall as an example, * * * development permission [should] be conditioned upon the owner's willingness to provide for expressive entry. Large-scale shopping malls invariably must pass through an extended planning process, often in the form of an application for a variance, special exception, or rezoning; during this period the community and developer negotiate the terms that will lead to the permit or zoning change. In the past, such negotiations have involved restrictions on the routing of traffic flow, the amount and location of off-street parking, the activity near the boundary with neighboring properties, and the building's architectural style. Even an as-of-right development often must meet similar conditions. Whether development approval results from a negotiated or an as-of-right process, linking approval to a satisfactory arrangement for expressive activity would not increase significantly community power over a developer's land-use autonomy.

* * *

IV
Constitutional Limitations

* * * [U]nder the Courts' current jurisprudence, neither the takings clause of the fifth amendment nor

---

[192] See Restatement (Second) of Torts §§ 176–207 (1965).

[200] 307 Or. 674, 773 P.2d 1294 (1989).

the free-speech clause of the first amendment bars the courts or legislators from establishing an expressive right of entry onto a private "public forum."

A. The Takings Clause

Pruneyard Shopping Center v. Robins[258] might seem to lay to rest any claim that the takings clause protects the private owner against uncompensated use of its property as a public forum. Writing for the entire Court in this regard, Justice Rehnquist noted that the literal "taking" of the owner's right to exclude others from its premises, in itself, did not become a "'taking' in the constitutional sense." The landowner must show that the restriction forces it alone "to bear public burdens which, in all fairness and justice, should be borne by the public as a whole." In *Pruneyard* the mall owner's burden—tolerating signature gatherers on its property—did not exceed the threshold that would necessitate constitutional relief: the project was a vast commercial complex opened to the public; time, place, and manner controls could minimize any interference with the mall's commercial functions; and no evidence demonstrated unreasonably impaired value or use. When the owner's minimal hardship was balanced against the appellees' enhanced exercise of free expression and petition, the Court deemed that no taking had occurred.

Yet the question remains as to whether a common-law or regulatory expressive entry right would face a more stringent takings examination than did the entry in *Pruneyard.* Analytically, it should make no difference that the entry would rest on nonconstitutional grounds, although at the margin a justice's response to a common-law or regulatory right of entry might not be the same as to one buttressed by the state's first amendment provision. However, the Court's treatment of the takings question in two post-*Pruneyard* decisions, *Loretto v. Teleprompter Manhattan CATV Corp.*[264] and *Nollan v. California Coastal Commission,*[265] raises doubts about whether nonconstitutional claims would receive equivalent treatment. In each case, an entry onto private land that was forced upon a recalcitrant owner by regulation was deemed to be a taking. This section asserts that neither of these later cases has compromised *Pruneyard* and that the federal Constitution poses no obstacle to a state common-law or legislative solution.

* * *

The path to reconciling the Court's decisions in *Loretto, Pruneyard,* and *Nollan* lies neither in the Marshall distinction between the continuous presence of a "foreign" body, nor in the Scalia search for the permanent loss of the private owner's right to exclude others. The logical consistency in these cases is provided by the nature of the private property to which the regulatory servitude was attached. The apartment building in *Loretto* and the beach front in *Nollan* were within their owners' exclusive possession. In the two instances, the owners had yielded none of their autonomy; until the state acted to create access, the public was not privileged to enter. By contrast, the mall owner in *Pruneyard* already had compromised its exclusionary privilege because the public had a general invitation to enter the mall. In fact, the heavier the public response to the invitation, the greater the center's potential sales, rentals, and profits. Having considerably diluted its autonomy, the owner thereby had weakened its position to complain about the presence of expressionists whose activity—subject to the owner's reasonable time, place, and manner controls—would add little physical burden or other disruption to the center's normal daily traffic.

There is good reason to assert that the Court, behind its formalistic utterances about permanent occupation or the loss of the right to exclude, sees this distinction as factually relevant. The *Nollan* footnote that distinguishes *Pruneyard* also states that the owner in *Pruneyard* "had already opened his property to the general public." Similarly, in *Loretto,* Justice Marshall writes that the Pruneyard owners "had already invited the general public" on their property. Thus, where the private owner has lifted the barriers against the public, by extending a generalized invitation to enter the premises, state action to expand the invitee class does not become a fatal taking. The marginal intrusion is de minimis and, with time, place, and manner regulations, the owner can control the added activity so that it does not interfere unduly with the center's normal activity.

The second way to reconcile the *Pruneyard* outcome with *Loretto* and *Nollan* relates to the purpose for which entry is sought. Although the taking question might seem not to depend upon how the premises are to be used by the speaker since the owner faces a loss of autonomy over the property in

---

[258] 447 U.S. 74 (1980).
[264] 458 U.S. 419 (1982).
[265] 483 U.S. 825 (1987).

any event, the preferred status of political speech helps to explain the Court's readiness in *Pruneyard* to trivialize the property loss. Weighed against the owner's abstract autonomy interest, an entry to engage in political activity achieves a favorable balance. The first amendment may not protect the entry, but it enshrines the expressive values that entry seeks to advance. By contrast, the entry that the Court disapproved of in *Nollan*—while extending the benefits of nature to a larger public—does not involve constitutionally preferred values.

The activity in *Loretto*, the installation of a cable television system, involves an aspect of speech since the New York City regulation would facilitate the cable company's access to the building tenants, resulting in reduced capital expenditures for the speech transmitter and lower service charges for the speech consumer. Whether the transmitter or the consumer is considered, however, the *Loretto* issue is not about the curtailment of speech—service certainly will continue whether the regulation stands or falls; rather, *Loretto* concerns—and then only marginally—the cost of providing and receiving speech. In this sense, cable service is much like telephone service where it is assumed that the utility must pay to extend its wires onto private lands even though this eventually may add to the cost of carrying telephonic speech.

* * *

CONCLUSION

This Article is informed by steadfast faith in political talk. As that talk becomes ever more costly, the need to preserve the domain for cheap talk and grassroots political activity becomes imperative if we wish to enjoy a vital, participatory democracy. If speech—the immediate target of every oppressive regime—is muted, none of our other cherished liberties ultimately can survive.

As the role of the constitutionally protected public forum diminishes (because the Supreme Court has chosen to define public forum narrowly even as more of the gathering places of modern America have become privately owned), other legal approaches to preserve an endangered domain must be sought. The promise of *Pruneyard*, which would have opened shopping malls to political activity, has foundered on the reluctance of most state courts to read their constitutions as providing access to privately owned lands. Speech advocates, therefore, must search elsewhere to fuel their struggle. State common-law limitations on property owners' powers and state regulatory schemes calling for expressive access are two sources for the struggle.

Inherent in this effort is a revised conception of what it means for a forum to be public in today's world. Balancing the need to preserve our free "market place of ideas" against the realistic expectations of the owners of modern "market places" results in a jurisprudence that is true to speech and property alike. Certainly, property should not become a vehicle by which speech is stifled.

Note

Given the confused legacy left by *Pruneyard Shopping Center v. Robins,* 447 U.S. 74 (1980) and *Nollan v. California Coastal Commission*, 483 U.S. 825 (1987), which of the following state trespass decisions would survive constitutional attack:

1. A decision confirming the right of a client of James Nollan, who is a lawyer, to walk on the beach by Nollan's house quietly carrying a picket sign protesting the way Nollan handled his case.

2. A decision dismissing a trespass prosecution brought against a person for walking in front of Nollan's house over a sidewalk. The sidewalk was built with public funds under a local ordinance requiring every homeowner, in order to get a building permit, to dedicate a specified part of the house lot along the street in front of the dwelling for use by pedestrians.

F. Public Land Use Controls Since World War II

This part reviews three sets of materials. The first, harking back to the formative era of zoning regulation described in Part II(C), reviews the operation of zoning and housing policies during the post

World War II building boom. The massive development of residential suburbs in this time period came under attack in the most densely populated states during the 1960's. The famous *Mt. Laurel* litigation led to major reforms in three eastern states—New Jersey, New York and Massachusetts. A review of the effectiveness of those reforms will be found in the second section. This part of the anthology concludes with a look at modern zoning practices, particularly the ubiquitous tendency of zoning authorities and real estate developers to make "deals" about urban planning.

1. Post World War II Land Use Policies: Suburban Subsidies and Segregation of the Urban Poor

The modern structure of land use was established after World War II. The construction of the interstate highway system, the collapse of streetcar networks, middle class mortgage guarantee programs and the enormous growth in housing demand during the baby boom permanently altered the American landscape. Millions of (mostly white) Americans escaped from the poverty of the Depression and moved to new housing tracts. The lives of those left behind in the cities presented an increasingly noticeable, and for a time, unacceptably impoverished contrast. This picture is portrayed in two excerpts. The first is from Kenneth T. Jackson's classic book CRABGRASS FRONTIER: THE SUBURBANIZATION OF THE UNITED STATES, which tells the tale lying behind the zoning structure subjected to searching review during the 1970's and 1980's in cases like *Southern Burlington County N.A.A.C.P. v. Township of Mt. Laurel.** The other excerpt, by Lawrence Friedman, is a compelling history of public housing entitled *Public Housing and the Poor.* These materials should be read with the background materials on the Realist era, found earlier in this anthology in Part II(C), in mind. For additional reading in this area, see the wonderful article by Martha Mahoney, *Law and Racial Geography: Public Housing and the Economy in New Orleans*, 42 STAN. L. REV. 1251 (1990).

---

*The case led to two huge sets of opinions emanating from the New Jersey Supreme Court, one at 67 N.J. 151, 336 A.2d 713 (1975) and the other at 92 N.J. 158, 456 A.2d 390 (1983).

Kenneth T. Jackson, Crabgrass Frontier: The Suburbanization of the United States 191, 193, 195–199, 203–208, 214–215, 238–245 (1985)**

Federal Subsidy and the Suburban Dream: How Washington Changed the American Housing Market

Government and Housing Before 1933

Although housing involves the largest capital costs of any human necessity, for the first three centuries of urban settlement in North America the provision of shelter was not regarded as an appropriate responsibility of government—whether that body was a colonial assembly or a state legislature, a town meeting or a city council, a Parliament in London or a Congress in Washington.

* * *

Not until the advent of the Great Depression in 1929 did the American attitude toward government intervention shift in a fundamental way. The prolonged and mammoth economic catastrophe * * * inflicted crippling blows on both the housing industry and the homeowner. Between 1928 and 1933, the construction of residential property fell by 95 percent, and the expenditures on home repairs fell by 90 percent. In 1926, which may be taken as a typical year, about 68,000 homes were foreclosed in the United States. In 1930 about 150,000 non-farm households lost their property through foreclosure; in 1931, this increased to nearly 200,000; in 1932 to 250,000. In the spring of 1933, when fully half of all home mortgages in the United States were technically in default, and when foreclosures reached the astronomical rate of more than a thousand per day, the home financing system was drifting toward complete collapse. Housing prices predictably declined—a typical $5,000 house in 1926 was worth about $3300 in 1932—virtually wiping out vast holdings in second and third mortgages as values fell below even the primary claim. Moreover, the victims were often middle-class families who were experiencing impoverishment for the first time.

* * *

The Home Owners Loan Corporation

On April 13, 1933, President Roosevelt urged the House and the Senate to pass a law that would protect the small homeowner from foreclosure, relieve him of part of the burden of excessive interest and principle payments incurred during a period of higher values and higher earning power, and declare that it was national policy to protect homeownership. The measure received bipartisan support. * * * The resulting Home Owners Loan Corporation (HOLC), signed into law by FDR on June 13, 1933, was designed to serve urban needs; the Emergency Farm Mortgage Act, passed almost a month earlier, was intended to reduce rural foreclosures.

The HOLC * * * refinanced tens of thousands of mortgages in danger of default or foreclosure. It even granted loans at low-interest rates to permit owners to recover homes lost through forced sale. Between July 1933 and June 1935 alone, the HOLC supplied more than $3 billion for over one million mortgages, or loans for one-tenth of all owner-occupied, non-farm residences in the United States. Although applications varied widely by state * * * nationally about 40 percent of eligible Americans sought HOLC assistance.

The HOLC is important to history because it introduced, perfected, and proved in practice the feasibility of the long term, self-amortizing mortgage with uniform payments spread over the whole life of the debt. In the nineteenth century, a stigma attached to the existence of a mortgage; well-established families were expected to purchase homes outright. After World War I, however, rising costs and increasing consumer debt made the mortgage a more typical instrument for the financing of a home. Indeed, housing became extraordinarily dependent on borrowed money, both to finance construction and to finance the final purchase. During the 1920s, a boom period in home building, the typical length of a mortgage was between five and ten years, and the loan itself was not fully paid off when the final settlement was due. Thus, the homeowner was periodically at the mercy of arbitrary and unpredictable forces in the money market. When money was easy, renewal every five or seven years was no problem. But if a mortgage expired at a time when money was tight, it might be impossible for the homeowner to secure a renewal, and foreclosure would ensue. Under the HOLC program, the loans were fully amortized, and the repayment period was extended to about twenty years.

Aside from the larger number of mortgages that it helped to refinance on a long-term, low-interest basis, the HOLC systematized appraisal methods across the nation. Because it was dealing with problem mortgages—in some states over 40 percent of all HOLC loans were foreclosed even after refinancing—the HOLC had to make predictions and assumptions regarding the useful or productive life of housing it financed. Unlike refrigerators or shoes, dwellings were expected to be durable—how durable was the purpose of the investigation.

With care and extraordinary attention to detail, the HOLC appraisers divided cities into neighborhoods and developed elaborate questionnaires relating to the occupation, income, and ethnicity of the inhabitants and the age, type of construction, price range, sales demand, and general state of repair of the housing stock. The element of novelty did not lie in the appraisal requirement itself—that had long been standard real-estate practice. Rather, it lay in the creation of a formal and uniform system of appraisal, reduced to writing, structured in defined procedures, and implemented by individuals only after intensive training. The ultimate aim was that one appraiser's judgment of value would have meaning to an investor located somewhere else. In evaluating such efforts, the distinguished economist C. Lowell Harriss has credited the HOLC training and evaluation procedures "with having helped raise the general level of American real estate appraisal methods." A less favorable judgment would be that the Home Owners Loan Corporation initiated the practice of "red lining."

This occurred because HOLC devised a rating system that undervalued neighborhoods that were dense, mixed, or aging. Four categories of quality—imaginatively entitled First, Second, Third and Fourth, with corresponding code letters of A, B, C and D and colors of green, blue, yellow, and red—were established. The First grade (also A and green) areas were described as new, homogeneous, and "in demand as residential locations in good times and bad." Homogeneous meant "American business and professional men." Jewish neighborhoods, or even those with an "infiltration of Jews" could not be considered "best" any more than they could be considered "American."

The Second security grade (blue) went to "still desirable" areas that had "reached their peak," but were expected to remain stable for many years. The Third grade (yellow or "C") neighborhoods were usually described as "definitely declining," while the Fourth grade (red) neighborhoods were defined as areas "in which the things taking place in C areas have already happened." * * * [B]lack neighborhoods were invariably rated as Fourth grade, but so also were any areas characterized by poor maintenance or vandalism. * * *

The Home Owners Loan Corporation did not initiate the idea of considering race and ethnicity in real-estate appraisal. Bigotry has a long history in the United States, and the individuals who bought and sold houses were no better or worse than the rest of their countrymen. Realtors were well aware of the intense antagonisms which attended the attempts of middle-class black families to escape from ghetto areas, and their business practices reflected their observations. Indeed, so common-place was the notion that race and ethnicity were important that * * * the socioeconomic characteristics of a neighborhood determined the value of housing to a much greater extent than did structural characteristics.

* * *

The HOLC simply applied these notions of ethnic and racial worth to real-estate appraising on an unprecedented scale. With the assistance of local realtors and banks, it assigned one of the four ratings to every block in every city. The resulting information was then translated into the appropriate color and duly recorded on secret "Residential Security Maps" in local HOLC offices. The maps themselves were placed in elaborate "City Survey Files," which consisted of reports, questionnaires, and workpapers relating to current and future values of real estate.

* * *

Even more importantly, HOLC appraisal methods, and probably the maps themselves, were adopted by the Federal Housing Administration.

The Federal Housing Administration

No agency of the United States government has had a more pervasive and powerful impact on the American people over the past half-century than the Federal Housing Administration (FHA). It dates from the adoption of the National Housing Act on June 27, 1934. * * * [I]t was intended "to encourage improvement in housing standards and conditions, to facilitate sound home financing on reasonable terms, and to exert a stabilizing influence on the mortgage market." The primary purpose of the legislation, however, was the alleviation of unemployment, which stood at about a quarter of the total work force in 1934 and which was particularly high in the construction industry.

* * *

The FHA effort was later supplemented by the Servicemen's Readjustment Act of 1944 (more familiarly known as the GI Bill), which created the Veterans Administration (VA) program to help the sixteen million soldiers and sailors of World War II purchase a home after the defeat of Germany and Japan. Because the VA very largely followed FHA procedures and attitudes * * *, the two programs can be considered as a single effort.

Between 1934 and 1968, and to a lesser extent to the present day, both the FHA and the VA * * * have had a remarkable record of accomplishment. Essentially, they insure long-term mortgage loans made by private lenders for home construction and sale. To this end, they collect premiums, set up reserves for losses, and in the event of a default on a mortgage, indemnify the lender. They do not build houses or lend money. Instead, they induce lenders who have money to invest it in residential mortgages by insuring them against loss on such instruments, with the full weight of the United States Treasury behind the contract. And they have revolutionized the home finance industry in the following ways:

Before the FHA began operation, first mortgages were limited to one-half to two-thirds of the appraised value of the property. * * * Thus, prospective home buyers needed a down payment of at least 30 percent to close a deal. By contrast, the fraction of the collateral that the lender was able to lend for an FHA-secured loan was about 93 percent. Thus, down payments of more than 10 percent were unnecessary.

Continuing a trend begun by the Home Owners Loan Corporation, FHA extended the repayment period for its guaranteed mortgages to twenty-five or thirty years and insisted that all loans be fully amortized. The effect was to reduce both the average monthly payment and the national rate of mortgage foreclosure. The latter declined from 250,000 nonfarm units in 1932 to only 18,000 in 1951.

FHA established minimum standards for home construction that became almost standard in the industry. These regulations were not intended to make any particular structure fault-free, nor even to assure the owner's satisfaction with the purchase. But they were designed to insure with at least statistical accuracy that the dwelling would be free of gross structural or mechanical deficiencies. * * * Since World War II, the largest private contractors have built all their new houses to meet FHA standards, even though financing has often been arranged without FHA aid. This has occurred because many potential purchasers will not consider a house that cannot earn FHA approval.

* * * Under the FHA * * * program, * * * there was very little risk to the banker if a loan turned sour. Reflecting this government guarantee, interest rates fell by two or three percentage points.

These four changes substantially increased the number of American families who could reasonably expect to purchase homes. Builders went back to work, and housing starts and sales began to accelerate rapidly in 1936. They rose to 332,000 in 1937, * * * and to 619,000 in 1941. This was a startling lift from the 93,000 starts of 1933. After World War II, the numbers became even larger, and by the end of 1972, FHA had helped nearly eleven million families to own houses and another twenty-two million families to improve their properties. It had also insured 1.8 million dwellings in multi-unit properties. And in those same years between 1934 and 1972, the percentage of American families living in owner-occupied dwellings rose from 44 percent to 63 percent.

* * *

Unfortunately, the corollary to this achievement was the * * * hastened decay of inner-city neighborhoods by stripping them of much of their middle-class constituency. In practice, FHA insurance went to new residential developments on the edges of metropolitan areas, to the neglect of core cities. This occurred for three reasons. First, although the legislation nowhere mentioned an antiurban bias, it favored the construction of single-family projects and discouraged construction of multi-family projects through unpopular terms. * * *

Second, loans for the repair of existing structures were small and for short duration, which meant that a family could more easily purchase a new home than modernize an old one. * * *

The third and most important variety of suburban, middle-class favoritism had to do with the "unbiased professional estimate" that was prerequisite to any loan guarantee. Required because maximum mortgage amounts were related to "appraised value," this mandatory judgment included a rating of the property itself, a rating of the mortgagor or borrower, and a rating of the neighborhood. The aim was to guarantee that at any time during the term of the mortgage the market value of the dwelling would exceed the outstanding debt. * * * And * * * the Federal Housing Administration allowed personal and agency bias in favor of all-white subdivisions in the suburbs to affect the kinds of loans it guaranteed—or, equally important, refused to guarantee.

* * *

Reflecting the racist tradition of the United States, the Federal Housing Administration was extraordinarily concerned with "inharmonious racial or nationality groups." It feared that an entire area could lose its investment value if rigid-white-black separation was not maintained. Bluntly warning, "If a neighborhood is to retain stability, it is necessary that properties shall continue to be occupied by the same social and racial classes," the *Underwriting Manual* openly recommended "subdivision regulations and suitable restrictive covenants" that would be "superior to any mortgage." Such covenants * * * were a common method of prohibiting black occupancy until the United States Supreme Court ruling in 1948 (*Shelley v. Kraemer)* that they were "unenforceable as law and contrary to public policy." Even then, it was not until 1949 that FHA announced that as of February 15, 1950, it would not insure mortgages on real estate subject to covenants. Although the press treated the FHA announcement as a major advancement in the field of racial justice, former housing administrator Nathan Strauss noted that "the new policy in fact served only to warn speculative builders who had not filed covenants of their right to do so, and it gave them a convenient respite in which to file."

* * *

Not until the civil-rights movement of the 1960s did community groups realize that red lining and disinvestment were a major cause of community decline and that home-improvement loans were the "lifeblood of housing." In 1967 Martin Nolan summed up the indictment against the FHA by asserting, "The imbalance against poor people and in favor of middle-income homeowners is so staggering that it makes all inquiries into the pathology of slums seem redundant." * * *

In 1966 FHA drastically shifted its policies with a view toward making much more mortgage insurance available for inner-city neighborhoods. Ironically, the primary effect of the change was to make it easier for white families to finance their escape from areas experiencing racial change. At the same time, the relaxed credit standards for black applicants meant that home improvement companies could buy properties at low cost, make cosmetic improvements, and sell the renovated home at inflated prices approved by FHA. Many of the minority purchasers could not afford the cost of maintenance, and FHA had to repossess thousands of homes. The final result was to increase the speed with which areas went through racial transformations and to victimize those it was designed to help. The only people to benefit were contractors and white, middle-class homeowners who were assisted in escaping from a distress position.

* * *

13
The Baby Boom and the Age of the Subdivision

* * *

Characteristics of Postwar Suburbs

However financed and by whomever built, the new subdivisions that were typical of American urban development between 1945 and 1973 tended to share five common characteristics. The first was peripheral location. * * * By 1950 the national suburban growth rate was ten times that of central cities, and in 1954 the editors of *Fortune* estimated that 9 million people had moved to the suburbs in the previous decade. * * *

The few new neighborhoods that were located within the boundaries of major cities tended also to be on the open land at the edges of the built-up sections. * * *

The second major characteristic of the postwar suburbs was their relatively low density. * * * [B]etween 1946 and 1956, about 97 percent of all new single-family dwellings were completely detached, surrounded on every side by their own plots. * * * Moreover, the new subdivisions allotted a higher proportion of their land area to streets and open spaces. * * * This design of new neighborhoods on the assumption that residents would have automobiles meant that those without cars faced severe handicaps in access to jobs and shopping facilities.

This low-density pattern was in marked contrast with Europe. * * * Nowhere in Europe was there the land, the money, or the tradition for single-family home construction.

The third major characteristic of the postwar suburbs was their architectural similarity. * * * In order to simplify their production methods and reduce design fees, most of the larger developers offered no more than a half-dozen basic house plans, and some offered half that number. The result was a monotony and repetition that was especially stark in the early years of the subdivision, before the individual owners had transformed their homes and yards according to personal taste.

* * *

The fourth characteristic of post-World War II housing was its easy availability and thus its reduced suggestion of wealth. To be sure, upper income suburbs and developments sprouted across the land, and some set high standards of style and design. * * * But the most important income development of the period was the lowering of the threshold of purchase. * * *

The fifth and perhaps most important characteristic of the postwar suburb was economic and racial homogeneity. The sorting out of families by income and color began even before the Civil war and was stimulated by the growth of the factory system. This pattern was noticeable in both the exclusive Main Line suburbs of Philadelphia and New York and in the more bourgeois streetcar developments which were part of every city. The automobile accentuated this discriminatory "Jim Crow" pattern. * * * But many pre-1930 suburbs * * * maintained an exclusive image despite the presence of low-income or minority groups living in slums near or within the community.

* * * What was unusual in the new circumstances was not the presence of discrimination * * * but the thoroughness of the physical separation which it entailed. * * *

The economic and age homogeneity of large subdivisions and sometimes entire suburbs was almost as complete as the racial distinction. Although this tendency had been present even in the nineteenth century, the introduction of zoning * * * served the general purpose of preserving residential class segregation and property values. In theory zoning was designed to protect the interest of all citizens by limiting land speculation and congestion. And it was popular. * * *

In actuality zoning was a device to keep poor people and obnoxious industries out of affluent areas. And in time, it also became a cudgel used by suburban areas to whack the central city. * * * [I]n suburbs everywhere, North and South, zoning was used by the people who already lived within the boundaries of a community as a method of keeping everyone else out. Apartments, factories, and "blight," euphemisms for blacks and people of limited means, were rigidly excluded.

While zoning provided a way for suburban areas to become secure enclaves for the well-to-do, it forced the city to provide economic facilities for the whole area and homes for people the suburbs refused to admit. Simply put, land-use restrictions tended to protect residential interests in the suburbs and commercial interests in the cities because the residents of the core usually lived on land owned by absentee landlords who were more interested in financial returns than neighborhood preferences.

* * *

By 1961, when President John F. Kennedy proclaimed his New Frontier and challenged Americans to send a man to the moon within the decade, his countrymen had already remade the nation's metropolitan areas in the short space of sixteen years. * * * In an era of low inflation, plentiful energy, federal subsidies, and expansive optimism, Americans showed the way to a more abundant and more perfect lifestyle. Almost every contractor-built, post-World War II home had central heating, indoor plumbing, telephones, automatic stoves, refrigerators and washing machines.

There was a darker side to the outward movement. By making it possible for young couples to have separate households of their own, abundance further weakened the extended family in America and ordained that most children would grow up in intimate contact only with their parents and siblings. * * *

Critics regarded the peripheral environment as devastating particularly to women and children. The suburban world was a female world, especially during the day. Betty Friedan's 1968 classic *The Feminine Mystique* challenged the notion that the American dream home was emotionally fulfilling for women. * * *

[But t]he young families who joyously moved into the new homes of the suburbs were not terribly concerned about the problems of the inner city * * * or * * * social critics. They were concerned about their hopes and dreams. * * * The single-family tract house * * * whatever its aesthetic failings, offered growing families a private haven in a heartless world. If the dream did not include minorities or the elderly, if it was accompanied by the isolation of nuclear families, by the decline of public transportation, and by the deterioration of urban neighborhoods, the creation of good, inexpensive suburban housing on an unprecedented scale was a unique achievement in the world.

Note

Now that you have read the excerpt from Jackson's book, would you make any changes in the reasoning of *Village of Euclid v. Ambler Realty Co.*, 272 U.S. 365 (1926)?

Lawrence M. Friedman, *Public Housing and the Poor: An Overview*, 54 CAL. L. REV. 642–647, 649, 651–653 (1966)*

Public housing became a reality in the United States only in the days of the New Deal. There were some gingerly steps toward public housing during the First World War, and a few more in the states in the Twenties, but a serious, living program had to wait for the days of the great depression. The major piece of federal legislation on housing was the Wagner-Steagall Act of 1937 which, despite a gloss of amendments, remains on the statute books today, hardly altered in its basic design. * * * In the years since then, public housing has become a familiar aspect of the urban landscape. By the end of 1965 every state had some public housing units in planning or operation, and more than 2,100,000 people lived in low-rent public housing. * * *

But to judge by some newspaper and magazine accounts—and even by the words of housing experts—the public housing program had betrayed its fond expectations. In 1937 Catherine Bauer, a highly respected expert on housing, praised the Wagner-Steagall Act as "progressive legislation"—a hopeful first step toward the goal of good housing for all.[12] Twenty years later, in 1957, Miss Bauer returned to the subject in an article in *Architectural Forum*. The title was significant: "The Dreary Deadlock of Public Housing."[13] She found little to praise in the program as it had evolved. Rather, she saw rigidity and paternalism in management, crudity and segregation in project design, and a deplorable fragmentation of over-all housing policy. In the following issue of the magazine, eleven housing experts commented on her article and made suggestions for change.[14] Not one of the eleven disagreed with her general thesis: that the public housing movement was stagnant; that politically the program was at a standstill; that existing projects were badly conceived and perhaps did more harm than good; and that the whole program needed radical reformation. This was the twentieth anniversary of the Wagner-Steagall Act.

It was a bad time for the image of public housing. Harrison Salisbury, Russian correspondent for the *New York Times*, came home to write his reactions to the domestic scene. What he saw in New York's housing projects profoundly shocked him—for example, the "stench of stale urine that pervades the elevators" in Fort Greene Houses, Brooklyn.[15] He had other things to report about the "new ghettos," as he called them. They were "human cesspools worse than those of yesterday." Fort Greene and similar projects were "monsters, devouring their residents, polluting the areas about them, spewing out a social excrescence which infects the whole of our society." The slums themselves had rarely felt such a tongue lashing.

Salisbury's conclusions were published in book form and widely read. They were by no means the last attack on public housing. * * *

Public housing does not totally lack defenders, but they have spoken softly of late. It is hard to think of any prominent housing figure outside of government who defends the program as it is. Politically the program has little appeal. Appropriations for additional units have been grudgingly voted in Congress; time and time again requests have been scaled down. What is perhaps more significant, authorizations have often gone begging because local government agencies have not been interested in applying for federal grants * * *. * * * The unpopularity of public housing need not be left to oblique inference. In scores of cities and small towns, public housing has been put to the test by the voters. Where it is legally possible, opponents have demanded referenda on the questions. In a distressing number of cases, bond issues to finance the program have failed or public housing has been voted out of town.

Where does the trouble lie? Is it in the conception, the shape of the public housing program? Is it in its mode of administration? Perhaps the problems lie in both. The indictment is clear: Public housing, ostensibly designed to clear the slums and to alleviate the sufferings of the poor, has failed to do either. We turn now to the facts.

---

[12] *Now, at Last: Housing*, New Republic, Sept. 8, 1937, pp. 119, 121.

[13] Bauer, *The Dreary Deadlock of Public Housing*, Architectural Forum, May 1957, p. 140.

[14] *The Dreary Deadlock of Public Housing—How to Break It*, Architectural Forum, June 1957, p. 139.

[15] SALISBURY, THE SHOOK-UP GENERATION 74 (1958).

I
THE PUBLIC HOUSING PROGRAM: CONCEPTION AND DESIGN

* * *

It would be a mistake to suppose (if anyone did) that the Wagner-Steagall Act arose solely out of a gradual persuasion of decent-minded people that the slums were odious, crowded, and evil, and that the federal government had a duty to relieve the sufferings of the poor. The social and economic conditions in the slums provided the opportunity, the background, and much of the emotive power of the law. Yet reformers had long dreamed in vain of public housing. And the slums were surely no worse than they had been in the nineteenth century, though possibly they were larger.

In 1937 the country was suffering from a deep and dangerous depression. Fully one-quarter of the work force was unemployed during the worst days of the depression. In the spring of 1933, thirteen to fifteen million were unemployed. Millions of families were barely making a living. The number of "poor people" in the country had vastly increased; indeed, many of the "poor people" were formerly members of the middle class, who had enjoyed prosperity in the twenties. They retained their middle-class culture and their outlook, their articulateness, their habit of expressing their desires at the polls. There were, therefore, millions of candidates for public housing who did not belong (as later was true) to the class of the "problem poor"; rather they were members of what we might call the submerged middle class. The attractiveness of public housing was enormously enhanced because the potential clientele was itself enormous, composed of millions of relatively articulate citizens, angry and dispirited at their unjust descent into poverty. Public housing was not supported by the dregs of society; a discontented army of men and women of high demands and high expectations stood ready to insist on decent housing from government or at least stood ready to approve and defend it. The political climate was receptive to federal planning and federal housing—not so much as a matter of radical ideology, but out of a demand for positive programs to eliminate the "undeserved" privations of the unaccustomed poor.

Moreover, business was stagnant in the thirties. Programs of social welfare and relief were tested by their ability to create new jobs and prime the business pump as much as by their inherent welfare virtues. Public works programs were exceedingly popular for this reason. A vast federal program of housing building naturally received the enthusiastic support of manufacturers of building supplies and workers in the building trades. The normal opposition to "socialized" housing made its appearance in debate, but it was weak and somewhat muted. Nonetheless, business support for the act was conditioned upon the act being so structured as to avoid any actual government competition with business. Homes would be built only for those who could not possibly afford to buy them on their own. A clear wall must separate the public and private sector. This too was only partly ideological. Government, it was felt, should not cut into the markets of private industry; it must stimulate fresh demand and make fresh jobs—otherwise the effect of the program on the economy would be wasted.

During the depression the volume of private housing construction was very low. In 1925, 900,000 housing units were constructed; in 1934, only 60,000. Yet in one sense no housing shortage developed. During much of the depression, plenty of apartments stood vacant. People who were poor doubled up with relatives, lived in "Hoovervilles" and shanties, returned to rural areas, and in general failed to consume the housing supply. Rents were extremely low. The high vacancy rate posed a potential danger for the program. If public construction increased the housing supply during a period in which many dwellings stood vacant, rents would decrease still more and vacancies would increase. In a decade willing to kill baby pigs and impose acreage controls on farmers, one could hardly expect to see government flooding the housing market with new units. And in fact, the Wagner-Steagall Act was careful to avoid the problem of over-supply. No units were to be built without destroying "dwellings . . . substantially equal in number to the number of newly constructed dwellings provided by the project." This provision—the so-called "equivalent elimination" provision—killed two birds with one stone. It neutralized potential opposition from landlords and the housing industry by removing the danger of oversupply; at the same time, by making slum clearance a part of the law, it appealed to those whose desire for public housing stemmed from their loathing of the slums and slum conditions. The Wagner-Steagall Act was thus shaped by the force of concrete social conditions; what emerged was a program geared to the needs of the submerged middle class, tied to slum clearance, and purged of any element of possible competition with business.

* * *

If this general analysis is correct, what would happen to public housing if a rising standard of living released the submerged middle class from dependence on government shelter? Public housing would be inherited by the permanent poor. The empty rooms would pass to those who had at first been disdained—the unemployed, "problem" families, those from broken homes. The program could adapt only with difficulty to its new conditions, because it had been originally designed for a different clientele. To suit the programs to the needs of the new tenant would require fresh legislation; and yet change would be difficult to enact and to implement precisely because the new clientele would be so poor, so powerless, so inarticulate. The political attractiveness of public housing would diminish. Maladaptations to reality in the program would disenchant housing reformers; they would declare the program a failure and abandon it to search out fresh cures for bad housing and slums.

All this is precisely what happened * * *.

The new tenants were precisely those who had the least power in our society, the least potent voice in the councils of city hall. The middle-class masses, moreover, were spending their sweat and treasure in a wild flight from the slums and their residents. Now that they had attained the status of suburban property owners, they had no intention of giving up their property values and their hard-won status by allowing their former neighbors (and even less desirable people) to move in. The slums were not to follow them to the suburbs. Race and income prejudice was by no means confined to the suburbs. It flourished in the city, too, particularly in the little enclaves of frame houses that formed ethnically homogeneous, proud, and self-contained neighborhoods. These subcities would also resist public housing in their midst. Public housing no longer meant homes for less fortunate friends, and neighbors, but rather, intrusions of "foreigners," the problem poor and those least welcome "forbidden neighbors," the lower class Negro. Public housing not only lost its political appeal but what was left of the program was confined to the core of the city. Public housing remained tied to slum clearance and rebuilding out of necessity. The suburbs and the middle-class areas of the city had shut their doors. Vacant land could not be used for sites unless the land happened to lie in skid row or a Negro neighborhood.

* * * Costs and enmity of the outside world squeezed the buildings into the heart of the slums. The ratio of Negroes to whites increased radically. The whites streamed out. By the early 1950's, project managers had to learn to cope with "problem" families. The texture of life in the projects changed for the worse; since more delinquent families lived in them, they were the locus for more and more delinquency. The attention of the public was now directed to public housing not as a hopeful program of reform but as the site of public folly and private decay—vandalism, crime and unrest. The sordid facts of life in public housing merely reinforced the passionate resistance of the rest of the city to public housing projects. Who wanted such places in their neighborhood? It was a vicious cycle. And when the intellectual community looked out its windows and saw the projects in the distance—drab, ugly blocks of cement standing like soldiers—when they observed that public housing built ghettos for Negroes and despondent classes, they, too, called for a halt. Right and left wings, oddly enough, agreed that the program had outlived its utility; both called for a curtailment of fresh building. Some have even urged the abandonment of existing projects, and Charles Abrams has called it a fiction that "public housing must be owned by the city forever," a fiction which, if lived by, would result in public housing becoming the "concentrated retreats" of the "saddest and bitterest assemblage of mortals ever permitted a foothold on earth."[50]

---

[50] ABRAMS, THE CITY IS THE FRONTIER 37-38 (1965).

Note

Does Reich's *New Property*, excerpted in Part II(D) of this anthology, have any solutions for the public housing problems described by Lawrence Friedman?

2. Attacks on Exclusive Residential Suburbs: *Mt. Laurel* at the End of the Century

The *Mt. Laurel* litigation in New Jersey* is the most often discussed set of cases resolving disputes over "snob-zoning" in the suburbs. The two decade long process of legislation and litigation has overshadowed the efforts of other states to deal with similar problems. Indeed, quite some time before the New Jersey Supreme Court issued the first of its *Mt. Laurel* opinions, Massachusetts took legislative steps to try to resolve some of the same problems. Paul Stockman's recent review of the impact of that and later legislation provides some evidence of the impact of the reform movement. For additional material on the history of exclusionary zoning, *see* Lawrence G. Sager, *Insular Majorities Unabated:* Warth v. Seldin *and* City of Eastlake v. Forest City Enterprises, Inc., 91 HARV. L. REV. 1373 (1978); *Developments in the Law: Zoning*, 91 HARV. L. REV. 1427 (1978).

Southern Burlington County N.A.A.C.P. v. Mt. Laurel, 67 N.J. 151, 336 A.2d 713 (1975); *Oakwood at Madison, Inc. v. Township of Madison*, 72 N.J. 481, 371 A.2d 1192 (1977); *Southern Burlington County N.A.A.C.P. v. Mt. Laurel*, 92 N.J. 158, 456 A.2d 390 (1980); *Hills Development Co. v. Township of Bernards*, 103 N.J. 1, 510 A.2d 621 (1986).

Note (Paul K. Stockman), *Anti-Snob Zoning in Massachusetts: Assessing One Attempt at Opening the Suburbs to Affordable Housing*, 78 VA. L. REV. 535–539, 542–557, 559–564, 572–577, 579–580 (1992)*

INTRODUCTION

By all accounts, America remains in the midst of an "affordable housing crisis." Middle-income Americans in many parts of the country are finding that high housing costs deny them the opportunity to own a home, the classic and enduring symbol of the American Dream. The level of homeownership, after rising for decades, fell throughout the first half of the 1980s,[3] as younger, first-time buyers were increasingly forced out of the market. Those who can afford to buy often face crushing mortgage payments, leaving them vulnerable to even small economic disruptions. As a result, the number of renters has increased, as have the problems facing renters. Real rents, adjusted for inflation, rose 18% between 1975 and 1983. Correspondingly, rent burdens dramatically increased; the median rent burden grew from 20% of income in 1970 to 29% of income in 1983. Nearly half of the poorest quartile of renters devoted over half of their income to rent; almost 27% paid more than three-quarters of their income for housing.

One of the most significant causes of this housing crisis has been the financial impact of government regulations on the cost of constructing new housing units.[12] Locally imposed zoning regulations are among the most costly types of regulatory regimes. In particular, many communities use zoning laws to raise indirectly the cost of housing, thus screening out the socioeconomically "undesirable," or those who cost the community more than they generate in tax revenues. Such exclusionary zoning practices are not new, nor are calls for reform. Starting in the 1960s, scholars and policymakers examined exclusionary zoning in depth and suggested a variety of methods to eliminate it. Most such attempts were

[3] See H. James Brown & John Yinger, Home Ownership and Housing Affordability in the United States: 1963–1985, at 6–7 (1986) * * *.

[12] * * * See generally William A. Fischel, The Economics of Zoning Laws (1987) * * *.

unsuccessful, falling prey to suburban political pressures.[16]

With the rapid increases in housing prices, the problems of exclusionary zoning have risen to new prominence. Exclusionary zoning once served merely to keep out the poor; now it constrains the dreams of even the middle class. Many children of the suburbs find that they no longer can afford to live in the communities where they grew up. Teachers, firemen, and policemen often cannot live among those they serve because of the restrictive costs of housing.

Although attempts to "open up the suburbs" have largely failed, one of the earliest programs remains in force. Enacted in 1969, the Massachusetts Low and Moderate Income Housing Act[19] was the first state legislation to address directly suburban exclusionary zoning. The new challenges created by the current affordable housing crisis have made an assessment of its effectiveness timely. To the extent the Act creates a coherent and effective regime, it serves as a model for other states grappling with the current housing crisis.

* * *

I. THE CAUSES AND EFFECTS OF EXCLUSIONARY SUBURBAN ZONING

A. The Origins of Suburban Snob Zoning

The exclusionary effect of zoning regulations has been apparent from the very beginning. In *Ambler Realty Co. v. Village of Euclid,*[24] the first constitutional challenge to zoning laws, the trial court struck down Euclid's zoning ordinance, finding that its effect was "to classify the population and segregate them according to their income or situation in life." The United States Supreme Court reversed, upholding the town's exclusion of apartments from single-family residential neighborhoods and essentially permitting socioeconomic segregation.

Two related historical developments highlight the especially pernicious aspects of zoning and illustrate how the process reduces the overall welfare of an urban community. First, the social geography of the American city fundamentally shifted. In the preindustrial city people of all socioeconomic groups lived together because workers needed to be within walking distance of their jobs. Improvements in transportation—streetcars, railroads, and ultimately automobiles—eliminated this need. Accordingly, the middle and upper classes evacuated to newer, more pastoral suburban areas, relegating the center cities to recent immigrants and to the poor. After the World Wars, this process accelerated dramatically, and it continues today.

Second, the city's political geography changed as well. At first, expanding cities annexed the outlying areas. Near the end of the last century, however, newer suburban areas resisted such annexation into the largely immigrant, usually poorer, often machine-led cities. This reticence increased as states imposed restrictive municipal annexation laws and permissive municipal incorporation laws. This ultimately splintered the metropolitan unit, creating a "crazy-quilt" of separate, often tiny municipalities. Neighborhood-like units thus could erect legal boundaries to enforce their own parochial interests.

These developments created a perverse set of incentives to exclude outsiders. Groups of people, particularly the upper and middle classes, sorted themselves into socially and economically homogeneous residential communities, which formed distinct and independent local governments. These suburban political units then adopted strict zoning ordinances designed to ensure the uniformity of their communities.

* * *

C. The Harmful Effects of Exclusionary Zoning

Suburban exclusionary zoning does much more than simply raise housing costs * * *. Most strikingly, such practices regressively redistribute the costs of local government. When the city contained all socioeconomic groups, all groups contributed to city programs. As suburbanization evolved, however, the middle and upper classes escaped that burden by fleeing into suburban enclaves sheltered from the city's taxing power. * * * The working class and the poor who remained in the city were left to shoulder a disproportionate share of these costs.

This is especially unfair, given that, under the best of circumstances, cities are more expensive to operate than suburbs or rural towns. City expenses,

---

[16] The National Commission on Urban Problems' ("Douglas Commission") 1968 report contained one of the most influential accounts of exclusionary zoning. See National Comm'n on Urban Problems, Building the American City 199–253 (1969) [hereinafter Building the American City]. For a detailed history of the attempts to address exclusionary zoning, see Michael N. Danielson, The Politics of Exclusion 159–322 (1976).

[19] Act of Aug. 23, 1969, ch. 774, 1969 Mass. Acts 712 (codified at Mass. Gen. Laws Ann. ch. 40B, §§ 20–23 (West 1979 & Supp.1991)). * * *

[24] 297 F. 307 (N.D.Ohio 1924), rev'd, 272 U.S. 365 (1926).

moreover, further increase as the city becomes poorer. Poorer families tend to have more school-age children who must be publicly educated. Poorer neighborhoods often have higher crime rates, more unemployment, increased drug addiction, and lower health standards. In addition, they generally require greater police and fire protection. The ultimate effect is that the lion's share of the metropolitan governmental expense is funded by those least able to pay.

In the worst case scenario, suburban flight threatens the city's financial viability. Employers seeking lower expenses have moved a massive number of city jobs into the suburbs. This practice only compounds the regressive social costs of exclusion because suburban communities that welcome the employers refuse to allow construction of modestly priced housing for the workers. As a result, the supply of entry-level jobs is taken from those people who need them most. Many of the urban poor do not even seek such jobs, and those who do face time-consuming and costly "reverse commutes."

These regressive effects ultimately harm everyone. Employers, having committed themselves to suburbia with long-term capital expenditures in the hopes of decreasing costs, face increased production costs as a result of exclusionary zoning practices. In many high-cost areas, employers have difficulty recruiting entry-level personnel. They often must pay wage premia and in some cases have resorted to privately busing workers from the cities to suburban jobsites. Some employers even have problems recruiting managers and executives because of high housing costs. Furthermore, even when employers find the workers, absenteeism and turnover rates are higher in the suburban sites. Ultimately these costs are passed on and reflected in the cost of the produced goods and services. Thus, in a significant way, exclusionary suburban practices cost everyone money.

Exclusionary practices not only burden city centers but have other intracommunity economic effects. Zoning rules benefit the earlier residents of a community at the expense of the later arrivals. First, a wealth effect occurs because "the assignment of rights under zoning is an important form of homeowners' wealth. . . . Thus an 'overgenerous' assignment of rights to (original) homeowners may result in more restrictive land use controls."[68] Second, local communities (obviously) have a monopoly over zoning. Professor William Fischel writes:

> [M]onopoly power by the community enables it to raise land prices, and thus housing prices, above the market equilibrium by restricting the supply of sites more than either landowners or a competitive set of communities would. This increases the wealth of community residents who are homeowners prior to the adoption of the restrictions.[70]

This redistribution is regressive because a suburb's earliest residents, who typically enact the zoning laws, tend to be wealthier than the later arrivals. The benefits of zoning thus "accrue chiefly to some of the wealthiest members of our society." * * *

In addition, suburban exclusionary zoning, by reducing residential density, creates another cluster of harmful effects, * * * the costs of sprawl. Low-density development increases construction costs and operating expenses and also can increase pollution, create other adverse environmental effects, and waste energy resources. The results of one study "show a surprising consistency: 'planning' to some extent, but higher densities to a much greater extent, result in lower economic costs, environmental costs, natural resource consumption, and some personal costs for a given number of dwelling units."[76] Sprawl also carries personal costs, most notably the value of the extra time spent commuting.

Finally, exclusionary zoning not only creates direct economic shifts but carries substantial nonpecuniary costs as well. There are serious demoralization costs generated by social immobility and social unrest. Low- and moderate-income people concentrated in economically segregated neighborhoods are denied the full range of opportunities available to the middle and upper classes.

* * *

In short, exclusionary zoning further polarizes an already divided society.

II. The Massachusetts Zoning Appeals Regime

A. The Origins of the System

Academicians and policymakers turned their attention to exclusionary zoning, which had quietly existed for decades, as urban decay and social unrest grabbed headlines in the 1960s. The national problems confronting these scholars and politicians did not spare Massachusetts. Moreover, the problems caused by the shortage of affordable housing and the

---

68 Fischel, supra note 12, at 136–37.

70 Id. at 141.

76 Real Estate Research Corp., The Costs of Sprawl 6 (1974) * * *.

jobsite-residence mismatch were exacerbated by the loss of thousands of existing affordable housing units, as urban renewal and highway programs displaced thousands of low- and moderate-income city dwellers.

Concerned about these problems, the Massachusetts Senate in 1967 commissioned the Legislative Research Council to investigate whether localities used zoning power unjustly. The council determined that restrictive suburban zoning practices adversely affected the supply of low- and moderate-income housing and urged action. The findings of the Douglas Commission and the President's Committee on Urban Housing echoed the council's view.[90]

The Massachusetts legislators responded to these findings by introducing five bills during the 1969 legislative session that would restrict local zoning power. These bills were referred to a joint Committee on Urban Affairs, which then released a legislative report and a consolidated bill in June, 1969. * * *

The bill was fiercely contested, becoming the hottest issue of the legislative session. It ultimately passed only because of what Emily Reed has termed "a fortuitous convergence of political issues and circumstances."[95] The key to passage was the formation of an unlikely coalition—a rather unholy alliance—between liberals and the more conservative representatives of Boston's working class ethnic neighborhoods. * * * This coalition united solely because of the events surrounding the passage of a 1966 bill addressing race relations. Through the efforts of suburban liberals, the legislature passed a racial imbalance bill that outlawed de facto segregation and that mandated, in effect, desegregation of the Boston public schools. This bill was strongly opposed by the politicians from Boston's white neighborhoods, who felt that the law was being shoved down their throats by liberal suburban legislators. Three years later, they had not forgotten this episode and saw the 1969 housing bill as an opportunity to seek retribution against the suburban liberals. They sought vengeance and to an extent succeeded: the bill was enacted in August, although it cleared the Senate by only two votes.

B. The Massachusetts Act

* * * The Act applies to "low and moderate income housing" but defines that category narrowly to encompass "any housing subsidized by the federal or state government under any program to assist the construction of low or moderate income housing . . . whether built or operated by any public agency or any nonprofit or limited dividend organization."

The Act creates a two-step administrative process. First, it consolidates the permit application and hearing process: "Any public agency or limited dividend or nonprofit organization proposing to build low or moderate income housing may submit to the [local zoning] board of appeals . . . a single application to build such housing in lieu of separate applications to the applicable local boards." The local zoning board of appeals must hold a public hearing within thirty days. The zoning board of appeals then has the power to issue a comprehensive permit and may attach to it any conditions and requirements. If the zoning board of appeals fails to convene a hearing as prescribed, or fails to render a decision on the comprehensive permit within forty days after the close of hearings, the comprehensive permit is deemed granted. If a comprehensive permit is issued, aggrieved parties may obtain immediate judicial review.

If an application for a comprehensive permit is denied, or granted with conditions and requirements that appear to make the project "uneconomic," the second phase of the Act's administrative process begins. The applicant may appeal the adverse local decision to the state Housing Appeals Committee ("HAC"), an administrative body established within the Department of Community Affairs of the Executive Office of Communities & Development. Within twenty days, the HAC begins a formal administrative hearing; a decision must be issued within thirty days of the end of the hearing.

As its primary inquiry, the HAC must decide whether the action of the local zoning board of appeals is "consistent with local needs." Local action will be conclusively presumed consistent with local needs if the municipality has met one of the following numerical thresholds: at least 10% of the city's local housing consists of low- and moderate-income housing; subsidized housing occupies more than 1.5% of the community's total land area; or the grant of a permit will result in the construction, within the span of a year, on the larger of ten acres or .3% of the locality's total land area. The city bears the burden of demonstrating that it has met a statutory threshold.

---

[90] See Building the American City, supra note 16; President's Committee on Urban Housing, A Decent Home (1969) * * *.

[95] Emily F. Reed, Tilting at Windmills: The Massachusetts Low and Moderate Income Housing Act, 4 W. New Eng. L. Rev. 105, 108 (1981). * * *

If the city has not satisfied one of these quotas, local action still may be "consistent with local needs" under two conditions. First, the locality must prove "that there is a valid health, safety, environmental, design, open space, or other local concern" supporting its denial or imposition of uneconomic conditions. Second, the municipality must further establish that these concerns outweigh the "regional housing need." In such an instance, "regional housing need" is strongly presumed to outweigh local planning considerations.

C. Coordinated Developments in Anti-Snob Zoning

The Act has not been the sole tool used to reduce the problems associated with exclusionary practices. Judicial decisions, executive orders, and regulatory initiatives all have played significant roles in expanding and clarifying the scope of the Act as originally written.

Progress under the Act was limited for the first several years as the Act's constitutionality and scope remained unsettled. In particular, it was unclear whether the Act conferred the power on local boards to override local zoning regulations. The Massachusetts Supreme Judicial Court finally resolved these questions in the 1973 landmark case *Board of Appeals v. Housing Appeals Committee.*[124]

In *Housing Appeals*, the court affirmed the HAC's order granting construction permits to low-income housing developers in the towns of Hanover and Concord. In so doing, the court upheld the Act's constitutionality and, in examining the legislative history, explicitly concluded that "the Legislature has given the boards the power to override local exclusionary zoning practices."

Even after *Housing Appeals*, municipalities continued to resist and to delay significant progress in implementing the Act. Angered by this intransigence on the part of affluent suburban areas, Governor Edward J. King promulgated Executive Order 215 in 1982, directing all state agencies to withhold "discretionary development-related financial assistance" to communities that are "unreasonably restrictive of new housing growth" because of exclusionary measures. Under the order, funds will be denied even if the state is acting only as "a mere conduit for federal funds." * * *

Executive Order 215, although powerful in its own right, represents only one half of a "carrot and stick" housing regime. Various state subsidy programs make production of affordable housing more attractive to developers as well as to local communities. The key feature of such programs is the promotion of mixed-income development, rather than the traditional, greatly feared, strictly low-income "projects." Three of the most important subsidy programs are the Homeownership Opportunity Program ("HOP"), the State Housing Assistance for Rental Production ("SHARP"), and the Tax-Exempt Loans to Encourage Rental Housing ("TELLER").

* * *

Furthermore, in response to the 1989 report of the Special Commission Relative to the Implementation of Low and Moderate Housing Provisions, the Department of Community Affairs promulgated regulations establishing a new Local Initiative Program ("LIP"). Critics complained primarily that the HAC too narrowly defined "low and moderate income housing," excluding all affordable housing not monetarily subsidized by the federal or state government. Such a definition provided cities with little incentive to undertake housing initiatives which do not require direct state or federal financial assistance.

The 1990 regulations explicitly recognize that technical assistance given by the Department of Community Affairs is a subsidy that makes recipient projects "low or moderate income housing" within the scope of the Act. Communities participate in LIP by requesting that developments be certified by the department as "Local Initiative Units" or "Comprehensive Permit Projects." Thus, privately developed affordable housing units may contribute to the town's ten percent affordable housing "quota."

LIP also indirectly addresses the concern that towns often build relatively noncontroversial elderly housing, while ignoring the greater need for family housing. The new regulations expressly state that "[t]he most critical needs in the Commonwealth are for family and special needs housing in general and low-income family housing in particular." To this end, the regulations prohibit the grant of otherwise-permissible approvals if housing "is unresponsive to local and regional housing needs" or if such approval would raise the proportion of subsidized elderly housing in the community to more than five percent of the total housing stock.

III. An Assessment of the Massachusetts Zoning Appeals Regime

Critics sharply dispute the effectiveness and wisdom of inclusionary housing programs in general and

---

[124] 294 N.E.2d 393 (Mass. 1973).

the Massachusetts zoning appeals system in particular. Although such criticisms are valuable and merit discussion, it is misleading to evaluate the Massachusetts scheme only by raising and assessing individual criticisms. At the outset, one must recognize that any attempt to socioeconomically diversify suburbia must confront the enormously strong symbolic appeal of localism. At the same time, an inclusionary program must not offend another broad strain of American thought that views municipalities with justifiable suspicion. A program like the Massachusetts regime therefore will generate considerable controversy. What some view as an infirmity in a legislative schema, however, may represent a necessary trade-off required to achieve an important policy goal. In short, any program that aspires to even modest success must "straddle the fence," maintaining a balance between competing social and moral visions.

With this in mind, * * * assess * * * the Massachusetts regime's ability to satisfy and to balance a series of often-conflicting goals * * *: (1) An inclusionary zoning program should socioeconomically integrate a suburban community in a process that is both incremental and self-limiting to prevent overcorrection; (2) An inclusionary zoning program should create as much affordable housing as possible, ideally meeting the region's need for low- and moderate-income housing; (3) An inclusionary zoning program should not give rise to counterproductive side effects; (4) The substance and procedure of an inclusionary zoning program should facilitate the consideration of legitimate local concerns; (5) An inclusionary zoning program should be relatively easy and inexpensive to administer, minimizing delays and total development costs on local and state treasuries.

It should be emphasized, however, that a successful inclusionary housing program cannot focus solely on the creation of affordable housing. The location of affordable housing should be a primary concern as well. Any suburban inclusionary program that ignores or minimizes the importance of the location of housing will have only limited success at great cost. The essential and central purpose of inclusionary zoning programs therefore must be the effective integration of the suburbs, to the greatest extent possible, even if the houses and apartments thereby generated do not meet completely the demand for affordable housing.

A. Achieving Optimal Suburban Integration

* * *

The challenge * * * is to heterogenize as much as possible while keeping potential adverse consequences de minimis. Even some of the strongest advocates of opening the suburbs admit that "enough homogeneity must be present to allow institutions to function and interest groups to reach workable compromises."[173] After studying the problem Richard Babcock and Fred Bosselman concluded:

> [A] balance of housing goals must be established at a level that will maintain a reasonable amount of various types of housing in each community and not exceed a hypothetical tipping point. Moreover, some assurance needs to be given to local communities that the "reasonable" number of apartments or mobile homes they might be willing to accept is not the nose of the camel—the advance guard of an inundation that will turn the community rapidly into a suburban slum.[174]

* * * Therefore, a program recognizing these concerns, designed to ensure the preservation of middle-class mores and to avoid passing the "tipping point," may meet with considerable success.

Other critics of inclusionary programs fear that the programs will be unsuccessful in achieving true heterogeneity and instead will merely "disperse ghettoes."[177] Low- and moderate-income suburban housing, they argue, will be spatially isolated, "set off in the 'corner' of the various suburbs." These concerns have been addressed largely by the increased reliance on mixed-income developments as a source of affordable suburban housing. Furthermore, house-by-house integration is not essential to the effective operation of an inclusionary program. Anthony Downs, for example, favors integration at the neighborhood level, not at the block level, to maximize access to jobs and schools while allowing lower-income families to reside near one another.

* * *

Essentially, the Massachusetts zoning regime operates as recommended by Babcock, Bosselman, and Downs. A community that meets the statutory minima is assured that no more housing will be built

[173] Herbert J. Gans, People and Plans 175 (1968).

[174] Richard F. Babcock & Fred P. Bosselman, Exclusionary Zoning: Land Use Regulation and Housing in the 1970s at 116 (1973).

[177] Paul M. Vaughn, Note, The Massachusetts Zoning Appeals Law: First Breach in the Exclusionary Wall, 54 B.U.L. Rev. 37, 70 (1974).

against its wishes. Furthermore, the ten percent threshold is low enough to ensure continued middle-class dominance and to prevent the problems some critics fear will result from heterogenization. In this instance, the law implicitly sacrifices full attainment of the regional housing need in favor of constructing a program that will successfully promote a moderate level of heterogeneity. All things considered, the Act is an effective vehicle for achieving reasonable and stable levels of suburban heterogeneity.

* * *

IV. An Evaluation of the Practical Effectiveness of the Massachusetts Zoning Appeals Regime

The zoning appeals regime in place in Massachusetts *can* be effective in creating a significant level of affordable housing in the suburbs. Showing that the system has been effective, however, is a different matter entirely. Empirical results, to the extent available, show mixed results that lead to wildly varied conclusions about the Act's effectiveness.[241] * * * The debate among housing experts is, in effect, over whether the glass is half empty or half full. Considering the compromising approach inherent in the system, this disagreement probably is inevitable.

At first, progress was very slow. Developers, towns, and the HAC were reluctant to move until reassured about the Act's constitutionality. By mid-1973, only six comprehensive permits had been issued, and construction was underway on only four projects—roughly 400 units—earmarked for the elderly. The HAC had received twenty-five appeals and had issued five decisions.

After the decision in *Board of Appeals v. Housing Appeals Committee* quelled doubts about the Act's constitutionality, things began to move more quickly. By late 1975, over 7,500 units were planned, pending, under construction, or occupied. Still, only 1,108 units had been completed and occupied. By 1979, there had been 111 proposals to construct 14,639 units; 3,600 units had been completed, and another 2,000 were under construction or in the final stages of planning. Eighty-two of Massachusetts' 351 municipalities had received at least one application for a comprehensive permit.

During the 1980s, progress under the Act further accelerated, due in part to the new housing incentives. Executive Order 215 also prompted new activity; the threat (or reality) of lost funding prodded into action many municipalities that once assumed an ostrich-like posture and ignored Chapter 774's existence altogether. The rapid housing price increases of the 1980s also may share responsibility for the new activity, instilling a new sense of urgency. Moreover, despite continued opposition, it appeared that many communities began to resign themselves to reality and haltingly recognized an obligation to meet local housing needs. Indeed, this gradual attitudinal evolution had been going on for some time. As HAC Chairman Murray Corman explained:

> "[T]he early hostility of municipal officials to the very existence of the zoning appeals law has subsided as they see that the procedures of the Committee are open and even-handed, do not represent any state effort to "railroad" through new housing projects, and in the initial cases at least have involved projects that will benefit primarily low-income residents of the suburbs where they are to be built."[259]

By 1989, 33,884 units had been proposed via comprehensive permit applications. Of these, 20,623 are currently built and occupied or will be shortly.

These figures, however, may underestimate the impact of the Act on the construction of affordable housing. In many cases, it appears that the Act has stimulated the liberalization of zoning laws, thereby allowing construction of subsidized housing as of right. Emily Reed's study of the Act's effectiveness in the Springfield Standard Metropolitan Statistical Area ("SMSA") buttresses this conclusion.[262] By 1979, only 300 units had been constructed in the SMSA pursuant to the Act, out of 944 that were proposed. Between 1970 and 1978, however, 11,615 new subsidized housing units had been built in the SMSA. Of these, 3,439 were built in suburban areas. Eight of the twenty-one communities had constructed their entire subsidized housing stock subsequent to the Act's enactment. The amount of subsidized housing in seven other communities more than tripled between 1970 and 1978.

* * *

[241] For instance, one commentator argues that the Act is merely "tilting at the exclusionary zoning windmill by addressing a phantom cause of an unexplained phenomenon." Reed, supra note 95, at 132. By contrast, another has declared it the "first breach in the exclusionary wall." Vaughn, supra note 177, at 37.

[259] Michael N. Danielson, The Politics of Exclusion 306 (1976).

[262] See Reed, supra note 95, at 131. * * *

The success of the zoning appeals process in increasing suburban diversity is more difficult to appraise. On the surface, progress seems dismally slow: in 1988, the most recent year for which information is available, only twenty-eight of Massachusetts' 351 cities and towns had met the statutory criteria. Ninety-five communities had no subsidized housing at all. This category, moreover, includes many of the state's wealthiest communities.

Such figures, however, understate the progress that has been made. When the Act was passed in 1969, only two localities—the city of Boston and the town of Malden—met the statutory minima. In addition, there has been significant progress that is not reflected in the figures: a number of towns that do not satisfy the Act's targets nonetheless have doubled or tripled the number of subsidized units within their borders since the mid-1980s. Further, many of those localities without subsidized housing are small rural communities; only six of the 225 cities and towns with populations greater than 5,000 have no subsidized units. Many housing specialists close to the issue in Massachusetts rate the program a success. "Without the law," commented one Boston real estate lawyer, "there would be virtually no affordable housing being built in [the] suburbs."[275]

V. Conclusion

To praise the Massachusetts scheme for its progress, however, is not to suggest that it needs no improvement. Indeed, a number of refinements could greatly increase its effectiveness. First, the Act should guard more closely against overconstruction of elderly housing at the expense of family housing, extending LIP limits to encompass all localities. Although a more accurate determination of actual need could be obtained by substituting a more complex fair-share calculation, the five-percent limit written into LIP is easy to administer and coordinates well with the other statutory minima.

More importantly, the system needs further safeguards against delay. Some delay is, of course, a necessary evil. At present, however, the process is so time-consuming that its effectiveness is compromised. First, the local consolidated hearing should be streamlined. Although the deadlines built into the Act constrain localities to a degree, the hearing process continues to cause significant delays. Hearings can last for days and, with adjournments, can drag on interminably. Therefore, there should be a strict limit, such as a thirty-day limit, on the amount of time that can elapse between a hearing's commencement and its closure, including adjournments. Because this time limit would be for the benefit of the developer, however, the developer should retain the option of tolling it.

* * *

Finally, appeals to the courts from HAC decisions—often frivolous and interposed merely for delay—should be strongly discouraged. Although the deferential standard of review provides reasonable assurance that the HAC's decision will stand, it does not relieve an applicant from the burdens and delays involved in litigating the appeal. Other measures are needed to streamline the appellate process. * * * In * * * extreme cases * * * there should be a credible threat of sanctions against the appealing locality. Alternatively, or additionally, when the HAC wins on appeal, it should be entitled to recover attorneys' fees for the cost of defending itself.

In sum, increases in the level of suburban heterogeneity and the amount of suburban affordable housing under the Massachusetts zoning appeals regime have been slowly realized and incremental. The suburbs still are, to a disturbing extent, monolithic and exclusionary; there still is an urgent need for more affordable housing. And the political obstacles still seem insoluble. Nonetheless, the Act has made substantial progress over a twenty-one year period. Considering the extreme difficulties confronting any attempt at suburban inclusion—the allure of localism, the growing political strength of exclusionary suburbs, the cynicism about what is now derisively called "social engineering"—this balanced and measured way of addressing the issue offers a feasible method of resolving the pervasive problems generated by suburban fragmentation and exclusion. With the modifications suggested above, the Massachusetts anti-snob zoning regime can stand as a model to other states, demonstrating that a cautious and moderate approach can indeed help resolve a seemingly intractable problem.

---

[275] Andrew J. Dabilie, Many Communities Lag on Affordable Housing, Boston Globe, Nov. 15, 1988, at 27.

3. Zoning in the Modern Era: Dealing in Value "Owned" by the Public

Once the basic structure of zoning was approved in *Village of Euclid v. Ambler Realty Co.*, governments obtained control over large amounts of valuable rights to develop property. The adoption of general zoning statutes subjected huge amounts of wealth to regulation. In addition, day to day decisions made by thousands of zoning agencies across the country on variances and other exceptions to zoning rules were often the make or break factors in real estate deals. Today, most zoning battles are played out transaction by transaction. Carol Rose, in *Planning as Dealing: Piecemeal Land Controls as a Problem of Local Legitimacy*, both describes the nature of the problems that such individuated land use actions present, and suggests a theoretical structure for analyzing piecemeal zoning actions. For further reading in this area, *see* Judith Welch Wegner, *Moving Toward the Bargaining Table: Contract Zoning, Development Agreements, and the Theoretical Foundations of Government Land Use Deals*, 65 N. CAR. L. REV. 957 (1987).

Carol M. Rose, *Planning and Dealing: Piecemeal Land Controls as a Problem of Local Legitimacy*, 71 CAL. L. REV. 837, 839–848, 893–912 (1983)*

Land use control in America has always been an intensely local area of the law. Modern land use law, with its roots in the turn-of-the-century City Beautiful movement, was intended to deal especially with the growing population concentrations of urban localities. From the beginning, those localities and their governments were implicitly deemed the appropriate agencies for planning and ordering the physical development associated with their own startling growth. But during the last two decades, judges and legal scholars have shown increasing doubt that local governments make land development decisions fairly and rationally that is, with a reasonable distribution of burdens among individuals, and with the care and deliberation commensurate with the long-term implications of land development.

This doubt stems from several causes and takes different forms. Much of the criticism concentrates on the extralocal effects of local land use decisions, particularly the exclusion of low income outsiders, and the shifting of environmental problems to neighboring communities.[4] But an older criticism has cut even deeper, and is the subject of this Article. It is that we need a new jurisprudence of local land decisions, not because of the external consequences of those decisions—serious though they may be—but because local governments cannot be trusted to deal

[4] The increased vulnerability of local land regulations is attributable in part to the civil rights movement and antipoverty efforts of the 1960's. These efforts focused attention on the cumulative consequences of what had until then seemed to be benevolent land controls: local "tight little islands," in their over-concentration on adequate space and on capacious and well-built single family homes, in effect used land decisions to exclude the minorities and the poor who could only afford more modest quarters. R. BABCOCK, THE ZONING GAME 58–59, 149–52 (1966); Sager, Tight Little Islands: Exclusionary Zoning, Equal Protection and the Indigent, 21 STAN. L. REV. 767 (1969).

From a different perspective, environmentalism heightened national awareness of other consequences of local land use decisions allowing too much new development, e.g., downstream siltification, increased auto fumes, and the loss of historical landmarks and fragile ecosystems. *See, e.g.,* R. HEALY & J. ROSENBERG, LAND USE AND THE STATES 17–29 (2d ed. 1979); F. POPPER, THE POLITICS OF LAND USE REFORM 46–55 (1981); U.S. COUNCIL ON ENVTL. QUALITY, THE QUIET REVOLUTION IN LAND USE CONTROL 1–3 (1971).

* * *

fairly or carefully even in land decisions with only local consequences.

Since the middle 1960's, legal scholars have complained that local land decisions can make a mockery of orderly and predictable planned development. Individual land decisions, the critics say, amount to deals with landowners and developers; these deals gut the local plan (if indeed any exists) and are merely ad hoc impulse choices that neither safeguard the surroundings for present and future residents, nor enable those residents and would-be developers to predict future actions.

These critics object most to the piecemeal changes in local land regulations: the all-pervasive "variance," the "conditional use permit," or the small-scale "rezoning" ordinance. These small adjustments are the everyday fare of local land regulations. Whatever the formal designation, any of these ad hoc adjustments alters preexisting general regulations governing the use of some individual parcel or other finite area within the community. Each such change is small on its face, appearing to have little effect outside the immediate community and to concern only the individual developer, the neighboring owners, and the local government.

The problem with these small changes, critics charge, is that they are so difficult to control. Judicial review of small changes is limited. Traditionally, they were tested only within the ample girth of a loose reasonableness standard. This was particularly true where individual properties were reclassified through actual amendments to the ordinances; these rezonings, as "legislative" acts, were insulated from close review by the courts, which required only that they not be arbitrary.[11] But the arbitrariness standard cannot really control small changes. It is too broad to treat seriously the fairness claims of the individual property owners with interests at stake in piecemeal changes, and it fails to account for the cumulative effect of many nonarbitrary decisions that seem to shave away, in salami slices, any larger concepts underlying the original, more general land regulations.

Thus, the traditional legislative reasonableness standard is inadequate to assure fairness and due consideration. Minor regulatory changes seem impervious to other, nonjudicial controls as well, including most of the land use reform ideas of the last decade. The state and regional controls in the so-called "Quiet Revolution" statutes [of the last decade] are meant to monitor only the regional impact of local changes, not to disturb local discretion over individual parcel changes lacking wider ramifications. Similarly, new state statutes requiring environmental review of proposed changes only add to local discretion over piecemeal changes * * *. Another set of ideas, the self-styled "deregulation" proposals, embraces a variety of approaches, but they all envision a fairly high residue of local regulatory authority, and some even aim at freeing local discretion from state or regional supervision.[15] Finally, there is considerable academic interest in proposals to reform local land use and control small changes by structuring regulations to copy a hypothesized market model of private transactions; but these proposals have not had great practical impact to date, perhaps because they would require a forbidding array of changes in current land use regulatory practice.[16]

How, then, to satisfy critics' charges that local governments make piecemeal changes unfairly and carelessly? The courts, urged on by academic commentators, have developed one much-discussed reform model to control these changes, which I call "plan jurisprudence." The model first postulates that some form of plan is necessary. Then, drawing heavily on administrative law doctrines, it regards all piecemeal changes as "judicial" or "quasi-judicial." According to this model, then, piecemeal land use decisions must conform to standards set out in preexisting plans; moreover, because the individual decision applies a general standard to a specific instance, the decision is to be made according to adjudicative procedures.

As we shall see, plan jurisprudence has generated much discussion—particularly of its leading case, *Fasano v. Board of County Commissioners*[17] —but its actual influence has been limited. In some jurisdictions it has been adopted completely; in others, it has been ultimately applied only in certain forms of piecemeal changes; in still others, it has

---

[11] Village of Euclid v. Ambler Realty Co., 272 U.S. 365, 395 (1926). * * *

[15] Perhaps the best-known and most persistent advocate of deregulation is Bernard Siegan. *See* B. SIEGAN, LAND USE WITHOUT ZONING (1972); Siegan, *Non-Zoning in Houston*, 13 J.L. & ECON. 71 (1970).
* * *

[16] The best known is Ellickson, *Alternatives to Zoning: Covenants, Nuisance Rules, and Fines as Land Use Controls*, 40 U. CHI. L. REV. 681 (1973), which proposes a substitution of local "nuisance boards" for the present apparatus of zoning.
* * *

[17] 264 Or. 574, 507 P.2d 23 (1973).

been rejected entirely. Newer statutes have been similarly mixed: the American Law Institute's Model Land Development Code calls for the quasi-judicialization of piecemeal changes, but is ambiguous as to plan conformity. On the other hand, some new state statutes mandate planning and "consistency" of land regulations with plans, but are silent as to the quasi-judicial character of individual decisions.

These hesitations about plan jurisprudence suggest it may have both practical and theoretical defects, and that it may not ensure that local land use decisions are fair and careful. In this Article I will argue that plan jurisprudence fails to solve the problems it sets out to meet, and instead creates new ones, particularly by its advocacy of an outmoded version of local land planning. We need some other approach to test the reasonableness of these decisions.

My thesis is that piecemeal local land decisions should not be classed as either "legislative" or "judicial"; these rubrics are drawn from a separation-of-powers doctrine more appropriate to larger governmental units. Piecemeal changes are quintessentially local matters, and any jurisprudential test of the reasonableness of piecemeal changes must identify and build upon the factors that lend legitimacy and institutional competence to local decisionmaking. In this Article I undertake that task. I will begin by analyzing plan jurisprudence, so as to point out its flaws and to draw on its merits. In Part I, I discuss the assertion of judicial control over piecemeal changes, especially in plan jurisprudence's ideal type, *Fasano*, and then explore *The Federalist* No. 10 as a doctrinal background for *Fasano*'s underlying suspicion of the validity of local land decisions. I will then trace the specific development of plan jurisprudence from some specialized issues in zoning in the 1950's and 1960's, issues that crystallized *Federalist*-type objections to local decisionmaking by illuminating certain problems of fairness and due consideration in local land decisions.

* * *

In Part IV, I will * * * develop an alternative jurisprudence of piecemeal changes. This jurisprudence treats piecemeal changes as dispute mediations, and tests fairness and due consideration in the light of the local opportunity for participation or departure. I attempt to develop standards that refine the processes local governments actually use, that encourage the use of up-to-date planning techniques, and that generally heighten the institutional competence of these local decisions. Finally, in the Conclusion I comment on why land use decisions have invariably been committed to local governments.

* * *

I

Plan Jurisprudence as Reform

A. *The Assertion of Judicial Control Over Piecemeal Changes*

Piecemeal changes in land use worry critics because they are hard to control. This Part looks at two ways in which plan jurisprudence seeks to control small changes. First, it examines judicial enforcement of conformity to a plan. It then takes a historical look at how the plan itself became favored as a way of solving problems of fairness and due consideration.

1. Traditional Planning Law and Plan Jurisprudence

* * *

The planning idea is not new, although it has only recently been taken seriously. In fact, the preference for "structured" land decisions harks back to one of the oldest methods of assuring both fairness and due consideration in local land use regulation. The Department of Commerce's Standard Zoning Enabling Act (SZEA), first published in 1922 and adopted by most states over the next few years, required that local land use controls be "in accordance with" a general plan. This plan presumably would be created by the local planning commission, whose impartiality and technical expertise would ensure the durability and rationality of the overall plan. The plan, in turn, would ensure the rationality and stability of the ordinances that implemented it. It was widely assumed that localities could indeed set their goals far in advance, that changes in land regulation would therefore seldom be necessary, and that citizens would not face fluctuations in the status of their own or their neighbors' land.

But both in law and in practice these assumptions proved false. The courts did little to establish advance planning as a legal prerequisite for local land regulation. They noted that the Standard Planning Enabling Act was issued several years after the SZEA, that it had been much less widely adopted, and concluded that state legislatures adopting the SZEA could not have meant to require an independent plan as a prerequisite to local zoning. Following the example of the leading Supreme Court case of

Village of Euclid v. Ambler Realty Co.,[34] courts regarded the zoning ordinances (and their amendments) as "legislative" acts, which were to be upheld unless they were clearly arbitrary and unreasonable.

The idea of a plan as an independent control on local regulation only began to take hold in the 1950's, when federal urban aid programs began to require (and fund) local planning as a condition to grants-in-aid. Even then, the courts were reluctant to require a plan as a prerequisite to actual regulation; well into the 1950's they routinely upheld zoning ordinances and amendments which disclosed some "plan" in themselves.

Experience also quickly confounded any expectation that stable regulations would flow automatically from well-considered long-term plans. Controls soon became ad hoc responses to individual development proposals. Local officials encouraged this pattern by zoning areas for uses less intense than those expected, then altering regulations on a parcel-by-parcel basis—sometimes after striking a bargain with the individual developer. The real estate industry understood this process well, and frequently conditioned land purchases on changes in existing zoning.

As this pattern of land regulation through piecemeal changes became uncomfortably obvious, the idea of a plan to guide actual land decisions took on renewed force. Within the last decade, a number of states have begun to sharpen the older SZEA requirements by adopting mandatory planning statutes, and by requiring that local land use controls be "consistent" with local plans. These new planning statutes generally require local governments to plan, and may even prescribe "elements" or subjects about which the local governments must have plans, but they set no substantive criteria against which to test the local plan.

Even procedurally, they are general: they require each community to consider its own locally defined goals, and then to state those goals in such a way as to direct future decisions. Beyond this, the mandatory planning and the planning consistency statutes prescribe no particular procedure that the local government must follow.

It was the courts, rather than the legislatures, that first took a further procedural step and judicialized local land use regulations. That is, instead of seeing small changes as legislative acts that are judicially reviewable only for arbitrariness, courts began to say that in making changes, local governmental bodies were acting in judicial or quasi-judicial capacities.[42]

2. The Fasano *Case*

Fasano v. Board of County Commissioners[43] is the leading case in the quasi-judicialization of local land decisions. I use *Fasano* and its *Federalist* underpinnings to show how and why courts thought they should enforce conformity to a plan. This 1973 Oregon case involved a small change: the rezoning of a thirty-two acre parcel to permit mobile homes. According to the traditional jurisprudence of planning and zoning, the local council's rezoning ordinance would be cast as a "legislative" act, whatever the size or scope of the parcel rezoned; and as such it enjoyed a strong presumption of validity.[44] But the *Fasano* court, clearly concerned that a local government's unrestrained discretion might lead to sweetheart deals with developers, rejected the traditional presumption favoring legislative acts. Instead, the court took an administrative law approach to the local decision, labelling this decision judicial rather than legislative.

The court's reasoning had two separate strands. The first, and more developed, concerned the nature of the piecemeal land decision itself; the second, the character of the decisionmaking body. As to the nature of the change itself, the *Fasano* court distinguished individual parcel rezonings from adoption of general plans or general land use controls. The latter are broad policy decisions, the court reasoned, and are properly viewed as legislative; but the former apply preexisting policy standards—embodied in the general plan itself—to an individual parcel. Such rezonings entail the consideration of what administrative law calls "adjudicative facts"—that is, specific details about specific properties brought forth by specially interested parties; and they entail the application of standards (i.e., the plan) to the facts presented. According to *Fasano*, such decisions are judicial rather than legislative. Therefore, in making these decisions, the local governmental body should operate with at least some of the procedural trappings of a court: it should act as an impartial

---

34 272 U.S. 365 (1926).

42 Golden v. City of Overland Park, 224 Kan. 591, 584 P.2d 130 (1978); City of Louisville v. McDonald, 470 S.W.2d 173 (Ky. 1971); Fasano v. Board of County Comm'rs, 264 Or. 574, 507 P.2d 23 (1973); Fleming v. City of Tacoma, 81 Wash. 2d 292, 502 P.2d 327 (1972) (en banc).

43 264 Or. 574, 507 P.2d 23 (1973).

44 Such rezonings, as "legislative" ordinances, are presumed to be valid, and are overturned only if arbitrary and capricious. *See, e.g.*, * * * Cheney v. Village 2 at New Hope, Inc., 429 Pa. 626, 241 A.2d 81 (1968) * * *.

tribunal and receive no ex parte contacts; it should allow the interested parties to present and rebut evidence; it should make decisions on a record, together with appropriate findings; judicial review of its decisions should be stricter than the traditional loose review for mere legislative arbitrariness, and should instead require substantial evidence to support the decision, with the burden on the local government to show plan conformity.

In concluding that some zoning ordinances were judicial rather than legislative, the *Fasano* court also suggested a second strand of reasoning, relating to the nature of the local decisionmaking body. The court rejected the argument that a local government's rezoning decision was legislative simply because it was undertaken by an elected council, and remarked that local governing bodies could not be equated with state or national legislatures. Indeed, the court's bold recharacterization of the local ordinance depended on seeing the local decisionmaking body not as a full "legislature," but rather as something less. A full state or national legislature may adopt legislation even on highly individualized subjects without special quasi-judicial hearings; these are required only of "subordinate bodies" such as administrative agencies.

This less developed strand of *Fasano*—the treatment of a local governing body as something less than a full legislature—is thus critical to its functional administrative law analysis of the local government's land regulations. But the court's discussion of this central issue is remarkably cryptic as to why a local representative body, at least in some of its decisions, is not a legislature but is more akin to an administrative body.

It is all the more important to ask this question because *Fasano* so sharply intrudes into the entire structure of local decisionmaking on land use matters. As I have argued, local governments from the outset had dealt with land development on a piecemeal, bargaining basis. In challenging and restructuring this bargaining process, *Fasano* broke with a pervasive pattern.

Moreover, *Fasano*'s challenge rests on a troublesome suspicion of local legislative bodies, and is related to a long line of legal doctrines that have limited the powers of local government—unduly so, in the eyes of some commentators. Let us then pursue that crucial undeveloped portion of *Fasano* : In what way is a local governing body not fully a legislature?

B. The Federalist *No. 10 and Local Land Decisions*

* * *

As one pair of administrative law authors has said, the American understanding of governance through separate branches was "developed by Locke and Montesquieu and refined by Madison." Madison's chief refinement has to do precisely with the legislature, and with the qualities that make a legislature's decisions fair and reliable. His celebrated *The Federalist* No. 10 merits study here, for it suggests why a local elected government should not always be seen as a legislature.

Madison's essay begins with the argument that the chief obstacle to fairness in a legislative body is "faction": the tendency of one interest group to impose its will at the expense of others. The antidote to faction, Madison says, lies in a constituency of sufficient size and variety; *The Federalist* No. 10 argued that the great advantage of the "extended republic" (i.e., the proposed national government) was that it would contain such a variety of interests that no one "faction" could tyrannize the others. Where the constituency is large, action is possible only through persuasion and coalitions of interest groups. Through a pattern of shifting alliances and vote trading, every interest can obtain at least partial satisfaction in the legislature of the "extended republic."

That all of the participating parties can expect some satisfaction of at least some of their desires is one assurance of fairness in legislation. Fairness is also advanced by the conditions that attend coalition-building itself: no interest group can safely go for the jugular of another, because all know that they may need to call on each other in different coalitions. Thus the very expectations built into the coalition-building process impose a modicum of mutual forbearance on the various interest groups.

* * *

But this justification of large legislatures' decisions contains an implicit criticism of small-scale government: A legislative body drawn from too small or too homogeneous a constituency may be dominated by a single interest or faction. Factional domination may take varying forms. One is sheer corruption, made possible in smaller representative bodies because a limited number of persons have influence which must be bought. Another possibility is domination by a few who are perceived by others as the powerful. The decisions of these few can affect many within the community; others must curry their favor, and even larger interests find difficulty in organizing against their "cabals." Finally, and perhaps most feared by Madison, is the factional domination created by a popular "passion"—sometimes a sudden whim, sometimes a longstanding prejudice—that carries a majority before it. Under any of these various forms of factional domination, all of which are far more likely to occur in a smaller legislature than in a larger one, a dominant group may subject others to sudden destruction or to permanent political disability.

* * *

However much or little local governments may structurally resemble the *Federalist* legislature in general, they are very unlikely to be restrained by the *Federalist* safeguards in making specific piecemeal land decisions. In making these decisions, which involve only a few interested parties meeting only on single issues, legislatures are restrained neither by a coalition-building process that assures the fairness of the decisions, nor by a clash of interests that gives time for sober consideration. Courts should therefore not assume that these safeguards have worked. If these decisions are to be found reasonable, the finding requires some alternative source of fairness and due consideration.

It seems, then, that any model suggesting that local governments are just like larger legislative bodies is unrealistic. It follows that courts should not give local governments' ad hoc land decisions the deference they accord to measures taken by state legislatures. *Fasano*'s plan jurisprudence attempts to solve the problem by agreeing that the local government is not a true legislature; rather, it is more like a court, and its decisions should therefore be made according to judicial standards. The substantive standards for these adjudicative decisions derive from the locality's own plan; the procedures derive from the courts.

But the skittishness of some jurisdictions about *Fasano* suggests that some courts find that quasi-judicialization is also inappropriate for controlling at least some piecemeal changes, and that we should seek alternatives to plan jurisprudence. This Article will argue that the better approach is to abandon analogies to the separate branches, and to fashion tests of fairness and due consideration that are based directly on the "dealing" character of piecemeal changes. Before arguing this thesis, however, I shall examine the history of the recent revival of the plan as a device to structure and test local land use discretion, for that history clarifies the precise nature of the problems that modern plan jurisprudence attempts to address.

C. A Historical Excursion into Plan Jurisprudence: Of Variances and Referenda

Although the civil rights and environmental movements, pointing as they did to unfairness toward outsiders in the local land use regulation process, undoubtedly had some role in reviving the idea of a general plan, it was the internal problems in local administration that provoked the criticism and analysis ultimately reflected in plan jurisprudence. Among these problems, the most prominent were the notoriously leaky variance process and the worrisome questions surrounding referenda on land use decisions. The next two Subsections trace the history of the issues involved in controlling variances and referenda.

1. Variances and the Quasi-Judicialization of Land Use Decisions

In the early SZEA model of land use control, the variance process allowed exceptions from general zoning regulations where, due to special circumstances, the owner of a particular property would suffer special hardship by the strict application of the general ordinance, and where relaxing the regulation would not be "contrary to the public interest." In such hardship cases, the possibility of getting a variance allayed charges that the general ordinance was an unconstitutional "taking" of property.

Even in the early years of zoning, however, one of the leaders of the city planning movement complained that variance boards granted variances simply when they thought no harm would be done.[75] During the mid-1950's and 1960's, academic studies of the variance process confirmed this pattern: Zoning adjustment boards granted variances in a seemingly haphazard fashion, disregarding both the statutory standards of special hardship or unique circumstances and such procedural niceties as notice to interested parties, establishment of a record, and statements of findings.

* * *

While some commentators attributed the variance flood to the rigidity of the general zoning ordinances, they also proposed a narrower solution to the variance problem: variance boards should be held to the procedures of "quasi-judicial" or "administrative"

[75] E. BASSETT, ZONING: THE LAWS, ADMINISTRATION AND COURT DECISIONS DURING THE FIRST TWENTY YEARS 142 (2d ed. 1940). * * *

bodies—terms that were often used interchangeably. The position had several arguments in its favor. First, the SZEA required minutes in variance proceedings and allowed decisions to be appealed to a court; this implied that a board's record should at least be sufficient for a court to review. Second, board members were usually appointed and had duties comparable to those of administrative officers—applying the statutory standards of hardship and unique circumstances to individual cases. Finally, and perhaps most important, quasi-judicial procedures might counterbalance zoning boards' tendency to be, as one court delicately put it, "insufficiently insulated" from developers seeking variances.

There were, however, certain problems with this characterization of the variance board's duties. "Unnecessary hardship" and "special circumstances" scarcely seemed to be matters calling for special administrative expertise, and the criterion "not contrary to the public interest" seemed even less to be a standard applied quasi-judicially. * * *

The vagueness of the variance criteria, and the lay status of the variance boards suggest that these boards were less expert administrators than representative groups of concerned but fair-minded citizens, compromising and smoothing conflicts among neighbors. The boards' own activities certainly suggested that they saw their duties as being akin to a mediating forum for development requests and neighbors' protests. They attempted to take into account genuinely interested objections, they granted requests where no such objections appeared or where the grant accorded with other uses in the vicinity, and they often mollified objectors by making conditional grants. Their real flaw, on this "mediation" view, was their frequent failure to notify and grant a hearing to potential objectors.

If this view of board-as-mediator had prevailed, we might have seen a very different jurisprudence of local land use matters. But it did not. By the 1960's the general wisdom held that in order both to preserve an overall zoning scheme and to protect the parties immediately interested, variances should be guided through procedures more rigorous than developer pressure as tempered by neighborhood uproar. Administrative law models suggested an analogy of the variance to quasi-judicial procedures, and perhaps it is not surprising that the courts grasped the analogy, at least to the extent of requiring records and findings that related variance decisions to what were considered the applicable standards. If nothing else, such procedures gave the courts a stable point of departure in reviewing variance proceedings.

Meanwhile, in two celebrated articles in the mid-1950's, Charles Haar extended the variance criticism to the zoning ordinance itself, arguing that unless bound to the standards of a preexisting plan, zoning ordinances too could be passed merely to grant special favors or to accommodate developers' pressures.[100] Haar's articles were the first major critiques of the courts' treatment of the relationship between planning and zoning. Even though the SZEA required that land use controls be "in accordance with a comprehensive plan," Haar argued, the courts had vitiated that requirement by viewing it as satisfied if the zoning ordinance was citywide, or covered a variety of uses, or indeed was merely "well-considered." Haar contended that the plan should be viewed as a "constitution," and that zoning ordinances should be judged by their conformity with it.

Some courts began to find Haar's ideas useful in reviewing challenged zoning ordinances. The difference between variances and small zoning amendments had always been blurred in practice; localities had long used the two techniques as more or less interchangeable methods to arrive at piecemeal changes. If variances required adherence to standards and findings, why should amendments be treated differently? Thus, as in the case of variances, plan conformity offered the courts a way to structure their review of these rezoning ordinances, particularly when the neighbors challenged the ordinance on vague public interest grounds. From the point of view of the courts, plan conformity saved them from resting on their own unaided version of the "public interest," and instead channeled their review along procedural lines. Moreover, requiring the community to adhere to its own prior plan seemed to increase fairness to the neighbors, not only by protecting them against surprise, but also by giving them a starting point for their legal arguments.

Later commentators, going beyond Haar's view of the plan as a guide to legislation, easily took the next procedural step: If the plan was the standard for zoning, then individual rezoning ordinances were not legislative decisions but quasi-judicial applications of the plan, and the decisionmakers should be held to

[100] Haar, *"In Accordance with a Comprehensive Plan,"* 68 HARV. L. REV. 1154 (1955); Haar, *The Master Plan: An Impermanent Constitution*, 20 LAW & CONTEMP. PROBS. 353 (1955).

quasi-judicial procedures.[106] The basic argument these commentators made was that in rezoning individual parcels, city councils essentially acted as judges, measuring specific facts against the standards of the plan.

These commentators distinguished individual parcel rezonings from large-scale citywide rezonings on the basis of the familiar administrative law distinction between legislative and adjudicative subject matter: large-scale rezonings involved policy decisions balancing great multitudes of facts, and were thus appropriate for legislative treatment, whereas small-scale rezonings involved particular parties and limited number of facts, which should be measured against the preexisting general policies. Commentators also referred to political considerations suggestive of *The Federalist* No. 10 to support the distinction: general rezonings affected large numbers of citizens, who would let their councilmen know their views and therefore would protect themselves through the ordinary political process; but in small-scale rezonings, the number of interested parties was limited, and those among them with contacts might have grossly disproportionate political influence. As in the variance context, there loomed behind the small-scale rezoning the specter of the influential developer, from whom the neighbors needed refuge in a quasi-judicial forum whose decisions met the standards of the duly considered plan.

Thus by the early 1970's, a perception that localities were yielding too easily to haphazard development pressures had brought courts and commentators well along toward plan jurisprudence. Some courts not only required that local land use decisions conform to an independent plan, but also recharacterized at least some of * * * those decisions as quasi-judicial, not legislative. Apparently, they thought that local legislatures were no stronger than variance boards in standing up to the factional influence of development pressure. To protect a semblance of due consideration, as well as the neighbors' interests, they began to hold the local decisionmakers to another procedural model—i.e., the quasi-judicial application of a preexisting plan.

2. Referenda and the Problem of Controlling Majoritarian Rule

In the variance context, the developers represented a "factional" influence of special economic interests. But the voters themselves sometimes seemed to represent another type of faction—that of popular prejudice or caprice. Indeed, voter decisions rather than developer influence generated a second set of worries about local land use administration: Could zoning changes be made by referenda or even more troublesome, by initiative? Could the voters reject the city council's zoning amendments, or, to up the ante, could they come up with zoning amendments of their own? And if they could do either, what happened to the idea of zoning according to a general plan?

* * *

These problems again focused attention on the general plan as the existing policy to be carried out administratively. As several courts noted, amendments by popular vote could destroy piecemeal the comprehensive and harmonious scheme that zoning was designed to promote. A second issue was the procedural suitability of a popular vote on an individual's property, where popular emotions were unrestrained even by ordinary city council processes. The planning commission reports, the public hearings, and the collegial discussion and decisionmaking were all dispensed with.

State courts had grappled with these issues for several years when the United States Supreme Court made two major constitutional decisions upholding local referenda. Both concerned voter objections to multifamily housing projects. First, in its 1971 decision in *James v. Valtierra*,[112] the Court upheld California's requirement that subsidized low-income housing projects be approved by local referenda. Then, in its 1976 decision in *City of Eastlake v. Forest City Enterprises, Inc.*,[113] the Court upheld a local charter amendment adopted by referendum after the city council rezoned to permit a multifamily housing project; the charter amendment required that any future rezoning pass a fifty-five percent referendum majority. The Ohio Supreme Court had held that this referendum procedure violated due process requirements, since a referendum made the

---

[106] In 1966, Richard Babcock took this view in his popular and influential critique of local land practice, R. Babcock, The Zoning Game, 158 (1966). Two years later, the American Law Institute (ALI), in its first tentative draft of a new Model Land Redevelopment Code, strongly suggested that local governing councils, like local variance boards, should be held to quasi-judicial proceedings in small-scale land decisions. Model Land Dev. Code §§ 3-106, 8-104, 8-202 (Tent. Draft No. 1, 1968). * * *

[112] 402 U.S. 137 (1971).

[113] 426 U.S. 668 (1976).

rezoning decision "dependent upon the potentially arbitrary and unreasonable whims of the voting public." But the United States Supreme Court reversed, noting that the Ohio court had ruled that rezonings were legislative rather than administrative acts. The local council merely acted for the people in such legislative acts, the Court reasoned, and the sovereign people could constitutionally reserve to itself a type of decision that otherwise would have been made by the local council in its legislative capacity.

It might seem that *Eastlake* leaves to the states the characterization of local land changes. So viewed, the case might well allow a state to characterize piecemeal changes as neither legislative nor judicial but as something else—a point to which I shall return. But the Court's discussion of the "legislative" rubric, together with Justice Stevens' dissenting citation of *Fasano* and its "judicial" characterization of piecemeal changes, directed the ensuing academic and legal discussion into conventional separation-of-powers channels, where the only choices among processes are legislative and judicial (or an administrative variant of the latter).

Certainly *Valtierra* and *Eastlake* did not settle the controversy over zoning amendments by popular vote; on the contrary, the decisions only fueled the debate. Academic commentators criticized *Eastlake*'s "reserved powers" argument, and commented on the procedural due process problems entailed in leaving complex decisions (particularly on such subjects as public housing) to an overheated populace; no one could realistically expect that the people at large—as distinguished from their city councils—would hold hearings, sift through reports, debate issues, or record their views on the relevant evidence and appropriate conclusions. *Eastlake* critics also pointed out that a decision by referendum was especially unlikely to be guided or restrained by the local general plan.

These considerations led some state courts, even after *Eastlake*, to invalidate referenda on land use decisions; they saw the issues as administrative or even judicial rather than legislative. Whichever characterization they used, these state courts held that nonlegislative decisions were to be made by fixed processes according to the standards already set out in the plan.

But if the land use changes were not legislative for purposes of a referendum, then why should they be legislative when made by a city council? The council members, after all, were bound to be swayed by the interests of their constituents. This anomaly bolstered the step taken in *Fasano*: the treatment of all small-scale land use decisions not as legislative acts but as quasi-judicial decisions, so that even elected representatives must follow courtlike procedures in applying the overall policies of the plan to individual properties.

Indeed, the referendum cases pointedly illustrated why individual land changes might require some check on arbitrariness, regardless of whether these changes were made by variance boards or elected councils or the citizens themselves. Perhaps the most important feature of the referendum discussion was that it justified *The Federalist's* mistrust of the militant local community as a type of faction. Referenda on housing projects were particularly troubling, but even the shopping center cases showed how an aroused local populace could trample the legitimate property expectations of an individual owner or developer. To check unfairness to the individual owner, and to halt the seeming irrationality of piecemeal changes, some courts turned to procedures involving some version of consistency with a larger plan. The content of any given plan seemed less important in these discussions than the need to restrain local action by some legal standard set out in advance, which the courts could call upon as a test of reasonableness.

Thus at least two strands of zoning decisions and commentaries urged plan jurisprudence as a control on local land use decisions. The variance and referenda cases, turning as they did on developer demands at the one extreme and popular pressures at the other, illustrated the potentially "factional" nature of piecemeal changes, as well as their particular vulnerability to partial judgments, haste, and lack of consideration or fairness.

The courts' and commentators' analyses of these two problems suggested quasi-judicial application of a general plan as a solution. Like the discretion-structuring model from administrative law, this solution seemed to safeguard carefulness and fairness where the ordinary legislative process might fail. In addition, it was ideal for judical review. It prescribed readymade standards in the form of a local plan, thus relieving the courts from having to invent substantive public interest criteria for themselves. At the same time, it enabled them to prescribe a familiar and regularized adjudicative procedural form for the local decisionmakers. Thus, plan jurisprudence clarified for the courts both the substance and the procedure for review of local piecemeal changes, and did so in such a way as to permit considerable judicial control over all these troublesome "deals."

* * *

[Professor Rose then turns to a critique of the quasi-judicial approach to land use decisions, arguing that this approach envisions an outdated and rigid concept of planning, and that it ignores the value of the much more fluid give-and-take that acutally exists in local decisionmaking.]

IV

AN ALTERNATIVE JURISPRUDENCE: PIECEMEAL CHANGES AS MEDIATION

Local land regulations, including piecemeal changes, must all meet a variety of substantive requirements in federal and state law. Thus they must not violate first amendment rights, they must provide due process, and they must comply with legislative or judicial mandates to take on regional responsibilities, particularly those of helping to care for low income needs.[260] But one lesson from plan jurisprudence is that even when these larger requirements are met, locally determined piecemeal changes may still be ill-considered or unfair, and the courts cannot rely on a traditional notion of legislative "reasonableness," or on *Federalist* arguments for institutional competence. Although this Article rejects the adjudicative model adopted by plan jurisprudence, it shares plan jurisprudence's goal: a mediation model too should strive to assure fairness and due consideration.

The terms "fairness" and "due consideration" both take meaning from the context in which they arise. We have seen that in a large legislature these qualities result from a clash of interests leading to temporary stasis. In local piecemeal changes, the meaning of fairness and due consideration should arise from the elements that legitimize local government. From the alternate tradition in American political thinking, we may identify those elements as participation and withdrawal—or, in Hirschman's terms, the combination of voice and exit.[261] These elements should guide a jurisprudence of local mediations toward the goals of fairness and due consideration. * * *

A. *Due Consideration as Voice*

Plan jurisprudence abandons the legislative clash of interests as a guarantor of due consideration, and instead sets forth two questions for assessing whether a given piecemeal change was adequately considered. First, it asks whether the change process followed the deliberative processes of a court or quasi-court; second, whether the change follows from an earlier deliberative process, that is, from the previously adopted "general plan." A mediation model, unlike plan jurisprudence, attempts to assure due consideration through a pattern of voice—through hearing from interested parties and attempting to arrive at an accommodation acceptable to them within the framework of larger community norms.

* * * [M]ediation has its own rhythm for working out accommodations, and a court should ask if the mediation sequence has been followed when it tests whether a result was duly considered—whether interested parties had enough opportunity to participate. At least three basic stages can be delineated: (1) identification of disputants; (2) exploration of issues; and (3) explanation of outcome.

In plan jurisprudence the stages appear as notice, hearings, and findings; and while these suggest too close an adherence to a judicial prototype, a mediative jursiprudence can use and flesh out that prototype. But it can also use other modern planning ideas, notably environmental impact analysis.

1. *Identification of Disputants and Sources of Dispute*

Disputes over proposed land use changes may not be immediately obvious, and failure to inquire into latent disputes and to locate potential disputants may abort the accommodation that mediation should create. One way to bring out latent disputes is notice to persons possibly interested in the change. Indeed, the persons who receive notice are those perceived by the community to have some stake in the piecemeal change. Plan jurisprudence itself grew out of, *inter alia*, the older variance proceedings, where some objectors had too little opportunity to voice objections, particularly if local boards ignored notice and hearing requirements. Current enabling statutes and local ordinances require that piecemeal changes proceed only after notice to interested groups, and after some hearing to allow them to object. Courts have quite rightly taken these requirements extremely seriously, however discomforting they may be.

---

260 *See*, e.g., Southern Burlington County NAACP v. Township of Mt. Laurel, 67 N.J. 151, 336 A.2d 713 (1975); Berenson v. Town of New Castle, 67 A.D.2d 506, 415 N.Y.S.2d 669 (1979); * * *.

261 Alfred O. Hirschman, EXIT, VOICE AND LOYALTY: RESPONSES TO DECLINE IN FIRMS, ORGANIZATIONS AND STATES (1970)

A mediation model suggests that when notice is given and no objections are raised, the courts have little reason to second-guess a local board's approval of a piecemeal change, and indeed the presumption should favor the proposed change. If one of the functions of a jurisprudence of piecemeal changes is to assure "voice" in the sense of a considered accommodation of differences, in the absence of differences one seeking change should be able to go forward.

There may, however, be some circumstances in which lack of objection is not a reliable indicator of general consent. At times many parties may have an interest, but the interest of any individual may be weak. Land developments whose effects are cumulative or most likely to be felt in the future often fail to arouse objections strong enough to raise the full range of potential disputes. Preexisting plans and studies may reveal such objections, as well as others that absent disputants might raise.

Modern impact analysis suggests another method for raising potential disputes. In California and elsewhere, the courts have held that land use change permits are "government projects" effectively requiring some impact review of all discretionary grants of private proposals. Although such rulings have been criticized as extending too far the idea of "government project," they make more sense where the procedures for regulatory change take the form of mediated negotiations of disputes. Threshold environmental review (i.e., the determination whether some proposed change will have a significant impact) inquires into potential objections when simple notice will fail to disclose or deal with them. As the courts have recognized, failure to identify those objections can short circuit the impact review process—just as it can hamper mediation.

2. Exploration of Issues

Plan jurisprudence rightly recognizes that small-scale land changes require a forum and a process for confronting factual and normative issues. Quasi-judicial proceedings, however, provide too limited a range within which the parties can exchange information. The literature of negotiation and mediation suggests that the confrontation of issues may take much more varied and vivid forms than can be encompassed by judicial proceedings. At the outset, for example, the parties may engage in posturing and name-calling behavior that delineates the outer extremes of their respective positions. This is an expression of voice certainly familiar in the annals of piecemeal land changes. In the later stages of negotiation the parties may construct "bids" or packages of solutions. These confrontations and explorations assist a successful, mutually acceptable solution; but they are certainly not suitable for a courtlike process of direct and cross-examination.

Other planning and regulatory processes, however, further the exchange of information. Hearings, for example, are a standard requirement in many land use changes. And here too, environmental impact review may be extremely helpful in airing issues. The stated purposes of these reviews, aside from the substantive goal of preserving the nebulously defined "environment," are essentially procedural: to publicize issues, to draw in interested parties, to examine alternative solutions, and to satisfy the public that the issues have been fully explored. Just as important, they give interested persons a sense of participation in the decision, either personally or through the auspices of like-minded others.

* * *

Interest representation and particularly impact review have been criticized for merely transposing "capture" from the regulated interests to other partisan and self-appointed "public interest" groups, and for causing delay and expense that verges on deadlock. But in a local setting the problems of incompleteness and paralysis may be less significant than they are for the "extended republic" and its vast bureaucracy. "Capture" itself may be less threatening in local mediation where even partisan authorities can be restrained by the threats of voice and exit—that is, the threats that the disputants may either pack the hearing room, or pull their business out of town altogether. Then too, the local community's smaller size narrows the range of interest groups that may intervene, thus leaving less opportunity for domination by the self-appointed guardians, or for the interminable delay and expense that accompany an effort to hear too many points of view.

In any event, some delay may well be useful to a local decision. For one thing, it prevents rash decisions about land uses—decisions whose consequences will last a long time. In a sense, the delay is like that which accompanies a clash of interests in a larger legislature: both prevent hasty decisions that might overlook a larger common good.

Moreover, the seemingly wasteful noise and repetition of impact review may have other uses. Patient collection of views, even if they are repetitious, serves a "venting" function that ultimately helps the disputants to accept a decision. While law-and-economics critiques rightly point out that the costs of process may outweigh the benefits in results, a lack of voice also carries real costs, however difficult they may be to quantify. Information leading to more lasting or indeed more efficient accommodations may be lost; and lacking a way to measure the relative costs of environmental effects, we may depend primarily on voice to keep us informed of costs and benefits. Then too, without voice, those defeated in final resolution may begrudge the short shrift they received and may be lost to useful civic participation in the future. On a less idealistic note, disgruntled losers may also litigate—at costs even higher than those of mediation.

A mediation model thus puts interest representation proposals to good use at the local level, employing them to make voice effective. These proposals suggest the value of voice in mediation: These techniques expand issues and give time for a range of arguments and explorations of the dispute, even when those explorations are emotionally charged. Standard planning devices too can give evidence of efforts to expand issues—the hearings, the reports and so on. But again, we should not be misled (as some courts have been) by a jurisprudence that fixes merely on the formal presence of a plan and plan consistency; formal devices may impede an exploration of issues rather than assure it.

3. Explanation

Plan jurisprudence calls for standards and records showing in specific form two general features common to dispute resolution methods: first, the resolution should be based on norms; and second, some disclosure must be made of the relationship between the relevant norms and the actual conclusion.

Plan jurisprudence, however, suggests that a record should contain only matters relevant to fixed preexisting standards rather than the free-form discussions in land changes, in which disputants refer to a wide variety of policy considerations and to tradeoffs among them. Moreover, if the "standard" is a vague or inconsistent plan, a mere reference to it may conceal rather than disclose the normative bases for a specific decision.

A mediation model of land changes recognizes the need for explanation, and suggests a different approach to normative disclosure. Acknowledging that not all norms can be satisfied at once, and that some may have to be weighed against others, a mediative approach would require that norms and tradeoffs be disclosed and explained case-by-case. Some standard planning techniques encourage a local body to do this. Findings may help. Impact analysis is especially appropriate for such disclosure, since it involves not only an issue-expanding review process, but also an ultimate explanation of norms and tradeoffs in an impact statement.

Explanation furthers due consideration in two ways. First, it reinforces and encourages an exploration of issues and potential accommodations; the very fact that decisionmakers have to explain outcomes may encourage them to think of alternatives and mitigations. Second, explanation ultimately helps to reconcile the parties. Some persons in a mediation may lose in whole or in part—developers may have to put shrubs around the shopping center; the neighbors may have to put up with the shopping center itself. But they all may be at least partially mollified if they know the reasons; like the opportunity for "venting," explanation treats seriously the objections of those who ultimately have to acquiesce in the outcome.

In sum, in inquiring whether a piecemeal land change was duly considered, a court should focus on voice in mediation and ask whether the local body went through the steps of identifying disputants, exploring issues, and explaining results. But doubts about piecemeal changes do not concern only due consideration or voice. Even when a local body goes through the steps of voice we may still think that the result is unfair to an individual. In the next Section, I turn to the meaning of fairness in local mediation.

B. Fairness and Exit

What does it mean to say that a governmental body has acted fairly? Clearly, fairness means different things in different contexts.

* * *

According to contract analysis, there are at least two aspects to fairness: fairness of result (that is, as a restraint on distribution, or more particularly on redistribution), and fairness in the bargaining arrangements (that is, as a restraint on surprise or duress).

In the following subsections, I will discuss the various meanings of fairness in piecemeal changes from both of these contract perspectives, but will argue that of the two, the latter is more important in local land regulations. It is also more interesting because on close analysis, the idea of fairness as "no surprise" brings us back to Hirschman's concept of exit: the party who is not surprised, and who can choose to avoid the deal, is the party who can ultimately exit.

1. Fairness as a Distributive or Redistributive Restraint

The use of "takings" clauses of federal and state constitutions is a major litigative vehicle for checking unfairness in local land regulation. Usually, the party raising the takings claim is the disappointed project initiator; neighbors or others opposing a development, because of their more diffuse and less direct property interests, have less frequently mounted such claims.

The root of a takings claim is that some public act has placed on an individual or group too high a proportion of some burden—a burden which all (or at least some larger portion of the community) should bear. Takings doctrine is thus essentially a limitation on redistributions or redefinitions of property rights that harm particular individuals.

* * *

[F]ederal takings doctrine, while it acts as some substantive check on the fairness of local land decisions, sets a very wide horizon within which those decisions can adjust property claims.

The neighbors' counterpart to a takings claim appeals to the locality's plan. This appeal to locally defined standards has traditionally come not from the proponent of change, but from the neighbors who opposed some deal that was in fact struck. Indeed, it was precisely these neighbors' claims that there should be some "public interest" test of variances and zoning changes that led the courts to the plan jurisprudence, and that brought the courts to see the locality's own plan as a substantive standard against which to measure the individual bargain. I have recounted at length the difficulties of relying on the advance plan; most relevant here are the facts that the plan itself may be vague or unfairly redistributive. Thus, a "general plan" is a highly dubious limitation on unfair redistribution.

In sum, given the way these doctrines have developed, the antiredistributive concept of fairness provides only very loose checks on local government discretion. Takings claims leave very wide latitude to the locality; and local general plans are too easily manipulable to act as serious limitations.

But plan jurisprudence does direct our attention to a second perspective on fairness. In holding that land changes should be based on some earlier defined local standards, plan jurisprudence uses predictability, or protection from surprise, as another criterion of fairness.

A somewhat similar movement—from fairness as a substantive check on redistribution to fairness as largely procedural predictability—emerges from the economic analysis in some of the academic land use reform proposals. The next subsection focuses on these proposals.

2. From Redistributive Fairness to Predictability: Lessons from the Market-Mimicking Model

Market-mimicking proposals generally take the position that land regulation outcomes should as closely as possible track the decisions that, but for "market failure," would be made through private transactions. The chief object of these proposals is to maintain (or restore) the efficient allocation of goods normally associated with market transactions, and many proponents take a skeptical stance toward expansive dispute settlement procedures, believing that these could be so costly as to produce inefficient net results.

But market-mimicking models nevertheless do have some surprising similarities to a mediation model. Their stress on exchange suggests that the land use change may encompass various types of quid pro quo, and thus implies that disputes may be settled with different packages of accommodations, rather than through the all-or-nothing outcome reached by a court applying a given standard. More important for present purposes, market proposals have some important lessons about the meaning of fairness in making piecemeal changes. Although these proposals appear to treat fairness as a brake on redistribution, on closer analysis their concept of fairness is protection from surprise.

At first glance, market-mimicking proposals seem to deal with fairness, if at all, as a substantive limitation on redistribution. This is because market transactions—the model to be emulated—involve trading rather than sheer wealth transfer. In economic models, therefore, regulations require us where possible to pay for what we want rather than allowing us simply to take it from others. For example, Robert Ellickson has suggested that piecemeal changes be regulated by an expanded version of traditional nuisance law; his proposed local "nuisance boards" would provide a public forum for working out private control of the adverse "spillover" effects of individual land uses. As in market transactions, individuals would be required to signal their preferences and pay accordingly.[311] Other scholars have formulated land regulations that would act as a different kind of market substitute: regulations would serve as brokerage devices, to charge and compensate for the otherwise unadjusted "wipeouts" and "windfalls" that so often accompany land development.[312]

---

[311] Ellickson, *supra* note 16.

[312] *See generally*, D. HAGMAN & D. MISCZYNSKI, WINDFALLS FOR WIPEOUTS (1978) * * *.

Municipalities have begun to apply market-mimicking theory in their own ways, arguing that various new developments have external costs to the public, and that fairness requires that these costs should be offset by "amenities" or charges imposed on the new development to benefit the existing community. Thus, some San Francisco officials, for example, hope to require new office developers to build housing and perhaps even to pay transportation fees for the office workers attracted to new office structures, or to provide art work and mini-parks to compensate for the shadows and gloom their structures will create. In variations on this theme, some municipalities have "paid" land owners for the maintenance of uneconomic historic structures or open spaces, or for the development of low income housing, by permitting these owners to exceed bulk limitations on their other properties.

City governments find such devices attractive because they may eliminate or reduce their own expenditures for public amenities; but developers have greeted such devices with outrage. This reaction should at least suggest that fairness problems in local land use decisions are not completely solved by using the market-mimicking approach.

First, market models may neglect considerations of fairness altogether, since they may seek only efficient solutions. An efficient regulation, when defined as one in which benefits outweigh costs, may involve unfair redistribution, since the individual may lose a great deal even though his costs are outweighed by social benefits. Perhaps more fundamental is an ambiguity about the meaning of the external harms that market-mimicking regulations supposedly address. Proponents of various market models concede the difficulties of defining "externality;" and the pricing of external harms or benefits that, by definition, never appear in a market, is an intractable difficulty of the market-mimicking approach. So long as the local governmental body decides the definition and price of harms and benefits, it can manipulate the market model and exploit the potential for abuse that led to reform proposals in the first place.

* * *

[P]lanning[, therefore,] is desirable, as plan jurisprudence holds. Planning documents, particularly vague and general end-state plans, may not be particularly good bases for prediction. But planning in the more modern conception—that is, as continuous and careful reevaluation of resources and goals—may enhance predictability in the way that ordinary language or ordinary patterns of change do. Rolling planning activities protect citizens from sharp discontinuities in land use control and can give notice to interested parties about the possible piecemeal changes affecting a given property. Indeed, planning itself may improve if the courts see plans not as talismans to which regulations must conform, but simply as evidence of foreseeability. Such treatment encourages communities to think ahead and to publicize their intentions, and in fact to weigh how they expect to develop. If they do so, the greater predictability of current mediations can rebut the charge of unfairness.

* * *

But there is still another step entailed in using predictability as a basis for fairness. One protects oneself against the predictable evil by not participating in the risky venture, by not purchasing the property that needs the seldom-granted zoning change. It is precisely because exit is relatively available at local governmental levels that predictability can test fairness. While predictability makes exit possible, the likelihood of exit acts as a check on local bodies: they will want to act reasonably so that potential developers will not decide that any investment in their community is simply too costly. As one law and economics commentator has observed, land use changes occur in a climate of regulation, and if developers are aware of the climate they can account for it in private arrangements; it is only the unforeseen governmental action that is unfair. Implicit in this view, of course, is the presupposition that one who does not like what is going on may leave or never enter the market in the first place.

* * *

Thus, just as the courts should look for voice in testing due consideration, so they should look for exit in testing for fairness—most notably, for signs that a change was predictable, giving the parties an opportunity to get out of harm's way if they did not wish to bear the risks.

Conclusion: Why Local Land Use Control?

In this Article I have attempted to link piecemeal land changes to a non-*Federalist* "alternative tradition" in American political thinking. This tradition legitimizes local decisionmaking by reference to the smallness of local communities, in contradistinction to the largeness of *The Federalist*'s extended republic. It suggests that the proper mode of ensuring reasonableness, in the sense of fairness and due consideration, is the refinement of the local potential for exit and voice, rather than the attempt to make a local body act like a court when it cannot act like a large legislature. As the elements of a new reasonableness standard, the test of due consideration should be based on popular participation in the steps of a mediation process, and the test of fairness should be based on predictability—the latter test made effective particularly by the opportunity for exit.

Still remaining is the question of why we so frequently entrust land use decisions to local governments or even to neighborhoods, where fairness and due consideration cannot rest on *Federalist* assurances, but must rely on opportunities for exit and voice.

* * *

The symbolic meanings and values attached to aesthetic tastes vary enormously and are based on polycentric criteria not easily standardized. It may be that we do not want to entrust decisions about such matters to coalition-building legislatures at all, preferring these decisions to be made by people we trust because we have chosen to live with them, and because we sense our influence on them. Moreover, we may prefer that such decisions be made individually. It is not enough to trade a shopping center here for an apartment project there; we want individual consideration of each on its merits. This may also be true of education, the other major subject Americans regularly entrust to local units: we are not willing to make decisions about our children through coalition building, but rather we want particularized consideration of individual proposals by people whose judgment we trust and whom we can influence through consultation. These are decisions where quality matters especially, and we want them made where we have voice—or the ultimate possibility of exit.

All this is no more than speculation. But if there is anything to it, we will be dealing with substantial local influence over land use decisions for a long time to come. That this local influence requires some safeguards beyond legislative coalition building was the main contribution of plan jurisprudence. But the principles that we use to guide local land use controls should bear some relation to an underlying rationale for local government. This Article has meant to suggest what that rationale might be and some of the principles that follow from it.

NOTE

In *Collard v. Incorporated Village of Flower Hill*, 52 N.Y.2d 594, 421 N.E.2d 818, 439 N.Y.S.2d 326 (1981), a property owner obtained a rezoning of his land and was allowed to proceed with a construction project, provided that certain conditions were made binding upon future use of the property by the filing of a declaration of covenants in the recording system. One of the conditions imposed was that no alterations or additions to any of the buildings on the land be made in the future without the permission of local authorities. When a successor owner challenged the conditions imposed on the land, the *Collard* court refused to treat the rezoning, which effected only the one parcel, as spot zoning and approved the actions of the land use authorities absent a showing of capricious behavior. How would Rose handle this dispute?

G. The Takings Dilemma

1. The Origins of the Takings Dilemma: *Pennsylvania Coal v. Mahon*

The majority opinion of Justice Holmes and the dissent of Justice Brandeis in *Pennsylvania Coal Company v. Mahon* have set the parameters for almost a century of debate over the meaning of the Due Process and Takings Clauses in the Constitution. Joseph DiMento has written an engaging article on the history of the Supreme Court's handling of the case. His work begins our journey through the modern takings debates. For additional material on *Mahon*, *see* Carol M. Rose, Mahon *Reconstructed: Why the Takings Issue is Still a Muddle*, 16 Land Use & Environment L. Rev. 3 (1985).

Joseph F. DiMento, *Mining the Archives of* Pennsylvania Coal: *Heaps of Constitutional Mischief*, 11 J. LEGAL HIST. 396–397, 401, 405–408, 413–420 (1990)*

I. INTRODUCTION

A source of much of the analysis of the taking issue in United States jurisprudence is *Pennsylvania Coal v. Mahon.*[1] Both the majority opinion written by Justice Oliver Wendell Holmes and the dissent written by Justice Louis Brandeis have been cited on innumerable occasions and have generated unending and non-converging commentary on when government regulation gives rise to a taking. The opinions are classics, outlining several major differences in these justices' views of the state's power to regulate uses of property.

* * *

The archival material on *Coal* is fascinating. It elucidates the interplay among members of the Court as [it] * * * was carried out in civilized, courteous, formal written ways. Furthermore, it sheds light on the less formal interactions, those not recorded in working correspondence within the Court, but in conversations and letters of the Justices. In the case of *Coal* the record is sufficient to offer a rare picture of the process by which an opinion develops. * * * In addition to being of historical interest, this background can provide understanding of the nuances of the words chosen in *Coal*, in turn to better understand the Court's positions on regulatory takings. Finally, mining of the archival material on *Coal* gives a glimpse into the alleged influences of personal characteristics and age and sickness on the doctrinal contributions of Justice Holmes and offers a rare example of a condescending evaluation of the great justice by his colleague, Justice Brandeis.

* * *

The Coal *Controversy Described*

The *Coal* case involved application of the Kohler Act, a Pennsylvania statute which made it unlawful "so to conduct the operation of mining anthracite coal as to cause the caving-in, collapse, or subsidence of" a described series of public buildings and structures or structures "used in the service of the public" and "[a]ny dwelling or other structure used as a human habitation, or any factory, store, or other industrial or mercantile establishment in which human labor is employed." An exception existed if the coal extractor was the owner of the surface estate. The case arose in equity as a challenge to prevent the Pennsylvania Coal Company from mining property for which it had executed a deed which conveyed the surface estate but reserved the right to remove the coals under the estate. Pennsylvania common law recognized three different estates in land used in mining: the surface right; ownership of subjacent minerals; and the so-called Third Estate which was the right of support by the subjacent strata. The Third Estate could be held, transferred, and conveyed by a party who had no right in the other estates. The Mahons were the owners of the surface estate and their deed stipulated that they accepted the property at risk. They waived * * * their right to damages resulting from coal mining.

* * *

THE DEVELOPMENT OF THE ARGUMENTS

Justice Holmes and Justice Brandeis developed their opinions in very different ways. The Holmes drafts number only four including the final Opinion which is exactly the same as the penultimate draft except for a citation. Brandeis, on the other hand, fills the Supreme Court file folder for the case with at least ten separate drafts including the final Dissent.

* * *

Something transpired between the * * * first two printed drafts and the Opinion to cause Mr. Justice Holmes to double its scope, both in physical size and in substantive reach.

* * * Holmes received a letter from Chief William H. Justice Taft dated December 2, 1922 in which Taft stressed the danger of creating distinctions between private houses, on the one hand, and streets and schools, on the other, a distinction made only in the first two Holmes drafts. Taft took a strong procompensation position and he anticipated the use by Justice Brandeis of the distinction between acquisi-

[1] 260 U.S. 393 (1922).

tion of rights to protect private as opposed to public uses.

The Taft letter was also sent to Justices Van Devanter, McReynolds, McKenna and Sutherland and covered by the note: "I know I agreed to acquiesce in Mr. Justice Holmes opinion as revised by us all, but on reading it, my original qualms returned, and I have written Justice Holmes the enclosed . . ." * * *

> My brethren made the suggestion of changes in your opinion in the Pennsylvania Subsidence cases and I acquiesced; but a further reading of the opinion as changed brings back my original qualms and they are these. I have no objection to the general principle that the character and extent of the public purpose in curtailing values incident to property may justify the exercise of the police power without compensation in one case when a less clear and pronounced public purpose might not do so in another. But in the case before us where the statute applies to streets and school houses as well as private buildings, and when we may reasonably anticipate the bringing of such cases before us, indeed when friends of the Court have thrust them on us, it seems to me unwise and likely to create a wrong impression of what we are likely to do in such cases to stress the distinction as this opinion does, unless we intend to recognize and enforce the distinction in the cases to come. Now to me such distinction in this class of cases would have no weight, because I don't think the public may take such an estate for itself and for a direct public use any more than it can by legislation take it for a private dwelling. I agree that an instance frequently quoted of [sic] overwhelming for the taking of property without compensation is where in a general conflagration it is necessary to burn houses to stop the spread of the fire. So, too, the destruction by the army in time of war of private property in the train of war is another instance. But no such case is here. The public acquired its right in the streets and in the schoolhouses and public buildings with the same defect in its title as to full enjoyment that is present in that of the dwelling owner in this case, and I cannot for the life of me see why the public should not pay for such an estate exactly as the householder must. It is better to pay and the process of condemnation for it is easier and more direct. I venture to think that when Mr. Justice Brandeis draws up his dissenting opinion, he will improve the opportunity to make this distinction, unnecessary as it seems to me and embarrassing in reference to coming cases, quite awkward for the Court. He will, moreover, rely on the Cole Pillar case which is not considered by the Court in this opinion. Of course, if the Court thinks the distinction is one which will lead to a different conclusion in the case of streets and municipal school buildings, all I have said is beside the point and I should write a concurring opinion. But if not, then I think we ought to face the question now, or at least not suggest a distinction which we have no purpose to make use of in this class of cases. I ask your kindly consideration of this view.

Holmes replied on the same day:

> Dear Chief: Your letter commands my sympathy, and I should be prepared to smash the whole Act. As my secretary suggests, this does not seem to be an exigency different in kind from that for laying out the way in the first place. But I supposed I was to confine myself to this particular case. Perhaps it should be well to bring it up in conference?
>
> * * *

* * *

The Taft correspondence must have been influential. Several of its main points are found in the penultimate version and the Opinion. These are points which are absent from the first two drafts. First, the Pillar case[84] is mentioned, whereas it is not cited nor discussed in the first two versions. The Opinion and the post-Taft correspondence draft, but not the first two drafts, make note of the "exceptional case . . . blowing up a house to stop a conflagration." And the Opinion and the almost identical immedi-

---

[84] Scranton v. Peoples Coal Company, 256 Pa. 332 (1917). * * * It * * * concluded that an "abutting owner cannot remove minerals from or adjacent to an established highway in such manner as to cause subsidence or other injury thereto; . . . to do so is a nuisance . . . * * *. * * *

Decided the same day as *Scranton* * * * was Commonwealth v. Clearview Coal Co., 256 Pa. 328 * * *. Here, the deed to the property contained a clause reserving the coal and minerals to the grantor, and grantee waived support of the surface. In this opinion * * * [the court concluded] that the school district's route to securing the district's building was by condemnation of the supporting coal. * * *

ately preceding draft express Taft's concern with subsequent suits—Holmes now address [sic] the general validity of the Act. The two earlier drafts do not.

* * *

THE JUSTICES' EVALUATIONS OF *COAL*

Holmes on Holmes

In his correspondence with both professional and social associates, Justice Holmes made several comments on his Opinion in *Coal* and reactions to it. * * *

As a general summary statement, Justice Holmes thought that his Opinion was misunderstood, that he might have made it more clear so as to emphasize the central issue of the rights the public has in certain specified contexts, and that the focus in the commentary on his Opinion on a particular analytical concept (average reciprocity of advantage) was misplaced.

* * *

Holmes in a New Year's Eve (1922) letter to Pollock argued that his Opinion did not rely on average reciprocity of advantage as a general ground, but only to explain certain cases:

> . . . I was surprised to receive a number of letters—increased by puff in the New Republic, that made me repeat that when you get to the top of a hill there is nothing left but to come down. I used to think that the main-spring was broken by 80, although my father kept on writing. I hope I was wrong for I am keeping on in the same way. I like it and want to produce as long as I can. I enclose one of my last decisions that you may judge whether there is any falling off. It was unpopular in Pennsylvania of course. Brandeis's dissent speaks as if what I call average reciprocity of advantage were made the general ground by me. No so. I use that only to explain a particular case. My ground is that the public only got on to this land by paying for it and that if they saw fit to pay only for a surface right they can't enlarge it because they need it now any more than they could have taken the right of being there in the first place. Perhaps it would have been well if I had emphasized more the distinction between the right of the public in places where their right to be there is unqualified and their right where they only get any *locus standi* by a transaction that renounced what they now claim.

Despite his post-Opinion protestation, Justice Holmes may have earlier been searching for an enticing phrase such as "average reciprocity of advantage." As to its origins, Holmes used it in other opinions.[102] Writing to Harold J. Laski on December 22, 1922, Holmes said of the phrase:

> * * * In this one I send I coined the formula "average reciprocity of advantage" which I think neatly expressed the rationale of certain cases—not of all as Brandeis did vainly talk in his dissent that I sent you before.

Holmes recognized that his opinion would be unpopular with some people. To Mrs. Gray on December 26, 1922, he wrote, after again expressing pleasure at the "great puff" in the New Republic (referring to an article which described him "as vigilant for the Union, for which he fought at Ball's Bluff and Antietam and Fredericksburg and equally watchful of needed scope for the state"): "However, it is not all cake and ale. I wrote a decision that I knew would be unpopular and I received an article yesterday written I should think by an ass or an angry man, telling how incompetent was my discourse." * * * But as to observers in general and Justice Frankfurter in particular (who, Holmes reports * * *, would normally write him about his important opinions and did not for *Coal*, "probably feeling an unnecessary delicacy about saying that he disagrees"), the disagreement did not have a major impact on his self assessment:

> But nevertheless when the premises are a little more emphasized, as they should have been by me, I confess to feeling as much confidence as I often do. I always have thought that old Harlan's decision in *Mugler v. Kansas* was pretty fishy. But I am not going to reargue the matter now.

Holmes went on to indicate that he was not impressed with the *New Republic* editorial written on the opinion. That piece characterized the opinions in *Coal* as an "intellectual battle of giants," one which Brandeis ultimately won:

> In the present case Justice Brandeis' view seems the superior statesmanship. It is frankly a qualification of a property right, but as this spinning globe comes to have living upon it more and more human beings, it is inevitable that the freedom of action of these individuals

---

[102] In the October, 1922 term Holmes wrote a short opinion in which he talked about but did not rely on, average reciprocity of advantage. * * * The case involved a party wall statute * * *. * * * Jackman v. Rosenbaum, 260 U.S. 22 * * * (1922).

> must become more and more limited. For property rights of the kind here in question are, as Justice Holmes has himself well said, merely rights to course of conduct.

Holmes attributes the editorial to Atcheson [sic] although it was an anonymous piece. Holmes had reason to believe that the source of the editorial was Dean Acheson who was secretary to Justice Brandeis in an earlier term.

Brandeis on Holmes

Brandeis was not gentle with Justice Holmes on the *Coal* opinion. Felix Frankfurter's notes of conversations he had with Brandeis report a request to Brandeis to account for the Holmes position in the case:

> I account for it by what one would think Holmes is last man to yield to—class bias. He came back to views not of his manhood but childhood. I recalled when I saw that opinion that there is one of the indices of [illegible] namely a denial of a heretofore conspicuous trait—a refined man becomes gross, a sensitive man does an act of injustice, etc. Here is Holmes in a case where you would have thought he above all men could be insured against reaching the result he did.

Brandeis' explanation also noted that property interests "got him" when Holmes was weak:

> [Undated] L.D.B.: Heightened respect for property has been part of Holmes' growing old. The *Mahon* case is a deep constitutional sentiment although they cut [caught] him when he was weak (after Holmes' prostate operation) & played him to go whole hog. But he said to me recently "I suppose miserliness is legitimate incident of age" a propos of accumulating & buying bonds. He is deeply worried about exhaustion of resources . . . intellectually he may try to rid himself of undue regard for property but emotionally he can't & it comes hard.

Regarding the importance of the prostate operation, Harvard Law school Professor Thomas Reed Powell also cited it as an explanation of what he considered an aberration in the Holmes record.

* * *

Coal may also have been one of the cases, which because it did not represent to Holmes new areas of major inquiry, Holmes wished to quickly move along. Brandeis knew that Holmes was often in a rush to circulate his opinions.

* * *

[S]peaking of the *Jackman* opinion,[124] the source of Holmes' average reciprocity of advantage concept and cited in the Brandeis *Coal* dissent, Brandeis said to Frankfurter: "Take that case. He actually voted & wrote the other way in that case. The great difficulty is his desire for speed. That always was a point of pride with him. Now it's a vice. He & McKenna run a race for diligence of finishing an opinion assigned to either. Holmes can't bear not to have case done the same day its given to him."

* * *

CONCLUSION

The archival analysis of *Coal* adds one small piece to a mosaic of the decision styles of two leading Supreme Court justices. It also adds to an understanding of the taking issue but not, I fear, in a manner which makes the constitutional doctrine less confused or muddled.

As is the case with many kinds of data, the interpretation of primary historical information of *Coal* is heavily influenced by the theoretical goggles through which it is viewed. Legal realists, doctrinal purists, and critical thinkers will see very different implications in the chronicling presented in this article.

Some of what we know from the archives is easy to summarize:

1. In weighing the legality of government action, although Brandeis balanced the public interest more heavily than did Holmes, for long periods in their judicial careers the two justices had similar views on property regulation: they generally supported governmental activities involving property control, especially when justified on a theory of nuisance avoidance. Indeed, for Holmes *Coal* was somewhat of an anomaly (at least in outcome), except to the extent that it culminated the concern for evaluating regulation in context and solidified his views both that degree of control and economic harm was a central concern and that regulation must have its limits.
2. Justice Holmes' position on the legal significance of *Coal* changed, fairly dramatically, in the process of his interactions with other

[124] 260 U.S. 22 (1922). * * *

justices, notably Taft, during the writing of the Opinion. * * *

3. Justice Holmes thought that his Opinion was generally misunderstood by contemporary commentators.

4. During the hearings on *Coal* and the writing of the Opinion, Justice Holmes was experiencing a recovery from a painful illness and operation.

5. Justice Brandeis worked several drafts of *Coal*, called up many cases, did considerable research, as he cut and pasted numerous approximations to what would be his final Dissent.

* * *

The implications of this summary * * * are * * * not simply drawn. The reported facts do, nonetheless, invite speculation. It seems clear that, regardless of legal interpretative theory applied, the historical and continuing importance placed on the conceptual framework Holmes employed in *Coal* needs to be viewed in light of knowledge about how the words and phrases in the Opinion were chosen. It certainly does not appear that some of the language which commentators and advocates have found powerful was written, by Holmes, with the self-consciousness and direction that its use suggests. * * * The Holmes story suggests that his choice of [the] words [average reciprocity of advantage] was not as precise as the tone of his Opinion would imply. In fact, it is the most general statement, that on regulation going "too far," which fits most comfortably into the most well-developed Holmes position on limitations of the police power. Furthermore, his earlier and his subsequent judicial opinions on property regulation reinforce the idea that, in outcome, *Coal* stands somewhat by itself, that it was not a new and central statement the justice wished to make on property regulation.

* * *

A second conclusion is tempting to draw although the record is insufficient to allow doing so with confidence: the combination of aging and illness may have been influential as Holmes wrote his Opinion. These factors, as his friend Brandeis contemporaneously noted, may have affected—not deep-seated philosophical views—but his ability to apply evolving principles, to have a "sure aim," to attend to the complexities of a case which he did not consider of major import, to reply to the long Taft intervention.

* * *

NOTE

Should DiMento's story about the formulation of the opinions in *Pennsylvania Coal v. Mahon* have any impact on the way present Supreme Court Justices use the case as precedent in their own opinions? What of Justice Rehnquist's dissent in *Penn Central Transportation Co. v. New York City,* 438 U.S. 104 (1978), where he writes:

> Only in the most superficial sense of the word can this case be said to involve "zoning." Typical zoning restrictions may, it is true, so limit the prospective uses of a piece of property as to diminish the value of that property in the abstract because it may not be used for the forbidden purpose. But any such abstract decrease in value will more than likely be at least partially offset by an increase in value which flows from similar restrictions as to use on neighboring properties. All property owners in a designated area are placed under the same restrictions, not only for the benefit of the municipality as a whole but also for the common benefit of one another. In the words of Mr. Justice Holmes, speaking for the court in *Pennsylvania Coal v. Mahon*, there is "an average reciprocity of advantage."

2. Eminent Domain and the Takings Dilemma in the Modern Era

The literature on modern takings jurisprudence is hopelessly vast. It is simply impossible to provide a representative sampling of the material. I have selected four articles. In the first, Thomas Merrill's *The Economics of Public Use*, the author discusses the requirement that condemnations must be for a "public purpose" and attempts to impose a rational structure on the meaning of that requirement by using economic analysis. Merrill is followed by Michelman's classic piece, *Property, Utility, and Fairness: Comments on the Ethical Foundations of "Just Compensation" Law*, which provided the jurisprudential and linguistic* backbone for Justice Brennan's majority opinion in *Penn Central Transportation Company v. City of New York,* 438 U.S. 104 (1978), approving the application of New York City's historical preservation rules to Grand Central Terminal. The third article, Jerold Kayden's *Zoning for Dollars: New Rules for an Old Game?*, discusses the conservative trends evident in recent Supreme Court cases, especially *Nollan v. California Coastal Commission.*This section concludes with Jeremy Paul's *The Hidden Structure of Takings Law*, which serves two functions. First, it summarizes or cites a number of the seminal articles written in this area, easing the burden of selecting materials for this segment of the anthology. And second, Paul argues, in a very qualified fashion, for a return to theories of property definition closely related to the "republicanism" this volume opened with. It therefore provides a nice sense of closure to this part of the anthology on the present status of property law.

For material on the history of transferable development rights and the *Penn Central* litigation, *see* Norman Marcus, *Air Rights in New York City: TDR, Zoning Lot Merger and the Well-Considered Plan*, 50 BROOKLYN L. REV. 867(1984); John Costonis, *The Chicago Plan: Incentive Zoning and the Preservation of Urban Landmarks*, 85 HARV. L. REV. 574 (1972). For additional material on *Nollan v. California Coastal Commission* and the recent conservative trend of the Supreme Court, *see* Margaret Jane Radin, *The Liberal Conception of Property: Cross Currents in the Jurisprudence of Takings,* 88 COLUM. L. REV. 1667 (1988); Frank Michelman, *Takings*, 1987, 88 COLUM. L. REV. 1600 (1988).

*Michelman invented the idea of a "distinctly perceived, sharply crystallized, investment-backed expectation" used by Brennan to define the core idea of property invasion prevented by the Constitution.

a. The Public Purpose Requirement

Thomas W. Merrill, *The Economics of Public Use*, 72 CORNELL L. REV. 61–68, 70–89, 93–98, 101–102, 108–114 (1986)*

The fifth amendment to the United States Constitution, as well as most state constitutions, provides that private property shall not be taken "for public use" unless just compensation is paid. American courts have long construed this to mean that some showing of "publicness" is a condition precedent to a legitimate exercise of the power of eminent domain. Thus, when a proposed condemnation of property lacks the appropriate public quality, the taking is deemed to be unconstitutional and can be enjoined. In practice, however, most observers today think the public use limitation is a dead letter. Three recent decisions, upholding takings that courts would very likely have found impermissible in the past, support this view.

In the first case, *Poletown Neighborhood Council v. City of Detroit,*[3] the Michigan Supreme Court approved the city of Detroit's plan to condemn a 465-acre tract of land and reconvey it on favorable terms to the General Motors Corporation (GM) for

[3] 410 Mich. 616, 34 N.W.2d 455 (1981).

construction of an automobile assembly plant. GM had previously announced its intention to relocate certain Detroit-based manufacturing operations if the city did not provide a new plant site. The purported public benefits of the condemnation (the "public use") included retaining over 6,000 jobs, preserving tax revenues, and avoiding the social deterioration caused by a declining industrial and population base. The Poletown Neighborhood Council, representing approximately 3,400 area residents whose homes, shops, and churches were to be bulldozed to make way for the plant, opposed the project, claiming it did not satisfy the public use requirement. Over two vigorous dissents, the Michigan Supreme Court held the proposed taking a legitimate public use.

The second case, *City of Oakland v. Oakland Raiders*,[7] sustained an even more unconventional exercise of eminent domain. The Oakland Raiders professional football team, after failing to renew its stadium lease with the city of Oakland, announced that it intended to move to Los Angeles. The city responded by seeking to condemn the intangible contractual rights associated with the Raiders' franchise, including player contracts. The city apparently contemplated operating the team for a brief period while seeking a private owner willing to keep the team in Oakland. Although not deciding conclusively that the proposed taking served a public use, the California Supreme Court held that neither the plan's exotic object—the intangible contractual rights of a professional sports team—nor the possibility of a resale to a private party precluded an exercise of eminent domain.[8]

Finally, *Hawaii Housing Authority v. Midkiff*[9] is probably the most important of the three cases, because it is the United States Supreme Court's first pronouncement on the meaning of "public use" since *Berman v. Parker*[10] was decided in 1954. At issue in *Midkiff* was the constitutionality of the Hawaii Land Reform Act of 1967, which allows persons renting homes in development tracts of five or more acres to condemn their landlord's interest and thereby acquire an estate in fee simple. A unanimous Court, citing figures suggesting that land ownership in Hawaii is highly concentrated, sustained the Act as a constitutional means of "[r]egulating oligopoly and the evils associated with it," in particular the inability of renters to purchase homes at a "fair" price. Although declaring that courts play a role in enforcing the public use clause, and that a "purely private taking" would be unconstitutional, the Court nonetheless characterized the historical judicial posture as one of extreme deference: "where the exercise of the eminent domain power is rationally related to a conceivable public purpose, the Court has never held a compensated taking to be proscribed by the Public Use Clause."

These three decisions suggest several common themes. First, and most clearly, they suggest that modern courts will tolerate very wide-ranging uses of eminent domain. Legislatures may use eminent domain to promote the construction of a privately owned factory (*Poletown*), to force a favored tenant to remain in a government-owned facility (*Oakland Raiders*), or to engage in "land reform" (*Midkiff*). Second, the cases suggest that modern courts are exceedingly deferential to legislative definitions of a permissible public use. Indeed, *Midkiff* hints that the public use analysis parallels the "minimum rationality" standard applied to equal protection and substantive due process challenges to economic legislation. Third, and perhaps most important, the cases suggest that courts have no theory or conceptual foundation from which meaningful standards for judicial review of public use issues might originate. Instead, the cases are filled with cliches regarding the "breadth" and "elasticity" of the "evolving" concept of public use, language indicating a dearth of theory—or perhaps a lack of any desire to develop one.

From an economic perspective, the extreme deference to legislative eminent domain decisions reflected in these cases is puzzling. After all, eminent domain entails coerced appropriation of private property by the state, and there is an important difference between coerced and consensual exchange. Consensual exchange is almost always beneficial to both parties in a transaction, while coerced exchange may or may not be, depending on whether the compensation is sufficient to make the coerced party indifferent to the loss. The distinction is equivalent to that drawn by Guido Calabresi and Douglas Melamed[19] between property rules, which allow an owner to protect a right or entitlement from an unconsented

[7] 32 Ca.3d 60, 646 P.2d 835, 183 Cal. Rptr. 673 (1982).

[8] * * * After more proceedings, the court of appeals ultimately held the proposed taking violated the commerce clause. City of Oakland v. Oakland Raiders, 174 Cal. App. 3d 414, 220 Cal. Rptr. 153 (1985). * * *

[9] 467 U.S. 229 (1984).

[10] 348 U.S. 26 (1954).

[19] *See generally,* Calabresi & Melamed, *Property Rules, Liability Rules, and Inalienability: One View of the Cathedral*, 85 HARV. L. REV. 1089 (1972).

taking by securing injunctive relief, and liability rules, which afford protection only through an ex post award of damages. It seems peculiar that in the eminent domain area, which so often parallels private law doctrine, courts have effectively declared that liability rules alone shall protect all private property rights.

In Part I of this article, I propose an explanation for the extreme judicial deference we see in public use cases. The underlying source of this deference, I suggest, is a historical focus on ends rather than means. Public use analysis has traditionally examined the ends of a government taking—the purpose or use to which property will be put once acquired. With the transition from the minimalist state to the activist state, however, courts have become increasingly uncomfortable in defining the correct or "natural" ends of government. Not surprisingly, therefore, courts have adopted a hands-off posture regarding questions of public use. In contrast, the property rule/liability rule distinction familiar to economists regards eminent domain as a means of achieving governmental ends. From this perspective, eminent domain offers just one of several possible means of acquiring resources, ranging from voluntary exchange at negotiated prices at one extreme to confiscation without compensation at the other. In this view, even if courts refuse to challenge legislative decisions about the ends to which property is put, they still might, and perhaps should, play some role in choosing the appropriate means to reach those ends.

After restating the relevant choice in public use cases as one between means, I attempt in Part II to construct a theory that would guide judicial review of a legislature's choice of eminent domain as a means. Drawing on economic analysis, I argue that eminent domain's purpose is to overcome barriers to voluntary exchange created when a seller of resources is in position to extract economic rents from a buyer. This "thin market" setting, as I will call it, can lead to monopoly pricing by the seller, to unacceptably high transaction costs, or to both. This conception of eminent domain's purpose is not new,[22] but I attempt to explore the basic idea, and certain important qualifications to it, more thoroughly than have others. This exploration produces two models of eminent domain: what I call the "basic model" and the "refined model." Each model carries different implications for judicial review of the exercise of eminent domain. The basic model sanctions virtually unlimited judicial deference to the legislature whereas the refined model supports heightened judicial scrutiny in certain limited circumstances.

Judicial theory is one thing; judicial decisions are another. Notwithstanding the tradition of judicial deference associated with the public use limitation, I seek in Part III to determine whether judicial decisions actually reflect a sensitivity to the choice-of-means issue. To this end, I survey all indexed federal and state appellate opinions since 1954 involving a contested public use issue. The results show that state courts are much less deferential to legislative declarations of public use than one would expect in light of *Poletown*, *Oakland Raiders*, and *Midkiff*. In fact, state court enforcement of the public use limitation has generally increased since 1954. Moreover, the survey strongly confirms the basic model of eminent domain, and partially corroborates the refined model.

Finally, in the concluding section, I return to *Poletown*, *Oakland Raiders*, and *Midkiff*, and consider how courts might resolve those cases under the economic models developed in Part II.

I

The Means-Ends Problem

Drawing on Calabresi and Melamed's model, one may isolate four possible rights that a citizen might have when faced with an attempted government taking. At one extreme, the citizen would have no entitlement; the government could take his property without his consent and without compensation. This is a citizen's plight when the government legitimately exercises its power to tax or its police power. A second possibility is that a liability rule would protect a citizen's property; the government could take the property without his consent, but would have to pay compensation. This describes a taking by eminent domain. A third possibility is that a property rule would protect a citizen's property; the government could take the property only with the citizen's consent, i.e., if he agreed to sell it to the government. This is the rule generally followed when government acquires chattels or employment services. Finally, a fourth possibility is that the government could not acquire a citizen's property by any means. This situation occurs if the proposed acquisition serves a

---

22 *See* R. Posner, Economic Analysis of Law §§3.6-.7 (3d ed. 1986) * * *; Michelman, *Property, Utility and Fairness: Comments on the Ethical Foundations of "Just Compensation" Law*, 80 Harv. L. Rev. 1165, 1175-76 (1967) * * *.

purpose or end not permitted by the Constitution, for example, the purchase of votes or the services of a slave.

A clear distinction exists between the first three of these rules—no entitlement, liability rule, and property rule—and the fourth, which completely bars government acquisitions of property. The first three rules define different means of achieving permissible government ends. The fourth, however, effectively demarcates a sphere of impermissible government ends. In fact, the means-ends distinction inherent in the Calabresi-Melamed framework suggests that judges may ask two questions of any proposed government acquisition. First, the ends question: is the government acquiring the resources for a constitutionally permissible purpose? Second, the means question: if the purpose is permissible, should the government proceed by police power regulation, eminent domain, or voluntary exchange in the marketplace?

The two questions present sharply different inquiries. The ends question asks what the government plans to do once the property is obtained. This inquiry, in turn, requires a clear conception of the legitimate functions or purposes of the state. May the state promote employment by subsidizing the construction of a privately owned factory? May it own a professional football team or undertake land reform? The answers to such questions demand an exercise in high political theory that most courts today are unwilling (or unable) to undertake. The means question, by contrast, is narrower. It asks where and how the government should get property, not what it may do with it. For example, the means approach accepts that a state may own a professional football team. It then asks: how should the state acquire the team? Must it purchase the team through voluntary negotiations? Or may the state coerce a transfer by condemning the team? Or may it simply commandeer the team under its police power? The means approach, of course, is also "political" in that it concerns state actions that will advance or retard conflicting interests. Nevertheless, the means approach demands a more narrowly focused and judicially manageable inquiry than the ends approach.

In deciding public use cases, courts nearly always pose the issue in terms of ends rather than in terms of means. Perhaps the constitutional language is responsible for this focus. The fifth amendment provides, "nor shall private property be taken for public use, without just compensation." This phrasing suggests that the government may exercise the power of eminent domain, but only if it puts the property acquired to a public use, that is, an end that is sufficiently "public" in nature.

The focus on ends also figures into the two judicial tests most often relied upon to define "public use." Under the narrower test, public use means literal use by the public. Under this test, a taking must yield a facility physically accessible to some segment of the public. By contrast, the broader test requires only that the taking produce a public benefit or advantage. This test roughly equates public use with "public interest." Although courts have almost unanimously resolved this interpretive dispute in favor of the broader public interest view, the main point for present purposes is that both tests look to the ends of the taking, not whether eminent domain is an appropriate means to achieve those ends.

The distinction between ends and means clarifies several developments associated with the jurisprudence of public use. First, it helps explain the emergence of language of extreme judicial deference in the last thirty years. Given that courts have understood the public use doctrine to refer to the ends of government, the question naturally arises: which institution is better suited to determine permissible ends—the courts or the legislature? In a society committed to majoritarian rule, not surprisingly the answer has been the legislature.

Here, as elsewhere, the crisis in democratic theory generated by judicial opposition to the New Deal provided the critical event. As late as 1930 the Supreme Court still clung to the position that legislative declarations of public use were subject to de novo judicial review. After a change in Court personnel produced a fundamental shift in judicial attitudes, however, the Court did an abrupt about-face and implied that the public use determination is exclusively for the legislature. This reversal ultimately produced Justice Douglas's formulation in *Berman v. Parker*: "Subject to specific constitutional limitations, when the legislature has spoken, the public interest has been declared in terms well-nigh conclusive." As long as courts regard the public use doctrine as a limitation upon permissible government ends, this extreme rhetoric of deference to legislative judgments will no doubt persist.

* * *

The most important insight to be gained from the distinction between ends and means * * * is that the public use limitation might be recast or reinterpreted to perform a different role. Rather than concerning itself with government ends, the public use limitation might serve to restrict a legislature's choice of means. I am not suggesting that it is somehow wrong, as a matter of first principles, to inquire about the ends to which government will put condemned property. Rather, the point is that the American judiciary is unlikely soon to assume the task of closely scrutinizing legislative judgments about the legitimate ends of government. Given also that the choice of means question is an analytically distinct and important inquiry, it is worth asking whether the public use limitation can be reformulated as a choice of means doctrine, and if so, whether the judiciary should have a role in reviewing the exercise of eminent domain from this perspective.

* * *

II

EMINENT DOMAIN AS A MEANS: AN ECONOMIC APPROACH

The literature addressing the public use issue from an economic perspective suggests three possible analytical models. I will briefly consider the first two, only to set them aside in favor of the third. Elements of the first two, however, ultimately reappear, "through the back door" as it were, under my "refined" version of the third approach.

The first economic model of public use, endorsed by Frank Michelman,[43] involves a straightforward comparison of costs and benefits. This model would have a court calculate all costs associated with an exercise of eminent domain, including the costs of compensation, and compare them with the taking's expected benefits. If the benefits exceed the costs, the court would deem the taking to serve public use; conversely, if the costs exceed the benefits, it would deem the taking to serve an unconstitutional private use.

The cost-benefit model of public use raises several problems. The first relates to measurement. How can courts accurately measure a taking's projected benefits, many of which will be intangible and speculative? A second problem involves the question of proper institutional roles. Presumably, the legislature has concluded that a taking's benefits exceed its costs. Are courts somehow better suited to make such a determination? Finally, the most telling problem, from this article's perspective, is that the cost-benefit calculus demands an inquiry into the ends of the taking rather than the choice of means. The cost-benefit approach explicitly adopts wealth maximization as the proper end, or at least one proper end, of government. Once again, I do not argue that the cost-benefit model is necessarily wrong. The problem is simply that the American judiciary, for reasons related to democratic theory, is not presently inclined to enforce directly any conception of limited government ends.

A second economic model of public use, recently advocated by Richard Epstein,[44] involves the public goods concept. Public goods, in their pure form, possess two properties: jointness in supply and impossibility of exclusion. In particular, because of the latter attribute, the market generates fewer public goods than generally thought desirable. Hence, theorists have long viewed public goods as an appropriate object of governmental action. Under the public goods model, a court would ask whether an exercise of eminent domain is designed to procure a public good. If so, the court would deem the taking to serve a public use; if not, the court would deem the exercise an unconstitutional taking for a private use.

As with the cost-benefit approach, the public goods model presents several difficulties. First, a definitional problem: there are very few "pure" public goods—goods of a kind that consumption by one does not diminish in some measure consumption by others. With most goods, consumption by one necessarily excludes, at least partially, consumption by someone else. Moreover, one can say that any activity that generates positive externalities—keeping one's lawn mowed, for example—shares the quality of public goods. Thus, the public goods analysis can be either very restrictive or very broad, depending on how the term is defined. Again, however, the main failing of the public goods model, at least for present purposes, is that it directs attention to ends rather than means. It asks whether government will use acquired property to provide a public good, not whether nonconsensual means are necessary to acquire the property.

The third economic model of public use derives from the property rule/liability rule distinction introduced by Calabresi and Melamed. From this perspective, eminent domain provides a mechanism that allows government to convert property rules into liability rules. This model presumes that property rules work well where low transaction costs make consensual exchange of resources practical. Liability rules, on the other hand, are necessary where high transaction costs render consensual exchange diffi-

[43] Michelman, *supra* note 22, at 1241.

[44] R. EPSTEIN, TAKINGS: PRIVATE PROPERTY AND THE POWER OF EMINENT DOMAIN 166–69 (1985).

cult. Applied to eminent domain, this analysis suggests that where a functioning market for a resource exists, the public use doctrine should require that government use that market. In contrast, where barriers to market exchange render such acquisition problematic, the doctrine should permit government to use its power of eminent domain. Importantly, the property rule/liability rule model of public use has the virtue of addressing eminent domain as a means. The distinction focuses on the conditions of the market in which property is acquired, not on its postacquisition use.

In the remainder of this section, I use the property rule/liability rule distinction to develop a basic model of the role of courts in determining eminent domain's proper scope. I then qualify the basic model in light of three persuasive economic objections. Taken together, these qualifications yield what I call the refined economic model of the judicial role in public use cases.

A. The Basic Model

The purpose of eminent domain is analogous to that of other liability rules, in that eminent domain applies where market exchange, if not impossible to achieve, is nevertheless subject to imperfections. To illustrate the point, consider the most common situation in which we see the exercise of eminent domain: a public or private project requiring the assembly of numerous parcels of land. Suppose, for example, that an oil refining company wants to construct an underground pipeline to transport crude oil from a producing field to a refinery several hundred miles away. Suppose further that only one feasible pipeline route exists. Without an exercise of eminent domain, the company must obtain an easement from each of hundreds of contiguous property owners. Each owner would have the power to hold out, should he choose to exercise it. If even a few owners held out, others might do the same. In this way, assembly of the needed parcels could become prohibitively expensive; in the end, the costs might well exceed the project's potential gains.

Some have described the above assembly problem in terms of monopoly-regulation.[50] In the pipeline example, each owner is a monopolist, effectively dominating a resource needed to complete the project. Each owner can thereby engage in monopoly pricing, that is, can set his price well above the opportunity cost of the needed resource. The result: fewer oil pipelines will be constructed, and those few that are built will cost a higher than optimal price.

Alternatively, others have described the assembly problem in terms of transaction cost economics.[51] Because each parcel owner has the power to hold out, each may be tempted to bargain strategically to appropriate some of the pipeline profit. On the other hand, the oil company—the sole buyer in the easement market—may also bargain strategically to appropriate most of the pipeline's gains to itself. The problem thus is really one of bilateral monopoly. Such strategic bargaining in a bilateral monopoly situation increases the project's transaction costs, and if the transaction costs approach or exceed the project's gains, the pipeline may never be built.

In the final analysis, whether one describes the assembly problem in terms of antitrust economics or transaction cost economics does not matter. In either case, the underlying predicament is the same: market conditions allow the seller to seek economic rents, that is, to charge a price higher than the property's opportunity cost. The oil pipeline hypothetical illustrates the potential for rent seeking. The opportunity cost of any one landowner's interest is near zero. But when this interest combines with other similar interests to form a right of way for a pipeline, its potential value becomes considerable. The difference between these two sums—the property's negligible opportunity cost and its value as part of the pipeline project—represents a potential economic rent to the seller.

Assembly projects, however, do not exhaust a seller's rent seeking opportunities. For example, rent seeking can occur when a buyer wants access to land that he already owns, but which is surrounded by the seller's land. It can also arise when a buyer needs to expand an existing site by acquiring adjacent land; when the buyer will lose undepreciated improvements if he does not acquire certain property from the seller; or when the seller owns property uniquely suited for some undertaking by the buyer, such as a promontory for a lighthouse or a narrows for a bridge. I will hereinafter refer to any situation where a seller can extract economic rents from a buyer as a "thin market." Conversely, I will call any situation where market conditions do not allow a seller to extract economic rents from a buyer a "thick market."

Whatever a thin market's source, its potential for engendering rent seeking may make it economically efficient to confer the power of eminent domain on a

[50] R. POSNER, *supra* note 22, § 3.6, at 49 * * *.
[51] *See* Michelman, *supra* note 22, at 1174.

buyer. On the one hand, we know that eminent domain would transfer the resource to a higher-valued use, because its value in the new use exceeds its value in every existing possible use (its opportunity cost); otherwise the seller could not extract an economic rent. On the other hand, if this transaction were left to the market, monopoly pricing (or strategic bargaining) could lead to a suboptimal quantity of the resource being acquired, or could even prevent the transaction from taking place at all.

Before completing discussion of the basic model, however, we must consider another important factor. So far we have focused exclusively on what might broadly be termed the transaction costs of market exchange. But we must also consider the administrative costs of eminent domain, and compare these costs with the costs of market exchange in either thick or thin market settings.

There is reason to believe, at least in thick market settings, that eminent domain is more expensive than market exchange. First, and most important, legislatures must authorize the exercise of eminent domain. It is thus necessary to persuade a legislature to grant the power of eminent domain, or, if a general grant of the power already exists, to persuade officials to exercise it. Second, the due process clauses of the fifth and fourteenth amendments, as well as local statutes and rules, impose various procedural requirements upon the exercise of eminent domain. At a minimum, these include drafting and filing a formal judicial complaint and service of process on the owner. Third, nearly all jurisdictions require at least one professional appraisal of the condemned property, something generally not done (or not done as formally) in a private sale. Finally, both court-made and statutory law guarantee a person whose property is subject to condemnation some sort of hearing on the condemnation's legality and the amount of compensation due. Of course, the parties to condemnation proceedings, like the parties to most civil litigation, typically settle before a trial. But the possibility of trial clearly increases the expected administrative costs of condemnation.

Given what might collectively be called the "due process" costs of eminent domain—obtaining legislative authority, drafting and filing the complaint, serving process, securing a formal appraisal, the possibility of a trial and appeal, and so forth—it is safe to conclude that, in a thick market setting, eminent domain is a more expensive way of acquiring resources than market exchange. This conclusion has important implications for the basic model. In effect, it means that the decision whether to use eminent domain should be, from an economic perspective, self-regulating. In thick markets, where the model initially suggests that eminent domain is inappropriate, the acquiring party should in fact utilize market exchange because eminent domain would consume more resources. Conversely, in thin market settings, where the model suggests that it is appropriate to use eminent domain, the acquiring party should in fact use eminent domain, so long as the administrative costs are less than the costs of market exchange.

* * *

The assumptions of the foregoing analysis are concededly open to question. In particular, we cannot assume that the condemnor will always act to minimize its costs—especially if the condemnor is the government. However, several considerations render cost-minimizing behavior by the condemnor as realistic as any other assumption, at least in the long run.

* * *

First, in many cases the condemnor is not the government, but rather some entity such as a public utility exercising a delegated power of eminent domain. Such a privately owned entity may be constrained by capital markets to seek to minimize its costs. Moreover, even if the government is the condemnor, the taking's beneficiary will often be a private entity, which would not undertake the expense of persuading the government to exercise the power of eminent domain unless these lobbying costs were lower than the costs of a market transaction.

Second, casual observation suggests that when governments acquire interests in land they prefer, if possible, to do so by market transactions. Government officials frequently complain about the costs and delays of eminent domain. Moreover, in many contested public use cases we read that the majority of parcels in a tract have been acquired by voluntary exchange or settlement, with only one or two holdout landowners forcing the government to resort to eminent domain. One might explain this preference for voluntary negotiation on the ground that private property owners simply give up in the face of a government threat to use eminent domain. But it also suggests that the government views eminent domain as a cumbersome and expensive process to be avoided if at all possible.

Finally, if we look at the broad range of government resource acquisitions, rather than solely at land acquisitions, we see that in markets that are clearly thick—office supplies, for example—the government almost invariably proceeds by market exchange. The principal exception occurs during wartime, when the need to accumulate vast amounts of material on short notice leaves the government vulnerable to rent seeking. But this exception only proves the rule. In the vast majority of cases, government does not use eminent domain in thick markets because market exchange is less expensive than condemnation.

If, as the basic model suggests, the decision to use the power of eminent domain is essentially self-regulating, this holds important implications for judicial review of public use issues. Most obviously, there would seem to be little point in courts second-guessing legislative and executive determinations of public use. Judicial review would add only uncertainty and expense * * *. It is simply not clear, a priori, that this tighter rationing of eminent domain is desirable.

In sum, the basic model suggests that courts, in setting the limits of eminent domain, should ensure that just compensation is paid and enforce the due process "tax"—the legislative and constitutional requirements that push the administrative costs of eminent domain above the costs of market exchange in thick market settings. Otherwise, the basic model suggests that courts need do nothing to limit the use of eminent domain. Thus, the basic economic model reinforces the principle, enunciated in *Berman* and *Midkiff,* that courts should give virtually complete deference to legislative determinations of public use.

B. The Refined Model

Despite the basic model's appealing simplicity, with its thick market/thin market distinction and its modest conception of the judicial role, the model raises a number of troubling economic and noneconomic questions. To avoid unduly complicating the argument, I will discuss only the economic objections.

The broadest and best-known economic objection to eminent domain is that it is unnecessary.[72] The critics who raise this objection first note that acquiring parties generally use eminent domain to assemble large tracts of land. They then point out that real estate developers and others are frequently able to assemble such parcels by using buying agents, option agreements, straw transactions, and the like. If private developers and the like can get by without eminent domain, the critics ask, then why cannot the government?

This broadscale objection meets with two answers. First, simply because the market can overcome the assembly problem (and presumably other thin market problems) some of the time, this does not mean that market mechanisms, by themselves, always produce optimal land assembly. The market may work well enough for shopping centers and commercial office buildings, but these projects entail relatively small amounts of land, are not strictly site-dependent, and often generate very high gains from trade. It does not necessarily follow that market mechanisms would work for such things as interstate highways, wilderness areas, or urban renewal projects. As the number of parcels and/or the site-dependence increases, the opportunities for rent seeking multiply. Moreover, if a project's expected gains are modest, it may not generate enough additional wealth to buy off the rent seekers. Therefore, limiting government to consensual exchange in all cases would almost certainly reduce the total supply of public goods in a way that, on balance, harms society.

Second, although buying agents, option agreements, and straw transactions may work well for private developers, it is unclear whether government can use these devices effectively. The necessary ingredient of these techniques is secrecy, and governments, at least in an open society like the United States, are not very good at keeping secrets. Moreover, even if governments could keep secrets, the combination of secret land acquisitions and the need to buy off holdouts raises a serious danger of corruption. One can easily imagine government officials charged with engaging in secret land assembly tipping off potential sellers about a project, or buying off sellers at exorbitant prices in return for kickbacks. It is one thing for a private developer to decide when to buy off a holdout and at what price. It is quite another when a government purchasing agent, spending taxpayers' money, makes these decisions without public oversight. To avoid this specter of corruption, government may have to use eminent domain under circumstances where a private developer, with his own money and guile, could use the market.

The broadscale denial of the need for eminent domain therefore fails. Nevertheless, I believe that there are three narrower economic objections that have greater merit. Each objection requires a partial modification of the basic model, and a corresponding refinement of the model's conception of the judicial role.

---

[72] *See* R. Posner, Economic Analysis of Law § 3.5, at 43–44 (2d ed. 1977) * * *.

1. Uncompensated Subjective Losses

The basic model posits that eminent domain is designed to increase social wealth by facilitating certain transactions that otherwise would not take place, or that would take place only at an inefficiently high cost. Eminent domain, to use a familiar metaphor, is an instrument for increasing the size of the pie. But eminent domain also contains an implicit decisional rule for allocating the gains and losses associated with these forced transactions. This rule, manifested in eminent domain's compensation requirement, dictates that a condemnee is entitled to the fair market value of his property in its highest and best use other than the use proposed by the condemnor. In other words, the condemnee is entitled to an award equal to the opportunity cost of his contribution to the condemnor's project, no more and no less.

This opportunity cost compensation formula, however, fails to compensate the condemnee for all of his losses. The formula awards the condemnee what he would obtain in an arm's length transaction with a third party, but does not compensate him for the subjective "premium" he might attach to his property above its opportunity cost. In some cases, such as those involving undeveloped land, there may be no subjective premium. But in other cases, the premium may be quite large and may reflect several potential concerns: a condemnee may have a sentimental attachment to the property, or may have made improvements or modifications to accommodate his unique needs, or may simply wish to avoid the costs and inconvenience of relocation. In addition, other personal losses which do not "run" with the property, such as lost goodwill, consequential damages to other property, relocation costs, and attorney fees, are also not compensable.

This failure to compensate for subjective losses indicates that the basic model, which emphasizes the self-regulating character of eminent domain, may break down. If the subjective loss is large enough, the condemnee's loss may exceed the additional wealth generated when eminent domain is used to overcome barriers to exchange in thin markets.

* * *

The foregoing concerns counsel a qualification of the basic model's core conception of the judicial role. Specifically, they suggest that courts should closely scrutinize the decision to condemn whenever an owner's subjective losses are high. For example, courts might apply a cost-benefit analysis in these circumstances, upholding an exercise of eminent domain only if the taking's "surplus value," or the total value of the condemned resources to the condemnor net of compensation, exceeds the condemnee's uncompensated subjective loss. This approach, however, runs into all the difficulties of measurement and comparative institutional advantage associated with judicial cost-benefit analyses generally. More realistically, courts could simply scrutinize cases where subjective losses appear to be high to insure that these losses are not "excessive" relative to the project's probable surplus. In effect, courts would provide a condemnee faced with large subjective losses an additional "trump card," in the form of a higher probability that the project would be enjoined as failing the public use requirement. This additional leverage should induce the government to increase its settlement offer, thus offsetting, at least in part, the subjective losses.

2. Secondary Rent Seeking

A second objection to the opportunity cost compensation formula is that it encourages rent seeking by condemnors. Eminent domain almost always generates a surplus—a resource's value after condemnation is almost always higher than before. The present compensation formula allocates 100% of this surplus to the condemnor, and none to the condemnee. Commentators have questioned such a division on fairness grounds.[84]

There are several conceivable justifications for awarding the entire surplus to the condemnor, rather than requiring restitution of all or part of the surplus to the condemnee. By giving the surplus to the condemnor, we provide an incentive to use eminent domain. In the case where the government directly undertakes public works projects that enjoy broad political support this additional incentive may be unnecessary, although a rule of restitution would put a higher price tag on government projects, and would probably reduce their number. In the case of profit-oriented entities, however, restitution could eliminate the use of eminent domain altogether. Profit-seeking condemnors would no longer be able to capture the added value from improvements brought about through condemnation. In effect, the surplus from eminent domain functions here much as profit does in the market. If we assume that in the long run citizens will be on both sides of eminent domain proceedings—either as condemnees or as taxpayers

---

[84] *See* R. Epstein, *supra* note 44, at 163 * * *.

and ratepayers—then a rule that encourages value-maximizing exchanges through eminent domain may leave them better off than would a rule that provides for restitution or apportionment of the surplus.

In addition, a rule of restitution would require some method of measuring the surplus generated by an exercise of eminent domain. Gains from trade or surplus, like subjective values, are notoriously difficult to measure. Thus, under a rule of restitution, either the administrative costs of eminent domain would rise, or some arbitrary measurement rule would emerge that would almost certainly produce distorted incentives.

Finally, awarding all of the surplus to the condemnor is perhaps not as unfair as first appears. The surplus generated by a condemnation may be caused in a but-for sense by both the condemnor and the condemnee. But in most cases the condemnee is merely a passive participant, an involuntary supplier of capital. The active agent, the supplier of the idea and initiative, is the condemnor. The labor theory of property may be out of fashion, but as between a condemnor and a condemnee, the condemnor is typically more responsible for, and hence arguably deserving of, the surplus generated by the project.

Despite these justifications, there is legitimate reason for concern about allocating the condemnation's entire surplus to the condemnor. The present rule may produce a kind of secondary rent seeking of its own, as competing interest groups attempt to acquire or defeat a legislative grant of the power of eminent domain. In this way, eminent domain, an instrument designed to overcome rent-seeking behavior associated with thin markets, may inadvertently produce the very type of socially inefficient resource allocation it was designed to avoid. Indeed, in the extreme, the expenditures undertaken to obtain or defeat a grant of eminent domain could completely offset the expected surplus that would be generated by the use of eminent domain.

* * *

The danger of secondary rent seeking suggests that it may be appropriate to add a second qualification to the basic model. In cases where eminent domain is most likely to foster secondary rent-seeking behavior—where one or a small number of persons will capture a taking's surplus—courts should closely scrutinize a decision to confer the power of eminent domain. Cases involving delegation of eminent domain to one or a few private parties, or involving condemnation followed by retransfer of the property to one or a few private parties, present the primary situations where such secondary rent seeking is likely to occur.

3. Market Bypass

In addition to the foregoing limitations derived from eminent domain's compensation formula, there is a third objection that would apply even if questions of compensation never produced distorted incentives. Suppose a buyer facing a relatively thick market for a resource declines to engage in market exchange, but later changes his position such that, ex post, he faces a thin market. Should eminent domain be available to buyers who have either deliberately or negligently bypassed a thick market exchange?

* * *

Clearly, a buyer who takes all reasonable and prudent steps while engaging in thick market exchange, only to later face the need for further exchange in a thin market, should be allowed to use eminent domain. On the other hand, a buyer who intentionally bypasses a thick market by taking action * * * that leaves him in a thin market should not be allowed to use eminent domain. Disallowing eminent domain under such circumstances is necessary to prevent the transformation of all property rules into liability rules.

* * *

III

Case Survey

Although courts almost invariably discuss the public use issue in terms of government ends, *Poletown*, *Oakland Raiders*, and *Midkiff* suggest that courts have no theory as to what those ends might be. Indeed, courts seem to have abandoned the idea that they should articulate and enforce a conception of permissible government ends. Nevertheless, one still finds state courts declaring that a proposed taking does not serve a public use. This state of affairs—no agreement on general principles, frequent statements of broad deference, and intermittent holdings of no public use—has led several courts and commentators to a kind of legal realist despair.

* * *

Nonetheless, the judiciary's failure to articulate either a coherent theory of public use or a theory of the judicial role in enforcing the public use limitation does not imply that public use cases are wrongly decided from an economic perspective. The very absence of coherent legal doctrine effectively allows courts to justify any result that strikes them as intuitively correct. With this thought in mind, I undertook a fairly large survey of appellate opinions concerning contested public use issues to determine whether the outcomes of these cases are consistent with the economic models developed in Part II. My operating hypothesis was that courts operating in a common law fashion, although interpreting an open-ended constitutional provision rather than fashioning rules of common law per se, would tend to embrace efficient results.

A. Description of the Survey

To test both the basic and refined versions of the economic model, I surveyed all reported appellate cases decided between *Berman v. Parker* and January 1, 1986, that involved a contested public use question.

* * *

Before discussing specifics, a few general observations about the survey are in order. First, virtually all the cases involved acquisitions of interests in land—either fees simple or easements. * * * That eminent domain is almost exclusively confined to real property markets is not surprising, because thick markets usually exist for other forms of property such as natural resources, consumer goods, securities, and the like. * * *

Second, of the 308 opinions in the sample, 261, or 84.7%, held that the proposed taking served a public use; conversely, 47, or 15.3%, held that it did not. Given *Berman*'s and *Midkiff*'s assertion that a legislative public use determination is virtually dispositive of the issue, the relatively high number of cases finding no public use is somewhat surprising. The apparent anomaly disappears, however, once we separate federal decisions from state decisions. Although the survey contained only 17 federal cases, each upheld a legislative public use determination, suggesting that lower federal courts have been faithful to *Berman*'s deferential standard of review. State courts, on the other hand, seem more willing to depart from *Berman*'s virtual abandonment of judicial review. Looking at the state appellate decisions alone, we find that 16.2%, roughly one in six, held that a proposed taking did not serve a public use.

Third, the survey failed to reveal any clear regional patterns. The 47 cases holding that a taking did not serve a public use are spread fairly evenly from across the country. * * *

Finally, the survey did disclose a clear—and surprising—temporal pattern. When we divide the survey cases into five-year periods, we find that the total number of public use cases is fairly constant, ranging from 42 to 61 cases in each period from 1954–1985. But the percentage of cases holding that a taking does not serve a public use generally increases throughout the 31-year period. The percentages are as follows: 1954–1960, 11.8%; 1961 1965, 12.5%; 1966–1970, 13.1%; 1971–1975, 13.7%; 1976–1980, 21.4%; and 1981–1985, 20.4%. These figures suggest that, most commentary notwithstanding, judicial enforcement of the public use requirement is not a thing of the past. On the contrary, it is generally on the rise.

B. Testing the Basic Model

The survey revealed that contested public use cases tend to fall into certain recurrent categories. Significantly, each category reflects what I have termed a thin market situation: the condemnor would be susceptible to a seller's rent seeking behavior if an open market transaction were attempted. After the cases revealed these recurrent categories, I reexamined the cases labeling each as either "clearly" falling into one of the categories or "arguably" falling into one of the categories. Table 1 summarizes the results.

* * *

TABLE 1

CATEGORIZATION OF CONTESTED PUBLIC USE CASES

	Clearly	Arguably	Total	% Total Holding Public Use
Assembly	143	42	185	90.3
Expanding Existing Facilities	25	16	41	85.3
Landlocked Property	16	25	41	75.6
Unique Property	9	5	14	100.0
Specific Capital Already Invested	7	7	14	85.7
Thick Market	7	6	13	15.3
Total	207	101	308	84.7

* * *

* * *, [W]e find that of the clearly classifiable cases, 200, or 96.6%, involved some sort of thin market; of the total sample of cases, 295, or 95.8%, arguably involved a thin market. These figures forcefully confirm the basic economic model. Regardless of courts' conclusions about whether a taking is for a public use, condemnors rarely use the power of eminent domain unless it is necessary to overcome barriers to voluntary market exchange—monopoly pricing or strategic bargaining. Thus, if we adhere to the basic model and ignore the refined model's three qualifications, eminent domain is in effect self-regulating.

The distinction between thin and thick markets is also useful in predicting appellate definitions of public use. In the five thin market categories, courts held that a taking serves a public use at a fairly consistent rate, ranging from 75.6% (landlocked property) to 100% (unique property), with the largest single category (assembly) coming in at 90.3%. In the few thick market cases (13 in total), courts found a public use only 15.3% of the time. These numbers suggest that the basic model at least partially explains the pattern of decisions reached by courts in deciding what constitutes a public use.

* * *

Can the refined model do even better? * * *

Unfortunately, the data in the appellate opinions did not allow me to make these estimations in a very precise manner. * * * Consequently, I did not obtain a satisfactory case sample presenting the first and third factors.

* * *

Conclusion

Explaining public use in terms of choice of means seems moderately successful, at least as a positive model for predicting the outcome of contested public use cases. In concluding, I consider how courts might apply this perspective as a normative standard. To do so, I return to the three cases that introduced this study: *Poletown*, *Oakland Raiders*, and *Midkiff*.

The basic model posits that eminent domain seeks to overcome thin market barriers to negotiated exchange. The basic model also posits that beyond assuring proper procedures and just compensation, courts need not intervene to limit the exercise of eminent domain, because the higher administrative costs associated with eminent domain render it essentially self-regulating. Nevertheless, it is instructive to ask how the three cases might have come out if the deciding courts had explicitly employed the thin market/thick market distinction in determining the limits of eminent domain.

Poletown presents a straightforward assembly problem. Hence, it easily conforms to the basic model. Because of holdouts, General Motors would have encountered tremendous difficulties had it tried to acquire a 465-acre tract in the middle of a major urban area by voluntary negotiation. Without eminent domain, GM would almost certainly have built the plant elsewhere, or at least not built it on the same scale.

Oakland Raiders presents a unique property case, and is thus also consistent with the basic model. The number of National Football League franchises is artificially restricted: the league, which controls the formation of new franchises, has created only 28 to date, and seems reluctant to add new ones. Realistically, Oakland had only one source for an NFL lessee for its stadium—the Raiders—making the case a classic example of bilateral monopoly. Moreover, the Raiders had been based in Oakland for approximately 20 years, and the residents of the area had developed a strong identification with the team—thus entailing a kind of reverse subjective loss when the Raiders sought to leave.

Midkiff appears at first blush to be another unique property case; after all, the Supreme Court's opinion emphasized that Hawaii's supply of residential property had been "artificially" restricted, and suggested that the price of single family homes had soared beyond the reach of most would-be purchasers. However, the Court's figures suggest that the residential home market in Hawaii is neither a monopoly nor a cartel, and is thus not subject to noncompetitive pricing. In all probability, the litigants and the Court mistakenly equated a "housing shortage" caused by high demand with oligopolistic pricing by sellers. Moreover, regardless of whether high demand or oligopoly caused Hawaii's high housing prices, the eminent domain solution would not provide the renters with any significant measure of relief. The opportunity cost compensation formula requires that the renters pay the same high prices in just compensation that they would pay in a market transaction. Of course, if oligopolistic pricing was the problem, then over the long run the use of eminent domain might sufficiently atomize the market that prices would come down. But if high prices in the current market are the problem, renters would have no incentive to use eminent domain, because the measure of compensation—fair market value—would also reflect these high prices.

One should always pause before attributing a seemingly futile purpose to a statute. Perhaps a better explanation for the Land Reform Act is that it addressed a specific capital problem. From this perspective, the refusal of Hawaii's land magnates to sell their land in fee simple did not motivate the statute; rather, it was motivated by their transfer of the land through long-term ground leases that were either coming due or up for renegotiation. The expiration or renegotiation of the ground leases rendered tenants with substantial capital investments in the property vulnerable to rent-seeking behavior by landlords. A landlord could charge a lease-renewal price that included not only the unimproved land's opportunity cost, but also the value of improvements previously paid for by the tenant. The Land Reform Act would have represented a rational response to this problem. In fact, there is evidence that tension between landlords and tenants over lease renewals was a contributing factor in the statute's enactment.

Thus, under the basic model's thin market/thick market distinction, all three cases present proper occasions to exercise eminent domain. True, an opinion sustaining these takings under the basic model would be drafted quite differently from those the courts actually produced. But an opinion written from the basic model's vantage point would at least embody a coherent vision of eminent domain as a means, and would thus possess a degree of intellectual credibility. This is more than can be said for the decisions in *Poletown*, *Oakland Raiders*, and *Midkiff*.

As one might expect, the analysis under the refined model is a good deal more complex. *Poletown* involves both high subjective value and secondary rent seeking. The taking displaced thousands from their homes and businesses and destroyed a community irreplaceable at any cost. The uncompensated subjective loss was undoubtedly large. Furthermore, the condemnation transferred the property to a single entity, General Motors, and accordingly presented a high potential for secondary rent seeking. Under the refined model, both factors suggest that heightened judicial scrutiny was appropriate.

Whether the ex post gains from assembly of the Poletown plant site would outweigh the costs in terms of lost subjective value and incentives for future secondary rent seeking is difficult to determine. To measure the surplus generated by the plant one would have to consider enhanced property values created by assembly of the plant site and the plant's positive and negative externalities, such as more or better jobs and additional pollution. One would then have to subtract the subsidies given to GM in the form of tax abatements and below-market prices for retransfer of the real estate. The uncertainties inherent in such an analysis are patent. Nevertheless, a court could perhaps rationally conclude that an accurate accounting would show that the surplus from the taking offsets the plan's uncompensated subjective losses.

When the potential for secondary rent seeking enters the picture, however, the *Poletown* decision looks increasingly dubious—especially if the grant of eminent domain was just one of many subsidies designed to influence GM's plant location decision. Such subsidies could easily degenerate into bidding wars between states and localities competing for plant sites, bidding wars that might simply cause transfer payments from one class of citizens to another (subsidies have to be paid out of taxes) rather than ensure efficient siting decisions. Only very large ex post gains from plant sites would justify this kind of inducement to rent-seeking behavior. Thus, under the refined model, we can perhaps conclude that *Poletown* was wrongly decided. It must be stressed, however, that all of the evidence demanded by the model is unavailable, and a confident assertion on this score is simply impossible.

Oakland Raiders also seems to involve uncompensated subjective losses and a high potential for secondary rent seeking. Most NFL owners probably view their team as not only a business venture, but as a personal hobby as well. Thus, one can reasonably conclude that Al Davis, owner of the Raiders, would incur uncompensated subjective losses if stripped of his ownership rights in the team. Given that the condemnation also involved players' and coaches' contracts, we should also consider the possibility that the players and coaches attached subjective value to playing for Davis. In addition, *Oakland Raiders* presents an open invitation to secondary rent seeking. A general practice of allowing municipalities to condemn corporate franchises to prevent businesses from relocating elsewhere could easily foster abuses, as municipalities sought to use eminent domain to keep businesses offering high-paying jobs and tax dollars from relocating. The risk of abuse would rise even further if a city could condemn a corporate franchise by simply securing personal jurisdiction over corporate officers or quasi-in-rem jurisdiction over some of its assets. If this were possible, Detroit would not be limited to condemning plant sites to induce GM to remain in the city. It could conceivably condemn some other auto company, Honda of America for example, and simply sell it to the highest bidder that agreed to relocate in Detroit—unless, of course, that company was not condemned by some other city first.

It follows from the foregoing that *Oakland Raiders* should also be subject to heightened scrutiny under the refined model. Here again, we must draw some difficult inferences about the surplus generated by the project to decide whether the taking should survive such scrutiny. Note that the city was seeking to condemn a viable business. If that business can internalize the value of all the benefits it produces, there would be no surplus, because all of the business's value would be included in the price a willing buyer would pay. After paying the required compensation, the city would be no better off than before. If the franchise produces positive externalities, however, then condemning the team and forcing it to stay in Oakland would conceivably generate a surplus.

Although a professional sports franchise may do a fairly good job of capturing the value it produces (fan enthusiasm translates into ticket sales, concession sales, television revenues, and so forth), undoubtedly some externalization exists. If nothing else, the franchise's market value would not reflect increased newspaper sales to sports fans, hotel rentals to teams and media personnel, and so forth. There is also the ineffable element of civic pride that a successful professional sports team offers a town. In the aggregate, the external community benefits probably exceed the subjective loss to the franchise's owners. On the other hand, as with *Poletown*, the surplus would not likely justify the rent seeking that could follow from a general practice of allowing cities to condemn corporate franchises. So, when we add together both the subjective losses and the potential for secondary rent seeking, *Oakland Raiders*, like *Poletown*, was probably wrongly decided under the refined model.

At first blush, *Midkiff* involves none of the refined model's qualifying factors. The gentry of Hawaii may derive a certain psychological benefit from the size of its holdings, but it probably views any particular parcel as fungible wealth. Thus, the condemnees probably cannot claim great uncompensated subjective losses. Moreover, because triggering the takings mechanism required petition by one-half of the renters in a tract, or 25 renters, whichever is less, the Land Reform Act does not satisfy the conditions that suggest a high probability of secondary rent seeking. The benefits of "land reform" will necessarily be spread among a sizeable group of people.

If the earlier speculation about the true purpose of the Act is correct, however, *Midkiff* may involve a market bypass problem. Persons purchasing homes subject to long-term ground leases should be aware of the date the leases are due to expire. Moreover, if the purchaser improves the leased land, he should be aware of the potential for rent-seeking behavior by the landlord when the lease comes up for renewal. Some possible responses to the limited duration of the ground lease would be to insist on a discounted price for improvements (if the improvements have been purchased separately) or a discounted ground rental (if the improvements are to be made by the tenant himself), or to negotiate a lease renewal or renewal option well before the original lease's termination. In other words, when the renter makes his initial commitment of capital, he faces a relatively thick market. Only later, when lease termination is imminent and the renter has invested a great deal in improvements, does he face a thin market. This suggests that the renters in *Midkiff* who sought to condemn their landlord's reversionary interest negligently bypassed opportunities for thick market exchange.

However, two other considerations, both quite speculative, suggest that even if *Midkiff* presents a market bypass situation, that fact perhaps should not invalidate the taking. First, although commercial tenants seem to cope successfully with the problems of longterm lease renewal, the experience may be relatively novel for residential tenants, especially if they have emigrated from parts of the continental United States where such leases are uncommon. Thus, the "negligence" in the *Midkiff* market bypass may not be very great. Second, as in any case involving specific capital in the form of structures, the renter's subjective premium guarantees at least some surplus from condemnation. Taking these factors into consideration, perhaps a more complete account of the facts in *Midkiff* could justify the taking under even the refined model. Here again, however, the reported decision simply does not provide enough information to apply the model with confidence. If the legal system were to adopt the refined model as a normative standard, clearly courts and lawyers would have to develop a different kind of record as a basis for appellate review.

In sum, under the basic model, *Poletown*, *Oakland Raiders*, and *Midkiff* were rightly decided; under the refined model the result is less clear, but possibly two and arguably all three were wrongly decided.

* * *

b. The Police Power and the Takings Clause

Frank I. Michelman, *Property, Utility, and Fairness: Comments on the Ethical Foundations of "Just Compensation" Law,* 80 HARV. L. REV. 1165, 1224–1239 (1967)*

We have * * * been searching for a useful and satisfying way to identify the "evil" supposedly combated by the constitutional just compensation provisions, and have * * * suggested equating it with a capacity of some collective actions to imply that someone may be subjected to immediately disadvantageous or painful treatment for no other apparent reasons, and in accordance with no other apparent principle, than that someone else's claim to satisfaction has been ranked as intrinsically superior to his own.

The discussion has * * * shown why avoidance of this evil is not the same thing as avoidance of all social action having capricious redistributive effects. The reasons begin with the universal acknowledgment that some collective constraint on individual free choice is necessary in order to minimize the frustrations produced by people's concurrent quests for fulfillment, and to exploit fully the potential benefits from human interaction; and that social control, therefore, can ultimately lead to fuller achievement by each of his own ends. It is true that collective action which depends for its legitimacy on such understandings must look ultimately to the furtherance of *everyone's* attainment of his own ends, without "discrimination," and that this latter requirement would most obviously be met if a way were found to distribute the benefits and costs associated with each collective measure so that each person would share equally in the net benefit. But such perfection is plainly unattainable. Efficiency-motivated collective measures will regularly inflict on countless people disproportionate burdens which cannot practically be erased by compensation settlements. In the face of this difficulty, it seems we are pleased to believe that we can arrive at an acceptable level of assurance that *over time* the burdens associated with collectively determined improvements will have been distributed "evenly" enough so that everyone will be a net gainer. The function of a compensation practice, as here viewed, is to fulfill a strongly felt need to maintain that assurance at an "acceptable" level to justify the general expectations of long-run "evenness." If one feels impelled to refer this need back to a social interest in maximizing production, what we have called a utilitarian approach to compensation will be the result. If, however, the need is accepted on its own terms and for its own sake, as simply rooted in the condition of being a human person, then justice or fairness, rather than utility, will seem to be the key to compensation. The two approaches may lead to different results in some situations, but in general decisions made under their guidance turn on much the same factors—the disproportionateness of the harm a measure inflicts on individuals, the likelihood that those harmed were in a position to extract balancing concessions, the clarity with which efficiency demands the measure, and so forth. In what follows, I shall often treat the two approaches as parallel, and use the word "fairness" to signify also that apparent evenhandedness which a utilitarian approach may be understood as requiring.

If it truly is important for a society to subordinate its pursuit of efficiency to a discipline aimed at preventing outrages to fairness, then it may be worth asking whether the constitutional just compensation provisions present any hazard to sound social functioning. These provisions attract attention as the visible, formal expressions of society's commitment to fairness as a constraint on its pursuit of efficiency. The question is whether their magnetism is an energizing force, or a mesmerizing one. If it induces the habit of waiting upon the courts to administer a fairness discipline, and if courts are less than fully equal to the task or cannot perform it without serious damage to their effectiveness in other spheres, then there is cause for concern.

To argue at length for the unamazing proposition that the true purpose of the just compensation rule is to forestall evils associated with unfair treatment, is to imply that the proposition, for all its obviousness, is insufficiently understood or recognized in practice. We should, then consider carefully the extent to which the "fairness" or utility rationale is already reflected, even if inexplicitly, in the judicial doctrines which presently compose the main corpus of our just compensation lore. My conclusion is that these doctrines do significantly reflect the line of thought which has been elaborated in these pages, and that this approach, indeed, derives some indirect support from its power to explain much that is otherwise mysterious about the doctrines. Nevertheless, the courts fall too far short of adequate performance to be left without major assistance from other quarters.

A. Physical Invasion

It will be recalled that the factor of physical invasion has a doctrinal potency often troublesome on two counts. First, private losses otherwise indistinguishable from one another may, as in the flight nuisance cases, be classified for compensability purposes according to whether they are accompanied by a physical invasion, even though that seems a purely fortuitous circumstance. Second, purely nominal harms such as many which accompany street-widening or subterranean utility installations—are automatically deemed compensable if accompanied by governmental occupation of private property, in apparent contradiction of the principle that the size of the private loss is a critically important variable. Both these seeming oddities may now seem easier to understand.

Actually, physical use or occupation by the public of private property may make it seem rather specially likely that the owner is sustaining a distinctly disproportionate share of the cost of some social undertaking. Moreover, there probably will be no need, in such a case, to trace remote consequences in order to arrive at a reasonable appraisal of the gravity of the owner's loss—a loss which is relatively likely to be practically determinable and expressible as a dollar amount. Furthermore, to limit compensation to those whose possessions have been physically violated, while in a sense arbitrary, may at least furnish a practical, defensible, impersonal line between compensable and noncompensable impositions—one which makes it possible to compensate on some occasions without becoming mired in the impossible task of compensating all disproportionately burdened interests.

* * *

But this justification for a physical criterion is really rather weak. The capacity for such a criterion to minimize settlement costs is beyond question, but its capacity to distinguish, even crudely, between significant and insignificant losses is too puny to be taken seriously. A rule that no loss is compensable unless accompanied by physical invasion would be patently unacceptable. A physical invasion test, then, can never be more than a convenience for identifying *clearly compensable* occasions. It cannot justify dismissal of any occasion as *clearly noncompensable.* But in that case, the significance of the settlement-cost saving feature is sharply diminished. We find ourselves accepting the disadvantage of a test requiring compensation on many occasions where losses in truth seem relatively insignificant and bearable, in return for the convenience of having a simple way to identify some—but by no means all—compensable occasions. This seems a questionable bargain.

There may be a way of shoring up the physical invasion test—viewing it as a way of identifying some but not all compensable occasions we are inclined to take a utilitarian rather than an "absolute" view of fairness. This requires some reflection on psychic phenomena. Physical possession doubtless is the most cherished prerogative, and the most dramatic index, of ownership of tangible things. Sophisticated rationalizations and assurances of overall evenness which may stand up as long as one's possessions are unmolested may wilt before the stark spectacle of an alien, uninvited presence in one's territory. The psychological shock, the emotional protest, the symbolic threat to all property and security, may be expected to reach their highest pitch when government is an unabashed invader. Perhaps, then, the utilitarian might say that as long as courts must fend with compensability issues, to lay great stress on the polar circumstance of a permanent or regular physical use of occupation by the public is sound judicial practice—even though, at the same time and in a broader view, to discriminate on such a basis seems unacceptably arbitrary.

It is this evident arbitrariness which seems to require outright disapproval of the physical invasion criterion if we judge it by the standards of "absolute" fairness. For, true as may be the utilitarian controller's judgment that physical invasion raises special risks to the sense of security he wishes to inculcate, the rational actors of the fairness model must be expected to see that the relevant comparison is between large losses and small losses—not between those which are and are not accompanied by partial evictions.

B. Diminution of Value

Earlier we found it hard to understand why compensability should be thought to turn on a comparison of the size of the claimant's loss with the preexisting value of that spatially defined piece of property to which the loss in value seems to be specifically attached. It can now be suggested that judicial reliance on such comparisons reflects a utilitarian approach to compensability, as qualified by some special behavioral assumptions.

The method of identifying compensable harms on the basis of the degree to which "the affected piece" of property is devalued offers several parallels to that of discriminating on the basis of physical invasion. Both methods, though they seem obtuse and illogical so long as the purpose of compensation is broadly stated to be that of preventing capricious redistributions, gain in plausibility given the more refined statement that the purpose of compensation is to prevent a special kind of suffering on the part of people who have grounds for feeling themselves the victims of unprincipled exploitation. Moreover, the appeal of both methods rests ultimately in administrative expediency, in their defining classes of cases whose members will (a) usually be easy to identify and (b) usually, under certain behavioral suppositions, present a particularly strong subjective need for compensation.

As applied to the diminution of value test, these statements require explanation. We may begin by noticing a refinement, not mentioned earlier, which might initially seem only to deepen the mystery. It will be recalled that Justice Holmes, writing for the Court in the famous *Pennsylvania Coal* case,[111] held that a restriction on the extraction of coal, which effectively prevented the petitioner from exercising certain mining rights which it owned, was a taking of property and so could be enforced only upon payment of compensation. Holmes intimated strongly that the separation in ownership of the mining rights from the balance of the fee, prior to enactment of the restriction, was critically important to the petitioner's victory. But why should this be so? We can see that if one owns mining rights only, but not the residue of the fee, then a regulation forbidding mining totally devalues the owner's stake in "that" land. But is there any reason why it should matter whether one owns, in addition to mining rights, residuary rights in the same parcel (which may be added to the denominator so as probably to reduce the fraction of value destroyed below what is necessary for compensability) or residuary rights in some other parcel (which will not be added to the denominator)?

The significance of this question is confirmed by its pertinency to many comparable judicial performances. There is, for example, the widespread rule requiring compensation to the owner of an equitable servitude (such as a residential building restriction) when the government destroys the servitude's value by acquiring the burdened land and then using that land in violation of the private restriction embodied in the servitude. Vis-á-vis the servitude owner, the government cannot be said in the narrow sense to have "taken" any property. It has not, as in the air easement cases, engaged in an activity which would be an actionable eviction if privately instigated. It is not affirmatively exploiting any prerogative formerly held by the owner of the servitude. It is simply engaging in activity which, absent the servitude, might have been a nuisance; but government does not usually come under an automatic obligation to compensate whenever it maintains a nuisance. Yet many courts award compensation to persons deprived by government action of the benefits of private building restrictions, without asking any questions about how much value, or what fraction of some value, has been destroyed. Thus, government activity, on land adjacent to the complainant's, which would otherwise give rise to no claim to compensation, may support such a claim if it violated a building restriction of which the complainant is a beneficiary. If a justification exists for such a difference in treatment, it would seem to be that one's psychological commitment to his explicit, formally carved out, appurtenant rights in another's land is much more sharply focused and intense, and much nearer the surface of his consciousness, than any reliance he placed on his general claim to be safeguarded against nuisances. This proposition, if valid, would not affect the "fairness" of noncompensation, but it means that a utilitarian, with his eye on the

---

[111] Pennsylvania Coal Co. v. Mahon, 260 U.S. 393 (1922).

actual long term psychological effects of his decisions, will be wary of denying compensation to the affronted servitude owner.

* * *

The "fraction of value destroyed" test, to recapitulate, appears to proceed by first trying to isolate some "thing" owned by the person complaining which is affected by the imposition. Ideally, it seems, one traces the incidence of the imposition and then asks what "thing" is likely to be identified by the owner as "the thing" affected by this measure? Once having thus found the denominator of the fraction, the test proceeds to ask what proportion of the value or prerogatives formerly attributed by the claimant to that thing has been destroyed by the measure. If practically all, compensation is to be paid.

All this suggests that the common way of stating the test under discussion—in terms of a vaguely located critical point on a sliding scale—is misleading (though certainly a true representation of the language repeatedly used by Holmes). The customary labels—magnitude of the harm test, or diminution of value test—obscure the test's foundations by conveying the idea that it calls for an arbitrary pinpointing of a critical proportion (probably lying somewhere between fifty and one hundred percent). More sympathetically perceived, however, the test poses not nearly so loose a question of degree; it does not ask "how much," but rather (like the physical-occupation test) it asks "whether or not"; whether or not the measure in question can easily be seen to have practically deprived the claimant of some distinctly perceived, sharply crystallized, investment-backed expectation.

C. Balancing

Earlier it was argued that while the process of striking a balance between a compensation claimant's losses and "society's" net gains would reveal the *efficiency* of the measure responsible for those losses and gains, it would be inconclusive as to compensability. By viewing compensation as a response to the demands of fairness we can now see that the "balancing" approach, while certainly inconclusive, is not entirely irrelevant to the compensability issue.

What fairness (or the utilitarian test) demands is assurance that society will not act deliberately so as to inflict painful burdens on some of its members unless such action is "unavoidable" in the interest of long-run, general well-being. Society violates that assurance if it pursues a doubtfully efficient course and, at the same time, refuses compensation for resulting painful losses. In this situation, even a practical impossibility of compensating will leave the sense of fairness unappeased, since it is unfair, and harmful to those expectations of the property owner that society wishes to protect, to proceed with measures which seem certain to cause painful individual losses while not clearly promising any net social improvement. In short, where compensability is the issue the "balancing" test is relevantly aimed at discovering not whether a measure is or is not efficient, but whether it is *so obviously* efficient as to quiet the potential outrage of persons "unavoidably" sacrificed in its interest. This conclusion does not, of course, detract from our earlier conclusion that even the clear and undisputed efficiency of a measure does not sufficiently establish its fairness in the absence of compensation.

D. Harm and Benefit

For clarity of analysis the most important point to be made about asking whether a restrictive measure requires a man to "benefit" his neighbors or only stops him from "harming" them is that this distinction (insofar as it is relevant and valid at all) is properly addressed to an issue different from, and antecedent to the issue of "compensation" as we have now come to view it. We concluded earlier that the harm-benefit distinction was illusory as long as efficiency was to be taken as the justifying purpose of a collective measure. But we have for many pages past been treating the compensation problem as one growing out of a need to reconcile efficiency with the protection of fair, or socially useful expectations. The issue we have been trying to clarify does not exist apart from the collective pursuit of efficiency. In this scheme of things, the office of the harm-benefit distinction cannot be to help resolve that issue. But the distinction, properly understood, does have a related use. It helps us to identify certain situations which, although in most obvious respects they resemble paradigm compensability problems, can be treated as raising no compensation issues *because the collective measures involved are not grounded solely in considerations of efficiency.*

The core of truth in the harm-prevention/benefit-extraction test—and the reason for its strong intuitive appeal—emerges when we recognize that some use restrictions can claim a justification having nothing to do with the question of what use of the available resources is the most efficient. If someone, without my consent, takes away a valuable possession of mine, he is said to have stolen and is called a thief. When theft occurs, society usually will do what it can to make the thief restore to the owner the thing stolen or its equivalent, either because "commutative justice" so requires or because it is felt that there will be an intolerable threat to stable, productive social existence unless society sets its face against the unilateral decisions of thieves that they should have what is in the possession of others. The case is not essentially different if I own a residence in a pleasant neighborhood and you open a brickworks nearby. In pursuit of your own welfare you have by your own fiat deprived me of some of mine. Society, by closing the brickworks, simply makes you give back the welfare you grabbed; and, since you were not authorized in the first place to make distributional judgments as between you and me, you have no claim to compensation. The whole point of society's intervention negates any claim to compensation.

The point, then, is that the appeal of the tendered distinction between antinuisance measures and public benefit measures lies in the fact that the activities curbed by the first sort of measure are much more likely to have been "theft-like" in their origin than are activities restricted by the second sort. Measures of the "public benefit" type can usually be justified *only* in terms of efficiency, a justification which leaves the compensation issue unresolved, while "antinuisance" measures may be justified by considerations of commutative justice, or of the protection of orderly decision making, which negate any possible claim to compensation.

It should be clear, however, that no sharp distinction is thus established between the types of measures. Activity which is obviously detrimental to others at the time regulations are adopted may have been truly innocent when first instigated. Failure to act upon this plain truth is responsible for some of the most violently offensive decisions not to compensate. The brickyard case is the undying classic.[121] The yard is established out of sight, hearing, and influence of any other activity whatsoever. The city expands, and eventually engulfs the brickyard. The brickmaker is then ordered to desist. That order reduces the market value of his land from 800,000 dollars to 60,000 dollars. There is no question here of disgorging ill-gotten gains; brickmaking is a worthy occupation, and at the time of its establishment the yard generated no nuisance. No incompatibility with any use of other land was apparent. To say that the brickmaker should have foreseen the emergence of the incompatibility is fantastic when the conclusion depending from that premise is that we may now destroy his investment without compensating him. It would be no less erratic for society to explain to a homeowner, as it bulldozed his house out of the way of a new public school or pumping station, that he should have realized from the beginning that congestion would necessitate these facilities and that topographical factors have all along pointed unerringly in the direction of his lot.

Just as the compensation issue raised by an ostensibly nuisance-curbing regulation cannot always be dismissed by assuming that the owner's claim is no stronger than a thief's or a gambler's, so conversely it will often be wholly appropriate to deny compensation because that assumption does hold, even though the measure occasioning the private loss seems to fall within the class of restrictions on "innocent" activity for the enrichment of the public.

Suppose I buy scenic land along the highway during the height of public discussion about the possibility of forbidding all development of such land, and the market clearly reflects awareness that future restrictions are a significant possibility. If restrictions are ultimately adopted, have I a claim to be compensated in the amount of the difference between the land's value with restrictions and its value without them? Surely this would be a weak claim. I bought land which I knew might be subjected to restrictions; and the price I paid should have been discounted by the possibility that restrictions would be imposed. Since I got exactly what I meant to buy, it perhaps can be said that society has effected no redistribution so far as I am concerned, any more than it does when it refuses to refund the price of my losing sweepstakes ticket.

In sum, then, it would appear that losses inflicted by "nuisance prevention" may raise serious questions of compensation, while losses fixed by "public benefit" measures may not even involve any redistribution. If that is so, then surely we ought to be wary of any compensation rule which treats as determinative the distinction between the two types of measures. Such a rule has overgeneralized from relevant considerations which are somewhat characteristic of, but not logically or practically inseparable from, measures in one or the other class. If the relevant considerations can be kept in view without the oversimplified rule, then the oversimplified rule is merely a menace to just decision and should be dismissed.

---

[121] Hadacheck v. Sebastian, 239 U.S. 394 (1915).

Clarity of analysis is, at any rate, greatly improved by treating these considerations as logically antecedent to compensability issues. If efficiency-motivated social action has a painfully uneven distributional side-effect, the issue of compensability must be faced and resolved. But social action which merely corrects prior, unilaterally determined redistributions, or brings a deliberate gamble to its denouement, raises no question of compensability. The true office of the harm-prevention/benefit-extraction dichotomy is, then, to help us decide whether a potential occasion of compensation exists at all. If one does, the compensability discussion must proceed from that point.

Jerold S. Kayden, *Zoning for Dollars: New Rules for an Old Game? Comments on the* Municipal Art Society *and* Nollan *Cases,* 39 Wash. U. J. Urb. & Contemp. L. 3-8, 30-51 (1991)*

Faced with mounting social needs and continuing fiscal constraints, more and more cities "mint" money through their zoning codes to finance a wide array of public amenities. Through the land use regulatory technique formally known as "incentive zoning," cities grant private real estate developers the legal right to disregard zoning restrictions in return for their voluntary agreement to provide urban design features such as plazas, atriums, and parks, and social facilities and services such as affordable housing, day care centers, and job training. Since its inception some thirty years ago,[1] incentive zoning has enjoyed broad support from developers and their attorneys, avoiding the legal challenges commonly brought against land use regulations requiring the provision of public amenities.

* * * [A] 1987 * * * decision * * * from the United States Supreme Court [has] * * * fixed an ominous cloud over certain applications of incentive zoning. * * * In *Nollan v. California Coastal Commission,*[4] the Court struck down a state agency's request to a private landowner for a public easement, using reasoning that appears to apply to incentive zoning. * * * The [case] * * * concerns a couple desiring to build a home on the California coast and does not even mention the words "incentive zoning." Nonetheless, [the] decision * * * [poses a] troubling question to advocates of the technique's recent efforts to encourage private provision of social facilities and services: what is the relationship between the government-offered incentive and the developer-provided amenity? Not surprisingly, the case * * * suggest[s] that the more tenuous the relationship, the more suspect the exercise.

This article explores the extent to which [this] * * * decision * * * undermine[s] incentive zoning. First, the article canvasses the empirical record of incentive zoning. Next, the article critiques the analyses of the * * * decision * * * insofar as [it applies] * * * to the technique. Moreover, the article argues that statutory and constitutional analysis of exercises of incentive zoning for "unrelated amenities" should not differ from that accorded incentive zoning for "related amenities." Finally, the article concludes that ameliorative public policies should address the legitimate concerns raised by the "unrelated amenities" question.

I. Empirical Record of Incentive Zoning

Many large and medium size cities throughout the United States employ incentive zoning. New York City pioneered its use in 1961, allowing construction of ten square feet of additional office space in exchange for each square foot of plaza, and three

1 New York City's 1961 zoning resolution, a massive rewrite of the city's (and the country's) first zoning ordinance of 1916, introduced the incentive zoning concept. See * * * Barnett, *Introduction to Part III: Case Studies in Creative Urban Zoning*, in The New Zoning: Legal, Administrative and Economic Concepts and Techniques 127 (N. Marcus & M. Groves eds. 1970) [hereinafter The New Zoning].

4 483 U.S. 825 (1987).

bonus office square feet in exchange for each square foot of arcade. New York's list of bonusable amenities expanded during the 1960s and 1970s to include through-block arcades, covered pedestrian spaces, elevated walkways, and theatres. Developers responded favorably to the city's enticements. More than two-thirds of all major office buildings constructed between 1963 and 1975 received zoning bonuses. Statistics compiled for that twelve-year period indicate that the city granted more than 12 million square feet of bonus office space to ninety-one buildings.

Other cities tailored incentive zoning to fit their specific environments. San Francisco, California, for example, offered zoning bonuses to encourage developers to provide rooftop observatories for tourists. Anchorage, Alaska provided incentives for climate-controlled plazas and courtyards. Miami, Florida developed incentives to encourage retail activity at street level. Cincinnati, Ohio granted incentives for historic preservation of important structures.

While cities used incentive zoning during the 1960s and 1970s principally to stimulate construction of "urban design" amenities such as plazas and arcades, more recent applications of the technique encourage "social" amenities such as low-income housing, day care centers, cultural facilities, and job training. Newton, Massachusetts allows larger residential apartment complexes than otherwise permissible in order to obtain low and moderate-income housing.[15] Seattle, Washington offers floor area bonuses to office developers who provide day care facilities and affordable housing. Hartford, Connecticut gives bonuses to encourage job training and the provision of visual and performing arts spaces.

As individuals have begun to understand better the connection between land use regulations and the quality of local physical environments, criticism of incentive zoning has increased. Where zoning administration was once left to planning-oriented professionals, zoning today excites neighborhood activists, political leaders, and newspaper reporters. Government approval of new development routinely triggers complaints that streets and sidewalks are already too congested, that neighborhoods have lost their human scale, and that indispensable open space is disappearing. Because incentive zoning definitionally tampers with baseline zoning rules by allowing developers to construct buildings larger than otherwise permitted, the technique has become a lightning rod for general discontent with local land use policies.[20]

The central criticism alleges that incentive zoning corrupts orthodox planning and zoning models by persuading planners to greenlight otherwise undesirable projects solely to obtain the privately financed amenities. Zoning expresses conclusions about theoretically objective physical planning criteria such as street, sidewalk, sewer, and water pipe capacity; light and air availability at ground level; and compatibility of new buildings with the existing neighborhood. Thus, any overriding of that zoning, no matter what the proposed amenity, intrinsically delegitimizes the entire regulatory system. This critique gains particular currency when the amenity is geographically or conceptually unrelated to the development project obtaining the incentive. For example, while the community-at-large benefits from the provision of affordable housing or an arts center, the neighborhood immediately surrounding the bonused project suffers from greater congestion and loss of light and air attributable to the bonus office space. Good physical planning, underpinned by objective criteria, is sacrificed on the altar of unrelated amenities. Consequently, one set of city residents or employees unfairly suffers for the benefit of all.

Additionally troubling to some is incentive zoning's inherent dependence on a philosophy of sanctioned bribery, abiding a private sector that can "buy" its way out of legal restrictions. If the public amenities are so important, goes the argument, then government should require developers to provide them without a zoning payoff, or alternatively, should finance them from tax revenues.[22]

In defense of incentive zoning, it first must be observed that physical planning objectives arguably undermined by the technique are not the only interests important to communities. Other values, including those represented by social amenities, contribute to the quality of life. For example, a city might resolve that it will tolerate taller buildings and

[15] See Iodice v. City of Newton, 397 Mass. 329, 491 N.E.2d 618 (1986).

[20] In the early 1980s, two of incentive zoning's most fervent practitioners, New York City and San Francisco, significantly reduced their reliance on the technique, in part because of its inherent bias toward additional development to provide desired amenities. * * * In contrast, economically depressed cities anxious to stimulate job creation and local tax revenues usually view any development whatsoever as an asset. * * *

[22] Still other criticisms focus on the inferior design quality of amenities that actually have been provided, * * * and the excessive financial value of incentives actually awarded to developers in relation to the financial cost of amenities. * * *

greater congestion in return for more low-income housing and day care facilities. Furthermore, most land use regulatory decisions, not just incentive zoning transactions, pose difficult tradeoffs between neighborhood and citywide concerns. The placement of a drug treatment center in one neighborhood, for example, will disproportionately burden that neighborhood for the good of the whole city. Similarly, the zoning of one district for one class of use may adversely affect property values in that area relative to other areas. Moreover, the sanctioned bribery criticism could apply to any government program of inducement to the private sector, not just incentive zoning. Finally, the technique enjoys a superior track record for creating amenities which otherwise might not exist.

* * *

III. The *Nollan* Case

* * *

The facts of *Nollan* are central to the inquiry. Pat and Marilyn Nollan leased, with an option to buy, a small beachfront lot containing a 521 square foot bungalow, located north of Los Angeles on the Pacific coast in Ventura County. Wanting to replace the bungalow with a new 1,674 square foot two-story single-family home,[107] the Nollans applied to the California Coastal Commission for the required coastal development permit. The Commission granted the permit, subject to the condition that the Nollans provide an easement allowing the public to walk north and south on their beach between the mean high tide line and their seawall.[109] The Commission imposed the easement condition because it found that the new house would block views to the ocean, would contribute to "a 'wall' of residential structures [preventing the public] psychologically . . . from realizing a stretch of coastline exists nearby that they have every right to visit," and would add to private use of the coast. The Nollans sued the Commission, arguing that the imposition of the permit condition effected a taking of their private property in violation of the fifth amendment's just compensation clause.

In its five-to-four decision, the United States Supreme Court sided with the Nollans. Writing for the majority, Justice Scalia found that the easement condition failed to substantially advance the same assumed legitimate state interests harmed by construction of the new house, and thus violated the just compensation clause. He first asserted that the Commission could not have demanded outright the conveyance of an easement had the Nollans simply maintained their existing bungalow use, because government actions causing a "permanent physical occupation" defeat the landowner's cardinal property right to exclude others.[114] Thus, he continued, the question for the Court was whether requiring the conveyance of the easement as a condition for issuing a land use permit altered the constitutional judgment.

Assuming the legitimacy of the Commission's declared public purposes, Justice Scalia reasoned that the Commission either could have refused permission altogether to construct the new house if construction would "substantially impede" such purposes,[116] or could have attached a condition to the

---

[107] In order to exercise their purchase option, the Nollans were required by deed restriction to demolish the bungalow and replace it with a new structure. * * * Apparently included in the original subdivision and conveyancing agreements for a large land holding along the coast, this restriction operated to ensure that all lot owners built and maintained quality properties, in effect a good neighbor policy.

[109] Under California law, the historic mean high tide line demarcated the boundary between private and public domains. Thus, at low tide, the public could walk along the coast, between the low and high tide lines, without trespassing on the Nollans' beach. At high tide, however, beachcombers would have to swim north and south, insofar as the only beach above water would be on the Nollans' property. At its maximum distance, the Nollans' seawall lay 10 feet east of the mean high tide line. The easement condition would make it easier for the public to walk directly between the Faria County Park public beach, one quarter mile up the coast from the Nollans' beach, and the Cove public beach, 1,800 feet to the south.

[114] * * * See, e.g., Loretto v. Teleprompter Manhattan CATV Corp., 458 U.S. 419 (1982). * * *

[116] Presumably to flag the "economic viability" prong of just compensation clause jurisprudence, Justice Scalia's majority appended the caveat, "unless the denial would interfere so drastically with the Nollans' use of their property as to constitute a taking." (citing Penn Central Transp. Co. v. New York City, 438 U.S. 104 (1978)); see, e.g., Agins v. City of Tiburon, 447 U.S. 255, 260 (1980). As a boiler-plate reminder that owners are generally entitled to economically viable use of their property, no matter how significant the public purpose underlying the regulation, the caveat is virtually axiomatic. See, e.g., Agins, 447 U.S. at 260; Pennsylvania Coal Co. v. Mahon, 260 U.S. 393, 415 (1922). As an ironclad guarantee of property rights in all cases, however, the caveat conflicts with the idea that owners are not entitled to economically viable use of their property if such use causes a nuisance or similarly harms the public interest. See * * * Hadacheck v. Sebastian, 239 U.S. 394 (1915); Mugler v. Kansas, 123 U.S. 623 (1887). Indeed, one may argue that such uses are not part of the

construction that "serves the same governmental purposes as the development ban." Thus, in service of the Commission's stated goals of protecting the public's ability to see the beach, overcoming the "psychological barrier" caused by coastal development, and preventing congestion on the public beaches, the Commission could have banned the new house, or imposed, for example, the following conditions actually suggested by Justice Scalia: height and width limitations, a fence ban, or most remarkably because it would constitute a permanent physical occupation, a requirement that the Nollans provide "a viewing spot on their property for passersby with whose sighting of the ocean their new house would interfere."[118] Because the actual easement condition failed to advance any of the asserted purposes—permitting people to walk along the Nollans' beach would not mitigate burdens on visual access to the ocean caused by the new house, or presumably, address the two other Commission goals—the Court struck down the condition.

A. *The* Nollan *Rationale and Incentive Zoning: Voluntariness Denied*

At first glance, *Nollan* would appear to have little relevance to incentive zoning. Where the technique involves landowners who voluntarily provide amenities in return for incentives, were not the Nollans forced to provide the beach access easement? Appearances can be deceiving. The majority's rationale effectively recasts the voluntary operation of all incentive zoning transactions. Consequently, the opinion threatens to prohibit exercises of the technique for unrelated amenities.

Justice Scalia argued that, because "the right to build on one's own property—even though its exercise can be subjected to legitimate permitting requirements—cannot remotely be described as a governmental benefit," the Commission's attempt to trade the new house permit for the beach easement could not a priori reflect a "voluntary exchange." If his predicate "right to build on one's own property," subject to "legitimate permitting requirements," means nothing more than the boilerplate right to use one's property, subject to government regulations serving the public interest, then this part of his argument is axiomatic. The theory that the sovereign grants private property rights, making them "governmental benefits," and thus can take all of them away without compensation, is upended by the express language of the just compensation clause and the legion of Supreme Court opinions interpreting its scope.

As a matter of logic, however, it does not follow from Justice Scalia's "right to build" axiom that a "voluntary exchange" of property rights for public amenities could never take place, in *Nollan*, or more broadly, in other land use cases involving special permits with conditions. The definition of "voluntariness" is fraught with conceptual and linguistic challenges. On what basis did Justice Scalia determine that the exchange of the new house for the beach easement amenity was not voluntary? He neither reviewed the statutory framework governing the Commission's issuance of coastal permits to establish the matter of right property use, nor canvassed the Nollans' expectations regarding their property. Furthermore, Justice Scalia did not elucidate a core constitutional property rights theory rendering such inquiries nugatory. Instead, he appears to have assumed *sub silentio* that the "right to build . . . subject to legitimate permitting requirements" included construction of the Nollans' new

---

individual's private property right at all. Thus, to the extent that substantial impediments to legitimate public purposes arising from the Nollans' new house might be analogized to a nuisance, a ban on the new house might not effect a taking even under the economic viability analysis.

[118] Justice Scalia's declared willingness to countenance a public viewing spot on the Nollans' front lawn (presumably equipped with oversized steel binoculars on stanchions that cost a quarter per view) should be treated warily. After all, it must be remembered, the Court only assumed the legitimacy of the Commission's visual access public purpose constituting the predicate for upholding a ban on the new house, or alternatively, a viewing spot condition.

Taken at face value, however, Justice Scalia's approval of a physical invasion invites further speculation. Previously, he argued that, had the Nollans retained the existing bungalow, the Commission could not have required outright the easement, because government actions causing a "permanent physical occupation" defeat the owner's property right to exclude others. What if, however, the definition of a nuisance altered over time to cover uses of private property blocking significant views? At that point, one might suppose, the Commission could ban the existing offending bungalow (assuming it blocked the view), just as government banned the existing brick yard use in Hadacheck v. Sebastian, 239 U.S. 394 (1915), and the existing brewery use in Mugler v. Kansas, 123 U.S. 623 (1887), without running afoul of the Constitution. * * * Property owners have never enjoyed a private property right to maintain nuisances. * * * Under this analysis, a government-authorized physical invasion condition imposed on an existing use of property that served the same interest as a ban on the existing use would be equally constitutional under Justice Scalia's reasoning.

house, thereby converting the beach easement into a requirement imposed upon a right.

Thus defined, Justice Scalia's unremarkable axiom becomes a novel constitutional principle: owners are entitled to whatever property use government conditionally authorizes as a matter of constitutional right, subject only to conditions serving the same public interest as that served by prohibiting the conditional use. Even if the Commission assumedly could have banned the new house altogether, its conditional willingness to allow it "constitutionalized" the Nollans' right to the house. At that point, a house for beach easement trade definitionally could not reflect a "voluntary exchange," because the Commission could not trade something to which the Nollans were already entitled.

Justice Scalia's property rights approach reduces the rest of his opinion to a foregone conclusion, commanding a constitutional analysis no different than when government directly imposes burdens on matter of right development. As a general rule, government may not force landowners to solve problems not of their own making. Otherwise, the just compensation clause's fundamental purpose, to ensure that individuals do not bear burdens more properly borne by society at large, would be thwarted. To prevent this occurrence, the clause's heavy machinery roars into action and limits government to the appending of burdens proportionally addressing harms or needs which the proposed development has generated. The Commission could no more compel the Nollans to provide the beach easement than it could compel them to provide a small maritime museum, because neither of these amenities mitigates the harm to the Commission-declared public interest in visual access assumedly caused by the conditional property use of a new house. Justice Scalia's string citation of twenty state court mandatory subdivision exaction and impact fees cases, in which providing amenities is a precondition to any development whatsoever, merely underscores the understanding that he viewed the beach easement as an imposition on a right. His choice of words is similarly pointed. For example, he stated that, "[u]nless the permit condition serves the same governmental purpose as the development ban, the building restriction is not a valid regulation of land use but an out-and-out plan of extortion." Framed in such terms, the debate would naturally shift from whether to how much of a relationship would be required.

Applied to incentive zoning, however, Justice Scalia's reasoning produces nothing less than a radical reconception. To fully appreciate this impact, it is helpful to recapitulate the paradigmatic incentive zoning transaction. By universally accepted definition, incentive zoning posits that the landowner voluntarily, as opposed to mandatorily, provides the public amenity. Through express statutory language, the technique establishes two tiers of governmental regulation of private property use. Landowners are entitled as a matter of right to a first tier maximum zoning-defined density without obligation to provide amenities. At their option, landowners seek the incentive of exceeding that maximum zoning-defined density, in return for their agreement to provide specified amenities. Government invents ex nihilo development rights above the first tier and offers them strictly in its discretion.[130] Landowners solicit such rights only if they envision a financial benefit in the tradeoff between the incentive's value and the amenity's cost. Private and public participants alike would agree that bonus development rights do not belong to the landowner until the exchange is consummated.

What makes incentive zoning voluntary, then, is that landowners may remain at the first tier with no obligation to ascend to the second tier and tender the desired public amenity. This touchstone of voluntary provision has made irrelevant the frequent resort to courts enveloping mandatory land use regulations of subdivision exactions, linkage, and inclusionary zoning, each of which requires private developers to provide public amenities before they can develop at all.[132] In any event, prior to *Nollan*, just compensa-

[130] One way to conceptualize these rights is that they reside in a public development rights bank, whose assets may be sold to individual property owners in return for desired public amenities. Another way is to assume that the city decides to sell unused air rights above publicly owned buildings and land. Public policy questions aside, it is clear that private owners have no constitutional claim of right to these development rights. Owners end up with larger buildings, the city with whatever amenities it wants, a scenario essentially no different from what would occur if incentive zoning were used for unrelated amenities.

[132] See, e.g., Associated Home Builders v. City of Walnut Creek, 4 Cal. 3d 633, 94 Cal. Rptr. 630, 484 P.2d 606 (exactions), appeal dismissed, 404 U.S. 878 (1971); * * * Board of Supervisors v. DeGroff Enterprises, 214 Va. 235, 198 S.E.2d 600 (1973) (inclusionary zoning); Jordan v. Village of Menomonee Falls, 28 Wis. 2d 608, 137 N.W.2d 442 (1965) (fees), appeal dismissed, 385 U.S. 4 (1966). See

tion clause jurisprudence would not have favored legal challenges from landowners involved in incentive zoning transactions. As long as such owners retained a first tier property use reasonable within the meaning of the clause, then the voluntary nature of an incentive zoning deal would *a fortiori* defeat a traditional takings claim.

As applied, Justice Scalia's majority opinion stands for the proposition that the Constitution, as the Court interprets it, does not recognize incentive zoning's paradigm of "voluntariness." By thinking about the bonus development rights residing between the first and second tiers as the owner's private property, instead of newly created rights, the opinion vitiates the technique's operating presumption of owners who voluntarily provide amenities in return for such rights. In the end, *Nollan*'s constitutional right to the second tier overrules incentive zoning's statutory right only to the first. This is not to say that developers may now march into city hall and demand second tier development rights without amenity obligation. But, by enmeshing private property rights with governmental prerogatives, *Nollan* creates the constitutional justification for overriding city hall's judgment about which legitimate state interests it may promote. The Court invalidated a government land use permit with conditions because the condition (amenity) was unrelated to the burden which additional development (incentive) imposed on a legitimate state interest. Thus, the Court could similarly strike down exercises of incentive zoning for such unrelated amenities as low-income housing, theatres, and job training because, like the beach easement, such amenities do not serve the same legitimate police power purposes as a refusal to grant the bonus floor area incentive in the first place. Specifically, such amenities fail to mitigate the negative impacts of congestion, light and air loss, and overburdened capital infrastructure generated by bonus floor area.

B. *Unconstitutional Conditions*

A companion analytical framework for evaluating Justice Scalia's related amenities requirement springs from the doctrine of unconstitutional conditions. Under that doctrine, government generally may not attach to benefits or permissions conditions that infringe upon constitutional rights, even though government has no initial obligation to grant such benefits or permissions. A gloss on the doctrine is that "germane" conditions, i.e., conditions related to the benefit or permission, are preferred to non-germane conditions. Thus, assuming that the Commission had no obligation to grant permission to build the new house in the first place, the Commission nonetheless could not condition such permission on the forfeiture of the just compensation clause right to be free from government-authorized physical invasions, any more than it could ask the Nollans to forego first amendment free speech rights. On the other hand, Justice Scalia's "viewing spot," no less an "unconstitutional" physical invasion than the beach easement, would survive as a condition germane to the Commission's declared visual access goal.

Although *Nollan* is facially about a condition on a government permit, and although Justice Scalia impressed a first amendment unconstitutional conditions analogy,[140] the case does not unambiguously

---

also * * * Ellickson, *The Irony of "Inclusionary" Zoning*, 54 S. Cal. L. Rev. 1167 (1981) * * *.

Unlike landowners who voluntarily participate in incentive zoning transactions, however, neighbors of bonused developments may have ample reason to file suits. After all, it is their light and air and sidewalks and streets which are impacted. * * * Would they be able to file a just compensation clause action against the transaction when their property rights are only indirectly affected? * * *

[140] Analogizing the Commission's actions to a state law that "forbade shouting fire in a crowded theater, but granted dispensations to those willing to contribute $100 to the state treasury," Justice Scalia observed that, while "requiring a $100 tax contribution in order to shout fire is a lesser restriction on speech than an outright ban, it would not pass constitutional muster." For him, the $100 "shout fire" treasury contribution condition would be unconstitutional because it (like the beach easement) lacked any relationship to the underlying purpose served by the ban, to wit, preventing panic in the theater (like preventing impairment of the Commission's goal of preserving visual access to the coast).

This is a gossamer analogy. Would Justice Scalia truly be satisfied if the state earmarked the money to an extra police detail to quell the panic or to a special fund to recompense the trampled for their injuries? The constitutional standard for reviewing regulation of speech is different than that employed for reviewing regulation of property. Speech restrictions are subject to the highest level of judicial scrutiny. Property restrictions, even post-*Nollan*, are subject to lesser scrutiny, although some might wish it otherwise. * * * Unlike the government's ubiquitous role in defining permissible property uses, the government's role in regulating speech is strictly limited to the margins. When government willingly allows an exception to the "shout fire" ban, for a related or unrelated $100 contribution, it intrinsically demonstrates that the ban itself is not strictly necessary. In contrast, while public goals furthered by a new house ban are undercut when an exception allowing construction is granted, a more lenient standard of constitu-

fit the unconstitutional conditions doctrine mold. In particular, an unconstitutional conditions analysis conflicts with Justice Scalia's property rights approach because it posits that the owner has no entitlement whatsoever to the new house, even as it demands germane conditions. On the other hand, the property rights approach posits that the Nollans enjoy a right to the new house, and thus may not be directly burdened with obligations addressing harms to the public interest which their development does not cause. Justice Scalia's express statement that "the right to build on one's own property . . . cannot remotely be described as a governmental benefit," and the implicit equation of the right to build with the Nollans' right to the new house, instead suggest an analysis deriving from direct burdens on constitutional rights rather than unconstitutional conditions. His citation of state subdivision exaction and impact fee cases employing the direct burden analysis sustains this view. Although Justice Scalia assumed for purposes of discussion that the Commission could have denied permission for the new house altogether, that authority was itself limited by constitutional dictates protecting underlying private property rights. *Nollan* surely does not trigger unconstitutional conditions doctrine in its purest and most intriguing form, where government has no constitutional obligation whatsoever to give permission or grant a benefit, such as National Endowment for the Arts awards or housing tax credits, but is nonetheless prevented from attaching non-germane restrictions requiring relinquishment of constitutional rights. In the end, however, both the property rights and unconstitutional conditions approaches would generally restrict government to requests for related (germane) amenities.[144]

C. *The* Nollan *Facts and Incentive Zoning: A Way to Limit the Rationale*

While the *Nollan* rationale enervates the exercise of incentive zoning for unrelated amenities, it would be rash to sound the death knell. The reason is that, while the facts of the case superficially lend themselves to the technique's argot, the Court did not squarely face a traditional incentive zoning transaction. It is true that the Nollans sought to build a house larger than that which the pertinent land use regulations authorized as a matter of right. Further, the Commission wanted to obtain beach access for the public. Just as a private developer applies for a floor area bonus in return for providing a plaza or low-income housing, the Nollans applied for a floor area bonus which the Commission would grant in exchange for the beach access amenity. This linguistic characterization glosses over several points. To begin with, the Court never explored or discussed the statutory matter of right use. While the Nollans needed a development permit in order to replace the existing bungalow with a new house, the Commission did not have unbounded discretion to grant or deny the permit. As long as their proposed house met announced statutory criteria, the Nollans would have received the permit. On the basis of the available record, one may therefore contend that the Nollans were statutorily entitled to their new house.

More significantly, neither the Nollans nor the Commission conceived or argued the case in the armature of incentive zoning. With lawsuit as testament, the Nollans themselves would be the first to bridle at any "voluntary" styling.[150] They were, after all, only asking to substitute a new home for an old one, not to develop a fifteen-unit condominium project. The Commission never asserted in incentive zoning terms that it was trading the new house for the unrelated amenity of the beach easement.[151]

---

tional review may tolerate a balancing of disparate public interests. * * *

[144] Attempts to distinguish between a "germaneness" requirement drawn from unconstitutional conditions cases and a "relationship" requirement drawn from subdivision exaction and impact fee cases ultimately are beside the point. * * * Justice Scalia makes clear in *Nollan* that government may not ask landowners to address problems which their own development does not create. His test comes in two parts: (1) does the proposed development substantially impede promotion of legitimate state interests justifying denial of the development; and (2) if so, then government may require the developer to mitigate the harm caused by the proposed development. For the land use lawyer, this test broadly sounds just like the traditional subdivision exaction test.

[150] In any event, linguistic presentations alone are deceiving. Just as the Nollans' interaction with the Commission can be described in incentive zoning's voluntary language, commonplace incentive zoning transactions can be couched in "mandatory" terminology. After all, in order to obtain the incentive of a FAR bonus, a developer is forced to provide adjacent subway improvements. Words frequently reflect and convey normative, rather than empirical, conceptions (penalty vs. nonsubsidy; right vs. privilege).

[151] Would there be anything wrong with the Commission deciding it is willing to tolerate harm A (less visual access to the coast) in return for benefit B (more beach access)? * * *

Instead, it maintained that the beach easement sufficiently related to the impact of the new house to pass constitutional muster.[152]

What, then, would the Court do if cleanly presented with incentive zoning for unrelated amenities? The * * * "Tale of Two Cities" presents a useful test case. In that Tale * * * city planners and elected officials meet to establish zoning FARs for the city's central business district. After reviewing governmental fiscal requirements and traditional physical planning concerns, the officials set a base matter of right maximum zoning of fifteen FAR. Thus far, even Justice Scalia would concede that private property owners are not constitutionally entitled to anything more than that level of development, assuming the FAR restriction provides owners reasonable use of their property within the meaning of the just compensation clause.

As the meeting progresses, the planners make various incentive zoning proposals. Under one, owners would receive three FAR floor area bonuses for plazas and arcades. The planners justify this bonus on the basis that the plazas and arcades would more than make up for deleterious impacts caused by the bonus floor space. Another proposal offers three FAR floor area bonuses for low-income housing, theatres, and day care centers. Some planners oppose this proposal on the grounds that the amenities fail to mitigate the incentive's negative physical impacts. Others respond, however, that notwithstanding such impacts, the city is on balance better off with these amenities. Following contentious debate, the city adopts only the second incentive zoning proposal. Thus, the city intentionally decides to accept greater congestion and less light and air in order to obtain an alternate set of public benefits.

Does the Constitution bar the city from making this choice? Two principal objections come to mind. First, government will manipulate the base matter of right zoning FAR to a lower level than otherwise necessary in order to obtain amenities at no marginal physical planning cost. Justice Scalia himself verbalized the danger of such manipulation and, Rashomonlike, portrayed another vision of the Tale.[156] In his over-leveraged city, the planners and elected officials might set a base FAR at an artificially low twelve rather than a planning-supported fifteen, and then offer three FAR bonuses in exchange for desired amenities. Alternatively, they might downzone a district's existing FAR from fifteen to twelve, and then offer incentives for amenities that allow developers to achieve the original fifteen. The sole reason for selecting the twelve FAR in both cases would be to fire up incentive zoning's economics without incurring the additional congestion, light and air, and other physical planning costs incurred with FARs in excess of fifteen. The city would have its cake, a fifteen, rather than eighteen, FAR central business district density, and eat it too, because developers would have provided desired amenities. At that point, the three FAR would no longer constitute a true bonus, and the situation would be no different than had the city zoned a fifteen FAR and directly burdened owners with amenity requirements. Not only could Justice Scalia express lofty concerns about a "lesser realization of the land use goals" served by the "more lenient (but nontradeable) development restrictions" of the fifteen FAR, but, more significantly, he could correctly assert that property rights had been unconstitutionally appropriated. Although Justice Scalia is correct as to the real world possibility of the over-leveraged city, his scenario does not rise to the level of a judicially noticeable fact justifying a blanket conclusion about whose property rights are at stake. Justice Scalia sounds a bit like a character from another Dickens story, the Ghost of Christmas Future, warning about things that might but do not have to be. Ever vigilant to the over-leveraged city scenario, courts can and should sift the evidence to assure that incentive zoning ordinances feature real incentives.

The second objection is that government's willingness to sacrifice physical planning goals served by the base FAR regulation demonstrates a lack of

---

[152] Indeed, under the prevailing lenient standard of review prior to *Nollan*, the Commission was probably correct. * * * The Court's myopic concentration on view blockage, only one of several proffered Commission justifications, and not surprisingly the one with the least connection to the beach easement, largely predetermined the judicial outcome. * * *

[156] * * * Justice Scalia stated:

> One would expect that a regime in which this kind of leveraging of the police power is allowed would produce stringent land-use regulations which the State then waives to accomplish other purposes, leading to lesser realization of the land-use goals purportedly sought to be served that would result from more lenient (but nontradeable) development restrictions. Thus, the importance of the purpose underlying the prohibition not only does not justify the imposition of unrelated conditions for eliminating the prohibition, but positively militates against the practice.

* * *

seriousness about such goals. If such goals are expendable, goes the argument, then so is the base regulation. In a world of scarce resources, however, cities routinely decide to advance one public interest over another, even though each interest may be important. Governing is centrally about choices from a basketful of apples and oranges. When a city openly, seriously, and intentionally chooses a mixture of more low-income housing and more congestion over a mixture of less congestion and less low-income housing, then that city has engaged in routine decision-making. Nothing in the just compensation clause elevates the goals underlying the base regulation to a more sacred position than the goals underlying the unrelated amenities. Interestingly, a ban on unrelated amenities interferes not only with the preferences of city mothers and fathers, but potentially with those of property owners as well. Given the choice between the "unrelated" beach easement and the "related" viewing spot, for example, the Nollans might very well have selected the beach easement. In the typical incentive zoning transaction, the developer's choice between related and unrelated amenities would reduce to an economic calculus in which developers, in return for a bonus, would prefer to provide an inexpensive unrelated amenity rather than an expensive related one.

Any constitutional assessment of incentive zoning under the just compensation clause ultimately falls prey to the circularity of private property rights definitions. Determination of rights depends on the level of government regulation, and the level of government regulation depends on avoiding improper infringement of private property rights. The idea that owners are constitutionally entitled to use their property as they see fit, but subject to government regulation promoting the health, safety, morals, and general welfare of its citizens, yields scant insight. Incentive zoning plays in the twilight of this guarantee, mixing two scenarios of the public interest with two levels of private property rights. The fundamental purpose of the just compensation clause, to ensure that individuals do not bear burdens more properly borne by society at large, proves equally unhelpful. Contingent upon one's assessment of who owns property rights nominally created by incentive zoning, the technique either does or does not impose such burdens when it attempts to encourage unrelated amenities.

Justice Scalia proffers no convincing theory to justify constitutional attribution of the bonus rights to the owner. Moreover, *Nollan* itself does not involve a classic incentive zoning transaction. Consequently, Justice Scalia's opinion represents a weak basis upon which to upset widespread acceptance by local governments and private developers of the technique. As long as Justice Scalia's over-leveraged world remains a case-by-case proposition, the technique does not deny landowners rights which should be ascribed to them. In the end, the result in *Nollan* is most understandable when described as a case about a family wanting to replace an old house with a new one. The five members of the Court majority thought this "right" to the new house could not be encumbered with obligations having nothing to do with the new house. Extending that proposition to the barter world of incentive zoning would likely surprise some, if not all, members of Justice Scalia's majority as much as it would surprise regular practitioners of the technique.

IV. The Need for Rules for Unrelated Amenities

The constitutional acceptance of incentive zoning for unrelated amenities should not obscure the technique's potential shortcomings and the resulting importance of policy guidelines. Questions of who gains and who loses demand explicit and rigorous examination, especially as the disconnection between an incentive's burden and an amenity's benefit increases. In order to make informed judgments about whether to support or oppose the tradeoff between congestion here and low-income housing there, citizens need full disclosure about the nature of the bargain.[162]

---

[162] It is not certain, however, that sunshine and resulting greater participation by the public will inevitably result in better or more equitable decisions. * * * Local governments may be captive of majorities or powerful neighborhood groups that refuse incentive zoning's cost of greater development for its benefit of unrelated amenities such as low-income housing. * * * Not surprisingly, incentive zoning's array of amenities and incentives have generally been clustered in high-income areas containing office buildings and market-rate housing, not in low-income neighborhoods. Furthermore, discussions in the sunshine sometimes encourage political rhetoric masking difficult choices. For example, when discussions of health and safety regulations quantitatively assign life and death rates to specific levels of regulation, elected officials understandably treat the issue as political dynamite. In a similar fashion, one wonders whether closer public scrutiny of the tradeoff between an intermittent shadow over Central Park and the extra public services provided from the additional revenue

Furthermore, incentive zoning, no less than land policy at all levels of government, should strive toward ideals of fairness and equity in its administration. Incentive zoning's burdens and benefits should be evenly distributed throughout a city in accordance with zoning's bedrock principle of according equal and uniform treatment to similarly situated landowners. No single area should bear a disproportionate share of bonus floor area, nor enjoy a disproportionate share of amenities. Rough equality would assure what Justice Holmes, in a different context, called the "average reciprocity of advantage," a catch-all concept fundamental to the legality and acceptance of all government restrictions on private property.[164] This concept, however, is not a call for exact equality. Just as commonplace zoning regulations or historic preservation laws routinely saddle one landowner or one area with burdens not shared by everyone else, incentive zoning will similarly burden some more than others.

The technique's administration may profit from government experience garnered in the NIMBY[166] and LULU[167] era, in which local planners strategically disperse throughout a city problematic, yet needed, land uses such as drug treatment centers, homeless shelters, and jails. Similarly, state governments have undertaken to apportion such unpopular uses as hazardous waste treatment plants and prisons among different towns, and even have offered compensating public benefits of additional state aid, which some describe as bribes, in order to encourage local acceptance. The purpose of these efforts is to assure individuals and neighborhoods that they are being treated fairly when government distributes benefits and burdens.

V. Conclusion

In usual circumstances, incentive zoning and courtrooms are strangers. The two principals, private developer and government, see the technique through spectacles of self-interest. Under utilitarian calculations, the private developer seeks to maximize the amount of development on a fixed quantity of land and enters an incentive zoning deal if the value of additional building rights exceeds the amenity's cost. Confronting decreased federal support and louder cries for social services, local governments view incentive zoning as an off-budget mechanism to meet public needs. As long as the "over-leveraged" city remains largely fictional, both principals will continue to support this exercise of zoning authority. In one respect, the * * * *Nollan* case * * * confirm[s] this reality. * * * [N]either the plaintiff owners nor the defendant government would likely characterize the beach easement as voluntary in any "incentive zoning" sense. Nonetheless, the * * * [case has] the potential for chilling the technique's use.

* * *

of a larger building would result in a more equitable or efficient decision.

164 See Pennsylvania Coal v. Mahon, 260 U.S. 393 (1922) * * *.

166 NIMBY stands for "not in my back yard."

167 LULU stands for "locally undesirable land uses."

Note

But for a problem in obtaining publication rights, I would have inserted here an excerpt from Margaret Jane Radin's article, *The Liberal Conception of Property: Cross Currents in the Jurisprudence of Takings,* 88 COLUM L. REV. 1667 (1988).* I highly recommend that it be read. In that article Radin coined the phrase "conceptual severance" to describe the tendency of those, such as Justice Scalia in *Nollan*, wishing to narrow the regulatory authority of local governments to describe a particular part of a parcel as the "property" subjected to restraint and then to find that "property" has been "taken" in violation of the Constitution. Those preferring an expansive view of government power to control use of property, such as Justice Brennan in the *Penn Central* litigation, tend to assume that the asset that should be subjected to takings analysis includes all of the assets on the regulated site. Radin views conceptual severance as an artifice that makes it possible for judges to evade resolving the basic question—whether it is "appropriate to make this particular person bear the cost of this particular government action for the benefit of this particular community."

* The article is going to be included in an anthology of Radin's work to be published in the near future. The anthology publisher would not allow any use of the work here.

But this debate about language also plays out other difficult issues. For example, Bruce Ackerman, in PRIVATE PROPERTY and the CONSTITUTION (1977) argues that use of common property labels in takings cases is the talk of Ordinary Observers—those who simply apply an unsophisticated, lay vision of standard property bundles to takings disputes. Ackerman prefers the work of Scientific Policymakers, who look behind ordinary labels by using some form of structured analysis. Ackerman's preference for Scientific Policymakers is, in turn, subjected to a searching critique by Philip Soper, in *On the Relevance of Philosophy to Law: Reflections on Ackerman's Private Property and the Constitution*, 79 COLUM L. REV. 44 (1979). Soper argues that any Scientific Policymaker will have to take the perceptions of Ordinary Observers into account. For regardless of the form of structured analysis a policymaker imposes on takings analysis—be it economics, ethics or politics—the attitudes of citizens about value, morality and democracy will be crucial to resolution of the dispute.

Does Kayden's argument, at the end of his article, that zoning ought to follow the "bedrock principle of according equal and uniform treatment to similarly situated landowners" solve the linguistic dilemma presented by conceptual severance, or by the degree of sophistication brought to a dispute by a decision maker? If different people view the consequences of land use regulation differently, then how are we to resolve the dispute in an equal and uniform way? Carol Rose suggests, in *Planning and Dealing: Piecemeal Land Controls as Problem of Local Legitimacy*, excerpted in Part III(F)(3) of this anthology, that mediation models should be used to resolve small scale land use disputes. Does this help? Is she wise to search for a set of procedural devices designed to settle differences of opinion over land use issues, rather than to urge judicial imposition upon land use officials of a particular form of structured analysis satisfactory to a Scientific Policymaker?

Jeremy Paul, *The Hidden Structure of Takings Law*, 64 S. CAL. L. REV. 1393, 1409–1411, 1416–1419, 1423–1425, 1522–1539, 1542–1548 (1991)*

I. PROPERTY AND THE POSITIVISM PROBLEM

The concept of property holds two special places at the heart of American law. As the basis of our economic system, private property law can be viewed as the set of rules we use to resolve conflicts among individuals concerning control over tangible and intangible resources. These rules establish, for example, my right to live quietly in my house, although they might also deny me a chance to build a restaurant on my lot. More generally, they help define the interests I can ask courts to protect and the entitlements with which I may enter the world of commercial exchange.

Property law, however, performs a second, equally vital role. Not only can one citizen invoke property claims to enlist the state in a struggle against another, but each citizen can call upon property law to protect herself against actions of the government itself. The fifth amendment specifically prohibits takings of property for public use without just compensation. Therefore a concept of property is necessary to render the Constitution an effective safeguard against excessive governmental interference with individual life.

At first glance, property's twin roles seem entirely complementary. Each citizen can be described as having a set of property rights that grant control over certain resources and protect the citizen from both neighborly and governmental intrusion. The image of the individual homeowner whose land is secure against all forms of trespass best conveys this notion of property.

The constitutional component of property law, however, confronts an obvious dilemma, whose relationship to private law property issues too often remains obscure. This dilemma can best be illustrated with an example * * *. Suppose a dangerously powerful government wishes to occupy a piece of land for a public theater displaying patriotic tributes to its leaders.[40] If the law gives government absolute power to define property rights, what prevents the state from telling the so-called owner of this land that the right to use or to sell the land is not "property," and that the owner therefore has no right to compensation when the government claims the land for the theater? In more general terms, how can government simultaneously be responsible for establishing the property rights of the citizenry and also be entrusted not to render its constituents helpless when conditions dictate defining property rights so as to benefit public officialdom? In property theory, this might be called the problem of positivism.[41]

* * *

B. Property Models

American law has responded forcefully to the need for property concepts to supplement the structures that protect against an oppressive state. Two opposing sets of ideas have occupied center stage in the development of a substantive theory of property that would prevent government's power to define from becoming the power to destroy.

* * *

1. *Physicalism*

* * * At its core is the idea that certain aspects of social practice, such as physical possession of previously unowned resources, demand legal recognition. Its genius lies in the understanding that if property rights could generally be derived from social life rather than created by the legal system, courts would then be freed from the dilemma of having simultaneously to define property rights and protect them against excessive government intervention.

* * *

The physicalist model forms the basis for one apparent solution to the positivism problem. It stems from the idea that the legal system should give formal recognition to what has occurred, usually without violence, in the social world. A woman who has farmed and encircled land deserves to keep it; a man who captures a fox deserves his bounty. Moreover, the model draws strength from common-sense categories used to determine which things are actually possessed by individual claimants. People own land, homes and animals but not necessarily stocks or radio frequencies. The beauty of this approach is that it appears to find property rights in factual questions (who got there first?) and principles (protect the existing occupant) so general and uncontroversial that the courts' role as definers of property rights seems to disappear.

The model also suggests methods for enforcing property right. Once physical things are awarded, they become synonymous with "property" and are protected against theft and trespass. * * * Every lawyer undoubtedly recognizes that this simplistic model is an abysmally poor description of contemporary property law. In reality, neighbors are permitted some types of physical interference, and physical invasions do not perfectly correspond to government accountability. What is ignored is the extent to which the physicalist model remains a foundation upon which much of contemporary law is built.

* * *

2. *The Market Model*

* * *

The key here is sequence. Possibilities for government overreaching created by the government's power to define property rights are drastically reduced if property rights are defined before the compensation issue arises. The fact that courts are theoretically asked to define and enforce property rights simulta-

---

40 * * * Takings doctrine is superficially structured so that the validity or public nature of governmental purpose is a threshold question. * * * Prevailing judicial attitudes, however, grant extraordinary deference to legislative determinations of public purpose where compensation is awarded. Hawaii Housing Authority v. Midkiff, 467 U.S. 229 (1984), Berman v. Parker, 348 U.S. 26 (1954); City of Oakland v. Oakland Raiders, 32 Cal.3d 60, 646 P.2d 835, 183 Cal. Rptr. 673 (1982); Poletown Neighborhood Council v. City of Detroit, 410 Mich. 616, 304 N.W.2d 455 (1981). * * * Accordingly, a landowner would have great difficulty preventing a compensated seizure if the only objection was that the land would be used for public tributes. * * *

41 The appellation "positivism" is used to evoke the central difficulty of any legal theory that defines law as the commands of the sovereign. * * *

neously is unimportant because this will almost never occur in fact. Instead, courts will first set the rules by which the conduct of private actors is governed and then require the government to pay compensation when public needs demand that the rules be changed. This vision of property as formally stabilizing entitlements so as to permit investment and exchange closely parallels the guiding spirit of neo-classical economics, hence the name market model.

* * *

Again, however * * * markets depend heavily on the hazy differentiation between settled and unresolved legal issues. Consider the problems for the market model posed by a constitutional challenge to a land use regulation alleged to be overly burdensome. One explication of the market model suggests that, because the land was not formally restricted prior to the challenged ordinance, the rules have changed and compensation is required. This approach searches for settled law consistent with the underlying notion that everything is permitted unless explicitly forbidden. It has the market model's advantage of preventing the government from using its power of definition to its own benefit. But it is untenable in practice. This version of the market model would require compensation whenever the government restricted land use or any other previously unregulated activity. Accordingly, it has been repeatedly rejected by the nation's courts.

* * *

III. TAKINGS' LESSONS

* * *

The point here * * * is not to offer a solution to the takings dilemma. Indeed, were an "answer" proposed, many readers would * * * rush * * * to identify the numerous flaws that any programmatic suggestions would no doubt entail. More important, * * * physicalist and market models of property are built deeply into the fabric of our thought and our law. It would be naive and arrogant to believe that the conflicts between them could somehow be immediately transcended if we simply thought hard enough about the problem. Finally, any well-crafted approach to the takings clause would require not only a theory of property and a theory of what constitutes unfair individual sacrifice, but also a theory of constitutional law that explained the proper role of judges in enforcing the ambiguous guarantees within the Bill of Rights. The development of such a theory, however, is well beyond the scope of this Article.

But the absence of a magic bullet that would somehow make the takings problem go away does not leave us without conclusions or direction. We know first that we should be suspicious of so-called unifying answers to the takings controversy, and we should be suspicious in a particular way. Unified theories must be carefully scrutinized to determine the extent to which they rely on one model of property at the expense of another. We know further that appeals to generalized concepts like "fairness" run the risk of simply reproducing our deep-seated conflicts rather than moving us toward a desirably flexible approach. In addition, we have reason to believe that the takings controversy would benefit from judicial efforts to identify substantive components that are contained within the notion of "property" deserving of constitutional protection. The hope is that the current multi-factor test might be supplemented with a vision of the values property serves in a democratic republic.

Ultimately, however, the takings clause poses an almost imponderable question. How can the same government which is to protect the property rights of the citizenry be charged with creating and altering those rights? The takings clause is designed to remind us of this question and never to allow the government to act without examining whether indeed it has gone "too far." In this sense defining the takings question is itself "the answer" and a detailed understanding of the riddles the question poses is our best protection against both majoritarian tyranny and the illegitimate claims of the economically entrenched.

A. THE MISGUIDED QUEST FOR UNIFYING THEORIES

The Court's inability to move beyond ad hoc inquiry and the undeniable difficulty of reconciling the Court's takings cases have provided an irresistible challenge to scholars, who seek to impose order upon this chaos. Many have attempted to find an overarching test, model, or theory that would describe how the Court has or, more boldly, should resolve controversies under the takings clause.[341]

[341] *See, e.g.,* R. EPSTEIN, TAKINGS: PRIVATE PROPERTY AND THE POWER OF EMINENT DOMAIN (1985); Costonis, *Presumptive and Per Se Takings: A Decisional Model for the Taking Issue*, 58 N.Y.U. L. REV. 465 (1983); Humbach, *A Unifying Theory for the Just-Compensation Cases: Takings, Regulation and Public Use*, 34 RUTGERS L. REV. 243 (1982);

These efforts to find a "unifying" approach have deeply enriched our collective understanding of the takings problem. This strategy is doomed, however, to at least partial failure.

Andrea Peterson, in her recent insightful and provocative study of the takings clause,[342] argued that the Court has tended to deny compensation whenever the government has advanced a plausible claim that new restrictions on a particular use of property stem from the public's belief that the use is morally wrong. Thus, laws banning liquor sales are essentially upheld because the Court could accept that the public finds such sales morally repugnant. In contrast, the Coastal Commission's actions in *Nollan* were unconstitutional because the public does not find moral fault with building a private beach house. Cases like *Penn Central* are difficult because the public may or may not believe that it would be wrong to destroy a landmark in pursuit of profit. Overall, Professor Peterson concludes that the moral justification for the government's conduct is at the core of a "unified set of principles" the Court uses to resolve takings cases.

Although Professor Peterson clearly expressed the caveat that she intended a descriptive rather than a normative account of the takings decisions, many may find that her formulation merely restated rather than advanced the question. If the key issue in takings cases is whether the individual has been called upon to make an unfair sacrifice to the collective, Professor Peterson has merely suggested that a sacrifice is not unfair if the public believes a citizen would be wrong not to make it. What little she says about how the public is to determine what conduct is morally wrong only adds to the puzzle. She not only grants the public authority to condemn conduct that contradicts preexisting norms but also to change those norms at any time. Thus, a rent control ordinance would seem to be an unconstitutional taking under her theory because the public does not really believe it is wrong to charge market rents. However, Professor Peterson can defend rent control through her notion of "civic obligation," which holds that citizens have an obligation to make special sacrifices to maintain the community. She thus avoids the extreme conclusions of scholars like Richard Epstein by giving the public permission to find anything (or nothing) morally wrong. On this view, Professor Peterson leaves us in almost the same position from which we started.

Professor Peterson's approach is subtle and powerful, however, despite her inability to limit the public's judgments of wrongdoing and her broader unwillingness to embrace a normative framework. She has devised a sophisticated version of the sequentialist (or market) model that she hopes will subdue the takings question. Professor Peterson envisions the public first forming a judgment concerning whether a particular use of property is morally wrong. This judgment is manifested through operation of the legislative branch and is largely independent of constitutional law. Then, only after this judgment has been made, the Court determines whether the legislature is acting to implement the public's value judgments. In this way, the positivism problem disappears, because the Court is no longer responsible for any tough decisions concerning the nature of property. It merely reaffirms the community's pre-existing value choices.

Like all market model solutions, Professor Peterson's approach gains considerable stability from reliance on preexisting values determined outside the Court. This approach has enormous appeal for a Court wishing to escape the burden of defining core constitutional values. Judicial disagreements under Peterson's system do not hinge on whether the Constitution protects a particular right, such as the right to charge market rent. Instead, judges will focus the debate only on whether the public that adopted rent control "reasonably believed" that landlords would be wrong to charge anything above the new rents. At the same time, however, Professor Peterson avoids traditional market-model rigidity because the preexisting values she relies on are not fixed legal rules but rather the ever-changing mores of the community. Thus, her approach leaves courts free to approve or condemn a wide range of government practices simply by offering differing accounts of community norms.

Professor Peterson's sophisticated market-model strategy appears to offer us the best of both worlds. The Court gains the appearance of objectivity by

---

Peterson, *The Takings Clause: In Search of Underlying Principles Part I—A Critique of Current Takings Clause Doctrine,* 77 CALIF. L. REV. 1301 (1989); Peterson, *The Takings Clause: In Search of Underlying Principles Part II—Takings as Intentional Deprivations of Property Without Moral Justification,* 78 CALIF. L. REV. 55 (1990); Sax, *Takings and the Police Power,* 74 YALE L. J. 36 (1964); Sax, *Takings, Private Property and Public Rights,* 81 YALE L. J. 149 (1971). * * *

[342] Peterson, Part I, *supra* note 341; Peterson, Part II, *supra* note 341.

looking outside itself to find the relevant standards to define an unconstitutional taking. These objective standards are formed prior to constitutional adjudication and thus satisfy the crucial sequential element of separating the constitutional decisions from the definition of fundamental property rights. At the same time, because community standards conform to something approaching a legal scholar's idea of property within constitutional adjudication, the Court under Professor Peterson's scheme can escape the blatant arbitrariness of relying on physicalism to resolve takings disputes. As a bonus, the Court gets a framework flexible enough to support a variety of outcomes. No wonder the Court's decisions can be persuasively described as fitting within the Peterson framework. Indeed, Professor Peterson's work may be the most compelling descriptive account to date.

The problem is that taken normatively, Professor Peterson's account, like all versions of the market model, underestimates the difficulty of sequentially separating what are supposedly independent decisions. She would have the public decide when it is wrong for citizens to make certain uses of property and then have the Court scrutinize legislative enforcement of these public value judgments. But upon what basis is the public to make such decisions? Either the public gains knowledge on the morality of property usage from some source other than the Constitution and the courts, or judicial decisions will ultimately play a key role in shaping public attitudes. In the former hypothetical case, a Court that gave free reign to an unguided public would run the risk of losing sight of any constitutional norms. After all, the takings clause cannot serve as a protection of individual rights if the courts defer to mercurial majority beliefs. It is much more likely that Court decisions will significantly determine what the public believes is right to do with one's property. If this is true, then the Peterson account may lead to a circular argument. For now, Court deference to public sentiment will in significant part be Court deference to its own decisions of an earlier era. Thus, the Court will have abdicated its role as articulator of public values in exchange for adherence to its own earlier pronouncements. The positivism problem will have reappeared.

Professor Sax's equally thoughtful effort at a unified description of takings clause jurisprudence runs the opposite risk of relying on physicalism at the expense of market ideas. Sax's initial perception is that even a typical nuisance suit between neighbors has takings implications.[357] If the court rules for the plaintiff who alleges nuisance, the defendant can argue that the judicial ruling constitutes a taking. Alternatively, a ruling that no nuisance exists leaves the plaintiff with the plausible takings argument. Sax notes, however, that traditional takings law is unlikely to be sympathetic to either side because courts adjudicating nuisance disputes are typically seen as establishing property rights rather than taking them from one side or the other. Thus, Sax asks the obvious question: Can the principle that immunizes judicial nuisance rulings from close takings scrutiny be extended to sanction a wider array of government conduct?

Sax's answer is that many government regulations share a common thread with judicial nuisance determinations. He notes that just as courts use nuisance law to prevent one party's use of land from having adverse "spillover" effects on the land of a neighbor, so government regulations, for example, those prohibiting pollution, restrict owners from adversely affecting the rights of the public as a whole. Thus, Sax concludes that any government regulation designed to prevent "spillover" effects is not an unconstitutional taking, even if it deprives an owner of 100% of that owner's property value. The problem, of course, is in defining "spillover effects."

Sax's examples suggest that the key determinant is whether the government is barring a property owner from a use of the property that will tangibly affect what occurs outside the owner's boundaries. Thus, a strip mining regulation that prevents a mining company from causing subsidence of nearby property is not a taking because, if the miners are left unchecked, their actions will "spillover" to nearby land. In contrast, a government edict that an owner must provide land for an airport runway is a Saxian taking because the owner might wish to use the land for other purposes, such as a personal residence, that would have no direct impact outside the physical boundaries.

At first glance, there is significant irony in Sax's attempt to limit government's power by focusing on "spillover" effects. The obvious physicalism inherent in the "spillover" metaphor appears in the same article where Sax wants to redraw the line between "mine" and "thine" so as to remove the emphasis placed on physical boundaries. Viewed through the

---

[357] Sax, *Takings, Private Property and Public Rights*, *supra* note 341.

lens of the positivism problem and our property models, however, Sax's solution is entirely understandable.

Sax's goal is to use the government's power to define property in the first instance as a wedge to expand its power to engage in what is commonly thought of as regulation. He relies then on the market model's familiar inability to specify a time at which property rights are established and after which further government actions constitute change. Sax correctly points out that the market model cannot work if all existing rules establish constitutionally protected property. Sax wants the Court to look not only at the explicit legal rules in effect at the time of the challenged regulation but also at an unspecified background rule that prohibits any property owner from using land to harm another. However, if harm is defined too broadly, this approach threatens to undo the market model so completely that the notion of private property is called into question.

Sax, then, must search for a definition of harm that is broad enough to permit the government wide latitude to regulate private land uses but not so broad as to permit the government to say, for example, that a landowner's decision not to build a post office on his or her land harms the neighbors who need one. Sax's concept of spillover effects is precisely tailored to fit this demand. It is extraordinarily broad in that Sax wants to allow the government to prevent any use of property that will interfere with the legitimate uses of neighbors or the public. Thus, Sax would not require compensation for landowners located near a naval gunnery range even if the noise rendered the private land virtually uninhabitable. His reasoning is that the government is only making use of its own resource (a commonly held bay) and is not responsible for the impact on adjacent lands. At the same time, however, Sax would not allow the navy to store goods on shoreland adjacent to the bay because that would involve using another citizen's land rather than merely the government's own resources.

Such primitive physicalism, however, undermines Sax's own crucial insights concerning the interdependence of property uses. First, there is only a very small correlation between whether an owner's intended activity will affect what others do within their boundaries and whether the claimant's activity is illegitimate. On one hand, Sax's position would seem to grant government unbounded authority to prohibit landowners from building. Neighbors could argue that any construction would block the view from their adjacent land and thus that all construction would have "spillover effects." On the other hand, Sax's position would seem to call for compensation in *Loretto*[369] because the building owner would presumably have nonspillover uses for the space occupied by the cable box, and thus the government could not rely on its power to adjudicate conflicts among neighbors. It seems doubtful that Sax would wish to endorse either position.

But Sax is trapped in the position of using physicalism to differentiate spillover from nonspillover effects precisely because he seeks an "objective" way to protect private property from his own powerful attack. Sax relies on the difficulty of separating the government's power to define property from some supposedly more limited power to regulate it. He wants the power of definition to include any instance when the government is arguably mediating between conflicting uses rather than imposing a specific use on an unwilling citizen. The problem, as Sax recognizes, is that any government regulation can be described as accommodating conflict. An ordinance requiring that land be kept vacant to limit neighborhood congestion certainly fits this characterization.

* * *

Ultimately what Sax gains in perceived objectivity, he loses in plausibility. Sax's limited definition of property's core does not correspond to whether a citizen seeks protection for illegitimate activity. More important, he embraces the physicalist definition of spillovers at the expense of any constitutional protection for those who rely on existing rules. He seeks to persuade us that the government can change any rule at all, provided it can describe newly prohibited conduct as creating a conflict that restricts uses within other boundaries. At the same time, government must keep hands off any planned use, no matter how trivial or expected the loss, as long as the use will not bleed across physical property lines. Beyond his desire for a familiar spot to anchor some notion of property against his own positivist tidal wave, however, Sax offers little to convince us that he has located the correct dividing line. In short, Sax again offers physicalism as an alternative to the traditional market model. But his ideas must be rejected, because of both physicalism's flaws and the market model's strengths.

---

[369] Loretto v. Teleprompter Manhattan CATV Corp., 458 U.S. 419 (1982).

Finally, consider Professor Humbach's effort to unify takings clause jurisprudence.[371] He begins with the classic lawyer's approach of dividing the prerogatives of ownership into mutually exclusive categories. In the first group, which he calls *rights*, Humbach places the legal causes of action available to owners to prevent others from interfering with their property. The prototypical example is the right to prevent a neighbor from trespassing upon one's land. In contrast, Humbach's second set of property's attributes consists of the *freedoms* available to owners to make use of their own property. Here Humbach refers to the freedom to build upon one's land or use it for particular activities.

Humbach builds upon his right/freedom distinction to reach a seemingly simple formula. When the government takes rights, as it does in the case of the typical condemnation of land for a post office, the government must pay just compensation. But when the government limits freedoms, as it does when it zones land to prohibit more than one home per acre, no compensation is necessary. Humbach defends this formula both as a descriptive account of the Court's actual practice and as a necessary accommodation to the practicalities of modern government.

The problems with the right/freedom distinction, however, are numerous and severe. First, there is the difficulty of maintaining the distinction in the face of multiple characterizations of the same events. Thus, Humbach classifies the property owner's ability to exclude others as a right because it involves the owner's authority to invoke the power of the state to prevent others from acting. Surely, however, the owner might also claim a right (as opposed to a freedom) to build, if the issue is whether a neighbor may physically interfere with the planned construction. Second, there is the problem that the distinction may not answer any of the hard questions. Humbach concedes, for example, that sometimes a restriction on a freedom may be so great as to amount in substance to a deprivation of right. Indeed, he argues that the overlap between loss of rights and mere deprivation of freedoms is the genesis of the "too far" test. But if only a "too far" test can meaningfully distinguish between loss of right and deprivation of freedom, one must wonder whether the distinction has advanced our understanding. Finally, and most importantly, the right/freedom distinction does not correspond to the issues normally at stake in takings litigation. Thus, a citizen can be unexpectedly and severely damaged by the loss of a freedom, as in the case of an outright ban on construction, whereas the loss of a right can be trivial, as in a case like *Loretto*. It is not surprising then, that the Court has not moved toward explicit adoption of Professor Humbach's suggestion.

What is noteworthy, however, is the extent to which Professor Humbach is correct in offering the right/freedom distinction as a rough account of Supreme Court precedent. Humbach has combined the market and physicalist models in a way that will tend to point them in the same direction. The trick lies in the familiar pattern whereby the preexisting rules at the core of the market model themselves often spring from physicalist roots. Thus, Humbach persuasively advocates compensation for the loss of the right to stop neighbors from crossing boundaries precisely because it is clearly already settled that a landowner may go to court to prevent trespass. Trespass rules, in turn, are themselves likely to be settled precisely because they rely on the physicalist distinctions at the core of a basic private property system. In contrast, prior to zoning, the legal system is unlikely to have carefully considered what an owner might build. Absent a physical conflict between uses, courts would have had little reason to adjudicate the limits on landowner freedom. Thus, Humbach can allow the government freely to alter permissible uses without creating as direct a challenge to preexisting rules. In short, Humbach offers a distinction between rights and freedoms that appeals to preexisting rules while simultaneously protecting physicalist rights such as the right to exclude.

The easy congruence Humbach finds between physicalism and the market model, however, is largely an illusion. Moreover, it is an illusion that obscures the values at stake in takings controversies. The problem is that Humbach's right/freedom distinction cannot be linked to any recognizable purpose of the takings clause, once the distinction is considered in light of the broad range of situations that raise takings issues. The key is the lack of a readily available, noncontroversial method for establishing the rights that the Constitution protects. Consider, for example, Congress's passage of the antitrust laws. These laws clearly restricted freedoms that business owners formerly had to conduct business in certain ways. Humbach, however, would see no taking issue because only so-called freedoms were lost. Now suppose, however, that Congress chooses to repeal

---

[371] Humbach, *supra* note 341.

the antitrust laws. If a small business owner loses a right to sue larger competitors, who engage in predatory pricing, this might force the small owner out of business. Here, under Humbach's terminology, the small business owner has a stronger case for compensation since that person has lost a right to prevent others from acting. The crucial question then is why the repeal of the antitrust laws evokes greater constitutional sympathy than their original enactment. In more general terms, why do conscious governmental decisions to structure economic life not raise the same sorts of takings issues as decisions to alter an already recognized structure?

* * *

In the end, Humbach's right/freedom approach breaks down for the same reason that all attempts to find a unified approach to takings inevitably fail. Humbach wishes to completely separate the supposedly private law process of the creation of rights from the public law process of the constitutional protection of already existing rights. The appeal of Humbach's position lies in a convincing effort to find an overlap between that market-like vision and property's physicalist roots. But because the overlap between market and physicalist ideas is not complete, and because both are deeply entrenched as our collective solution to the positivist dilemma, Humbach's approach cannot ultimately succeed. As long as we remember that the takings problem is not merely a problem of which already-created rights deserve protection but also a problem of deciding how and which rights have been created, a unified approach to takings law will never work. We should all stop trying to find one.

B. THE INCOMPLETENESS OF GENERALIZATIONS

The most tempting alternative to unified theories is the attempt to capture the conflicting strands of takings jurisprudence within broad formulations of principle that point toward relevant considerations without necessarily determining or predicting outcomes. Professor Michelman's classic work represents the pinnacle of this approach, and he has already so successfully described its strengths and weaknesses that little will be added here.[383] It is worth recalling some of what Michelman has taught us, however, so as to avoid an overly optimistic attitude toward general, abstract solutions. More important, our experience with a Michelman-influenced Court fully vindicates Michelman's suspicions concerning the judicial tendency to translate general formulations into mechanistic rules. Indeed, as this Article demonstrates, the Court's attraction to formal models of property has enabled it to employ a so-called flexible, ad hoc test without confronting its own role in assessing the fairness of particular governmental actions.

Michelman identified two general considerations at the heart of takings jurisprudence. First, Michelman focused on a utilitarian conception of private property that excludes capricious redistributions as inconsistent with the secure expectations necessary for investment and initiative. At first glance, this perspective might suggest a complete ban on uncompensated governmental interference with private property. But Michelman rightly explained that a committed utilitarian would not want to block public projects when the efficiency gains of those projects are sufficient to outweigh the costs to uncompensated victims but still less than the settlement costs involved in reimbursing those harmed by the project. Thus, Michelman argued that utilitarianism suggested a practice whereby compensation would be awarded if the demoralization costs of failing to compensate exceed the settlement costs of arranging for compensation.[387]

Second, Michelman suggested that judicial compensation practice might be explained in terms of fairness to the victim. Thus, extrapolating from Rawls's theory of justice, Michelman asks courts to imagine themselves in the position of a patient person suffering the impact of an uncompensated redistribution. Would it be possible to convince this person that it was fair for him or her to bear the project's costs using the argument that in the long run, he or she, or persons similarly situated, would benefit from similar projects that would have been blocked by a stringent compensation rule? If so, then compensation need not be awarded.

Michelman's approach provides the best explanation for the fact that the Court often permits the

---

[383] Michelman, *Property, Utility, and Fairness: Comments on the Ethical Foundations of "Just Compensation" Law*, 80 HARV. L. REV. 1165 (1967).

[387] Michelman defined demoralization costs as including not only the costs to the victims of a particular governmental project but also costs to others resulting from the knowledge that their property was less secure against governmental redistribution. Moreover, he was careful to make clear that no project would go forward if both settlement costs and demoralization costs were greater than gains from the project.

government to diminish citizens' holdings without paying compensation. Not surprisingly, conservatives have been arguing with Michelman about this ever since.[389] What everyone tends to forget is Michelman's own well-expressed caveats concerning the possibility of judicial application of general standards of utility and fairness. He worried, for example, that they may be "inescapably vague" and that "fairness as a standard may simply be too difficult for courts to grasp and apply successfully."

What we can now add, with 20/20 hindsight, is precisely the way in which standards like utility and fairness have turned out to be vague. We can also describe the content that courts will likely impart to such standards in an effort to conform simultaneously to the need for clear judicial guidelines and the desire for just outcomes. It will come as no surprise that market and physicalist ideas dominate our understanding of utility and fairness within the context of takings law.

Consider first the root of Michelman's utilitarian description of compensation practice. To oversimplify, Michelman suggests that courts have, and should, award compensation when the demoralization costs of not compensating are high. However, courts cannot measure demoralization costs without a baseline notion of property against which to judge how severely expectations have been disrupted. Michelman suggests two such notions. First, demoralization costs will be high when the citizens perceive that the government has physically invaded or actually taken an entire parcel of property or other tangible item. Second, demoralization costs will be high when the government alters explicit legal rules that have given rise to "sharply crystallized" expectations. For example, if a new zoning ordinance negates the effect of a previously issued building permit, the landowner will have a stronger compensation claim than if the same ordinance merely prevents the owner from proceeding with future building plans. The correspondence between Michelman's baselines and the physicalist and market models is clear.

Michelman attributed these two cases of high demoralization to aspects of human psychology. However, that psychology is itself a product of a collective struggle to create a concept of property that fits into a judicially enforceable package. Why are demoralization costs high when physical space is invaded or an entire item taken rather than when any large loss is inflicted? The answer lies partly in citizens' efforts to make sense of their holdings in terms of a conceptual model they can apply to many different situations. Physical boundaries form the most basic, comprehensible model. Why are people particularly upset when government disrupts "sharply crystallized" expectations? Again, part of the answer is that the government's breaking of explicit promises directly conflicts with the idea that some allocations of property are already decided such that the government is not free to reconsider them without compensating those harmed by the change. Thus demoralization costs are high when government departs from the market model.

The bottom line is that judicial focus on general considerations like utility runs the risk of merely duplicating society's existing ideas about property. If those ideas are themselves confused and contradictory, as this Article has suggested, then judicial evaluation of takings cases is unlikely to escape the confusion. As we have seen, the Court's application of its * * * test has been riddled with appeals to competing models of property. But this is exactly what one would predict, if the judicial task is to decide when compensation is due based on society's general perceptions of which uncompensated losses are demoralizing and which uncompensated takings are unfair. How precisely are citizens to know when to be demoralized or justly aggrieved if they do not assess their own experience in light of a model of property that applies universally rather than to their situation alone? If this is so, the Court seems to be the social institution best positioned to interact with the citizenry while providing guidance through construction of its own normative view of property. In the end, the greatest danger of appeals to general considerations is that they may allow the Court to forget that part of its constitutional role.

* * *

C. THE GROUNDS FOR HOPE

The real question then is whether the riddles posed by our allegiance to conflicting views of property can be escaped at all. The most obvious improvement would involve coming to terms with the absence of a "set formula" for takings decisions so that our current state of affairs need no longer pejoratively be judged "ad hoc." Indeed, given the complexities described here, the Court already deserves credit for its willingness to approach takings controversies on a case-by-case basis. As we have

[389] *See, e.g.*, R. EPSTEIN, *supra* note 341.

seen, however, particularistic calculations unguided by normative goals run a substantial risk of depending on the precise global theories that case-by-case analysis was meant to reject. Accordingly, the task facing future judges and commentators is to attempt a richer description of takings controversies that will more directly address the competing values at stake.

Although there is hardly space here to attempt such a description, it may be a fitting conclusion to consider two familiar strands of property theory that hold promise in light of the demonstrated inadequacies of the physicalist and market models. The first would involve judicial specification of concrete aspects of human existence that the takings clause is designed to protect. Thus, rather than embarking upon global protection of all physical objects, courts might note certain objects, such as one's home, that a constitution would sensibly mark out as deserving of special protection.[405] A second, related strategy would entail judicial separation of those aspects of private property deemed essential to the creation of a community and those an existing community would adopt as useful to further other purposes. Pursuing this strategy, courts might seek to ascertain and protect the amount and types of property citizens need to participate meaningfully in a self-governing society.

The ingredient linking these strategies is that they depend upon identifying constitutional norms at what might be called an intermediate level of generality. Candid assessment of takings jurisprudence requires us to doubt the possibility of capturing a universal model of property that would resolve the positivism problem. Nor can we easily retreat to analysis of particular circumstances without a guide to which circumstances point in which direction. The strategies suggested here seek to create a doctrinal framework that helps to identify, but does not determine, when private claims to economic stability fit within the Constitution's contemplated safeguards.

The problems with this enterprise are grave and come from both directions. On one hand, it is extraordinarily difficult to provide enough content to an abstract formulation so that it does not merely restate the problem. The Court's reliance on expectations analysis demonstrates this. At the same time, to the extent the Court openly attempts to develop a normative theory of constitutionally protected property, it risks challenges to its underlying legitimacy as an applier, not maker, of law.

Consider first the strengths and weaknesses of a substantive standard that arises out of the concrete needs of affected citizens. Suppose, for example, that the Court found the real lesson of the takings clause to be that citizens who have managed to carve out ownership of a place to live should not be deprived of their homes without receiving the resources necessary to find similar quarters and the chance to reconnect with the community that only a home can provide. In more abstract terms, this might be described as a constitutional right to shelter. What it would do for takings jurisprudence is to place the Court squarely in the role of giving substantive content to the constitution's vague command that "property" not be taken without just compensation.

The initial legitimacy of protecting personal residences above other well-recognized forms of property would, of course, be open to question. Since the Constitution does not differentiate among kinds of property, why can the Court? By now, however, this first-stage objection is insignificant. The entire twentieth-century history of takings clause jurisprudence involves judicial efforts to distinguish protected from unprotected economic rights, and the proposed emphasis on individual homes would be merely one more chapter in that history.

A second question is whether there is any basis at all for protecting selected substantive rights, like a right to shelter. Here a detailed account would involve inquiry into precisely those situations the framers and ratifiers had in mind when enacting the takings clause. A safe guess, however, is that the paradigm case of land taken for a public project often involved loss of a family farm or homestead, and that in any event the image of a dispossessed family has always affected the rhetoric surrounding protection for private property. The point, of course, is not that there is a clear case for special constitutional protection for the loss of a private home. Rather, the emphasis here is on the advantages of asking this type of question.

A takings jurisprudence that differentiated among types of property based on the extent to which that property met core human needs would involve an explicit attempt to answer the question that everyone, including the Court, sees at the heart of the takings problem. If the takings clause is about preventing the government from demanding unfair

---

[405] *See generally*, Radin, *Property and Personhood*, 34 STAN. L. REV. 957 (1982) * * *.

sacrifice, the Court has no choice but to be involved in defining what is fair. The only question is whether the Court continues to pretend that it can articulate principles universal enough to defy dissent, or whether it will instead attempt to defend certain aspects of property as more central to the idea of constitutional protection. Perhaps the most significant advantage of the latter approach is that it would directly focus disagreements on the competing values at stake in takings controversies. Moreover, providing increased protection for selected property rights, such as a right to shelter, would bring some of the traditional benefits of permitting the citizenry to guide behavior, and it would enable us to predict more accurately what the Court is likely to do.

Imagine the *Nollan* case, for example, being fought out in Court on the issue of whether the Nollans' contemplated beach house was sufficiently like a primary residence such that California's ability to regulate construction should be subject to strict constitutional limits. Unlike any current formulation of takings doctrine, this approach would consider whether the Nollans planned to live in the house all year or whether this is a vacation retreat. Should this not be a crucial factor in determining whether the Nollans are being asked to sacrifice too much for collective welfare? Moreover, the public would learn more about the nature of constitutionally protected property from an opinion that defended the Nollans' right to build in this particular context, as opposed to one that simply assumed that right as part of an undefined political philosophy.

Ultimately, however, a judicial effort to derive property law from a set of core human needs will prove empty and ungrounded unless it can be linked to a political theory concerning the role property serves in constituting the republic. There may be many reasons why people need shelter more than speculative profits, or why a personal residence belongs high on the list of desired resources. The constitutional question, however, is why the takings clause should be interpreted to place courts in the position of making special efforts to prevent the other branches from taking a person's home without paying compensation. Thus, it is necessary to identify a political (that is, group-focused) as opposed to a personal (that is, individual-focused) definition of what is meant by an unfair sacrifice.

It is not difficult to discern that the crucial political question involved in evaluating constitutional claims to property is whether it is possible to identify the aspects of property that people need to make the society work, as opposed to those society grants so as to work *better*. One theory along these lines might stress the role of certain aspects of property, such as a place to live and other essential items, as the economic ingredients a citizen needs to participate freely in collective affairs. Land ownership was once a qualification for voting, and it is crucial to remember that the takings clause protects political as well as economic rights. Accordingly, courts have reason in every takings case to ask whether the government's power to alter economic rights risks depriving a citizen of the economic means to form independent political judgments, or worse still to strip political opponents of the wherewithal to combat government policy.

The advantage of this "republican" approach is that it again forces courts to return to the question of what values underlie the constitutional protection of property. Once more, courts can abandon the search for a unified definition of property and explicitly adopt a multi-factor approach that seeks to define what constitutes an unfair sacrifice. Now, however, unfair sacrifices may be judged by evaluating the extent to which government policy threatens to take economic resources that the citizen physically possesses, that the rules protect, *and* that the citizen needs to be part of the political community. In other words, the protected baseline may be set by constitutional norms as well as by independent visions of property law.

It will be no easier to establish the content of republican norms than it might be to identify those aspects of property that correspond to core human needs. Who is to say what level of property the Constitution protects as a mechanism for ensuring independent political dialogue? The point is that as long as the Court persists in avoiding the task of articulating some substantive vision of property, it will remain trapped in the hopeless vacillation between inadequate models that this Article has described in detail. Moreover, the prospect of judicial articulation of property's normative content holds a significant additional advantage. The question of which property interests the Constitution protects will become more explicitly linked to substantive discussions concerning the nation's distribution of resources. A Court that explicitly recognizes its power to approve or disapprove legislative alterations of the status quo based on a normative choice among different models of property can hardly pretend to be neutral concerning the nature of its choice.

In the end, of course, the takings clause is an unlikely source of inspiration for an inquiry into society's appropriate distribution of resources. The takings clause comes into play only after some distribution is in place, and courts are asked whether government may disturb that distribution. Any sophisticated analysis of distributional questions would thus involve an inquiry into the law that creates property rights as well as the law that takes them away. But if this exhaustive study has proven anything, it is that nowhere in our jurisprudence do we get a better look at society's struggle to define an overarching vision of property than we do in takings law. Takings law shows us the models of private property that capture our imagination and that inform our collective vision concerning the nation's distribution of entitlements. It shows us that our society defines property in many different ways and that we are deeply divided over which kinds of property the Constitution protects.

What has united us to this point is the goal of maintaining a society where a majority vote to demand individual sacrifice is not always sufficient justification to demand individual compliance. What each generation must decide for itself, therefore, is which kinds of sacrifice constitute the price of civilization and which sacrifices are themselves uncivilized. The framers and ratifiers passed on the takings clause as a permanent reminder of this fundamental question. In the end, it is this question that is the "answer" to the takings controversy. The problem with our current law is not its failure to answer this timeless question. Instead, the search for a unified answer ironically prevents us from continuing to ask it.

Note

A number of the excerpts in this anthology have taken positions on the value of predictability in legal norms. The famous "ad hoc" statement of Justice Brennan in his majority opinion in *Penn Central* has led to a long debate on the wisdom of seeking well understood rules as opposed to relying upon case-by-case factor analysis. Compare the views on this question taken by Jeremy Paul in the article excerpted just above with those of Jennifer Nedelsky in *Law, Boundaries, and The Bounded Self* [Part II(A)]; Carol Rose in *Crystals and Mud in Property Law* [Part III(C)]; C. Dent Bostick in *Land Title Registration: An English Solution to an American Problem* [Part III(C)]; Susan French in *Perpetuities: Three Essays in Honor of my Father* [Part III(F)]; and Robert Ellickson, in *Alternatives to Zoning: Covenants, Nuisance Rules and Fines as Land Use Controls* [Part IV(B)].

Part IV
Thinking About Property in the Next Century

As the materials in Part II suggested, various theoretical justifications for the existence of property have come under severe attack in this century. By the time Christopher Stone wrote *Should Trees Have Standing?*, excerpted in Part II(D) of this anthology, it was standard fare for academics to state that legal rights and economic value were determined by actions of the state. It is therefore not surprising that debates over how the state should behave have dominated thinking about property in the last two decades.

Some have responded to the historical problems with property as a concept by declaring the very idea to be passé. The first section of this part contains an example of that perspective. Others have attempted to rebuild "property," often by calling upon old concepts and reworking them. Jeremy Paul, for example, returns to republicanism at the end of *The Hidden Structure of Takings Law*, the last article in the prior section of this anthology. Much of the debate surrounding this reconstruction project turns on attitudes toward property and history. That discussion often refers to the work of Robert Nozick and John Rawls. Those who, like Rawls, are willing to disturb the status quo or impose ongoing obligations to share, are quite likely to argue that government has a continuing obligation to redistribute economic goods and services for the benefit of the least well off segments of society. Giving credence to the justness of prior distributions of wealth, as Nozick does, requires a low tolerance for government efforts to redistribute wealth. Materials in the final two sections of the anthology sample the work of Nozick and Rawls, as well as other legal commentary on this debate. For additional materials on the relationships between history and property, *see* Gregory Alexander, *Time and Property in the American Republican Legal Culture*, 66 N.Y.U. L. REV. 273 (1991); John Stick, *Turning Rawls Into Nozick and Back Again*, 81 NW. L. REV. 363 (1987); Margaret Jane Radin, *Time, Possession, and Alienation*, 64 WASH. U. L. Q. 739 (1986); Richard Epstein, *Past and Future: The Temporal Dimension in the Law of Property,* 64 WASH. U. L. Q. 667 (1986).

A. The Death of "Property"

Thomas C. Grey, *The Disintegration of Property*, in PROPERTY: NOMOS XXII (J. Roland Pennock & John W. Chapman, eds.) 69-85 (1980)*

I

In the English-speaking countries today, the conception of property held by the specialist (the lawyer or economist) is quite different from that held by the ordinary person. Most people, including most specialists in their unprofessional moments, conceive of property as *things* that are *owned* by *persons*. To own property is to have exclusive control of something—to be able to use it as one wishes, to sell it, give it away, leave it idle, or destroy it. Legal restraints on the free use of one's property are conceived as departures from an ideal conception of full ownership.[1]

By contrast, the theory of property rights held by the modern specialist tends both to dissolve the notion of ownership and to eliminate any necessary connection between property rights and things. Consider ownership first. The specialist fragments the robust unitary conception of ownership into a more shadowy "bundle of rights." Thus, a thing can be owned by more than one person, in which case it becomes necessary to focus on the particular limited rights each of the co-owners has with respect to the thing. Further, the notion that full ownership includes rights to do as you wish with what you own suggests that you might sell off *particular aspects* of your control—rights to certain uses, to profits from the thing, and so on. Finally, rights of use, profit, and the like can be parceled out along a temporal dimension as well—you might sell your control over your property for tomorrow to one person, for the next day to another, and so on.

Not only can ownership rights be subdivided, they can even be made to disappear as if by magic, if we postulate full freedom of disposition in the owner. Consider the convenient legal institution of the trust. Yesterday A owned Blackacre; among his rights of ownership was the legal power to leave the land idle, even though developing it would bring a good income. Today A puts Blackacre in trust, conveying it to B (the trustee) for the benefit of C (the beneficiary). Now no one any longer has the legal power to use the land uneconomically or to leave it idle—that part of the rights of ownership is neither in A nor B nor C, but has disappeared. As between B and C, who owns Blackacre? Lawyers say B has the legal and C the equitable ownership, but upon reflection the question seems meaningless: what is important is that we be able to specify what B and C can legally do with respect to the land.

The same point can be made with respect to fragmentation of ownership generally. When a full owner of a thing begins to sell off various of his rights over it—the right to use it for this purpose tomorrow, for that purpose next year, and so on—at what point does he cease to be the owner, and who then owns the thing? You can say that each one of many right holders owns it to the extent of the right, or you can say that no one owns it. Or you can say, as we still tend to do, in vestigial deference to the lay conception of property, that some conventionally designated rights constitute "ownership." The issue is seen as one of terminology; nothing significant turns on it.

What, then, of the idea that property rights must be rights in things? Perhaps we no longer need a notion of ownership, but surely property rights are a distinct category from other legal rights, in that they pertain to things. But this suggestion cannot withstand analysis either; most property in a modern

---

*Reprinted by permission of New York University Press from *Property* (NOMOS XXII), edited by J. Roland Pennock and John W. Chapman. Copyright © 1980 by New York University.

[1] *See* the excellent explication of the "ordinary" conception of property in Bruce A. Ackerman, *Private Property and the Constitution* (New Haven and London, 1977), pp. 97-100, 113-67. * * *

capitalist economy is intangible. Consider the common forms of wealth: shares of stock in corporations, bonds, various kinds of commercial paper, bank accounts, insurance policies—not to mention more arcane intangibles such as trademarks, patents, copyrights, franchises, and business goodwill.

In our everyday language, we tend to speak of these rights as if they attached to things. Thus we "deposit our money in the bank," as if we were putting a thing in a place; but really we are creating a complex set of abstract claims against an abstract legal institution. We are told that as insurance policy holders we "own a piece of the rock;" but we really have other abstract claims against another abstract institution. We think of our share of stock in Megabucks Corporation as part ownership in the Megabucks factory outside town; but really the Megabucks board of directors could sell the factory and go into another line of business and we would still have the same claims on the same abstract corporation.

Property rights cannot any longer be characterized as "rights of ownership" or as "rights in things" by specialists in property. What, then, *is* their special characteristic? How do property rights differ from rights generally—from human rights or personal rights or rights to life or liberty, say? Our specialists and theoreticians have no answer; or rather, they have a multiplicity of widely differing answers, related only in that they bear some association or analogy, more or less remote, to the common notion of property as ownership of things.

Let me briefly list a number of present usages of the term property in law, legal theory, and economics.

1. The law of property for law teachers and law students typically is the whole body of law concerned with the use of land, title registration and transfer, the financing of real estate transactions, the law of landlord and tenant, public regulation of land use (including zoning and environmental regulation), and public subsidy and provision of low-income housing. The only thing these doctrines have in common with each other is that they concern real estate as distinguished from other aspects of the economy.

2. Lawyers (and some economists) identify property rights with rights *in rem* (rights good against the world), as distinguished from rights *in personam* (rights good against determinate persons). This distinction does not fit closely with popular notions of property; for example, the rights to life, bodily security, and personal liberty protected by criminal laws against murder, assault, and kidnapping are on this account "property rights." Neither the application of the distinction nor its purpose is very clear; for example, *in personam* contract rights shade into property rights as they become freely assignable, and assumable, and as "interference with contractual relations" is recognized as a tort.[4]

3. Some economists seem to adopt, implicitly, a purposive account of property, including among property rights all and only those entitlements whose purpose (in some sense) is to advance allocative efficiency by allowing individuals to reap the benefits and requiring them to bear the costs generated by their activities. Again, on this account rights to life, liberty, and personal security are included within the field of property. On the other hand, legal entitlements to transfer payments, such as are conferred by welfare and social security laws, are presumably excluded.[5]

4. By contrast, some modern legal theorists have stressed that a traditional purpose of private property has been to protect security and independence, and that public law entitlements to social minima serve this purpose in the modern economy, and hence should be considered a "new property."[6] This view has been embodied in the construction the courts have given to the constitutional requirement that persons not be "deprived of . . . property without due process of law." Protections offered to property have been extended to entitlements conferred by, for example, welfare and public education law.[7]

5. Another contrasting view of property is suggested by the prevailing interpretation of another constitutional provision, the prohibition against "taking" private property except for a public purpose and upon the payment of just compensation. Here, the kind of property that can be taken is confined to those conglomerations of rights that, in the popular mind, have been reified into "things" or "pieces of property." Thus, the Supreme Court recently held that designation of Grand Central Station as a historic monument and the consequent prohibition of construction of a skyscraper over the station, did not "take" any property of the landowners—the right to

---

[4] For the *in rem* vs. *in personam* distinction, see, e.g., Felix Cohen, "Dialogue on Private Property," 9 *Rutgers Law Review* 373–74 (Fall 1954).

[5] See, e.g., Richard Posner, *Economic Analysis of Law*, 2d. ed. (Boston and Toronto, 1977), pp. 27–31; * * *.

[6] See Charles A. Reich, "The New Property," 73 *Yale Law Journal* 733 (April 1964).

[7] Goldberg v. Kelly, 397 U.S. 254 (1970); * * *.

use the airspace over the building, an economically valuable entitlement, was not sufficiently thing-like to be subject to the just compensation requirement.[8] (This body of "takings" law, which most nearly corresponds to popular conceptions of property as thing ownership, is difficult to rationalize in the terms of modern legal and economic theory.)

6. Another specialized usage distinguishes between "property" and "liability" rules according to the nature of the sanctions imposed upon their violation. Property rules are enforceable by injunction or criminal sanctions or both—sanctions designed to prevent violation even when it would be cost justified in terms of market valuation. Liability rules are enforced only by the award of money damages, measured by the market valuation of the resources lost to the victim. This conception departs widely from popular usage; thus, a person's ownership of his car, for example, is protected by both liability rules (tort doctrines of conversion and liability for negligent damage to property) and property rules (criminal laws against theft).[10]

The conclusion of all this is that discourse about property has fragmented into a set of discontinuous usages. The more fruitful and useful of these usages are those stipulated by theorists; but these depart drastically from each other and from common speech. Conversely, meanings of "property" in law that cling to their origin in the thing-ownership conception are integrated least successfully into the general doctrinal framework of law, legal theory, and economics. It seems fair to conclude from a glance at the range of current usages that the specialists who design and manipulate the legal structures of the advanced capitalist economies could easily do without using the term "property" at all.

II

It was not always so. At the high point of classical liberal thought, around the end of the eighteenth century, the idea of private property stood at the center of the conceptual scheme of lawyers and political theorists.

* * *

It is not difficult to see how the idea of simple ownership came to dominate classical liberal legal and political thought. First, this conception of property mirrored economic reality to a much greater extent than it did before or has since. Much of the wealth of the preindustrial capitalist economy consisted of the houses and lots of freeholders, the land of peasant proprietors or small farmers, and the shops and tools of artisans.

Second, the concept of property as thing-ownership served important ideological functions. Liberalism was the ideology of the attack on feudalism. A central feature of feudalism was its complex and hierarchical system of land tenure. To the rising bourgeoisie, property conceived as a web of relations among persons meant the system of lord, vassal, and serf from which they were struggling to free themselves. On the other hand, property conceived as the control of a piece of the material world by a single individual meant freedom and equality of status. Thus Blackstone denounced the archaisms of feudal tenure. The French Civil Code marked the culmination of a revolution that abolished feudal property. Hegel wrote that the abolition of feudal property in favor of individual ownership was as great a triumph of freedom as the abolition of slavery.[20] Jefferson contrasted the free allodial system of land titles in America with the servile English system of feudal tenure.

Third, ownership of things by individuals fit the principal justifications for treating property as a natural right. In England and America, the dominant theory was Locke's rightful property resulted from the mixing of an individual's labor with nature.[22] The main rival to Locke's theory within liberal thought was the German Idealist conception of Kant and Hegel, who saw original property resulting from the subjective act of appropriation, the exercise of the individual will over a piece of unclaimed nature. On this view, property was an extension of personality. Ownership expanded the natural sphere of freedom for the individual beyond his body to part of the material world.

III

We have gone, then, in less than two centuries, from a world in which property was a central idea mirroring a clearly understood institution, to one in which it is no longer a coherent or crucial category in our conceptual scheme. The concept of property and

[8] Penn Central Transp. Co. v. New York City, 438 U.S. 104 (1978).

[10] This usage was introduced by Guido Calabresi and A. Douglas Melamed, "Property Rules, Liability Rules, and Inalienability: One View of the Cathedral," 85 *Harvard Law Review* 1089 (1972).

[20] Hegel, *Philosophy of Right*, trans. W.W. Dyde (London, 1896), pp. 65–68.

[22] Locke, *Second Treatise of Government* (London, 1964), chap. 5, "Of Property."

the institution of property have disintegrated. I want to offer first a partial explanation of this phenomenon, and then some suggestions about its political significance.

My explanatory point is that the collapse of the idea of property can best be understood as a process internal to the development of capitalism itself. It is, on this view, not a result of the attack on capitalism by socialists, and not a result of the modifications of laissez-faire that we associate with the coming of a mixed economy or a welfare state. Rather, it is intrinsic to the development of a free-market economy into an industrial phase. Indeed, it is a factor contributing to the declining prestige, the decaying cultural hegemony, of capitalism. To say this is not to deny that the causation may run the other way as well. The decline of capitalism may also contribute to the breakdown of the idea of private property, so that the two phenomena mutually reinforce each other; but my purpose is to isolate a sense in which the disintegration of property follows from the workings of an idealized market economy.

The development from an economy of small property owners to an industrial economy proceeds by the progressive exploitation of the *division of labor or function* and the *economies of scale*. This development can be pictured as taking place through a series of free economic transactions, with the state playing only its classically liberal, neutral, facilitative role. Proprietors subdivide and recombine the bundles of rights that make up their original ownership, creating by private agreement the complex of elaborate and abstract economic institutions and claims characteristic of industrial capitalism, particularly the financial institutions and the industrial corporations. With very few exceptions, all of the private law institutions of mature capitalism can be imagined as arising from the voluntary decompositions and recombination of elements of simple ownership, under a regime in which owners are allowed to divide and transfer their interests as they wish.

The few aspects of the modern private economy that require state action beyond the enforcement of private agreements are the newer forms of originally acquired intangible entitlements, such as patents, copyrights, and trademarks on the one hand, and on the other hand the privilege of corporate limited liability against tort claims. (Limited liability against claims by employees and creditors could be created by contract, as could the rest of the structure of the modern corporation). The intangible entitlements are of nontrivial but relatively peripheral significance to the functioning of mature capitalism. And although the corporation is the central institution of the modern economy, it is not likely that the corporate economy would collapse without limited liability in tort.

The transformation of a preindustrial economy of private proprietors into an industrial economy by the process suggested here presupposes that the entrepreneurs, financiers, and lawyers who carry the process through have the imagination to liberate themselves from the imprisoning concept of property as the simple ownership of a thing by an individual person. They must be able to design new forms of finance and control for enterprise, which can take maximum advantage of the efficiencies of scale and division of function, forms that fractionate traditional ownership and that create claims remote from tangible objects. Similarly, if the process is to go forward smoothly, the courts will have to free themselves from stereotypes about the appropriate forms of control over the economic resources of the community, stereotypes founded on an economy of artisans, tradesmen, and family farms.

The creation of new forms of enterprise and new structures of entitlements would require doctrinal formulation, at least by lawyers and courts. And where law, business, and finance are subjects of theoretical study, these new legal structures of economic organization would eventually become the focus of examination by commentators and scholars, particularly as they come to replace older forms of property as the chief economic institutions of the society. Leaving ideological considerations aside for the moment, it would not be surprising if the replacement of thing-ownership by abstract claim structures in the real world should eventually lead some theorists to the kind of analysis of the concept of property I sketched in the first section. Even if the analysis did not go that far, the basic need to teach lawyers the technical tools of their trade would suggest, if not require, some movement toward a bundle-of-rights formulation of property, as against the historical and popular thing-ownership conception. The main point is that all of these developments—the new economic structures, the legal forms through which they are organized, and the theoretical analysis of property that they suggest—can be plausibly seen as entirely *internal* to the capitalist market system; entirely consistent with full loyalty to that system; in no way fueled by the ethics, politics, or interests of socialism, collectivism, paternalism, or redistributive egalitarianism.

I must repeat that this account is not offered as an accurate narrative of historical events. (No society has practiced as pure an economic liberalism as this; industrial development has been subsidized, retarded, and actively shaped by government throughout.) But this account is intended to abstract out a plausible *partial* explanation, based on simplified assumptions, of the collapse of the idea of property between 1800 and today. I now want to turn to the ideological factors this simplified account has left out. If the internal logic of the market tends to fragment the concept of property in the ways I have suggested, what does a recognition of this development mean in political terms?

IV

The dissolution of the traditional conception of property erodes the moral basis of capitalism. Capitalism has commonly been conceived, by friends and enemies alike, as a system based on the existence and protection of private property rights. Given this conception, the view that property rights have intrinsic worth must strengthen the case for capitalism—at least so long as "property rights" are viewed as a single coherent category. But the phenomenon of the "death of property" breaks the connection between simple thing-ownership and the legal entitlements that make up the framework of the capitalist organization of the economy. And it is simple thing-ownership that has been justified in classical liberal theory, and I think in popular consciousness, as having intrinsic worth.

The theories that support an intrinsic moral right to property can be roughly divided into the labor and personality justifications for private ownership. The labor theory expresses the intuition that the individual owns as a matter of natural right the valued objects he has made or wrested from nature. Thus, the farmer naturally owns the land he has cleared and the crops he has grown; the artisan owns the tools he has fashioned, the raw materials he has gathered, and the products he has made. The idealist "personality" theory rests on the different but no less powerful idea that human beings naturally come to regard some objects as extensions of themselves in some important sense. This idea gains its intuitive force from the way most people regard their homes, their immediate personal effects, and other material things that play a double role as part of their most immediate environment in daily life and at the same time as expressions of their personalities.

Insofar as capitalism connotes a general regime of protection of private property, it enlists these still potent justifications on its side. Conversely, attacks on capitalism engender the sense of outrage that most people feel at a threat to their simple possessions and the immediate fruits of their labor. Marx and Engels realized this well when they sought to dissociate the socialist case for abolition of private property from any threat to the security of ordinary possessions.

> We communists have been reproached with the desire of abolishing the right of personally acquiring property as the fruit of a man's own labor. . . . Hard-won, self-acquired, self-earned property! Do you mean the property of the petty artisan and of the small peasant, a form of property that preceded the bourgeois form? There is no need to abolish that; the development of industry has to a great extent already destroyed it, and is destroying it daily.[29]

I have argued in this essay that we no longer have any coherent concept of property encompassing both simple thing-ownership, on the one hand, and the variety of legal entitlements that are generally called property rights on the other. If correct, this argument means that the forceful intuitions behind the moral arguments for simple thing-ownership can no longer be as readily transferred to the legal institutions of the capitalist economy, as they could when private property was a clearly comprehended unitary concept.

Of course, the legitimacy of capitalism does not rest solely, or perhaps even predominately anymore, on the notion of intrinsic moral rights to private property. Especially among the professionals and intellectuals for whom the breakdown of the concept of property is most likely to be apparent, the moral basis of capitalist institutions is likely to be found in other, more instrumental, values. Thus, capitalism is more commonly defended today on the basis of its capacity to produce material well-being and its tendency to protect personal liberty.

However, the belief that capitalist economic organization is especially protective of personal liberty is itself linked in a subtle way to the traditional conception of property. The connection is suggested by the theory of capitalist private law offered by the Austrian legal sociologist Karl Renner.[31] Renner

---

[29] Marx and Engels, *The Communist Manifesto*, trans. Moore (Chicago, 1969), pp. 41-42.

[31] What follows is a quite free interpretation of the argument of Renner's *The Institution of Private Law and Their Social Functions*, ed. O. Kahn-Freund, trans. A. Schwarzschild (London, 1949). Renner's discussion at pp. 81-95 captures the main thrust of his theory.

described the fundamental structure of the capitalist legal order as made up of two basic elements: the right of ownership and the right of personal liberty. Ownership defines the relationship between man and nature, which consists of the control by separate individuals of separate parcels of the material world. The right of personal liberty defines the relations between persons—a relation of independent equality, in which each person is free to do as he likes, consistent with respect for the rights of others. The interaction of the two rights creates a structure in which atomistic individuals stand, on the one hand, in a vertical relation of domination to the things they own, and on the other hand, in a horizontal relation of mutual independence to all other individuals. The only legal relations among the individuals, then, are those created by their voluntary agreements.

The ideological significance of this simple and compelling picture of civil society is that it masks the existence of private economic power. The only relation of domination it recognizes is the relation of *dominium* or ownership over things. The danger of domination over persons—infringement of liberty—arises only when the state and public law are introduced, creating the power of sovereignty, or *imperium*. Thus, liberty can be threatened only by the state, and by the state only in its public law role, not in its role as neutral enforcer of the private law relations of ownership and contract.

This structure depends for its plausibility upon the obsolete thing-ownership conception of property. Acceptance of the bundle-of-rights conception breaks the main institutions of capitalist private law free from the metaphor of ownership as control over things by individuals. Mature capitalist property must be seen as a web of state-enforced relations of entitlement and duty *between persons*, some assumed voluntarily and some not.

Given this conceptual shift, the neutrality of the state as enforcer of private law evaporates; state protection of property rights is more easily seen as the use of collective force on behalf of the haves against the have-nots. It then becomes a matter of debate whether the private centers of the unregulated capitalist economy, on the one hand, or the augmented state machinery of a socialist or mixed system, on the other, pose the more serious threat to personal liberty. The conflict between capitalism and socialism can no longer be articulated as a clash between liberty on the one side and equality on the other; both systems must be seen as protective against different threats to human freedom.

V

The breakdown of the traditional conception of property serves at the same time to undermine traditional Marxism, and to suggest that the natural development of industrial capitalism is toward a mixed economy. To put the point briefly: private property need not be *abolished* by revolution if it tends to *dissolve* with the development of mature capitalism.

Marxists have tended to view the transition from capitalism to socialism as necessarily a convulsive, qualitative transfer of ownership of the means of production from the bourgeoisie to the proletariat—revolution. This revolution might under certain historical circumstances take place peacefully, but the end of capitalism cannot, on a Marxist view, be gradual or partial. There can be no compromise or halfway house between forms of social system; people live either under capitalism or under socialism.

This world view is strongly compatible with a thing-ownership conception of property—indeed, perhaps influenced and reinforced by such a conception. Marxist definitions of the forms of social system tend to focus on who owns the means of production. Marxists sometimes note that this does not necessarily mean formal or juridical ownership, but rather real or economic ownership. Nevertheless, both real and formal ownership have in common an all-or-nothing character. Something owned is either mine or thine, but not a little bit of each.

The Marxist approach is then substantially undermined by the demonstration that the category of all-or-nothing ownership has become increasingly unimportant as a form of legal thought in modern capitalist economies, where legal control over resources is increasingly fragmented into particularized entitlements. This fragmentation of property is most strikingly evident with respect to the large publicly held corporations that control the chief means of production. I am not speaking here primarily of the much-debated "separation of ownership and control." The growth of power of non-shareholding management is only one aspect of the more general phenomenon of the dispersion of lawful power over the resources involved in a modern corporation. Not only managers and common shareholders, but also other classes of shareholders, directors, bondholders, other creditors, large suppliers and customers (through contractual arrangements), insurers, government regulators, tax authorities, and labor unions—all may have some of the legal powers that would be concentrated in the single ideal thing-owner of classical theory.

There are clear structural similarities between this multiple institutional control and the mechanisms often suggested for controlling socialist enterprises—workers' councils, hired expert managers, central planners, suppliers, and buyers, each with influence, none with anything that might be called total power. Once the perspective of ownership is abandoned and the focus of inquiry shifts to particular legal rights and duties, on the one hand, and actual practical control, on the other, it seems natural to suppose that under any social system a variety of individuals, institutions, and interests are likely to share both the legal and the actual power over anything so complex as a major productive enterprise.

On this view, capitalism and socialism become, not mutually exclusive forms of social organization, but tendencies that can be blended in various proportions. Important differences between profit-oriented market exchange and political collective decision as methods of organizing and operating enterprises remain. But the idea that natural necessity somehow imposes a stark choice between organizing an economy according to one or the other mode becomes less plausible, once the single-owner presupposition is dropped.

I do not want to overstate the extent to which the breakdown of classical property theory undercuts Marxist socialism. The central theoretical feature of Marxism remains the view that capitalist society is fundamentally divided into two sharply distinct and irreconcilably opposed classes, the bourgeoisie and the proletariat. Once this picture of society is accepted, it becomes a matter of detail that economic resources are controlled through complex and overlapping legal forms. As long as all rights of ownership are held within a compact and identifiable bourgeois class, it makes sense to characterize capitalism as ownership of the means of production by the bourgeois class as a whole. What analysis of the disintegration of property does is to indicate how totally Marxism depends upon the dubious reifications of its theory of class division and class struggle.

VI

The substitution of a bundle-of-rights for a thing-ownership conception of property has the ultimate consequence that property ceases to be an important category in legal and political theory. This in turn has political implications, which I have explored in the last two parts of this chapter. I believe that history confirms the centrist political tendency of the attack upon traditional conceptions of property. The legal realists who developed the bundle-of-rights notion were on the whole supporters of the regulatory and welfare state, and in the writings that develop the bundle-of-rights conception, a purpose to remove the sanctity that had traditionally attached to the rights of property can often be discerned.[40]

The same point is illustrated by the most influential recent theoretical work on questions of economic justice, John Rawls's *A Theory of Justice*. The concept of property rights plays only the most minor role in the monumental treatise, which on the whole displays a welfare state liberal orientation toward questions of the organization of economic life.

I would want to deny, however, that the account and explanation of the breakdown of the concept of property offered here is in the last analysis ideological, in the pejorative sense of a mystifying or false apologetic. The development of a largely capitalist market economy toward industrialism objectively demands formulation of its emergent system of economic entitlements in something like the bundle-of-rights form, which in turn must lead to the decline of property as a central category of legal and political thought.

Note

If "property" as a concept is no longer viable, is there anything about a house which makes it worth special attention as a thing of value?

---

[40] The "bundle-of-rights" conception of property appears in well-articulated form for the first time (insofar as I have discovered) in Wesley Hohfeld, "Some Fundamental Legal Conceptions as Applied in Judicial Reasoning," 23 *Yale Law Journal* 16 (1913). Thereafter, it became part of the conceptual stock-in-trade of the legal realist movement, often with a strong implication that "private" and "public" property were not as different as traditional property theory would suggest. See, e.g., Cohen, op. cit., n. 4 above, pp. 357–59.

B. Minimalist Government: Neo-Conservatism and *Laissez Faire*

The jurisprudential foundation for late twentieth century neo-conservative thinking about minimalist government and property law was set by Robert Nozick's ANARCHY, STATE AND UTOPIA. Among those taking up from where Nozick left off is Richard Epstein, whose book TAKINGS: PRIVATE PROPERTY AND THE POWER OF EMINENT DOMAIN has become the analytical starting point for discussion of the meaning of the Constitution's takings clause. Much of the neo-conservative debate over land use controls was anticipated by Robert Ellickson in his now classic article, *Alternatives to Zoning: Covenants, Nuisance Rules and Fines as Land Use Controls*, published the year before Nozick's book. An excerpt from Ellickson's article, which paints a less radical vision of land use controls than Epstein, concludes this section.

Robert Nozick, ANARCHY, STATE AND UTOPIA 149–155 (1974)*

Chapter 7
Distributive Justice

The minimal state is the most extensive state that can be justified. Any state more extensive violates people's rights. Yet many persons have put forth reasons purporting to justify a more extensive state. * * * I shall focus upon those generally acknowledged to be most weighty and influential, to see precisely wherein they fail. In this chapter we consider the claim that a more extensive state is justified, because necessary (or the best instrument to achieve distributive justice. * * *

The term "distributive justice" is not a neutral one. Hearing the term "distribution," most people presume that some thing or mechanism uses some principle or criterion to give out a supply of things. Into this process of distributing shares some error may have crept. So it is an open question, at least, whether *re*distribution should take place; whether we should do again what has already been done once, though poorly. However, we are not in the position of children who have been given portions of pie by someone who now makes last minute adjustments to rectify careless cutting. There is no *central* distribution, no person or group entitled to control all the resources, jointly deciding how they are to be doled out. What each person gets, he gets from others who give to him in exchange for something, or as a gift. In a free society, diverse persons control different resources, and new holdings arise out of the voluntary exchanges and actions of persons. There is no more a distributing or distribution of shares than there is a distributing of mates in a society in which persons choose whom they shall marry. The total result is the product of many individual decisions which the different individuals involved are entitled to make. Some uses of the term "distribution," it is true, do not imply a previous distributing appropriately judged by some criterion (for example, "probability distribution"); nevertheless, despite the title of this chapter, it would be best to use a terminology that clearly is neutral. We shall speak of people's holdings; a principle of justice in holdings describes (part of) what justice tells us (requires) about holdings. * * *

THE ENTITLEMENT THEORY

The subject of justice in holdings consists of three major topics. The first is the *original acquisition of holdings*, the appropriation of unheld things. This includes the issues of how unheld things may come to be held, the process, or processes, by which unheld things may come to be held, the things that may come to be held by these processes, the extent of what comes to be held by a particular process, and so on.

We shall refer to the complicated truth about this topic, which we shall not formulate here, as the principle of justice in acquisition. The second topic concerns the *transfer of holdings* from one person to another. By what processes may a person transfer holdings to another? How may a person acquire a holding from another who holds it? Under this topic come general descriptions of voluntary exchange, and gift and (on the other hand) fraud, as well as reference to particular conventional details fixed upon in a given society. The complicated truth about this subject (with placeholders for conventional details) we shall call the principle of justice in transfer. (And we shall suppose it also includes principles governing how a person may divest himself of a holding, passing it into an unheld state.)

If the world were wholly just, the following inductive definition would exhaustively cover the subject of justice in holdings.

1. A person who acquires a holding in accordance with the principle of justice in acquisition is entitled to that holding.

2. A person who acquires a holding in accordance with the principle of justice in transfer, from someone else entitled to the holding, is entitled to the holding.

3. No one is entitled to a holding except by (repeated) applications of 1 and 2.

The complete principle of distributive justice would say simply that a distribution is just if everyone is entitled to the holdings they possess under the distribution.

A distribution is just if it arises from another just distribution by legitimate means. The legitimate means of moving from one distribution to another are specified by the principle of justice in transfer. The legitimate first "moves" are specified by the principle of justice in acquisition. Whatever arises from a just situation by just steps is itself just. The means of change specified by the principle of justice in transfer preserve justice. As correct rules of inference are truth-preserving, and any conclusion deduced via repeated application of such rules from only true premises is itself true, so the means of transition from one situation to another specified by the principle of justice in transfer are justice-preserving, and any situation actually arising from repeated transitions in accordance with the principle from a just situation is itself just. The parallel between justice-preserving transformations and truth-preserving transformations illuminates where it fails as well as where it holds. That a conclusion could have been deduced by truth-preserving means from premises that are true suffices to show its truth. That from a just situation a situation *could* have arisen via justice-preserving means does *not* suffice to show its justice. The fact that a thief's victims voluntarily *could* have presented him with gifts does not entitle the thief to his ill-gotten gains. Justice in holdings is historical; it depends upon what actually has happened. We shall return to this point later.

Not all actual situations are generated in accordance with the two principles of justice in holdings; the principle of justice in acquisition and the principle of justice in transfer. Some people steal from others, or defraud them, or enslave them, seizing their product and preventing them from living as they choose, or forcibly exclude others from competing in exchanges. None of these are permissible modes of transition from one situation to another. And some persons acquire holdings by means not sanctioned by the principle of justice in acquisition. The existence of past injustice (previous violations of the first two principles of justice in holdings) raises the third major topic under justice in holdings: the rectification of injustice in holdings. If past injustice has shaped present holdings in various ways, some identifiable and some not, what now, if anything, ought to be done to rectify these injustices? What obligations do the performers of injustice have toward those whose position is worse than it would have been had the injustice not been done? Or, that it would have been had compensation been paid promptly? How, if at all, do things change if the beneficiaries and those made worse off are not the direct parties in the act of injustice, but, for example, their descendants? Is an injustice done to someone whose holding was itself based upon an unrectified injustice? How far back must one go in wiping clean the historical slate of injustices? What may victims of injustice permissibly do in order to rectify the injustices being done to them, including the many injustices done by persons acting through their government? I do not know of a thorough or theoretically sophisticated treatment of such issues. Idealizing greatly, let us suppose theoretical investigation will produce a principle of rectification. This principle uses historical information about previous situations and injustices done in them (as defined by the first two principles of justice and rights against interference), and information about the actual course of events that flowed from these injustices, until the present, and it yields a description (or descriptions) of holdings in society. The principle of rectification presumably will make use of its best estimate of subjunctive information about what would have occurred (or a probability distribution over what might have occurred, using the expected value) if the injustice had not taken place. If the actual description of holdings turns out not to be one of the descriptions yielded by the principle, then one of the descriptions yielded must be realized.

The general outlines of the theory of justice in holdings are that the holdings of a person are just if he is entitled to them by the principles of justice in acquisition and transfer, or by the principle of rectification of injustice (as specified by the first two principles). If each person's holdings are just, then the total set (distribution) is just. * * *

HISTORICAL PRINCIPLES AND END-RESULT PRINCIPLES

The general outlines of the entitlement theory illuminate the nature and defects of other conceptions of distributive justice. The entitlement theory of justice in distribution is *historical;* whether a distribution is just depends upon how it came about. In contrast, *current time-slice principles* of justice hold that the justice of a distribution is determined by how things are distributed (who has what) as judged by some *structural* principle(s) of just distribution. A utilitarian who judges between any two distributions by seeing which has the greater sum of utility and, if the sums tie, applies some fixed equality criterion to choose the more equal distribution, would hold a current time-slice principle of justice. As would someone who had a fixed schedule of trade-offs between the sum of happiness and equality. According to a current time-slice principle, all that needs to be looked at, in judging the justice of a distribution, is who ends up with what; in comparing any two distributions one need look only at the matrix presenting the distributions. No further information need be fed into a principle of justice. It is a consequence of such principles of justice that any two structurally identical distributions are equally just. (Two distributions are structurally identical if they present the same profile, but perhaps have different persons occupying the particular slots. My having ten and your having five, and my having five and your having ten are structurally identical distributions.) Welfare economics is the theory of current time-slice principles of justice. The subject is conceived as operating on matrices representing only current information about distribution. This, as well as some of the usual conditions (for example, the choice of distribution is invariant under relabeling of columns), guarantees that welfare economics will be a current time-slice theory, with all of its inadequacies.

Most persons do not accept current time-slice principles as constituting the whole story about distributive shares. They think it relevant in assessing the justice of a situation to consider not only the distribution it embodies, but also how that distribution came about. If some persons are in prison for murder or war crimes, we do not say that to assess the justice of the distribution in the society we must look only at what this person has, and that person has, and that person has, * * * at the current time. We think it relevant to ask whether someone did something so that he *deserved* to be punished, deserved to have a lower share. Most will agree to the relevance of further information with regard to punishments and penalties. Consider also desired things. One traditional socialist view is that workers are entitled to the product and full fruits of their labor; they have earned it; a distribution is unjust if it does not give the workers what they are entitled to. Such entitlements are based upon some past history. No socialist holding this view would find it comforting to be told that because the actual distribution A happens to coincide structurally with the one he desires D, A therefore is no less just than D; it differs only in that the "parasitic" owners of capital received under A what the owners are entitled to under D, namely very little. This socialist rightly, in my view, holds onto the notions of earning, producing, entitlement, desert, and so forth, and he rejects current time-slice principles that look only to the structure of the resulting set of holdings. (The set of holdings resulting from what? Isn't it implausible that how holdings are produced and come to exist has no effect at all on who should hold what?) His mistake lies in his view of what entitlements arise out of what sorts of productive processes.

We construe the position we discuss too narrowly by speaking of *current* time-slice principles. Nothing is changed if structural principles operate upon a time sequence of current time-slice profiles and, for example, give someone more now to counterbalance the less he has had earlier. A utilitarian or an egalitarian or any mixture of the two over time will inherit the difficulties of his more myopic comrades. He is not helped by the fact that *some* of the information others consider relevant in assessing a distribution is reflected, unrecoverably, in past matrices. Henceforth, we shall refer to such unhistorical principles of distributive justice, including the current time-slice principles, as *end-result principles* or *end-state principles.*

In contrast to end-result principles of justice, *historical principles* of justice hold that past circumstances or actions of people can create differential entitlements or differential deserts to things. An injustice can be worked by moving from one distribution to another structurally identical one, for the second, in profile the same, may violated people's entitlements or deserts; it may not fit the actual history.

Richard Epstein, TAKINGS: PRIVATE PROPERTY AND THE POWER OF EMINENT DOMAIN 331–342, 344–348 (1985)*

CONCLUSION

Philosophical Implications

A Summing Up

* * * My central concern in this concluding chapter is not with the legal status of the takings clause, but with the larger questions of normative political theory: what are the intrinsic merits of the eminent domain provision when it is stripped of its present constitutional authority? If we were now in a position to organize a government from scratch, would its constitution include an eminent domain clause as interpreted here? My thesis is that the eminent domain approach, as applied both to personal liberty and private property, offers a principled account of both the functions of the state and the limitations upon its powers.

Representative government begins with the premise that the state's rights against its citizens are no greater than the sum of the rights of the individuals whom it benefits in any given transaction. The state qua state has no independent set of entitlements, any more than a corporation has rights qua corporation against any of its shareholders. All questions of public right are complex amalgams of questions of individual entitlements, so the principles of property, contract, and tort law can be used to explain the proper extent of government power. These rules determine the property relationships among private individuals, which are preserved when the state intervenes as an agent on one side of the transaction. These entitlement principles obey very simple rules of summation and hence apply with undiminished vigor to large-number situations involving modifications of liability rules, regulation, and taxation. A system of private rights provides an exhaustive and internally consistent normative baseline of entitlements against which all the complex schemes of governance can be tested. As there are no gaps in rights when ownership is first established, no gaps emerge when private ownership is transformed by state intervention, whatever its form.

The state, however, cannot simply arise (even conceptually) out of a series of voluntary transactions from an original distribution of rights. Free riders, holdouts, and radical uncertainty thwart any omnibus agreement before its inception. The question then arises, what minimum of additional power must be added for the state to become more than a voluntary protective associate and to acquire the exclusive use of force within its territory? The eminent domain analysis provides the answer: the only additional power needed is the state's right to force exchanges of property rights that leave individuals with rights more valuable than those they have been deprived of. The specter of the unlimited Hobbesian sovereign is averted by two critical limitations upon the nature of the exchanges that the state can force. First, the eminent domain logic allows forced exchanges only for the public use, which excludes naked transfers from one person to another. Second, it requires compensation, so everyone receives something of greater value in exchange for the *rights* surrendered.

In the final analysis the two conditions blend into one, because the power to coerce is limited to cases in

---

*Reprinted by permission of the publishers from TAKINGS: PRIVATE PROPERTY AND THE POWER OF EMINENT DOMAIN by Richard Epstein, Cambridge, Mass.: Harvard University Press, Copyright © 1985 by the President and Fellows of Harvard College.

which positive-sum games may go forward with a pro rata division of the surplus they generate. It is always easy to construct examples whereby some individuals with distinctive personal tastes will be worse off in fact, because they will lose the power to rape, kill, pillage, and plunder. Yet the baseline for forced exchanges is individual entitlements to personal autonomy, not individual preferences regardless of their content. Aggrieved parties cannot complain if they lose under the state something they were not entitled to against other individuals as a matter of right. No requirement of unanimous consent prevents the move to a system of governance. The single pervert cannot block the state. Once organized, the state has the power to govern because within its own territory it has the monopoly of force sufficient to protect all persons against aggression in all its forms. Finally, by a system of unbiased judges (long recognized as part of the tradition of natural justice) the state insures that all disputes can be resolved. The gains of final adjudication are the substantial gains of social order, while the errors tend to be randomly distributed, so all persons share pro rata in the surplus created.

This eminent domain framework does not depend upon a hidden assumption that before the formation of a government all individuals, real or hypothetical, reside in a "state of nature." Quite the contrary, political theory is quite unintelligible if it assumes that prior to the establishment of a government, individuals have no common language, no conception of right and wrong, no common culture or tradition, and no means of socialization outside the state. The question of the state is narrower than is sometimes supposed. The state is not the source of individual rights or of social community. It presupposes that these exist and are worth protecting, and that individuals reciprocally benefit from their interactions with one another. A unique sovereign emerges solely in response to the demands to preserve order. The state becomes a moral imperative precisely because there is something of value that is worth protecting from the unbridled use of force by those who forsake tradition, family, and friends. A set of forced exchanges from existing rights does not create the original rights so exchanged; like the constitutional vision of private property, forced exchanges presuppose them. A forced exchange does not create culture and sense of community, it protects them by removing the need for compelling or allowing everyone to act as a policeman in his own cause. The state arises because the rates of error and abuse in pure self-help regimes become intolerable. The strength of a natural law theory is in its insistence that individual rights (and their correlative obligations) exist independent of agreement and prior to the formation of the state.

Rival Theories

To get some sense of the power of the eminent domain approach, it is instructive to compare this view with two rival theories that have been very influential in recent times, theories with which it has both important similarities and important differences. These theories are the ones associated with the work of Robert Nozick in *Anarchy, State, and Utopia* and that of John Rawls in *A Theory of Justice.* After reviewing them, I shall consider whether the theory of eminent domain is consistent with a vision of civic virtue in public life or is nullified by past acts that violate the theory itself.

NOZICK

Nozick's theory incorporates the first part of the eminent domain approach in its respect for the principles of individual rights. Nozick relies heavily upon "historical" principles of justice to account for the institution of private property and the inequalities in wealth it engenders. At one time those principles were widely accepted in both common and constitutional discourse. Nozick's rules of acquisition have close affinity to the first-possession rules of property. His principles of rectification cover the terrain of the law of tort, and those of transfer cover the law of contract. One great attraction of his normative theory is its powerful congruence with basic social institutions and human practices which provides a convenient data base on which to examine its implications. Another strong point is that by striking a responsive chord, the theory requires no great cost to be legitimated, because people do not need to be persuaded to abandon their customary moral views, as they would to embrace a highly abstract theory (like Rawls's) that cuts against the grain and commits them to outcomes they cannot understand by procedures they sorely distrust.

But there are difficulties with Nozick's theory. The first concerns its origin and the status of individual rights. Nozick follows closely in the Lockean and common law tradition, for his historical theory of justice begins with the proposition that ownership is acquired by taking possession of an unowned thing. Nonetheless, the proposition that possession is the root of title is not a necessary truth. The linkage between possession and title can be denied without self-contradiction. Arguably, all things in an initial position are subject to some form of collective ownership. Some nondeductive procedure must be available to let us choose between competing visions of the correct original position. Nozick's view depends upon an intuitive appreciation of the need for autonomy and self-determination. In one sense his position looks like a bare assertion: private property and personal liberty are important because they are important or because they are inherent in human nature. Such efforts at self-justification are always uneasy, but they are not for that reason wrong. One way to look at Nozick's simple theory is to ask what the world would look like if the popular conception of autonomy was abandoned. On what grounds could one categorically condemn murder, rape, mayhem, theft, and pillage? Our instincts of revulsion are so powerful that one is loath to adopt a theory of individual rights that rests solely upon the shifting sands of utilitarian calculation. Slavery by conquest is regarded as a categorical evil. Do we want even to consider the argument that slavery is justified if the agency costs of control and supervision are small in comparison with the resource gains from subjecting an incompetent slave to the will of a competent master? Or is the incompetence of one person only an argument for guardianship by another? Is it really an open question whether the parent-child relationship is one of guardianship or ownership? Simple faith may not serve as the ideal foundation of an ethical society, but it may be much better than the next best alternative.

* * *

The original position taken * * * by Nozick has enormous appeal. Everyone does own himself, and no one owns any external things, and there are natural status obligations of support within the family. Nonetheless, Nozick's libertarian theory fails in its central mission because it cannot justify the existence of the state. Its chief weakness is that it views all entitlements as absolute, so all forced exchanges are ruled out of bounds, regardless of their terms. Yet without forced exchanges, social order cannot be achieved, given the holdout and free rider problems. Nozick presents a wonderful discussion of the invisible-hand mechanisms that lead to the creation of multiple collective protection associations. But no invisible-hand mechanism explains the emergence of an exclusive sovereign within any given territory. The need for forced exchanges makes this last leap from many associations to a single state, and the eminent domain argument supplies this step. Individual entitlements are respected always as claims for compensation and frequently, but not uniformly, as absolutes.

There are still some limits on what the eminent domain theory can do. It cannot explain *which* protective association should become the exclusive one; for example, the place of honor might be awarded to the association with the most members. (Even here the specification of the territory can be decisive in choosing between rival claims.) The critical point is that any association which assumes power is hemmed in by a nondiscrimination provision: it owes the same obligations toward outsiders that it owes to its own members. Exploitation is made more difficult, if not precluded, when those who are bound without their consent must on average be left better off in their entitlement than before. The libertarian theory augmented by a willingness to tolerate some forced exchanges is vastly richer than a libertarian theory that wholly shuns them.

RAWLS

* * *

Rawls's contractarian theory permits a richness of discussion that cannot be generated by simple libertarian premises, but it is open to powerful and familiar criticisms of a different sort * * *. First, it is quite impossible to understand Rawls's use of contract as it relates to abstractions. Contract within the private law is an effort to vindicate the unique tastes of discrete persons who are far more concerned with their particular places and preferences than with the general social good. * * * Voluntary exchanges presuppose that in general every person has reliable information as to what he values and how much he values it or, at least, that he has better information about those things than those who would limit his choices. Trades are a positive-sum game because each person attaches greater value to what he receives than to what he surrenders. To argue for contracts by disinterested, indeed disembodied, persons is simply to strain a metaphor beyond its breaking point. By removing all traces of psychological struggle and individual self-interest, the theory departs radically from any plausible view of the private agreements based upon personal knowledge that lie at its analogical root. The metaphor of contract is best dropped altogether from Rawls's conception, because a single composite individual could do everything that is required of a contracting group. Indeed it is only the residual allure of the contract idea of consensus that drives Rawls to consider the preferences of hypothetical groups. By the terms of his theory, the choice of the single mean (or median?) person should suffice as well.

* * *

The eminent domain approach meets * * * these objections to Rawls's theory. The eminent domain theory does not have to deal with the entitlements of lifeless abstractions. Instead of relying upon a set of complex procedures to generate the needed substantive rights, it starts with a substantive account of individual rights, beginning with first possession and covering every aspect of the use and disposition of property. * * *

The eminent domain approach also eliminates the need to resort to hypothetical persons with incomplete personal knowledge. All persons are treated as their own masters, who are entitled to the full benefits of their natural talents and abilities. When a person takes possession of that which was previously unowned, he does not do so both as an agent for himself *and* as trustee for all other persons with claims upon him. He does so only for himself. In contrast, the Rawlsian approach regards the distribution of original talents (and hence the gains derived from their application) as morally arbitrary, the product of luck, and thus worthy of no protection. The opposition to Locke's view that each person owns his own labor cannot be more vivid.

Rawls's position * * * gives each person a lien upon the product of every other person, so that the personal destinies of all persons, present and future, are forever intertwined. His position forces upon every individual obligations that run contrary to biological instincts of egoism, whereby some special genetic linkage, such as parent to child, helps explain why one person takes into account another's gain or loss. The strong opposition between obligations within the family and within society at large is largely suppressed in Rawls's picture of human obligation. It is as if every person enjoyed the fruits of his own labor by leave of some central authority, so taxation becomes no longer a charge on individual wealth for supplying public goods but an efficient means for the state to reclaim the product of human talents that it already owns as trustee for the public at large. This conception strikes at the very heart of personal self-definition and individual self-expression. It presupposes the kind of detachment from, and impartiality toward, self that no human being emerging from his evolutionary past of remorseless self-interest can hope to achieve. Each person becomes so enmeshed in the affairs of others that even heroic efforts will never get them out. The theory is advanced in the cause of freedom, but the totalitarian abuse that it risks should be evident, for what happens if the wrong people gain control of the central machinery of social control?

* * *

This collectivization * * * leads to the very types of management problems that well-functioning markets seek to avoid. If an individual does not own himself, then there is the classic agency-cost question, because he must bear all the costs of his own labor while retaining only some portion of the gain. When everyone perceives the conflict between production and yield, the problems become additive. If individual misfortune is socialized, then some common pool must be formed to determine what fraction of each risk each person must bear. This pooling is designed to remove arbitrary individual differences that are distasteful to risk-averse parties. But the diversification of this risk comes at a very high cost. Transactional freedom is reduced because no one has clear title to anything that he wishes to purchase or sell, so property rights remain ill defined over time. The system downplays the natural, if imperfect, form of risk pooling provided by family and religious units.

* * *

CIVIC VIRTUE

A final critique of the eminent domain theory comes from a very different quarter. It is often said that a theory that stresses the importance of private property and the fragility of government institutions ignores the role of civic virtue—devotion to public service, protection of the weak, advancement of the arts, participation in public life—which is central to understanding the highest aspirations of political life. To be sure, there is nothing wrong with a view of the world that treats the renunciation of force and fraud as the noblest of human endeavors. * * * But civic virtue in public affairs is akin to happiness in private affairs. To make it the direct end of human conduct is to guarantee that it will not be obtained. Discreet indirection becomes the order of the day. As personal happiness is the by-product of a rich and productive life, so civic virtue is the by-product of sound institutional arrangements. The eminent domain approach works toward civic virtue, not by trumpeting its evident goodness, but by creating a sound institutional environment where it can flourish.

Consider the point that virtue and poverty do not go well together. * * * Civic virtue * * * depends upon sufficient personal liberty, security, and wealth to keep most people far from the thin edge. What set of institutions will tend to guarantee these political conditions? The first is the facilitation of voluntary transactions, which are generally positive-sum games, because people deal only with their own property. The second is control of legislatures, which have a propensity for negative-sum games because they allow people to deal in the property of others.

* * *

PAST INJUSTICES

* * *

In the simplest case A owns property, which is then taken by B. C then takes the property from B. The question is whether the infirmity in B's title is sufficient to defeat his action to recover possession of the thing from C. The common law answer is no. * * * If B cannot recover from C, there is no way to prevent C taking the thing from B in the first place.

The doctrine of *relative title*, then, is the common law response to the problem. B by his wrong has title superior to all the world save A and those persons who claim through A. Let C, a stranger, take B's property, and B may recover it or its proceeds. Yet both of these actions may be trumped by A, either by a suit against B or a direct action against the party in possession. Nor does the story end there. B may die and leave his cause of action to D. C may die and leave his property to E. To the extent of assets descended, D has a cause of action against E, as the relative title extends across persons and across generations.

Still, A or his successor cannot always have the right of action. With property titles as with contract claims, some statute of limitations is needed to wipe ancient titles off the books. * * * [B]arring old claims is the price worth paying to protect valid titles against ceaseless attack. The social gains from forcing quick resolution of disputes are so enormous that everyone is better off with the limitations than without it. * * * Once the flawed title is cleared by a statute of limitations, the normal process of mutually beneficial transactions can improve everyone's lot, notwithstanding the initial deviation from the ideal position.

Robert C. Ellickson, *Alternatives to Zoning: Covenants, Nuisance Rules, and Fines as Land Use Controls*, 40 U. CHI. L. REV. 681–684, 687–691, 693–694, 696–699, 703–705, 711–714, 716–719, 724–726, 728–733, 761–762, 764, 766–768, 772–775, 777–780 (1973).*

With increasing frequency commentators have been urging greater reliance on the market mechanism to allocate resources in a variety of fields. There has been relatively little examination, however, of the extent to which decentralized mechanisms can be used to handle the controversial social problem of conflicts among neighboring landowners.[2] Land development in urban areas is one of the most regulated human activities in the United States. In recent decades, public regulation of urban land has increased sharply in incidence and severity, but dissatisfaction with the physical appearance and living arrangements in American cities continues to grow. Despite the evident shortcomings of present public regulatory schemes, even those commentators who propose reliance on the market mechanism in other areas tend to concur with the prevailing view that increased public planning is the most promising guide for the growth of cities. This article advances a different thesis: that conflicts among neighboring landowners are generally better resolved by systems less centralized than master planning and zoning.

* * *

I. EXTERNALITIES AND SYSTEMS FOR THEIR INTERNALIZATION

Economists assert that if the market remains free of imperfections, market transactions will optimally allocate scarce resources. They do not maintain that the distribution of these optimally-allocated re-

---

[2] The leading articles advocating market-oriented solutions to land use problems include: Coase, *The Problem of Social Cost*, 3 J. LAW & ECON. 1 (1960); Siegan, *Non-Zoning in Houston*, 13 J. LAW & ECON. 71 (1970) * * *.

sources among specific individuals will necessarily be just. If injustices in distribution arise, most economists urge that they be corrected by direct cash transfer payments, rather than through more indirect attempts at redistribution. According to this economic model, optimally efficient patterns of city development would evolve naturally if urban land development markets were to operate free of imperfections; city planning or public land use controls would only make matters worse from an efficiency standpoint. Since market forces would generate the most efficient land use, the basic decision for policy makers would be the distribution of urban pleasures among residents, with adjustments preferably made through cash transfer payments.

Land development markets, however, are not perfect and in reality city development is far from optimal. Economists regularly use land markets to illustrate that where transactions or activities entail "externalities" or "spillovers"—that is, impacts on nonconsenting outsiders—suboptimal resource allocation will often result. Although beneficial externalities can also impair efficient allocation, this article deals primarily with externalities harmful to nonconsenting outsiders. Welfare economists have urged that harmful externalities be "internalized" to eliminate excessive amounts of nuisance activity. Internalization is said to be accomplished through devices that force a nuisance-maker to bear the true costs of his activity. Internalization of harmful spillovers in land development often requires some departure from what this article calls a laissez faire distribution of property rights, an imaginary legal world where each landowner can choose to pursue any activity within the boundaries of his parcel without fear of liability to his neighbors or governmental sanction. These departures range from those that are compatible with the continuance of private markets to those that seek to supplant the market mechanism altogether; thus, systems for internalizing harmful spillovers range from relatively decentralized ones that emphasize private ordering to others that are highly collectivized and rely on mandatory decrees.

* * *

II. Criteria for Evaluating Land Use Control Systems

How are intelligent choices to be made from this array of alternative actions? Problems of resource allocation have been attacked with the greatest conceptual rigor by economists. They generally judge the impact of social policies by two basic standards: efficiency and equity.[21] A measure is inefficient if it is likely to waste resources, that is, allocate scarce goods and services in a suboptimal manner. Equity, however, is a function of the distribution of resources, or who ends up with what share of the wealth. For example, uninternalized harmful spillovers from land use activities may not only result in inefficiencies, but may also cause redistributions of wealth that are perceived as unjust. Following other legal scholars who have applied welfare economics to problems of external cost, this article employs efficiency and equity as the two basic criteria for evaluating land use control systems.

The notion of efficiency requires some dissection. When a conflict among neighboring land use arises, three reasonably distinct types of resource diminutions may occur, singly or in combination. First, harmful externalities decrease the utility and thus the value of neighboring property. To keep the terminology as simple as possible, this factor will be called *nuisance costs.* Under a laissez faire distribution of property rights, these costs would probably be very high. A second possible source of resource diminutions will be termed *prevention costs.* This category includes nonadministrative expenditures made, or opportunity costs incurred, by either a nuisance maker or his injured neighbor to reduce the level of nuisance costs. Prevention costs will tend to be higher when either or both of the parties are compelled to undertake specific steps than when they are permitted to select voluntarily among available preventive measures. Finally, *administrative costs* may also diminish resources. This term will be used to encompass both public and private costs of getting information, negotiating, writing agreements and laws, policing agreements and rules, and arranging for the execution of preventive measures.

If administrative costs are zero, optimal resource allocation is achieved when the sum of nuisance

[21] The production and distribution of wealth, however, are not the sole societal concerns. Land use control policies, particularly highly centralized ones, can severely threaten individual liberty, a value not sufficiently recognized in economic theory. This analysis devotes little space to liberty issues, not because of unimportance, but because the deprivations of liberty caused by land use regulations, or uninterrupted nuisances, are rarely perceived as severe. * * *

costs and prevention costs is minimized. It will rarely be efficient to eliminate all nuisance costs, since that action will ordinarily require unacceptable levels of prevention costs. A major city could easily extinguish all nuisance costs from gas stations by banning them within city limits. Such a measure, however, would involve high prevention costs as all motorists would have to take long, annoying trips to the suburbs to service their cars. Prevention costs in this instance would probably far exceed the eliminated nuisance costs, and overall efficiency would not be enhanced.

The weighing of nuisance costs and prevention costs is further complicated by the fact that in reality administrative costs are not zero. All land use control systems involve some form of administrative costs. These costs may be collectivized through government, as in the case of salaries for zoning officials, or borne directly by private persons, as in the case of the costs of inculcating good manners, arranging for the installation of preventive devices, litigating nuisance suits, or deciphering zoning codes. The overall goal from an efficiency standpoint is the minimization of the sum of nuisance costs, prevention costs, and administrative costs.

The goal of equity, however, complicates matters considerably; an efficient policy may be an unfair one, particularly when the gains of the policy are not distributed to those injured by its imposition. Because they have found no theoretically sound basis for making interpersonal comparisons of utility, many economists believe that they can at best only describe the wealth transfer effects of a policy, but that they cannot assess the fairness of those transfers. Thus, they either ignore the issue of equity or defer to courts and legislatures. The legal profession can certainly provide guidance to those institutions, and most legal scholars writing on welfare economics have been careful to consider equity criteria in their analysis. The degree of unfairness of a system obviously cannot be quantified and persuasive arguments about fairness issues are hard to construct; nevertheless legal scholars must confront an issue so central to law.[30]

III. An Evaluation of Zoning

* * *

A. Zoning and Efficiency

Despite the difficulty of discussing the uncoordinated practices of over 9,000 local governments, the basic structure of zoning and present knowledge about its effectiveness will support some general observations about its likely efficiency as a land use control system.

1. *Reduction in Nuisance Costs.* Since zoning inevitably results in considerable prevention and administrative costs, large reductions in nuisance costs would have to be forthcoming for zoning to be deemed efficient. At present, zoning administrators either ban or greatly restrict the location of highly desirable uses. Where a noxious use is permitted, planning officials generally try to place it adjacent to activities not particularly vulnerable to the type of harm caused by that use. For example, most zoning ordinances cluster industrial uses, often placing the cluster adjacent to railroad tracks. Similarly, apartment zones are commonly placed next to highways, perhaps on the assumption that if apartment dwellers must tolerate the noise coming through the party walls of their building, they should not be especially sensitive to the hum of nearby automobiles. Most ordinances also set aside large areas exclusively for single-family homes, a land use perceived as particularly vulnerable to external harm.

These locational decisions unquestionably reduce the nuisance costs that would occur if land uses were randomly distributed. Nonzoning allocations, however, may also be better than random. Urban land markets automatically reduce nuisance costs far below the level that would be found with random land use distribution. Industrial plants are not attracted to prime residential areas; instead they naturally congregate along railroad tracks, just where zoning is likely to put them. * * * Thus, even if a zoning system is more efficient than random land use, it does not necessarily follow that it reduces nuisance costs more than the market mechanism.

---

[30] Professor Michelman has proposed as a standard of fairness that requiring a person to bear a loss is not unfair if he should be able to perceive that refusing compensation to people in his situation is likely to promote the welfare of people like him in the long run. Michelman, *Property, Utility, and Fairness: Comments on the Ethical Formulation of "Just Compensation" Law,* 80 HARV. L. REV. 1165, 1223 (1967). * * * His test is obviously linked to efficiency considerations. * * * Michelman's standard for fairness is analogous in many respects to John Rawls's second basic principle of a just society: "social and economic inequalities, for example, inequalities of wealth and authority, are just only if they result in compensating benefits for everyone, and in particular for the least advantaged members of society." J. RAWLS, A THEORY OF JUSTICE 14–15 (1971). Both the Michelman and Rawls approaches show a kinship in many respects to the classical economic notion of Pareto optimality.

* * *

2. *Prevention Costs.* The great danger, however, is not that the drafters of zoning ordinances will fail to eliminate nuisance costs, but that they will try to eliminate them all. The pertinent goal is minimization of the sum of nuisance, prevention, and administrative costs. If zoning is directed solely toward eliminating nuisance costs, planners will impose land use controls so restrictive as to create inefficiently high prevention costs.

* * *

In most communities, for example, zoning ordinances are designed to promote the interests of single-family homeowners, often a majority of the voting population. This constituency generally prefers strict zoning controls, a policy that eventually causes a buildup of market demand for some development not permitted by existing zoning regulations. When this demand becomes large enough, the prodevelopment forces are usually able to finance a winning campaign for a relaxation of control, and an outbreak of new land development follows. This pattern of long pauses in development, followed by bursts of activity, can create substantial inefficiency in the land development industry. For example, a prospective tightening of zoning restrictions on high-rise apartment buildings in New York City caused construction of an artificially high number of apartments in the early 1960's. This overbuilding was a major cause of the 75 percent drop in private apartment construction in Manhattan from the first half of the 1960's to the second. The economic effects of this artificial boom-and-bust cycle were probably great enough to impede the efficient functioning of local construction firms and cause suboptimal employment of labor in the building trades. Similarly, the pendulum cycle of zoning may require architects and civil engineers to incur the expense of revising plans already on their drawing boards in order to accommodate the latest shift in political winds.

* * *

3. *Administrative Costs.* The most conspicuous administrative cost of zoning is the direct cost of operating a public planning agency. Local governments, however, are tightfisted in budgeting for their planning staffs, and direct public costs are actually quite low. The Manvel survey found that, in 1967, total spending by municipalities for planning, zoning, and subdivision regulation was $70 million, only 61¢ per capita for the cities involved.[56] That amount is less than half of the spending on building code administration.

* * *

The private administrative costs necessitated by zoning systems far exceed the public costs. Developers of urban land, and traders of urban property, must investigate any public land use restrictions governing development. The existence of zoning means that builders, land speculators, civil engineers, architects, financial institutions, lawyers, and others involved in land development must maintain libraries of local land use regulations and spend time studying them. These information costs are greatly increased by the rapid changes in the regulations.

* * *

The total public and private administrative costs of zoning are far from insubstantial. These costs, when added to the high prevention costs zoning is likely to involve, may be so great that an entire zoning ordinance is inefficient; that is, the reduction in nuisance costs is less than the concomitant prevention and administrative costs. This occurrence is probably extremely common in the United States. Thus, other internalization devices are likely to be better equipped to deal with many problems now handled by zoning. Nevertheless, the efficiency of zoning as an internalization device varies with the specific type of externality at issue. This article will suggest * * * that mandatory regulations may indeed be the most efficient device for dealing with a few pervasive land use problems.

B. Zoning and Equity

Zoning can promote equity by prohibiting unneighborly acts, thereby protecting some landowners from privately inflicted losses. As it is usually operated, however, zoning is an inequitable system; the Achilles heel of zoning is that it does not correct the changes in wealth distribution it causes. When a zoning decision increases the value of a parcel, the owner is generally not obligated to disgorge the increased value. Conversely, when a zoning action reduces property values, an owner is not compensated for any losses unless he can obtain a judicial decision that the ordinance constitutes an unconstitutional "taking."

* * *

The inequities of zoning are not limited to its effects on landowners. Recent legal commentary about zoning has emphasized its potential as a

---

[56] A. Manvel, Local Land and Building Regulations 29 (National Commission on Urban Problems Research Report No. 6, 1968).

vehicle for segregation of racial minorities and low income groups.[83] In highly balkanized metropolitan areas, exclusionary policies, if widespread enough, may cause substantial inefficiencies by widely separating housing for working-class families from industrial jobs opportunities and may be unfair to excluded groups. Not surprisingly, small governments do seek to keep social and fiscal undesirables out of their communities entirely. Employing land use regulations to segregate racial groups predates the pioneering New York [zoning] ordinance. Some of the earliest reported cases involving controls having the effect of zoning dealt with devices designed to set apart the Chinese in California and Blacks elsewhere; these overt racial classifications have not survived constitutional scrutiny.[87]

The separation of families by income, however, is still abetted by many zoning ordinances, primarily through minimum lot size, lot frontage, and floor area requirements for residences, and the total exclusion of apartments and mobile homes. Needless to say, income discriminations often have racial ramifications. Lawsuits attacking these practices have primarily alleged violations of equal protection and use of the police power for invalid purposes, with relatively little success except in Pennsylvania[90] and New Jersey.[91] Legislative action to deal with exclusionary zoning has been taken only in Massachusetts and California.

In the United States zoning generally works to the detriment of the poor and near-poor, racial minorities, and renters; it operates for the benefit of the well-to-do, particularly homeowners, by artificially increasing the supply of sites on the market usable only for expensive homes and thus reducing their cost. The City of Los Angeles in effect prohibits its citizens of average income or less, and all would-be apartment dwellers, from living in the Santa Monica Mountains by restricting land use there to single-family homes on large lots. Market forces might have caused the Mountains to be inhabited primarily by the well-to-do, but not as exclusively so.

* * *

With the inherent shortcomings of zoning as a backdrop, this analysis now turns to the fundamental issues that underlie land use conflicts—the proper distribution of rights among landowners and optimal systems for their enforcement. That investigation will lead to the construction of an alternative model to zoning that alleviates the impact of the problems * * * just discussed without causing greater ones.

IV. Covenants, Merger, and Other Consensual Systems of Land Use Regulation

The construction of a more privatized land use control system begins with an examination of the implications of a laissez faire distribution of property rights. In that imaginary legal world, landowners would be free to use their land in any manner without fear of legal consequence. The government in such a society would provide a collective system for enforcement of privately negotiated agreements, but would itself impose no standards on land use. How would a landowner be expected to act under these conditions? If good manners were not a characteristic of this society, the landowner would realize that externalities were preventing him from maximizing his welfare. He would notice that his neighbors rarely generated external benefits through activities like fine architecture or landscaping. Further, he would observe that some of his neighbors were often causing him substantial harm that could be sharply reduced by relatively minor modifications, a shade on a neighbor's bright light, a filter on his smokestack, or a fence around his junkyard.

Following the realization that some internalization device would tend to enhance their welfare, landowners can be expected to try two types of voluntary transactions, merger and the partial exchange of rights. A merger is effected when a landowner is prompted to buy his neighbor's land in fee simple absolute. If there are no financing problems, this outcome is likely where the administrative costs of acquisition and unilateral rule making are less than the costs of bargaining for and enforcing a more limited exchange of rights. Merger is often the device

---

[83] *See, e.g.,* L. Sagalyn & G. Sternlieb, Zoning and Housing Costs (1973); Lefcoe, *The Public Housing Referendum Case, Zoning, and the Supreme Court,* 59 Calif. L. Rev. 1384 (1971); Sager, *Tight Little Island: Exclusionary Zoning, Equal Protection, and the Indigent,* 21 Stan. L. Rev. 767 (1969) * * *.

[87] Yick Wo v. Hopkins, 118 U.S. 356 (1886); Buchanan v. Warley, 245 U.S. 60 (1917) * * *.

[90] * * * Appeal of Kit-Mar Builders, 439 Pa. 466, 268 A.2d 765 (1970) * * *; Appeal of Girsh, 437 Pa. 237, 263 A.2d 395 (1970) * * *; National Land & Inv. Co. v. Koh, 419 Pa. 504, 215 A.2d 597 (1965) * * *.

[91] * * * Oakwood at Madison, Inc. v. Township of Madison, 117 N.J. Super 11, 283 A.2d 353 (1971) * * *. [Editor's Note: This article was written shortly before the New Jersey Supreme Court decided Southern Burlington County N.A.A.C.P. v. Township of Mt. Laurel, 67 N.J. 151, 336 A.2d 713 (1975).]

used by a landowner to internalize his own beneficial externalities, perhaps because the present legal system fails to provide any reliable alternative method of internalizing such spillovers. Good examples of internalization through merger are the "new town" developments recently undertaken by private land developers. The entrepreneur places improvements such as golf courses, lakes, and community centers near the center of his holding; ownership of the surrounding land allows the developer to internalize the increases in adjacent land values that result from the improvements.

The neighboring owners may decide not to merge but rather negotiate a lesser exchange of rights, enforcing the exchange through mechanisms provided by the government. For some consideration, a landowner might submit to restrictions on the use of his land or agree to be bound by affirmative obligations to carry out specific activities like mowing grass or maintaining a fence. Existing property law provides for enforcement of many agreements of this type, including covenants, leases, easements, and defeasible fees. Covenants serve as a representative example of these consensual transactions between landowners; this category encompasses affirmative and negative obligations and is perhaps the most prevalent type of private agreement between neighbors.

Covenants negotiated between landowners will tend to optimize resource allocation among them. In other words, the reduction in future nuisance costs to each party will exceed the sum of prevention and administrative costs each agrees to bear, with all costs discounted to present value. * * *

In addition to promoting efficiency, covenants will not usually cause unfair wealth transfers among landowners. Absent fraud, duress, and the like, a party will not agree to a contract that he perceives as unfair. Thus, assuming equal bargaining power and information, consensual covenants will not involve inequitable gains or losses to any party.

Covenants cause problems, however, when they impose external costs on third parties, creating suboptimal resource allocation and unfairness. The classic American example of this nature was the widespread use of covenants to prevent the sale of residential property to Blacks. Restrictive racial covenants, particularly when widespread, impose opportunity costs on Black home buyers by restricting their market. More difficult to measure, but unquestionably present, are the costs of segregation to society in general. Anti-Black covenants are unfair because they single out a small population group for permanent exclusion; the inequity is compounded because Blacks have suffered from other artificially imposed disadvantages. The courts understandably struck down such agreements on constitutional rights or public policy grounds.[124]

* * *

One limitation on the greater use of covenants is high administrative costs. Standard forms could reduce drafting costs to parties and information costs to participants in land markets, who now must decipher private land use restrictions. Information costs could also be reduced by simplifying, through modernization of the indexing of land records, the process of finding the covenants applicable to a specific parcel. More definite exposition of termination doctrines might also reduce administrative costs. When a common covenant scheme governs many parcels, high administrative costs may prevent landowners from organizing to terminate the scheme even though the prevention costs of the scheme exceed its reduction in nuisance costs. Courts have attempted to solve this problem by terminating those covenants where neighborhood conditions have changed. Liberal application of this doctrine results, however, in excessive litigation. State legislatures could help solve the problem by establishing standard termination procedures and maximum life spans for covenants; legislative rules would also permit courts to depart from perverse requirements such as "privity of estate" and "touch and concern" for the running of covenants. These judicially created rules are designed to prevent the accumulation of legal cobwebs on land parcels; the invocation of these rules, however, often ignores the intent of the parties. Procedures to remove stale covenants systematically after several decades would interfere less seriously with freedom of contract and tend to reduce administrative costs.

* * *

Systems of covenants are an ideal system of land use regulation in major developments undertaken by single owners. The administrative costs involved are minimal since the developer drafts the covenants unilaterally and buyers must accept them. In such cases, public intervention is necessary only at the margins of the parcel since most nuisance problems are internalized. The usefulness of private ordering

---

124 *See* * * * Shelley v. Kraemer, 334 U.S. 1 (1948). Whether narrowly drawn covenants to protect ethnic neighborhoods should also be illegal is a more difficult question.

in these situations is recognized, to some extent, by PUD zoning provisions. Since the land development industry is becoming increasingly dominated by larger firms, covenants should play a more important role in the future.

Even if covenant law were sensibly modernized, however, covenants could play only a limited role in older, established neighborhoods where land ownership is highly fractionated. Except for the simplest problems involving a few neighbors, land owners rarely meet as a group to draft agreements governing land use. Aside from privity of estate requirements that currently discourage such neighborhood mobilization, the costs of organizing many people are apparently too high, and the risk of freeloaders too great, for private bargaining to take place.

Thus, although covenants are an attractive device, they are not feasible in many neighborhoods. To deal with harmful externalities in these areas, the original assumption of a laissez faire distribution of property rights must be reconsidered. Even if the initial placement of rights is altered to a different distribution, landowners can still gain by trading rights. Consensual systems like covenants are valuable tools for private adjustment of any initial rights distribution.

V. Assigning Rights Among Landowners: A Reformulation of Nuisance law

More efficient and more equitable resource allocation will sometimes be achieved by altering the laissez faire distribution of property rights so as to place the risk of loss from external harms on the landowner carrying out the damaging activity. * * * Common law doctrines * * * have long assigned property rights to deter unneighborly acts. At common law, landowners were held to an absolute duty to provide lateral support for their neighbors' land. * * * Less tangible interferences such as noise, fumes, aesthetic blight, or vibration may be handled under the law of nuisance. Since most potential conflicts in modern urban environments involve these less tangible interferences, nuisance law provides the most important source of common law rules for shifting the risk of loss for external harms.

* * *

1. *Assigning Rights to Promote Efficiency: A Preliminary General Rule.* Efficient resource allocation is accomplished through the minimization of the sum of nuisance costs, prevention costs, and administrative costs arising from land use conflicts. A party compelled to bear a nuisance cost can be expected to adopt all preventive measures he perceived as efficient. A measure will appear efficient to a party if its prevention cost and the administrative cost of carrying it out are less than the reduction in nuisance costs achieved. Prevention costs cannot be diminished by shifting the assignment of rights; those costs are only affected by technological innovation. Legal rules may, however, affect the administrative costs involved in the execution of a specific preventive measure. Rights should therefore be assigned to reduce administrative costs in order to increase the number of preventive measures that parties perceive to be in their self-interest. Four guidelines can help reduce administrative costs; none is controlling, but each helps in assigning legal rights when other factors are neutral.

The first guideline is *knowledge.* It will help to assign the risk of loss to the party facing the lowest information costs. Legal rules should focus on the party who has, or can most cheaply acquire, relevant information on the risks of future nuisance costs, and who can most cheaply assess available preventive measures. The object of this guideline is minimizing expenditures of resources on information.

The second guideline is *organization.* It will help to place the risk of loss on the class of parties likely to have the lowest organization costs, usually the one with the fewest members. This assignment will reduce the costs of internal organization and policing against freeloaders that arise when many parties must negotiate the division of costs of damage payments or preventive measures.

The third guideline is *control.* When the risk of loss is assigned to the parties in control of the properties where the most efficient preventive actions can be taken, the administrative costs of executing the preventive measures will be reduced.

The final guideline is *simplicity of rules.* Other things being equal, simple rules of liability are preferable to more complex ones since they reduce the costs of determining the distribution of rights in specific cases.

These guidelines can now be used to generate rules of liability for nuisance cases. The process can begin with the following general rules of nuisance liability: if a physical change on B's property results in a diminution of the value of A's property, B should have to compensate A for that loss. This rule for liability of landowners is overbroad and will be qualified. As a general rule, however, it is more in accord with the guidelines for efficiency than the laissez faire distribution of property rights discussed earlier.

* * *

2. *Toward a Tripartite System of Internalization: The Unneighborliness Requirement.* The general rule of host landowner liability for harmful externalities must be qualified in order to operate yet more efficiently. A landowner can reduce the welfare of his neighbors either by undertaking harmful activities or by terminating beneficial conditions that had previously existed on his property; the analysis thus far has dealt with only the former situation. A layman would regard a smokestack or billboard as "theft" of neighborhood enjoyment that should be tagged with liability or proscribed. He would perceive quite differently, however, the demolition of an architectural landmark or the construction of a housing development on a beautiful vacant meadow. These latter acts would no doubt diminish neighboring property values, yet a layman would not characterize the acting landowner as a thief of neighborhood enjoyment, but perhaps as a former "Good Samaritan" who has understandably become tired of bestowing "windfalls" on his neighbors. Thieves, the layman would probably say, should be liable for the damage they cause, but lapsed Good Samaritans should not.

The wisdom of attaching any operational significance to this linguistic distinction has been a matter of considerable controversy. Some commentators have criticized the distinction on the ground that it cannot be determined which party is causing harm to the other.[172] * * * In ordinary speech, however, people constantly distinguish "harms" from "benefits." Evaluative terms like good, bad, beneficial, and harmful are easily used because people have remarkably consistent perceptions of normal conditions and thus can agree in characterizing deviations from normalcy. In any community, observers empirically establish standards of normal conduct for repetitive activities; people largely agree on normal clothes styles or normal behavior in public places. Similarly, there is considerable agreement on the identification of normal land uses, a category virtually certain to include characteristics of modestly priced residential developments. A specific land use is characterized in ordinary speech as beneficial when it would have a more positive than usual impact, and harmful when it would have a more negative than usual impact, on the values of normal surrounding properties assuming a laissez faire distribution of property rights.

* * *

Normalcy has become a central concept in law as well as language, but the reasons for this importance have not yet been adequately explored. This article contends that normalcy is often used as a legal standard because the concept promises substantial efficiencies. In order to promote economically productive behavior that cannot be easily achieved by bargaining and to satisfy community desires to reward virtuous activities, legal rules should seek to transfer wealth from those whose actions have unusually harmful external impacts and to those whose actions are unusually beneficial to others. That pattern of transfers is now accomplished through a tripartite set of rules incorporating the normalcy standard: meritorious behavior is sometimes rewarded through quasi-contract doctrines and other devices, normal behavior is treated neutrally, and substandard behavior is penalized through liability rules and other sanctions.

* * *

This article assumes that a tripartite legal approach to land use spillovers is more efficient than a unitary one. Proper internalization for the owner of a beautiful meadow or a beautiful building is then best accomplished through some reward system; his termination of those beneficial activities is deterred by concern about losing those rewards. Since the rules being formulated here are limited to the liability side of a tripartite system, imposition of host landowner liability must be limited to instances in which he undertakes subnormal activity. According to the simplicity of rules guideline, the addition of the element of subnormalcy to the prima facie case for nuisance will raise administrative costs in cases where the element is contested. Indeed, many students of tort law feel the added costs of the analogous fault requirement in negligence cases has undermined the viability of that system of liability, particularly in automobile accident cases. Fact finding in nuisance cases, however, is generally cheaper than in accident cases because the damaging condition is usually continuing; the administrative costs of a counterpart to the fault requirement should therefore be less.

The following modification in the general rule of host landowner liability is proposed to establish the tripartite system: a change in land use should result in liability of the host landowner only if the change is perceived as unneighborly according to contemporary community standards. In cases where only part of a complex land use is unneighborly, only the damage done by its unneighborly aspects should be compen-

[172] Coase, *Social Cost*, *supra* note 2, at 34–35. * * *

sable. For example, if a gas station blocks a scenic view, but a typical residence would also have blocked the view, damages from view blockage should not be included in the gas station's liability.

An unneighborliness test is a democratic and dynamic method of assuring that neighbors of an enterprising landowner do not receive excessive endowments of property rights. The unneighborliness concept is analogous to the emphasis on unreasonableness in current nuisance law, but the latter test is avoided here since it has been used in far too many situations to protect host landowners from liability, often by courts trying to avoid the harshness of injunctive relief.

* * *

Under the system described above, an aggrieved landowner establishes a prima facie case for nuisance when he shows that his neighbor has damaged him by carrying on activities, or harboring natural conditions, perceived as unneighborly under contemporary community standards. To determine whether a prima facie case against a proposed grocery can be made out by homeowners in the Santa Monica Mountains, one would have to investigate perceptions of groceries as neighbors in Los Angeles County. Groceries are relatively rare land uses, and they must be perceived as unneighborly since they are barred, along with other commercial uses, by most restrictive covenants in modest residential areas in Los Angeles. A grocery should thus be treated as a nuisance in that region. This treatment can be accorded because groceries are not so common that imposing liability on them will result in inefficiently numerous claims, the danger inherent in imposing liability for normal land uses.

VI. A Tentative Sketch of a More Privatized System of Land Use Regulation

* * * There remains the problem of selecting appropriate devices for correcting * * * imperfections in market operations. This article proposes that private nuisance remedies become the exclusive remedy for "localized" spillovers—that is, those that concern no more then several dozen parties. Private nuisance remedies, however, are not the optimal internalization system for all types of harmful spillovers from land use activity; in particular private remedies are likely to be an inefficient means of handling insubstantial injuries from "pervasive" nuisances that affect many outsiders. More centralized systems for internalizing pervasive harms may be capable of achieving savings in administrative costs that outweigh the inevitable allocative inefficiencies of collective regulation. This article will suggest that fines be assessed by a public authority to internalize insubstantial injuries from those pervasive nuisances that present a reasonably objective index of noxiousness. These fines would complement the nuisance remedies that would remain available to persons able to show substantial injury from the pervasive problem. Lack of an objective index of noxiousness may justify imposition of mandatory standards on pervasive nuisance activity, but such an approach is usually justified only when the public authority is willing to impose standards retroactively. To develop and administer these systems, this article proposes creation of a specialized metropolitan body.

A. The Superiority of Nuisance Law for Localized Harms

Many land use activities now constrained by zoning ordinances raise only localized threats that would be better handled through private nuisance remedies supplemented by covenants and good manners. The system of private nuisance law outlined above avoids the allocative inefficiencies threatened by mandatory regulations or injunctions. It relies upon a decentralized policing system that is triggered more efficiently than a centralized system, and it can easily be used to internalize existing nuisances, not merely future ones. It also assures the availability of compensation to parties substantially injured by nuisances.

The major drawback of the nuisance approach is potentially excessive administrative costs. Even in localized conflicts, the costs of assessing and distributing payments * * * might be so high as to make the nuisance approach inferior to one of its alternatives. Some economies should be possible, however, through proper structuring of the public administrative apparatus used for handling nuisance disputes. Land use conflicts arise frequently in urban areas and present specialized and repetitive issues. A single adjudicative authority[, a Nuisance Board,] with exclusive jurisdiction over these cases could resolve them with greater facility and consistency than courts of general jurisdiction.

* * *

Some examples will illustrate how the nuisance system might apply to localized problems now regulated by zoning.

* * *

Intermixtures of different land uses. The paramount purpose of zoning is the segregation of land uses into different districts; as discussed earlier this segregation causes allocative inefficiencies, requires frequent and expensive amendments, and makes equitable administration impossible. Since more privatized alternatives than use zoning are available, use zoning should be discontinued. The nuisance system, however, despite its general advantages, is unlikely to be the best method of handling pervasive land use conflicts. Harmful spillovers from heavy uses like steel mills may be so widespread that the administrative costs of private nuisance remedies renders inefficient and impracticable use of that system as an internalization device.

Use zoning, however, is not the only available response to the problem of pervasive nuisances. Rather than rely on use zoning, municipalities should deal with uninternalized pervasive harms through fines, varying in magnitude from zone to zone, and selected uniform mandatory standards. The effect of this change would not be radical. The threat of suboptimal location of heavy uses was greatly exaggerated in the early zoning literature; market transactions naturally segregate land use to a remarkable extent. Heavy uses in Houston, where there is neither zoning nor a fine system, appear to be as spatially segregated as in most zoned cities.

In addition, use zoning is not primarily concerned with pervasive conflicts. For example, most zoning ordinances try to segregate multi-acre estates from modest subdivisions, single-family residences from multifamily developments, and all residential units from light commercial and industrial uses. The nuisance system, buttressed by private covenants, is likely to be superior to zoning for handling conflicts involving these kinds of uses. First, use zoning is an overreaction to the need to control micro-neighborhood conditions. Although homeowners may believe that construction of a nearby apartment building will depress property values, there is little evidence to support such fears. Even where intermixture of uses does result in substantial external losses, those losses are usually localized. In addition, proximity to certain uses may entail benefits that offset external costs; for example, commercial and industrial uses provide opportunities for shopping and employment.

The familiar example of a grocery in the Santa Monica Mountains can be used to demonstrate how a Nuisance Board could handle conflicts between residential and commercial uses. After examining metropolitan sentiment, the Board would probably classify groceries as an unneighborly land use. Nevertheless, because of the benefits of proximity to groceries, it is unlikely that more than a score or so of the grocery's neighbors could prove substantial harm from its operation. If the parties could not reach a private settlement, the uncompensated neighbors could take their case to the Nuisance Board either to collect damages or to purchase the closing of the grocery. This approach would be much more likely than the present system to assure the optimal number of groceries, as well as uses like multifamily dwellings, in the Mountains. Undoubtedly the nuisance system will permit groceries to externalize some insubstantial pervasive costs, but allocative perfection—the adoption of all efficient preventive measures—is too administratively burdensome to be desirable.

* * *

B. The Necessity of More Collective Internalization Systems for Pervasive Harm

A pervasive nuisance may inflict substantial harm on nearby neighbors and also cause legally insubstantial injuries to a large number of more distant parties. Entitlement to nuisance remedies assures those suffering large injuries compensation for their losses. Use of nuisance remedies to internalize the insubstantial pervasive harms, however, would pose an intolerable administrative burden. One of the more collective internalization systems—fines, regulatory taxes, mandatory standards, mandatory prohibitions—may prove to be a more efficient intervention by eliminating the task of assessing and distributing many small awards. It might be suggested that insubstantial, pervasive harms should be left uninternalized. Although these injuries are individually insubstantial, however, the total harm may be significant; thus, major allocative efficiencies should be possible if any appropriate internalization device can be found. In addition, when a nuisance is pervasive, the administrative costs of forcing internalization are likely to be justified because of efficiencies of scale of policing; centrally enforced internalization of localized insubstantial injuries, however, is less likely to be efficient.

An informed choice among the more collective systems for internalization would be primarily based on empirical examination of each system's relative administrative costs, and potential for allocative damage. Since many of the options have not been tried, policy prescriptions at this point are necessarily tentative. This analysis suggests, however, that in many instances fines should be tried in the place of mandatory standards and prohibitions as a means of regulating pervasive nuisances.

1. *Uniform Standards Enforced Solely through Fines.* Welfare economists have historically favored fines as solutions to problems of external cost. Unlike mandatory standards and prohibitions, fines can be applied retrospectively to existing nuisances without imposing the drastic prevention costs that deter

many zoning administrators from eliminating nonconforming uses. Fines are also more flexible than mandatory regulations since a landowner is free to buy, in effect, the right to violate an inefficient standard. A system of fines requires establishment of standards for imposition of the fines, rules for calculating their amounts, and an administrative structure for assessment and collection.

Standards can take either of two forms: performance standards, setting performance levels to be achieved, or specification standards, detailing exact technologies that are, and are not, acceptable. * * * Performance standards are often praised in the literature, but are useful only when the allocative flexibility they permit justifies the additional administrative costs, to both the regulator and the regulated, of measuring compliance with the standards. A desirable combination is thus the establishment of a general performance standard and, in addition, the articulation of examples of complying and noncomplying technologies.

The unneighborliness requirement is a general performance standard and may function well as a general standard for identifying conduct to be fined. Fines on activities meeting an unneighborliness test will discourage below normal conduct; * * * the fining of normal conduct is rarely efficient because of the frequency of these offenses, and the efficient way to induce above-normal behavior is usually through rewards. Just as administrative costs in nuisance cases can be reduced by regulations identifying unneighborly activities in a jurisdiction, the Nuisance Board should be authorized to write standards for fines and should recognize the advantages of a high degree of specificity in its regulations.

Administrative simplicity is a paramount consideration in structuring the calculation of fines. For distributional reasons, substantially injured landowners should be permitted to pursue their nuisance remedies. To avoid "overinternalization" the fines must then be calculated to cover only the insubstantial, and thus incompensable, losses inflicted by the pervasive unneighborly activity. * * *

Monetary penalties could be individually calculated to internalize the precise damage inflicted on the actual neighbors of the offensive activity, the "regulatory taxes" approach, or they could be "fines" based solely on the nature of the offending landowner's conduct, with the mix of surrounding uses assumed to be normal. Fines are simpler, and thus often will be the preferable approach; for example, pollution charges cannot feasibly be calculated to equal the actual external damage of each polluter. A middle ground might be best. A regulatory agency might obtain greater allocative efficiency, at additional administrative cost, by combining the two approaches and varying assessments for violations of standards according to the geographic zone in which the offending activity occurs. The amount of the fine would be an estimate of the pervasive damage a violation would normally cause in that mapped zone. Fines against unusually tall buildings, for example, would be greater in hilly areas or along coast lines than elsewhere, but would be uniformly assessed within each zone. Varying fines among zones would reintroduce some of the arbitrariness and discrimination typical of current zoning systems. The distributional effects of determining the boundaries of zones for fines, however, would not be nearly as dramatic as under current zoning decisions. Present restrictions on heights determine whether or not a skyscraper can be built; zones for fines would affect only the developer's cost of construction, not his right to build.

* * *

Although fines are an attractive land use control, they are not necessarily the best system for all types of pervasive nuisances. Fines work best as an internalization device when the harmful activity presents a simple and objective index of noxiousness; the amount of the fine is then easily keyed to that index. If no such index exists, the administrative costs of calculation will be higher, and the amount of individual fines are likely to be so arbitrary that courts will have a difficult time preventing graft and discrimination. Even where a simple, objective index can be applied, rapid changes in index variables may make fines unworkable by requiring maintenance of expensive monitoring devices.

* * *

2. *Mandatory Enforcement of Uniform Standards and Prohibitions.* When an activity that causes pervasive harm presents no reasonably objective indexes of noxiousness * * * mandatory enforcement of minimum standards may be the best method for limiting damage * * *. Mandatory standards involve great risks, however, and such a system should be compared to the laissez faire approach that is preferable when there is no cost-justified mechanism for internalizing pervasive nuisance injuries. In addition, mandatory standards raise difficult equity issues when they are nonuniform, either among zones or over time due to prospective application. To be fair, standards should generally apply across a given metropolitan area and, except where obviously inefficient, should be retroactive as well as prospective. Since mandatory restraints on normal behavior are politically unpopular, retrospective mandatory stan-

dards are rarely aimed at activities that are not perceived as unneighborly. * * *

Mandatory standards may be the best land use control system for regulating activities like subdivision design. Subdivision activity may pervasively disrupt the community road, utility, and drainage networks. There is no apparent simple index for assessing fines against violations of normal standards on subdivision design, and regulatory taxes that equal the actual damage inflicted would be both expensive to calculate and difficult for courts to scrutinize. The current system of mandatory subdivision standards is often discriminatory in that new subdivisions are commonly required to be above-normal in quality. This discrimination could be avoided by making uniform subdivision standards, where efficient, applicable to both new and existing subdivisions, and by refraining from prospective controls mandating above-normal conduct.

* * *

VII. CONCLUSION

The most prevalent systems of land use control in the United States are neither as efficient nor as equitable as available alternatives. Detailed mandatory zoning standards inevitably impair efficient urban growth and discriminate against migrants, lower classes, and landowners with little political influence. The elimination of all mandatory zoning controls on populations densities, land use locations, and building bulks is therefore probably desirable. The alternative proposed in this article relies primarily on a variety of less centralized devices to internalize the external costs of unneighborly land use activities.

* * *

The proposed approach is superior to zoning in achieving the fundamental goals of a land use control system—efficiency and equity. Greater reliance on decentralized internalization devices reduces the potential for high prevention costs inherent in centralized approaches. Although the administrative costs of the proposed combination of remedies might be greater than in a system relying heavily on zoning controls, that difference is likely to be more than compensated for by allocative efficiencies. To assure equity, arbitrary geographic zones for standards that are too elusive for effective judicial review should be avoided; extensive use of zones has resulted in the serious amounts of graft and discrimination that now plague zoning. Finally elimination of mandatory population density controls can correct the regressive distributional effects of existing zoning standards.

Note

Ellickson, like his more politically liberal peers, pays quite a bit of attention to the problem of exclusionary zoning. As you know, New Jersey opted to impose a highly structured regulation of zoning to guarantee that local governments would accept their "fair share" of least cost housing. *Southern Burlington County N.A.A.C.P. v. Township of Mt. Laurel*, 67 N.J. 151, 336 A.2d 713 (1975); *Southern Burlington County N.A.A.C.P. v. Township of Mt. Laurel*, 92 N.J. 158, 456 A.2d 390 (1983). Ellickson prefers to remove density, lot size and building size restrictions altogether and leave disputes over use to Nuisance Boards. Even if, as Ellickson suggests, such Nuisance Boards covered an entire metropolitan area rather than each small town, would they be likely to allow least cost housing in existing residential neighborhoods? To whatever extent they would restrain such development more than construction of standard housing, do you think Ellickson would favor adoption of any additional regulations?

C. Government and Community: Civic Republicanism Revisited

Since the publication of John Rawls' A THEORY OF JUSTICE, excerpted to open this section, a large literature has developed on the mutual responsibilities of individuals within communities and on the obligations of government to care for the economic well-being of the body politic. Three articles, already widely recognized as classics, are excerpted here. In the first, *Market-Inalienability*, Margaret

Jane Radin argues that the concept of personhood, when properly thought of as an idea of human flourishing within a community, requires that use of markets be restricted. The more intimately connected with human flourishing an item of value is, the less likely it is that markets should be allowed. Radin is followed by Joseph Singer's *The Reliance Interest in Property*, and William Simon's *Social-Republican Property*. Both Singer and Simon argue that relationships create and require economic understandings. Singer focuses on the ways in which people's long term expectations about economic relationships should be used to formulate legal policy. Simon uses classical and sometimes contradictory notions of equality and individual participation in government to develop a new understanding of the meaning of social-republican property.

In a related set of articles, excerpted in other parts of this anthology, law and economics theory has been used to argue that those with a cooperative frame of mind will succeed less well in a standard market economy unless they work in group settings. Two of the best are by Carol M. Rose, *Women and Property: Gaining and Losing Ground*, 78 VA. L. REV. 421 (1992), and Stewart Sterk, *Neighbors in American Land Law*, 87 COLUM. L. REV. 55 (1987).

JOHN RAWLS, A THEORY OF JUSTICE 11–15, 284–287, 293 (1971)*

THE MAIN IDEA OF THE THEORY OF JUSTICE

My aim is to present a conception of justice which generalizes and carries to a higher level of abstraction the familiar theory of the social contract as found, say, in Locke, Rousseau, and Kant. In order to do this we are not to think of the original contract as one to enter a particular society or to set up a particular form of government. Rather, the guiding idea is that the principles of justice for the basic structure of society are the object of the original agreement. They are the principles that free and rational persons concerned to further their own interests would accept in an initial position of equality as defining the fundamental terms of their association. These principles are to regulate all further agreements; they specify the kinds of social cooperation that can be entered into and the forms of government that can be established. This way of regarding the principles of justice I shall call justice as fairness.

Thus we are to imagine that those who engage in social cooperation choose together, in one joint act, the principles which are to assign basic rights and duties and to determine the division of social benefits. Men are to decide in advance how they are to regulate their claims against one another and what is to be the foundation charter of their society. Just as each person must decide by rational reflection what constitutes his good, that is, the system of ends which it is rational for him to pursue, so a group of persons must decide once and for all what is to count among them as just and unjust. The choice which rational men would make in this hypothetical situation of equal liberty, assuming for the present that this choice problem has a solution, determine the principles of justice.

In justice as fairness the original position of equality corresponds to the state of nature in the traditional theory of the social contract. This original position is not, of course, thought of as an actual historical state of affairs, much less as a primitive condition of culture. It is understood as a purely hypothetical situation characterized so as to lead to a certain conception of justice. Among the essential features of this situation is that no one knows his place in society, his class position or social status, nor does any one know his fortune in the distribution

*Reprinted by permission of the publishers from A THEORY OF JUSTICE by John Rawls, Cambridge, Mass.: The Belknap Press of Harvard University Press, Copyright © 1971 by the President and Fellows of Harvard College.

of natural assets and abilities, his intelligence, strength, and the like. I shall even assume that the parties do not know their conceptions of the good or their special psychological propensities. The principles of justice are chosen behind the veil of ignorance. This ensures that no one is advantaged or disadvantaged in the choice of principles by the outcome of natural chance or the contingency of social circumstances. Since all are similarly situated and no one is able to design principles to favor his particular condition, the principles of justice are the result of a fair agreement or bargain. For given the circumstances of the original position, the symmetry of everyone's relations to each other, this initial situation is fair between individuals as moral persons, that is, as rational beings with their own ends and capable, I shall assume, of a sense of justice. The original position is, one might say, the appropriate initial status quo, and thus the fundamental agreements reached in it are fair. This explains the propriety of the name "justice as fairness": it conveys the idea that the principles of justice are agreed to in an initial situation that is fair. The name does not mean that the concepts of justice and fairness are the same, any more than the phrase "poetry as metaphor" means that the concepts of poetry and metaphor are the same.

* * *

In working out the conception of justice as fairness one main task clearly is to determine which principles of justice would be chosen in the original position. To do this we must describe this situation in some detail and formulate with care the problem of choice which it presents. * * * It may be observed, however, that once the principles of justice are thought of as arising from an original agreement in a situation of equality, it is an open question whether the principle of utility would be acknowledged. Offhand it hardly seems likely that the persons who view themselves as equals, entitled to press their claims upon one another, would agree to a principle which may require lesser life prospects for some simply for the sake of a greater sum of advantages enjoyed by others. Since each desires to protect his interests, his capacity to advance his conception of the good, no one has a reason to acquiesce in an enduring loss for himself in order to bring about a greater net balance of satisfaction. In the absence of strong and lasting benevolent impulses, a rational man would not accept a basic structure merely because it maximized the algebraic sum of advantages irrespective of its permanent effects on his own basic rights and interests. Thus it seems that the principle of utility is incompatible with the conception of social cooperation among equals for mutual advantage. It appears to be inconsistent with the idea of reciprocity implicit in the notion of a well-ordered society. Or, at any rate, so I shall argue.

I shall maintain instead that the persons in the initial situation would choose two rather different principles: the first requires equality in the assignment of basic rights and duties, while the second holds that social and economic inequalities, for example inequalities of wealth and authority, are just only if they result in compensating benefits for everyone, and in particular for the least advantaged members of society. These principles rule out justifying institutions on the grounds that the hardships of some are offset by the greater good in the aggregate. It may be expedient but it is not just that some should have less in order that others may prosper. But there is no injustice in the greater benefits earned by a few provided that the situation of persons not so fortunate is thereby improved. The intuitive idea is that since everyone's well-being depends upon a scheme of cooperation without which no one could have a satisfactory life, the division of advantages should be such as to draw forth the willing cooperation of everyone taking part in it, including those less well situated. Yet this can be expected only if reasonable terms are proposed. The two principles mentioned seem to be a fair agreement on the basis of which those better endowed, or more fortunate in their social position, neither of which we can be said to deserve, could expect the willing cooperation of others when some workable scheme is a necessary condition of the welfare of all. Once we decide to look for a conception of justice that nullifies the accidents of natural endowment and the contingencies of social circumstance as counters in quest for political and economic advantage, we are led to these principles. They express the result of leaving aside those aspects of the social world that seem arbitrary from a moral point of view.

* * *

THE PROBLEM OF JUSTICE BETWEEN GENERATIONS

We must now consider the question of justice between generations. There is no need to stress the difficulties that this problem raises. It subjects any ethical theory to severe if not impossible tests. Nevertheless, the account of justice as fairness would be incomplete without some discussion of this important matter. The problem arises in the present context because the question is still open whether the social system as a whole, the competitive economy surrounded by the appropriate family of background institutions, can be made to satisfy the two principles of justice. The answer is bound to depend, to some degree anyway, on the level at which the social minimum is to be set. But this in turn connects up with how far the present generation is bound to respect the claims of its successors.

* * *

Finding a just savings principle is one aspect of this question. Now I believe that it is not possible, at present anyway, to define precise limits on what the rate of savings should be. How the burden of capital accumulation and of raising the standard of civilization and culture is to be shared between generations seems to admit of no definite answer. It does not follow, however, that certain bounds which impose significant ethical constraints cannot be formulated. As I have said, a moral theory characterizes a point of view from which policies are to be assessed; and it may often be clear that a suggested answer is mistaken even if an alternative doctrine is not ready at hand.

* * *

Now the contract doctrine looks at the problem from the standpoint of the original position. The parties do not know to which generation they belong or, what comes to the same thing, the stage of civilization of their society. They have no way of telling whether it is poor or relatively wealthy, largely agricultural or already industrialized, and so on. The veil of ignorance is complete in these respects. Thus the persons in the original position are to ask themselves how much they would be willing to save at each stage of advance on the assumption that all other generations are to save at the same rates. That is, they are to consider their willingness to save at any given phase of civilization with the understanding that the rates they propose are to regulate the whole span of accumulation. In effect, then, they must choose a just savings principle that assigns an appropriate rate of accumulation to each level of advance. Presumably this rate changes depending upon the state of society. When people are poor and saving is difficult, a lower rate of saving should be required; whereas in a wealthier society greater savings may reasonably be expected since the real burden is less. Eventually once just institutions are firmly established, the net accumulation required falls to zero. At this point a society meets its duty of justice by maintaining just institutions and preserving their material base.

* * *

We can now see that persons in different generations have duties and obligations to one another just as contemporaries do. The present generation cannot do as it pleases but is bound by the principles that would be chosen in the original position to define justice between persons at different moments of time. In addition, men have a natural duty to uphold and to further just institutions and for this the improvement of civilization up to a certain level is required. The derivation of these duties and obligations may seem at first a somewhat farfetched application of the contract doctrine. Nevertheless these requirements would be acknowledged in the original position, and so the conception of justice as fairness covers these matters without any change in its basic idea.

Margaret Jane Radin, *Market-Inalienability*, 100 HARV. L. REV. 1849, 1898–1917, 1936–1937 (1987)*

* * *

Two theories about freedom are central to the ideological framework in which we view inalienability: the notion that freedom means negative liberty, and the notion that (negative) liberty is identical with, or necessarily connected to, free alienability of everything in markets. The conception of freedom as negative liberty gives rise to the view that all inalienabilities are paternalistic limitations on freedom. The idea that liberty consists in alienability of everything in markets clashes with substantive requirements of personhood, making it difficult, for example, to argue against human commodification. In general, the commitment to negative liberty, like the commitment to the Kantian structure of persons versus objects, has caused confusion in liberal pluralism** and has exerted a pull toward universal commodification.***

Inalienabilities are often said to be paternalistic.[187] Paternalism usually means to substitute the judgment of a third party or the government for that of a person on the ground that to do so is in that person's best interests. For advocates of negative liberty, to substitute someone else's choice for my own is a naked infringement of my liberty. Freedom means doing (or not doing) whatever I as an individual prefer at the moment, as long as I am not harming other people. To think of inalienability as paternalism assumes that freedom is negative liberty—that people would choose to alienate certain things if they could, but are restrained from doing so by moral or legal rules saying, in effect, that they are mistaken about what is good for them.

To say that inalienabilities involve a loss of freedom also assumes that alienation itself is an act of freedom, or is freedom-enhancing. Someone who holds this view and conceives of alienation as sale through free contract is deeply committed to commodification as expressive of—perhaps necessary for—human freedom. Insofar as theories of negative freedom are allied to universal commodification, so are traditional discussions of inalienability in terms of paternalism. If we reject the notion that freedom means negative liberty, and the notion that liberty and alienation in markets are identical or necessarily connected, then inalienability will cease to seem inherently paternalistic. If we adopt a positive view of liberty that includes proper self-development as necessary for freedom, then inalienabilities needed to foster that development will be seen as freedom-enhancing rather than as impositions of unwanted restraints on our desires to transact in markets.

Joel Feinberg's discussion of the inalienable right to life[192] illustrates the traditional link between inalienability and paternalism, as well as the tension caused by the clash between negative liberty and substantive requirements of personhood. Feinberg distinguishes three conceptions of the inalienable right to life, which he calls "the paternalist," "the founding fathers," and "the extreme antipaternalist." In the view he calls paternalist, to say that the right to life is inalienable means that it is a nonrelinquishable mandatory right, one that ought to be exercised, like the right to education. In contrast, the view that Feinberg attributes to the founding fathers holds that the inalienable right to life is a nonrelinquishable discretionary right. It is discretionary because the individual may choose whether to exercise it. For example, the right to own property is a discretionary right because I may choose to own nothing; it is a nonrelinquishable discretionary right because I cannot morally or legally renounce the right to own property even if I choose not to own any. Feinberg concludes that the nonrelinquishable right to life is discretionary, not mandatory:

> [W]e have a right, within the boundaries of our own autonomy, to live or die, as we choose . . .. [T]he basic right underlying each is the right to be one's own master, to dispose of one's own lot as one chooses, subject of course to the limits imposed by the like rights of others. . . . In exercising my own choice in these matters, I am not renouncing, abjuring, forswearing, resigning, or relinquishing my right to life; quite the contrary, I am acting on that right by exercising it one way or the other.

**[Editor's Note: Radin, earlier in this article at p. 1858, defines liberal pluralists as "those who see a normatively appropriate but limited realm for commodification coexisting with one or more nonmarket realms. Pluralists often see one other normative realm besides that of the market, and partition the social world into markets and politics, markets and rights, or markets and families; but pluralists also may envision multiple nonmarket realms. For a pluralist, the crucial question is how to conceive of the permissible scope of the market."]

***[Editor's Note: Radin, earlier in this article at 1860, states that "universal commodifcation is characterized by universal market rhetoric and universal market methodology. In universal market rhetoric—the discourse of complete commodification—everything that is desired or valued is conceived of and spoken of as a 'good.' Everything that is desired or valued is an object that can be possessed, that can be thought of as equivalent to a sum of money, and that can be alienated. The person is conceived of and spoken of as the possessor and trader of these goods, and hence all human interactions are sales."]

187 Calabresi and Melamed's discussion of inalienability rules illustrates a typical use of the notion of paternalism. *See* Calabresi & Melamed, *Property Rules, Liaability Rules, and Inalienability: One View of the Cathedral*, 85 HARV. L. REV. 1089 (1972). Another illustration is Anthony Kronman's treatment of restrictions on alienation as a form of paternalism. *See* Kronman, *Paternalism and the Law of Contracts*, 92 YALE L.J. 763 (1983).

192 *See* Feinberg, *Voluntary Euthanasia and the Inalienable Right*, 7 PHIL. & PUB. AFF. 93 (1978).

This passage suggests that the right to life is discretionary because it is parasitic on negative liberty. But Feinberg does not say whether the underlying right to be one's own master is mandatory or discretionary. The omission points to an apparent contradiction in the argument, a contradiction that stems from a commitment to negative liberty. If the discretionary right to life is nonrelinquishable, as Feinberg claims is the founding fathers' view, then we can infer that the "basic right" to have discretion—liberty—must be mandatory: one cannot choose not to be one's own master, not to dispose of one's lot as one chooses. But to attribute this mandatory conception of liberty to the founding fathers would apparently be to attribute to them a form of positive liberty, a view that people can be required to be free. Hence, Feinberg attributes to the founding fathers a discretionary, not mandatory, view of the right to liberty. But if the right to liberty is indeed discretionary, then it seems I could choose not to be my own master, not to dispose of my lot as I choose, just as I could choose not to own property. And if I could choose that, I could choose not to have any of the other parasitic nonrelinquishable rights, like the right to life. The right to life would then be relinquishable.

This contradiction shows why a commitment to negative liberty pulls liberal pluralists toward universal commodification. The commitment to negative liberty usually attributed to the founding fathers forces those who hold it to choose between submerging a contradiction and moving toward conceiving of everything as relinquishable. If the intellectual descendants of the founding fathers want to maintain a nonrelinquishable discretionary right to life, they must adopt a mandatory right to liberty: we are not free not to be free. But adopting a mandatory right moves toward positive liberty, undermining the negative view that generates the nonrelinquishable, but discretionary, right to life. Holding firm to the view that liberty means negative liberty leads to a view that everything, including one's life, is relinquishable.

In this latter view, that of Feinberg's "extreme antipaternalist," the fully informed autonomous individual could sell herself into slavery or sell her right to life. Thus, the antipaternalist is a universal commodifier. This appears to be a more cogent view, once we grant that rights to life and property are parasitic upon an inalienable, but nonmandatory, right to negative liberty.

Might one hold fast to negative liberty and—contrary to the argument I have just given—still claim we are not free not to be free? This difficulty is the root of the tension between pluralism and negative liberty, and of the consequent pressure to give up pluralism. Mill's well-known attempt to argue against freedom to sell oneself into slavery directly poses this difficulty:

> [B]y selling himself for a slave, [a person] abdicates his liberty; he foregoes any future use of it beyond that single act. He therefore defeats, in his own case, the very purpose which is the justification of allowing him to dispose of himself . . .. The principle of freedom cannot require that he should be free not to be free. It is not freedom, to be allowed to alienate his freedom.[201]

The argument is obscure. It is hard to see why Mill thought it obvious that the principle of negative freedom could not require the "freedom not to be free;" only positive freedom clearly holds that a person must be free. In general, what in Mill's view is the connection between free alienation and freedom? (Why is alienation of freedom "not freedom"?) Most commentators have viewed Mill's argument against selling off one's freedom as a lapse into paternalism.

Neither in his conception of freedom nor in his conception of alienability does Mill appear to explain why human beings are noncommodifiable. One could understand him to imply that there is an unstated divide between the realm of the market (free trade) and the realm of politics (liberty). People must be free in order for a free political order to exist; they cannot be free without such a political order; hence, in the nonmarket realm they cannot, without contradiction, be free not to be free. This reconstruction makes Mill a pluralist, as indeed he apparently wished to be; but the reading is not very true to Mill in the way it relinquishes negative liberty.

Again, one way to avoid Mill's problem is to espouse universal commodification. The universal commodifier can hold on to negative liberty and avoid Mill's problem—espousing negative liberty while eschewing voluntary enslavement—because under universal commodification freedom itself is seen as monetizable and alienable. Those who tend toward universal commodification may indeed endorse voluntary enslavement.[205] Those who declare

[201] J. S. Mill, *On Liberty*, in THREE ESSAYS 126 (1975).

[205] Robert Nozick takes the extreme view: a "free system" will allow an individual "to sell himself into

human beings noncommodifiable must do so on the ground of postulated market failure (for example, transaction costs.)

We can now see why liberal pluralism should be reconceived. If we are to avoid the tendency toward universal commodification inherent in liberal pluralism, we must cease thinking that market alienability is inherent in the concept of property, and we must modify pluralism's commitments to negative liberty and Kantian personhood. In doing so, we must find a satisfactory way of deciding what market-inalienabilities are justified by the need to protect and foster personhood, and a way of understanding why these inalienabilities seem to us to be freedom enhancing.

V. Toward an Evolutionary Pluralism

In this Part, I develop a pluralist view that differs in significant respects from liberal pluralism. My central hypothesis is that market-inalienability is grounded in noncommodification of things important to personhood. In an ideal world markets would not necessarily be abolished, but market-inalienability would protect all things important to personhood. But we do not live in an ideal world. In the nonideal world we do live in, market-inalienability must be judged against a background of unequal power. In that world it may sometimes be better to commodify incompletely than not to commodify at all. Market-inalienability may be ideally justified in light of an appropriate conception of human flourishing, and yet sometimes be unjustifiable because of our nonideal circumstances.

A. Noncommodification and the Ideal of Human Flourishing

1. Rethinking Personhood: Freedom, Identity, Contextuality.—Because of the ideological heritage of the subject/object dichotomy, we tend to view things internal to the person as inalienable and things external as freely alienable. Because of the ideological heritage of negative liberty, we also tend to think of inalienabilities as paternalistic. A better view of personhood, one that does not conceive of the self as pure subjectivity standing wholly separate from an environment of pure objectivity, should enable us to discard both the notion that inalienabilities relate only to things wholly subjective or internal and the notion that inalienabilities are paternalistic.

In searching for such a better view, it is useful to single out three main, overlapping aspects of personhood: freedom, identity, and contextuality. The freedom aspect of personhood focuses on will, or the power to choose for oneself. In order to be autonomous individuals, we must at least be able to act for ourselves through free will in relation to the environment of things and other people. The identity aspect of personhood focuses on the integrity and continuity of the self required for individuation. In order to have a unique individual identity, we must have selves that are integrated and continuous over time. The contextuality aspect of personhood focuses on the necessity of self-constitution in relation to the environment of things and other people. In order to be differentiated human persons, unique individuals, we must have relationships with the social and natural world.

A better view of personhood—a conception of human flourishing that is superior to the one implied by universal commodification—should present more satisfactory views of personhood in each of these three aspects. I am not seeking here to elaborate a complete view of personhood. Rather, I focus primarily on a certain view of contextuality and its consequences: the view that connections between the person and her environment are integral to personhood. I also suggest that to the extent we have already accepted certain views of freedom, identity, and contextuality, we are committed to a view of personhood that rejects universal commodification.

* * *

A more positive meaning of freedom starts to emerge if one accepts the contextuality aspect of personhood. Contextuality means that physical and social contexts are integral to personal individuation, to self-development. Even under the narrowest conception of negative liberty, we would have to bring about the social environment that makes trade possible in order to become the persons whose freedom consists in unfettered trades of commodified objects. Under a broader negative view that conceives of freedom as the ability to make oneself what one will, contextuality implies that self-development in accordance with one's own will requires one to will certain interactions with the physical and social context because context can be integral to self-development. The relationship between personhood and context requires a positive commitment to act so as to create and maintain particular contexts of

---

slavery." R. Nozick, Anarchy, State, and Utopia 331 (1974).

environment and community. Recognition of the need for such a commitment turns toward a positive view of freedom, in which the self-development of the individual is linked to pursuit of proper social development, and in which proper self-development, as a requirement of personhood, could in principle sometimes take precedence over one's momentary desires or preferences.

Universal commodification undermines personal identity by conceiving of personal attributes, relationships, and philosophical and moral commitments as monetizable and alienable from the self. A better view of personhood should understand many kinds of particulars—one's politics, work, religion, family, love, sexuality, friendships, altruism, experiences, wisdom, moral commitments, character, and personal attributes—as integral to the self. To understand any of these as monetizable or completely detachable from the person—to think, for example, that the value of one person's moral commitments is commensurate or fungible with those of another, or that the "same" person remains when her moral commitments are subtracted—is to do violence to our deepest understanding of what it is to be human.

To affirm that work, politics, or character is integral to the person is not to say that persons cease to be persons when they dissociate themselves from their jobs, political engagements, or personal attributes. Indeed, the ability to dissociate oneself from one's particular context seems integral to personhood. But if we must recognize the importance of the ability to detach oneself, we must recognize as well that interaction with physical and social contexts is also integral to personhood. One's surroundings—both people and things—can become part of who one is, of the self. From our understanding that attributes and things can be integral to personhood, which stems mainly from our understanding of identity and contextuality, and from our rejection of the idea of commodification of the person, which stems mainly from our understanding of freedom, it follows that those attributes and things identified with the person cannot be treated as completely commodified. Hence, market-inalienability may attach to things that are personal.

2. Protecting Personhood: Noncommodification of Personal Rights, Attributes, and Things.—* * * We are now in a better position to understand how conceiving of personal things as commodities does violence to personhood, and to explore the problem of knowing what things are personal.

To conceive of something personal as fungible assumes that the person and the attribute, right, or thing, are separate. This view imposes the subject/object dichotomy to create two kinds of alienation. If the discourse of fungibility is partially made one's own, it creates disorientation of the self that experiences the distortion of its own personhood. For example, workers who internalize market rhetoric conceive of their own labor as a commodity separate from themselves as persons; they dissociate their daily life from their own self-conception. To the extent the discourse is not internalized, it creates alienation between those who use the discourse and those whose personhood they wrong in doing so. For example, workers who do not conceive of their labor as a commodity are alienated from others who do, because, in the workers' view, people who conceive of their labor as a commodity fail to see them as whole persons.

To conceive of something personal as fungible also assumes that persons cannot freely give of themselves to others. At best they can bestow commodities. At worst—in universal commodification—the gift is conceived of as a bargain. Conceiving of gifts as bargains not only conceives of what is personal as fungible, it also endorses the picture of persons as profit-maximizers. A better view of personhood should conceive of gifts not as disguised sales, but rather as expressions of the interrelationships between the self and others. To relinquish something to someone else by gift is to give of yourself. Such a gift takes place within a personal relationship with the recipient, or else it creates one. Commodification stresses separateness both between ourselves and our things and between ourselves and other people. To postulate personal interrelationship and communion requires us to postulate people who can yield personal things to other people and not have them instantly become fungible. Seen this way, gifts diminish separateness. This is why (to take an obvious example) people say that sex bought and paid for is not the same "thing" as sex freely shared. Commodified sex leaves the parties as separate individuals and perhaps reinforces their separateness; they only engage in it if each individual considers it worthwhile. Noncommodified sex ideally diminishes separateness; it is conceived of as a union because it is ideally a sharing of selves.

Not everything with which someone may subjectively identify herself should be treated legally or morally as personal. Otherwise the category of personal things might collapse into "consumer surplus": anything to which someone attached high subjective value would be personal. The question whether something is personal has a normative aspect: whether identifying oneself with something—constituting oneself in connection with that thing—is justifiable.

What makes identifying oneself with something justifiable, in turn, is an appropriate connection to our conception of human flourishing. More specifically, such relationships are justified if they can form part of an appropriate understanding of freedom, identity, and contextuality. A proper understanding of contextuality, for example, must recognize that, although personhood is fostered by relations with people and things, it is possible to be involved too much, or in the wrong way, or with the wrong things.

To identify something as personal, it is not enough to observe that many people seem to identify with some particular kind of thing, because we may judge such identification to be bad for people. An example of a justifiable kind of relationship is people's involvement with their homes. This relationship permits self-constitution within a stable environment. An example of an unjustifiable kind of relationship is the involvement of the robber baron with an empire of "property for power." The latter is unjustified because it ties into a conception of the person we can recognize as inferior: the person as self-interested maximizer of manipulative power.

There is no algorithm or abstract formula to tell us which items are (justifiably) personal. A moral judgment is required in each case. * * * I am suggesting that we relinquish the subject/object dichotomy and rely instead on our best moral judgment in light of the best conception of personhood as we now understand it.

B. Methods of Justifying Market-Inalienabilities

If some people wish to sell something that is identifiably personal, why not let them? In a market society, whatever some people wish to buy and others wish to sell is deemed alienable. Under these circumstances, we must formulate an affirmative case for market-inalienability, so that no one may choose to make fungible—commodify—a personal attribute, right, or thing. In this Section, I propose and evaluate three possible methods of justifying market-inalienability based on personhood: a prophylactic argument, assimilation to prohibition, and a domino theory.

The method of justification that correlates most readily with traditional liberal pluralism is a prophylactic argument. For the liberal it makes sense to countenance both selling and sharing of personal things as the holder freely chooses. If an item of property is personal, however, sometimes the circumstances under which the holder places it on the market might arouse suspicion that her act is coerced. Given that we cannot know whether anyone really intends to cut herself off from something personal by commodifying it, our suspicions might sometimes justify banning sales. The risk of harm to the seller's personhood in cases in which coerced transactions are permitted (especially if the thing sought to be commodified is normally very important to personhood), and the great difficulties involved in trying to scrutinize every transaction closely, may sometimes outweigh the harm that a ban would impose on would-be sellers who are in fact uncoerced. A prophylactic rule aims to ensure free choice—negative liberty—by the best possible coercion-avoidance mechanism under conditions of uncertainty. This prophylactic argument is one way for a liberal to justify, for example, the ban on selling oneself into slavery. We normally view such commodification as so destructive of personhood that we would readily presume all instances of it to be coerced. We would not wish, therefore, to have a rule creating a rebuttable presumption that such transactions are uncoerced (as with ordinary contracts), nor even a rule that would scrutinize such transactions case-by-case for voluntariness, because the risk of harm to personhood in the coerced transactions we might mistakenly see as voluntary is so great that we would rather risk constraining the exercise of choice by those (if any) who really wish to enslave themselves.

A liberal pluralist might use a prophylactic justification to prevent poor people from selling their children, sexual services, or body parts. The liberal would argue that an appropriate conception of coercion should, with respect to selling these things, include the desperation of poverty. Poor people should not be forced to give up personal things because the relinquishment diminishes them as persons, contrary to the liberal regime of respect for persons. We should presume that such transactions are not the result of free choice.

When thus applied to coercion by poverty, the prophylactic argument is deeply troubling. If poverty can make some things nonsalable because we must prophylactically presume such sales are coerced, we would add insult to injury if we then do not provide the would-be seller with the goods she needs or the money she would have received. If we think respect for persons warrants prohibiting a mother from selling something personal to obtain food for her starving children, we do not respect her personhood more by forcing her to let them starve instead. To the extent it equates poverty with coercion, the prophylactic argument requires a corollary in welfare rights. Otherwise we would be forcing the mother to endure a devastating loss in her primary relationship (with her children) rather than in the secondary one (with the personal thing) she is willing to sacrifice to protect the primary one. It is as if, when someone is coerced at gunpoint, we were to direct our moral opprobrium at the victim rather than the gun-wielder, and our enforcement efforts at preventing the victim from handing over her money rather than at preventing the gun-wielder from placing her in the situation where she must. Thus, this aspect of liberal prophylactic pluralism is hypocritical without a large-scale redistribution of wealth and power that seems highly improbable. Although we may nevertheless decide to ban sales of certain personal things, the prophylactic argument, insofar as it rests on equating poverty with coercion, cannot be the reason.

A second method of justifying market-inalienability assimilates it to prohibition. If we accept that the commodified object is different from the "same" thing noncommodified and embedded in personal relationships, then market-inalienability is a prohibition of the commodified version, resting on some moral requirement that it not exist. What might be the basis of such a moral requirement? Something might be prohibited in its market form because it both creates and exposes wealth- and class-based contingencies for obtaining things that are critical to life itself—for example, health care—and thus undermines a commitment to the sanctity of life. Another reason for prohibition might be that the use of market rhetoric, in conceiving of the "good" and understanding the interactions of people respecting it, creates and fosters an inferior conception of human flourishing. For example, we accept an inferior conception of personhood (one allied to the extreme view of negative freedom) if we suppose people may freely choose to commodify themselves.

The prohibition argument—that commodification of things is bad in itself, or because these things are not the "same" things that would be available to people in nonmarket relationships—leads to universal noncommodification. If commodification is bad in itself it is bad for everything. Any social good is arguably "different" if not embedded in a market society. To restrict the argument in order to permit pluralism, we have to accept either that certain things are the "same" whether or not they are bought and sold, and others are "different," or that prohibiting the commodified version morally matters only for certain things, but not for all of them. At present we tend to think that nuts and bolts are pretty much the "same" whether commodified or not, whereas love, friendship, and sexuality are very "different"; we also tend to think that trying to keep society free of commodified love, friendship, and sexuality morally matters more than trying to keep it free of commodified nuts and bolts.

A third method of justifying market-inalienability, the domino theory, envisions a slippery slope leading to market domination. The domino theory assumes that for some things, the noncommodified version is morally preferable; it also assumes that the commodified and noncommodified versions of some interactions cannot coexist. To commodify some things is simply to preclude their noncommodified analogues from existing. Under this theory, the existence of some commodified sexual interactions will contaminate or infiltrate everyone's sexuality so that all sexual relationships will become commodified. If it is morally required that noncommodified sex be possible, market-inalienability of sexuality would be justified. This result can be conceived of as the opposite of a prohibition: there is assumed to exist some moral requirement that a certain "good" be socially available. The domino theory thus supplies an answer (as the prohibition theory does not) to the liberal question why people should not be permitted to choose both market and nonmarket interactions: the noncommodified version is morally preferable when we cannot have both.

We can now see how the prohibition and domino theories are connected. The prohibition theory focuses on the importance of excluding from social life commodified versions of certain "goods"—such as love, friendship, and sexuality—whereas the domino theory focuses on the importance for social life of maintaining the noncommodified versions. The prohibition theory stresses the wrongness of commodification—its alienation and degradation of the person—and the domino theory stresses the rightness of noncommodification in creating the social context for the proper expression and fostering of personhood. If one explicitly adopts both prongs of this commitment to personhood, the prohibition and domino theories merge.

* * *

Rather than merely assuming that money is at the core of every transaction in "goods," thereby making commodification inevitable and phasing out the noncommodified version of the "same" thing (or the nonmarket aspects of sale transactions), we should evaluate the domino theory on a case-by-case basis. We should assess how important it is to us that any particular contested thing remain available in a noncommodified form and try to estimate how likely it is that allowing market transactions for those things would engender a domino effect and make the nonmarket version impossible. This might involve judging how close to universal commodification our consciousness really is, and how this consciousness would affect the particular thing in question.

C. The Problem of Nonideal Evaluation

One ideal world would countenance no commodification; another would insist that all harms to personhood are unjust; still another would permit no relationships of oppression or disempowerment. But we are situated in a nonideal world of ignorance, greed, and violence; of poverty, racism, and sexism. In spite of our ideals, justice under nonideal circumstances, pragmatic justice, consists in choosing the best alternative now available to us. In doing so we may have to tolerate some things that would count as harms in our ideal world. Whatever harms to our ideals we decide we must now tolerate in the name of justice may push our ideals that much farther away. How are we to decide, now, what is the best transition toward our ideals, knowing that our choices now will help to reconstitute those ideals?

The possible avenues for justifying market-inalienability must be reevaluated in light of our nonideal world. In light of the desperation of poverty, a prophylactic market-inalienability may amount merely to an added burden on would-be sellers; under some circumstances we may judge it, nevertheless, to be our best available alternative. We might think that both nonmarket and market interactions can exist in some situations without a domino effect leading to a more commodified order, or we might think it is appropriate to risk a domino effect in light of the harm that otherwise would result to would-be sellers. We might find prohibition of sales not morally warranted, on balance, in some situations, unless there is a serious risk of a domino effect. These will be pragmatic judgments.

1. The Double Bind.—Often commodification is put forward as a solution to powerlessness or oppression, as in the suggestion that women be permitted to sell sexual and reproductive services. But is women's personhood injured by allowing or by disallowing commodification of sex and reproduction? The argument that commodification empowers women is that recognition of these alienable entitlements will enable a needy group—poor women—to improve their relatively powerless, oppressed condition, an improvement that would be beneficial to personhood. If the law denies women the opportunity to be comfortable sex workers and baby producers instead of subsistence domestics, assemblers, clerks, and waitresses—or pariahs (welfare recipients) and criminals (prostitutes)—it keeps them out of the economic mainstream and hence the mainstream of American life.

The rejoinder is that, on the contrary, commodification will harm personhood by powerfully symbolizing, legitimating, and enforcing class division and gender oppression. It will create the two forms of alienation that correlate with commodification of personal things. Women will partly internalize the notion that their persons and their attributes are separate, thus creating the pain of a divided self. To the extent that this self-conception is not internalized, women will be alienated from the dominant order that, by allowing commodification, sees them in this light. Moreover, commodification will exacerbate, not ameliorate, oppression and powerlessness, because of the social disapproval connected with marketing one's body.

But the surrejoinder is that noncommodification of women's capabilities under current circumstances represents not a brave new world of human flourishing, but rather a perpetuation of the old order that submerges women in oppressive status relationships, in which personal identity as market-traders is the prerogative of males. We cannot make progress toward the noncommodification that might exist under ideal conditions of equality and freedom by trying to maintain noncommodification now under historically determined conditions of inequality and bondage.

These conflicting arguments illuminate the problem with the prophylactic argument for market-inalienability. If we now permit commodification, we may exacerbate the oppression of women—the suppliers. If we now disallow commodification—without what I have called the welfare-rights corollary, or large-scale redistribution of social wealth and power—we force women to remain in circumstances that they themselves believe are worse than becoming sexual commodity-suppliers. Thus, the alternatives seem subsumed by a need for social progress, yet we must choose some regime now in order to make progress. This dilemma of transition is the double bind.

The double bind has two main consequences. First, if we cannot respect personhood either by permitting sales or by banning sales, justice requires that we consider changing the circumstances that create the dilemma. We must consider wealth and power redistribution. Second, we still must choose a regime for the meantime, the transition, in nonideal circumstances. To resolve the double bind, we have to investigate particular problems separately; decisions must be made (and remade) for each thing that some people desire to sell.

* * *

VI. CONCLUSION

Market-inalienability is an important normative category for our society. Economic analysis and traditional liberal pluralism have failed to recognize and correctly understand its significance because of the market orientation of their premises. In attempting to free our conceptions from these premises in order to see market-inalienability as an important countercurrent to our market orientation, I have created an archetype, universal commodification, and tried to show how it underlies both economic analysis and more traditional liberal thinking about inalienability. As an archetype, universal commodification is too uncomplicated to describe fully any actual thinker or complex of ideas, but I believe consideration of the archetype and what it entails is a necessary corrective. The rhetoric of commodification has led us into an unreflective use of market characterizations and comparisons for almost everything people may value, and hence into an inferior conception of personhood.

* * *

To the extent that we must not assimilate our conception of personhood to the market, market-inalienabilities are justified. But market-inalienabilities are unjust when they are too harmful to personhood in our nonideal world. Incomplete commodification* can help us mediate this kind of injustice. To see the world of exchange as shot through with incomplete commodification can also show us that inalienability is not the anomaly that economics and more traditional liberalism conceive it to be. This perspective can also help us begin to decommodify things important to personhood—like work and housing—that are now wrongly conceived of in market rhetoric.

Market-inalienability ultimately rests on our best conception of human flourishing, which must evolve as we continue to learn and debate. Likewise, market-inalienabilities must evolve as we continue to learn and debate; there is no magic formula that will delineate them with utter certainty, or once and for all. In our debate, there is no such thing as two radically different normative discourses reaching the "same" result. The terms of our debate will matter to who we are.

*[Editor's Note: Radin, earlier in this article at 1917-1918, describes incomplete commodification. She writes: "One way to mediate the dilemma [of the double bind] is through what I shall call incomplete commodification. Under nonideal circumstances the question whether market-inalienability can be justified is more complicated than a binary decision between complete commodification and complete noncommodification. Rather, we should understand there to be a continuum reflecting degrees of commodification that will be appropriate in a given context. An incomplete commodification—a partial market-inalienability—can sometimes substitute for a complete noncommodification that might accord with our ideals but cause too much harm in our nonideal world."]

Note

Think about personhood and the developing right of publicity in which people may prevent use of their names or personalities for commercial purposes. Is the right of publicity designed to allow us to commodify our names or personalities, to allow us to preclude commodification of our names or personalities, or to choose either mode when it suits us?

Heirs may also claim a right of publicity in their deceased ancestors. Is this aspect of the right designed to protect the personhood of the living, the dead or both?

Joseph William Singer, *The Reliance Interest in Property*, 40 STAN. L. REV. 614–623, 632, 635–641, 652–653, 657, 661–663 (1988)*

I. THE PLANT CLOSING PROBLEM

A. The Setting

On April 28, 1982, the United States Steel Company demolished two steel plants at Youngstown, Ohio. The next day, a dramatic photograph in the New York Times showed four huge blast furnaces crumbling to the ground after being blown up by explosive charges. One plant, the Ohio Works, had been in operation since 1901; the second, the McDonald Works, since 1918. Together, the two plants employed 3,500 workers. After so many years of operation, the plants had become technologically obsolete. The management of the corporation faced a decision whether to modernize the plants or to abandon them and discharge the workers. On November 27, 1979, in a meeting in New York City, the board of directors of U.S. Steel decided to close both plants, along with a dozen other smaller facilities. The effects of that decision would be momentous. As noted by the Court of Appeals for the Sixth Circuit:

> For all of the years United States Steel has been operating in Youngstown, it has been a dominant factor in the lives of its thousands of employees and their families, and in the life of the city itself. The contemplated abrupt departure of United States Steel from Youngstown will, of course, have direct impact on 3,500 workers and their families. It will doubtless mean a devastating blow to them, to the business community and to the City of Youngstown itself. While we cannot read the future of Youngstown from this record, what the record does indicate clearly is that we deal with an economic tragedy of major proportion to Youngstown and Ohio's Mahoning Valley.[10]

In the face of this crisis, the local union representing the workers at the two plants took a series of actions to prevent the plants from closing and to protect the interests of the workers and the community. These actions included community organizing, picketing, sit-ins at corporate headquarters, contact with public officials in state and local government, attempts to bargain with the company, and finally, legal action. The initial theory of the lawsuit was that the local managers had explicitly promised the workers that the plants would not be closed as long as they were profitable and that the workers had relied on those promises to their detriment by agreeing to changed work practices to increase the plants' profitability and by foregoing opportunities elsewhere. After the lawsuit was filed, the union considered the possibility of buying the plants from the company and even began negotiations with company representatives. On January 31, 1980, however, David Roderick, Chair of the Board of Directors of U.S. Steel, announced to the press that the company would refuse to sell the plants to the union because such a purchase would be subsidized by government loans and would arguably result in unfair competition for U.S. Steel. The company's refusal to consider selling the plant to the union formed the basis of a second set of legal claims against the company in the litigation.

After an initial demonstration of sympathy to the union, the federal district judge, Judge Thomas Lambros, decided that U.S. Steel had no legal obligation to sell the plants to the union and could do whatever it wanted with the property. The Sixth Circuit affirmed this ruling on July 25, 1980. Roughly two years later, the company destroyed the plants.

The property issue addressed by both the district court and the court of appeals was expressed as a choice between the union's right to purchase the plant and the company's freedom to control it. The employees claimed that they had a legal right to buy the plant from the company while the company claimed that it had the legal right to do anything it wanted with the plant, including destroy it, without regard to the workers' or the community's interests. To recast the dispute in Hohfeldian terminology:[22]

---

[10] Local 1330, United Steel Workers v. United States Steel Corp., 631 F.2d 1264, 1265 (6th Cir. 1980).

[22] Wesley Newcomb Hohfeld, *Some Fundamental Legal Conceptions as Applied in Judicial Reasoning*, 23 YALE L.J. 16, 30 (1913) * * *. I use Hohfeldian terminology because it highlights the relational aspect of legal rights. Every legal

(1) The union claimed both (a) a power to purchase the plant with a correlative liability in the company to have the plant transferred against its will to the union for its fair market price and (b) a right to have the plant not be destroyed with a correlative duty on the company not to destroy the plant if the union sought to exercise its power to purchase. (2) The company claimed both (a) an immunity from having the plant taken away from it involuntarily even with compensation (with a correlative disability in the union to force the company to sell the plant to the union) and (b) a privilege in the company to destroy the plant with the union having no right to legal relief on that account.

B. Can Relationships Create Property Rights?

During the pretrial hearings in the United Steel Workers case, Judge Lambros listened to statements of the attorneys representing the union and the company. In the middle of one of those hearings, Judge Lambros delivered a statement charged with emotion.

> We are not talking now about a local bakery shop, grocery store, tool and die shop or a body shop in Youngstown that is planning to close and move out. . . .
>
> It's not just a steel company making steel. . . . [S]teel has become an institution in the Mahoning Valley. . . .
>
> Everything that has happened in the Mahoning Valley has been happening for many years because of steel. Schools have been built, roads have been built. Expansion that has taken place is because of steel. And to accommodate that industry, lives and destinies of the inhabitants of that community were based and planned on the basis of that institution: Steel.
>
> . . . .
>
> We are talking about an institution, a large corporate institution that is virtually the reason for the existence of that segment of this nation [Youngstown]. Without it, that segment of this nation perhaps suffers, instantly and severely. Whether it becomes a ghost town or not, I don't know. I am not aware of its capability for adapting.
>
> . . . .
>
> But what has happened over the years between U.S. Steel, Youngstown and the inhabitants? Hasn't something come out of that relationship, something that out of which—not reaching for a case on property law or a series of cases but looking at the law as a whole, the Constitution, the whole body of law, not only contract law, but tort, corporations, agency, negotiable instruments—taking a look at the whole body of American law and then sitting back and reflecting on what it seeks to do, and that is to adjust human relationships in keeping with the whole spirit and foundation of the American system of law, to preserve property rights. . . .
>
> The judicial process cannot survive by adhering to the attitudes of the 1800's. My daily function cannot be regulated by those persons that reach into the dungeons of the past and attempt to stranglehold our present day thinking by 1800 [sic] concepts.
>
> Were the framers of our Constitution or the judges of previous decades able to perceive the conditions that we find in America today and the reliance of a whole community and segment of our society on an institution such as the steel industry?
>
> Well, the easy solution is: "Well, we haven't dealt with it in the past. There is no precedent. You have no case. The case is dismissed. Bailiff, call the next case."
>
> Well, the law has to be more than mere mechanical acts. There has to be more than just form. There has to be substance.
>
> It would seem to me that when we take a look at the whole body of American law and the principles we attempt to come out with—and although a legislature has not pronounced any laws with respect to such a property right, that is not to suggest that there will not be a need for such a law in the future dealing with similar situations—*it seems to me that a property right has arisen from this lengthy, long-established relationship between United States Steel, the steel industry as an institution, the community in Youngstown, the people in Mahoning County and the Mahoning Valley in having given and devoted their lives to this industry.* Perhaps not a property right to the extent that can be remedied by compelling U.S. Steel to remain in Youngstown. *But I think the law can recognize*

---

entitlement correlates with a legal exposure in others. Every right in one person entails a potential or actual vulnerability in others. *See* Duncan Kennedy & Frank Michelman, *Are Property and Contract Efficient?*, 8 HOFSTRA L. REV. 711, 760 (1980) ("For every legal entitlement there is an equal and opposite legal exposure.").

the property right to the extent that U.S. Steel cannot leave that Mahoning Valley and the Youngstown area in a state of waste, that it cannot completely abandon its obligation to that community, because certain vested rights have arisen out of this long relationship and institution.

After this demonstration of concern by the judge, the steelworkers amended their complaint to include a claim based on property law along the lines suggested by Judge Lambros. The amended claim read:

> 52. A property right has arisen from the long-established relation between the community of the 19th Congressional District and Plaintiffs, on the one hand, and Defendant, on the other hand, which this Court can enforce.
>
> 53. This right, in the nature of an easement, requires that Defendant:
>
> a. Assist in the preservation of the institution of steel in that community;
>
> b. Figure into its cost of withdrawing and closing the Ohio and McDonald Works the cost of rehabilitating the community and the workers;
>
> c. Be restrained from leaving the Mahoning Valley in a state of waste and from abandoning its obligation to that community.

Despite his tentative conclusion that the company should have a continuing legal obligation to the community, Judge Lambros decided that no precedent for such a property right existed and that he lacked the power to create one. He reached this conclusion even though he had earlier defended the power of judges to recognize or create a new property right when social conditions and values had changed to warrant it. He saw the issue as a divergence of the company's moral and legal obligations. This disjunction existed because the federal court lacked the legal authority to change state property law to conform to the dictates of morality:

> United States Steel should not be permitted to leave the Youngstown area devastated after drawing from the lifeblood of the community for so many years.
>
> Unfortunately, the mechanism to reach this ideal settlement, to recognize this new property right, is not now in existence in the code of laws of our nation.

The Sixth Circuit also voiced "great sympathy for the community interest" reflected in the union's amended complaint. However, like Judge Lambros, the court concluded that such a property right did not exist, either in legislation or in the common law, and that the court lacked the authority to create it.

* * * I argue that the United Steel Workers case was wrongly decided. Judge Lambros' initial intuition about the correct legal result was better than his ultimate disposition. The courts should have recognized the workers' property rights arising out of their relationship with the company. Such a new legally protected interest would place obligations on the company toward the workers and the community to alleviate the social costs of its decision to close the plant. Protection of this reliance interest could take a variety of forms: It could grant the workers the right to buy the plant from the company for its fair market value; it could require the company to review possible modernization proposals to determine the feasibility and profitability of updating the plant; it could give workers access to information held by the company regarding operation of the facility; it could impose obligations on the company to make severance payments to workers and tax payments to the municipality to protect them until new businesses could be established in the community; it could require the company to assist in finding a purchaser for the plant; it could mean other things as well. The goal should be to identify flexible remedies that are appropriate to protect the workers' reliance interests.

Moreover, contrary to the conclusions of the judges in this case, precedent for the creation of property rights of the kind asserted by the union does exist. I do not want to be so disingenuous as to claim that recognition of such entitlements would not constitute a substantial change in the law, but I do want to assert that the legal system contains a variety of doctrines—in torts, property, contracts, family law and in legislative modifications of those common law doctrines—that recognize the sharing or shifting of various property interests in situations that should be viewed as analogous to plant closings. If I am right, the courts had access to enforceable legal rules based on principles that could have been seen as applicable precedent for extension of existing law by creation of this new set of entitlements.

* * * I argue that the judges in the United Steel Workers case failed to find these precedents and principles in the rules in force because they asked the wrong questions. They wrongly defined the issue as a search for the "owner" of the property. They then assumed that, in the absence of specific doctrinal exceptions to the contrary, owners are allowed to do whatever they want with their property. This approach is seriously misleading: Property rights are more often shared than unitary, and rights to use and dispose of property are never absolute. Moreover, this

approach takes our attention away from the relations of mutual dependence that develop within industrial enterprises and between those enterprises and the communities in which they are situated. Legitimate reliance on such relationships constitutes a central aspect of our social and economic life—so central that numerous rules in force protect reliance on those relationships. Although both the district court and the court of appeals sympathetically noted the legitimate interests of the workers and the community, and the long term relationships that had developed between U.S. Steel, the workers and the community, the courts deemed those interests irrelevant in defining property entitlements. Consideration of competing interests in access to resources and past reliance on relationships granting such access should be a central component of any legal determination of how to allocate lawful power over those resources.

* * * [In addition,] I argue that a wide variety of current legal rules can be justified in terms of an underlying moral principle that I call "the reliance interest in property." They include, for example, the rules about adverse possession, prescriptive easements, public rights of access to private property, tenants' rights, equitable division of property on divorce, and welfare rights. These currently enforceable doctrines encompass the full range of social relationships, from relations among strangers, between neighbors, among long-term contractual partners in the marketplace, among family members and others in intimate relationships, and finally, between citizens and the government. At crucial points in the development of these relationships—often, but not always, when they break up—the legal system requires a sharing or shifting of property interests from the "owner" to the "non-owner" to protect the more vulnerable party to the relationship. The legal system requires this shift, not because of reliance on specific promises, but because the parties have relied on each other generally and on the continuation of their relationship. Moreover, the more vulnerable party may need access to resources controlled by the more powerful party, and the relationship is such that we consider it fair to place this burden on the more powerful party by redistributing entitlements. I demonstrate that this principle currently exists in the legal system and I explore the different types of interests that I collectively refer to as "reliance." In each instance, the legal rules reflect a choice between the freedom of the stronger party to do whatever she wants with "her" property and the security of the weaker party who has relied on access to the other's property in the past or who has relied on the continuation of the relationship.

* * *

Finally, * * * I argue that our central concern in defining property rights in the context of plant closings should be to encourage desirable economic change without unnecessary social misery. To a large extent, this means developing institutions that are capable of generating trust among participants within common enterprises. This, in turn, requires us to focus on relations of power and vulnerability in social and economic life in general. We must confront directly questions about the distribution of power and wealth if we want to shape our institutional environment to create conditions of mutual trust.

* * *

II. Social Vision: Reliance on Relationships

* * *

The legal realist attack on individualistic property and contract theory fatally undermined the coherence of the free market model.[86] Yet the model has a life of its own and continues to dominate legal discourse. Nevertheless, in the twentieth century, both torts and contracts have changed in ways that reintroduce or expand altruistic or communal obligations to share both gains and losses. To the extent those fields are still understood to have a core of individualism surrounded by a periphery of altruism, the line between the core and the periphery is no longer clear. Moreover, to sophisticated thinkers, the absence of a general theory to separate the core from the periphery undermines the meaningfulness of the distinction. In the absence of a metatheory, neither torts nor contracts seems to have a core anymore; rather, every doctrinal issue recreates the contest between the competing social visions of individualism and altruism. Torts is characterized by a contest between the relatively more individualistic negligence principle and the relatively more altruistic strict liability principle. Contracts is characterized by a contest between the individualistic assent principle and the

---

[86] *See* Morris R. Cohen, *The Basis of Contract*, 46 HARV. L. REV. 553 (1933); Robert L. Hale, *Coercion and Distribution in a Supposedly Non-coercive State*, 38 POL. SCI. Q. 470 (1923); John P. Dawson, *Economic Duress—An Essay in Perspective*, 45 MICH. L. REV. 253 (1947); Morris R. Cohen, *Property and Sovereignty*, 13 CORNELL L.Q. 8 (1927); Oliver Wendell Holmes, Jr., *Privilege, Malice and Intent*, 8 HARV. L. REV. 1 (1894); Hohfeld, *supra* note 22; Walter Wheeler Cook, *Privileges of Labor Unions in the Struggle for Life*, 27 YALE L.J. 779 (1918).

altruistic principles of reliance, good faith, unconscionability, and remedies for unjust results of unequal bargaining power.

Property, on the other hand, remains, to a large extent, captive of the free market model based on the fundamental policy of promoting the free alienability of property by concentrating power over that alienation in the hands of existing owners. It is nonetheless true that numerous legal doctrines require redistribution of property interests when people have relied on relationships of mutual dependence. It is my purpose to bring property law into the twentieth century by describing the counterprinciple of reliance. While this will do no more than bring property law into line with torts and contracts, the effect should be to reconceptualize property law as everywhere reproducing the fundamental conflict between the alienability principle and the reliance principle. My goal is to bring to consciousness the peripheral doctrines and principles of property law that the free market social vision has marginalized and suppressed.

B. *What is Wrong with Free Market Assumptions*

* * *

Property interests can be divided in various ways, including: (1) over time (current versus future interests); (2) into co-ownership (joint tenancy, tenancy in common, partnership, corporations); (3) into leases (landlord/tenant relations); (4) into trusts (trustee/beneficiary); (5) into easements and covenants; and (6) into mortgages (mortgagor/mortgagee). Who owns the property in these cases? The landlord or the tenant? The trustee or the beneficiary? The mortgagor or the mortgagee? The question is meaningless. Just as the landlord, life tenant, defeasible fee owner, trustee, and fee simple owner may be "owners" of property, so may tenants, reversioners, trust beneficiaries, holders of future interests, and owners of easements. There are even cases in which it is difficult to identify anyone as the owner. Who owns a university? The board of trustees? The graduates? The students?

When several parties share legal rights in property, any identification of a single person as the "owner" is likely to be both arbitrary and misleading. It is arbitrary because we could just as easily identify someone else as the owner. It is misleading because it denies the existence of joint interests and the need to determine the legal relations among all the persons with legally protected interests in the property. The "owner's" rights are limited by the rights of others with entitlements in the property. Identifying the owner does not tell us who these other people are or what their rights are.

* * *

In the context of plant closings, the search for the owner of the plant is particularly inappropriate. No person or set of persons resembles the fee simple owner of a homestead. We identify the owner as the corporate entity only for the sake of convenience. It is useful for some purposes to conceptualize the corporation as an individual. But the reality is that corporate ownership provides a complicated legal mechanism for joint ownership and control of business property by large groups of people.

* * *

The image of the corporation as the fee simple owner of its own property is an image that has outlived its usefulness. A better paradigm would focus on the industrial relations between and among the thousands of persons who participate in the ongoing affairs of the business or who depend on its success. These persons include management, shareholders, workers and their families, suppliers, and government entities. The rights of these thousands of persons are only partly governed by contract. The business constitutes a network of ongoing relationships. The factory is a locus for this network.

Rather than ask who owns the property, we should ask who has a right to say something about the use or disposition of the property. If we ask this question, it turns out that in every case we will identify more than one person because property rights in corporate enterprises are always shared. Given this fact, the proper normative question then is how to allocate power among the persons with legally protected interests in the property.

* * *

C. *Property as Social Relations*

* * *

The free market model describes the world in terms of possessive individualism. This paradigm is derived from the traditional social contract theory of Hobbes and Locke. It pictures the world as made up of autonomous individuals. These individuals are understood as fundamentally separate from each other; they are alone in the world. They are basically self-interested, and their interests conflict. To protect themselves from each other, they band together to form the state. Once this system is set up, obligations have two main sources: commands of the state and voluntary agreements. Initially, the state allocates property rights and determines how they may be otherwise acquired. It also defines legally protected personal interests of security through tort law. After this initial definition and allocation of entitlements, individuals exercise their property rights or rights of personal freedom, limited only by the duty not to infringe on someone else's rights. Any further obligations are voluntarily assumed by agreement.

In this paradigm, rights are clearly defined at decision points: first, when the state defines personal rights of security and allocates property rights, and second, when people exchange services or property through voluntary agreement. Any obligation that cannot be traced to a full-fledged private contract or a clearly defined state obligation is seen as anomalous. This paradigm therefore understands individuals as connected to each other legally in only two ways: through the universal community of the state or through private agreements. The more fluid relationships of connection are banished to the realm of the family.

In contrast, the social relations approach assumes that there is a basic connectedness between people, instead of assuming that autonomy is the prior and essential dimension of personhood. If we see people as situated in relation to others, rather than as isolated and autonomous, our understanding of social life changes, and with it, our understanding of the source of legal obligations. In this view, people are never completely alone. They are situated in a complicated network of relations with others. Rather than relating to others either through the universal community of the state or through individual decisions to contract, people relate to each other in a range of ways. We can understand social relationships as comprising a spectrum, from relations among strangers, to relations among neighbors, to continuing relations in the market, to intimate relations in the family. This understanding of social relations relativizes the distinction between autonomy and community. We do not relate to others only through the mechanism of the whole community or through agreements between autonomous individuals. Rather, we can relate to others in ways that do not fit either of these polar categories, but through the more fluid, ongoing relationships of give and take that are characteristic of relations in the family and in associations.

Understanding people as situated in a spectrum of relationships with others allows us also to relativize the distinction between state coercion and private contractual freedom. This understanding therefore changes our understanding of the source of legal obligations. Many of the legal developments of the twentieth century can be described as recognition of obligations that emerge over time out of relationships of interdependence. These entitlements are neither fully articulated initially by clear state-imposed obligations nor by fully-executed and complete contracts. Rather, these obligations often are imposed to protect the interests of individuals in relying on the continuation of important relationships of interdependence. Moreover, these obligations are not created only at magic moments when decisions are made by the state or by contracting parties; instead, they may change as the relation between the parties changes.

* * *

The relational approach shifts our attention from asking "Who is the owner?" to the question "What relationships have been established?" The shift is partly a shift from focusing on the relation between the owner and the resources owned to the relation between the owner and non-owners who have benefited from the resources. But more important, the shift is from a perspective that focuses on the owner as an isolated individual whose presumptive control of the resource is absolute within her sphere of power to a perspective that understands individuals to be in a continuing relation to each other as part of a common enterprise. Rights are not limited to the initial allocation of property entitlements or the agreement of the parties, but emerge and change over the course of the relationship.

The relational idea forces us to turn our attention to facts that would otherwise be obscured. It allows us to take seriously Judge Lambros' intuition that property rights should be recognized from the long-standing relation between U.S. Steel, its workers, and the town. Rather than seeing the corporation and the workers in isolation, and assuming that the corporation has absolute freedom to dispose of "its" property as it sees fit, in the absence of a clear contractual obligation to the contrary, we can see the corporation and the workers as together having established and relied on long-standing relations with each other in creating a common enterprise. The rights of the members of the common enterprise cannot be fully articulated by reference to ownership rights defined a priori or by the explicit terms of written contracts. If workers are considered to be part of the corporation, rather than factors of production or hired hands, our analysis of property rights changes.

* * *

This image allows us to consider the moral character of that relationship and the obligations that should be imposed on the more powerful party to protect the interests of the more vulnerable party. It allows us to address as a legal matter the question that Lambros ultimately treated as non-legal, as a matter of morality. The relational idea does not tell us what to do, but it helps us define the issue of the case in a way that does not exclude consideration of the legitimate obligations of powerful parties to their partners in common enterprises.

* * *

If we accept the view of corporations as common enterprises, and if we accept the idea that owners of property have social obligations to the community and to those with whom they establish continuing relations of mutual dependence, then we can begin to talk about a new social vision that can orient our decisions about the social responsibilities of property owners. This social vision of property law will center on the image of protecting reliance on relationships constituting common enterprises. As a normative matter, we must therefore determine what responsibilities property owners should have to the community at large and to vulnerable persons with whom the owners have established continuing relationships. What values should inform our construction of these relationships?

Professor Radin has argued that we should make a fundamental moral distinction between personal and fungible property.[165] Fungible property is held for its exchange value; we value it because of our ability to use it to acquire goods or services of equal value. Personal property is held not primarily for its exchange value but because it is necessary to our sense of ourselves as persons and because of our emotional commitment to the relationships such property makes possible. She further argues that personal property should be granted greater protection than fungible property, and that we must make moral judgments about which sorts of resources should be classified as personal property.

In the context of plant closings, Radin would ask us to make moral judgments about the quality and importance of the relative interests of the company and the workers. The company is interested in plants for investment purposes—to make money. Plants are interchangeable from the point of view of corporate management; in Radin's terms, they are fungible. But from the standpoint of the workers and the community members, plants are not fungible. It is not the case that all jobs are equally good. Workers have an interest in remaining in their homes and in their jobs and using the skills they have acquired over many years of service to the company. They may be interested in maintaining work relations with others in the company—to continue working in the common enterprise. The workers are interested in their homes, their jobs, and in continuing the relationships that give them a sense of security and identity.

In a conflict between the workers' personal reliance interest in property and the company's fungible investment interest in controlling or destroying the plant, the workers' interest should prevail. This choice holds so long as it is sensible from an economic standpoint to encourage continued use of the plant and the range of legal alternatives open to the workers is not sufficient to protect their reliance interests.

I have argued that we should understand property as social relations, rather than through the lens of the free market model. Industrial enterprises comprise ongoing relationships of mutual dependence among all the members of the joint enterprise. The social relations approach asks us to be sensitive to the power inequalities within those relationships; some members of the common enterprise are more vulnerable than others. These inequalities are not natural; they are the direct result of the allocation of power determined by the assignment of legal entitlements. We should focus on the various ways in which vulnerable persons rely on relationships of mutual dependence. This perspective will give us a deeper understanding of how the legal system regulates economic life.

I have further argued that we should be committed to defining the social obligations of property owners toward the community at large and to those with whom the owner establishes continuing relations of mutual dependence. Those obligations are not fully specified in advance through pre-existing duties or contractual provisions, but emerge and change over the course of the relationship, as dependencies and legitimate expectations develop on the part of the more vulnerable party to the relationship.

If we take this view of property law, and ask the questions about reliance on relationships that it suggests, we will see and understand legal doctrine in ways that the judges in the United Steel Workers case did not. Because the social relations approach directs our attention in new ways, it allows us to redescribe property law in terms of the reliance principle.

---

165 Margaret Jane Radin, *Property and Personhood*, 34 Stan. L. Rev. 957, 959-60 (1982).

Note

In a portion of Singer's article not excerpted here, he summarizes a number of legal rules recognizing various reliance principles to make the point that community understandings are an important part of the American legal scene. Among the rules discussed are easements by estoppel, where courts decline to permit a property owner to terminate a license granted to another to use land if that action would be unfair to the non-owner. Thus, in *Stoner v. Zucker*, 148 Cal. 516, 83 P. 808 (1906), Singer argues in his article at 670–671, the owner was properly precluded from stopping use of an irrigation ditch that cost the non-owner a significant amount of money to build. He also notes that the ability of homeowners to rely upon their ability to redeem mortgages after default has often taken precedence over the investment interests of lenders, even in situations, such as installment land sale contracts like that in *Skendzel v. Marshall*, 261 Ind. 226, 301 N.E.2d 641 (1973), where the parties did not formally establish a mortgage relationship. *Id.* at 685–686. Peruse your property text for other cases that affirm Singer's idea that property rights emerge from ongoing relationships and expectations.

William H. Simon, *Social-Republican Property*, 38 UCLA L. REV. 1335–1350 (1991)*

INTRODUCTION

Economic democracy is the idea that the norms of equality and participation that classical liberalism confines to a narrowly defined sphere of government should apply to the sphere of economic life. Economic democracy thus entails a challenge to the classical liberal notion of property. In classical liberalism, property defines a realm of private enjoyment. No particular property right is a prerogative of, or a prerequisite to, citizenship, and the exercise of property rights by those who have them is not assessed in political terms.

One alternative to classical liberalism responsive to the ideal of economic democracy is classical socialism. Classical socialism opposes to the liberal notion of private property the notion of state property—property controlled by the officials of a democratically constituted state. Another alternative to classical liberalism inspired in part by the ideal of economic democracy is social democracy or welfare-regulatory liberalism. Social democracy retains the classical liberal notion of private property rights, but it both qualifies them by regulatory restrictions on their exercise and supplements them with welfare rights to minimal subsistence funded and administered through a tax-transfer system.

This essay is about aspects of a further alternative to classical liberalism inspired by the ideal of economic democracy. This alternative can be found in converging elements of the traditions of republicanism and market socialism. Like social democracy, the alternative rejects both state property and the unrestricted accumulation and exercise of private property rights. However, to a greater extent than social democracy, it pursues its concerns by encouraging a politically desirable primary organization of economic activity and distribution of income and wealth.

The distinctive notion of property in this alternative view is sometimes called social property in the market socialist tradition, but its simultaneous affinity with the republican tradition leads me to call it social-republican property. The distinctive feature of social-republican property is that it is held by private individuals subject to two types of conditions—one requiring that the holder bear a relation of potential active participation in a group or community constituted by the property, and another designed to limit inequality among the members of a group or community. Among the more familiar forms of social-republican property are interests in certain producer cooperatives and "limited equity" housing cooperatives.

In contemporary American society, the characteristics associated with social-republican property are routinely imputed to a narrow set of political or citizenship entitlements, such as voting rights, but these characteristics seem anomalous in private economic life. Nevertheless, there are some interesting examples of social republican property in the private sphere, and there has recently been a variety of proposals that would increase its importance there. Moreover, a variety of regulatory and welfare policies, such as certain forms of tax relief and rent control, create interests that resemble social-republican property and may be inspired by social-republican principles.

* * *

The essay's political purpose is to contribute to contemporary debates about radical economic reform, in particular to debates over the possibility of a "third way" between capitalism (both its classical liberal and social democratic versions) and socialism. The social-republican vision may be the closest thing we have to a reform model that is both distinguishable from the capitalist and socialist models and at least moderately institutionally concrete.

To be sure, the sophisticated contemporary response to the question of the "third way" is to assert the indeterminacy of all general reform models, and to insist that any plausible program for a particular economy would have to be an amalgam of a diverse variety of forms of property. General models do not generate concrete programs by themselves, and no single general model could plausibly serve as a unique inspiration for the restructuring of an entire economy. Nevertheless, general models inescapably influence even the most contextual thinking about particular reforms. Enlarging our repertory of general models thus seems likely to enhance the flexibility of our thinking and the range of particular alternative possibilities we can summon in appraising particular practices and institutions.

* * *

I. Republicanism, Market Socialism, and Property

* * *

Both republicanism and market socialism express or imply critiques of classical liberalism and corporate capitalism. They both suggest that the ideal of democracy implicit in classical liberal social arrangements is implausible because it tolerates too high a degree of material inequality and too circumscribed a scope of participation in decisions of collective significance. Moreover, both traditions criticize classical liberalism for legitimating and fostering a narrow egoism, which they see as a threat both to mutually beneficial cooperation and to an ambitious conception of personal development and expression.

Nineteenth-century and many later versions of republicanism and market socialism converge on some specific points of political economy that today seem dogmatic or confused, including a vision of the macrodynamics of capitalism that asserts an inexorable tendency toward increased inequality and volatility, a precapitalist hostility to interest-taking, and a categorical denial of the productivity of economic intermediaries and many other white collar occupations.

They also, however, converge on some points that retain considerable force. One central point of convergence challenges the line classical liberalism draws between public and private spheres. The liberal public sphere is in principle a realm of equality and participation; the liberal private sphere is in principle a realm of contract in which people with unequal endowments exchange productive efforts for consumption benefits. To republicans and market socialists, this structure subverts democracy in two ways. The wealthy can translate the resources acquired in the private sphere into power in the public sphere in ways that undermine equality and participation. At the same time, in the private sphere of work (and to a more ambiguous extent, the sphere of consumption) the nonwealthy are forced into experiences of dependence (to use the republican term) and alienation (to use the socialist term) that preclude personal and political autonomy.

The subordination that these doctrines deplore has several dimensions. One dimension is simply the need of those who lack property to submit to the often pervasive direction of those who have it in order to earn their livings. Another is the degradation and stultification that result from the need to spend nearly all one's time focused anxiously on securing basic material subsistence, with the consequence that one lacks the time and security to develop broader capacities, including the capacity for effective political participation. Still a third dimension is the way in which workers experience the operation of labor and capital markets as natural processes beyond human control. This occurs both because important social decisions have been removed from the agenda of collective deliberation and because the workers' experience as passive objects of economic forces undermines their capacity for autonomous participation in social decisions.

This critique of the private sphere expresses, not only opposition to inequality, but a commitment to public collective decisionmaking over private individual decisionmaking. It tends to see public collective decisionmaking as an expression of virtue and solidarity and hence both intrinsically more satisfying and conducive to better decisions. It tends to see private individual decisionmaking as an expression of corruption and alienation. Although the relations between institutions and attitudes are complex and often obscure, there is one straightforward sense in which collective public decisionmaking is associated with civic virtue and solidarity: it compels the participants to address each other in terms that appeal to common interests.

A further point of convergence of the republican and market socialist critiques is the contention that a plausible conception of democracy requires that political autonomy be grounded in the control of property, or more specifically, a particular kind of property—productive resources, or capital. Classical liberalism seems to deny political significance to the distribution of property; social democratic liberalism seems to focus its concern on guaranteeing the citizen a minimum level of consumption. In contrast, republicans and market socialists see broadly distributed property as a safeguard against the subversion of democracy by either a wealthy oligarchy or an aggressive state.

The critical norm of republican political economy is propertied independence—civic competence grounded in ownership of capital. The critical norm in market socialism is "social property"—productive resources controlled by workers in a participatory workplace but subject to important obligations to the larger society.

In addition to providing material security and protecting against subordination to either wealthy individuals or an impersonal market, social-republican property functions to promote political responsibility. Since the value of property is affected by collective decisions, property is a medium through which the consequences of such decisions are transmitted to individual citizens. Property thus serves as an inducement both to participate and to avoid reckless or opportunistic behavior.

Social-republican property can be distinguished from the more conventional notion of capital ownership, which might be called "liberal private" property, by two features: first, transfer or alienation restraints that confine control of the property to active or potentially active participants in a community constituted by the property, and second, accumulation restraints designed to limit inequality among members of such a community. These core features of social-republican property operate as restraints on the commodification and capitalization of relationships. They restrict the ability of the owner/citizen to fully monetize or liquidate her interest or to convert anticipated future benefits into present lump sums. They thus encourage the owner to view her interest as a stake in a particular long-term relationship.

Alienation restraints may contribute to the maintenance of a politically desirable distribution of wealth by preventing presumptively imprudent transfers likely to exacerbate disadvantage. They also serve as safeguards of the propertied independence essential to civic competence. We often think of alienation restraints on welfare benefits like Social Security as purely paternalistic, but from a social-republican point of view they have a more complex character. Like the prohibition against selling yourself into slavery, such restraints preclude individual choices, but they do so in the interest of preserving the individual's capacity for choice. Transfer restrictions also impede the formation of broad ranging markets that increase economic volatility and hence undermine the security essential to political autonomy. In addition, alienation restraints help confine control rights to active participants in the community, and preclude transfers that might threaten the social-republican character of the community—notably transfers to absentee owners or "speculators."

An explicit, exacting alienation restraint would entirely preclude individual members of the relevant community from transferring their property interests; a looser one would require the consent of the other members. In Yugoslav market socialism, capital is considered "social property," a category that differs from Soviet-style state property in that it contemplates that the possessors have broad discretion over the employment of the capital and some claim to the proceeds from it, but also differs from liberal private property partly in being more or less categorically nontransferable. In America, memberships in partnerships and cooperatives are typically not unilaterally transferable. Small businesses of many varieties often require the consent of remaining owners for transfers of ownership interests.

Another form of transfer restriction is a residency or usage requirement that conditions property rights on the owner residing on the property, making some productive use of it, or both. The law of some of the American Colonies made extensive use of conditions of occupation, settlement, and cultivation in defining both the acquisition and maintenance of land ownership; the Homestead Act of 1862 imposed settlement conditions on property interests in federal grants of western lands; the "prior appropriation" system of water law that predominates in the American West conditions ownership of water rights on continued use. In all these cases, the conditions appear to have been influenced by republican notions. (But this is not to say that they effectively implemented republican values; the Homestead restrictions were weak and weakly enforced; in the water law case, the recognition of corporate and absentee owners permits the conditions to be satisfied in ways that subvert republican goals.)

As either a substitute for or a complement of explicit transfer restrictions, both republicans and market socialists have often favored investments in resources that are relatively immobile. * * * The preference for immobile property is based partly on its tendency to be relatively stable in value, but more importantly on its tendency to give the owner a stake in the community likely to motivate political activity. Landowners, the French republican Anne Robert Jacques Turgot wrote, "are attached to the land by virtue of their property; they cannot cease to take an interest in the district where it is placed. . . . It is the possession of land . . . which, linking the possessor to the State, constitutes true citizenship. . . ." By contrast, proprietors of liquid, mobile capital "belong to no place."[14]

Nineteenth century theorists expanded the category of republican property, first to artisanal tools (and, inferentially, to skills) and then to small-scale industrial capital held by owner-operators. The theorists emphasized the politically significant qualities these forms of property shared with agricultural land—they were equally compatible with production by owners working at their own direction, and they were rooted in face-to-face local economic relations. Their immobility arose from the fact that their value depended heavily on the local presence of collaborators and customers. Thus, in addition to providing the material security needed for political independence, this type of property encouraged cooperation and fostered trust in a way that enhanced the people's capacities as citizens.

The two types of property most prominently condemned as incompatible with republican politics were financial property (securities) and slaves. Aside from the fact that they explicitly constituted subordination (of the wage-earner to the distant capitalist in the one case, of the slave to the master in the other), what these types of property had in common was their relative mobility. The traditional socialist and republican hostility to financiers, as well as to speculators and other intermediaries, is grounded in part on the notion that they introduce a degree of liquidity into economic relations that threatens the political structure of the community. Socialists and republicans attributed an astonishing range of morally corrosive effects to engagement in far-flung financial markets, including fraud and sexual licentiousness, most of which they explained at least in part by the failure of such property to anchor the individual in a local political community.

And one reason why republicans considered black slavery a threat to the independence of whites was that the comparative mobility of slaves as opposed to landed property discouraged slaveholders from making material or personal investments in local communities, and encouraged them to oppose politically the types of public investments necessary to a vital public culture. With their wealth in slave property, owners tended to treat land as a variable cost, cultivate extensively, and then move on as soil productivity declined, without developing local attachments.

Here the republican perspective resembles a notion * * * that impediments to easy exit from a community create inducements for internal participation in efforts to improve the community. Fixed, locally rooted investments create such impediments (without directly or categorically infringing liberty of personal movement).

The second distinctive feature of social-republican property involves restraints on accumulation designed to preserve equality. The classical republican instance of such restraints is the "agrarian law" of the Roman Republic that constrained (to a limited and disputed extent) the amount of land that a citizen could acquire. A central part of the constitution of Harrington's utopian Oceana was an agrarian law requiring the equal division of property among heirs at death and precluding citizens from acquiring during their lifetimes more land than the amount that would generate income of 2000 pounds per year.

---

[14] Quoted in W. SEWELL, WORK AND REVOLUTION IN FRANCE: THE LANGUAGE OF LABOR FROM THE OLD REGIME TO 1848, at 127–128 (1980).

Accumulation restraints figured commonly in 19th century reform models. To take one of the more radical examples, Thomas Skidmore, who influenced labor activists in New York in the 1830s, proposed a system under which property could be held privately only as a life estate, would revert to the state upon the holder's death, and would be redistributed each generation to young people in roughly equal allotments. A comparatively moderate instance was the provision (ineffectively enforced) of the Homestead Act of 1862 limiting the amount of public lands that might be acquired to a quarter section per claimant. The Federal Reclamation Act of 1902 imposed a limitation (much evaded and recently liberalized) of 160 acres on the size of individual holdings that might benefit from federally subsidized water.

A different type of accumulation restraint is expressed in the market socialist notion of "social property." Under this notion, individuals have claims on the income of the enterprise in which they work, but they cannot either individually or collectively sell the enterprise or its assets. I mentioned this above as a transfer restraint, but it can also be seen as an accumulation constraint. It prevents worker/owners from capitalizing the anticipated future income of the enterprise. As in Skidmore's conception, their ownership interest is in the nature of a life estate—here the "life" being their membership tenure in the enterprise—though in market socialism the remainder interest is typically ascribed to the enterprise and its future members rather than, as Skidmore proposed, to the state.

A further type of accumulation restraint limits the degree of inequality within an enterprise. A strict constraint would provide equal rights of control and income for each member of the enterprise. Contemporary American partnership law presumes this in the absence of contrary agreement for members of a partnership. Early American corporate charters commonly limited inequality by capping the number of votes a single shareholder could exercise. Some republican and market socialist programs mandate equal control and severely limit income inequality.

Yet another type of accumulation restraint common to many social-republican programs works indirectly and prospectively. This type includes arrangements involving insurance or cross-collateralization. Nineteenth century labor organizations, for example, often sought to provide health and unemployment insurance to their members. Many such programs were not funded on an actuarial basis and contemplated future charges on the more successful members to meet the needs of the others. Analogous accumulation constraints were imposed by arrangements in which groups of worker-entrepreneurs would jointly guarantee or collateralize credit. The legendary Farmer's Alliance program provided for cooperatives to purchase farm supplies with "joint notes" secured by mortgages of members' farms. Each farmer's wealth was thus made subject to creditor claims in the event that any of them should default.

In the small-firm industrial districts of the "Third Italy" that achieved dramatic success in the 1970s, among the various types of interfirm cooperatives—many of them sponsored by the Communist and Socialist parties—are credit cooperatives based on the cross-collateralization idea. The cooperatives, which are funded by membership fees and public subsidies, issue loan guarantees to their members that enable them to secure otherwise unavailable commercial bank financing. Another area in which the cross-collateralization approach appears today is cooperative (as opposed to condominium) housing, where individual owners typically pledge their ownership interests as security for their neighbors', as well as their own, debts.

Finally, the hostility in social-republican discourse to the corporate form of economic organization reflects in part the equality concerns underlying accumulation constraints. A central objection is that the corporation's ability to aggregate resources of far-flung absentee owners gives it political and economic advantages over local worker-owners. It can bring its outside resources to bear in the local political community in ways that give it disproportionate power. And because corporate owners are typically "absentees," they largely escape the local social externalities of their economic conduct (for example, unemployment and pollution), and thus are inclined to engage in activities that are inefficient in terms of the larger interests of the community. And social-republican rhetoric associates the corporate form with monopolistic market power that unfairly stifles local competition and exploits local business customers and suppliers. Thus, limitations and prohibitions of corporate business and political activity may be seen as social-republican accumulation restraints.

The equality commitment creates an important tension within republicanism. Historically, republicans have been ambivalent as to whether just distribution of property should be treated as a subject of politics or as a prerequisite to it. The prominence of equality in the republican vision suggests that it should be a focus of ongoing political debate and action. But to many republicans, fundamental distributive struggles entail an aggressive factionalism inimical to the spirit of civic virtue that republican politics requires, and strong equality commitments pose the threat of requiring an excessively powerful state. Thus, some have argued that republican politics is possible only after fundamental distributive issues have been settled, so that redistributive claims can be excluded from the political agenda. Many republicans, even some as radical as Tom Paine, have opposed ambitious redistribution schemes.

A frequent republican strategy of compromise—common to ancient Rome, revolutionary France and America, and 19th century America (as reflected in the minor land reform efforts of Reconstruction and the Homestead Act)—has been to focus efforts to achieve economic equality on the distribution of land conquered from outsiders or confiscated from the losing side in civil wars. Today, explicit accumulation restraints on capital arise most commonly as conditions on government or charitable grants, or on exemptions from taxes or regulations.

The tension over redistribution has been avoided in the socialist tradition by a relatively unqualified commitment to equality, but this commitment has been made at the cost of the plausibility of the doctrine. The failure to recognize the political dangers of charging the state with a strong permanent mission of economic leveling, and of making leveling a preeminent focus of politics, are among the most important reasons for the increasingly widespread rejection of socialism.

Thus, a critical task of a plausible vision of social-republican property is to reconcile its commitment to equality with a decentralized institutional structure and a political culture that recognizes the importance of distribution without being obsessed with it.

The social-republican vision and its notion of property are not always distinguishable from social democratic notions that have played a prominent role in mainstream thought throughout most of this century. Social democracy also has ambitious aspirations for equality and democracy. Moreover, it has proposed conceptions of property, not only in welfare benefits and regulatory fairness, but in membership in public and private institutions, including the workplace, that overlap with social-republican property.[37] Nevertheless, the distinction between the social democratic and social-republican visions is worth drawing.

In contrast to social-republicans, social democrats tend to focus their egalitarian and democratic concerns on regulatory and tax-transfer structures rather than on the structure of the primary processes of production and exchange. Their efforts to limit inequality in the primary distribution of wealth tend to stop after the equitable provision of education and the limitation of inheritance. Social democrats tend to believe that the ownership of capital, once the powers of ownership have been shrunk by their transfer and regulatory apparatus, is of relatively slight political importance. They are less likely than social-republicans to see the sphere of production as a realm of political expression. When they do attempt to apply democratic and egalitarian norms to the workplace, they are likely to prefer models of unionization and collective bargaining in investor-owned or state-owned firms to models of worker ownership.

Finally, social democrats tend to be relatively sympathetic to large-scale enterprise and concentrated capital (subject to regulatory restrictions and worker collective bargaining rights) and to find the social-republican vision of small-scale, owner-managed enterprise anachronistic and unattractive. While there may be some room in the social democratic view for social-republican property, such property plays a more marginal role there.

---

37 * * * Reich, *The New Property*, 73 YALE L. J. 733 (1964) * * *.

Note

Compare the social-republicanism of Simon to the civic-republicanism of Thomas Jefferson, as described by Stanley Katz in *Thomas Jefferson and the Right to Property in Revolutionary America* [Part II(A)] and John Adams, as exposed in his *Letter to John Sullivan* [Part II(A)].

Additional Bibliography

Additional reading suggestions are made throughout the anthology. These suggestions are listed here, alphabetically by author.

Ackerman, Bruce, *Private Property and the Constitution (1977).*

Alexander, Gregory, *Time and Property in the American Republican Legal Culture*, 66 N.Y.U. L. Rev. 273 (1991).

August, Ray, *The Spread of Community Property Law to the Far West*, 3 Western Leg. Hist. 35 (1990).

Bittker, Boris, *The Case of the Checker-Board Ordinance: An Experiment in Race Relations*, 71 Yale L. J. 1387 (1962).

Blumberg, Grace Ganz, *Cohabitation Without Marriage: A Different Perspective*, 28 UCLA L. Rev. 1126 (1981).

Bone, Robert G., *Normative Theory and Legal Doctrine in American Nuisance Law: 1850-1920*, 59 So. Cal. L. Rev. 1101 (1986).

Browder, Olin L., *The Taming of the Duty–The Tort Liability of Landlords*, 81 Mich. L. Rev. 99 (1982).

Burke, Joseph C., *The Cherokee Cases, A Study in Law, Politics, and Morality*, 21 Stan. L. Rev. 503 (1969).

Carol M. Rose, Mahon *Reconstructed: Why the Takings Issue is Still a Muddle*, 16 Land Use & Environment L. Rev. 3 (1985).

Chambers, Reid P., *Judicial Enforcement of the Federal Trust Responsibility to Indians*, 27 Stan. L. Rev. 1213 (1975).

Chused, Richard, *Married Women's Property Law, 1800-1850*, 71 Geo. L. J. 1359 (1983).

Coase, Ronald, *The Problem of Social Cost,* 3 J. L. & Econ. 1 (1960).

Costonis, John, *The Chicago Plan: Incentive Zoning and the Preservation of Urban Landmarks*, 85 Harv. L. Rev. 574 (1972).

Cunningham, Roger A., *The New Implied and Statutory Warranties of Habitability in Residential Leases: From Contract to Status*, 16 Urban L. Annual 3 (1979).

Epstein, Richard, *Possession as the Root of Title,* 13 Ga. L. Rev. 1221 (1979).

Epstein, Richard, *Covenants and Constitutions*, 73 Cornell L. Rev. 906 (1988).

Epstein, Richard, *Past and Future: The Temporal Dimension in the Law of Property,* 64 Wash. U. L. Q. 667 (1986).

French, Susan F., *Servitudes Reform and the New Restatement of Property: Creation Doctrines and Structural Simplification,* 73 Cornell L. Rev. 928 (1988).

Gates, Paul W., A History of The Public Land Policies (1965).

Gregory, Alexander, *The Dead Hand and the Law of Trusts in the Nineteenth Century*, 37 STAN. L. REV. 1189 (1985).

Hirsch, Hirsch & Margolis, *Regression Analysis of the Effects of Habitability Laws Upon Rent: An Empirical Observation on the Ackerman-Komesar Debate*, 63 CAL. L. REV. 1098 (1975).

Lewin, Jeff L., *Comparative Nuisance*, 50 U. PITT. L. REV. 1009 (1989).

Mahoney, Martha, *Law and Racial Geography: Public Housing and the Economy in New Orleans*, 42 STAN. L. REV. 1251 (1990).

Marcus, Norman, *Air Rights in New York City: TDR, Zoning Lot Merger and the Well-Considered Plan*, 50 BROOKLYN L. REV. 867(1984).

McDonald, Forrest, NOVUS ORDO SECLORUM: THE INTELLECTUAL ORIGINS OF THE CONSTITUTION (1985).

Mensch, Elizabeth, *The Colonial Origins of Liberal Property Rights*, 31 BUFF. L. REV. 635 (1982).

Merrill, Thomas, *Trespass, Nuisance, and the Costs of Determining Property Rights,* 14 J. LEGAL STUD. 13 (1985).

Michelman, Frank, *Takings, 1987,* 88 COLUM. L. REV. 1600 (1988).

Michelman, Frank, *Tutelary Jurisprudence and Constitutonal Property*, in LIBERTY, PROPERTY AND THE FUTURE OF CONSTITUTIONAL DEVELOPMENT (Ellen Frankel Paul & Howard Dickman, eds.)(1990).

Norgren, Jill, *Lawyers and the Legal Business of the Cherokee Republic in Courts of the United States, 1829-1835, 10* LAW & HIST. REV. 253 (1992).

Polinsky, A. Mitchell, *Resolving Nuisance Disputes: The Simple Economics of Injunctive and Damage Remedies*, 32 STAN. L. REV. 1075 (1980).

Posner, Richard, ECONOMIC ANALYSIS OF LAW 10-40 (1972).

Potter, Michael, *Racial Diversity in Residential Communities: Societal Housing Patterns and a Proposal for a "Racial Inclusionary Ordinance,"* 63 S. CAL. L. REV. 1151 (1990).

Power, Garrett, *The Unwisdom of Allowing City Growth to Work Out its Own Destiny*, 47 MD. L. REV. 626 (1988).

Rabin, Edward, *Rethinking Basic Assumptions,* 63 VA. L. REV. 1299(1977).

Radin, Margaret Jane, *The Liberal Conception of Property: Cross Currents in the Jurisprudence of Takings,* 88 COLUM. L. REV. 1667 (1988).

Radin, Margaret Jane, *Time, Possession, and Alienation*, 64 WASH. U. L. Q. 739 (1986).

Reich, Charles, *Beyond the New Property: An Ecological View of Due Process*, 56 BROOKLYN L. REV. 731 (1990).

Reichman, Uriel, *Residential Private Governments: An Introductory Survey*, 43 U. CHI. L. REV. 253 (1976).

Richards, J. Gregory, *Zoning for Direct Social Control*, 1982 DUKE L. J. 761.

Sager, Lawrence G., *Insular Majorities Unabated:* Warth v. Seldin *and* City of Eastlake v. Forest City Enterprises, Inc., 91 HARV. L. REV. 1373 (1978).

Siegel, Stephen A., *Understanding the Nineteenth Century Contract Clause: The Rule of the Property-Privilege Distinction and "Takings" Clause Jurisprudence*, 60 SO. CAL. L. REV. 1 (1986).

Singer, Joseph W., *Sovereignty and Property, 86 Nw. U. L.* REV. 1 (1991);

Singer, Joseph W., *The Legal Rights Debate in Analytical Jurisprudence From Bentham to Hohfeld*, Wisc. L. Rev. 975 (1982).

Smolla, Rodney A., *In Pursuit of Racial Utopias: Fair Housing, Quotas, and Goals in the 1980's*, 58 S. Cal. L. Rev. 947 (1985).

Soper, Philip, On the Relevance of Philosophy to Law: Reflections on Ackerman's Private Property and the Constitution, 79 Colum. L. Rev. 44 (1979).

Sterk, Stewart E. *Foresight and the Law of Servitudes*, 73 Cornell L. Rev. 956 (1988).

Stick, John, *Turning Rawls Into Nozick and Back Again*, 81 Nw. L. Rev. 363 (1987).

Townsend, *Congressional Abrogation of Indian Treaties: Reevaluation and Reform,* 98 Yale L. J. 793 (1989).

Ware, Leland B., *Invisible Walls: An Examination of the Legal Strategy of the Restrictive Covenant Cases*, 67 Wash. U. L. Q. 737 (1989).

Wegner, Judith Welch, *Moving Toward the Bargaining Table: Contract Zoning, Development Agreements, and the Theoretical Foundations of Government Land Use Deals*, 65 N. Car. L. Rev. 957 (1987).

Williams, Robert, *The Algebra of Federal Indian Law: The Hard Trail of Decolonizing and Americanizing the White Man's Indian Jurisprudence,* 1986 Wis. L. Rev. 219.

Winokur, James L., *The Mixed Blessing of Promissory Servitudes: Toward Optimizing Economic Utility, Individual Liberty, and Personal Identity*, 1989 Wis. L. Rev. 1.

____, *Developments in the Law: Zoning*, 91 Harv. L. Rev. 1427 (1978).

____, Note, *The Integration Ordinance: Honi Soit Qui Mal Y Pense*, 17 Stan. L. Rev. 280 (1965).

____, Note, *Tortious Interference With Contractual Relations in the Nineteenth Century: The Transformation of Property, Contract and Tort*, 93 Harv. L. Rev. 1510 (1980).

Case Index